Advanced Visual Basic® .NET
Programming Web and Desktop Applications in ADO.NET and ASP.NET

Advanced Visual Basic® .NET
Programming Web and Desktop Applications in ADO.NET and ASP.NET

David Gefen
Drexel University
Chittibabu Govindarajulu
Drexel University

Upper Saddle River, NJ 07458

Library of Congress Cataloging-in-Publication Data
CIP data on file

Vice President and Editorial Director, ECS: *Marcia Horton*
Senior Acquisitions Editor: *Kate Hargett*
Assistant Editor: *Sarah E. Parker*
Editorial Assistant: *Michael Giacobbe*
Vice President and Director of Production and Manufacturing, ESM: *David W. Riccardi*
Executive Managing Editor: *Vince O'Brien*
Assistant Managing Editor: *Camille Trentacoste*
Production Editor: *Lakshmi Balasubramanian*
Director of Creative Services: *Paul Belfanti*
Creative Director: *Carole Anson*
Art Director: *Jayne Conte*
Cover Designer: *Bruce Kenselaar*
Cover Art: *Chad Baker/Artville/Getty Images*
Art Editor: *Greg Dulles*
Manufacturing Manager: *Trudy Pisciotti*
Manufacturing Buyer: *Lisa McDowell*
Marketing Manager: *Pamela Shaffer*
Marketing Assistant: *Barrie Reinhold*

© 2004 Pearson Education, Inc.
Pearson Prentice Hall
Pearson Education, Inc.
Upper Saddle River, NJ 07458

Pearson Prentice Hall® is a trademark of Pearson Education, Inc.

Printed in the United States of America

10 9 8 7 6 5 4 3 2 1

ISBN 0-13-089367-6

Pearson Education Ltd., *London*
Pearson Education Australia Pty. Ltd., *Sydney*
Pearson Education Singapore, Pte. Ltd.
Pearson Education North Asia Ltd., *Hong Kong*
Pearson Education Canada, Inc., *Toronto*
Pearson Educación de Mexico, S.A. de C.V.
Pearson Education—Japan, *Tokyo*
Pearson Education Malaysia, Pte. Ltd.
Pearson Education, Inc., *Upper Saddle River, New Jersey*

This book is dedicated in loving memory to
David ben Yehezkiel of Varsha by David

and to

My parents, A. Govindarajulu (late) and G. Sakuntala,
who gave me the greatest assets of love and education by Chitti.

Table of Contents

CHAPTER 11   More on the Connected Layer   **390**

Preface

ABOUT THE AUTHORS

David Gefen is an Associate Professor of MIS at Drexel University. David was a senior MIS project manager in charge of the design, programming, implementation, and ongoing improvement of a large complex IT before entering academia. Prior to that he was a systems analyst, database administrator, and senior programmer. As a professor, he specialized in teaching database analysis and design, programming languages, and MIS management for the last six years. David won the distinguished *LeBow Excellence in Teaching Award* and the *Drexel University Faculty Teaching Award, Graduate Level*. Professor Gefen received his Ph.D. in Computer Information Systems from Georgia State University in 1997. He has over forty five refereed publications to his name, many of them in the top MIS journals.

Chittibabu Govindarajulu is an Assistant Professor of MIS at Drexel University. He has been teaching Visual Basic since 1996, the year he graduated from University of Mississippi with a Ph.D. in MIS. Professor Govindarajulu has an extensive publication record (over twenty five refereed publications), several of which are in top MIS journals. Before Ph.D. he served as a Deputy Contracts Officer in an Atomic Power Project where he oversaw development of purchase related information systems. Professor Govindarajulu specializes in teaching Windows and Web development courses using ASP, VB.NET, ASP.NET, ADO.NET, and Cold Fusion.

ABOUT THE BOOK

The idea for this book came when we realized how helpful the *hands-on theory application* approach we developed when teaching Visual Basic and Database Analysis and Design was to our students. In this method, theory is introduced within the context of its application and is then relearned through hands on application building whereby students end each class with after building at least one new application that demonstrates the material. The method is very much based on Dr. Gefen's industry experience. This is how Dr. Gefen used to train new programmers in his team. The book itself is based on a series of highly successful courses taught by the authors using this approach at the undergraduate and graduate level at Drexel University.

An advantage of this method is that students are not overloaded with many language and syntax details before they begin applying the concepts. Rather, students learn to apply these concepts as they are taught. This makes learning much easier by letting the students ground the theoretical concepts in an actual application and so getting a good feel for it. VB.NET is a unique and powerful language that is based on the .NET framework. It combines a fully object oriented language with a powerful graphical user interface. Teaching such a language requires detailed attention to both theory and hands-on practice because of the complexity of the theory, especially since students often learn VB.NET as their first programming language. This textbook was written with the recognition that special attention must be given to presenting the material in such a way that while being comprehensive in covering the theory part of the language and the extensive .NET architecture it is based upon, the presentation should still present the material in a manageable easy to understand manner.

Combining these needs, this book presents the successful *hands-on theory application* method combined with *extensive review labs*. These labs guide the student in a detailed manner in building an application that demonstrates the main topics discussed in that chapter. This method teaches the extensive VB.NET theory within the context of hands-on application building so that the student clearly understands the context to tie theory into. We wrote the book based on our experience that theory alone is hard to learn and that hands-on practice alone does not provide a sufficiently deep understanding of how to implement the language. Integrating these two perspectives enable the students see the big picture, the theory, at a high level, while still firmly rooted with their feet on the ground, applying this theory in code.

The book, although being an advanced VB.NET book, starts with a detailed review of the basics. We have discovered that students in advanced courses often require a review of the material they have learned earlier on in their academic endeavor. The comprehensive summary provides a necessary resource for an advanced course by summarizing and extending previously acquired knowledge. At the same time, this summary is also written in such a way that, beyond being a review, the book can serve as the first textbook in a series of VB.NET courses. The book then delves into more advanced topics, including file and directory management, access methods, graphics, and multi-threading, before dealing with the core material of ADO and ASP.

CHAPTER 1

An Essential Introduction

CHAPTER OBJECTIVES

After completing this chapter, students should have an understanding of the basic ideas behind

- Object orientation
- Properties, methods, Events, and classes
- Namespaces
- Event-driven programming
- Rapid application development
- Garbage collection

1.1   AIMS OF CHAPTER

This chapter begins by discussing the underlying object-oriented philosophy of VB.NET, demonstrated with a short example. The concept of Rapid Application Development (RAD) is introduced and explained in the context of a Windows application. Namespaces and a brief look at the .NET Architecture are also introduced.

A short lab exercise is added at the end of the chapter as a refresher. This lab is short because many of the programming concepts will be introduced in later chapters.

1.2   HOW TO USE THIS BOOK

The underlying philosophy of this textbook is to teach VB.NET programming theory within a strongly understood hands-on environment: When theory is introduced, it is tied directly to a programming context. The objective of this approach is that the student should *understand* the programming concepts and how to *implement* them.

As such, the book, although dealing with advanced topics, begins with review chapters. These chapters are a reference source that is written with the explicit intention of providing a lookup summary and the basis for several review classes prior to

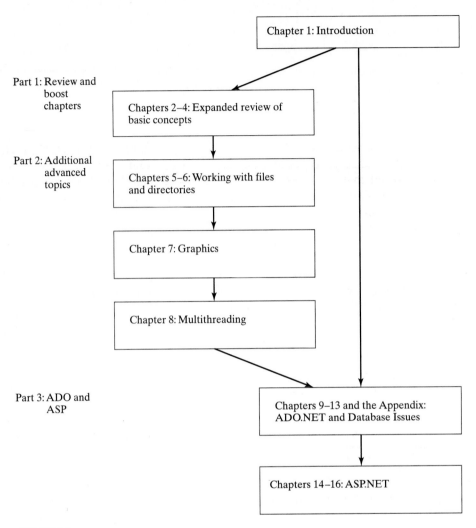

FIGURE 1.1
Diagram of textbook composition.

delving in the advanced topics. These chapters can be assigned as self-review chapters or can constitute an integral part of the course if an extended review is necessary. Having said that, since these chapters look into the review topics in greater depth than is typically discussed in many introduction courses, devoting class time to them might be a good idea.

Accordingly, the textbook essentially has three parts to it (Figure 1.1). Chapters 1 through 4 are review and boost chapters. Their objective is to review the topics that should have been covered in an introductory course to VB.NET, but to do so in a manner that greatly expands on these topics. It is essential that these chapters be reviewed because the remainder of the book assumes that knowledge has been well acquired. We actually recommend going through these chapters carefully and using them to strengthen student knowledge before going on to the next group of chapters. In a graduate-level course that encompasses both an introductory and an advanced VB.NET course, these chapters could replace the introductory textbook. Chapter 1 introduces some of the necessary background philosophy of VB.NET and the .NET Framework in general. Chapters 2, 3, and 4 discuss and exemplify the building blocks of VB.NET. Chapter 2 discusses data types and their application in variables, literals, constants, and Enums. Chapter 3 expands on Chapter 2 to discuss arrays, structures, control statements, and handling errors. With the knowledge that these basic building blocks have been covered, Chapter 4 proceeds to discuss objects and their application in VB.NET. Having said that these chapters cover material that is taught in introductory courses, it should be pointed out that this coverage is much broader than that taught in introductory courses, discussing topics such as building control arrays dynamically and recursive functions. Chapter 5 onward deals with more advanced VB.NET programming topics, such as input-output operations, threading, graphics, and a more detailed look at database and web programming through ADO.NET, and ASP.NET.

Each chapter is made up of two sections: applied theory and then one or more lab exercises. The applied theory section discusses and demonstrates the programming concepts of that chapter. The lab exercises take the student through a guided step-by-step lab in which one or more VB.NET projects are created that demonstrate the principles learned earlier in the applied theory section. Each guided lab section takes approximately between one and two hours. These lab exercises can be assigned as recitation, but should not be skipped. The lab exercises are more than mere regurgitation of the applied theory section. They also introduce new topics and are essential in both reviewing the material and giving the students something tangible with which to absorb the knowledge they acquired in the applied theory section. The labs also provide the students with a sense of accomplishment at the end of each lecture session, something along the lines of "I went in not knowing the material and look, now I can even build a Project that uses it."

1.3   THE UNDERLYING PHILOSOPHY OF OBJECTS

VB.NET is a fully object-oriented language. Object orientation is a programming philosophy in which everything is regarded as an object. A *Project* is an object. A *Form* is an object. A *Button* control is an object, and so on. An object can be thought of in a simplified manner, that will be expanded upon in Chapter 4, as an entity that exists in its own right. An *object* is a real thing. This entity (i.e., the object) encapsulates both data and functionality. The data of an object describe its *state*. These data are set through the *Properties* of the object either in the Properties window or directly through the code. These Properties can also be thought of as characteristics of the object, such as what is written in or on it (the Text property), its color, location, font, and size. Apart from data, the object also has predefined built-in functionality that is handled by *methods*. Methods can be functions or subroutines. We will discuss the difference between the two in Chapter 3. Everything about the object is handled with these Properties and methods. An object can also have the ability to know how to respond to certain things happening to it. For example, a *Button* can know when and how to respond to a click on it. Things that can happen to an object, such as clicking on it or

```
Private Sub Button1_Click _
       (ByVal sender As System.Object, ByVal e As _
       System.EventArgs) _
       Handles Button1.Click
```

FIGURE 1.2
Specifying which object handles which event.

changing its text, and that the object can know how to respond to, through code that has to be specially written, are called *Events*.

An object knows how to respond to an Event when its code explicitly specifies the name of the method that *handles* the Event (such as the command in Figure 1.2 dealing with the Button1 object that connects the Button1_Click method to the Button1.Click Event through the `Handles` keyword). If no method is explicitly connected to an Event, then the object will not respond to that Event. (Technically, it is possible to set Events also with the `addhandler` statement using a delegate. More on that in Chapter 3.)

An object is an instantiation of a class. A class is a definition, a potential or formation without substance, of what an object of that class can be. To make something "real" of a class, an object must be defined as an instantiation of it. For example, a Button control icon in the Toolbox is a class, a noninstantiated definition. The icon is a potential control that may or may not be added to a Form. It does not exist yet, either in the Form or anywhere else. But, when a Button control is placed on a Form by dragging it onto the Form, it creates an object. That object is an instantiation of the `Button` class within the Form. One of the great advantages of this object orientation is that new objects, such as a new Button in a Form, do not need to be created from scratch each time they are used. Rather, new objects can inherit from the class of objects they belong to. When a new Button control is placed on a Form, for example, it inherits the methods and Properties, together with their default values, of the class. This saves considerable time when programming and allows for both standardization and reuse of code. The ability to reuse code and create standardized units of code are a major benefit of object orientation.

All objects inherit either directly from a basic object class called "`System.Object`" or from a class that itself inherits either directly from `System.Object` or from another class that somewhere at the base of the inheritance tree does. This ensures that all the objects in VB.NET essentially behave the same way at their core.

Dragging the icon creates explicit code that is usually hidden. That code defines the Button as an instantiation of the `System.Windows.Forms.Button` class. In the code in Figure 1.4, a new object named `Button1` is defined as a member of the class in the line starting with the `Friend` keyword. (Actually, `Friend` is a modifier, as we will discuss in Chapter 4.) Then a new occurrence of the object is instantiated within the Form with the assignment statement and `New` keyword. This is one of the powerful tools of VB.NET, providing a graphical interface that automatically generates code.

An object, as we just said, has *Properties*, *methods*, and responds to *Events*. The Button, however, will do nothing on its own unless an Event on it occurs. This is true of all other controls, too. (Even the timer, which supposedly wakes up on its own every given interval, really responds to an Event.) That is why VB used to be known as an

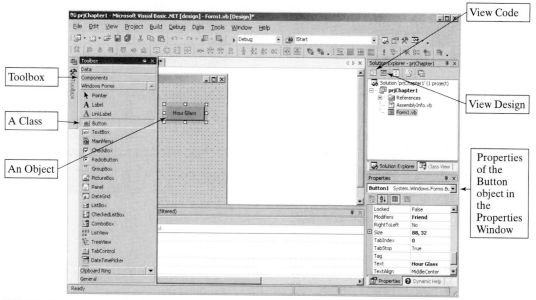

FIGURE 1.3
The IDE showing the Toolbox and other windows.

```
Friend WithEvents Button1 As _
        System.Windows.Forms.Button
        <System.Diagnostics.DebuggerStepThrough()> _
    Private Sub InitializeComponent()
      Me.Button1 = New _
          System.Windows.Forms.Button()
    . . .
```

FIGURE 1.4
The automatically generated code for the button

Event-Driven Language. It still is so, except that VB.NET is now also an object-oriented language. This is still a very convenient way of thinking when building a new Project in VB.NET. When new code is added, it should be added in a method that responds to an appropriate Event on a given object. For example, if a Button's size is to be doubled when it is clicked, then the method that handles this should be connected to the click Event of that specific Button.

It is also sometimes convenient to think of an object as a noun, its methods as verbs that specify what is does, and its Properties as specifying what it is, with included objects as sub-sentences. A Form is a noun. The Form can be hidden, a verb, with the `Hide` method, and its size can set with the `Size` property, as what it is. The Form can also contain a Button, an object within an object. The Button, too, is an object, a noun, which can also be hidden, a verb with an appropriate method `Hide`, and the order in which it is tabbed in the Form, what it is, can be changed through the `TabIndex` property.

Object			
Properties	Methods	Events	Objects within
🖼 TabIndex	≋◆ ToString	⚡ ChangeUICues	◆ Button2
🖼 TabStop	≋◆ Update	⚡ **Click**	◆ Button3
🖼 Tag	≋◆ Hide	⚡ ContextMenuChanged	◆ Button4
🖼 Text		⚡ CursorChanged	◆ Button5
🖼 TextAlign		⚡ DockChanged	◆ Button6
🖼 Top		⚡ DragDrop	◆ Button7
		⚡ DragEnter	

FIGURE 1.5
Contents of an object.

Figure 1.5 shows the contents of an object. Note the special icons that appear next to the Properties, methods, Events, and objects within. These icons appear throughout VB.NET next to the names of Properties, methods, Events, and other objects to graphically identify what each is. As can be seen in the diagram, Properties are identified by an icon of a hand pointing at a page, methods by a flying purple book, Events by a yellow lightning rod, and objects that are contained within the current objects by blue boxes. The bold font of the Event name specifies that this is the default Event of that object. Each one of these objects within has its own Properties and methods and may have Events that it can know how to respond to (*can* know rather than *know*, because only when code explicitly associates a method with an Event does the object know how to respond to it) and other objects within.

The latter category is an important aspect of object orientation. An object can contain other objects (as we just saw when we added a Button to a Form). A Project may contain Forms, and each Form may contain many controls, such as Buttons and labels. See the example in Figure 1.6.

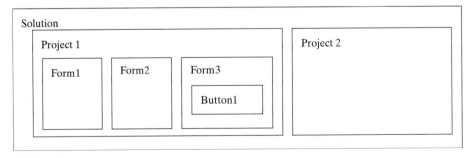

FIGURE 1.6
Solution and sample embedded objects.

1.4   A SHORT EXAMPLE

To demonstrate the topics covered up to now and maintain a good hands-on feeling, we will build a simple Windows application and explain these concepts through it. When we enter the Microsoft Development Environment of Visual Studio.NET, which is where we develop VB.NET applications, the start page appears. It has the more or less standard menu bar that many Windows applications have and its own set of appropriate shortcut icons just below it. The start page also contains links to URL with additional information and Dynamic Help with tutorials.

At this stage, there is only one current display—that of the Start Page, as illustrated in Figure 1.7. As we open more displays, more of these will appear in the tabbed control. This is very convenient because it will allow us later on to go back to any one of the displays we had opened, including the start page. The content of the other windows in the VB.NET development area will change in accordance with which display is currently the active one.

We will open a new Project by clicking the appropriate Button with that name. Doing so will open the New Project window. (See Figure 1.8.) There are many types of applications that VB.NET supports. These are called *templates* in VB jargon. In this chapter, we will focus on Windows applications. This type of application creates a Windows interface. A Windows interface is one where the application looks like a window with controls, such as Buttons, textboxes, labels, and the like. The start page and the new Project windows are both Windows applications. Choose Windows Application on the new Project window, as shown in Figure 1.8. Name the new application prjChapter1.

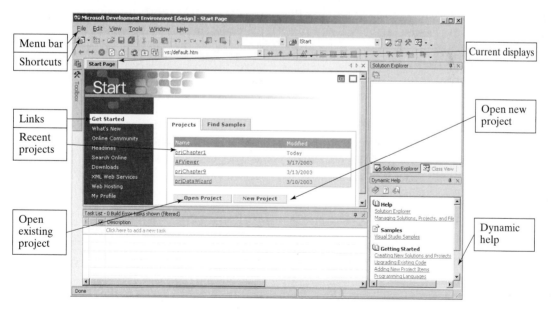

FIGURE 1.7
The Start Page.

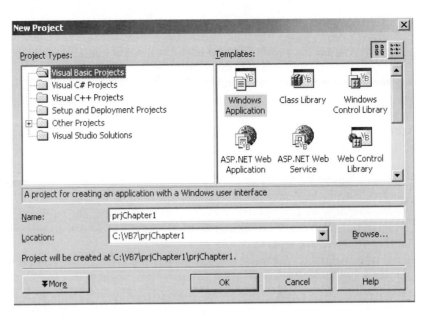

FIGURE 1.8
The New Project window.

Make sure that the left pane says Visual Basic Projects. Then click on the OK Button. The "prj" prefix is a customary prefix of Projects.

This will create a new Project with a Form named Form1. The Form is created with many default values set in its Properties. Its name, "Form1", is one of those default Property values. Other default Properties include the size of the Form, its background color (named `backcolor`), its cursor icon, and many others. All the Properties are explicitly inherited from the `System.Windows.Forms.Form` class by the `Inherits` command at the top of the Form's View Code window. The `Inherits` command also allows the Form to inherit all the methods and Events that have been previously defined in the `Form` class, which makes writing the code for our new Form much easier and faster. This inheritance also makes the Form more standardized with other Forms.

The code can be displayed either by double-clicking on the Form, which will bring you to the code that handles the Load_Form Event, by clicking on the View Code icon , or by choosing the appropriate menu item in the Window menu. The code is as follows:

```
Public Class Form1
    Inherits System.Windows.Forms.Form
```

The name Form1 is not really informative, so we will rename it `frmMyFirstForm` (Figure 1.9). *When renaming the Form make sure NOT to change the .vb suffix.* To rename the Form, click with the right mouse Button on the name of the Form in the Solution Explorer window, and from the dropdown menu select Rename. Do not change the name of the Form in the Properties window. Such a change will require more changes. We will discuss those changes in Chapter 2.

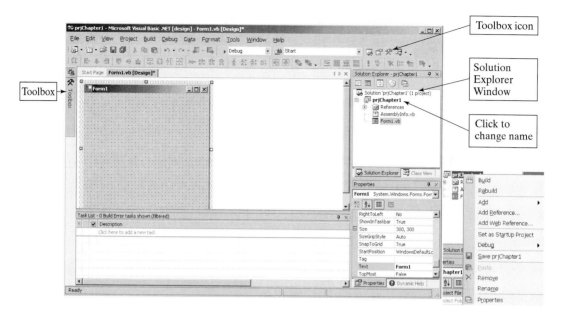

FIGURE 1.9
The Form Development IDE.

Next we will add a Button to the Form. The Button is a control in the toolbox. Click on the toolbox tab. (If the toolbox tab is not visible, it can be added through the View menu. Alternatively, clicking on the toolbox icon, ✖, will also open the toolbox.)[1] When the toolbox opens, double click on the Button to place it on the Form. Then set the Properties of the Button.

- Change `Anchor` to Right. This will cause the Button position in the Form to change automatically as the Form is resized so that the Button is always in the same position compared to the right-hand side of the Form.
- Change the `Cursor` to WaitCursor. This is the icon the cursor will have when it is placed on top of the Button.
- Change the `Text` to "Hour Glass". This is the caption that will appear on the Button.
- Change the `BackColor` to Hot Pink. Do this by clicking on the pulldown arrow and then selecting the appropriate color from the palette.

---

[1]The View menu is where all the windowpanes in the Microsoft Development Environment and tabs within these panes can be made visible. When a pane needs to be added, just click on the appropriate menu item. It is a good idea to always add the Task List. In this window all the typos and other syntax errors will be listed. Clicking on any syntax error item in this windowpane will automatically show the line with the error in it highlighted.

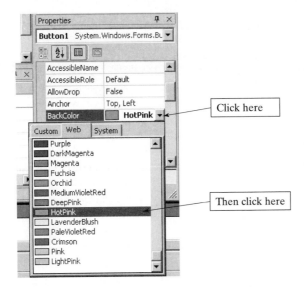

FIGURE 1.10
Back Color Properties Window.

Programming Note: The panels in the IDE, the integrated development environment, tend to get undocked and it is hard to get them docked again properly. If you need to get the panels and windows rearranged back to their original layout, and you will, the way to do it is with the Tools Menu and then the Options submenu. In the window that opens, click on the Reset Window Layout Button.

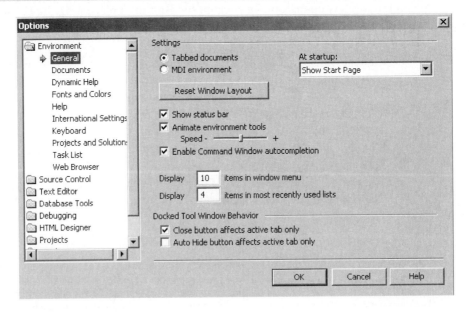

FIGURE 1.11
The Tools Option Window.

1.5   RAPID APPLICATION DESIGN

What we just did is known as Rapid Application Development (RAD). RAD is a software development environment and philosophy that supports developing code very quickly and without need to explicitly write all the code. When the Button was added to the Form it required no more than copying it from the toolbox, placing it, resizing it, and changing its Properties through a straightforward interface. In a non-RAD language, the same operation would require writing the explicit code that would define the Button as an object, instantiate it, and then set its Properties with assignment statement. You can actually see what this would entail in a non-RAD language when you examine the code that VB.NET generates automatically. Figure 1.12 illustrates what RAD looks like.

RAD saves a tremendous amount of time on programmer generated coding, by having that code generated automatically when the programmer uses the graphic interface. For example, in the example we just went through, a Button was dropped onto the Form and its Properties changed through an easy interface. There was no programmer coding involved. That code was automatically generated.

This is what non-RAD would have required to do the same for each control that is added to the Form. Clearly, RAD, as its name specifies, allows rapid interface development. The code syntax is explained in the inset boxes.

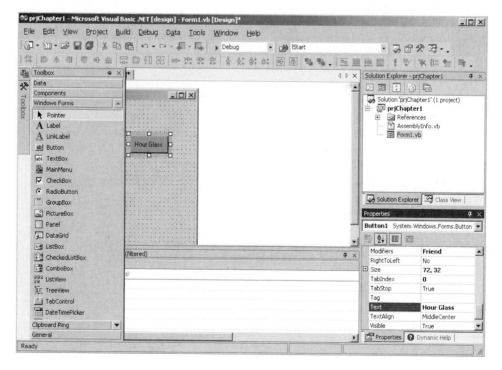

FIGURE 1.12
The Windows Forms Toolbox.

```
Friend WithEvents Button1 As System.Windows.Forms.Button
        <System.Diagnostics.DebuggerStepThrough()> _
    Private Sub InitializeComponent()
```

Create a new Button object as an instantiation of the Button class that resides in the System.Windows.Forms.Button class.

```
Me.Button1 = New System.Windows.Forms.Button()
Me.SuspendLayout()
'
'Button1
'
```

Set the Properties of the Button. Me in the code refers to the current class, in this case the current Form. Me.Button1.Anchor means the value of the Anchor property of Button1 in the current Form. (The value that is set into this property can be a literal value or it can be the value of another property, as in the next three lines, where the of AnchorStyles is set into the Anchor property of Button1.)

```
Me.Button1.Anchor = _
    System.Windows.Forms.AnchorStyles.Right
Me.Button1.BackColor = System.Drawing.Color.HotPink
Me.Button1.Cursor = _
    System.Windows.Forms.Cursors.WaitCursor
```

Alternatively, the value that is set in the property can be a literal (see Chapter 2), as in the line

Me.Button1.Name = "Button1"

or another object, as in

Me.Button1.Size = New System.Drawing.Size(96, 32)

where a new Point object is instantiated and its Properties copied into the Button's Location property.

```
Me.Button1.Location = New System.Drawing.Point(396, 40)
Me.Button1.Name = "Button1"
Me.Button1.Size = New System.Drawing.Size(96, 32)
Me.Button1.TabIndex = 0
Me.Button1.Text = "Hour Glass"
```

1.6   ARRANGING CLASSES INTO NAMESPACES

In the preceding brief code example, there is reference to many preexisting classes, including `System.Drawing` and `System.Windows.Forms`. Having so many classes requires a solid method of organizing, classifying, and managing them. The namespace is such a method. A namespace is like a library of classes. It arranges the classes of objects into a well-defined hierarchy of groups that can retain the uniqueness of each class' name. Thus, for example, all the math functionalities, or to be precise all the classes that make the math functionalities possible, are contained together in a special namespace called `System.Math`. This namespace is contained within a broader namespace called `System`. The `System` also happens to contain the `Drawing` namespace, which handles graphics and the `Form` namespace in which many of the controls reside. And so, the namespace hierarchy indicates that there is a system-wide library, or namespace, which contains system-related classes. Within this broad category, there are sub-categories, also namespaces, that deal with more specific groups of functionality (in this case, drawings, Forms, and math). We will get to know more namespaces as we progress through the book.

A single *assembly* (an assembly is where metadata about the VB solution is stored, discussed in Chapter 2) can and does contain references to many namespaces, some of which contain within them additional namespaces. All assemblies contain the `System` namespace and the `System.Object` class.

Having all these classes grouped together provides two basic advantages: First, arranging all the classes on the same subject together makes for better organization and faster searching for relevant classes. Second, two namespaces can have different classes with the same name without causing any confusion. The latter advantage is important in the context of the namespace created by each new Project. If Project A creates a new class called C and Project B also creates a new class called C, then by virtue of having C appear in two separate namespaces Project A will utilized its C and Project B will utilize its C without a mix up. Thus, by enforcing the placement of classes into namespaces VB.NET makes managing these resources and avoiding conflicts easier.

1.7   WHERE IT ALL FITS IN, AN OVERVIEW OF THE .NET ARCHITECTURE

Namespaces are part of the .NET framework. VB.NET, along with its sister language C# (pronounced C-Sharp), is the flagship programming language and software development environment of Microsoft's .NET Architecture. The .NET architecture has several components: ASP.NET, framework classes, and the common language runtime (CLR). ASP.NET allows the development of Web applications in the same manner as Windows applications. The framework classes are a set of libraries with predefined object classes that handle common functionality, such as math functions and graphics. Having these classes and objects available in predefined libraries makes reusing their code, rather than rewriting it every time, easier, faster, and more standardized. These framework classes are organized into namespaces. The third element, CLR, is an interface between the human readable VB.NET code and the operating system. CLR is a major component of VB.NET allowing it to support the RAD features that VB always supported while at the same time allowing the direct interaction with the operating system that was missing in previous versions of VB.

In the .NET Framework, all applications, regardless of the language they are written in—so long as these are supported by CLR—run in the identical runtime environment created by the CLR. All code run with the CLR is known as *managed code*, meaning that it is code that the CLR knows how to manage. Code from other languages is run in what is known as *unmanaged code*. Unmanaged code does not enjoy all the benefits that running under the .NET framework provides. Managed code can take full advantage of the .NET framework. A key advantage of the CLR is that it allows cross-language integration. That is, objects from different languages can talk to each other. CLR manages this through storing information within each Project in an *assembly* and by handling metadata (data about the application). The assemblies contain information about the objects, such as its name and identity, the files and other assemblies its needs, and all its external references. It is this metadata in information about the code that allows objects, even from different languages, to talk to each other during runtime. Other advantages of managed code are an automated management of memory through the garbage collection thread (more on that in Chapter 8).

The *Garbage Collector* keeps track of when each object was loaded and when it was last used. Objects that are no longer used are discarded to make way for new ones. The catch is that all this is done automatically and in the background as a separate thread without any control of the process being given to the program. Practically, it means that the application program never knows when an object will be de-allocated and hence cannot manage its own memory. The pro is that in most cases programmers do not want or need to get involved with these processes. (Nothing unusual there. Taking out the garbage is nobody's hobby. So, Mr. Nobody, the CLR, is assigned to do it.) It is worth taking a quick look at how this process is completed. The underlying principle of garbage collection is to identify unused objects and de-allocate them. However, at the same time a provision is made for objects that may not be used right now, but that are nonetheless used often. So, for example, a program-specific object that is used only once should be de-allocated as soon as possible, but one such as Sin, the trigonometric function of sine, should remain in memory even if it is not used right now because it is quite likely that it will be used soon. Retaining Sin in memory will save the resources needed to allocate it anew.

CLR manages all this garbage collection in a simple manner. When new objects are allocated with the New keyword, they are allocated memory. When the memory an application is given is used up, the CLR activates the garbage collection. When this process will wake up is unpredictable to the application programs although its parameters can be controlled through the methods in the GC namespace. The garbage collection identifies the objects that are no longer used and de-allocates them. The advantage of working in this manner is that the CLR releases unused memory in chunks. That makes for faster processing. (But note the caveat that CLR only knows about managed code use of an object, if the object is used by unmanaged code, the CLR may still de-allocate the object even if it is still in use. Avoiding this requires "cheating" on VB.NET. Objects can be kept alive, bypassing this process, with the KeepAlive method. This allows objects that are unmanaged by CLR to remain in memory.)

LAB 1.1: LAS-VEGAS 21

Lab Objectives:

This lab is to be a refresher lab. A more detailed walkthrough is provided in Chapter 2. The lab will deal with

1. a quick review of building simple applications with VB.NET,
2. review the Button, Picture, and TextBox controls,
3. using Forms and Modules.

Application Overview

The lab builds a Form that plays the card game 21. When the Form comes up only the Start Button is displayed. When it is clicked, the remaining buttons and textboxes appear. The Place a Bet Button generates three random numbers and places them in the three textboxes. If the sum of the numbers is 21, then a smiling face appears. For those who are impatient, the Cheat Button makes sure you win.

Part 1: Build the Form

Add a new Project and solution, name them **prjChapter1**, making the Project handle a Windows Form. Name the Form **frmLasVegas** (Figure 1.13).

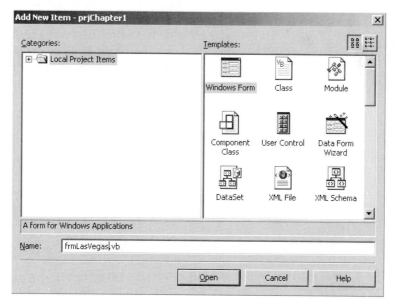

FIGURE 1.13
"The Add New Item Window."

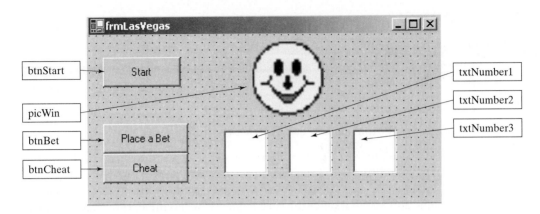

FIGURE 1.14
Las-Vegas 21 E caption.

Add the Buttons, textboxes, and picture as shown in Figure 1.14. You will need to set some of the Properties to make the Form appear as it does in the figure. Set the name of the Start Button to btnStart and its text to Start. We will discuss naming conventions in detail in Chapter 2. Suffice it for now to say that Buttons should start with btn, textboxes with txt, and pictures with pic. Set the name of the Place a Bet Button to btnBet and its text to Place a Bet. Make its Visible property False. This will make it invisible. Set the name of the Cheat Button to btnCheat and its text to Cheat. Set its Visible property also to False.

Add one textbox. Name it txtNumber1, and change its font size to 26 (Figure 1.15). This is done in two stages. First, click on the Font property. This will add a three dots icon, ⋯. Click on it, and in the Font window that will open change the size to 26. Just resizing the textbox will have no effect. Also make the Enabled property of the textbox False. This will mean that a value can be set in it through the code, but not through the interface. With this textbox ready, click on it and then on Edit Copy in the menu or on

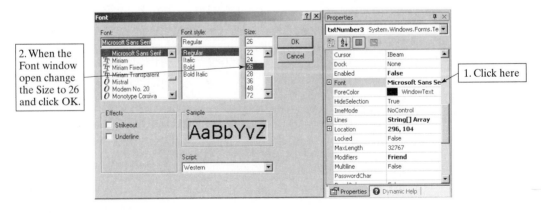

FIGURE 1.15
Setting the font size.

ctrl+C. Click on the Form and then on Edit Paste or ctrl+V. Do it twice to add two textboxes. The new textboxes will have the same Properties as the original one except for the name. Name the two textboxes txtNumber2 and txtNumber3.

Then add a picture control. Name it picWin, and make its `Visible` property False. Click on the `Image` property and when the three dots icon appears click on it. In dialog window that will open, go to the following path:

```
C:\Program Files\Microsoft Visual Studio.NET\Common7\Graphics\Icons\Misc
```

You may need to select a different path if VB.NET was installed on a different default directory than Program Files. Choose Face05. Click Open. Now the icon is placed in the Form, but must be resized. To allow it to be resized change the `SizeMode` property to `StretchImage`. Resize the picture, and place the controls on the Form as shown earlier.

Part 2: Adding the Code

When the Start Button is clicked, the other Buttons and the textboxes become visible. This requires changing their `Visible` property to True. Double-click the Start Button to open the code window with the skeleton code of the method that handles the click Event for btnStart:

```
Private Sub btnStart_Click(ByVal sender As System.Object, _
            ByVal e As System.EventArgs)_
            Handles btnStart.Click
End Sub
```

The code connects this method, a subroutine, to the Click Event on this Button. We will discuss how to attach methods to other Events in Chapter 2. At this stage, add the code that will assign the True value to the `Visible` Properties of the other Buttons and textboxes:

```
Private Sub btnStart_Click(ByVal sender As System.Object, _
            ByVal e As System.EventArgs)_
            Handles btnStart.Click
        txtNumber1.Visible = True
        txtNumber2.Visible = True
        txtNumber3.Visible = True
        picWin.Visible = True
        btnBet.Visible = True
        btnCheat.Visible = True
End Sub
```

Part 3: Adding the Rest of the Code

Placing a bet requires generating three random numbers and placing them in the three textboxes. We will skip forward a bit at this stage and just place the code. We will discuss *casting* (changing values from one data type to another) in Chapter 2 and the `Random` object in Chapter 3. Double-click on the Place a Bet Button and add the code. The `Private` and `End Sub` commands will be generated automatically. The rest of the code creates a new Random type object. These objects generate random numbers. The Random object, named here myRandom, is used to generate three random numbers between 0 and 10. (See Chapter 3 to learn how this is accomplished.) If the integer sum of the values in the Text property of the three textboxes adds up to 21, then the picture is made visible; otherwise the picture is made invisible. The CInt function casts a value into an integer with the code that follows:

```
Private Sub btnBet_Click(ByVal sender As System.Object, _
          ByVal e As System.EventArgs) Handles btnBet.Click

    Dim myRandom As Random = New Random()

    txtNumber1.Text = CInt(myRandom.NextDouble * 10)
    txtNumber2.Text = CInt(myRandom.NextDouble * 10)
    txtNumber3.Text = CInt(myRandom.NextDouble * 10)

    If CInt(txtNumber1.Text) + _
       CInt(txtNumber2.Text) + _
       CInt(txtNumber3.Text) = 21 Then
       picWin.Visible = True
    Else
       picWin.Visible = False
    End If

End Sub
```

Alternatively, rather than apply the NextDouble method, which returns a random double precision number between 0 and 1, the Next method can be used. The Next method returns an integer value within a range that is specified in its parameters. In the line of code that follows, the Next method will return a whole numbers, otherwise known as an integer, between 0 and 10. The underscore preceded by a space signals to VB.NET that the current command will span also to the next line:

```
txtNumber1.Text = myRandom.Next(0, 10)
```

The code in the Cheat Button is for those who have little patience;

```
Private Sub btnCheat_Click(ByVal sender As System.Object, _
          ByVal e As System.EventArgs) Handles btnCheat.Click
    Dim myRandom As Random = New Random()

    txtNumber1.Text = CInt(myRandom.NextDouble * 10)
    txtNumber2.Text = CInt(myRandom.NextDouble * 10)
    txtNumber3.Text = 21 - CInt(txtNumber1.Text) _
                    - CInt(txtNumber2.Text)

    picWin.Visible = True

End Sub
```

SUGGESTED HOME ASSIGNMENTS

Build a new Form with a Button on it. When the Button is clicked once, its background color, the BackColor property, should become red. When it is clicked again, its color should become green. When it is clicked a third time its color should become brown.

```
Button1.BackColor = System.Drawing.Color.
```

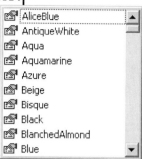

FIGURE 1.16
Color Values.

When it is clicked again the sequence should repeat itself starting with the red background color. The color is set by selecting a color from the System.Drawing.Color namespace as shown in Figure 1.16.

TEST YOURSELF

1. What is meant by an object-oriented language?
2. Discuss how Buttons can be included in a Form if they are objects.
3. What are Properties and methods?
4. Discuss how methods and Events relate to each other.
5. Discuss the relationship between objects and classes.
6. What is inheritance? Why is it needed?
7. How is VB.NET an Event-driven language?
8. What does the icon of a flying purple book represent?
9. What are templates?
10. What is the Anchor property?
11. What is RAD? Why is it useful?
12. What is the Me keyword in the code **Me**.Button1.Name = "Button1"?
13. How can Properties be set?
14. Discuss the concept of namespace.
15. What is System.Math?
16. Discuss the advantages of namespaces.
17. What is CLR?
18. What is managed code?
19. Discuss one problem with running unmanaged code in the .NET framework.
20. What is garbage collection?

Review of Variables, Constants, Data Types, and More

CHAPTER OBJECTIVES

After completing this chapter, students should Understand and be able to use

- Variables, constants, literals, and data types
- Data type conversion
- Numeric data manipulation
- Strings
- The `StringBuilder`
- The Date data type

> **Teaching Note:** This chapter can be taught either as a review chapter (one lesson) or as an integral part of the course, (in which case, together with the class exercises, it may account for more than one lesson). We recommend that it be taught and not skipped even in an advanced course, because the material it covers is handled in much greater detail than in introductory textbooks.

2.1   AIMS OF CHAPTER 2

Beginning with this chapter, the objective for this part of the book is to review what we expect students to know from an introductory course in VB.NET, on the one hand, and to extend that knowledge extensively so that students will have an appropriate advanced knowledge base, on the other. This should enable students who have not taken an introductory course in VB, but have some basic knowledge of it, to use the book.

    The chapter reviews some of the basic code-building blocks of VB.NET: variables, constants, data types, and literals. Arrays will be discussed in the next chapter, along with more advanced data structures that are typically not taught in introductory courses.

In keeping with the style of the book, this chapter's review will include explained example code that will be examined again in the hands-on part at the end of the chapter in which sample applications applying these issues will be built in guided line-by-line examples. The sample applications can be assigned as independent homework review assignments or as class recitation.

We recommend that even students who are familiar with VB.NET review this chapter just to make sure that they grasp the basic material we expect them to know.

2.2   VARIABLES, CONSTANTS, LITERALS, AND DATA TYPES

Variables are memory areas in which values can be stored, retrieved, and manipulated. *Constants* are the same as variables except that the value of a constant is set when it is declared, or dimensioned in VB terminology, and cannot be changed thereafter. A good programming habit is to use constants for values that will not be changed throughout the program, such as the value of π. Although a variable would do just as well in this case, keeping the value of π in a constant both increases the readability of the code and avoids possible glitches (bugs) when the value is changed inadvertently. Indeed, the value of π is available in the `System.Math` class as a constant named `PI`.

2.2.1   Naming Conventions and Data Types

Variables and constants come in many data types. These data types represent the kind of data that the variable or constant can hold, such as dates and numbers. Table 2.1 contains the main data types in VB.NET. In previous versions of VB, it was customary that the name of a variable or of a constant began with a lowercase three- or four-letter prefix that described the data type of the variable or constant. This is known as *Hungarian Notation*. Thus, a variable named `intCalc` would have been an integer type variable because the "int" at its beginning meant that it was customarily an Integer. The current documentation of VB.NET is ambivalent about continuing this practice, as were the examples in the documentations of previous versions of VB. Currently, there is no agreement as to whether this should remain the accepted practice in VB.NET, but we highly recommend it. Naming variables and constants, and this goes for controls and other objects too, with a prefix that describes their data type avoids misunderstandings and increases the readability of the code. As will be seen in the lab at the end of this chapter, adhering to the prefix rules makes applications more readable and makes adding control-related subroutines to forms much easier. (Some of the more common accepted prefixes are shown in the Table 2.1. It should be noted that VB does not enforce these agreed-upon standards.)

Some points need to be pointed out about Table 2.1. The `Integer` data type in versions of VB prior to VB.NET was equivalent to what is now called the `Short` data type. The `Long` data type prior to VB.NET was equivalent to what is now called the `Integer` data type. Beware of these changes when looking at code written with prior versions of VB. Dates, and by extension also time, are stored differently in VB.NET than in previous versions of VB. Dates are stored as the number of 100-nanosecond intervals, known

TABLE 2.1 Main Data Types in VB.NET

Data Type	Meaning	Suggested Standard Prefix	Memory Allocation	Default Initial Value
Boolean	Contains a True or a False value.	bool	2 bytes	False
Byte	Integer value between 0 and 255.	byt or byte	1 byte	0
Char	A single Unicode character represented as a value between 0 and 65535.	char	2 bytes	0
Date	Date and time from 0:00:00 January 1, 0001 through 11:59:59 PM December 31, 9999.	dat or date	8 bytes	1/1/0001 12:00:00 A.M.
Decimal	Contains a number with up to 29 digits. The value ranges from $79*10^{27}$ to $-79*10^{27}$ when no decimals are used. Can handle up to 28 digits right of the decimal point, but each decimal "uses up" one of the 29 digits.	dec	16 bytes	0
Double	A double-precision floating-point number between $4.94065645841246544E-324$ and $1.79769313486231570E+308$ for positive values, and between $-1.79769313486231570E+308$ and $-4.94065645841246544E-324$ for negative values.	dbl	8 bytes	0
Integer	An integer value (i.e., a whole number with no fraction) between $-2,147,483,648$ and $2,147,483,647$.	int	4 bytes	0
Long	An integer value between $-9,223,372,036,854,775,808$ and $9,223,372,036,854,775,807$.	lng	8 bytes	0
Object	An instantiation of an object (more on this later in the book).	obj		The value **Nothing**[2]
Short	An integer value between $-32,768$ and $32,767$.	srt	2 bytes	0
Single	A single-precision floating-point number between $1.401298E-45$ and $3.4028235E+38$ for positive values and between $-3.4028235E+38$ and $-1.401298E-45$ for negative values.	sng	4 bytes	0
String	An instantiation of a String object from the System.String class. Contains text or any other Unicode characters up to 2^{31} characters long. That is enough to hold approximately 2000 copies of this book.	str	The memory allocation of this data type changes dynamically.	Empty

[2]"Nothing" is a keyword in VB.NET. It is a value that can be assigned to an object. This value specifies that the object contains nothing.

as *ticks*, that have elapsed since midnight 1/1/0001 in the Gregorian calendar—rather odd when one considers that the Gregorian calendar did not exist prior to 10/15/1582.

2.2.2   Defining Variables and Constants

Variables and constants are identified by their name. There are very few limitations on variable and constant names: The name must be at most 255 characters long and must contain no spaces. Case is immaterial, and so the variable name strMyVariable and the variable name strMYVARIABLE are one and the same. By default, variables and constants must be defined prior to any reference to them. This default can be changed by writing the following statement in the first line of code:

```
Option Explicit Off
```

But doing so is highly unadvised. Allowing the default, **Option Explicit On**, can catch many typos and thus glitches in the code. Variables are *dimensioned* (declared) with the Dim or the Static statements; constants with the Const statement. More than one variable or constant can be defined with the same statement, although that may decrease the readability of the code. As a rule, we recommend that multiple variables be declared with the same statement only when they are logically related to each other. In that case, declaring them together would indicate to the reader that they have something in common.

Constants must be assigned a value when they are defined. The Dim and the Static statements can also assign an initial value to the variable, but only when one variable is being defined with that statement. The simplified syntax of these commands (simplified because variables and constants are defined with them) is as follows:

```
[Public | Private] Dim <variable-names> As <data-type> [= <initial-value>]
[Public | Private] Static <variable-names> As <data-type> [= <initial-value>]
[Public | Private] Const <constant-names> As <data-type> = <initial-value>
```

Since this is the first time we are introducing code syntax, let's take a closer look at the syntax we will use to introduce code throughout the book. In the foregoing lines, what appears within square brackets, [], is optional code. Parentheses, (), when included in the syntax, are part of the code. The horizontal line, |, means one of the list. The words enclosed within the greater-than/smaller-than signs are programmer code, such as variable names. Thus, in the preceding syntax, writing Public or Private is optional, but only one of the two keywords can be written. On the other hand, the keyword As must be written as is, while it is up to the programmer to decide what variable names to assign. The <initial-value> can be either a typed value, known as a literal, or the name of a variable or constant. The equals sign, =, is an assignment statement that is embedded within the other statements. The simplified syntax of the assignment statement alone is

```
<receiving-variable-names> = [<literal> | <variable> | <result of an operation>]
```

Accordingly, the following code will define two variables, I and J, as integer-type variables with the default initial value of 0 and strName as a string type variable with an initial value containing the literal string "David":

```
Dim I, J As Integer
Dim strName As String = "David"
```

Note the color coding that VB applies. Code in blue is reserved for keywords, such as Dim. Code in black is programmer-written code. Additionally, VB uses green to mark comments. (These are nonexecutables lines of code that are added solely for the benefit of increasing the readability of the code.) Comments, also known as remarks, are delineated with a single quote, '. Comments can also be specified with the keyword Rem at the beginning of the line. This can be done for the sake of compatibility with previous versions of VB, but it is much less readable.

Variables are recognized only after the Dim command in which they are declared. For that reason, it is advisable to place the Dim commands at the beginning of the subroutine or function. It also makes for better readability.

Programming Note: Although it is customary to name variables with the three-letter prefix of their data type, some shorthand coding has taken hold. Thus, it is common that I, J, K, x, and y, as well as several other letters are integer-type variables. The variables named x and y are typically integer coordinates in VB.NET.

Programming Note: Statements in VB.NET are typically line oriented. That is to say that each statement is on one line only. Occasionally, it contributes to the readability of the code if a very long statement is allowed to span more than one line. This avoids the need to scroll to the right when reading the code and also allows the statement to be broken down into meaningful segments. Statements span more than one line of code in VB when the current line ends with a space followed by an underscore, as in the following example:

```
txtOutput.Text = txtOutput.Text & _
txtInput.Text.Substring(0, CInt(txtLength.Text))
```

VB also allows more than one statement on one line of code by the insertion of a colon between the statements, as in the following example, where a timer is started and its interval set on the same line:

```
tmrStrings.Interval = 200 : tmrStrings.Start()
```

As in English, sometimes statements need to be grouped together to increase readability. (In English, we do this with a semicolon.) Except for special cases, grouping statements onto one line of code is not recommended.

The optional Public and Private keywords specify whether the variable or constant will have public access or will be recognized only within the section of code within which it is declared, respectively. There are actually more options besides these (more information on this topic can be found in the next chapters dealing with object orientation). The Public keyword can be applied only at the module, namespace, or file level; it cannot be used in a subroutine or function because that would violate the principles of object orientation. The Private keyword means that the variable or constant is recognized only within the block in which it is defined and in the nested blocks of that block. This is the de-facto default. In effect, Private variables are local to the block—module, subroutine, function, or even If block—within which they are declared. When the keyword Private is used, the Dim keyword may be omitted. In a Module, but not in a Form, a variable, and for that matter subroutines and functions, can be defined as Public. A Public variable is recognized throughout the project; that is to say, its *scope* is the entire project. The scope of a Private variable, on the other hand, is limited to the block it is declared in and all the blocks within it only. The same applies to Private subroutines and functions.

The Dim and the Static keywords both define variables, but with an important difference: A variable defined with the Dim keyword "ceases to exist" once it is out of scope (i.e., once the block of code it is defined within is no longer active), while a variable defined with the Static keyword continues to exist and hold its value until the next time the block it is defined in is active. What this means in practical terms is that the Static variable will retain its value from one execution of the section of code it is defined in to the next. Both Dim and Static variables may be assigned a starting value. The Dim command is also used to declare other object types.

Programming Note: Variables and constants cannot be named with VB.NET reserved words, such as End and Exit. VB.NET does allow a way around this limitation, as shown in the code that follows, where a variable named [end] is dimensioned and used. We strongly discourage this practice. In the following example, such a variable is dimensioned and then displayed in the Output window with the Console.Writeline command:

```
Dim [end] As String = "AAA"
Console.WriteLine([end])
```

Programming Note: If the Output window does not appear on the work area, add it by pulling down the View menu and selecting Other Windows. Then, from the submenu, select Output. Alternatively, simply type the keys Ctrl+Alt+O.

Programming Note: As in previous versions of VB, the data type of a variable can also be defined with an identifier. Thus,

```
Dim I%
```

will define an integer type variable. We strongly discourage that practice because it reduces the readability of the code.

2.2.3 Scope of Name Recognition

Once a variable is defined as `Private`, which is the default, it is recognized only within the code of the block that it was declared within. Thus, in the following code, the variables `I` and `K` will be recognized in all seven lines, but `J` will be recognized only within the `If` block, so the assignment statement J = 9 will fail because `J` is being referenced outside of its name recognition scope:

```
Dim I, K As Integer
I = 2
If I = 2 Then
    Dim J As Integer = 4
    I = 4
End If
J = 9
```

> **Programming Note:** Previous versions of VB worked differently. To begin with, variable `I` would have been a variant, a data type that no longer exists, and variable `J` would have been recognized throughout also beyond the If Block. And, the variable `J` would have been recognized even before the `Dim` statement it is declared with so long as it was referenced within the same subroutine, function, or module.

Variable names should be unique within a name recognition scope. Thus, the following code will return the error "`Variable 'I' hides a variable in an enclosing block`" in the second `Dim` statement because the variable `I` is already defined, even though the second definition is within a separate block:

```
Dim I As Integer = 2
If I = 2 Then
    Dim I As Integer = 4
End If
```

The reason for this error message is that, once a variable is defined, it is recognized within all the blocks that are contained in the block where is it defined. This applies also to the `If` block, and so the variable `I` has in effect been defined twice. The exception to this rule is when a variable is defined in an object or in a subroutine or function (i.e., within a larger object, such as a form). In the next example, the class Form1 defines two variables `I` and `J` and assigns them the starting values of 99 and 199, respectively. These variables are recognized with the subroutine Button1_Click because it is within the class of Form1. However, being a subroutine, Button1_Click can define a new variable `I`, which will be unrelated to the variable `I` that was defined in Form1. As a result, the output window will show 100 in one line and 199 in the next. In fact, the variable `I` that was defined in Form1 cannot be accessed any more in the Button1_Click subroutine, once variable `I` has been defined there, too—unless variable I in Form1 is defined as *Shared* (more on this in the next chapters dealing with object orientation) or is qualified with the prefix **Me** to specify that it is the `I` variable in the form class, as in the following code:

```
Public Class Form1

    Dim I As Integer = 99
    Dim J As Integer = 199

    Private Sub Button1_Click _
                ByVal sender As System.Object, _
                ByVal e As System.EventArgs) _
                Handles Button1.Click
        Dim I As Integer = 100
        Console.WriteLine(I)
        Console.WriteLine(J)
    End Sub
    ' This will reference the I variable in the Form Declarations
    Me.I = 10
End Class
```

2.2.4   Literals

Literals are typed values placed in the code. Without saying so, we have already seen a bit of these in the code that was introduced earlier in the chapter when we assigned an initial value to a variable. For example, the following statements will assign the literal 3 as an integer, the literal 4 as a string, and the literal 1/1/2002 as a date:

```
Dim intThree As Integer
Dim strFour As String
Dim datOne As Date
intThree = 3I ' The 'I' here means a literal of Integer type.
              ' Typically, such literal type indicators are omitted.
strFour = "4"
datOne = #1/1/2002#
```

As can be seen in the preceding code, the addition of a suffix "I" makes the literal an integer, while surrounding the value with double quotes makes it a string and with pound signs a date. Table 2.2 summarizes these character-assigned literals.

2.3   CASTING AMONG DATA TYPES

When data are assigned from one data type to another, either by assigning values from a variable or constant to another variable or constant, or when a literal is assigned to a constant or variable, it is possible that the data may not be convertible or that data may be lost in the process. Data may not be convertible, for example, when a nonnumeric text (such as the literal "yes") is assigned to one of the numeric data types, because the literal "yes" is not a numeric value. Data may be lost when the value is too big or too small for the range of values that the receiving variable or constant can hold, such as assigning the literal 40000 to a variable that is defined as a Short data type. By default, VB.NET does not check for such possible problems. This default is set with the statement

```
Option Strict Off
```

TABLE 2.2 Character-Assigned Literals

Literal Data Type	Character Assigned to Identify the Data Type of the Literal	Example
Byte	None	`Dim bytA As Byte = 123`
Char	Value enclosed with double quotes with a C suffix	`Dim charA As Char = "Q"c`
Date	Date enclosed within pound signs ##	`Dim datA As date = #12/2/2099#`
Decimal	A suffix of D	`Dim decA As Decimal = 12.34D`
Double	By default, any number with a decimal point will be a double. A number can be forced to be stored as an integer with a suffix of # or R	`Dim dblA As double = 12.34R` or `Dim dblA As double = 12.34` or `Dim dblA As double = 12.34#`
Integer	By default, any integer number will be an integer. A number can be forced to be stored as an integer with a suffix of I	`Dim intA As Integer = 12I` or `Dim intA As Integer = 12I`
Long	A suffix of L	`Dim lngA As Long = 123L`
Short	A suffix of S	`Dim srtA As Short = 12S`
Single	A suffix of F	`Dim sngA As Single = 12.34F`
String	Value enclosed within double quotes	`Dim strA As String = "David"`

Option Strict applies even when the preceding statement is not explicitly added to the code. Setting the option to Off will disable the automatic check that data may be lost. Turning the option off will result in disabling the conversion checks during typing and compilation. Conversion errors during runtime will thus result in a runtime error. With the option turned On, conversion checks are performed as the code is typed.

Needless to say, many conversions from one data type to another can always go through without a problem and without causing any data to be lost. This will happen, for example, when Integer data are assigned to a variable that is defined as a Double. Table 2.3 summarizes the conversions that are automatically accepted by VB.NET even when Option Strict is on. These are called *widening conversions*. As a rule, any numeric data type may be *cast* to another data type as long as the receiving data type has a larger range of values.

In all other assignment statements, the data must be converted explicitly if Option Strict is on. This is called *casting* in VB terminology. Casting is done through a set of functions whose name is composed of the letter "C" followed by the prefix name of the receiving data-type name, as shown in the Table 2.4. Of course, not every casting can work. Casting works only when the literal, expression, variable, or constant being cast contains a value that can be represented in the data type of the receiving variable. Thus, casting a nonnumeric value such as the literal string "abc" to a numeric data type such as Integer will not work. But casting the literal string "123" to an Integer will work, because the literal contains a numeric value even if it is a string.

TABLE 2.3 Conversions Automatically Accepted by VB.NET

Data Type	May Be Converted To
Byte	String and any numeric data type: Short, Integer, Long, Single, Double, and Decimal
Short	String, Integer, Long, Single, Double, and Decimal
Integer	String, Long, Single, Double, and Decimal
Long	String, Single, Double, and Decimal
Single	String, Double, and Decimal
Date	String

TABLE 2.4 Casting Functions

Casting Function	Objective
CBool	Casts a numeric value as False if it is 0 and True otherwise
CByte	Casts a numeric value to a byte *rounding* the value
CInt	Casts a numeric value to an integer *rounding* the value
CLng	Casts a numeric value to a long integer *rounding* the value
CSng	Casts a numeric value to a single
CDate	Casts a string that contains a valid date into a date type
CDbl	Casts a numeric value to a double
CDec	Casts a numeric value to a decimal
CStr	Casts any value to a string
CChar	Casts the first character of any string value to a character

In the following example, two literals are cast to a Boolean date-typed variable with the CBool function:

```
Dim bolExample As Boolean
bolExample = CBool(23)
bolExample = CBool("1")
```

Both conversions are valid because CBool casts any numeric value, whether the value is contained in a numeric data type or in a string. Interestingly, the result of this casting will be a Boolean value of True for any value except 0.

A related casting function is ToString. This function, which is a method of every data type class and of many objects, casts any value to a string:

```
Dim strExample As String, intExample As Integer
intExample = 99
strExample = intExample.ToString()
```

2.4   WORKING WITH NUMERIC DATA TYPES

Numeric variables handle the standard arithmetic operators: addition, subtraction, multiplication, exponentiation, and two kinds of division. In the following example, 200 is added to the variable I, which is then set to -100, another 100 is subtracted from it, the result is multiplied by 2, brought to the third power, divided by 4.5, and then integer-divided by 3:

```
Dim I As Double
I = I + 200 ' result is I = 200
I = - 100   ' result is I = -100
I = I - 100 ' result is I = 100
I = I * 2   ' result is I = 200
I = I ^ 3   ' result is I = 8000000
I = I / 4.5 ' result is I = 1777777.7777777778
I = I \ 3   ' result is I = 592592.0
```

Integer-divide is a divide that does not retain the remainder and, unlike a regular divide, can result in a zero-division exception.

The integer-divide operator is *not* equivalent to taking the integer result of a division, because of the rounding that cInt does. Also, note that integer-divide can result in a divide-by-zero exception, while division by zero with the division operator, /, will result in a value of infinity, #INF. The arithmetic operators are shown in Table 2.5.

VB.NET also adopted the accepted shorthand operators of C++ to denote doing an operator on the receiving variable as follows:

```
I += 200 ' result is the same as I = I + 200
I -= 200 ' result is the same as I = I - 200
I *= 200 ' result is the same as I = I * 200
I /= 200 ' result is the same as I = I / 200
I \= 200 ' result is the same as I = I \ 200
I *= 200 ' result is the same as I = I * 200
```

TABLE 2.5   Arithmetic Operators in VB

Operator	Meaning
+	Addition
−	1. Subtraction 2. Marking a number as negative
/	Division as a double data type
\	Integer-division
*	Multiplication
^	Exponentiation

Accordingly, the next example defines a new variable named dblCalc, which, in accordance with its name prefix is defined as a double data type. This variable is assigned an initial value of 10, is then doubled with a multiplication operator, and is doubled-again with a shortcut multiplication. Here is the code:

```
Dim dblCalc As Double = 10
dblCalc = dblCalc * 2
dblCalc *= 2
```

VB.NET also provides a Math namespace that contains many shared mathematical functions and constants. Being instantiations of *shared classes*, these functions and constants do not need to explicitly be included in the VB solution or explicitly instantiated. (Objects in Shared classes, as will be discussed in later chapters, are accessible without being explicitly included in the VB solution.) This class also includes Math.PI and Math.E, which are constants with a double data type value of π and of the base of the natural logarithm, respectively. And so, anywhere in a VB solution, a reference to Math.PI, for example, will be recognized. The Math class also contains a host of very useful functions. Some of these are summarized in Table 2.6.

In the next example, the variable dblCalc, which is defined as a Double data type, is first assigned the trigonometric value of the sine of the angle of two radians, which is provided as a parameter. (All the trigonometric operations in VB are in radians and measure angles counterclockwise. There are 2π radians in the circumference of a circle.) Next, the cosine value of two radians is assigned and then the tangent of two radians. Parallel to these three functions, VB.NET has the Math.Asin, Math.Acos, and Math.Atan that returns the angles in radians that will return the values returned by

TABLE 2.6   Some Useful Functions in the Math Class

Function	Description
Abs	Returns the absolute value of a number to the appropriate numeric data type
Ceiling	Rounds upward a Double data-type number to the smallest integer value that is equal to or larger than the parameter

Round	Rounds a number either to the closest integer or to the closest value with the given number of significant digits:
	`dblCalc = Math.Round(2.15) ' returns 2`
	`dblCalc = Math.Round(2.12345, 2) ' returns 2.12`

Log	Returns the natural logarithm of a number
Log10	Returns the base 10 logarithm of a number
Exp	Returns the exponent of a number, which is Math.E to the power of the parameter
Sqrt	Returns the square root of a number
Max	Returns the larger of two numbers to the appropriate numeric data type
Min	Returns the smaller of two numbers to the appropriate numeric data type

`Math.Sin`, `Math.Cos`, and `Math.Tan`. Simply put, if the value returned by `Math.Sin` (X) is Y, then `Math.Asin` (Y) is X. VB.Net also supports the hyperbolic trigonometric functions `Math.Sinh`, `Math.Cosh`, and `Math.Tanh`. Here is the code:

```
Dim dblCalc As Double
dblCalc = Math.Sin(2)
dblCalc = Math.Cos(2)
dblCalc = Math.Tan(2)
```

Programming Note: The `Min`, `Max`, and Abs are good examples of *polymorphism*, the ability of an object to respond differently to different types of input and yet retain the same meaning of the function. For example, `Abs` will return a value depending on the data type of the receiving variable or constant. The *IntelliSense* interface handles the situation as follows:

```
dblCalc = Math.Abs(2)
dblCalc = ▲ 1 of 7 ▼  Abs (value As System.SByte) As System.SByte
         value: A number in the range System.SByte.MinValue &lt; value (&lt;=) System.SByte.MaxValue.
```

2.5   WORKING WITH STRINGS

The `String` data type is designed to store and manipulate text, or to be precise Unicode characters. In Unicode, each character is represented by a number. That number is a unique identifier of that character regardless of the platform, program, or programming language. A `String` typed variable or constant can hold approximately 2^{31} characters, which is slightly above 2 billion characters. By definition, these `String` variables are variable-length, meaning that the length of the data held in a `String` typed variable will be the length of the data it contains. In other words, if a literal of 100 characters is assigned to a `String` typed variable, then that will be the length of the data the `String` typed variable will hold. If a literal of 1000 characters is then assigned to that same `String` typed variable, then the variable will hold a string that is 1000 characters long. Data will never be truncated to a given size when assigned to a `String` type data variable. That is because there is no fixed-length string data type in VB.NET.

Programming Note: In previous versions of VB, `String` typed variables could be assigned a fixed length so that the variable or constant would truncate down to size data that were too long or would pad with blanks data that were too short. That option is not included in VB.NET.

Values are assigned to a string data-typed variable the same way that they are assigned to any other variable: either as an initial value during dimensioning or with an assignment statement. Values can also be manipulated with the concatenation operator, &, to add to the end of a string. This is demonstrated in the next two commands, which assign the famous words from Lewis Carroll:

```
Dim strExample As String = "The Sun was shining on the sea, "
strExample &= "shining with all his might"
```

The operator combination &= means, as elsewhere in VB.NET, to perform the operator that precedes the = on the variable or object on the left. In this case, &= means concatenate (add a string to the end) the literal "shining with all his might" to the end of the variable strExample.

> **Programming Note:** In previous versions of VB, concatenation would also work with the + operator. This operator still works with VB.NET but is not recommended, because the + operator takes on a different meaning if the data are numeric. Therefore, using it to specify concatenation can cause confusion when reading the code.

Apart from concatenation, strings can be manipulated with a set of additional functions. (Although VB.NET still supports the previous VB6 string functions, this section will focus exclusively on the VB.NET methods.) Because these string operations are methods of the String class, they are written and activated as methods of an object rather than as functions usually are.

The Chars method returns the character that is in a given position within a string, the first character being at index 0:

```
Dim strExample As String = "The Sun was shining on the sea, "
Dim strResult As String
strResult = strExample.Chars(0) ' strResult will contain 'T'
strResult = strExample.Chars(5) ' strResult will contain 'U'
```

The Concat method, as its name implies, returns a string that is the concatenation of a set of parameter strings. Although syntactically correct, adding the Concat method to a string data type variable is meaningless. As the following code shows, this method is a method of the String class:

```
Dim strExample As String
strExample = String.Concat("abc", "def") 'this returns "abcdef"
strExample = String.Concat("a", "b", "c") ' this returns "abc"
```

The Concat method, however, will do nothing if its returned value is not assigned to a variable, as in the case of the following two commands:

```
strExample.Concat("abc")  ' this does nothing
strExample.Concat("abc", "def") ' this too does nothing
```

The Compare method is another method of the String class:

```
If String.Compare("aaaa", "abcd") < 0 Then ' True
If String.Compare("bbbb", "abcd") > 0 Then ' True
If String.Compare("aaaa", "aaaa") = 0 Then ' True
If String.Compare("ABC", "abc", True) = 0 Then ' True
```

This method compares two strings and returns an integer value that indicates whether the first string is larger, smaller, or equal to the second string. The method returns an integer value greater than zero, if the first string is smaller; a value that is smaller than zero, if the first string is bigger; and zero, if the two strings are equal. Optionally, the method can be overloaded with another parameter that specifies whether the comparison should ignore the case of the strings when comparing them. By default, lowercase characters are smaller than uppercase characters.

The documentation of VB.NET does not specify what exact value the Compare method returns, but as the following code shows, the method returns the values $-1, 1,$ and 0:

```
Console.WriteLine(String.Compare("Abc", "ABC"))
Console.WriteLine(String.Compare("ABc", "abc"))
Console.WriteLine(String.Compare("ABC", "abc", True))
```

Programming Note: The Console.WriteLine command is a convenient debugging tool. It writes to the output window, which can be accessed during debugging.

Some of the methods are rather superfluous, such as the Copy method, which just makes a copy of an existing string and behaves the same as a simple assignment statement:

```
Dim strExample As String = "The Sun was shining on the sea, "
Dim strResult As String
strResult = String.Copy(strExample)
```

Other methods are more useful, such as CopyTo, which breaks down a specified part of a string into an array of characters. This method receives four parameters: (1) the index of the first character (starting at position 0) from where to copy the characters; (2) the destination array of Characters, (3) from which entry in the character array to start filling in the results of the CopyTo; and (4) how many characters to copy. (More on arrays in the next chapter.) The syntax of this method is somewhat complex and so deserves a detailed look:

```
<string-variable> .CopyTo (<starting character number in the
                        string-variable> ,
                        <character-type array> ,
                        <starting entry in the character-type array> ,
                        <number of characters to copy> )
                {returns a string}
```

In the next example, eight characters from the third character onward in strExample will be copied into entries 2 and onward in chrExample:

```
Dim strExample As String = "0123456789abcde"
Dim chrExample(10) As Char
strExample.CopyTo(3, chrExample, 2, 8)
```

As a result of this statement, entries 0, 1, and 10 in chrExample will contain the value Nothing, while entries 2 through 9 will contain the values "3" through "a", respectively.

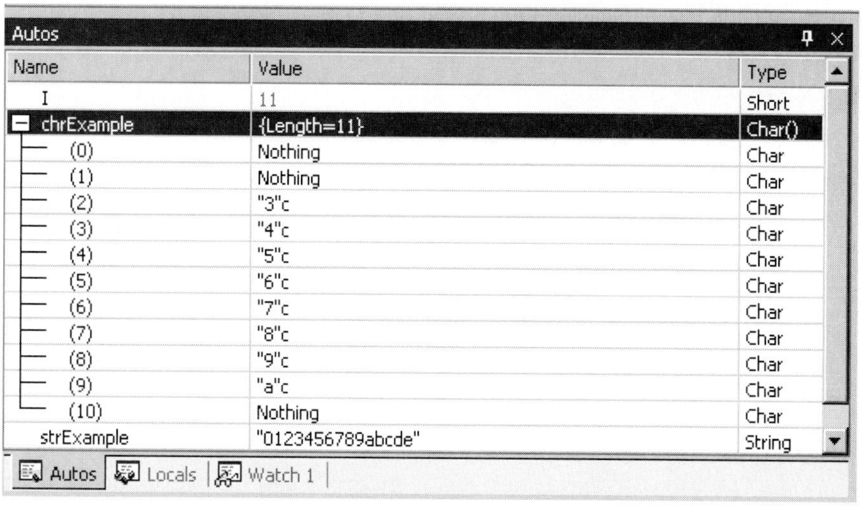

Autos			⏚ ×
Name	Value		Type
I	11		Short
⊟ chrExample	{Length=11}		Char()
├── (0)	Nothing		Char
├── (1)	Nothing		Char
├── (2)	"3"c		Char
├── (3)	"4"c		Char
├── (4)	"5"c		Char
├── (5)	"6"c		Char
├── (6)	"7"c		Char
├── (7)	"8"c		Char
├── (8)	"9"c		Char
├── (9)	"a"c		Char
└── (10)	Nothing		Char
strExample	"0123456789abcde"		String

🔍 Autos | 📋 Locals | 📋 Watch 1

FIGURE 2.1
Autos window.

As they change, these values can be conveniently viewed in the Autos window (Figure 2.1), which appears at the bottom of the screen during debugging.

The String class also contains a set of methods that edit the string data. All these methods, as well as the properties, equally apply to string literals. Among these are the EndsWith function that returns a True or False value depending on whether the last character in the string is the one specified as a parameter. Its counterpart, StartsWith, does the same for the first characters. The resulting code is

```
Dim strExample As String = "0123456789abcde"
Console.WriteLine(strExample.EndsWith("1"))     ' writes "False"
Console.WriteLine(strExample.EndsWith("e"))     ' writes "True"
Console.WriteLine(strExample.StartsWith("1"))   ' writes "False"
Console.WriteLine(strExample.StartsWith("0"))   ' writes "True"
```

Other editing commands include the Insert method, which inserts a substring into an existing string. Note, however, that since a new string object is created each time a string is changed, assigning a new value to the String variable with this method, as with any other method or operator, will actually result in a totally new object. The Replace method replaces all occurrences of one string with another, again creating a new string in the process. The ToLower and ToUpper methods return the lowercase and uppercase values of a string. The IndexOf method returns the position of the first occurrence of one string within another; the LastIndexOf method returns the position of the last occurrence of one string within another. The Length property returns the length of a string. These methods are illustrated in the following code:

```
Dim strExample As String = "0123456789abcde"
Dim strResult As String
Dim intLength As Integer
```

```
intLength = strExample.Length ' returns 15
strResult = strExample.Insert(2, " inserted string ")
strResult = strResult.Replace("inserted ", " confirmed")

' delete 4 characters starting from index 2
strResult = strResult.Remove(2, 4)

' strResult will contain only uppercase letters.
strResult = strResult.ToUpper()
' strResult will contain only lowercase letters.
strResult = strResult.ToLower()

intLength = strExample.IndexOf("89") ' returns 8

' Example with a literal
intPos = "232323232324232323".IndexOf("4")
```

The IndexOf and LastIndexOf methods can be overloaded (i.e., run with other sets of parameters) to refine the search. The syntax of these methods is

```
<string-variable | string-literal> {IndexOf | LastIndexOf}
                                   (<search-string> |<literal>
                                   [,<starting position> ]
                                   [,<number of positions to search> ]
                                   {returns an integer}
```

The following example shows how these methods can be used to search, beginning from a starting position in the string and restricting the search to a limited number of characters:

```
Dim intPos As Integer
strExample = "012012012012"
intPos = strExample.IndexOf("1") ' returns 1
intPos = strExample.LastIndexOf("1") ' returns 10

' looks for "1" but starts at the 4th character, returns 4
intPos = strExample.IndexOf("1", 3)
' looks for "1" but starts at the 4th character but searches
' only 2 characters, returns 4
intPos = strExample.IndexOf("1", 3, 2)
```

Another widely applied method is Substring. This method returns a substring (partial string) of the string variable or literal, starting at a given position and optionally limiting the length of the returned substring. When no limit is set on the number of characters to copy, the remainder of the string is copied, as in the following code:

```
Dim strExample As String = "0123456789abcde"
Dim strResult As String
strResult = strExample.Substring(3, 3) ' returns "345"
strResult = strExample.Substring(3) 'returns "3456789abcde"
```

The syntax of the method is

```
<string-variable | string-literal> Substring (<starting position> ]
                                     [,<number of positions to
                                       copy> ]
                                  {returns an integer}
```

Last but not least, the `String` class has a set of methods to trim and to pad strings to a given length. These methods are case sensitive, meaning that padding with the literal "a", for example, is not the same as padding with the literal "A". The `PadLeft` and the `PadRight` methods return a string of a given length; when the specified length of this string is larger than the original string, the method will add blanks to the left or the right of it, respectively. When the length parameter is the equal to or shorter than the length of the string, the whole string is returned, as in the following code:

```
Dim strExample As String = "0123"
strExample = strExample.PadLeft(6) ' will return      "  0123"
strExample = strExample.PadRight(7)' will then return "  0123 "
strExample = strExample.PadLeft(1) ' will return      "  0123 "
```

The two methods can also pad the original string with a specific Unicode character by adding a second parameter to the method:

```
Dim strExample As String = "0123"
          ' will return "aa0123"
strExample = strExample.PadLeft(6, "a")
          ' will then return "aa0123bb"
strExample = strExample.PadRight(8, "b")
```

The trim set of methods work in the opposite direction. The `TrimEnd` method truncates (shortens by trimming) a string value from the end of a string; the `TrimStart` method truncates the value from the beginning of a string; and the `Trim` method truncates the value from both the end and the beginning of a string. These methods are case sensitive, meaning that trimming the leading "a"s, for example, is not the same as trimming the leading "A"s. These methods are especially useful for deleting blanks from a string. The `TrimEnd`, `TrimStart`, and `Trim` method all use a space as their default parameter (the space is the most common application of these methods):

```
Dim strExample As String = " 01230 "  ' contains     " 01230 "
strExample = strExample.TrimEnd(" ")   ' will return " 01230"
strExample = strExample.TrimStart(" ") ' will return "01230"
strExample = strExample.Trim("0")      ' will return "123"
```

The `String` class also comes with a necessary constant, the `Empty` constant, which is akin to assigning it with an empty string within quotes, "":

```
strExample = String.Empty
```

2.5.1   Working Efficiently with Strings, the StringBuilder

When working with strings, it is important to remember that the string data type is not a base data type, such as an `Integer` is; rather, it is an instance of the `String` class. Thus, with all these methods, a method without a receiving string, as in the following example, is syntactically correct, albeit meaningless:

```
strExample.Insert(2, " inserted string ")
```

The foregoing method is syntactically correct because it creates a new string object; it is just that that new string is not assigned anywhere and is not named. Therefore, nothing happens.

Each time the value in a `String` data-type variable is changed, a new instance of the `String` class is created. This is in accordance with the object-oriented philosophy of VB.NET. Up to now, when we defined a new string-typed variable, we wrote

```
Dim strExample As String
```

That code is actually shorthand for

```
Dim strExample As New String
```

What the code says, as we will discuss in the chapter on object orientation, is that the object `strExample` is a new instance of the `String` class. As a desired side effect, this allows us to use many constructor methods belonging to the same `String` class. A constructor is a special type of method that is used to control how an object (remember, even a variable is actually an object) is initialized. A `Constructor` method is invoked when, and only when, the object is created. We already saw one such constructor:

```
Dim strExample As String = "01230"
```

Another constructor allows us to pass multiple occurrences of a character literal as the initial value:

```
Dim strExample As New String (CChar ("1"), 100)
```

In the latter case, the constructor will set the initial value of the new variable, actually an object, to one hundred 1's. This is possible because the string variable, being an object, can have many constructors. Another benefit of having string variables as objects is that *intelliSense* option can guide the programmer whenever a period is typed after the name of a string-type variable.

While all these benefits are useful, they come at a cost. Each time the value of a string-typed variable is changed, VB.NET creates a new instance of the object, which is very costly compared with the way other variables are managed. VB.NET provides a solution to this performance issue with the `StringBuilder` class. This class is in the `System.Text` namespace and is specifically designed to efficiently handle strings that change often. The `StringBuilder` is a string of characters with a size that is set when the object is instantiated through its `Capacity` property. This capacity is automatically increased when a string that is larger than the current capacity is assigned to the object. The actual size of the current value, which can be smaller than its capacity, is registered in its `Length` property. By default, the initial capacity of the object is 16 characters. When more than that is needed, the object will acquire more memory up to its maximum capacity of 2^{31} characters. As a string of characters, rather than a `String` data type, the `StringBuilder` is not recreated whenever a new value is assigned to it. This characteristic is called *mutable* in VB.NET terminology. It is one of the main benefits of the `StringBuilder`. As a direct consequence of being mutable, changes in the content of the object do not require reinstantiating it.

A `StringBuilder` can be dimensioned in many ways. The simplest way is without specifying any parameters, as done here to instantiate a new `StringBuilder` object with a default capacity of 16:

```
Dim strA0 As New System.Text.StringBuilder()
```

The initial capacity, as well as the maximum capacity, can also be set explicitly:

```
' initial capacity 100
Dim strA1 As New System.Text.StringBuilder(100)
' initial capacity is 100 and max capacity is 12000
Dim strA4 As New System.Text.StringBuilder(100, 12000)
```

Alternatively, an initial value can be assigned, with or without specifying the capacity:

```
' initial value set
Dim strA2 As New System.Text.StringBuilder("initial")
' initial value and size are set
Dim strA3 As New System.Text.StringBuilder("initial", 100)
```

Once the `StringBuilder` object has been dimensioned, it can be manipulated with a set of methods. Values are added with the `Append` method, which has many constructors, allowing the assignment of data to the object, regardless of the type. This is a novel feature of the `StringBuilder` object that is quite in contrast to the general philosophy of all other data types, which require an explicit data conversion. Thus, the following two commands will produce identical results:

```
strA0 = strA0.Append("12")    ' parameter data are a string
strA0 = strA0.Append(12)      ' parameter data are an integer
```

The preceding `Append` method adds data to the `StringBuilder` object. After executing either one of the two commands shown, the `Length` property will be 2, but the `Capacity` property will remain 16. This can be verified easily with the commands

```
Console.WriteLine(strA0.Length)    ' will print 2
Console.WriteLine(strA0.Capacity)  ' will print 16
```

The Append method can also be execute d to add multiple occurrences of a character. Note, however, that if a string with more than one character is passed as a parameter, only the first character of the string will be multiplied:

```
strA0 = strA0.Append("1", 10)  ' will append 10 ones to strA0
strA0 = strA0.Append("14", 10) ' This too will append 10 ones
```

This justifies special caution, because elsewhere throughout VB.NET such data-type conflicts are singled out when Option Explicit is On, but not so with the StringBuilder.

Other convenient methods are Insert, which inserts a string at a given position, any given number of times; Remove, which deletes a given number of characters from a given position; Replace, which replaces one string with another in the String-Builder, optionally specifying from where to begin the replacement and how many characters long to search; and the Chars property, which inserts a character at a given position. *As elsewhere in VB.NET, the first position in a* StringBuilder *is indexed zero, the second position is indexed 1, and so on.* Thus, one of the following commands will insert the string "abc" in the second position of strA1, shifting the remainder of the string to the right:

```
strA1 = strA1.Append(1234567890)' will contain "1234567890"
strA1.Insert(1, "abc")           ' will contain "1abc234567890"
strA1.Chars(2) = "d"             ' will contain "1adc234567890"
strA1.Remove(2, 2)               ' will contain "1a234567890"
strA1 = strA1.Remove(5, 4)       ' will remove 4 characters
                                 ' starting with the 5th
                                 ' position, result "1a23490"
```

Note that the Chars method works differently, just overriding whatever was there.

More complex things can be done with these methods. This is demonstrated in the following code:

```
strA1.Length = 0  ' empty the stringbuilder
strA1 = strA1.Append("0123456789") ' contains "0123456789"
strA1 = strA1.Insert(8, "AA", 2)   ' at position 8, insert
                                   ' "AA", 2 times. The
                                   ' result is "01234567AAAA89"
```

First, the StringBuilder is emptied by assigning the literal 0 to its Length property. Assigning the Nothing keyword will also work. Next, a string is assigned with the Append method. (Note the significance of doing so: Had an integer been assigned as before, then the leading zero would have been lost. Although the method, thanks to its many constructors that create its polymorphism, can accept both String data-type parameters and numeric ones, these different constructors are not treated the same.) The string "AA" is then inserted at position 8 twice.

This string can be modified, replacing every occurrence of the string "AA" with the string "BB" and then every occurrence of "BB" with "CC", but only searching from position 2 onward to a total length of 8 characters:

```
strA1 = strA1.Replace("AA", "BB")          ' replace AA with BB
                        ' the result will be "01234567BBBB89"
strA1 = strA1.Replace("BB", "CC", 2, 8) ' replace BB with CC
                        ' starting from position 2 and looking 8
                        ' characters forward the result will be
                        ' "01234567CCBB89". The last "BB" is not
                        ' replaced.
```

2.6   WORKING WITH DATES

As discussed earlier, time and date values are managed in a special data type, named Date. This data type stores the date and time combination in 64 bits that represent the elapsed time since midnight 01/01/0001. Date and time are assigned to a Date data-type variable or constant with an assignment statement, which can be included in the Dim statement. This value must be an actual valid date or a string that can be explicitly cast into a valid date and time. A convenient system-assigned value is Now, which returns the current date and time on the computer. The CDate function casts a string that contains a valid date into a date data type:

```
Dim datExample As Date = #1/1/2002#
datExample = #2/2/2002#
datExample = CDate("3/3/2003")
```

Because date and time requires special operations, the Date data type comes with a set of needed public properties that separate the date–time value into its components:

```
Dim datExample As Date
Dim strExample As String

datExample = Now  ' get local date and time on the computer

strExample = datExample.Day       'current day of the month
strExample = datExample.Month     'current month
strExample = datExample.Year      'current year

strExample = datExample.DayOfWeek 'day of the week, Monday is 1
strExample = datExample.DayOfYear 'days since January 1st

strExample = datExample.Hour      'current hour
strExample = datExample.Minute    'current minute
strExample = datExample.Second    'current second
strExample = datExample.Millisecond 'current millisecond

strExample = datExample.Ticks 'This is an internal representation
                              'of date and time in ticks, measured in
                              'units of 100 nanoseconds that elapsed
                              'since midnight 01/01/0001.
```

Date and time are manipulated also with a set of dedicated public methods whose name self-identifies what each does. In the next set of statements, date and time intervals are added, with a positive integer, and subtracted, with a negative one, with these methods:

```
datExample = datExample.AddTicks(10)
datExample = datExample.AddMilliseconds(-10)
datExample = datExample.AddSeconds(10)
datExample = datExample.AddMinutes(-10)
datExample = datExample.AddHours(10)
datExample = datExample.AddDays(-10)
datExample = datExample.AddMonths(10)
datExample = datExample.AddYears(-10)
```

The foregoing date and time methods can be applied with a method that applies to more than one date and time interval—something of a unified method. This more general method, Add, utilizes a TimeSpan value. The TimeSpan value contains four integers that represent in order days, hours, minutes, and seconds. Using the following method is somewhat less straightforward than employing the other methods:

```
Dim datExample As Date = #1/1/2002#
Dim MyTimeSpan As System.TimeSpan
MyTimeSpan = New System.TimeSpan(2, 3, 4, 5)
    ' add 2 days, 3 hours, 4 minutes, and 5 seconds
datExample = datExample.Add(MyTimeSpan)
```

A look at the Autos window shows the complexity of this new data type and why applying the previous set of methods might be easier. The Autos window (Figure 2.2) shows the components of the TimeSpan value.

Autos		⊉ ×
Name	Value	Type
⊟ MyTimeSpan	{System.TimeSpan}	System.T
⊞ System.ValueType	{System.TimeSpan}	System.V
TicksPerMillisecond	10000	Long
TicksPerSecond	10000000	Long
TicksPerMinute	600000000	Long
TicksPerHour	36000000000	Long
TicksPerDay	864000000000	Long
MillisPerSecond	1000	Integer
MillisPerMinute	60000	Integer
MillisPerHour	3600000	Integer
MillisPerDay	86400000	Integer
MaxSeconds	922337203685	Long
MinSeconds	-922337203685	Long
MaxMilliSeconds	922337203685477	Long
MinMilliSeconds	-922337203685477	Long
⊞ Zero	{System.TimeSpan}	System.T
⊞ MaxValue	{System.TimeSpan}	System.T
⊞ MinValue	{System.TimeSpan}	System.T
_ticks	1838450000000	Long
Ticks	1838450000000	Long
Days	2	Integer
Hours	3	Integer
Milliseconds	0	Integer
Minutes	4	Integer
Seconds	5	Integer
TotalDays	2.1278356481481482	Double
TotalHours	51.068055555555553	Double
TotalMilliseconds	183845000.0	Double
TotalMinutes	3064.0833333333335	Double
TotalSeconds	183845.0	Double
🖳 Autos 🖳 Locals 🖳 Watch 1		

FIGURE 2.2
Autos window.

Date and time values cannot be compared with or added to each other directly, because of the need to consider the components of time and date in the process. Hence, VB.NET provides a set of methods that handle date and time values. These are demonstrated in the next statements, which also introduce a new data type, the `TimeSpan`. This data type contains the difference between dates as a function of the `Subtract` method. In the following code, the difference between January 1, 2002, at 10:22:10 P.M. and December 31 of the same year at 11:59:59 P.M. is determined to be 364.03:37:49, that is, 364 days, 3 hours, 37 minutes, and 49 seconds, as printed in the Output window (variables with a `TimeSpan` data type—strictly speaking, these are objects—contain information about the difference in days, hours, minutes, seconds, and milliseconds):

```
Dim datEarly As New System.DateTime(2002, 1, 1, 20, 22, 10)
Dim dateLate As New System.DateTime(2002, 12, 31, 23, 59, 59)
Dim datDiff As System.TimeSpan

' date difference between the two dates
datDiff = dateLate.Subtract(datEarly)
Console.WriteLine(datDiff)
```

The `Days`, `Hours`, and `Minutes` properties can then be used to assign the difference registered in the timespan variable to a more workable data type:

```
Dim strDays As String
strDays = datDiff.Days()
```

Here, the `datDiff` object will actually contain a whole set of values, as can be seen in the `Local` window (Figure 2.3) during debug. In fact, the preceding command is actually referencing one of the many properties of this object.

A `TimeSpan` object can also be used to add date-time, although with more complexity than with the methods introduced earlier. In the following code, the `op_Addition` method is used to add a `TimeSpan` to a date:

```
Dim datOriginal As New System.DateTime(2002, 3, 4) ' 3/4/2002
' The timeSpan is 10 days, 9 hours, 8 minutes, and 7 seconds
Dim MyTimeSpan As New System.TimeSpan(10, 9, 8, 7)
Dim datResult As System.DateTime
' This will print 3/14/2002 9:08:07 AM
datResult = System.DateTime.op_Addition _
        (datOriginal, MyTimeSpan)
Console.WriteLine(datResult)
```

Notice how the `DateTime` object receives an initial value of only year, month, and day, compared with the previous example where it also received hours, minutes, and seconds. This *overloading* is possible because of the polymorphism of the `DateTime` object, which is achieved through its many constructors.

The `Compare` method compares two date–time objects. If the first date–time is smaller, the method will return a negative integer; if it is bigger, the method will return a positive integer; and if the two date–time values are equal, it will return an integer of

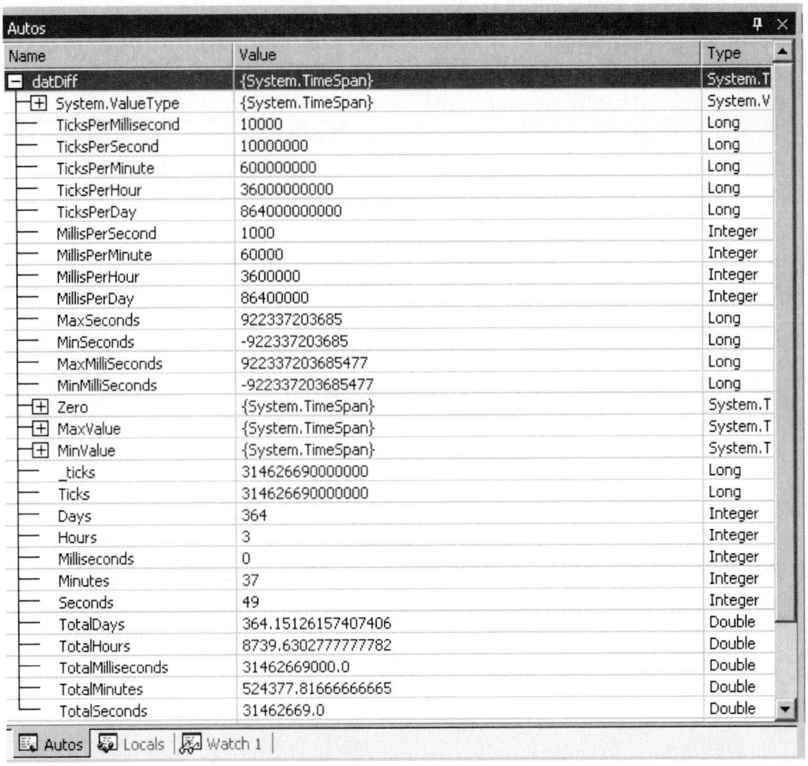

Autos		⊕ ×
Name	Value	Type ▲
⊟ datDiff	{System.TimeSpan}	System.T
⊕ System.ValueType	{System.TimeSpan}	System.V
TicksPerMillisecond	10000	Long
TicksPerSecond	10000000	Long
TicksPerMinute	600000000	Long
TicksPerHour	36000000000	Long
TicksPerDay	864000000000	Long
MillisPerSecond	1000	Integer
MillisPerMinute	60000	Integer
MillisPerHour	3600000	Integer
MillisPerDay	86400000	Integer
MaxSeconds	922337203685	Long
MinSeconds	-922337203685	Long
MaxMilliSeconds	922337203685477	Long
MinMilliSeconds	-922337203685477	Long
⊕ Zero	{System.TimeSpan}	System.T
⊕ MaxValue	{System.TimeSpan}	System.T
⊕ MinValue	{System.TimeSpan}	System.T
_ticks	314626690000000	Long
Ticks	314626690000000	Long
Days	364	Integer
Hours	3	Integer
Milliseconds	0	Integer
Minutes	37	Integer
Seconds	49	Integer
TotalDays	364.15126157407406	Double
TotalHours	8739.6302777777782	Double
TotalMilliseconds	31462669000.0	Double
TotalMinutes	524377.81666666665	Double
TotalSeconds	31462669.0	Double ▼

📋 Autos | 🔲 Locals | 🔲 Watch 1 |

FIGURE 2.3
Local window.

zero. Comparing dates and times is also done through a dedicated set of operators that
return a True or False value:

```
Dim datEarly As New System.DateTime(2002, 1, 1, 20, 22, 10)
Dim datLate As New System.DateTime(2002, 12, 31, 23, 59, 59)
Dim intResult As Integer

intResult = System.DateTime.Compare(datEarly, datLate)
Console.WriteLine(intResult) ' This will print -1

Dim bolResult As Boolean

bolResult = System.DateTime.op_Equality(datEarly, datLate)
Console.WriteLine(bolResult) ' This will print False

bolResult = System.DateTime.op_GreaterThan _
        (datEarly, datLate)
Console.WriteLine(bolResult) ' This will print False

bolResult = System.DateTime.op_GreaterThanOrEqual _
        (datEarly, datLate)
```

```
Console.WriteLine(bolResult) ' This will print False

bolResult = System.DateTime.op_Inequality(datEarly, datLate)
Console.WriteLine(bolResult) ' This will print True

bolResult = System.DateTime.op_LessThan(datEarly, datLate)
Console.WriteLine(bolResult) ' This will print True

bolResult = System.DateTime.op_LessThanOrEqual _
        (datEarly, datLate)
Console.WriteLine(bolResult) ' This will print True
```

Programming Note: Nonetheless, as in previous versions of VB, the date data type is unaware of some nonexistent dates throughout history. Accordingly, the following two commands are perfectly valid in VB.NET, although they reference dates that never existed:

```
Dim datNoDate As Date = #10/5/1582#
datNoDate.AddDays(2)
```

The calendar we use today jumps from Wednesday, October 4, 1582, to Thursday October 15, 1582, when the Gregorian calendar replaced the defunct Julian one, so the two dates cited never occurred.[3]

2.7   DETERMINING THE DATA TYPE DYNAMICALLY

When the value of a variable, a constant, or a literal is assigned to a variable, VB.NET automatically checks whether the data are of the same data type, unless Option Strict is turned Off. Nonetheless, it is often necessary to check within the code to determine whether the data can be cast correctly—that is, whether the data contain a valid value for the receiving variable. For example, a variable defined with a String data type can always receive a numeric value, but a variable defined with a Long data type will only be able to receive numeric strings from a String data-type variable. Thus, it may be necessary to verify that the String data-type variable contains a numeric value before it is assigned to the Long data-type variable. We will see an example of such a case in the lab at the end of the chapter. There are several functions in Visual Basic (returning a True or False value) that can be used before

---

[3]The calendar used in the West, and hence in most of the world (and in Visual Basic), is the Gregorian calendar. This calendar is based on the Julian calendar that was composed of sequences of three 365-day years followed by a 366-day year. This pretty close approximation is only about 11 minutes and 14 seconds off from the real length of a solar year. However, by the time of pope Gregory XIII, the calendar was evidently 14 days wrong (because the equinox was not on March 25th), so on October 5, 1582, the calendar was moved 10 days forward to October 15, 1582. Visual Basic is not aware of this historic event. So while an assignment of a date like #2/30/2000# will result in a runtime error, the assignment of #10/6/1582#, a date that never existed, will not result in any error! (England and its colonies, including what was later to become the United States, did not catch up till 1752, and Russia did not make the change until 1918, which is why the Russian October Revolution took place in November!)

an assignment statement is made in order to examine whether the data in a variable can be converted without error to another data type:

- IsNumeric (*expression*), which examines whether an expression is numeric, where the expression can contain a combination of strings, variables, operators, and keywords that produce a string, an object, or a number. The function returns a value of True if the expression can be converted to a Double data type and False otherwise.
- IsDate (*expression*), which returns a value of True if the expression is a valid Gregorian date and False otherwise, where an expression can contain a combination of strings, variables, operators, and keywords that produce a string, an object, or a date. (See the footnote in the preceding section on the known inaccuracies of how dates are managed in VB.)
- IsArray (*variable-name*), which returns a value of True if the variable is an array and False otherwise. (More details on arrays are found in the next chapter.)
- IsNothing (*variable-name*), which examines whether an object contains a value.

Accordingly, the statements

```
Console.WriteLine(IsDate("12/12/1919"))
Console.WriteLine(IsDate("12/12/19aa"))
Console.WriteLine(IsNumeric("12"))
Console.WriteLine(IsNumeric("12a"))
Console.WriteLine(IsNothing(strArray3))
```

will print

```
True
False
True
False
False
```

in the Output window.

Another useful function is TypeName. This function returns a string with the data-type name of the variable. When the parameter is an array (as we shall see in Chapter 3, arrays are declared with a parentheses after the variable name), the data type name is returned with parentheses. The following code is illustrative:

```
Dim strArray3(9) As String
Dim I As Integer
Dim intArray(10) As Integer
Console.WriteLine(TypeName(strArray3))    ' prints String()
Console.WriteLine(TypeName(I))            ' prints Integer
Console.WriteLine(TypeName(intArray))     ' prints Integer()
```

2.8   THE MESSAGE BOX

The Message Box is a convenient way of displaying messages to the user in a popup screen. The Message Box exists in VB in two equivalent versions: the `MsgBox` command and the `MessageBox.Show` command. In this section, we will demonstrate `Message-Box.Show`.

The `MessageBox.Show` command has at least one parameter: the message that will appear in the Message Box. Running the command shown below will pop up the Message Box that follows:

```
MessageBox.Show("Hi")
```

The second parameter, which is optional, contains the caption of the Message Box:

```
MessageBox.Show("Hi", "I am a Caption")
```

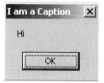

The third parameter, also optional, contains the Message Box Buttons. A Message Box can contain one of several combinations of buttons. (See Figure 2.4.). In contrast to the previous two examples of a Message Box, in this case, the program can handle the functionality that is embedded in the buttons. However, adding buttons requires some additional coding: A special object, a `DialogResult`, must be dimensioned. Into this object the result of executing the Message Box will be returned. In the following code, the third parameter specifies what combination of buttons will appear in the Message Box (Yes, No, and Cancel):

```
MessageBoxButtons.AbortRetryIgnore
MessageBoxButtons.OK
MessageBoxButtons.OKCancel
MessageBoxButtons.RetryCancel
MessageBoxButtons.YesNo
MessageBoxButtons.YesNoCancel
```

FIGURE 2.4
Message Box Buttons.

Clicking on any button in the Message Box will close it, but identifying which button was clicked requires the DialogResult object.

```
Dim myDialogResult As DialogResult
myDialogResult = MessageBox.Show("Hi", "I am a Caption", _
                                    MessageBoxButtons.YesNoCancel)
If myDialogResult = DialogResult.Yes Then
    Console.WriteLine("Clicked Yes")
End If
If myDialogResult = DialogResult.No Then
    Console.WriteLine("Clicked No")
End If
```

The fourth parameter, also optional, contains the icon that will appear in the Message Box. (See Figure 2.5.) A DialogResult object is not required if only one button was specified in the third parameter:

```
MessageBox.Show("Hi", "I am a Caption", _
            MessageBoxButtons.OK, _
            MessageBoxIcon.Information)
```

FIGURE 2.5
Icon that will appear in Message Box.

If, however, as in the previous example, more than one button is displayed in the Message Box, and it is necessary to discern which button was clicked, then a DialogResult object is required:

```
myDialogResult = MessageBox.Show("Hi", "I am a Caption", _
            MessageBoxButtons.YesNoCancel, _
            MessageBoxIcon.Information)

If myDialogResult = DialogResult.Yes Then
    Console.WriteLine("Clicked Ok")
End If
If myDialogResult = DialogResult.No Then
    Console.WriteLine("Clicked No")
End If
```

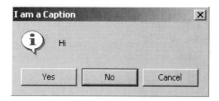

The fifth parameter, also optional, is only really relevant when several buttons are displayed in the Message Box. This parameter specifies which of the buttons will be the default one. If the parameter is omitted, then the first button is the default one. In the following code, the second button is set as the default button:

```
myDialogResult = _
    MessageBox.Show("Hi", _
        "I am a Caption", _
        MessageBoxButtons.YesNoCancel, _
        MessageBoxIcon.Information, _
        MessageBoxDefaultButton.Button2)
```

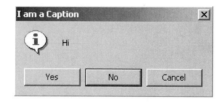

The last parameter, also optional, specifies the layout of the Message Box. The various options are shown in the following code:

```
myDialogResult = _
        MessageBox.Show("Hi", _
        "I am a Caption", _
        MessageBoxButtons.YesNoCancel, _
        MessageBoxIcon.Information, _
        MessageBoxDefaultButton.Button2, _
        MessageBoxOptions.RightAlign)
```

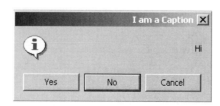

```
myDialogResult = _
        MessageBox.Show("Hi", _
        "I am a Caption", _
```

```
              MessageBoxButtons.YesNoCancel, _
              MessageBoxIcon.Information, _
              MessageBoxDefaultButton.Button2, _
              MessageBoxOptions.DefaultDesktopOnly)
```

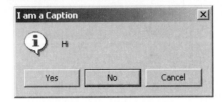

```
myDialogResult = _
              MessageBox.Show("Hi", _
              "I am a Caption", _
              MessageBoxButtons.YesNoCancel, _
              MessageBoxIcon.Information, _
              MessageBoxDefaultButton.Button2, _
              MessageBoxOptions.RtlReading)
```

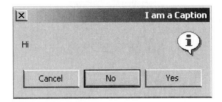

```
myDialogResult = _
              MessageBox.Show("Hi", _
              "I am a Caption", _
              MessageBoxButtons.YesNoCancel, _
              MessageBoxIcon.Information, _
              MessageBoxDefaultButton.Button2, _
              MessageBoxOptions.ServiceNotification)
```

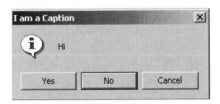

LAB 2.1: THE DATE DATA TYPE AND A QUICK REVIEW OF FORM DESIGN

It is assumed that the student has already built projects and forms in VB.NET and is
well versed in the content of the menus in VB.NET. The objective of reviewing these
topics in this lab is accordingly just to review what is assumed to be known already.
Nonetheless, the explanations should be sufficiently detailed also for a student new to
VB.NET who has limited prior experience.

Lab Objectives:

1. Review material

- IDE
- Working with Forms
- Button control
- Textbox control

2. Work with variables

- String variables
- Date variables
- Casting
- `CDate` function
- `CStr` function
- `IsDate` function
- `IsNumeric` function

3. Use controls

- Button
- Label
- TextBox
- Radio Button
- Group Box

4. Use properties

- Name
- Text
- Tab Index
- Size
- Font

Application Overview

In this lab, we will start with a quick overview of the VB.NET interface and, in doing so, will discuss building a simple form application. That demonstrates how `String` and `Date` variables and casting are used. The application also demonstrates simple date operations.

The application has two parts. In the first part, numbers are entered in a textbox one at a time. After each number is entered, a button is clicked. This button checks the input in the textbox, and if it is numeric, the code associated with this button will calculate and display, in another textbox, the current average of all the numbers entered so far. In the second part of the application, the form will accept two dates and then perform various date functions, depending upon which button has been clicked.

Part 1: A Quick Walkthrough the Interface of VB.NET

When you enter VB.NET, the first screen looks like the one in Figure 2.6. The Start window shows recent projects.

Click on the New Project button and the New Project window will open. This window contains the various languages the .NET framework supports (these languages are

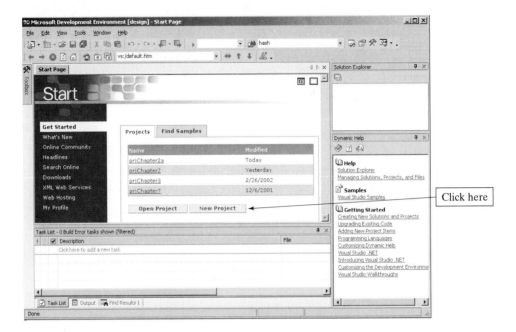

Click here

FIGURE 2.6
Start page.

called *Project Types* because the .NET is supposed to be a cross-language platform) and the *Templates* that each language supports. Choose Visual Basic Projects as the language and Windows Application as the template (Figure 2.7). Name the project **prjChapter2a** and specify in which folder it should be kept. In this example, the project will be kept in a folder called VB7 on the "C" drive.

Now the VB.NET work area (Figure 2.8) should be open. A quick look at the work area shows the menu bar on top and the tool bar just below it with convenient shortcuts equivalent to some of the more widely used menu items. In the center of the work area is the form itself. (The form is the window that will come up when the application is run.) Onto this form various controls can be added from the toolbox on its left. Clicking the toolbox will open it by expanding it to the right. (More details on the toolbox are found later in the section.)

On the right-hand side of the work area on the top are the Solution Explorer, Class View, Context, and Index windows. These four windows are pooled together in a tabbed control. Click the appropriate tab at the bottom of the shared window to open the appropriate window. As can be seen, the current active window is the Solution Explorer. The Solution Explorer shows the projects that are currently included in the solution and the current contents of each project. Currently, this being a new project, there are only three components in the current project. The project contains a list of the reference libraries that are included in the project. Clicking on the plus sign next to the References keyword will expand the display to show all the VB.NET libraries that are included in this project. By default, these libraries are System, System.Data, System.Drawing, System.Windows.Forms, and System.XML. Additional namespaces (you

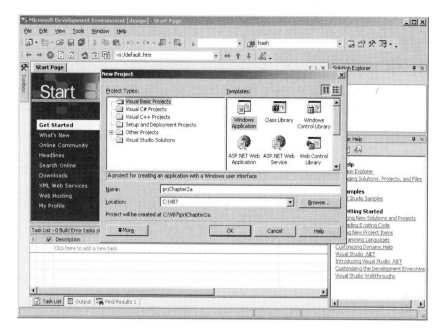

FIGURE 2.7
The New Project window.

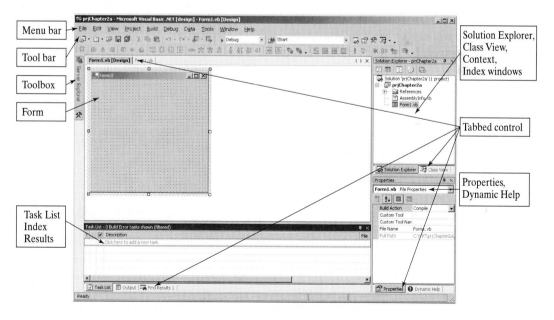

FIGURE 2.8
The Form Development IDE.

can conveniently think of these as class libraries) can be included with the Imports statement that will be discussed later in the book:

```
Imports System.Threading
```

The Solution Explorer also contains the *AssemblyInfo*. This file contains programmer- and system-managed information about the assembly. Double-clicking on the AssemblyInfo keyword will open a window with information about the assembly. This information will be presented in the same section of the work area as the form is displayed in. You can move among the windows presented in this section by clicking the appropriate tab at the top of the display. In general, because the VB.NET work area contains so much information in such a small space, the information is grouped into tabbed displays and the requested information is shown when the appropriate tab is clicked. Perhaps most importantly, the Solution Explorer contains the list of forms that are included in the project. Currently, there is only one form, named Form1. The name of the form will soon be changed to make it comply with the usual naming standard in VB.

The tab next to the Solution Explorer is the Class View. The Class View shows a more detailed description of the current contents of the project as added by the programmer. Currently, it will show the Form1 class. When clicked, the Form1 class will expand and show the list of subroutines and additional modules in the form. (Go to this window later as we add controls to the form, and notice how new entries are added to this list that correspond to the new subroutines.) The last two tabs are the tutorial and the help windows. These excellent windows are self-explanatory.

As a short detour, it is worth adding a Button to the form at this stage. Click on the toolbox. The toolbox will expand as shown in Figure 2.9 to display the available controls. These controls are grouped into five groups. The default group, which we will use now, contains the "standard" controls, such as the Button, the textbox, and many others that we will work with throughout the book. That group is called Windows Forms. Right at the top of the toolbox is the Data group. We will look at these extensively in the second part of the book. We will not deal much with the other groups in the toolbox.

Click the Button control, and then draw a Button on the form by marking the rectangle within which it will appear. The Button, once drawn, can easily be resized by expanding one of the little boxes that appear around the control when it is clicked once. The Class View will not yet contain any reference to the Button because no code is associated with it yet. However, once the Button is double-clicked and the appropriate subroutine added automatically in the Code window, then two new lines will appear in the Class View: In one line, an icon made of two turquoise boxes that represents the control will appear, and the other line will contain a purple-box icon that represents the subroutine which handles the default event of that control. (As explained in Chapter 1, an object contains properties and methods and responds to events.) The default event of a Button is that is it clicked. This default event is shown in the class view in Figure 2.10 as "Button 1_Click". We will take a detailed look at the code later in this section.

Below the Solution Explorer, Class View, Context, and Index windows appears another group of windows. These contain the Properties window and the Dynamic Help window, again both in one tabbed control. The Properties window shows the properties of the object that is currently being pointed at in the form. In this case, it will be the new Button that was just added. The Dynamic Help window contains another

FIGURE 2.9
Windows Forms Toolbox.

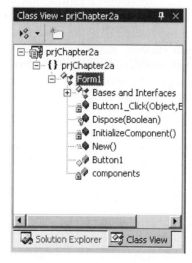

FIGURE 2.10
The Class View Window.

set of tutorials. We will discuss the Properties window in greater detail in this lab. By default, the Task window will not appear. To make it appear, press Ctrl + Alt + k.

At the bottom of the work area there is the Task List and Index Results. These, and additional windows with information about the current task, also appear in a tabbed control. All the syntax errors will appear in the Task List as they are typed. In this area, additional windows will appear during runtime to indicate the Call Stack, the Output window, the Watch window, and others.

Part 2: A Look at the Form

The first thing we need to do with the form is to rename it. Forms in previous versions of VB were recommended to start with an "frm" prefix. That was consistent with the prevailing VB programming philosophy in which each variable and each object should have a name that started with a three- or four-letter identifying prefix. Thus, all string variables started with "str", as we have done earlier in this chapter. VB.NET is a drastic departure from that philosophy in that everything in VB.NET is an object; therefore, in theory, a form is just as much an object as a Button or a variable. Consequently, there are those who recommend that there should be no identifying prefixes before any object types, including variables and forms. However, since the identifying prefixes clearly improve the readability of the code and make debugging easier, we will adopt the opinion that the VB prefix system should remain in VB.NET, especially as the casting functions (CStr, CInt, and the others) rely on these prefixes for clarity.

To rename the form (as in Figure 2.11) make sure the active tab in the center of the screen is "Form1.vb [Design]" by clicking on its tab. Then click once on the form itself to make it the active object, and go to the Properties window. In the Properties window, change the Name property to "frmLab2a". This will change the internal name of the form within VB.NET. Also change the Text property to "Lab 2a". This will change the caption of the form. Then go to the Solution Explorer and change the name of Form1 there, too. Do this by clicking with the right mouse button and selecting the Rename option. Then, change the name to "frmLab2a". This will change the ".vb" file name in which the form will be stored. *Do not delete the .vb suffix.*

This is not quite enough, though, because VB.NET does not cascade the change in the form name to the project properties. And so it is necessary to also change the startup object of the project manually to reflect the change we have just made to the form (Figure 2.12). To do this, click the project in the Solution Explorer with the right mouse button, and select the Properties menu item in the popup menu that will open. As you do so, the Property Pages window will open. In this window change the Startup Object to frmLab2a. You can use the Combo pulldown menu to save the typing. The Combo pulldown menu is an arrow that, when clicked, shows all the possible values.

Last, but not least, also change the name under which the form will be saved (Figure 2.13). Click on the tab for "Form1.vb [Design]", and in the Properties window, change the File Name property to frmLab2a. The caption of the tab "Form1.vb [Design]" will then change to "frmLab2a.vb [Design]".

Back in the Solution Explorer, click on the View Code icon, ▤, to show the code. This will open the code window and show a detailed listing of the code. We will look at that next. Note that the tab in the center of the screen changes to indicate that the code is being shown. You can see that through the name of the tab, "frmLab2a.vb", as opposed to the tab with the design of the form that is called "frmLab2a.vb [Design]". (See Figure 2.14.)

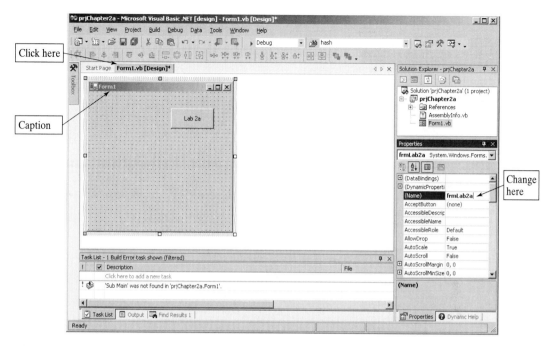

FIGURE 2.11
Renaming the form.

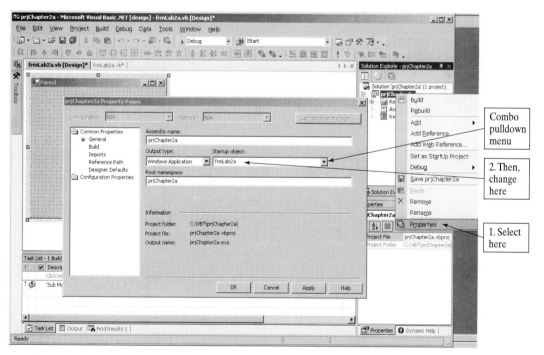

FIGURE 2.12
Changing the startup object.

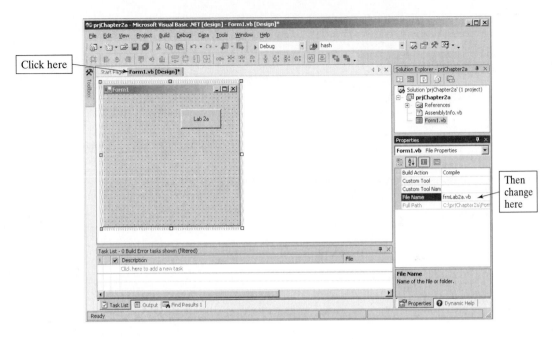

Click here

Then change here

FIGURE 2.13
Changing the name under which the form will be saved.

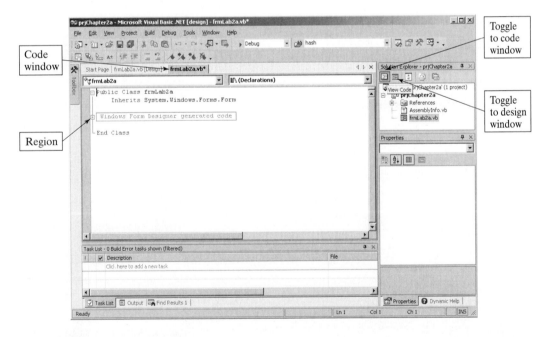

Toggle to code window

Code window

Toggle to design window

Region

FIGURE 2.14
The code window.

At this stage, it is worth taking a close look at the automatically generated code. The code window conveniently shows only the code that has been added explicitly to the form class. (The form is actually a class.) The code that was generated automatically is hidden within *Region*s. You can identify a *Region* by the icon of a plus sign enclosed in a box with a message next to it. The code that is exposed shows that the form we just created is a `Public Class`, meaning it can be accessed from anywhere in the project or the solution. We also see that the form inherits from the system class of `System.Windows.Forms.Form`. Additionally, we know the declaration of a subroutine to handle the Button we just created.

> **Programming Note:** A `Region` can be added into the code by typing the keyword `#Region` and its matching `#End Region` appropriately before the section that you want to allow being hidden. The *Region* can be given a caption by adding a string with the caption to the `Region` statement:
>
> ```
> #Region "Hide this button"
>     Private Sub Button1_Click(ByVal sender As System.Object, _
>             ByVal e As System.EventArgs) _
>             Handles Button1.Click
>     End Sub
> #End Region
> ```

This is a very convenient way to allow complicated code that is rarely changed to be hidden and yet accessible to other programmers.

Expand the *Region* by clicking on the icon with the plus sign enclosed in a box; all the code will be shown. The code that was automatically generated and hidden in a region by VB.NET is as follows (with explanations):

```
Public Class frmLab2a
    Inherits System.Windows.Forms.Form
```

This is the hidden region.

```
#Region " Windows Form Designer generated code "
```

The `New` subroutine is the standard entry point of any form in VB.NET.

```
Public Sub New()
    MyBase.New()

    'This call is required by the Windows Form Designer.
    InitializeComponent()

    'Add any initialization after the InitializeComponent() call

End Sub
```

```
'Form overrides dispose to clean up the component list.
Protected Overloads Overrides Sub Dispose (ByVal disposing As Boolean)
    If disposing Then
```

These are essential subroutines for handling the Form class. This one disposes of the form once it is closed. More on MyBase in the chapter dealing with the object-oriented aspects of VB.NET.

```
        If Not (components Is Nothing) Then
            components.Dispose()
        End If
    End If
    MyBase.Dispose(disposing)
End Sub

'Required by the Windows Form Designer
Private components As System.ComponentModel.IContainer

'NOTE: The following procedure is required by the Windows Form
    'Designer
'It can be modified using the Windows Form Designer.
'Do not modify it using the code editor.

Friend WithEvents Button1 As System.Windows.Forms.Button
<System.Diagnostics.DebuggerStepThrough()> Private Sub _
InitializeComponent()
```

Here is the code that sets the Properties of the form and the controls we added to it. Every control will appear here as well as any changes to its Properties, whether set in the Properties window or set by moving and resizing the control on the form.

```
    Me.Button1 = New System.Windows.Forms.Button()
    Me.SuspendLayout()
    '
    'Button1
    '
    Me.Button1.Location = New System.Drawing.Point(176, 24)
    Me.Button1.Name = "Button1"
    Me.Button1.Size = New System.Drawing.Size(104, 40)
    Me.Button1.TabIndex = 0
    Me.Button1.Text = "Button1"
    '
    'frmLab2a
    '
```

The Me keyword is the current form.

```
Me.AutoScaleBaseSize = New System.Drawing.Size(5, 13)
Me.ClientSize = New System.Drawing.Size(292, 273)
Me.Controls.AddRange(New System.Windows.Forms.Control() _
    {Me.Button1})
Me.Name = "frmLab2a"
Me.Text = "Lab 2a"
Me.ResumeLayout(False)

    End Sub

#End Region
#Region "Hide this button"
```

> Here is the code of the button we just added and the `Region` we created in the preceding programming note.

```
    Private Sub Button1_Click(ByVal sender As System.Object, _
            ByVal e As System.EventArgs) Handles Button1.Click
    End Sub
#End Region

End Class
```

Part 3: Designing the Form, Part 1

Go back to the design window, the one with a tab heading of "frmLab2a.vb [Design]"; delete Button1; then add the following Buttons, labels, and textboxes, renaming them according to Figure 2.15. Note the standard prefixes of the controls. Buttons start with "btn", textboxes with "txt", and labels with "lbl". Also, change the Text property of the controls according to what is shown in the diagram. (The Text property is what used to be called Caption in previous versions of VB.)

You will need to resize the form, too, so that it will more or less match Figure 2.15. You will also need to change the MultiLine property of the textboxes so that when you change their Height property, the change will take effect. *(Without changing the Mul-tiLine property, the height of a textbox will be determined by its font size. In the default case, the height will be 20 units. Changes made by resizing the control on the form or changes in the Height property will not take effect.)* The Height property is contained within the Size property. Click on the plus icon next to the Size property to reveal the Height property. The Size property is what is called an *ordered pair* of the Height and Width properties and will display the paired value when it is not expanded. Also change the Font Size property to a more readable size of 12. Repeat this process with all the textboxes. Or, as a shorter process, make the changes to the first textbox; then just copy and paste it. The changed properties will be copied to the new textbox. (In previous versions of VB, this would create a control array. That option does not exist in VB.NET.)

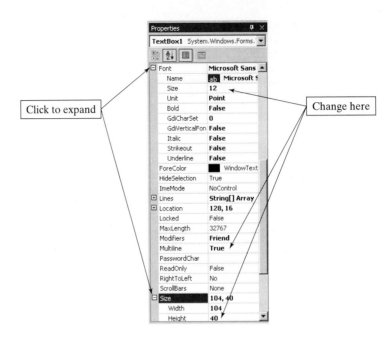

FIGURE 2.15
The Properties window.

Make txtAverage disabled; that is, allow it only to display values without allowing the user to change the value being displayed. This is done by changing the Enabled property to False. Also change the TabIndex property of txtNumber to 0 and of btnAverage to 1. The TabIndex property determines the order in which the controls will be tabbed through when the Tab key in the keyboard is clicked. The first control to get focus is the one with a TabIndex property of 0, the next will be the one with a TabIndex of 1, and so on. (It is worthwhile looking again at the hidden code in the form class and seeing how the additional controls have been added.) The form we will build is shown in Figure 2.16.

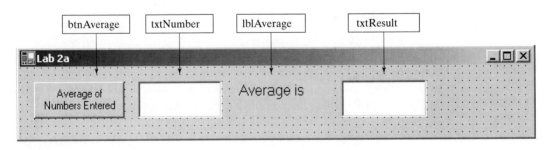

FIGURE 2.16
Lab 2a.

Part 4: Adding the Code, Part 1

Go back to the design window, and double-click btnAverage. This will open the Code window and automatically add a subroutine to deal with the Click event on that button. Add the following code to calculate the average:

```
Private Sub btnAverage_Click(ByVal sender As System.Object, _
        ByVal e As System.EventArgs) Handles btnAverage.Click
    Dim dblCalc As Double
    Static intHowManyNumbers As Integer = 0
    Static dblSum As Double = 0

    If IsNumeric(txtNumber.Text) Then
        dblSum = dblSum + CDbl(txtNumber.Text)
        intHowManyNumbers += 1
        dblCalc = dblSum / intHowManyNumbers
        txtResult.Text = CStr(dblCalc)
    End If
End Sub
```

This code is rather straightforward. Two static variables are declared to store the number of numbers entered and the current sum. These two variables must be static because their value must be retained from one execution of the subroutine to the next. Also declared is dblCalc, which will be used to calculate the average. It is declared with the Dim statement, because we do not need it to retain its value from one execution to another. Had dblCalc been declared with the Static statement, the code would have worked just as correctly, but its readability would have been impaired, because experienced programmers would have wrongly assumed that the variable needs to retain its value from one execution to another. The casting of the data from one data type to another is done explicitly with the CDbl and CStr functions. CDbl casts a value into a double-precision floating-point number. CStr casts a value into a string. Casting into a String data type is recommended for readability and to make sure that a person reading the code realizes the data type has changed, although with the default value of Option Strict being Off, the assignment operation that places dblCalc into the Text property will compile and work correctly. The data type of the data in the Text property of a textbox is a String.

In the preceding code, starting values are explicitly assigned to the two Static variables, although by default variables with a numeric data type have a starting value of 0. Of course, the code will work in a perfectly correct manner also without this assignment in the Static statement. Nonetheless, there are good reasons for doing so, including increases in readability of the code, making it absolutely clear also to those who may be unfamiliar with the default settings of VB.NET that the initial value is zero. More importantly, since there is no guarantee that the defaults of the language will not change when new versions come out (as happened with some of the default values in the transition from VB6 to VB.NET), doing so is a good way to avoid possible bugs in the future.

Any typos, and hence erroneous code syntax, will appear underlined with a wiggly line (as in Figure 2.17) in the Code window and will be explained in the Task List window. Double-clicking the error message in the Task List window will automatically point the cursor to the exact location of the error in the code. You can try this out by deliberately adding the following typo to the code:

```
txtResult1.Text == CStr(dblCalc)
```

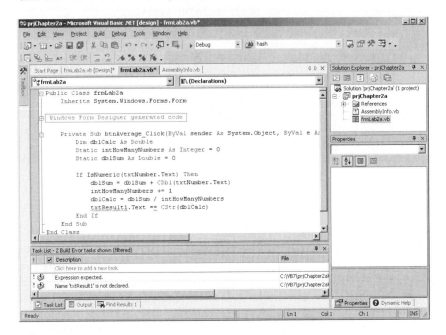

FIGURE 2.17
The Task List window highlighting errors in the code.

Correct the deliberate typo, and save the project and the form with the Save All menu in the File menu or with the Save All icon.

Programming Note: It is a good programming habit to always have the Task List window open when writing code. Doing so makes locating errors easier and faster. The default settings will not display this window. To display it, go to the View menu, and choose Other Windows in the menu list and then Task List in the secondary menu list. Alternatively, Ctrl + Alt + K will do the same.

Part 5: Designing the Form, Part 2

As has been explained, in the second part of the application the form will accept two dates and then perform various date functions on the date depending upon which button has been clicked. To add these additions to the form, resize it, and then add the additional buttons, labels, group box, and radio buttons. Change their names and text properties to correspond to the diagram in Figure 2.18. Name the Radio Buttons controls with a prefix of

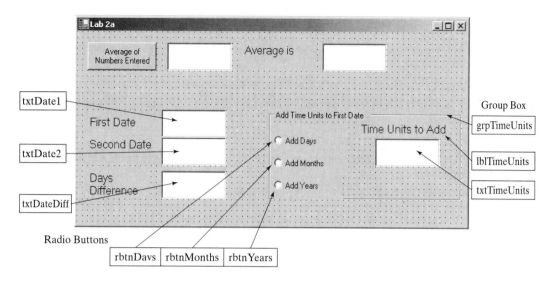

FIGURE 2.18
Extended Lab 2a.

"rbtn". (Radio Button controls in previous versions of VB were called Option Buttons and, accordingly, were assigned the prefix "opt".) Placing the three Radio Buttons together within one Group Box will result in the three being treated as one group, meaning that if one button is clicked, the other two will simultaneously be automatically un-clicked. On the bottom left-hand side of the form, the first date ("txtDate1") and second date ("txtDate2") textboxes are Enabled textboxes, while the bottom one ("txtDateDiff") is not.

Designing the Bottom Left-Hand Side of the Form

We will start with adding the functionality to the bottom left side of the form. Let's take a quick look first at what that part of the form does. When the cursor is tabbed out of the middle textbox, the one with an adjacent label of "Second Date", the difference in days between the dates that were entered into the textboxes adjacent to "First Date" and "Second Date" will be calculated. This, of course, will be done only provided that valid dates were entered first. Tabbing out is completed either by pressing the Tab key in the keyboard when the cursor is located on the specific textbox or by clicking the cursor anywhere else on the form after it was first located on the specific textbox.

Adding this functionality requires adding a subroutine that will respond to an event other than the default event of a textbox. Some words of explanation are needed here. A textbox, just like any other object in VB.NET, knows how to respond to many prespecified events. *One of these events is "Leave", which occurs when the textbox loses focus—that is, when it is tabbed out of.* The default event a textbox responds to, however, is TextChanged. That event is raised whenever the text in the textbox is changed, whether by the user or by the code. Consequently, when a textbox is double-clicked on a form, the subroutine that is automatically created in the Code window is the one that handles the TextChanged event. You can try this out by double-clicking on the top left-hand side textbox, the one named txtNumber. Doing so will automatically open the

FIGURE 2.19

Code window and show this code. Being the default event of the textbox control, this method is associated by VB.NET with the form itself, as can be seen at the top of the Code window.

It is thus necessary to circumvent this default handling in the case of this lab because any date value being entered one character at a time will, perforce, begin as an invalid date. Imagine entering the date 1/1/2004. When the first "1" is entered, the date is invalid, because "1" is not a valid date. The date will remain invalid also after entering "/" and even after entering the second "1" and the second "/", because "1/1/" is still an invalid date. Since we do not want to bother the user with message boxes declaring invalid dates while the date is still being entered, the date will be checked only after the user has entered the entire date. Doing so requires first changing the object that is at the center of attention in the code window. Clicking on the left-hand side combo (Figure 2.20), where the objects are listed, will show all the objects currently defined in the class of the form. *This, by the way, demonstrates why adhering to the methodology of assigning fixed prefixes to objects based on the object type is such a good idea. By adding this prefix, it takes no less than a quick glance to know the type of each control, which can otherwise be very confusing when a form has dozens of controls on it.*

Select "txtDate1"; then, on the right-hand side combo, you will see the list of events that this control can respond to. Note how the object in the left-hand side is

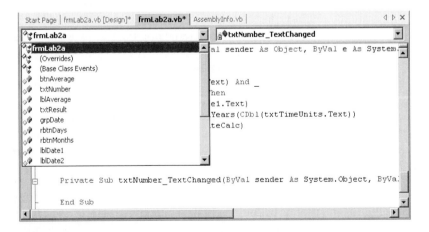

FIGURE 2.20
Objects within the form Lab 2a.

now "txtDate1", rather than the class "frmLab2a". In the right-hand side combo, you will see that the *current* event that is handled by this method is in bold font. If you do not change the Handles value in the subroutine (i.e., the method), then the bold font event will be the default event of that control type. In the case of a Button, this default will be Click.

Scroll up the list of events and double-click on Leave. This is the event that corresponds to tabbing out of a textbox or any other control for that matter. Once you do so, the display on the right-hand side combo will revert back to the class "frmLab2a".

> **Programming Note:** Changing the name of the subroutine alone (i.e., circumventing the preceding process) will not work. The subroutine will still be associated with the default event, even though its name says otherwise. This is a major departure from previous versions of VB.

To assign a different event to the subroutine, change the event name in the Handles *part of the command*, as shown in the following code, where, rather than handle a Click event, the subroutine will handle a DockChanged event:

```
Private Sub Button1_Click _
        (ByVal sender As System.Object, ByVal e As System.EventArgs) _
        Handles Button1.DockChanged
```

In the new routine, we will add the appropriate code to check that the data entered indicated a valid date. It makes sense to check this with the Leave event rather than with the default TextChanged event, because the latter will be raised each time a character is typed into the textbox. In addition, even if a valid date is eventually entered, the data will be an invalid date until almost the last digits are entered. (Entering the date 1/1/2002 will only register a valid date after the first 5 characters are entered.) The code will check whether the data in the Text property of the textbox (meaning the data

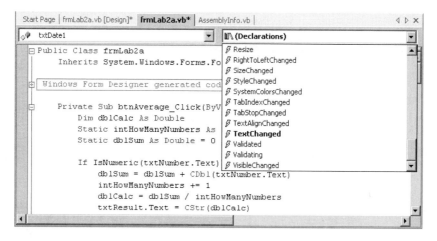

FIGURE 2.21
Events that can be handled by txtDate1.

that were entered into the textbox) is a valid date. This is checked with the IsDate function. If the data are not a valid date, then an appropriate message box will be created.

The MsgBox command has three optional parameters: the prompt, the button, and the title. The prompt is the message inside the message box, the button is the icon on its left, and the title is the caption at the top. The following code is illustrative:

```
Private Sub txtDate1_Leave(ByVal sender As Object, _
             ByVal e As System.EventArgs) Handles txtDate1.Leave
    If Not IsDate(txtDate1.Text) Then
        MsgBox("First date is not a valid date", _
            MsgBoxStyle.Critical, _
            "Date Error")
    End If
End Sub
```

The resulting message box will look like this:

"Next, add the code that will handle the Leave event, i.e., the code that will be executed when the Tab key is clicked while the focus (the current active control) is on the second button. There is nothing special about the code that results (all the methods and properties were discussed earlier):

```
Private Sub txtDate2_Leave(ByVal sender As Object, _
             ByVal e As System.EventArgs) Handles txtDate2.Leave

    Dim tsDiff As System.TimeSpan
    Dim dat1 As System.DateTime
    Dim dat2 As System.DateTime

    If Not IsDate(txtDate2.Text) Then
        MsgBox("Second date is not a valid date", _
            MsgBoxStyle.Critical, "Date Error")
    End If
    If IsDate(txtDate1.Text) And IsDate(txtDate2.Text) Then
        dat1 = CDate(txtDate1.Text)
        dat2 = CDate(txtDate2.Text)
        tsDiff = dat2.Subtract(dat1)
        txtDateDiff.Text = tsDiff.Days()
    End If

End Sub
```

Designing Form of the Bottom Right-Hand Side

On the right-hand side, there is a group box that contains three radio Buttons, a label, and a textbox. When one of the radio Buttons is clicked, then the related number of days, months, or years from the textbox will be added to the first date on the left-hand side of the form. The code will do this by responding to events on the radio Buttons. Here is the code for subroutine "rbtnDays":

```
Private Sub rbtnDays_CheckedChanged(ByVal sender As System.Object, _
        ByVal e As System.EventArgs) Handles rbtnDays.CheckedChanged

    Dim datCalc As Date

    If IsNumeric(txtTimeUnits.Text) And _
        IsDate(txtDate1.Text) And _
        rbtnDays.Checked Then
        datCalc = CDate(txtDate1.Text)
        datCalc = datCalc.AddDays(CDbl(txtTimeUnits.Text))
        txtDate1.Text = CStr(datCalc)
    End If
End Sub
```

In this code, the event is responding to the default event of the radio Button control, so no change in the event is needed. The code checks that the textbox contains a numeric value and that txtDate1 contains a valid date. The code also checks that the radio Button is checked, because the event will be raised also when the radio Button is unchecked. If these conditions are true, then the AddDays method will be used to change the date. Note how the casting is done whenever the data types are not the same.

The other two radio Buttons use the Click event. This event is raised only when the radio Button is clicked. You will need to associate the subroutine with the Click event, as was done earlier with the Leave event. In fact, applying the event saves the need to check the Checked property. Here is the code:

```
Private Sub rbtnMonths_Click(ByVal sender As Object, _
            ByVal e As System.EventArgs) Handles rbtnMonths.Click
    Dim datCalc As Date

    If IsNumeric(txtTimeUnits.Text) And _
        IsDate(txtDate1.Text) Then
        datCalc = CDate(txtDate1.Text)
        datCalc = datCalc.AddMonths(CDbl(txtTimeUnits.Text))
        txtDate1.Text = CStr(datCalc)
    End If

End Sub

Private Sub rbtnYears_Click(ByVal sender As Object, _
            ByVal e As System.EventArgs) Handles rbtnYears.Click
    Dim datCalc As Date
```

```
    If IsNumeric(txtTimeUnits.Text) And _
        IsDate(txtDate1.Text) Then
        datCalc = CDate(txtDate1.Text)
        datCalc = datCalc.AddYears(CDbl(txtTimeUnits.Text))
        txtDate1.Text = CStr(datCalc)
    End If

End Sub
```

Teaching Note: It is recommended at this stage to review the debugging tools available in VB.NET and the application of the F5, F9, F10, and F11 keys, as well as the Output, the Locals, and the Auto windows.

LAB 2.2: PRACTICING THE STRING DATA TYPE

Lab Objectives:
1. Work with strings

- ToUpper method
- Substring method
- Trim method
- Replace method
- Length property

2. Practice using controls

- Textbox
- Button
- Label
- Timer

Application Overview

In this lab, we will practice some of the string methods and will review the Timer control (Figure 2.22). When the project is run, the text "The quick brown fox jumped over the lazy dog" will appear in the txtInput textbox. When the btnLeft Button is clicked, the *x* leftmost characters from this string will be appended to the current multiline display of txtOutput, provided of course that txtLength contains a numeric value and that this value does not exceed the length of the string in txtInput. The btnRight Button will do the same, except that it will copy the *x* rightmost characters, while btnMid will copy from the middle of the string starting with the character whose number is stated in txtStart.

The Buttons below txtOutput work on the string displayed in txtOutput: btnTrim will trim the string, btnUpperCase will change the text to uppercase, and btnReplace will replace every occurrence of the text in txtReplace with the text in txtWith. The btnStart Button activates a timer that eats up the string in txtOutput, truncating the rightmost character every tenth of a second. The form and its controls are shown in Figure 2.22.

Part 1: Building the Form

Start a new solution with a Windows application. Name it **prjChapter2b**. Name its form **frmLab2b**. Then add the Buttons, labels, textboxes, and timer as shown in Figure 2.22,

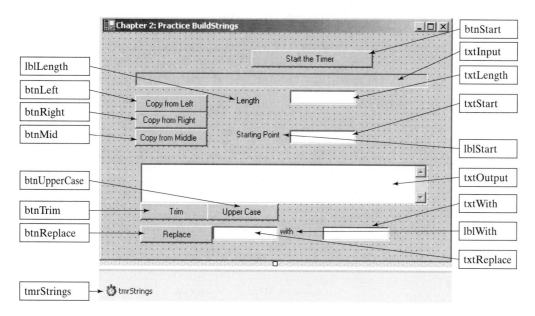

FIGURE 2.22
Timer control: "The Practice Build Strings Project".

naming them accordingly. Buttons start with "btn", labels with "lbl", textboxes with "txt", and the timer with "tmr". Make the txtOutput control multilined with vertical scrollbars by setting its properties accordingly. Finally, set the timer's Interval property to 100 and its Enabled property to False. Change the Text property of txtInput textbox to "The quick brown fox jumped over the lazy dog."

The Buttons btnLeft, btnRight, and btnMid use the Length property, the Substring method, and the & operator to check the input and then append the requested text. The code is as follows:

```
Private Sub btnLeft_Click(ByVal sender As System.Object, _
        ByVal e As System.EventArgs) Handles btnLeft.Click

    Dim strCalc As String = txtInput.Text

    If IsNumeric(txtLength.Text) Then
        If CInt(txtLength.Text) <= strCalc.Length Then
            txtOutput.Text = txtOutput.Text & _
                            txtInput.Text.Substring(0, _
                                CInt(txtLength.Text))
        End If
    End If
End Sub


Private Sub btnRight_Click(ByVal sender As System.Object, _
            ByVal e As System.EventArgs) Handles btnRight.Click

    Dim strCalc As String = txtInput.Text
```

```
        If IsNumeric(txtLength.Text) Then
            If CInt(txtLength.Text) <= strCalc.Length Then
                txtOutput.Text = txtOutput.Text & _
                            txtInput.Text.Substring ( _
                                strCalc.Length - _
                                CDbl(txtLength.Text), _
                                CDbl(txtLength.Text))
            End If
        End If
End Sub


Private Sub btnMid_Click(ByVal sender As System.Object, _
            ByVal e As System.EventArgs) Handles btnMid.Click
    Dim strCalc As String = txtInput.Text

    If IsNumeric(txtStart.Text) And IsNumeric(txtLength.Text) Then
        If CInt(txtStart.Text) + CInt(txtLength.Text) <= _
            strCalc.Length Then
                txtOutput.Text = txtOutput.Text & txtInput.Text.Substring _
                            (CInt(txtStart.Text), CInt(txtLength.Text))
        End If
    End If
End Sub
```

The Buttons btnTrim, btnReplace, and btnUpperCase use the Length property and the Trim, Replace, and ToUpper methods of the String class. Note that because these methods and the property belong to the String class, the data are copied from the textbox to a string variable first. The code is as follows:

```
Private Sub btnTrim_Click(ByVal sender As System.Object, _
            ByVal e As System.EventArgs) Handles btnTrim.Click
    Dim strCalc As String = txtOutput.Text

    txtOutput.Text = strCalc.Trim
End Sub

Private Sub btnUpperCase_Click(ByVal sender As System.Object, _
            ByVal e As System.EventArgs) Handles btnUpperCase.Click
    Dim strCalc As String = txtOutput.Text

    txtOutput.Text = strCalc.ToUpper
End Sub

Private Sub btnReplace_Click(ByVal sender As System.Object, _
        ByVal e As System.EventArgs) Handles btnReplace.Click
    Dim strCalc As String = txtOutput.Text

    txtOutput.Text = strCalc.Replace(txtReplace.Text, txtWith.Text)

End Sub
```

The timer is activated and deactivated by the btnStart Button, which also changes its caption (set by its Text property) according to the action it will perform on the timer.

The timer itself "eats up" the string in txtOutput with the Substring method of the String class, as in the following code:

```
Private Sub btnStart_Click(ByVal sender As System.Object, _
        ByVal e As System.EventArgs) Handles btnStart.Click
    If tmrStrings.Enabled = True Then
        tmrStrings.Enabled = False
        btnStart.Text = "Start the Timer"
    Else
        tmrStrings.Interval = 200
        tmrStrings.Start()
        btnStart.Text = "Stop the Timer"
    End If
End Sub


Private Sub tmrStrings_Tick(ByVal sender As System.Object, _
            ByVal e As System.EventArgs) Handles tmrStrings.Tick

    Dim strCalc As String = txtOutput.Text

    If strCalc.Length > 0 Then
        ' truncate the right most digit
        txtOutput.Text = txtOutput.Text.Substring(0, strCalc.Length - 1)
    End If

End Sub
```

SUGGESTED HOME ASSIGNMENTS

1. Build a new form that receives a date in a textbox, verifies that it is a valid date, and then displays its time components, separated by colons, in another textbox.
2. Build a new form that receives a text in a textbox and then displays the 5th and 10th characters of that text without using strings.
3. Build a new form that will receive four dates in separate textboxes and then show the average difference in days between dates.

TEST YOURSELF

1. Discuss the advantages of working with a Double data type to calculate numeric expressions rather than a String.
2. Why can a date not be increased by just adding 1 to it?
3. Discuss when it is correct to declare a constant rather than a variable.
4. What is Option Explicit?
5. Compare and contrast the Dim and the Static commands. When would you use each?
6. Why is there no equivalent of a Static command for constants?
7. Compare and contrast the outcome of using the Private and Public keywords when declaring a variable.
8. How can a command span more than one line of code? Why would you do so?
9. How can two commands be written on one line? Why would you do so?

10. What is *scope of name recognition*?

11. Why is the following code wrong?

```
I = 10
Dim I As Integer
```

12. What is `Console.Writeline`? When would you use it?

13. What is `Option Strict`?

14. What are *widening conversions*? Why should they always work?

15. What is casting? Why is it necessary? How is it done?

16. What will the following code do and why?

```
Dim I As Integer = -10

I = Math.Abs(I)
Console.WriteLine(Math.Sqrt(I))
Console.WriteLine(Math.Sqrt(CDbl(I)))
Console.WriteLine(Math.Sqrt(I) ^ 2)
Console.WriteLine(Math.Sqrt(CDbl(I)) ^ 2)
```

17. What will the following code do and why?

```
Dim I As Integer = 10
Console.WriteLine(Math.Round(Math.Sqrt(I)) ^ 2)
```

18. In VB6, there was a function named `Left` that returned the leftmost characters of a string. The number of characters was given as a parameter. How would you build such a function with VB.NET `Strings`?

19. What is the `StringBuilder`? Why is it necessary?

20. Write code using a `StringBuilder` that will do the equivalent of the `EndsWith` method of a `String`.

21. Write code using a `StringBuilder` that will perform the equivalent of the `IndexOf` method of a `String`.

Review of Arrays and Control Statements

CHAPTER OBJECTIVES

After completing this chapter, students should possess an understanding of the following topics:

1. Arrays
   - Defining arrays
   - Rank
   - Initializing arrays
   - Jagged arrays
   - The `Erase` statement, along with the `Sort` and `Join` methods
2. Structures
   - What they are
   - Defining structures
3. Enum
4. Control statements
   - If
   - Loops
   - Select Case
   - Subroutines
   - Functions
5. Handling errors
   - Try, Catch, and Finally
6. Review controls (in the lab)
   - Listbox
   - Building control arrays
7. Other topics
   - `Random` object type

Teaching Note: This chapter can be taught either as a review chapter, taking one lesson, or as an integral part of the course, in which case together with the class exercises it may account for three lessons. We recommend that it be taught and not skipped even in an advanced course, because the book handles material in much greater detail than introductory textbooks do.

3.1 AIMS OF CHAPTER

The objective of this chapter, as with the last one, is, on the one hand, to review the knowledge that we expect students who have taken an introductory course in VB.NET to possess and, on the other hand, to extend that knowledge so that the students will have an appropriate advanced knowledge base.

The chapter continues the review of variables—in particular, arrays. Discussed next are control statements: If, loops, and Select Case. These are accompanied by detailed examples of code and are reviewed again in the hands-on labs at the end of the chapter, in which sample applications applying the topics are built in guided line-by-line examples.

The chapter is designed to be taught either as the first lecture in the sequence of a really advanced class, or as the first set of lectures in a less advanced VB class. In the latter case, the chapter should be taught to review and expand upon material taught in previous courses. The lab in which control arrays are built dynamically should not be skipped. It is also a good review of algorithms.

3.2 ARRAYS

Arrays are a set of variables that are grouped together by a shared variable name and are differentiated by an indexed reference. In VB.NET terminology, we speak of an array as containing many *elements*, all of which are exactly the same data type. These elements can be arranged in a single dimension or into many dimensions. The number of elements in a single dimension of an array is called its *rank*. Each element in an array is created when the array is created and ceases to exist when the array does. Likewise, each element of the array is initialized with the default starting value of the array's data type. There can be up to $2^{64}-1$ elements in an array.

In the following example, an array named strArray contains 11 elements, all of the String data type, in one dimension, ranging from index 0 to index 10:

```
Dim strArray(10) As String
```

(There is no typo in the preceding code; there are 11 elements in the array, even though the statement explicitly defines a rank of only 10 elements.) The "10" specifies the *highest* element in that dimension. All arrays in VB.NET inherit from the System.Array type and can be cast into an object data type.

Programming Note: In the previous version of VB, as in many other programming languages, it was possible to specify in each dimension of an array either the number of elements or its starting and ending index value. This option no longer exists in VB.NET.

Individual elements in the array can then be referenced by their index. The index of the element is stated within parentheses. The index always starts at 0 in VB.NET, as shown in the following code:

```
strArray(0) = "a"                  ' place a value into the 1st element
strArray(1) = strArray(0) & "b"    ' place a value into the 2nd element
strArray(10) = "k"                 ' place a value into the 11th element
```

The code is quite misleading, however, because in previous versions of VB, it was possible to declare the starting value of an array both explicitly in the Dim statement itself and as a default in the project as a whole.

An array can also contain many *dimensions*, making them into matrixes. Elements in that case need to be referenced by a set of indexes, each of which refers to one of the dimensions. In the following code, a matrix with 11 by 11 by 11 elements is created and a value placed into the first element:

```
Dim strMatRix(10, 10, 10) As String
strMatRix(0, 0, 0) = "a" ' place a value into the 1st element
```

3.2.1   Explicit and Implicit Rank

The rank of an array can be specified explicitly, as just shown, or it can be specified "on the fly" and then resized dynamically. In the next two examples of code, two arrays are defined: a one-dimensional array first and a three-dimensional one second. Both arrays have unspecified rank. The addition of a pair of parentheses makes the variable into an array, and the addition of commas within the parentheses indicates the additional dimensionality:

```
Dim intArray() As Integer      ' An array of integers
Dim dblMatrix(,,) As Double    ' A three-dimensional matrix of double
```

However, it is necessary in this case to specify the rank of the array before it can be referenced, as the following code reveals:

```
intArray(1) = 10   ' This will not work, rank is not specified yet
```

The rank of the array is specified with the ReDim command. The ReDim command applies only to implicit rank arrays—that is, to arrays that were dimensioned without specifically stating their rank. The syntax of the ReDim command is

```
ReDim [Preserve] <array-name> (<integer specifying new-rank>)
```

The following command redimensions the array, changing its rank dynamically:

```
ReDim intArray(19)      ' Make the array contain 20 elements
```

There is an important caveat here: When an array is redimensioned, VB.NET will not guarantee that the data stored in its elements will not be lost. Guaranteeing that data will not be lost requires the addition of the Preserve keyword to the command:

```
ReDim Preserve intArray(19) ' Make the array contain 20 elements
```

That is how it works with a one-dimensional array. With a multidimensional array the ReDim command, however, works somewhat differently. It changes the rank only on the rightmost dimension, except for the first time a rank is specified for a matrix. Thus, the first three of the following commands are valid, but the fourth is not:

```
Dim dblMatrix(,,) As Double    ' A three-dimensional matrix of double

        ' This is valid as the first specification of matrix rank
        ' This will make the matrix 11 by 11 by 11
ReDim Preserve dblMatrix(10, 10, 10)

        ' This is valid, too, changing the rightmost dimension
        ' This will make the matrix 11 by 11 by 21
ReDim Preserve dblMatrix(10, 10, 20)

        ' But not this, because it is changing a higher dimension
        ' of an already specified matrix
ReDim Preserve dblMatrix(20, 10, 10)
```

The GetUpperBound method can be helpful in handling these redimensions:

```
Dim intArray() As Integer     ' An array of integers
Dim dblMatrix(,,) As Double   ' A three-dimensional matrix of double

ReDim Preserve dblMatrix(5, 10, 15)  ' this is legal
Console.WriteLine(dblMatrix.GetUpperBound(0))  ' Will print 5
Console.WriteLine(dblMatrix.GetUpperBound(1))  ' Will print 10
Console.WriteLine(dblMatrix.GetUpperBound(2))  ' Will print 15

ReDim intArray(10)
Console.WriteLine(intArray.GetUpperBound(0))   ' Will print 10
```

The method returns the upper bound of a given dimension of an array—in effect, one less than the number of elements, or rank, of that dimension. But the method works only when the array has been dimensioned, of course. The method works with both single- and multiple-dimension arrays. Its only parameter is the dimension number whose rank is to be returned.

Accordingly, when the rank of a certain dimension is not known, the GetUpperBound can be used to specify the rank of the dimensions that will not be changed. This can be done either through a variable or by writing the method directly in the ReDim command:

```
Dim I0, I1 As Integer
I0 = dblMatrix.GetUpperBound(0)
ReDim Preserve dblMatrix(I0, dblMatrix.GetUpperBound(1), 10)
```

In the next example, an array with 11 elements is dimensioned, each element is assigned its index number in the array, and then five additional elements are added. Note that there is no need to specify the data type in the ReDim statement—indeed, to do so would be a syntax error—because the ReDim statement cannot change the data type of the array. (The `For` statement is described in detailed elsewhere.) The `UBound` method returns the upper bound of the array. The code is as follows:

```
Dim bytExample(10) As Byte
Dim I2 As Integer
For I2 = 0 To 10
    bytExample(I2) = I2
Next

ReDim Preserve bytExample(15)
For I2 = 11 To UBound(bytExample)
    bytExample(I2) = I2
Next
ReDim Preserve bytExample(8)
Console.WriteLine(UBound(bytExample))
```

The second `ReDim` statement actually makes the array smaller. This is perfectly correct, even with the `Preserve` keyword. If the new rank of the array is larger than its original rank, then the new elements will contain the default value of the data type of the array; *if the new rank of the array is smaller than its original rank, then elements will be deleted from the array, even though it has the `Preserve` keyword.*

Programming Note: A seemingly inconsistent aspect of VB.NET is that the upper bound of an array, as returned by this method, is in effect smaller by 1 than its actual rank. Thus, the `console.writeline` command will print 8 in the output window while there are really 9 elements in the array.

Each time an array is redimensioned, the array, which is in fact an object, is deleted and then re-created. This can be extremely inefficient if arrays are redimensioned over and over again. In such cases, it is more advisable to create an array with a larger than necessary rank and to manage in a separate integer variable what the actual upper bound of the array is.

3.2.2 Initializing Arrays

Like any other variables, arrays can be assigned initial values. This is done in the case of an array in a slightly different manner than with a nonarray variable. Assigning an initial value requires defining a *new* instance of the object type:

```
Dim strArray() As String = New String() {"0", "1", "2", "3"}
```

The rank of the array cannot be specified explicitly; it is derived from the number of initial values that are provided in the list. This list must be specified within *braces*, {}, otherwise known as "wiggly parentheses." The order in which the initial values appear inside the braces will be the order in which they will be assigned to the elements in the array. An empty array will accordingly be defined by specifying an empty list within the braces. The braces must always be written, even when no initial values are assigned:

```
Dim strEmpty() As String = New String() {}
```

Alternatively, the rank of the array can be specified explicitly with the object type. In this case, the rank must exactly fit the number of initial values. Had the number 3 in the following statement been replaced by 2 or by 4, a compilation error would have resulted:

```
Dim strArray() As String = New String(3) {"0", "1", "2", "3"}
```

Multidimensional arrays can also be initialized in this manner, except that the initial values of each dimension need to be clustered together within another pair of braces in addition to the braces that cluster together all the initial values. An example of how to do that is

```
Dim strArray(,) As String = New String(1, 2) _
                {{"0.0", "0.1", "0.2"}, {"1.0", "1.1", "1.2"}}
```

In this example, the initial value of each element is the value of its identifying pair of indexes within the array. Accordingly, printing the elements

```
Console.Write(strArray(0, 0) & ",")
Console.Write(strArray(0, 1) & ",")
Console.Write(strArray(0, 2) & ",")
Console.Write(strArray(1, 0) & ",")
Console.Write(strArray(1, 1) & ",")
Console.Write(strArray(1, 2))
```

will show this display in the Output window:

```
0.0,0.1,0.2,1.0,1.1,1.2
```

Consistent with one-dimensional arrays, this dimensioning will produce exactly the same result:

```
Dim strArray(,) As String = New String(,) _
                {{"0.0", "0.1", "0.2"}, {"1.0", "1.1", "1.2"}}
```

> **Programming Note:** The keyword New can be used also with variables that are not arrays. In that case, it is a convenient way of assigning strings with a repeating value. In the following example, an initial value of 20 "A"s is assigned:
>
> ```
> Dim strMultiple As String = New String("A", 20)
> ```

3.2.3 Jagged Array

Occasionally, the number of elements in the lower (rightmost) dimensions of an array may be different, depending on the index of the higher (leftmost) dimensions of the array. The VB.NET documentation brings an excellent example of such a case: in a two-dimensional array of the days of the year indexed by the number of the month and the number of the day within the month, there will be a rank of 12 in the first dimension, corresponding to the twelve months, but a varying number of elements in the second dimension, because the number of days in a month changes depending on the month. (One could make it even more complex by including the additional complexity of accounting for February 29, but we will leave it at that.) VB.NET provides the tools to define and reference such an array, known as a *jagged array*.

In the next example, the code enables weight watchers to manage their daily calorie input in a jagged array. There is one crucial difference, however, between jagged arrays and regular arrays, and that is in the indexing method. Because the dimensionality of the arrays varies, two indexes must be specified. In the example, a jagged array is created with a rank of 12 in its highest dimension and an unspecified number of elements in the second dimension. The number of elements in the second dimension is set dynamically to the number of days in that month, given the specific year. This is done with the `DaysInMonth` method of the `DateTime` object, which returns a value as its name implies. Values are then assigned and read based on a double index. But before this can be done, it is imperative to instantiate the lower dimensions of the jagged array. The code is as follows:

```
' Only the top-level dimension is specified explicitly.
Dim intDailyCalorieLevel()() As Integer = {New Integer(11) {}}
Dim intMonth As Integer          ' Month number within year
Dim intDaysInMonth As Integer    ' Number of days within the month

For intMonth = 0 To 11
    intDaysInMonth = DateTime.DaysInMonth(Year(Now), intMonth)

    ' Instantiate the lower level of the jagged array.
    intDailyCalorieLevel(intMonth) = _
        New Integer(intDaysInMonth - 1) {}
Next

intDailyCalorieLevel(2)(0) = 2001
intDailyCalorieLevel(2)(1) = intDailyCalorieLevel(2)(0) + 10
```

3.2.4 The `Erase`, the `Sort`, and the `Join` Arrays Statements

The `Erase` statement and the `Sort` and `Join` methods are especially helpful when handling arrays. The `Erase` statement empties an array, in effect deleting the array to `Nothing`. When the dimensionality of the array is set dynamically, the `Erase` statement will cause the array to have no elements at all. In the following example, a new array, `strArray`, is defined with its rank set dynamically—a value is assigned to the second element of the array and then it is erased:

```
Dim strArray() As String = New String() {"0", "1", "2", "3"}
strArray(1) = "a"
Erase strArray
```

At this stage, the array has no elements in it. Referencing one of them will result in a runtime error. It is essential, therefore, to redimension the array before any elements in it can be referenced:

```
ReDim strArray(4)    ' strArray will otherwise have Nothing
strArray(0) = "a"
strArray(1) = "b"
strArray(2) = "c"
strArray(3) = "d"
```

The Join method concatenates the elements of an array into a string, optionally adding a separator between them. Join is a function. It returns an array of the joined arrays. Applying this method to the values assigned to strArray will print, in the Output window, a string that concatenates the values in the array:

```
Dim strValue As String

strValue = Join(strArray)
Console.WriteLine(strValue)              ' Will print "abcd"

strValue = Join(strArray, ", ")
Console.WriteLine(strValue)              ' Will print "a, b, c, d"
```

Programming Note: There is also a method named Join in the String class. It performs the same operation, except that the order of the parameters is opposite! In the following code, both strA and strC will contain "A, B":

```
Dim strA, strC As String
Dim strB() As String = {"A", "B"}
strA =      Join(strB, ",")
strC = strC.Join(",", strB)
```

The Sort method is an Array class method. It sorts the values in an array. The method has many overrides. In its simplest form, the Sort method will simply sort all the elements in an array, or it can sort only a range of elements. As the following code shows, the range of sorted elements can be limited with other overrides:

```
ReDim strArray(3)
strArray(0) = "9"
strArray(1) = "2"
strArray(2) = "0"
strArray(3) = "7"

Console.WriteLine(Join(strArray, ", ")) ' Will print "9, 2, 0, 7"
Array.Sort(strArray, 1, 2) ' sort 2 elements starting with element 1
Console.WriteLine(Join(strArray, ", ")) ' Will print "9, 0, 2, 7"

Array.Sort(strArray) ' simply sort all the elements in the array
Console.WriteLine(Join(strArray, ", ")) ' Will print "0, 2, 7, 9"
```

3.3   STRUCTURES

Variables can also contain user-defined data types. These are in effect structures that combine several variables into one encompassing unit. For example, a module or form handling a person's "buddies" may contain a structure that combines the friend's first name, last name, and address into one unit, thus showing that a friend's first name, last name, and address are associated in that they are all members of one overall unit. Structures are declared with the Structure command. Once they are declared, they can be applied as any other data type to specify the data type of variables. This is useful when many instances of the structure will be used, as in the case of managing all of one's buddies in an array where it is beneficial to show the association between first name, last name, and address explicitly. The simplified syntax of the Structure command is as follows:

```
Structure <structure-name>
      [Public | Private] <member-name> As <data-type>
      {[Public | Private] <member-name> As <data-type>}
End Structure
```

Note that between the `Structure` and the `End Structure` statements there must be at least one *member* declared. That member can be of any data type.

`Public` specifies that the *member* will be accessible outside the `structure`, while `Private` means that it will be recognized only inside the `structure`. This distinction is necessary because a `structure`, just like a class, can also contain methods. The most common of these would likely be the constructor method New. (Constructors and methods will be covered extensively in the next chapters.) The code that follows defines a new structure name, `Buddies`:

```
Public Class frmLoops
    Inherits System.Windows.Forms.Form

    Structure Buddies
        Public strFName As String
        Public strLNAme As String
        Public strAddr As String
    End Structure
End Class
```

When this structure is added to a form, it should be added at the Class level; it should not be declared in a subroutine.

Programming Note: Members within a structure cannot have initial values, except for constants. Once the structure is defined, it can be used just as any other data type:

```
Public myList(100) As Buddies
Public myFriend As Buddies
Public intFriendNumber As Integer
```

When it is referenced, however, the structure name should precede the member name:

```
myList(intFriendNumber).strFName = txtFName.Text
myList(intFriendNumber).strLNAme = txtLName.Text
myList(intFriendNumber).strAddr = txtAddr.Text
```

with VB.NET providing appropriate guidance accordingly through its *intellisense* interface, with methods in purple flying boxes and controls in stationary blue ones:

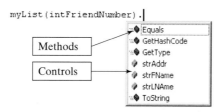

As can be seen, the preceding structure does behave much as a class does. Both have members, constructors, methods, properties, and so on. Indeed, a `structure` is rather similar to a class, which will be covered in later chapters on object orientation, except that structures cannot be inherited and cannot be terminated. Additionally, by default all structure members are `Public`, while members in a class are `Private`, and structures cannot be `Protected` or respond to events (more on that in the next chapters). Instead, a structure should be thought of as an extended user-defined combination of data types, and, just like any other data type (with the exception of the special case of the `String` data type—see Chapter 2), it does not require instantiation the way objects do. Indeed, a `structure` inherits from the `System.ValueType` class.

This is an important distinction. Different objects may reference the same data; therefore, when one object changes the data, the change will immediately and automatically be reflected in the other object, too. This is not the case with a structure. Like data types, structures are unrelated to each other. Thus, if an object in the VB code represents a file (as will we see in later in this book), then any changes made to that object will automatically carry over to the file and any changes in the file will be accessible to the object on the code. This is clearly not the case with a structure. Even when several variables are defined with the same structure, they are unrelated variables, just as two `Integer` type variables are independent of each other and changes in one do not carry over to the other.

> **Programming Note:** Declaring a structure with the keyword `Dim` is equivalent to declaring it with the keyword `Public`. This is a bit misleading, because usually the keyword `Dim` is equivalent to keyword `Private`. When a structure is intended to be private, declare it with the keyword `Private`.

Moreover, when a variable is declared as an object, it can refer to many different instances of that object that can be changed within the code with a simple assignment statement. This is not the case with a variable that is declared as a given structure data type. The latter variable will always be attached to the specific instance of that structure, much as a variable defined as an `Integer` will always refer to a specific data location. Thus, when the value of one object is assigned to another object, the data are not actually copied, but instead, a pointer is set so that the two objects point to the same data. Hence, any change to one variable will automatically be reflected in the other. When the value of a variable that is declared as a given structure data type is passed to another variable that is declared as the same structure data type, the actual values are copied; therefore, any change to one variable will *not* be reflected in the other. For the same reason, assigning `Nothing` to variable that is declared as a given structure data type will simply set its value to `Nothing`, while with an object such an assignment will disconnect the object from what it is pointing at. Thus, in the following code, `myList(1).strAddr` will contain "`Washington Rd.`":

```
myList(2).strAddr = "Washington Rd."
myList(1).strAddr = myList(2).strAddr
myList(2).strAddr = "Washington St."
```

Had `myList` been declared as an instantiation of an object, then `myList(1).strAddr` would have contained "`Washington St.`".

Programming Note: A comparison of two variables declared with the same structure as their data type must be completed one structure member at a time. The `Equals` method that compares the content of two objects does not work here.

3.3.1   Methods in Structures

Structures can also contain methods and constructors. We can extend the preceding structure statement to include a constructor—these are subroutines that are called with the keyword `New` and are used to initialize a new instance of an object, as shown by the following code:

```
Structure Buddies
    Public strFName As String
    Public strLNAme As String
    Public strAddr As String
    Public datDOB As Date
    Private intAge As Integer

    Public Sub New(ByVal datDOB As Date)

        If Not IsDate(Me.datDOB) Then
            datDOB = Now
        End If
        intAge = Now.Year - datDOB.Year
        Console.WriteLine(intAge)
    End Sub

End Structure
```

This constructor writes in the Output window the age of the friend by calculating the difference in years between the year of the current date as given by the `Now` function and the year of his or her date of birth. (We will go into methods and constructors in the next chapter dealing with object orientation.) As with any other constructor, this one is activated with the `New` method of the structure. Note that the constructor would not have been activated had we just accessed the structure through the `Dim` statement without adding the `New` keyword to the statement as follows:

```
Dim myFriend As New Buddies(#1/1/1970#)
```

3.3.2   Arrays Inside Structures

We saw in the preceding code that a convenient way of manipulating structures is to use them as the data type of an array. In that example, we dealt with a list of our buddies, and for each, we collected data on their first name, last name, and address. These three elements of data, being represented as members of a structure, were thus related so that the first name of a given friend was tied to his or her last name and address. We used the code

```
Public myList(100) As Buddies
```

It is sometimes necessary to add an array inside the structure itself. In an extension of this example, let us add the names of the children of each friend. Of course, each friend may have many children, so an array is necessary:

```
Structure Buddies
    Public strFName As String
    Public strLNAme As String
    Public strAddr As String
    Public strKids() As String
End Structure
```

The rank of the member is not and cannot be specified. The rank will be resolved automatically during runtime. As many instances as are referenced of the array within the structure will exist. Thus, in the following code, the first friend will have two children, while the second friend will have three:

```
Public myList(100) As Buddies

myList(0).strKids(0) = "Abe"
myList(0).strKids(1) = "Arnold"

myList(1).strKids(0) = "Mike"
myList(1).strKids(1) = "Michael"
myList(1).strKids(2) = "Michelle"
```

The index next to the variable name indexes the array of buddies. The index next to the member name indexes the child number within each friend. This can be a convenient and neat way to avoid jagged arrays without explicitly specifying the sets of ranks.

Programming Note: A better way of handling data structures is with the Dataset object and its related objects. More detail on those topics will be given in Chapters 11 through 13.

3.4   ENUM

Enums are the equivalent of an array of numbered constants (i.e., enumerated predefined values). Applying Enums is a convenient way of handling constant values that are referenced many times, such as a set of predefined colors, through an index. They are used extensively by the System methods of VB.Net. As with Structures, Enums cannot appear inside a method. They should be declared at the Class level. In the following example, an Enum is used to enumerate the day of the week (note that, as a numeric value, an Enum can be manipulated with arithmetic operators):

```
Public Class myExample
    Enum myWeek
        Sunday = 1
        Monday = 2
        Tuesday = 3
        Wednesday = 4
```

```
            Thursday = 5
            Friday = 6
            Saturday = 7
            NextSunday = 8
    End Enum

    Private Sub mySub ()
            Console.WriteLine _
                    ("If today is " & myWeek.Sunday)
            Console.WriteLine _
                    ("Then, tomorrow will be " & myWeek.Sunday + 1)
    End Sub
End Class
```

The Output window will show the enumerated value of the constant:

```
The value of today is 1
Tomorrow will be 2
```

3.5   CONTROL STATEMENTS, SELECTION

There are three types of control statements in Visual Basic: selection, repetition, and sequence. Selection commands are used to check whether a statement should be executed. Repetition commands are used to execute a block of statements many times. Sequence commands are used to execute sections of code in separate functions or subroutines.

There are two major selection statements in Visual Basic: If and Select. The If statement has two syntax options. The short format has only one then-statement and one optional else-statement:

```
If <condition> Then [<statement>][Else <else-statement>]
```

The block-form syntax supports several then-statements and several else-statements, but must be closed with an End If statement:

```
If <condition> Then
    [<statement>]
    {[<statement>]}
[Else
    [<else-statement>]
    {[<else-statement>]}]
End If
```

If the *condition* is true, then the *statements* are executed. If the *condition* is false and there is an Else clause, the *else-statements* are executed. Alternatively, the block syntax can contain the ElseIf keyword:

```
If <condition> Then
    [<statement>]
    {[<statement>]}
```

```
[ElseIf  <else-condition> Then
    [<else-then-statement>]
    {[<else-the-statement>]}]
End If
```

In the following code example, an If statement is used to toggle a timer on and off (if the timer is enabled, it is than disabled, and if it is disabled, it is then enabled), while at the same time changing the caption of the Button through its Text property:

```
If tmrStrings.Enabled = True Then
    tmrStrings.Stop()
    ' The timer can be stopped also by changing its Enabled property.
    ' tmrStrings.Enabled = False
    btnStart.Text = "Start the Timer"
Else
    tmrStrings.Start()
    btnStart.Text = "Stop the Timer"
End If
```

In the next example, the value of a number is examined to determine whether it is divisible by 5 and, if not, whether it is divisible by 3 and, if not, whether it is divisible by 2. (As we shall soon see, there is a more elegant way of doing that with the Select Case statement.) The following code uses the Mod operator, which divides the first number by the second number and returns the remainder:

```
    ' will write 0 because the remainder of 10/5 is 0
Console.WriteLine(10 Mod 5)
    ' will write 2 because the remainder of 12/5 is 2
Console.WriteLine(12 Mod 5)
```

The If statement will look like this:

```
If I Mod 5 = 0 Then
    Console.WriteLine(I & " divides into 5")
ElseIf I Mod 3 = 0 Then
    Console.WriteLine(I & " divides into 3")
ElseIf I Mod 2 = 0 Then
    Console.WriteLine(I & " divides into 2")
End If
```

Writing code this way can be quite cumbersome when there are many If clauses. There are more readable ways of writing such code. For example, when there are several values of a single expression being evaluated, it is preferable to use the Select Case statement:

```
Select Case <text-expression>
    Case <expression-list>
     {[<statements>]}
     {[Case <expression-list>
        [<statements>]}
```

```
   {[Case Else
        [<statements>]}
End Select
```

In the preceding syntax, *test-expression* is any numeric or string expression and *expression-list* is a list of one or more values, separated by commas, that are compared with the value in *test-expression*. Visual Basic examines whether *test-expression* matches the different Case clauses in the order they appear in the Select block. If *test-expression* matches the value or values in the *expression-list* of the Case clause, then the statements following that Case clause until the next Case clause are executed, and the next Case clauses are skipped, making the End Select the next executable statement. If *test-expression* does not match any of the Case clauses, then the statements following the Case Else clause, if it appears, are executed.

In the next example, *text-expression* contains an Integer type variable. The different Case clauses demonstrate three ways in which *expression-list* can be used. In the first Case clause, intValue is compared with a single value. In the second Case clause, intValue is compared with a list of values. In the third Case clause, intValue is compared with a range of values, and in the fourth Case clause, intValue is compared with a list and range of values. If intValue contains 10, then it will contain 99 after the select block has been executed. If intValue contains 20, then it will contain 25. Note that if intValue contains 10, the second Case clause will not be executed! If intValue contains any value between 30 and 40, then it will contain 40; and if intValue contains 80 or 90 or any value between 100 and 200, then intValue will contain 100. The code is as follows:

```
Dim intValue As Integer = 10
Select Case intValue
    Case 10
        intValue = 99
    Case 10, 20
        intValue = 25
    Case 30 To 40
        intValue = 40
    Case 80, 90, 100 To 200
        intValue = 100
End Select
```

The Select Case statement can also examine an *expression-list* with other conditions except equals. Doing so requires the inclusion of the Is keyword and an appropriate condition:

```
Select Case intValue
    Case Is < 10
        intValue = 99
    Case Is < 20
        intValue = 25
    Case Is < 30
        intValue = 40
End Select
```

In addition, the `Select` `Case` statement can examine other data types, such as `Strings`. An example of applying this command to strings is

```
Dim strValue As String = "95"
Select Case strValue
    Case Is = "10"
        strValue = "99"
    Case Is = "145", "20"
        strValue = 25
    Case Is > "30"
        strValue = "40"
    Case Else
        strValue = "100"
End Select
```

The `Case` `Else` clause will catch any value that is no caught by the preceding `Case` clauses. No `Case` clauses can follow the `Case` `Else` clause.

3.6   CONTROL STATEMENT LOOPS

Loops allow the execution of lines of code repeatedly and enable the limiting of this repetition on a condition. There are three types of loops in Visual Basic:

1. `For Next`
2. variations on the `Do` loop
3. `For Each Next`.

The `For Next` loop is the ideal technique for examining arrays or any sequence of values. The algorithm behind the `For Next` loop is simple:

1. At the `For` statement, complete the following steps:
   1.1 Place the *start* numeric value (it must be a numeric value, although it can be cast from a variable with a nonnumeric data type) into the *counter*. The *counter* must be a variable that can support numeric operations, one of the numeric data type.
   1.2 If the counter is within range of the *end* value, then enter the loop and execute the *loop-statements*. Otherwise, go to the statement after the `Next` statement without executing the *loop-statements*. The counter is within range of the *end* value if it is not larger than the *end* value and the *step* contains a positive numeric value, or if it is not smaller than the *end* value and the *step* contains a negative numeric value. If no *step* is specified, it is 1 by default.
2. Inside the `For` block, perform the following functions:
   2.1 Execute the *loop-statements* in the order they appear until the `Next` statement.
   2.2 If one of the *loop-statements* is `Exit For`, then go to the command after the `Next` statement.

3. At the Next statement (note that the Next statement will be executed only if Visual Basic entered the loop), follow these instructions:

   3.1 Add the *step* value to the *counter*. If there is no *step* specified in the For statement, then add 1.

   3.2 Go back and reperform the algorithm starting at step 1.2.

The syntax of the For Next loop is

```
For <counter> = <start-value> To <end-value> [Step <increment>]
          [<loop-statements>]
          [Exit For ]
          [<loop-statements>]
Next [<counter>]
```

If Step is omitted, the default *step* increment is 1. The *counter* at the Next statement is also optional: Adding or removing it has no executable effect. But if it is added, it must be the same as the *counter* in the For statement.

Programming Note: When a loop is completed after being executed at least once, the value in the counter variable will be one increment step value beyond the value stated in the end parameter.

Programming Note: Although this makes no difference in the way the code is run, when writing embedded loops (i.e., one loop within another), adding the counter at the Next statement makes the code more readable.

Programming Note: Changing the value of the counter variable within the loop will affect the number of times the loop is executed. This is not a recommended practice: It can confuse the person reading the loop. Moreover, in some programming languages (e.g., PL/1), changing the value of the counter variable within the loop may work in debug mode, but not when an Optimizer complier is used.

For loops are very useful for reading through an array. In the following code, a For loop is used to sum the values in all the odd-numbered elements of an array:

```
Dim intArray(10) As Integer
Dim intIndex As Integer
Dim intSum As Integer

For intIndex = 1 To 10 Step 2
    intSum = intSum + intArray(intIndex)
Next
```

In this loop, the counter variable, intIndex, is assigned the value 1. Then Visual Basic verifies that it is not larger than the end value of the loop, in this case 10. Since intIndex, being 1, is not larger, the command inside the For block is executed. At the Next statement, the value of intIndex is incremented by 2, the step value, and checked again if it is not larger than the end value. Since it is not, the statement inside the loop is executed again. This continues until the value of intIndex is no longer not larger than the end value. If the value of intIndex changes inside the loop, the new value will be checked at the Next statement. When the loop is completed, the counter variable, intIndex, will contain 11.

In the next example, a For Next loop is used to sum the elements of the same array, but from the highest indexed element to the lowest and only while the sum is smaller than 100:

```
For intIndex = 10 To 0 Step -1
    intSum = intSum + intArray(intIndex)
    If intSum >= 100 Then Exit For
Next
```

Note that the loop is exited by using the Exit For command. Assigning a value smaller than 1 to intIndex would have had the same effect, but only when there are no statements between that assignment statement and the Next statement.

The For loop is also a very useful for repeating an operation a prespecified number of times. In the following code, a For loop is used to calculate the factorial of a number (the factorial of a positive integer is the product of all the integers between 1 and that number; the factorial of 6, for example, is 1*2*3*4*5*6, which is 720):

```
intSum = 1
For I = 1 To 6
    intSum = intSum * I
Next
```

The For loop is also a convenient way to search through a list of values. In the following code, a List Box named lstBuddies is searched for a given value with a loop:

```
Dim I As Integer

lstBuddies.Items.Add("A")
lstBuddies.Items.Add("B")
lstBuddies.Items.Add("C")
lstBuddies.Items.Add("D")
lstBuddies.Items.Add("E")

For I = 0 To lstBuddies.Items.Count - 1
    If lstBuddies.Items.Item(I) = "D" Then
        Console.WriteLine("Located at entry " & I + 1)
        Exit For
    End If
Next

If I = lstBuddies.FindString("D") Then
    Console.WriteLine("Code works okay")
End If
```

In the foregoing code, the values of the List Box items are assigned with the Items.Add method. The Items.Count property contains the number of elements in the List Box. Because these items are indexed from 0, the loop goes up to the Items.Count value minus 1. The Items.Item(I) property contains the value in the item that is numbered "i". This whole code can of course be simplified by using the List

Box method `FindString`, which performs the same operation as the loop; that is why the last three lines of code verify the results obtained in the loop.[4]

> **Teaching Note:** We recommend running the preceding code while examining how the variables change in the Autos window. That will give the students an excellent hands-on feeling for how loops work.

3.7   SIMPLE LOOPS

In this section, we will utilize `For` loops. Recall that a `For` loop will perform the statements inside the For block a given number of times as controlled by an index (also known as a counter). The index is assigned a starting value, and then this index is checked against the end-value. If the index is within the range of the end-value, the statements inside the For block are executed in sequence. After performing the statements inside the For block, the `Next` command that closes the For block is executed. The `Next` command increments the loop index by the value in the `Step` clause (or by 1 is there is no `Step` clause). Then the index is checked again against the end-value. If the index is still within the range of the end-value, the statements inside the For block are executed in sequence once more.

The use of an index to control the For block is a powerful tool. It provides two major advantages: (1) the ability to perform a section of code a given number of times in a controlled manner and (2) the ability to number (i.e., to index) each execution of that section of code in an ascending or descending order. Both of these advantages appear in the following code:

```
Dim I As Integer
Dim intSum As Integer = 0

For I = 1 To 10
    intSum += I
Next
```

The preceding code adds up all the integer numbers between 1 and 10. We can see in this code these two major advantages cited. The statement inside the For block adds into the variable `intSum` the value of the variable I. This statement is performed 10 times, because the index of the loop, the variable `I`, controls the number of times the code inside the For block is executed. The index in effect says: count how many times the For block is entered by numbering the first entry 1 (this is its starting value) and

---

[4]Other convenient methods and properties of the List Box are as follows:

`SelectedIndex`	Returns the index of the selected item in the List Box.
`SelectedItem`	Returns the value of the selected item in the List Box.
`Sorted`	Returns a `True` value when the values of the items in the List Box are sorted. Setting this property to `True` will sort the items.
`GetSelected`	Returns `True` if the index is that of the selected item in the List Box.
`Items.Add`	Adds an item to a List Box.
`Items.Remove`	Removes an item from a List Box.

counting up to 10 (this is the end-value). As a direct result of this process, the variable I will also contain an index that specifies how many times the statements inside the For Block have been performed. The first time the code is executed, the index will be 1; the next time, it will be 2; and so on.

> **Programming Note:** In the foregoing code, the variable intSum is provided with an initial value of zero, even though, by default, that is the initial value of an Integer data type. This is done on purpose. Relying on the defaults of a language is not a good programming habit. These defaults might be different in other languages and may even change within the same language between one version of it and another—as actually happened with the transition from VB6 to VB.NET. It is a good programming habit to always explicitly declare the initial values.

If you run the code placing a Break Point on the For statement and advancing one command at a time by clicking on the F11 key on the keyboard, you can see how these numbers change in the Locals window. This window will open up automatically when the application is run. It is one of three in the lower left window pane. The Locals window shows what variables are currently defined and their values. When a value changes, it is painted in red. When the application is first run, the Locals window will show the initial values of the variables. As shown in Figure 3.1, when the next line to be executed (the one with a yellow arrow) is the For statement, the value of both integers is 0. (See circled portion of screen.)

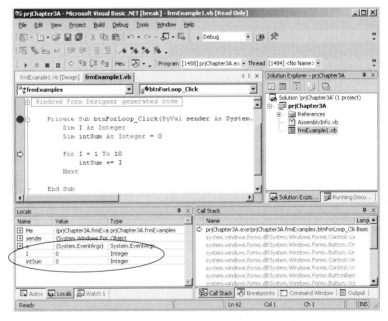

FIGURE 3.1
Initial Values in the For loop.

As F11 is clicked once, the value of the variable I is changed to 1 and shown as such in red in the Locals window (Figure 3.2).

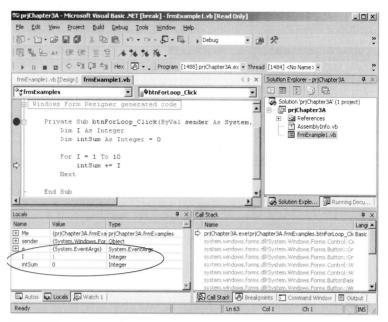

FIGURE 3.2
Values at the beginning of the first iteration of the For Loop.

If you continue clicking F11 and observing the way the values in the variables change in the Locals window, you will notice that the next time F11 is clicked the value of the variable intSum is incremented by 1, or, to be precise, by the value in the variable I. (See Figure 3.3.)

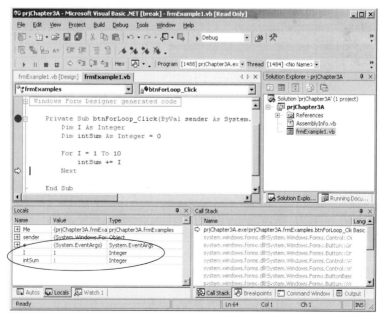

FIGURE 3.3
Values at the end of the first iteration of the For loop.

The next time F11 is clicked, the code inside the loop will be entered for a second time. But this time the variable I will contain the value 2 (Figure 3.4). That is what we mean when we say that the index of the loop—in this case, the variable I—indexes the execution of the code within the loop.

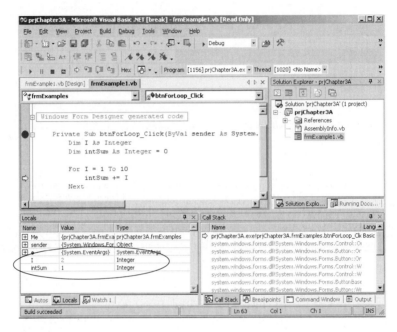

FIGURE 3.4
Values at the beginning of the second iteration of the For loop.

This pattern will continue, with the variable I containing the number of the current execution of the code. Since the loop is limited by the variable I to be executed only as long as the value in I is within the end-value of the loop, the variable I also controls the loop. So the loop will be executed 10 times in this case. The variable I will contain the value 1 the first time the code inside the loop is executed, the value 2 the second time the code inside the loop is executed, the value 3 the third time, and so on.

For *loops are an excellent way of performing the same operation over and over a given number of times while providing a self-incrementing index that can be used to identify each iteration.* We will apply this powerful tool in the next set of examples.

3.7.1 The Factorial of X

We already saw code that generates factorials, but a quick rehearsal looking at it in detail is beneficial. The factorial, X!, of a positive integer, X, is defined as the product of all the integers from 1 up to X. Only positive integers have factorials. And so, the factorial of 5 is 5! = 1*2*3*4*5, which is 120. The factorial of 10 is 10! = 1*2*3*4*5*6*7*8*9*10. Suppose you are asked to find the factorial of an unknown number. How would you go about finding it?

If you look at the factorial carefully, what you see is that it is composed of a set of multiplications. The product of these multiplications starts with 1 and is then multiplied by every integer greater than 1 in order, up to the integer value of X. Now that is precisely the logic of a For loop: Perform the code (in this case multiplication) a given number of times (the value of X), with an increasing value each time (the value of the loop index). That algorithm is performed by the form in Figure 3.5, which is provided in the CD.

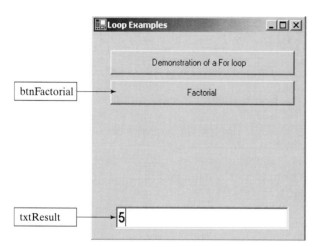
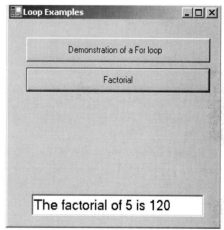

a) Entering the parameter for the Factorial Loop.

b) Result after clicking on the Factorial button.

FIGURE 3.5

Here is the code:

```
Private Sub btnFactorial_Click _
        (ByVal sender As System.Object, _
        ByVal e As System.EventArgs) _
        Handles btnFactorial.Click
' This subroutine handles a click event on the btnFactorial
' Button. When the Button is clicked, the value in the TextBox
' txtResult is checked to verify that it is numeric, integer,
' and positive. If it is, a For loop is used to calculate its
' factorial and display it back in the textbox.

        Dim I As Integer   ' Index of the loop
        Dim dblSum As Double = 1 ' Accumulator of the factorial
```

```
            If IsNumeric(txtResult.Text) And _
                   txtResult.Text <> "" Then
               ' A numeric value was entered

             If CDbl(txtResult.Text) = CInt(txtResult.Text) Then
                ' An integer was entered
               If CInt(txtResult.Text) > 0 Then
                  ' A positive integer was entered

                 For I = 1 To CInt(txtResult.Text) Step 1
                     dblSum *= I
                 Next

                 ' Place factorial result in the textbox
                 txtResult.Text = "The factorial of " & _
                                 txtResult.Text & _
                                 " is " & _
                                 CStr(dblSum)

              End If
           End If
        End If
     End Sub
```

The For Loop at the center of the code calculates the factorial by multiplying into dblSum, which has an initial value of 1, all the integers from 1 up to the value entered in the textbox. The loop in this case controls both the number of multiplications and the value that will be multiplied into dblSum.

3.7.2 Searching an Array

Another frequent application of For loops is searching for a given value in an array. In the next example, 10 random values between 10 and 20 are created and assigned to an array. Then another random number is created, and the array is searched to determine whether the last number exists in one of the array elements. If it does, the number of that element is displayed in the textbox.

The approach we will apply to write the algorithm will

1. break down the problem to a clear-cut statement of what the problem is
2. define what needs to be done to solve it
3. only when this is clear, make the transition into code.

The problem is to identify whether a random value exists in an array. What needs to be done to solve it is to examine the elements of an array in sequence. In plain English, the algorithm should look at the first element of the array. If the value is there, then present an appropriate message in the textbox and stop. Otherwise, advance to the next element in the array, if such an element exists, and repeat the operation as specified in the previous sentence. With that made clear, here is how the code could do the search. The For loop's index, the variable I, will serve as the index of the array, too.

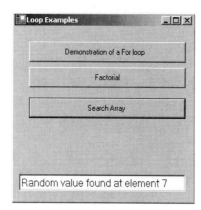

FIGURE 3.6
Searching an array.

That way, as the variable I progresses from 0 to 9, it will examine elements 0 through 9 in the array. If the random value was found, an appropriate message will be placed in the textbox. See the example in Figure 3.6. The code is as follows:

```
For I = 0 To 9
    If intArray(I) = intSearch Then
        txtResult.Text = _
            "Random value found at element " & CStr(I + 1)
    End If
Next
```

Here is the entire code:

```
Private Sub btnSearch_Click( _
  ByVal sender As System.Object, _
  ByVal e As System.EventArgs) _
  Handles btnSearch.Click
    ' This subroutine defines an array of integers,
    ' places random numbers between 10 and 20 into all
    ' its elements. Next, the application creates another
    ' random number within the same range and searches
    ' for it in the array.

    Dim intArray(9) As Integer
    Dim myRandom As New Random()
    Dim I, intSearch As Integer

    'Place random values into array
    For I = 0 To 9
        intArray(I) = myRandom.Next(10, 20)
    Next
```

The first part of the code utilizes a For loop to place random integer values ranging from 10 to 20 into elements 0 through 9 of the array. Here, as in the previous example, the index of the array, the variable I, is used both to control the number of times the code inside the `For` Block is executed and as an index inside the `For` Block that identifies different elements of the array in sequence. With that done, another random value is placed into the variable `intSearch` whose value is then searched for in the array. The search examines all the entries of the array in sequence with a `For` loop:

```
'Create the random value to be searched
intSearch = myRandom.Next(10, 20)

'Search for the value
txtResult.Text = "Random value not found"
For I = 0 To 9
    If intArray(I) = intSearch Then
        txtResult.Text = _
            "Random value found at element " & _
            CStr(I + 1)
    End If
Next
End Sub
```

3.7.3   Another Example of Searching an Array

Suppose we want to create an array with 1000 entries and place into each element its index value. How would we proceed to do so? Recall that the `For` loop is an ideal tool for performing a sequence of code a controlled number of times while providing an index that identifies each of those times. We can apply that property to fill the array. The command inside the For block will be executed 1000 times, because the index `J` will be need to be incremented by 1 1000 times altogether to go from 0 up to 999. The index `J` will in effect count the number of times that the code inside the For block is being executed. Since `J` is incremented by 1 each time, it can be used to assign values into all the elements of the array. The first time the loop is entered, `J` will be 0 and, using its value, element 0 in the array will receive the value 0. The next time the loop is entered, `J` will be 1 and, using its value, element 1 in the array will receive the value 1, and so on up to 999. The code is as follows:

```
' Here we define a loop and place into each element its index
Dim intArray(999) As Integer
Dim J As Integer

For J = 0 To 999
    intArray(J) = J
Next
```

If we now wished to sum the values in each 10th element in the array, we could use another loop to work our way through the array. This time the index will be incremented with a step of 10, meaning that if we apply this loop index as the index of the array, we will add into `dblSum` every 10th element. The first time the loop is entered, `J` will be 0, so the value inside element 0 of the array will be added into `dblSum`. The next time the loop is entered, `J` will be 10, so the value inside element 10 of the array will be added into `dblSum`, and so on. The code is

```
' Sum every tenth element
Dim dblSum As Double
For J = 0 To 999 Step 10
    dblSum += intArray(J)
Next
```

If we wished to sum only the elements containing an even value, we will again need a loop. This time, too, we will use its index as the index of the array:

```
For J = 0 To 999 Step 1
    If intArray(J) Mod 2 = 0 Then
        dblSum += intArray(J)
    End If
Next
```

3.7.4   A More Complex Example

In this example, we will create a 12-by-12 matrix and place into it the Multiplication Table. In this table, the value in each cell, in our case in each element of the matrix, is the product of its two indexes. For example, the value in element (8,9) represents the product 8*9 and so contains the value 73. To fill the matrix, we will need two loops. The algorithm here will reproduce the way such a table would be filled manually. Each row represents one number between 1 and 12 in order. Each column also represents one number between 1 and 12 in order. To fill in the table in an orderly manner, we should go through the rows one at a time, and in each row go through the columns one at a time to calculate the product and place it in the matrix. We will do the same thing here with For loops:

```
' Build Times Table
Dim intTimes(11, 11) As Integer
Dim intRow, intCol As Integer

' Go through the rows in sequence
For intRow = 0 To 11
    ' In each row go through the columns in sequence
    For intCol = 0 To 11
        ' And place the product in each cell
        intTimes(intRow, intCol) = intRow * intCol
    Next
Next
```

3.7.5   Identifying Prime Numbers

Another application to which For loops are well suited is identifying prime numbers. A prime number is a number that, among all integers, is divisible only by 1 and itself. That is, if we examined all the integers from 2 up to that number, not one integer should divide into the number with no remainder. See Example in Figure 3.7. The algorithm will do the same in a loop, examining whether the number is divisible by the current index

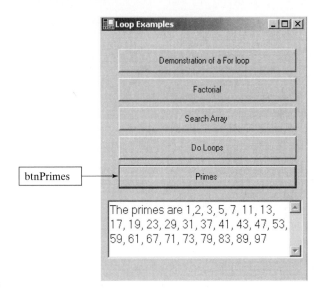

FIGURE 3.7
Identifying Prime Numbers.

of the loop, with this index running from 2 up the number examined. Actually, we will improve the algorithm by running the index till only half the number we are testing. To build the algorithm, we will

1. break down of the problem to a clear-cut statement of what the problem is
2. define what needs to be done to solve it
3. only when this is clear, make the transition into code.

This is how the code would work:

```
Private Sub btnPrimes_Click _
         (ByVal sender As System.Object, _
         ByVal e As System.EventArgs) _
         Handles btnPrimes.Click

         ' Show all the prime numbers between 1 and 100
         Dim I, J As Integer
         Dim bolPrime As Boolean

         ' 1 and 2 are special cases
         txtResult.Text = "The primes are 1,2"
```

The numbers 1 and 2 are special cases—1 by definition and 2 because it is the only even number that is prime. With the exception of these two numbers, only odd numbers 3 and greater can be prime, so the For loop should start with a start-value of 3 and have a Step of 2. That part is handled by the I loop. For each such number, and we will apply a For loop to examine the whole lot, it is necessary to examine all the integers from 2 and up until half the number. A number cannot be divisible without a remainder by any integer that is more than half its value. Examining the division is done by the J loop:

```
' Examine all the odd integers in the range.
' All even numbers above 2 cannot be prime.
For I = 3 To 100 Step 2
    'For each of these numbers examine if
    ' it is divisible by a smaller integer

    bolPrime = True
    For J = 2 To (I - 1) / 2 Step 1
```

Inside the J loop, the current index I is examined to check whether it is divisible by the current J. This is done with the Mod operator.[5] If Mod returns zero, then I is divisible by J without a remainder; hence, I cannot be prime. The code is as follows:

```
        If I Mod J = 0 Then
            ' I cannot be prime because it is divisible
            ' by a smaller integer, so leave the loop
            J = I
            bolPrime = False
        End If
    Next
    If bolPrime Then
        txtResult.Text &= ", " & CStr(I)
    End If
Next
End Sub
```

3.7.6 Do Loops

Do loops are used when a block of statements needs to be executed based on a condition, rather than based on a prespecified number of times. While For loops are especially equipped to handle the repetition of a sequence of code a given number of times, *Do loops are especially equipped to handle the repetition of a sequence of code when it is unknown how many times that section of code should be executed.* A good example of this is reading records from a file, as we will do later in the book. When reading records, it is unknown how many records there are. Controlling the loop with a For loop is therefore not practical. Rather, reading the records should continue while the end of the file has not yet been reached. That type of loop is what Do loops are especially adept at.

---

[5]Mod returns the remainder, so the code

```
I Mod J
```

will return the remainder of dividing I by J—for example,

```
10 Mod 3 = 1
10 Mod 4 = 2
10 Mod 5 = 0
```

There are three variants of Do loops: Do While, While, and Do Until loops. All three apply the same basic logic. The code inside the loop is executed if the condition is true, in the case of Do While and While, or as long as it is not true in the case of Do Until loops. Do While and While loops are just different syntaxes for the same operation. In this chapter, we will stick to Do While loops, because any function performed with Do Until loops can be handled with Do While loops by just adding the keyword Not before the condition.

A While or an Until clause can be added to a Do loop to specify the condition that limits its execution. The While and the Until clauses can be added either at the Do statement or at the Loop statement, but not at both. If the condition is examined at the Do statement, then the *do-statements* will be executed only if the condition permits it. If the condition is examined at the Loop statement, then the *do-statements* will be executed once regardless of whether the condition permits it, but will be executed again only as long as the condition permits it. Note that the While and the Until clauses are the opposite of each other: The *do-statements* will be executed when the While clause is True or when the Until clause is false. The syntax of the Do loop is

```
Do [{While|Unit} <condition>]
    [<do-statements>]
    [Exit Do]
    [<do-statements>]
Loop[{While|Unit} <condition>]
```

Alternatively, we have

```
Do
    [<do-statements>]
    [Exit Do]
    [<do-statements>]
Loop
```

In the following example, a Do loop is used to emulate a For Next loop that sums the elements of an array dimensioned with 1 to 10 elements:

```
I = 1
Do While I <= 10
    intSum = intSum + intArray(I)
    I = I + 1
Loop
```

In this code, the value 1 is assigned to the variable I. Then, because of the condition in the Do While loop, so long as I is smaller or equal to 10 the two statements inside the loop will be executed. In all, these two statements will be executed 10 times. Each time the two statements within the Do loop are executed, I is incremented by 1. By the time these two statements are executed 10 times, the value of I will be 11, and then the condition in the Do loop will no longer be True.

The `Do While` loop has an equivalent shorthand syntax that is widely used:

```
While <condition>
        [<do-statements>]
End While
```

with the shorthand syntax, this example would look like the following:

```
I = 1
While I <= 10
    intSum = intSum + intArray(I)
    I = I + 1
End While
```

> **Programming Note:** `Do While` and `Do Until` loops are the exact opposites of each other. `Do While` enters the loops so long as the condition is `True`, while `Do Until` enters it so long as the condition is `False`. In the interest of not getting too mixed up, it is a good habit to stick to one or the other.

3.7.7   More Examples with `Do` Loops

In this example, the objective is to identify how many occurrences of the letter "A" there are in a string. To create the algorithm, we will (1) break down of the problem to a clear-cut statement of what the problem is, (2) define what needs to be done to solve it, and (3) only when this is clear, make the transition into code.

The problem is to examine all the characters in a string of an unknown length with the purpose of counting how many of these characters are the letter "A". What needs to be done to solve it is to examine the characters one by one in sequence while there are still characters left in the string to be examined. In plain English, the algorithm does exactly what a `Do While` loop does: examine the current character inside the loop, provided that there are still characters to be examined. Also, inside the loop, after the character is examined, it is removed from the string so that the next character examined will be the next character in the string. Characters will be removed in the loop as long as there are still characters left. An alternative way of doing this is to use the `Chars` function. We already saw that function in this chapter, so we will demonstrate the algorithm with the `Substring` function here:

```
Do While strText.Length > 0  ' as long as there are still characters
    If strText.Chars(0) = "A" Then ' see if the current one is "A"
        intTotal += 1
    End If
    strText = strText.Substring(1)
Loop
```

By the same logic, a `Do Until` loop would have examined the same condition by changing the operator, either with

```
Do Until strText.Length = 0
```

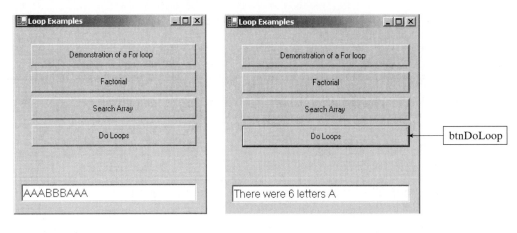

FIGURE 3.8

or with

Do Until Not strText.Length > 0

Figure 3.8 is an example of the application running.
The whole code is as follows:

```
Private Sub btnDoLoop_Click _
        (ByVal sender As System.Object, _ ]
        ByVal e As System.EventArgs) _
        Handles btnDoLoop.Click
    ' This subroutine demonstrates a Do Loop.
    ' The subroutine examines a string of unknown length;
    ' hence, the Do Loop is a good way of handling it, and
    ' returns the number of "A"s in it.
    ' The string is analyzed by examining its leftmost
    ' character and then truncating it.
    ' Note that "A" is not the same as "a".

    Dim I As Integer
    Dim intTotal As Integer = 0
    Dim strText As String

    strText = txtResult.Text
    Do While strText.Length > 0
        If strText.Chars(0) = "A" Then
            intTotal += 1
        End If
        strText = strText.Substring(1)
    Loop

    txtResult.Text = "There were " & CStr(intTotal) & _
        " letters A"
End Sub
```

3.7.8   `For Each` **Loops**

Another useful loop is the `For Each` loop. This loop allows the inspection of all the elements in a collection as though they were elements in an array. The `For Each` loop takes advantage of the fact that everything in VB.NET is an object; thus, any multiply occurring object is a group with a collection of items in it. Earlier in the chapter, we defined an array like this:

```
Dim intExp() As Integer = {3, 5, 7, 9, 11}
```

What we actually did was to create a group of objects that happen to be integer-type variables grouped together under the same name with an identifying index. We can take advantage of this arrangement by defining another variable, this time as an object:

```
Dim intExpEllement As Object
```

Then we can use the new variable to explore the array as though it were a group of objects. This is done with the `For Each` loop, in which each object is treated as an element in a group. The code uses the `ToString` method to display the string value of the object. Without the `ToString` method, the `Output` window will show the data type of the object. In this case, the `Output` window will show that the data type is integer:

```
For Each intExpEllement In intExp
    Console.WriteLine(intExpEllement.ToString)
Next
```

The syntax of the `For Each` loop is

```
For Each <element> In <group>
        [<each-statements>]
      Exit For
        [<each-statements>]
    Next
```

3.8   CONTROL STATEMENTS SEQUENCE COMMANDS

3.8.1   Subroutines and Functions

Subroutines, which are also known as `Sub` procedures, and functions are indivisible units of code which contain a group of statements that perform a predefined activity and that should be activated as one unit. There is a theoretical distinction between functions and subroutines: Subroutines are called and return no value, while functions are activated by assigning the value that they return. Both subroutines and functions are in fact methods. This can been seen in the Code window, which displays the subroutines that handle the events on the various controls of a form, as discussed in the lab of Chapter 2.

3.8.2   Subroutines

Subroutines are *invoked* (i.e., activated) either with the Call statement or just by name. The following two statements invoke a subroutine named One:

```
Call One()
One()
```

Subroutines are defined with the Sub statement. Everything between the Sub statement and the End Sub statement is called the *Sub Block*. All the code within this Sub Block is accessible only by calling the subroutine. Both subroutines and functions cannot be nested. There cannot be a subroutine defined inside the Sub Block of another subroutine.

A subroutine may receive *parameters* (i.e., values that are passed to it for processing) when it is invoked. Parameters are separated by commas. These parameters when received by the subroutine are technically called *arguments*. There is no practical limit to the number of parameters a subroutine may receive.

The *arguments* are defined in the Sub statement in a manner equivalent to declaring them as regular variables. Arguments can either be declared in the Sub statement with an explicit data type or left as the default object. VB.NET, however, requires that either all the *arguments* be typed (given a specific data type, such as Integer) or all *arguments* be untyped (and thus be objects). When the subroutine is called, the value in each *parameter* is assigned to its corresponding *argument*. That is, the value of the first *parameter* is assigned to the first *argument*, the value of the second *parameter* is assigned to the second *argument*, and so on. This is done even when the *parameter* has a different data type than the *argument*. This is done automatically, requiring no explicit casting statement, which is in stark contrast to the way VB.NET treats regular assignment statements!

The *arguments* can be defined either as ByRef of as ByVal, with the default being ByVal. When an *argument* is defined ByVal, it receives the value passed to it from its corresponding *parameter* but is a totally different and unrelated variable. Any changes made to the value of an *argument* are totally invisible to its corresponding *parameter* just as such changes would be after any other assignment statement between two variables. (Note that this may not always be the case when the *argument* and *parameter* are both objects referencing an external object such as a database.)

When an *argument* is defined ByRef it becomes as though it were one and the same as its corresponding *parameter*, and thus any changes made to the value stored in an *argument* are carried over to its corresponding *parameter* and are available even after the subroutine is ended. This used to be the default in VB, but with the transition to a fully object-oriented environment in VB.NET, it is no longer the default.

In the next sample code a subroutine named mySub is defined. The subroutine receives two arguments, conveniently named in the example argument1 and argument2. Both arguments are defined as Integers. It is a good programming habit to always define the data type explicitly. As explained in Chapter 2, defaults may change. Therefore, programs relying on default values may encounter unexpected glitches or bugs when the vendor-defined defaults change—and they do, as is evident from the transition from VB6 to VB.NET. The first argument is defined with the option ByRef, while the second is defined with `ByVal`. In the subroutine, both arguments are assigned the value 10. There is no `Dim` or equivalent statement to define the arguments, because the arguments are already defined in the `Sub` statement. The value of each argument is written to the `Output` window. The code is as follows:

```
Private Sub mySub(ByRef argument1 As Integer, _
                  ByVal argument2 As Integer)
    argument1 = 10
    argument2 = 10
    Console.WriteLine("Argument 1 is " & argument1)
    Console.WriteLine("Argument 2 is " & argument2)
End Sub
```

The subroutine is activated with the `Call` statement. The number of parameters passed to it in the `Call` statement must correspond to the number of arguments. (There are some exceptions to that rule, such as when the subroutine can be overloaded, as we already saw in Chapter 2.) After calling the subroutine, the values of the two parameters are written to the `Output` window:

```
Private Sub myCallingSub()
    Dim parameter1, parameter2 As Integer
    Call mySub(parameter1, parameter2)
    Console.WriteLine("Parameter 1 is " & parameter1)
    Console.WriteLine("Parameter 2 is " & parameter2)
End Sub
```

As would be expected, the `Output` window shows that `parameter1` has changed, while `parameter 2` retained its original value:

```
Argument 1 is 10
Argument 2 is 10
Parameter 1 is 10
Parameter 2 is 0
```

A word of caution: VB.NET is extremely lax in enforcing its casting when the data type of a parameter does not match the data type of its corresponding argument. In fact, even when the parameter and the argument have different data types, any changes made to an argument that is defined with the `ByRef` option will carry over to its corresponding parameter. This circumventing of the casting checks is done without warning from VB.NET. Indeed, even after changing the data types of the arguments as follows, exactly the same output will be written to the `Output` window. Here is the code:

```
Private Sub mySub(ByRef argument1 As String, _
                  ByVal argument2 As String)
```

3.8.3   Overloading a Subroutine

We mentioned earlier that the number of *parameters* passed to a subroutine should match the number of *arguments* it defines, and that *overloading* is an exception to that rule. Overloading is when a subroutine or a function can receive different kinds of parameters.

We have seen overloading in Chapter 2. One way of achieving overloading with sub-routines is when parameters are made optional. (There are more ways of overloading a subroutine. These are discussed in the chapter on object orientation.) Overloading a subroutine by applying an optional parameter is done by adding the keyword Optional before the argument, as in the following code:

```
Private Sub mySub(ByRef argument1 As String, _
                  ByVal argument2 As String, _
                  Optional ByVal argument3 As Integer = 10)
```

With the Sub statement written in this way, the next Call statements will be syntactical-ly correct:

```
Call mySub(parameter1, parameter2)
Call mySub(parameter1, parameter2, 10)
Call mySub(parameter1, parameter2, parameter3)
```

Argument3 in the overloaded subroutine is optional and has a default value of 10. When no parameter matches the argument, this will be the default value of the argu-ment. It is imperative to add a default value when the argument is optional.

The default value of the argument can then be an indicator specifying the func-tionality of the subroutine:

```
Private Sub mySub(ByRef argument1 As String, _
                  ByVal argument2 As String, _
                  Optional ByVal argument3 As Integer = 10)

    If argument3 = 10 Then
        argument1 = 10
        argument2 = 10
    Else
        argument1 = argument3
        argument2 = argument3 + 10
    End If
    Console.WriteLine("Argument 1 is " & argument1)
    Console.WriteLine("Argument 2 is " & argument2)
End Sub
```

3.8.4   Private, Public, Friend, Shared, and Protected Subroutines

Subroutines can be Private, Public, Friend, or Protected. These keywords specify the availability of the subroutine to other modules. When the subroutine is Private, it is ac-cessible only within its declaration context. In the preceding code, when defined within a class of given form, such subroutines will be recognized only within that specific form.

When the subroutine is Public, it is accessible also beyond the class it is defined within. These subroutines are not limited to the class they are defined within and can be activated also not through it. This is also shown graphically in the Code window, where there is no icon of a lock next to the subroutine name. See Figure 3.9. To avoid misunderstandings and to increase the readability of the code, subroutines should be defined as Public only when there is a reason why they should be called from outside the class they are defined in.

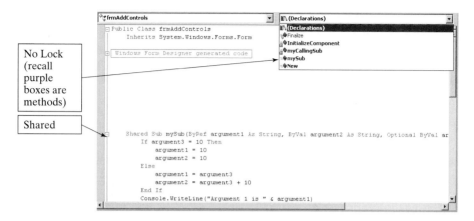

FIGURE 3.9
Code Window with Shared subroutine.

Another keyword is Shared. When the subroutine is Shared, there is no need to instantiate it before executing it. A subroutine can be Shared whether it is Private, Public, Friend, or Protected.

When the subroutine is Public, it is accessible also outside the class it is defined within, but the subroutine is still associated with the class it is defined within. There will be no lock icon next to a public subroutine either. When the subroutine is Protected it is accessible also from within its own class or a class derived from it. When the subroutine is Friend, it is accessible from anywhere within the assembly that their class is defined within. When the subroutine is a Protected Friend, it is accessible from anywhere within the assembly that their class is defined within or from classes that are derived from the class itself.

The simplified syntax of the Sub statement is

```
[{Private|Public|Protected|Friend|Protected Friend]} Sub <sub-name>
   [<arguments>]
```

3.8.5 Functions

A function is also an indivisible unit of code that contains a group of statements that perform a predefined activity, except that functions can also return a value and are activated by referencing their name. For example, the NextDouble method of the Random class is a function that returns a double-precision random number:

```
Dim objRandom As New Random()
Dim dblRandom As Double = objRandom.NextDouble
```

Functions are defined with the Function keyword and with the data type of the returned value:

```
[{Private|Public|Protected|Friend|Protected Friend]} Function
   <sub-name> [{<arguments>)]
[As <data-type-of-returned-value>]
```

Otherwise, the definition is equivalent to that of Subroutines.

The arguments and the application of overriding through optional arguments applies equally well with functions. The data type of the returned value can be any of the data types supported by VB.NET. The value that a function returns is set in one of two ways: either by assigning the value to the function name in an explicit assignment statement or with the Return statement. Both options are demonstrated in the code below. The code first defines a new function named Factorial that will return the factorial of an integer that is passed to it as an argument. If the argument is greater than zero, then the factorial is calculated with a For loop and the factorial returned with the Return statement. Otherwise, the value 1 is returned by assigning it to the function name.

It should be stressed that returning a value with the Return statement is not the same as assigning it to the function name. After the Return statement is executed, the function ends. After a value is assigned to the function name, the remainder of the function code is executed until the End Function or Return statement is reached. Following is some sample code:

```
' Activate the function
Dim I As Integer = Factorial(10)
Console.WriteLine("The factorial of 10 is " & CStr(I))

Private Function Factorial(ByVal intNumber As Integer) As Double
    Dim I As Integer
    Dim dblSum As Double = 1

    Console.WriteLine("Argument is " & intNumber)
    If intNumber > 0 Then
        For I = 1 To intNumber
            dblSum = dblSum * I
        Next
        Return (dblSum)

        ' This statement will never be executed
        Console.WriteLine("After R")
    Else
        Factorial = 1
        ' This statement will be executed
        Console.WriteLine("After assigning value")
    End If
End Function
```

A function is invoked by referencing its name or by calling it, but when a function is called, it does not return a value:

```
Private Sub Button3_Click(ByVal sender As System.Object, _
            ByVal e As System.EventArgs) Handles Button3.Click
    Console.WriteLine("Factorial is " & Factorial(9))
    Call Factorial(8)

End Sub
```

Programming Note: VB.NET allows the programmer to call also functions and treat functions as though they were subroutines, in effects overriding the function as a subroutine. This is not a recommended practice because it detracts from the readability of the code.

3.8.6 Recursive Functions

A function can also call itself. This is called a recursive function. The Factorial function is one example in which using a recursive function is appropriate, albeit should be avoided because of the difficulty in reading how recursive functions work. To make Factorial recursive we need to examine its inner workings. By definition, the factorial of N, written as N!, is N multiplied by (N-1)! unless N is 0, in which case the factorial is 1. In other words, to calculate N!, we need to examine whether N is zero. If it is, then the function returns 1. If it is not, then the function should return N multiplied by factorial of N-1. Written in VB.NET code, this is what it would look like:

```
Private Function factorial(ByVal dblNumber As Double) As Double
    If dblNumber <= 1 Then
        Return (1)
    Else
        Return (dblNumber * factorial(dblNumber - 1))
    End If
End Function
```

Activating the function with the code

```
Console.WriteLine(factorial(9))
Console.WriteLine(factorial(5))
```

would result in the factorials being written in the Output window:

```
362880
120
```

3.9 CATCHING AND HANDLING ERRORS

Occasionally, when statements are executed, they may perform illegal operations, such as dividing an integer by zero, or incur certain types of events that are not handled by the code, such as when reading beyond the end of a file. In these cases it is better if the VB.NET code can catch the error and handle it within the program, rather than let VB.NET catch and handle it as a run-time error. The Try and Catch statements do exactly that.

The Try statement and its accompanying End Try statement define a Try block. Any error occurring within this Try block will be caught and suspended, and execution of the code will be transferred to the code after the Catch statement. All statements after the one where the error occurred will be ignored. The code in the Catch block (i.e., after the Catch statement) will be executed only if an error occurred. A short example is called for. In the following code, the variable I will be assigned the values 1, then 2, and then 3 (it will never be assigned the value 10, because no error was caught):

```
Dim I As Integer
Try
    I = 1
    I = 2
    I = 3
Catch
    I = 10 ' This statement will not be executed
End Try
```

Programming Note: VB.NET still supports the On Error statements of VB6. In VB6, whenever an error in a section of code occurred, execution of the code would resume at the latest On Error statement that was encountered. The On Error statement had three possible options:

```
On Error Resume Next      Ignore the error entirely
On Error 0                Turn the last On Error off
On Error Go To <label>    Resume execution at a given command
                          in the code identified by a label,
                          (i.e., by a label-name followed by a colon).
```

VB.NET supports this archaic way of handling exceptions only for backward compatibility. It is highly recommended not to use it anymore.

The variable I will be assigned the value 10 in the next section of code. Here, a division by zero will raise an error that will be caught by the Catch statement. Once the Catch statement is activated, the remainder of the code in the Try block that precedes the Catch statement will be ignored. Thus, the variable I will be assigned the value 1 and then 10, but never 3. The code is as follows:

```
Dim I As Integer
Try
    I = 1
    I = I / 0 ' This will raise an error and execution will resume
              ' in the Catch block

    I = 3 ' so this statement will not be executed
Catch
    I = 10
End Try
```

Programming Note: The Catch statement can be set to handle specific types of errors. In such a case, there can be many Catch statements within the same Try block. We will discuss more on this in the chapters dealing with database connectivity.

Sometimes, it is also necessary to have a section of code that will always be executed, regardless of whether an error is caught. That section of code appears after the `Finally` statement, which is optional. In the following code, the variable `I` will always end up with the value 99:

```
Try
    I = 1
    I = I / J ' This may raise an error
    I = 3 ' If an error is raised this will not be executed
Catch
    I = 10
Finally
    I = 99 ' But this will always be executed
End Try
```

Programming Note: It is always better in terms of performance to check for an error, such as division by zero, *before the operation* is done, rather than relying on `Try` and `Catch` to catch the error. The following code is illustrative:

```
Dim I, J As Integer
Try
    ' This is the better way to handle division by zero
    If J <> 0 Then
        I = I / J
    Else
        I = 0
    End If
Catch
    ' this is not an efficient way to handle division by zero
    I = 0
End Try
```

The `Exit Try`, like any other Exit command, results in leaving the current block. The next command to be executed will be in the `Finally` section of the block. The `Exit Try` command cannot appear in the `Finally` section of the block. The following code demonstrates the flow of execution:

```
Try
    Console.WriteLine("This line will be printed first")
    Exit Try
    Console.WriteLine("This line will never be printed")
Catch
    Console.WriteLine("This line will never be printed")
Finally
    Console.WriteLine("This line will be printed second")
End Try
Console.WriteLine("This line will be printed third")
End Sub
```

Sometimes, it is also necessary to throw an exception—that is, to emulate a runtime error in the code. This may happen if an unmanageable situation arouse and it would be thus necessary to cease the current section of code immediately and leave it while generating an appropriate error message. For example, suppose a subroutine suddenly found that a user is trying to perform a privileged operation like deleting a file. In such an extreme case, the subroutine should drop all it is doing and stop. Note that exceptions like that should be thrown only in extreme cases. It is much more efficient to handle unexpected values with If statements, although in that case, as in the example, it is more readable to throw an exception that signifies a total error and requires a total stop. Exceptions are thrown with the Throw statement. If there is a specific error, and there should be if you are throwing an exception, the error message is passed through a special object, the System.Exception. In the following code, if the variable intUserCode has the value 2 (and let us suppose for the sake of the example that such a value must not occur), then an exception with an appropriate message is created as a new implementation of the System.Exception class:

```
If intUserCode = 2 Then Throw _
              New System.Exception("An exception has occurred.")
```

Many exceptions can be thrown within the same Try Block. To handle this, the Catch statement can be parameterized to deal with specific exception. A sequence of Catch statements works the same way as a Select Case statement does: Only the statements within an appropriate Catch are executed, and only one Catch can handle the exception. The Catch statement is parameterized to filter which exceptions it handles with the When keyword. In the following code, the Output window will show the message "Error 3":

```
Try
    I = 3
    Throw New System.Exception()

Catch expCode As Exception When I = 2
    Console.WriteLine("Error 2")
Catch expCode As Exception When I = 3
    Console.WriteLine("Error 3")
Catch
    Console.WriteLine("Other Error")
End Try
```

Note that expCode is defined through the Catch statement as an instance of the System.Exception class, which, as its name implies, handles exceptions.

Alternatively, the value of the System.Exception object can be used and examined and its Message property used to pass a specific error message. In the code that follows, if the variable I has the value 3, then a message of "100" is passed through the exception and "100" will be printed in the Output window. If the variable I has the value 100, then a message "Error 3" will be printed in the Output window. Otherwise, a more general message will be passed through the Message property and printed as "Unidentified Error" in the Output window. Here is the code:

```
Try
    If I = 3 Then
        Throw New System.Exception("100")
    Else
        Throw New System.Exception("Unidentified Error")
    End If

Catch expCode As Exception When I = 100
    Console.WriteLine("Error 3")
Catch expCode As Exception
    Console.WriteLine(ExpCode.Message)
End Try
```

Of course, that is not a very efficient way of handling errors. The Catch option is much more appropriate when it handles different system errors differently, as in the following code:

```
Catch expCode As System.IO.EndOfStreamException
    ' Reached end of IO Stream
Catch IOExcep As System.IO.IOException
    ' IO Error
```

The syntax of the Try block is

```
Try
  <statements>
[Throw [New System.Exception ([<message> | Exception])]]
  <statements>
[Exit Try]
[Catch [<exception-code>]
   [<statements that handle a specific exception code>]]
[Catch [<exception-code>]
   [<statements that handle a specific exception code>]]
[Catch [<other exception-code>]
   [<statements that handle a specific exception code>]
[Finally
   [<statements that will always be executed>]]
End Try
```

A Try block must have at least one Catch or a Finally statement.

3.10   STRUCTURED EXCEPTION HANDLING

A Try block is intended to catch errors during runtime. These errors can be raised by VB.NET itself when an instruction fails, such as a division by zero or trying to read from a closed database, or when an error exception is explicitly thrown in the code with the Throw statement, as shown earlier.

Since it is necessary on occasion to handle exceptions even of the same exception-code differently in different parts of the code, VB.NET also provides the ability to have Try blocks nested within each other in a hierarchy. A simple example of this would be adding a separate Try block within a subroutine to handle a certain command in a special manner, overriding exception handling at the subroutine level Try block. For example, as we will see in Chapter 12, in a subroutine that accesses a database, it may be necessary to handle database access exceptions differently: catching, but ignoring, an error when trying to close a Dataset prior to reopening it, but catching and handling all subsequent exceptions with a Message Box thereafter. In this manner, errors that are not problems that need to be handled, such as attempting to close an already closed Dataset, can be ignored, while other errors are brought to the attention of the user. In the next example, the Close method is written within its own Try block. This inner Try block will catch any exception that is thrown within it, so these exceptions will not be handled by the outer Try block. However, any other statement thereafter that will cause an exception to be thrown will be handled by the outer Try block.

As a rule, exceptions are caught and handled by the Try block within which resides the statement that caused the exceptions, unless that Try block cannot handle that type of exception. Only when the Try block cannot handle an exception is it passed to a Try block higher in the hierarchy. Accordingly, in the following code, had the Catch statement been limited to a certain exception-code, rather than being a catchall, and had the exception been an exception other than the one specified in the Catch statement, then that exception would have been passed to the outer Try block for handling:

```
Try
    Try
        myConnection.Close() ' in case it is being reopened
    Catch
    End Try

    myConnection.ConnectionString = SqlConnection1.ConnectionString
    myConnection.Open()
Catch e1 As Exception
    MessageBox.Show(e1.Message)
End Try
```

To recapitulate, when an exception in a statement is thrown, the associated exception is passed first to the Try block that contains the statement where it occurred. If that Try block can handle it, all is clear. But, if that Try block cannot handle it, for example, because the Try Block has no Catch statement to handle the specific exception code, then the exception is passed to a higher level Try block. That higher level Try block can be, as shown in the preceding code, in the same subroutine, or the higher level Try block can be higher still, in another subroutine. In the latter case, it is possible to construct a hierarchy of Try blocks so that a subroutine handles only errors it knows how to, while passing all other errors to the subroutine that called it. This is demonstrated in the following code:

```
Private Sub One()
    Try
```

```
        If IsNumeric(txtInput.Text) Then
            Call Two(CInt(txtInput.Text))
        End If
    Catch e1 As Exception
        MessageBox.Show(e1.Message)
    End Try
End Sub

Private Sub Two(ByVal I As Integer)
    Try
        I = 2 * I / I
    Catch e1 As OverflowException
        I = 0
    End Try
End Sub
```

In the preceding code, subroutine One has a Try Block that handles all exceptions. Subroutine Two has a Try Block that handles only a special type of numeric operation exception, namely, an overflow exception. (This exception is thrown when
trying to assign to a variable a value that is too big for it. In VB.NET, dividing by zero
will return infinity. Integers cannot hold infinity.) If an exception is thrown in subroutine Two, the Try block within that subroutine will be the first to have a chance at catching it. If the Try block in this subroutine can handle the exception, it will. Then
subroutine One will never be aware of any problem in subroutine Two. But since, in
this case, only an overflow exception can be handled by the Try block in subroutine
Two, any other exception will be passed on to the higher level Try block, which, because
subroutine One called subroutine Two, will be the Try block in subroutine One. Accordingly, because of the way the subroutines are nested, overflow exceptions in subroutine Two will be handled by assigning zero to the variable, while all other exceptions
will result in a Message Box displayed through subroutine One.

This hierarchy of Try blocks can be quite confusing if the code is not written really
well. Imagine we add another subroutine, say, subroutine Three. This subroutine also
calls subroutine Two, but has its own unique way of handling exceptions. If any exception except for an overflow occurs in subroutine Two, the result will be assigning a
string to the text property of the textbox. Accordingly, the same exception in subroutine Two can be handled in two different ways, depending on which subroutine was the
calling one. This is something that should be avoided when possible, perhaps by the following code:

```
Private Sub Three()
    Try
        Call Two(CInt(txtInput.Text))
    Catch
        txtInput.Text = "Value entered should be numeric"
    End Try
End Sub
```

Actually, to be precise, even when only one Try block is written, there is a hierarchy. The uppermost level of catching exceptions is handled by VB.NET itself. When we

write a Try block, what in effect happens is that our Try block "catches" the exception before it reaches the exception handling of VB.NET. Since the exception is caught, VB.NET ignores it. If, however, there is no appropriate `Catch` statement in the Try block, then, because the Try block did not catch the exception, it will be passed to a higher level. In this case, the exception handling of VB.NET.

3.11   A QUICK LOOK AT DELEGATES

Delegates are objects that can be employed to call methods of other classes when the class or method needs to be resolved dynamically at runtime. While invoking a delegate is somewhat equivalent to invoking a subroutine or a function in another class, there is a major difference. A delegate is resolved (a pointer to the invoked method is set) at runtime, while a subroutine or function is resolved at compile time. This means that the actual method that will be invoked with the delegate can be changed during the execution of the code. A delegate can reference both `Shared` and instance methods. Instance methods are methods that must be instantiated before they can be invoked. Delegates are also known as *type-safe function pointers*.

Delegates are needed when an object raising an event cannot know in advance what method should be invoked, for example in a client server environment where the client is linked only during execution to the server. The delegate will need to resolve which method in which class is appropriate and then forward the event to it. The appropriate method is resolved when applying a delegate by getting its address with a *constructor* and then invoking the method at that constructor address. This highlights a major difference between employing delegates and a Select Case statement that chooses among methods: With a delegate, the methods are left unresolved until runtime; when a method is invoked, it is resolved at compilation time. Because the delegate must be resolved at runtime with all the additional overhead that comes with it, it is advisable to refrain from applying delegates where methods can be invoked without it. An exception is when writing applications with ASP.NET, a topic that will be discussed in Chapter 14.

Delegates are created with the `Delegate Sub` statement:

```
Delegate Sub myDelegatingSub(ByVal X As Integer)
```

With this done, instances of the new delegate can be declared with the `Dim` statement:

```
Dim subDelegate As myDelegatingSub
```

The actual method that will be invoked with these instances can be set dynamically with the `AddressOf` constructor. The constructor receives one parameter, which contains the name of the class and the name of the method:

```
subDelegate = AddressOf cls1.subtest
```

Then, the method is invoked with the `Invoke` method:

```
subDelegate.Invoke(intNumber)
```

The entire code is as follows:

```
Public Module mod1

    Public Class clsTest2
        Delegate Sub myDelegatingSub(ByVal X As Integer)

        Shared Sub subTest2(ByVal intNumber As Integer)
            Dim cls1 As clsTest
            Dim e1 As New System.EventArgs()
            Dim subDelegate As myDelegatingSub

            cls1 = New clsTest()
            Select Case intNumber
                Case Is = 1
                    subDelegate = AddressOf cls1.subtest
                    subDelegate.Invoke(intNumber)
                Case Is = 2
                    subDelegate = AddressOf cls1.subTest2
                    subDelegate.Invoke(intNumber)
                Case Is = 3
                    Dim myfrm As New frmDelegates()
                    subDelegate = AddressOf myfrm.subplace
                    subDelegate.Invoke(intNumber)
                    myfrm.Show()
            End Select
        End Sub
    End Class

    Public Class clsTest
        Public Sub subTest(ByVal X As Integer)
            MessageBox.Show("1  " & X)
        End Sub
        Public Sub subTest2(ByVal X As Integer)
            MessageBox.Show("2  " & X)
        End Sub
    End Class

End Module
```

In the preceding code, the Delegate statement is declared at the Class level. It is then instantiated in the subTest2 subroutine, where a constructor is set dynamically to one of several methods in another class. The same principle can be applied to the creation of a new instance of an existing form, as shown in the last Case of the Select Case statement.

LAB 3.1: LOOPS AND THE LIST BOX

Lab Objectives:
1. Practice For loops
2. Start new forms from within a running form
3. Review arrays

4. Review structures
5. Review the List Box
   - SelectedItem
   - Items.Add.

Application Overview

The application handles a list of buddies. This list is handled in a array that has a structure as its data type. The details of each friend are entered in the top right-hand side textboxes, except for age, which is calculated in the application. When the Add Friend Button is clicked, the friend is added to the list of buddies in the array. The first name of all the buddies is displayed in the List Box. When a first name is clicked in the List Box, the data about the appropriate friend are extracted from the array and are displayed back in the textboxes. At this stage, the age of the friend is calculated. Below the List Box there are two Buttons. The Remove Friend Button will remove the friend from the array and rebuild the display in the List Box. The Next Lab Button will close this form and open the form for the next lab in this section.

Part 1: Building the Form

Start a new solution with a new project, and name it **prjChapter3a**. Rename the form **frmListbox**. (See the lab in Chapter 2 on how to change both the name of the form and the .vb file in which it is stored.) Add the controls Figure 3.10 to the form, and name them accordingly so that you can follow the code in Part 2. Set the Text property of the form, the labels (name these as you wish), the Buttons, and the List Box. Make the Enabled property of txtAge False. That way its text can be seen, but not changed. You might also want to change the Font property of the textboxes by clicking the three dots next to the Font property of each.

The form should look like Figure 3.11.

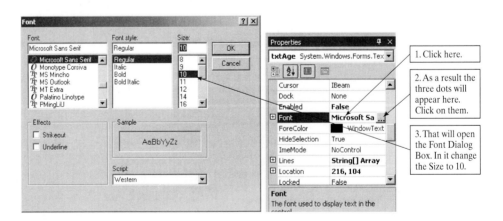

FIGURE 3.10
The Font Property Window.

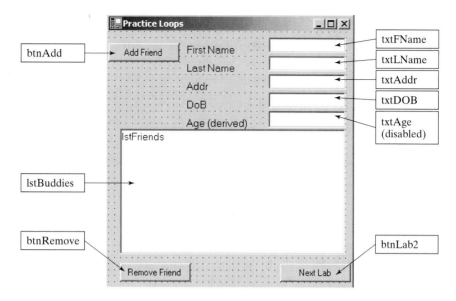

FIGURE 3.11
Lab 3.1.

Part 2: Adding the Structure

In the public class section of the code, add the structure. The structure must be added here so that it will be recognized in all the methods (=subroutines) of the form (=class). The members of the structure must be `Public`, or else they will not be accessible outside the structure box (i.e., outside the code that is enclosed between the `Structure` and the `End Structure` statements). Also in this section, add `myList` as an array with the preceding structure as its data type, and add an integer data typed variable that will be used to handle the number of elements in the array. Again, this code must appear in the public class section of the code so that it can be accessible throughout the class:

```
Public Class frmListbox
    Inherits System.Windows.Forms.Form

    Structure Buddies
        Public strFName As String
        Public strLNAme As String
        Public strAddr As String
        Public datDOB As Date
        Public intAge As Integer
    End Structure

    Public myList(100) As Buddies
    Public intFriendNumber As Integer
```

Part 3: Adding the Rest of the Code

When the Add Friend Button is clicked, the data in the textboxes are assigned into a new element of the MyList array. If, however, the data entered as date of birth are not valid, they are ignored. If the data denote a valid date, then the age of the friend is calculated as the difference in years between today's date, given by the Now function, and the year of the date of birth. The year is given in the Year property of any Date type variable. Having updated the array, the first name is added to the List Box and the index of the current element in the array is incremented by 1. The code is as follows:

```
Private Sub btnAdd_Click(ByVal sender As System.Object, _
        ByVal e As System.EventArgs) Handles btnAdd.Click

    If intFriendNumber > 100 Then
        MsgBox("Too many buddies")
        Exit Sub
    End If

    myList(intFriendNumber).strFName = txtFName.Text
    myList(intFriendNumber).strLNAme = txtLName.Text
    myList(intFriendNumber).strAddr = txtAddr.Text

    If IsDate(txtDOB.Text) Then
        myList(intFriendNumber).datDOB = CDate(txtDOB.Text)
        myList(intFriendNumber).intAge = _
              Now.Year - myList(intFriendNumber).datDOB.Year
    End If

    lstBuddies.Items.Add(myList(intFriendNumber).strFName)
    intFriendNumber = intFriendNumber + 1
End Sub
```

When any of the first names in the List Box are clicked (*selected*, in VB.NET terminology), the application will copy the data from the appropriate entry in the array back to the textboxes. Two properties of the List Box are used here: the SelectedItem property, which contains the text of the item that is clicked, and the SelectedIndex property, which contains the index of the selected item. Since the items are added to the List Box in the same order they are added to the array, the SelectedIndex will also be the element index of that friend in the array.

The lstBuddies.Items.Add statement adds an item to the List Box. A List Box contains a *collection* of Items. These Items are the lines presented in the List Box. The Items collection has a set of methods that handle the items in the collection. One of these methods is Add. Its objective is to add an item to the end of the Items collection. Other methods that are frequently applied include Clear, to empty the collection of its items, and Remove, to remove an item. Here is the code:

```
Private Sub lstBuddies_SelectedIndexChanged( _
                    ByVal sender As System.Object, _
                    ByVal e As System.EventArgs) _
                    Handles lstBuddies.SelectedIndexChanged

    If lstBuddies.SelectedIndex <> -1 Then
        txtFName.Text = lstBuddies.SelectedItem
```

```
            txtLName.Text = myList(lstBuddies.SelectedIndex).strLNAme
            txtAddr.Text = myList(lstBuddies.SelectedIndex).strAddr
            txtDOB.Text = CStr(myList(lstBuddies.SelectedIndex).datDOB)
            txtAge.Text = CStr(myList(lstBuddies.SelectedIndex).intage)
        End If

    End Sub
```

When the Remove Friend Button is clicked, the friend whose first name was clicked is removed from the array and the List Box display is rebuilt. The friend is identified by his or her first name. The array is read in sequence until the friend is found, and then the element is deleted by moving the elements after it forward one place in the array. Once this is done, the array is cleared and the items are added back to it:

```
    Private Sub btnRemove_Click(ByVal sender As System.Object, _
                    ByVal e As System.EventArgs) Handles btnRemove.Click
        Dim I, J As Integer
        For I = 0 To intFriendNumber
            If myList(I).strFName = lstBuddies.SelectedItem Then
                For J = I To intFriendNumber
                    myList(J) = myList(J + 1)
                Next
                intFriendNumber = intFriendNumber - 1
                J = intFriendNumber + 1
                I = intFriendNumber + 1
            End If
        Next

        lstBuddies.Items.Clear()
        For I = 0 To intFriendNumber - 1
            lstBuddies.Items.Add(myList(I).strFName)
        Next

    End Sub
```

The last Button hides the current form and opens the next one in the chapter. This is accomplished by creating a new instance of the second form (which, like anything else, is an object) and activating it. With that done, the current form is hidden. You will get an error when you reference frmLoops, because the form has not yet been created. (It is recommended that you leave this section of the code until after you add the form at the beginning of the next lab.) Here is the relevant code:

```
    Private Sub btnLab2_Click(ByVal sender As System.Object, _
                    ByVal e As System.EventArgs) Handles btnLab2.Click
        Dim frmNew As New frmLoops()

        frmNew.Show()
        Me.Hide()

    End Sub
End Class
```

Demo Run

Run the application, and add the details of one friend (in this case, John Doe of 1 Rd City One, born on January 1, 2003). (See Figure 3.12.)

FIGURE 3.12
Lab 3.1. Specify new friend details.

Click Add Friend, and the friend has been added (Figure 3.13).

FIGURE 3.13
Lab 3.1. Add the friend.

Let's add several more friends (Figure 3.14).

FIGURE 3.14
Lab 3.1. Application after more friends were added.

Now if we click a friend in the List Box, the age will appear as in Figure 3.15.

FIGURE 3.15
Lab 3.1 - Select friend.

If we then click on the Remove Friend Button, the friend will disappear. (See Figure 3.16.)

FIGURE 3.16
Lab 3.1 Remove friend.

LAB 3.2: LOOPS, FACTORIALS, AND THE LIST BOX

Lab Objectives:

1. Practice `For` loops.
2. Review `Select Case`
3. Review arrays
4. Review the List Box
   - `SelectedItem`
   - `Items.Add.`

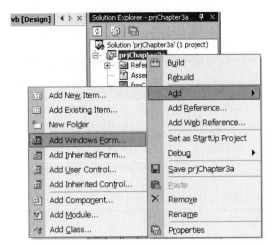

FIGURE 3.17
Adding a Windows form through the
Solution Explorer.

Application Overview

The second application in this chapter receives a number in a textbox and checks whether it is a positive integer that is smaller than 100. If it is, the factorial of that number is calculated and the distribution of the digits in the factorial is displayed in the List Box.

Part 1: Building the Form

Add a new Windows Form to the project by clicking with the right mouse Button on the Project and then selecting Add and Add Windows Form (Figure 3.17).

In the dialog that will open, type the name of the new form where it now says Form1.vb. Make the new form's name **frmLoops** (Figure 3.18), and click Open.

In the new form, add the controls shown in Figure 3.19 and name them accordingly. Set the Text property of the form, the labels (name these as you wish), the Buttons, and the List Box. You might also want to change the Font property of the textboxes.

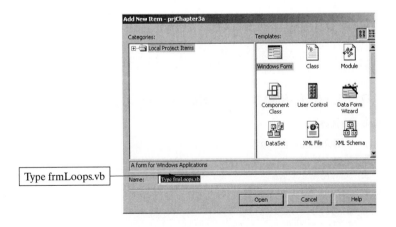

Type frmLoops.vb

FIGURE 3.18
Specifying form name in Add New Item dialog.

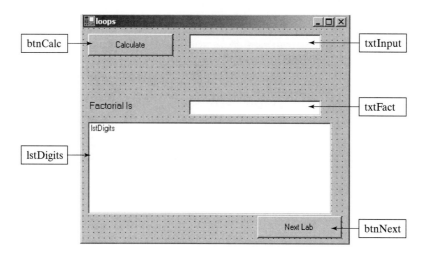

FIGURE 3.19
Lab 3.2.

Part 2: Adding the Code

The functionality of this lab is concentrated in one Button: Calculate. When the Button is clicked, the List Box is cleared and the text in the top textbox is checked to verify that it is a number. Then a `Select Case` is used to identify wrong values. If none are found, then a function to calculate the factorial is invoked. The returned value of the function is placed in the second TextBox and then the number is broken down to its digits. The digits are handled one at a time by taking the remainder of a division by 10. This remainder, the singles digit, is conveniently also the index of an array where the number of occurrences of each digit is stored. The contents of that array is displayed in the List Box. Here is the code:

```
Private Sub btnCalc_Click(ByVal sender As System.Object, _
             ByVal e As System.EventArgs) Handles btnCalc.Click
    Dim dblInput As Double
    Dim intInput As Integer
    Dim I As Integer
    Dim dblSum As Double

    Dim intDigit(9) As Integer

    lstDigits.Items.Clear()  ' clear the List Box

    If Not IsNumeric(txtInput.Text) Then
        txtFact.Text = "Enter a number"
        Exit Sub
    End If

    dblInput = CDbl(txtInput.Text)
    intInput = CInt(dblInput)
    If dblInput <> intInput Then
        txtFact.Text = "Enter an integer"
        Exit Sub
    End If
```

```
Select Case intInput
    Case Is < 0
        txtFact.Text = "Negative number"
    Case Is >= 100
        txtFact.Text = "Too big"
    Case Else
        dblSum = Factorial(intInput)
        txtFact.Text = dblSum

        Do While dblSum > 0
            I = dblSum Mod 10   ' take right digit
            intDigit(I) += 1
            dblSum = (dblSum - I) / 10    ' truncate right digit
        Loop

        For I = 0 To 9
            If intDigit(I) > 0 Then
                lstDigits.Items.Add(" The digit " & I & _
                " appears " & intDigit(I) & " times.")
            End If
        Next
End Select
End Sub

Private Function Factorial(ByVal intNumber As Integer) As Double
    Dim I As Integer
    Dim dblSum As Double = 1

    If intNumber > 0 Then
        For I = 1 To intNumber
            dblSum = dblSum * I
        Next
        Return (dblSum)
    Else
        Factorial = 1
    End If
End Function
```

As in the previous lab, the last Button closes the current form and opens the next one in the chapter. This is completed is by creating a new instance of the second form, which like anything else is an object, and activating it. With this done, the current form is made hidden. You will get an error when you reference frmLoops, because the form has not been created yet. (It is recommended to leave this section of the code until after you add the form in the beginning of the next lab.) The code is

```
Private Sub btnNext_Click(ByVal sender As System.Object, _
                ByVal e As System.EventArgs) Handles btnNext.Click

    Dim frmNext As New frmSort()

    frmNext.Show()
    Me.Hide()

End Sub
```

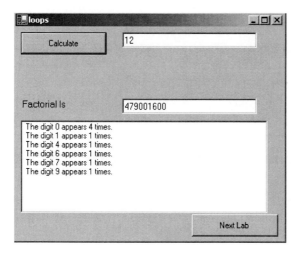

FIGURE 3.20
Lab 3.2 Application demonstration.

Application Demo

Let's run the application and see what the factorial of 12 is (Figure 3.20).

LAB 3.3: SORT AND DYNAMIC CONTROL ARRAYS

Lab Objectives:

1. Practice For loops
2. Practice Do loops
3. Review arrays
4. Study the Random Class
5. Build *Control Arrays* dynamically
6. Set Control properties from within the code.

Application Overview

The application generates 24 textboxes dynamically when the Set the Board Button is clicked and placed a random value between 0 and 100 in each. New random numbers are generated when the Random Numbers Button is clicked. The numbers are sorted with a bubble-sort algorithm when the Sort Button is clicked and then sorted again with the Sort method when the Verify Button is clicked.

> **Teaching Note:** It would be a good idea to discuss sort algorithms with the class as part of this lab.

Part 1: Building the Form

Add a new Windows form to the project by clicking with the right mouse Button on Project and then selecting Add and Add Windows Form. Name the form frmSort. Then add the four Buttons as shown in Figure 3.21.

Part 2: Adding Textboxes Dynamically

The code will dynamically create 24 textboxes on the form. Because these textboxes need to be recognized throughout the form class, they need to be declared first in the

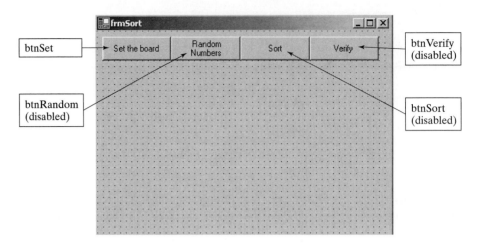

FIGURE 3.21
Lab 3.3.

`Declarations` section of the class. The textboxes are defined as an array; note that the data type of the array is a control type:

```
Public Class frmSort
    Inherits System.Windows.Forms.Form
    Dim txtNumber(23) As TextBox
```

The Set the Board Button will generate these textboxes and place them on the form. First, to help keep track of the `Location`, two variables are declared: `intCol` and `intRow`. `Location` is a structure used to specify the location of a control on a form. The two variables specify the column and row of the location in which each textbox will be placed. Also declared at this stage is `myRandom`, an instance of the Random class, and we will use it to generate a sequence of random numbers:

```
Private Sub btnSet_Click(ByVal sender As System.Object, _
                ByVal e As System.EventArgs) Handles btnSet.Click

    Dim intRow As Integer = 30
    Dim intCol As Integer = 100

    Dim I As Integer
    Dim myRandom As New Random()
```

Having done all the preparatory work, we are ready to generate the textboxes, one at a time. Being declared in an array, the `For` loop is a very appropriate way of doing this. Each textbox in turn is first instantiated as a new instance of the `TextBox` class:

```
For I = 0 To 23
    txtNumber(I) = New TextBox()
```

Then, its font is set as a new instantiation of the `Font` class. There are many possible overriding instantiations of this class. In the following code, we are setting its font name and size:

```
txtNumber(I).Font = New Font("Times New Roman", 10)
txtNumber(I).Size = New Size(20, 20)   ' width and height
```

The location of the textbox is then set as the `Point`; this, too, is an instantiation of a structure that is defined by the `intCol` and `intRow` variables:

```
txtNumber(I).Location = New Point(intRow, intCol)
```

Now that the textbox exists and has a location, it is added to the form as a new control. `Controls` is a collection of control objects in the form. The `Me` keyword specifies the current active form. The `Add` method adds the control to the form:

```
Me.Controls.Add(txtNumber(I))
```

With the textbox in the form, the application generates a random number between 0 and 100. The function `myRandom.NextDouble` returns a double-precision fraction between 0 and 1. Multiplying it by 100 and casting it to an integer will thus result in a random integer value between 0 and 100:

```
txtNumber(I).Text = CStr(CInt(myRandom.NextDouble * 100))
```

With this textbox completed, the location of the next one needs to be calculated:

```
intRow += 30
If intRow >= 30 + 6 * 30 Then
    intRow = 30
    intCol += 30
End If
Next
```

With all this done, the other Buttons can be enabled:

```
btnRandom.Enabled = True
btnSort.Enabled = True
btnVerify.Enabled = True

End Sub
```

Part 3: Adding the Rest of the Code

The Random Numbers Button generates a new set of random values:

```
Private Sub btnRandom_Click(ByVal sender As System.Object,_
                ByVal e As System.EventArgs) Handles btnRandom.Click

    Dim I As Integer
    Dim myRandom As New Random()
```

```
For I = 0 To 23
    txtNumber(I).Text = CStr(CInt(myRandom.NextDouble * 100))
Next

End Sub
```

The Sort Button sorts the values in the textboxes. The sort algorithm is called bubble-sort. The bubble-sort algorithm examines all the elements in the array in sequence and places the largest in the rightmost element. However, as it does so, it also sorts the elements to the left. In other words, as the current element, representing the largest value so far, is moved to the right by switching it with a smaller element, the smaller element is also placed in its correct location in the sorted array. As a result, by the time the largest element has been placed in the rightmost element, all the elements to its left have also been sorted. Here is an example of how this algorithm would work:

The algorithm compares card "9" with card "4":

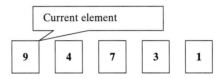

Card "9" is larger so the two are switched. There is no reason to check whether the elements to the left of the switched pair are sorted, because there are no elements there:

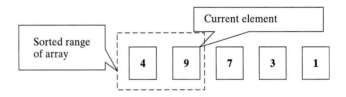

Now card "9" is compared with the next card:

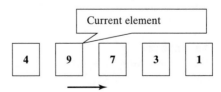

Card "9" is larger, so the two are switched:

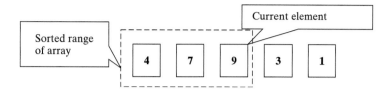

Bubble sort now examines whether "7" is in its correct position:

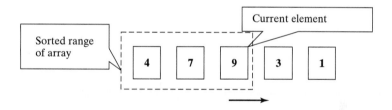

It is, so card "9" is compared with the next card:

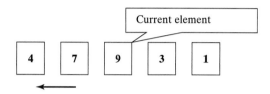

Again, card "9" is larger and the two are switched:

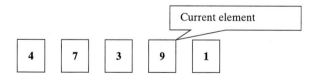

Now card "3" is compared with the previous card:

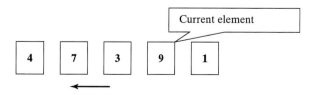

The two cards are not in order, so they are switched:

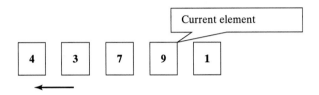

Now card "3" is compared again with the previous card:

It is switched again:

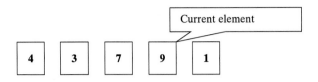

Now that card "3" is in its correct position, the comparisons continue with card "9":

The two cards are not in the correct order, so they are switched. Card "9" is in the correct position now, but card "1" is not yet in its correct position:

Now card "1" is compared with the previous card:

It is switched:

Now card "1" is compared with the previous card:

It, too, is switched:

Now card "1" is compared with the previous card:

It is switched:

Finally, it is switched, too:

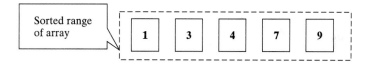

Sorted range of array

The array is now sorted. It takes a bubble sort, on average, $\log_2(N)$ comparisons and switches to sort an array with N elements. Here is the code that does it (note that the Text of the textboxes is copied to an array of integers for the comparison):

```
Private Sub btnSort_Click(ByVal sender As System.Object, _
                    ByVal e As System.EventArgs)  _
                    Handles btnSort.Click

    Dim intNumbers(23) As Integer
    Dim I, J As Integer
    Dim intcalc As Integer

    For I = 0 To UBound(intNumbers)
        intNumbers(I) = CInt(txtNumber(I).Text)
    Next

    For I = 0 To UBound(intNumbers) - 1
        If intNumbers(I) > intNumbers(I + 1) Then
            intcalc = intNumbers(I)
```

```
                    intNumbers(I) = intNumbers(I + 1)
                    intNumbers(I + 1) = intcalc
                    For J = I To 1 Step -1
                        If intNumbers(J) < intNumbers(J - 1) Then
                            intcalc = intNumbers(J)
                            intNumbers(J) = intNumbers(J - 1)
                            intNumbers(J - 1) = intcalc
                        Else
                            J = 0
                        End If
                    Next
                End If
        Next

        For I = 0 To UBound(intNumbers)
            txtNumber(I).Text = CStr(intNumbers(I))
        Next

    End Sub
```

The Verify Button also sorts the textbox array, but with the Sort method:

```
    Private Sub btnVerify_Click(ByVal sender As System.Object, _
                    ByVal e As System.EventArgs) Handles _
                        btnVerify.Click
        Dim intNumbers(23) As Integer
        Dim I, J As Integer
        Dim intcalc As Integer

        For I = 0 To UBound(intNumbers)
            intNumbers(I) = CInt(txtNumber(I).Text)
        Next

        intNumbers.Sort(intNumbers)

        For I = 0 To UBound(intNumbers)
            txtNumber(I).Text = CStr(intNumbers(I))
        Next
    End Sub
```

Application Demo

Let's start the application. (See Figure 3.22.)

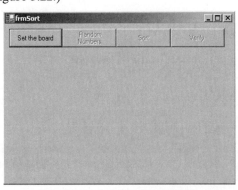

FIGURE 3.22
Initial form in Lab 3.3.

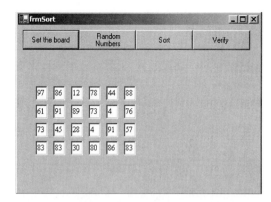

FIGURE 3.23
Lab 3.3 After clicking Set the Board.

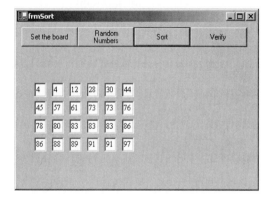

FIGURE 3.24
Lab 3.3 After Clicking Sort.

Click Set the Board. This generates the 24 textboxes and places random values into them, as shown in Figure 3.23.

The Sort Button and the Verify Button will sort the control array as in Figure 3.24.

LAB 3.4: SINE AND COSINE

Lab Objectives:
1. Practice `For` loops
2. Practice functions and subroutines
3. Algorithmic thinking.

Application Overview

The application will receive a number in the textbox, representing a number of radians,[6] and calculate its Sine or its Cosine, depending on which Button is clicked. The Cosine Button will call a subroutine to do this, while the Sine Button will activate a function. Both subroutine and function will utilize a factorial function. The formulas of

---

[6]Radians are an equivalent method of specifying the degrees of an angle. There are 2π radians in a whole circle, which corresponds to 360°. As such, 3.14 radians corresponds approximately to 180°, and 3.14/6 = .5233... radians is approximately 30°. The Sine of .5233 should therefore be .5 a d the Cosine should be about 0.866.

both Sine and Cosine are especially suited for For loops. Both are the sum of a mathematical series.

Part 1: Building the Form

Add a new Windows form to the project by clicking with the right mouse button on the Project and then selecting Add and Add Windows form. Name the form frmSineCosine. Then add the controls shown in Figure 3.25. Make txtResult multilined and with a vertical scrollbar by changing its MultiLined property to True and its Scrollbar property to Vertical.

Part 2: Add the Cosine Code

The Cosine Button will call a subroutine that will calculate the Cosine, in radians, of the number that was entered in the textbox and then will display the answer in the same textbox:

```
Private Sub btnCosine_Click(ByVal sender As System.Object, _
        ByVal e As System.EventArgs) Handles btnCosine.Click
    ' This part of the project calls a subroutine
    ' that will display the cosine of a number
    ' entered in the TextBox.
    If IsNumeric(txtResult.Text) And _
    txtResult.Text <> "" Then
        Call cosine(CDbl(txtResult.Text))
    End If
End Sub
```

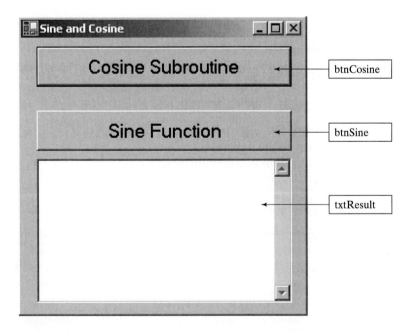

FIGURE 3.25
Lab 3.4.

The subroutine Cosine will take advantage of the repeating nature of the mathematical series that defines a Cosine. The Cosine is defined as a series of elements that are each made up of the radian parameter to the power of an even number and then divided by the factorial of that even number. These even number are ordered in such a way that each elements handles the next even number in sequence after the number in the previous element of the series. These elements are iteratively subtracted from the series or added to it. The series starts with 1.

For example, the Cosine of 0.98 radian is found as

$$\text{Cosine}(0.98) = 1 - ((0.98^2)/2!) + ((0.98^4)/4!) - ((0.98^6)/6!) + ((0.98^8)/8!) - \text{etc.} \approx .557.$$

This type of a series is ideal for a `For` loop. Recall that a `For` loop controls the number of times a section of code within the For block is executed and also provides an index of what iteration number is currently being executed. The code uses this functionality to control adding the first 50 elements to the Cosine series, while taking advantage of the `For` loop index to calculate the value of the current element in the series. The `For` loop index starts at the starting value of the loop and is incremented by the `Step` value. In the next example of the index code, starts with 2 and is incremented by 2. In doing so, it performs the code inside the For block with `For` loop index values of all the even numbers between 2 and 100. These `For` loop index values will determine the value of the element that will be added to the series in this execution of the code within the For block.

Note that the series adds and subtracts elements iteratively: subtracting the first, adding the second, subtracting the third, adding the fourth, and so on. We will apply a small trick to handle this. The variable `intSign` is an integer with a starting value of -1. Each iteration of the `For` loop, its value will be multiplied by -1. In that way, its value will start at -1, will then change to 1 in the next iteration, then to -1 in the next, and so on. This flip-flop will let us add or subtract the current element from the values accumulated so far by just adding the current element but multiplied by `intSign`.

The factorial itself, being a commonly used section of code in this project, will be a function. Recall that a function returns a value. That value will be plugged into the formula of the current element with the following code:

```
Private Sub cosine(ByVal dblAngle As Double)
    ' A Cosine of a radian is
    ' cosine(x) = 1- (x^2 / 2!)+(x^4 / 4!)-(x^6 / 6!)+ (X^8 / 8!)…
    ' this subroutine will show the value in the textbox while
    ' generating the factorial with another function

    Dim I As Integer
    Dim intSign As Integer = -1
    Dim dblCalc As Double = 1

    For I = 2 To 100 Step 2
        dblCalc += intSign * dblAngle ^ I / factorial(I)
        intSign *= -1
    Next

    txtResult.Text &= "The radian cosine of " & _
                    CStr(dblAngle) & " is " & CStr(dblCalc)
End Sub
```

The factorial is defined as the sum of all the integers up to the one in question. In the following code, it is calculated with a recursive function:

```
Private Function factorial(ByVal intX As Integer) As Double
    Dim I As Integer
    Dim dblCalc As Double = 1

    If intX > 1 Then
        For I = 2 To intX
            dblCalc *= I
        Next
    Else
        dblCalc = 1
    End If
    factorial = dblCalc
End Function
```

To see how this recursive function operates, note that the factorial of 1 is, by definition, 1. The factorial of any other number is that number multiplied by the factorial of the previous integer. For example, the factorial of 5 is 5*4!. To calculate the value of $n!$, the function multiplies n by its own returned value of $n - 1$. If the parameter passed to the function was 5, then the function will return 5 multiplied by the returned valued of the factorial of 4. To calculate the factorial of 4, the function will return 4 multiplied by the factorial of 3. To calculate the factorial of 3, the function will return 3 multiplied by the factorial of 2. To calculate the factorial of 2, the function will return 2 multiplied by the factorial of 1, which is 1.

Part 3: Add the Sine Code

The sine of a radian is calculated much in the same way, except that the elements are made up of odd numbers and the series starts with the radian value, rather than 1. The remainder of the algorithm in the function is the same as in the cosine example. In this example, the subroutine that handles the Sine Button will activate a function and display its returned value in the textbox:

```
Private Sub btnSine_Click(ByVal sender As System.Object, _
        ByVal e As System.EventArgs) Handles btnSine.Click
    ' This subroutine will check that the TextBox
    ' contains only a single positive number and if it
    ' does then it will activate a function to
    ' return the sine of that number in the TextBox
    If IsNumeric(txtResult.Text) And _
    txtResult.Text <> "" Then
        txtResult.Text = "The Sine of " & _
            txtResult.Text & " radians is " & _
            CStr(sine(CDbl(txtResult.Text)))
    End If
End Sub
```

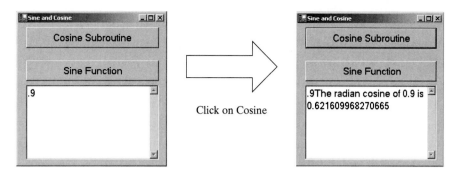

FIGURE 3.26
Running Lab 3.4.

```
Private Function sine(ByVal dblAngle As Double) _
    As Double
    ' Sine is defined as a series
    ' sine(x) = x - (x^3/3!) + (x^5/5!) - (x^7/7!) + (X^9/9!)
    ' this function will return an estimate of sine(x)

    Dim I As Integer
    Dim intSign As Integer = 1
    Dim dblCalc As Double = 0

    For I = 1 To 100 Step 2
        dblCalc += intSign * dblAngle ^ I / factorial(I)
        intSign *= -1
    Next
    Return (dblCalc)
End Function
```

Application Demo

Run the application and enter .9 in the textbox (Figure 3.26).

LAB 3.5: A CALCULATOR

Lab Objectives:
1. Practice subroutines
2. Algorithmic thinking.

Application Overview

The calculator accumulates numbers and handles the basic arithmetic operators. Because all the digits are treated basically the same, as are the operators, it is an ideal application for demonstrating the need and advantage of subroutines.

Part 1: Building the Form

Add a new Windows Form to the project by clicking with the right mouse button on the Project and then selecting Add, and Add Windows Form. Name the form frmCalculator.

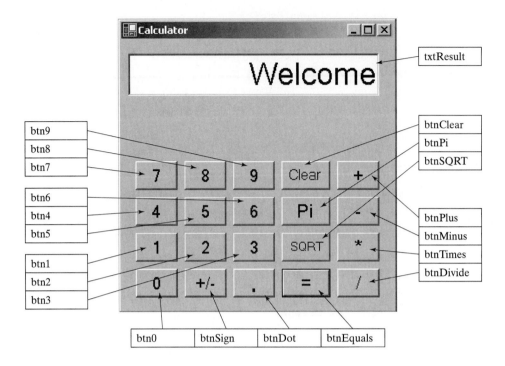

FIGURE 3.27
Lab 3.5.

Then add the controls shown in Figure 3.27. Make the Font size properties appropriately large and add the text property value in txtResult.

Part 2: Accumulating Numbers

The functionality handled by the calculator can be divided into two primary sections: accumulating numbers from the digits and performing the operators on these numbers. We will handle accumulating numbers first.

Essentially, when a digit Button is clicked, the previously accumulated number should be multiplied by 10 and this digit added to the accumulated value, unless the Dot Button has been clicked, in which case we add to the accumulated number the current digit divided by 10 to the power of the occurrence of this digit, since the Dot Button was clicked. Here is an example to clarify the logic. Suppose the buttons were clicked in this sequence: btn9, btn1, btn8, btnDot, btn7, btn3, and then btn4. The number shown in the display should be 918.734. And this is how the algorithm will do it: We will name the accumulated number dblAcc1 and the power of 10 by which we divide a digit as dblAcc3. Table 3.1 shows only the values as they change.

What is evident from this algorithm is that all the 10 digits are treated the same, except for a parameter of what specific value to add. This makes the algorithm an ideal candidate for a subroutine with a parameter that specifies what the actual digit is.

Let us first define some variables in the General Declarations section. These variables will be referenced in many subroutines and so must be defined where their

TABLE 3.1   Tracking Key Variables as an Accumulated Number is Being Created.

Button Clicked	Accumulated Number	Divide by to add decimal	Indicator if adding a fraction	Explanation
	dblAcc1	dblAcc3	bolDot	
Starting values	0	10	False	These are the starting values.
Clicked on 9	= 0*10 + 9 = 9			The value accumulated so far is 9.
Clicked on 1	= 9*10 +1 = 91			Multiply the previously accumulated number by 10, and add the current digit.
Clicked on 8	= 91*10 +8 = 918			Multiply the previously accumulated number by 10, and add the current digit.
Clicked on Dot			True	Mark that, from now on, when accumulating this number, add the digits as decimals.
Clicked on 7	= 918 + 7 /10 = 918.7	10*10 = 100		Add the current digit divided by 10 to the accumulated number. Thus, 7 will be added as .7. The division is by 10 because that is what dblAcc3 indicates. Having done that, multiply dblAcc3 by 10 so that the next digit will be divided by 100 before being added.
Clicked on 3	= 918.7 + 3 / 100 = 918.73	100*10 = 1000		Add the current digit as 0.03. Increment dblAcc3 so that the next digit will be added in units of thousandths.
Clicked on 4	= 918.73 + 4 / 1000 = 918.734	1000*10 = 10000		

scope of name recognition will allow them to be recognized throughout the class. The other variables will be discussed later on. The code is as follows:

```
Public Class frmCalculator
    Inherits System.Windows.Forms.Form

    Dim bolDot As Boolean
    Dim dblACC1, dblACC2 As Double
    Dim dblACC3 As Double = 10
    Dim strOp As String
```

The ten digit Buttons do essentially the same, calling the subroutine with a parameter that corresponds to their text.

```
Private Sub btn0_Click(ByVal sender As System.Object, _
    ByVal e As System.EventArgs) Handles btn0.Click
      Call add_num(0)
End Sub

Private Sub btn1_Click(ByVal sender As System.Object, _
    ByVal e As System.EventArgs) Handles btn1.Click
      Call add_num(1)
End Sub

Private Sub btn2_Click(ByVal sender As System.Object, _
    ByVal e As System.EventArgs) Handles btn2.Click
      Call add_num(2)
End Sub

Private Sub btn3_Click(ByVal sender As System.Object, _
    ByVal e As System.EventArgs) Handles btn3.Click
      Call add_num(3)
End Sub

Private Sub btn4_Click(ByVal sender As System.Object, _
    ByVal e As System.EventArgs) Handles btn4.Click
      Call add_num(4)
End Sub

Private Sub btn5_Click(ByVal sender As System.Object, _
    ByVal e As System.EventArgs) Handles btn5.Click
      Call add_num(5)
End Sub

Private Sub btn6_Click(ByVal sender As System.Object, _
    ByVal e As System.EventArgs) Handles btn6.Click
      Call add_num(6)
End Sub

Private Sub btn7_Click(ByVal sender As System.Object, _
    ByVal e As System.EventArgs) Handles btn7.Click
      Call add_num(7)
End Sub

Private Sub btn8_Click(ByVal sender As System.Object, _
    ByVal e As System.EventArgs) Handles btn8.Click
      Call add_num(8)
End Sub

Private Sub btn9_Click(ByVal sender As System.Object, _
    ByVal e As System.EventArgs) Handles btn9.Click
      Call add_num(9)
End Sub

Private Sub btnDot_Click(ByVal sender As System.Object, _
    ByVal e As System.EventArgs) Handles btnDot.Click
      bolDot = True
    End Sub
```

Here is the algorithm that actually accumulates the number and displays it in the textbox:

```
Private Sub add_num(ByVal intNumber As Integer)
    If bolDot Then
        dblACC1 = dblACC1 + intNumber / dblACC3
        dblACC3 *= 10
    Else
        dblACC1 = dblACC1 * 10 + intNumber
    End If
    txtResult.Text = CStr(dblACC1)
End Sub
```

Part 3: Operators

The second part of the functionality handled by the calculator is performing the operators. As with the digits, the functionality of the operators also overlaps. Essentially, when an operator button is clicked, the previous operators needs to be executed between the current accumulated number and the previously accumulated number. Suppose the buttons were clicked in this sequence: btn9, btnDot, btn7, btnPlus, btn1, btnMinus, btn8, btn3, and btnEquals. The calculator will accumulate the number 9.7 until btnPlus is clicked. Once that button is clicked, a new number will start being accumulated, but the Add operation will not be performed yet, because the second number has not yet been entered. Only when btnMinus is clicked, signaling that the second number has been completely accumulated, will the Add operation be executed. In this manner, when an operator button is clicked, regardless of which operator it is, the previous operators will always be executed. Again, this is a degree of shared functionality that justifies putting all the code in one place, a subroutine.

Table 3.2 shows how these values will be handled. In addition to the variables we saw with the last table, we will add dblAcc2 that will hold the previously accumulated number, and strOp that will hold the previous operators.

Because the algorithm is the same for all five operators, all will call the same subroutine. The only difference is in the parameter that is passed:

```
Private Sub btnPlus_Click(ByVal sender As System.Object, _
        ByVal e As System.EventArgs) Handles btnPlus.Click
    Call Action("+")
End Sub

Private Sub btnMinus_Click(ByVal sender As System.Object, _
    ByVal e As System.EventArgs) Handles btnMinus.Click
    Call Action("-")
End Sub

Private Sub btnTimes_Click(ByVal sender As System.Object, _
    ByVal e As System.EventArgs) Handles btnTimes.Click
    Call Action("*")
End Sub
```

TABLE 3.2 Tracking Key Variables as an Accumulated Number Is Being Created

Button Clicked	Currently Acc. Number dblAcc1	Stored Acc. Number dblAcc2	Divide By to Add Fraction dblAcc3	Indicator If Adding a Decimal bolDot	Previous Operator strOp	Explanation
Starting values	0	0	10	False	""	These are the starting values.
btn9	= 0*10+9 = 9					The value accumulated so far is 9.
btnDot				True		Indicate that the next digit is a decimal.
btn7	= 9 + 7/10 = 9.7		= 10*10 = 100			Add 7 as a decimal, in units of tenths.
btnPlus	0	9.7	10	False	"+"	1. Perform the previous operator on both numbers. In this case, just assign the current accumulated number to the stored accumulated number. 2. Display this value in the textbox. 3. Set the currently accumulated number to its starting values, including the value in bolDot. 4. Save the current operator in strOp so that the next time an operator is clicked, the operation executed between the two numbers will be Plus.
btn1	1					
btnMinus	0	10.7	10	False	"−"	1. Perform the previous operator on both numbers; in this case, add 1 into 9.7. 2. Store this value as the Stored Accumulated 3. Display this number in the Number textbox. 4. Set the Currently Accumulated number to its starting values, including the value in bolDot.

TABLE 3.2 (*Continued*)

Button Clicked	Currently Acc. Number	Stored Acc. Number	Divide by to add fraction	Indicator if adding a decimal	Previous Operator	Explanation
	dblAcc1	dblAcc2	dblAcc3	bolDot	strOp	
						5. Save the current operator in strOp so that, the next time an operator is clicked, the operation that will be executed between the two numbers will be Minus.
btn8	8					
btn3	= 8*10+3 = 83					
btnEquals	0	= 10.7−83 = −72.3	10	False	"="	1. Perform the previous operator on both numbers, in this case, subtract 83 from 10.7. 2. Store this value as the Stored Accumulated Number. 3. Display this number in the textbox. 4. Set the Currently Accumulated number to its starting values, including the value in bolDot. 5. Save the current operator in strOp so that, the next time an operator is clicked, this will be the operation that will be executed.

```
Private Sub btnDivide_Click(ByVal sender As System.Object, _
    ByVal e As System.EventArgs) Handles btnDivide.Click
    Call Action("/")
End Sub

Private Sub btnEquals_Click(ByVal sender As System.Object, _
    ByVal e As System.EventArgs) Handles btnEquals.Click
    Call Action("=")
End Sub
```

Performing the actual operator is done in the subroutine:

```
Private Sub Action(ByVal strCurrentOp As String)
    Select Case strOp
        Case Is = "+"
            dblACC2 = dblACC2 + dblACC1
            dblACC1 = 0
        Case Is = "-"
            dblACC2 = dblACC2 - dblACC1
            dblACC1 = 0
```

```
        Case Is = "/"
            dblACC2 = dblACC2 / dblACC1
            dblACC1 = 0
        Case Is = "*"
            dblACC2 = dblACC2 * dblACC1
            dblACC1 = 0
        Case Is = "="
        Case Else
            dblACC2 = dblACC1
            dblACC1 = 0
    End Select
    strOp = strCurrentOp
    txtResult.Text = dblACC2
    bolDot = False
    dblACC3 = 10
End Sub
```

Part 4: Additional Operators and Constants

The Clear Button resets the current accumulated number:

```
Private Sub btnClear_Click(ByVal sender As System.Object, _
    ByVal e As System.EventArgs) Handles btnClear.Click
    dblACC1 = 0
    dblACC2 = 0
    dblACC3 = 10
    bolDot = False
    strOp = ""
    txtResult.Text = ""
End Sub
```

The Pi Button sets the current accumulated number to π:

```
Private Sub btnPi_Click(ByVal sender As System.Object, _
        ByVal e As System.EventArgs) Handles btnPi.Click
    'dblACC1 = 3.1419265359
    dblACC1 = Math.PI
    dblACC3 = 10
    bolDot = False
    txtResult.Text = dblACC1

End Sub
```

The SQRT Button sets the current accumulated number to its square root. There are many ways of doing this. It can be done with the SQRT function. In this example, it is done with the logarithm of the number:

```
Private Sub btnSQRT_Click(ByVal sender As System.Object, _
        ByVal e As System.EventArgs) Handles btnSQRT.Click
    dblACC1 = Math.Exp(Math.Log(dblACC1) / 2)
    dblACC3 = 10
```

```
        bolDot = False
        txtResult.Text = dblACC1
End Sub
```

SUGGESTED HOME ASSIGNMENTS

1. Write a function that receives two integers and returns the starting digit in the first number of the second number. For example, if the function received the numbers 1234967 and 96, it will return 4. If the second number is not included within the first, the function will return −1.
2. Write the same, but as a subroutine with three parameters where the third parameter is the result of the examination.
3. Write a `For` loop that can replace a `Do While` loop.

TEST YOURSELF

1. What is an array? Give several examples when an array is necessary and makes programming much easier. (*Hint*: Think of the sort algorithm.)
2. What is the rank of this array?

   ```
   Dim strArray(10) As String
   ```

3. What will the following statement do?

   ```
   strArray(10) = "k"
   ```

4. When would you use implicit ranking?
5. Give examples of when you would use `ReDim`
6. What does the `Preserve` keyword mean?
7. What will this statement do?

   ```
   Dim strArray() As String = New String() {"0", "1", "2", "3"}
   ```

8. What will this statement do?

   ```
   Dim strArray(,) As String = New String(1, 2) _
                   {{"0.0", "0.1", "0.2"}, {"1.0", "1.1", "1.2"}}
   ```

9. What are *jagged arrays*? When are they used?
10. The `Join` method joins elements of an array into one string. Write code that will do the same using only a `For` loop. (*Hint*: You will need to examine the upper bound of the array).
11. What are structures? Why are they necessary?
12. Is a `Private` member of a Structure available outside the Structure block? What is it used for.
13. Write code using `If` statements to check when the "tens" digit of a number is and to write its type (10s, 20s, 30s, etc.) in the `Output` window.
14. Write the same code with the `Select Case` statement. Why is this preferable.
15. Using a `For` loop write code that will generate the *N*th power of a given number using only the multiply and add operators.
16. Do the same, but use only the add operator.

17. What will be the value of I after this loop is completed?

```
For I = 10 To 0 Step -1
Next
```

18. What will be the value of I after this loop is completed?

```
For I = 10 To 0 Step 1
Next
```

19. What will be the value of I after this loop is completed?

```
For I = 10 To 20 Step 9
Next
```

20. What is SelectedIndex?

A Detailed Look at Object Orientation

CHAPTER OBJECTIVES

After completing this chapter, students should possess

1. An understanding of the Object-Oriented Programming concepts of

   - Encapsulation
   - Inheritance
   - Polymorphism

2. An understanding of how OOP concepts are implemented in VB.NET.
3. Knowledge how to create classes and their Properties, methods, and Events.
4. The ability to use *instances* of the classes in Projects.
5. An understanding of additional OO topics that aid in the development of software

4.1 AIMS OF CHAPTER

The main focus of this chapter is to introduce *object-oriented concepts* and explain how VB.NET implements these concepts. Starting with the .NET version of Visual Basic, object orientation is completely supported with the exception of multiple inheritances. Also, VB.NET is entirely based on object-oriented design. Object-oriented design is a powerful tool that helps to reuse code, thus reducing redundant development efforts. The careful design of objects is vital in OOP. Neither very few objects that have a broader scope nor too many objects that have narrow scope are desirable. A sound knowledge of subprograms and functions is necessary before reading this chapter.

4.2 OBJECT-ORIENTED PROGRAMMING

4.2.1 Introduction

Object-oriented programming (OOP) is about modeling objects. An object is a real world entity such as a person, place, object, or an event and it is implemented as a package that contains information and methods/events that act on this information. Traditional programming concentrates on how different objects work with each other. In OOP, the focus is on modeling objects in terms of defining their properties, determining data requirements, and designing the events/methods they use. In Visual Basic, controls such as textboxes and option buttons are class objects by definition. Suppose that a textbox named `txtLastName` is added to the form interface. This initiates the code `Friend WithEvents txtLastName As System.Windows.Forms.TextBox` to be placed in the `Windows Form Designer generated code` section to create an instance of the `TextBox` class. Once a class is designed, instances of the class (also known as objects) can be used in various project modules, thus eliminating the need to recode. When a textbox is added to a form, properties can be set and certain events such as `Leave` and `Click` can be coded and methods such as `Focus` may be used. Class objects are used in a similar way. When these properties, events, or methods are used, it is not crucial to know how Visual Basic implements them, but to know what happens when they are invoked. It is necessary, however, to understand OO terminologies and concepts to appreciate what happens "behind the scenes." While limited code reuse can be achieved through the use of subprograms and functions, OOP offers additional features such as (a) *encapsulation*, (b) *polymorphism*, and (c) *inheritance*.

4.2.2 Encapsulation

A class definition contains a description of its properties (data), and/or methods that act on the data, and/or event definitions. Thus, a class instance (object) is self-contained. External project modules cannot add new properties (data), events, or methods to the object. This characteristic of objects is known as *encapsulation*. Once a class is defined with its associated properties, methods, and events, other project modules can use instances of the class (objects) without concern as to how the class handles its data. Hence, encapsulation sometimes is also known as *data-hiding*.

4.2.3 Polymorphism

Polymorphism is the ability to create procedures that can operate on objects from more than one class. It also allows the methods and properties in different classes have the same name even if those methods/properties perform different tasks. The lab section will discuss how polymorphism is implemented in VB.NET.

4.2.4   Inheritance

Inheritance is the ability of a subclass[7] to inherit properties and methods of a super-class.[8] For example, if a superclass Employee has a Public method Salary, its subclass, ContractEmployee (for contract employee) will also inherit the public method, Salary. Additionally, another class created from the ContractEmployee subclass will inherit all the public properties, methods, and events of both the ContractEmployee subclass and Employee superclass. Although earlier versions of Visual Basic did not support inheritance, starting with VB.NET it is supported. In some cases, it is useful to create a generic superclass with common properties and methods, and subclasses that contain specific properties and methods that apply only to the subclasses.

The next section defines *namespaces* and how classes are created and instantiated in Visual Basic. The hands-on lab demonstrates in detail the creation of Employee class and two subclasses ContractEmployee and FullTimeEmployee derived from the Employee class. Also, client code that instantiates these objects is presented.

4.3   NAMESPACES AND CLASSES

In VB.NET, everything such as forms and message boxes are classes. Namespaces are a way to organize similar classes together. For example, form classes are present in Systems.Windows.Forms namespace and collections are found in the Systems.Collections namespace. Namespaces help organize classes in a structured fashion. When a new project is designed and developed, all the code of the project is placed inside a namespace in VB.NET. If no namespace is supplied explicitly for the code, a namespace based on the project name is automatically generated and the code is actually placed inside that namespace.

Because namespaces can be nested, an application can have more than one namespace. For example, an inventory application can have a high-level namespace called Inventory and other nested namespaces such as Inventory.Electronics, Inventory.Mechanical, and Inventory.Civil within the Inventory namespace. Since all the code is present inside namespaces, classes are defined inside them. Suppose we want to instantiate an object of the class Part contained inside Inventory.Civil namespace. The code to accomplish this would be as follows:

```
Dim objPart As New Inventory.Civil.Part
```

As can be seen, namespaces can be addressed directly. However, the code can get lengthy and hard to read. Another way is to use the Imports keyword:

```
Imports Inventory.Civil

Dim objPart As New Part()
```

In the preceding code, the Imports keyword makes it unnecessary to reference the namespace in the Dim statement. Although the Imports keyword makes the code simpler, care should be taken if more than one namespace has class declarations that have

---

[7]A subclass is a class derived from another class.
[8]A superclass is a parent class from which other classes can be derived.

the same name. In the inventory application, all the nested namespaces may have a class called `Part`. In such cases, the following code will not work:

```
Imports Inventory.Civil
Imports Inventory.Electronics
Imports Inventory.Mechanical

Dim objPart As New Part
```

The alternative would be to *alias* namespaces as in the following code:

```
Imports Cvl = Inventory.Civil
Imports Elc = Inventory.Electronics
Imports Mec = Inventory.Mechanical

Dim objPart As New Cvl.Part
```

This code is still simple and easy to read. By default, all the class definitions are contained within its root namespace. If a class needs to be defined in a specific namespace, then the `Namespace` keyword must be used:

```
Namespace NewNamespace

    Class NewClass

    End Class

End Namespace
```

Because of the block structure, many namespaces can be declared in a single source file. Also, classes of the same namespace can be created in more than one source file. Finally, the scope of namespaces is local by default.

4.4   DESIGNING AND USING A CLASS MODULE

This section focuses on creating class modules (including subclasses), setting their properties, defining the events and methods for them with examples. To begin, create a new `Windows Application` (by selecting `File`, `New`, `Project`, and then `Visual Basic Projects` from `New Project` dialog box). To add a new class module, select `Project`, `Add Class`, and `Class` from the `Add New Item` dialog box (Figure 4.1).

When a new class is added, VB.NET assigns a default filename `Class1.vb` as can be seen in the `Solution Explorer` window. In VB.NET, files have a `.vb` extension. The file type (Form, Class, Module) is determined by the *content* of the file and not by its extension. For example, in the `Solution Explorer` window, the name of the form file is `Form1.vb`. The code window for the class module shows

```
Public Class class1

End Class
```

Class definitions are coded inside the `Public Class...End Class` block structure. Because of this block structure, multiple class definitions are allowed in one class file. By contrast, in VB 6.0 each class definition needs to be saved in a different file. The only requirement is that each class definition should have its own `Public Class...End Class` block structure.

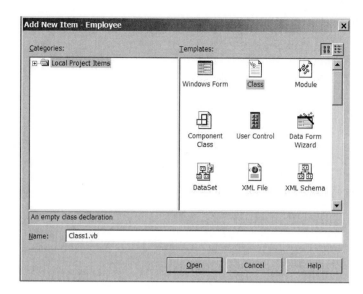

FIGURE 4.1
Adding a new class.

For illustration purposes, consider an Employee class with typical properties such as SSN, Last Name, and Rank. The sections that follow illustrate how properties and methods are defined and how to declare events.

4.4.1 Class Properties

In order to define a property for a class module, the Public Property...End Property structure should be used. This structure allows setting a value for the property as well as accessing the current value of the property. For example, the code for SSN property of the Employee class would be

```
Private mstrSSN As String

Public Property SSN() As String
    Get
        Return mstrSSN
    End Get
    Set(ByVal Value As String)
        mstrSSN = Value
    End Set
End Property
```

Note that mstrSSN is a local module-level variable used to set value for or retrieve the current value of public property SSN. Intuitively, it is clear that the Set...End Set structure should be removed in order to make the SSN property read only. Also, the ReadOnly keyword must be used to achieve this status:

```
Public ReadOnly Property SSN() As String
    Get
        Return mstrSSN
    End Get
End Property
```

Similarly, to allow for modifications only to the SSN property, the `WriteOnly` keyword must be used:

```
Public WriteOnly Property SSN() As String
        Set(ByVal Value As String)
            mstrSSN = Value
        End Set
End Property
```

VB.NET also allows the creation of default properties for classes. However, the default property must be a property array. This was done mainly to reduce confusion in code. For example, the following code is ambiguous, since it is not clear whether the variable is assigned the object or the object's default property:

```
Variable = Object
```

Making the default property a property array clears up this confusion. The following code demonstrates the definition of a default property, SSN (note the required use of the `Default` keyword):

```
Private mstrSSN(0) As String

Default Public Property SSN(ByVal Index As Integer) As String
        Get
            Return mstrSSN(Index)
        End Get
        Set(ByVal Value As String)
            mstrSSN(Index) = Value
        End Set
End Property
```

This is clear, since `Variable = Object(0)` means that the default property of the object is assigned to the variable. The code `strEmployeeSSN = objEmployee(0)` would assign the default property value to the `strEmployeeSSN` variable.

4.4.2   Class Methods

Methods of a class are created using `Sub` and `Function` keywords. A function must return a value, whereas a sub procedure need not. To check whether the input values (SSN and Rank) are valid (for the `Employee` class), the following function can be declared in the `Employee` class:

```
Public Function CheckData() As Boolean
        If mstrSSN.Length = 11 And (mintRank <= 5 And _
        mintRank >= 1) Then
            Return True
        Else
            Return False
        End If
End Function
```

This function checks the number of characters entered for SSN (it does not check whether numbers were entered) and the value of Rank property. If both are within allowable limits, the function returns True.

4.4.3 Overloading Methods

VB.NET allows for an interesting feature where methods can be *overloaded*. More than one method can have the same name in a class definition. Consider designing a method to compute salary for employees. Since the contract employees are paid hourly, their salary calculations are different from regular employees. Instead of having two methods with different names to compute salaries for employees, VB.NET allows the creation of two methods with the same name. However, there are restrictions: (1) The arguments of the methods should be of different data type or the number of arguments should be different in those methods; (2) the Overloads keyword must be used. For example, the function CheckData presented earlier can be split into two functions. In the following code, SSN and Rank property values will be set only when CheckData function returns True:

```
Private mstrSSN As String, mintRank As Integer

Public Property SSN() As String
      Get
            Return mstrSSN
      End Get
      Set(ByVal Value As String)
         If CheckData(Value) Then
             mstrSSN = Value
         End If
      End Set
End Property

Public Property Rank() As Integer
      Get
            Return mintRank
      End Get
      Set(ByVal Value As Integer)
         If CheckData(Value) Then
             mintRank = Value
         End If
      End Set
End Property

Private Overloads Function CheckData(ByVal strSSN _
As String) As Boolean
      If strSSN.Length = 11 Then
            Return True
      Else
            Return False
      End If
End Function
```

```
Private Overloads Function CheckData(ByVal intRank _
As Integer) As Boolean
        If intRank <= 5 And intRank >= 1 Then
            Return True
      Else
            Return False
      End If
End Function
```

These two functions have the same name and it is syntactically perfect, since the argument data types are different and the function declarations use the `Overloads` keyword. The scope of these functions can also be different: one can be of `Public` scope and the other `Private`. Several classes in VB.NET have overloaded methods. For example, the `MessageBox` class has 12 overloaded `Show` methods. Note that the above overloaded functions are `Private` in scope. Hence, it can be accessed only by procedures of the class and not by client code outside the class. The different scopes properties and methods of a class can have are as follows:

1. `Private`: The property or method can be used only by code within the class.
2. `Public`: The property or method can be used by code outside the class.
3. `Friend`: The property or method can be used by code within a project or component.
4. `Protected`: The property or method can be accessed by code in the class and by code in the subclasses derived from the parent class.
5. `Protected Friend`: This is same as having both `Friend` and `Protected` scopes.

4.4.4   Methods Overriding

When a subclass is designed based on a superclass, it automatically inherits all the public properties and methods of the superclass. However, there may be a situation where the subclass needs to implement its own version of the method(s) it inherited. This is allowed through the use of `Overrides` keyword. Also, the original method definition in the superclass must have the `Overridable` keyword. This offers greater flexibility in the subclass design. The following example illustrates this concept:

```
Public Class SuperClass
   --- Property Definitions ---
   Public Overridable Function Compensation() As Long
      --- Code ---
   End Function
End Class

Public Class SubClass
      Inherits SuperClass

      Public Overrides Function Compensation() As Long
         --- Code ---
      End Function
End Class
```

Note the use of `Inherits` keyword in the subclass definition. This is required to indicate the superclass from which the subclass inherited its properties and methods. It is important to remember that the subclass inherits all the public properties and methods except the *Constructor* method. The subclass must implement its own constructor method. Constructor method is explained in the next section. A subclass can have additional properties, methods, or events necessary for its functionality. As mentioned earlier, a class derived out of a subclass will inherit not only the properties and methods of the subclass, but also will inherit the properties and methods of the superclass. Again, the constructor method is the exception. This is how Inheritance is implemented in VB.NET. Note that in VB.NET subclasses cannot inherit from more than one superclass.

4.4.5   Class Events

Classes can have event definitions, but the event handler should be defined in the client code. A subclass derived from a superclass will also inherit the event definitions, provided that those events are public. Both the class and its subclasses can raise this event. The following example illustrates this feature:

```
Public Class SuperClass
    Public Event MainEvent()
    --------------------------
    Public Sub DoSomething()
        ----
        RaiseEvent MainEvent()
    End Sub
End Class

Public Class Subclass
    Inherits SuperClass
    --------------------------
    Public Sub DoSomeotherthing()
        ----
        RaiseEvent MainEvent()
    End Sub
End Class
```

In order to instantiate a class that has public event definitions, the `WithEvents` keyword should be used. Also, the scope of the class instance cannot be local. It should be at least at the Form level. Refer to the Lab 4.1 for a detailed look at the event handler code. Remember that it is the responsibility of the client code (a project that uses instances of the class) to implement the event handler for all the events declared in the class definition. To understand this, consider the `textbox` class. This class contains definitions for methods such as `Clear` and `Focus`. But, it contains only declarations for events such as `Enter` and `Leave`. The event handlers for these events should be defined (coded), if necessary, in the client code that uses the `textbox` class instance. If no event handlers are coded for, say `Enter` event of a textbox, nothing happens when textbox receives focus. Similarly, even if the `MainEvent` is raised, nothing happens and no exception occurs if the event handler is not present in client code.

4.5 LIFECYCLE OF AN OBJECT

Objects created based on a class have a life cycle. When an object is created or in other words when a class is instantiated, it can be initialized at the same time. VB.NET offers an object constructor method called New. The code in the constructor method is called first before any other code in the class. To prevent an exception from being raised, the New method, which is optional, if defined, has to be placed above all other code in a class declaration as shown in the following code:

```
Public Class Class1
       Public Sub New()
             Object Initialization code
       End New
       ---Property definitions---
       ---Method Definitions---
End Class
```

Since the constructor method can accept parameters, an object can be initialized with data as it is being created. The following code is illustrative:

```
Public Class SomeClass
       Private msngBonus As Single
       Public Sub New (ByVal sngBonus As Single)
            msngBonus = sngBonus
       End Sub
       ---Other definitions---
End Class
```

Client Code

With the public class defined above, we can dimension and instantiate an object of that class. In the code below this is done in the client code.

```
Dim objNew As New SomeClass(sngBonus)
```

Passing sngBonus to the constructor method initializes the object objNew. To provide flexibility in design, multiple constructor New methods are allowed in a class definition:

```
Public Class SomeClass
       Private msngBonus As Single
       Public Sub New (ByVal sngBonus As Single = 0)
           msngBonus = sngBonus
       End Sub
       Public Sub New()
           msngBonus = 0
       End Sub
       ---Other definitions---
End Class
```

Client Code

In the following client code, both `Dim` statements that instantiate the class are syntactically correct, since the `SomeClass` has two constructor methods:

```
Dim objNew As New SomeClass
--------------------------
Dim objNew2 As New SomeClass(sngBonus)
```

The `msngBonus` variable in the class definition will be set to zero if a parameter is not used to instantiate the class. Else `msngBonus` will receive the value of the parameter. The keyword `Overloads`, which is used in other class methods, is not allowed in the constructor method.

When an object has completed its useful purpose, setting its reference to `Nothing` destroys it. However, the object is not destroyed immediately (deterministic finalization). VB.NET has a garbage collection mechanism that runs a task periodically to look for objects that do not have any reference. This is referred to as nondeterministic finalization. Hence, it is possible that the resources locked up for an object are not released immediately. Although, the garbage collection can be invoked manually it consumes more resources and hence not advisable. In summary, while it is clear when an object will be created, it is not so obvious when it will be destroyed.

A lab exercise is presented in the next section that defines a super class called `Employee` and two subclasses `ContractEmployee` and `FullTimeEmployee` derived from the super class. The classes implement the topics covered so far such as class definitions, property and method definitions, constructor methods, overriding methods, and overloading methods and client code that creates, uses, and destroys the objects based on subclasses.

LAB EXERCISE 4.1

Lab Objectives

1. Create Class Modules
2. Understand Property definitions
3. Understand class Methods

   - Constructor
   - Overriding
   - Overloads

4. Understand class Events
5. Create Instances of Objects
6. Inherits Statement
7. Encapsulation and Polymorphism

Lab Overview

This lab focuses on designing a superclass, `Employee`, and two subclasses, `ContractEmployee` and `FullTimeEmployee`, derived from the superclass. A superclass is also referred to as a base class and a parent class. Similarly, a subclass is also known as a child class. The Employee class will have the following properties: SSN, LastName, FirstName, Address, Age, and Rank. A public event ErrorEvent() will be raised if inappropriate values are supplied to SSN and Rank properties. To compute compensation, a method called Compensation will be defined. Since compensation computations are different for contract, regular managerial, and regular non-managerial employees, this method will be an overridable method and the subclasses (ContractEmployee and FullTimeEmployee) will have their own version of this method. The subclasses will also have additional properties defined to meet their needs.

Part 1: Designing the Employee Class

Start a new VB.NET Project by selecting File, New, Project, VB Projects and then Windows Application. Before classes can be used in client code, they need to be defined. Add a new class module, and name it Employee.vb. Remember that all code modules will have a .vb extension. The file type is determined by the contents of the file and not by the file extension.

Next step is to add code to the class module. The first two lines of code make sure that variables are declared and that the variable data-type usage is followed strictly. Next, code for property definitions should be added. Complete the module as follows:

```
Option Explicit On  'Declare Variables
Option Strict On 'Explicit Data types

Public Class Employee

    'Event Definition for ErrorEvent
    Public Event ErrorEvent(ByVal objName As String)

    Private mstrSSN As String
    Private mstrLastName As String
    Private mstrFirstName As String
    Private mstrAddress As String
    Private mintRank As Integer

    Private mintAge As Integer
    Public Property SSN() As String
        Get
            Return mstrSSN
        End Get
        Set(ByVal Value As String)
            If Value.Length < 11 Then
                RaiseEvent ErrorEvent("SSN")
            Else
                mstrSSN = Value
            End If
        End Set
    End Property

    Public Property LastName() As String
        Get
```

```
            Return mstrLastName
        End Get
        Set(ByVal Value As String)
            mstrLastName = Value
        End Set
    End Property

    Public Property FirstName() As String
        Get
            Return mstrFirstName
        End Get
        Set(ByVal Value As String)
            mstrFirstName = Value
        End Set
    End Property

    Public Property Address() As String
        Get
            Return mstrAddress
        End Get
        Set(ByVal Value As String)
            mstrAddress = Value
        End Set
    End Property

    Public Property Age() As Integer
        Get
            Return mintAge
        End Get
        Set(ByVal Value As Integer)
            mintAge = Value
        End Set
    End Property

    Public Property Rank() As Integer
        Get
            Return mintRank
        End Get
        Set(ByVal Value As Integer)
            If Value > 5 Or Value < 1 Then
                RaiseEvent ErrorEvent("Rank")
            Else
                mintRank = Value
            End If
        End Set
    End Property
```

In the Employee class definition, the event ErrorEvent is defined first. This event should be Public in scope and will be raised by the code in the class if invalid values are supplied to the SSN and Rank properties. Next, local variables to be used only by the class module for property settings are declared. Since they are declared before any property/method declarations, these variables are available to all procedures within the class module.

This is followed by six `Public Property` definitions for SSN, LastName, First-Name, Address, Age, and Rank respectively. Note the `Get` and `Set` statements in each property setting. Also, the `Public` keyword for each property definition is required to enable code outside the class gain access to the property. The property structures for SSN and Rank check whether the input values are valid. If valid, the properties are assigned corresponding values. If not, the event `ErrorEvent` is raised. Remember that the actual event handler to handle the error will be designed in the client code (presented later in this lab).

Next, to understand class methods design a `Public` function to compute compensation. This method (`Compensation`) does not have any code, since the subclasses that inherit the method will have their own version of it. The code is as follows:

```
Public Overridable Function Compensation() As Long
    'This Function will be overriden by
    'code in Subclasses.
End Function
End Class
```

Note the keyword `Overridable`. This keyword is a must so that a subclass derived from the `Employee` class can have its own implementation of this method. This concludes `Employee` class definitions. (Note the `End Class` at the bottom.) In summary, the `Employee` class contains six properties, an event definition, and a method.

Since the `Employee` class is a generic class for employees, its usefulness is limited for contract employees and others. For example, pay rate and hours information that is crucial for computing pay for contract employees is absent in `Employee` class definition. This is so because such information is not required to compute pay for regular managerial employees. Hence, while defining the parent `Employee` class, care should be taken only to include properties and methods that are common for *all* employees. If contract employees and others require special processing, then appropriate subclasses (based on the parent class) with additional properties should be designed. Such subclasses are presented next.

Part 2: The `ContractEmployee` Subclass

The `ContractEmployee` subclass inherits the properties and methods of the `Employee` class. However, since the compensation computation is different for contract employees, additional properties are defined. Also, the `Compensation` method of `Employee` class is overridden by the subclass version of the method.

Continue to add the following code after the `Public Class...End Class` block for `Employee` class (remember that multiple class declarations are allowed in a single file):

```
Public Class ContractEmployee
   Inherits Employee
Private mintHours As Integer
Private msngPayRate As Single
```

```
Public Property Hours() As Integer
    Get
        Return mintHours
    End Get
    Set(ByVal Value As Integer)
        mintHours = Value
    End Set
End Property

Public Property PayRate() As Single
    Get
        Return msngPayRate
    End Get
    Set(ByVal Value As Single)
        msngPayRate = Value
    End Set
End Property
```

Note the `Inherits` keyword in the beginning. With this declaration, `ContractEmployee` inherits the six properties, the event definition, and the method of `Employee` class. In addition, the subclass has two Properties (`Hours` and `PayRate`) of its own. Again, these two properties are `Public` in scope so that client code can access them. Finally, a procedure to compute salaries for contract employees should be added. The keyword `Overrides` is required to override the method the subclass inherited. The calculations show that contract employees receive an increased pay rate if they worked more than 40 hours per week:

```
Public Overrides Function Compensation() As Long
    If mintHours > 40 Then
        Return CLng((msngPayRate * 40) + (msngPayRate * 1.5 * _
(mintHours - 40)))
    Else
        Return CLng(msngPayRate * mintHours)
    End If
End Function
End Class
```

The `FullTimeEmployee` Subclass

This is another subclass that inherits from the `Employee` class. In addition to the inherited properties, event and method, the subclass has two additional properties and the constructor method, `New`. The code is

```
Public Class FullTimeEmployee
Inherits Employee

    Private msngSalary As Single
    Private msngBonus As Single
    Private mintOTHours As Integer

    Public Sub New(ByVal intHrs As Integer)
        If intHrs > 40 Then
```

```
                        mintOTHours = intHrs - 40
                Else
                        mintOTHours = 0
                End If
        End Sub
```

The constructor `New` method is the first method in the definition of the `FullTimeEmployee` subclass. As mentioned earlier, the constructor method must be defined before any other method. This method is used to initialize an object created from this class. The method uses one parameter—`intHrs`. Suppose that full-time employees who are managers are not paid for overtime and that nonmanagers are paid for overtime hours. Hence, when the object based on this class is instantiated, it is initialized with overtime hours. If the object is for a manager, the parameter `intHrs` is set to zero. For a nonmanager employee, `intHrs` is assigned the number of hours worked. Thus, the constructor method is useful in initializing the object. Two new `Public` properties are defined next, for `Salary` and `Bonus`, respectively:

```
        Public Property Salary() As Single
                Get
                        Return msngSalary
                End Get
                Set(ByVal Value As Single)
                        msngSalary = Value
                End Set
        End Property

        Public Property Bonus() As Single
                Get
                        Return msngBonus
                End Get
                Set(ByVal Value As Single)
                        msngBonus = Value
                End Set
        End Property
```

Next, the subclass needs to implement its own version of the method `Compensation`. The pay is computed differently for manager and nonmanager employees, since nonmanagers are paid for overtime in addition to salary and bonus. Hence, the `Compensation` method uses two overloaded functions. As mentioned earlier, this is possible in VB.NET through the use of the `Overloads` keyword. The code is as follows:

```
        Public Overrides Function Compensation() As Long
                'Call method based on OT Hours
                Dim intOTHours As Integer = mintOTHours

                If intOTHours > 0 Then
                        Return CalcSalary(intOTHours)
                Else
                        Return CalcSalary()
                End If
        End Function
```

On the basis of the value of intOTHours, one of the two functions CalcSalary (parameter) or CalcSalary() will be invoked. These functions are presented in the following code:

```
Private Overloads Function CalcSalary() As Long
    'For Manager Employee

    Return CLng(Salary + Bonus)
End Function

Private Overloads Function CalcSalary(ByVal Hours As Integer)
As Long
    'For Non-Manager Employee

    Dim sngHourlyRate As Single = Salary/180

  Select Case mintOTHours
      Case Is <= 10
          Return CLng(Salary + Bonus + mintOTHours * 1.25 * _
          sngHourlyRate)
      Case Is <= 20
          Return CLng(Salary + Bonus + mintOTHours * 1.5 * _
          sngHourlyRate)
      Case Is <= 30
          Return CLng(Salary + Bonus + mintOTHours * 1.75 *
          _ sngHourlyRate)
      Case Else
          Return CLng(Salary + Bonus + mintOTHours * 2 * _
          sngHourlyRate)
  End Select

End Function
End Class
```

Note the Overloads keyword and End Class statement in the preceding code. The code segment completes the FullTimeEmployee subclass definition.

For a manager employee, the first CalcSalary function will be used. Nonmanager employees will be paid different rate depending on the number of overtime hours worked using the algorithm in the second function. Both the functions are Private in scope and hence available only to the code in the FullTimeEmployee class and not to code outside the class. Only the public Compensation method is exposed to outside client code. In order to understand how classes are instantiated and used, a client application is presented next.

Part 4: Designing the Form

In this section, a Windows form with the required controls and the associated code will be designed. Depending on user inputs appropriate class objects will be created, used, and destroyed. The form is shown in Figure 4.2. Name the form frmClass. The form has three group box controls, three buttons, and labels among others. The first group box contains textboxes to collect information such as SSN, Last Name, and Rank. The second group box is designed to collect information for contract employees. It has a check box that, if checked, will show additional controls to enter rate-per-hour and

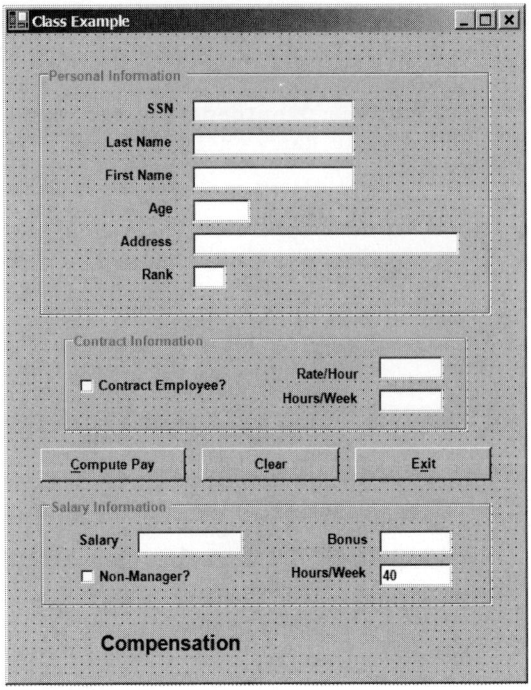

FIGURE 4.2
The frmClass Form.

hours-worked information. At the same time, the last group box's controls, designed to input regular employee information, are made invisible. Such designs are considered user friendly and show only the appropriate controls to the user. Similarly, if the nonmanager check box is checked, the controls in the middle group box are made invisible. The form at different states is shown in Figures 4.3 and 4.4.

Start adding code with the event handler for the event ErrorEvent that will be raised by the Employee class. The objCoEmployee_ErrorEvent handles the error raised by the Employee class whenever invalid values are supplied for the SSN and Rank properties. Although no object of the Employee class will be instantiated, objects created from classes such as ContractEmployee and FullTimeEmployee can also raise the event since these classes inherit the event definition from the Employee class. The error handler event accepts one parameter strObj that contains the name of the property that was supplied with incorrect values. If this event is raised, then a message box is displayed with appropriate message and the value of Boolean variable mstrErr is set to True indicating that the property value is invalid. Note that objCoEmployee_ErrorEvent handles both objCoEmployee.ErrorEvent and objFTEmployee.ErrorEvent.[9]

First consider the scenario for a contract employee. The user enters the required data in the text-box controls and then clicks on the check box for contract employee.

---

[9]The objects objCoEmployee and objFTEmployee are instances of the classes ContractEmployee and FullTimeEmployee, respectively.

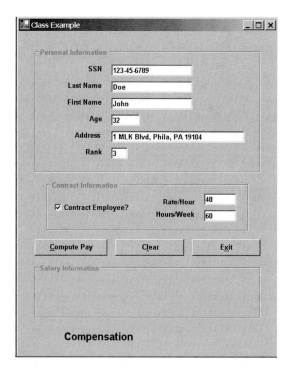

FIGURE 4.3
Data entry for contract employee.

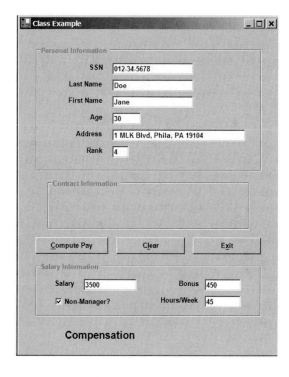

FIGURE 4.4
Data entry for nonmanager employee.

Additional textbox controls now appear for rate and hour inputs (coded to appear using the `chkContract.CheckedChanged` event). After inputs are provided, clicking on the compute button invokes the `btnCompute.Click` event. These events are examined next. As usual, the variables are declared in the beginning of the class definitions for the form. Since the classes have events, appropriate objects should be declared with the `WithEvents` keyword. Objects with `WithEvents` keyword are not allowed in local declarations. Hence, they are declared with `Private` scope and thus available to all code in the form class. The objects (`objCoEmployee` and `objFTEmployee`) are not actually created yet. As the following code shows, the keyword `New` is missing from their declaration:

```
Public Class frmClass
    Inherits System.Windows.Forms.Form

    Private WithEvents objCoEmployee As ContractEmployee
    Private WithEvents objFTEmployee As FullTimeEmployee
    Private mstrErr As Boolean

    Private Sub objCoEmployee_ErrorEvent(ByVal strObj As String) Handles _
    objCoEmployee.ErrorEvent, objFTEmployee.ErrorEvent
        'This handles the errors raised by the object

        MessageBox.Show(strObj & " incorrect")
        mstrErr = True
    End Sub

    Private Sub btnCompute_Click(ByVal sender As System.Object, ByVal e _
    As System.EventArgs) Handles btnCompute.Click
        'Instantiate necessary classes, set Properties and invoke methods

        Dim strSSN As String = txtSSN.Text
        Dim strLastName As String = txtLastName.Text
        Dim strFirstName As String = txtFirstName.Text
        Dim strAddress As String = txtAddress.Text
        Dim intAge As Integer = CInt(txtAge.Text)
        Dim intRank As Integer = CInt(txtRank.Text)
```

In the `btnCompute_Click` event handler, variables are declared and assigned appropriate values from the textboxes. If the check box for contract employee is checked, the `If` structure creates a new object of type `ContractEmployee` class. The properties of the superclass, `Employee`, are available to the object `objCoEmployee`, and they are assigned appropriate textbox values. The next step is to determine whether the input values are valid. Another `If` structure checks the value of Boolean variable `mstrErr`:

```
If chkContract.Checked Then
    'Instantiate ContractEmployee Class
    objCoEmployee = New ContractEmployee()

    objCoEmployee.SSN = strSSN
    objCoEmployee.LastName = strLastName
    objCoEmployee.FirstName = strFirstName
    objCoEmployee.Age = intAge
    objCoEmployee.Rank = intRank
```

```
If mstrErr = False Then
      objCoEmployee.Hours = CInt(txtHours.Text)
      objCoEmployee.PayRate = CSng(txtRate.Text)

      'Finally Compute Compensation
      lblCompensation.Text = _
      FormatCurrency(objCoEmployee.Compensation)
End If
objCoEmployee = Nothing
mstrErr = False
```

If the input data are correct, mstrErr's value will still be False, hence, rate and hour data are assigned to the properties of the object and pay is computed by invoking the Compensation method. This information is then formatted to display as currency using the FormatCurrency built-in function and assigned to the output label lblCompensation. If input values are invalid, no calculations are performed. Finally, the object is set to Nothing so that it can be destroyed during the next garbage collection process. Also, mstrErr variable is reset. Figure 4.5 shows an example for a contract employee. The following important concepts should be noted:

1. The object objCoEmployee is an instance of the ContractEmployee class.

2. Since ContractEmployee is a subclass of the Employee class, all the properties of Employee class are available to ContractEmployee and hence to objCoEmployee object.

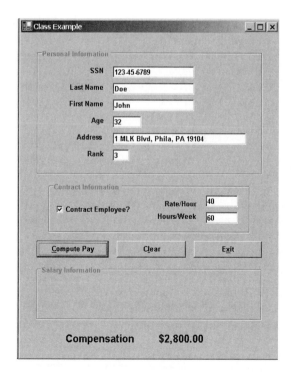

FIGURE 4.5
Contract employee example.

3. The properties available to objCoEmployee are SSN, LastName, FirstName, Address, Age, Rank, PayRate, and Hours.

4. The method available to objCoEmployee is Compensation.

5. The event declaration available to objCoEmployee is ErrorEvent.

6. objCoEmployee uses these properties, the method, and the event handler to compute pay for the contract employee.

7. After the calculations are complete, the object is set for destruction. Remember that the object may not be destroyed immediately. It will be actually destroyed during next garbage collection process.

If the check box for contract employee was not checked, then an object of FullTimeEmployee class is created. Note that the object is immediately initialized with the overtime hours worked. This is an important concept, since a constructor method is involved here. If the employee is a manager, the overtime hours will be set to zero.[10] The code is as follows:

```
Else
    objFTEmployee = New _
    FullTimeEmployee(CInt(txtNonManagerHours.Text))

    objFTEmployee.SSN = strSSN
    objFTEmployee.LastName = strLastName
    objFTEmployee.FirstName = strFirstName
    objFTEmployee.Age = intAge
    objFTEmployee.Rank = intRank

    If mstrErr = False Then
        objFTEmployee.Salary = CSng(txtSalary.Text)
        objFTEmployee.Bonus = CSng(txtBonus.Text)
        lblCompensation.Text = _
        FormatCurrency(objFTEmployee.Compensation)
    End If
    objFTEmployee = Nothing
    mstrErr = False
End If

End Sub
```

By initializing the object using the constructor method, a declaration of another public property for overtime hours is avoided. After the new object is created, appropriate values are assigned to its properties and the pay is computed using the Compensation method. This method invokes the appropriate private function CalcSalary to compute pay. Note that invalid values for SSN and Rank will invoke the error handler objCoEmployee_ErrorClick. Figure 4.6 shows an example for a full-time employee. The method Compensation has been defined in different classes, and it performs different functions, based on the class instantiated. This is polymorphism.

---

[10]The Text property of txtNonManagerHours should be assigned 40 during design time.

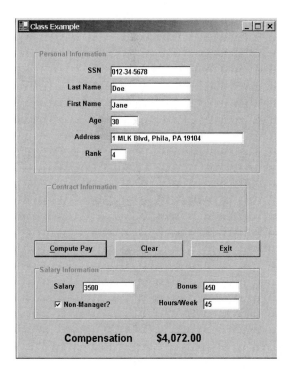

FIGURE 4.6
Full-time employee example.

Again, several concepts should be noted:

1. The object objFTEmployee is an instance of the FullTimeEmployee class.
2. All the properties of Employee class are available to FullTimeEmployee and hence to objFTEmployee object.
3. The properties available to objFTEmployee are SSN, LastName, FirstName, Address, Age, Rank, Salary, and Bonus.
4. The method available to objFTEmployee is Compensation.
5. The event declaration available to objFTEmployee is ErrorEvent.
6. objFTEmployee, similar to objCoEmployee object, uses these properties, the method, and the event handler to compute pay for the contract employee.
7. The object uses the constructor method New to initialize the object by passing a parameter of hours worked to the method.

To complete coding the form, add events for the check boxes chkContract and chkNonManager. The respective CheckedChanged event code is as follows:

```
Private Sub chkContract_CheckedChanged(ByVal sender As System.Object, _
    ByVal e As System.EventArgs) Handles chkContract.CheckedChanged
    'Make controls visible/Invisible based on checkbox state

    If chkContract.Checked Then
        lblRate.Visible = True
```

```
            lblHours.Visible = True
            txtRate.Visible = True
            txtHours.Visible = True
            chkNonManager.Visible = False
            txtSalary.Visible = False
            txtBonus.Visible = False
            lblBonus.Visible = False
            lblSalary.Visible = False
        Else
            lblRate.Visible = False
            lblHours.Visible = False
            txtRate.Visible = False
            txtHours.Visible = False
            chkNonManager.Visible = True
            txtSalary.Visible = True
            txtBonus.Visible = True
            lblBonus.Visible = True
            lblSalary.Visible = True
        End If
    End Sub

    Private Sub chkNonManager_CheckedChanged(ByVal sender As _
        System.Object, ByVal e As System.EventArgs) Handles _
        chkNonManager.CheckedChanged
        'Make controls visible/Invisible based on checkbox state

        If chkNonManager.Checked Then
            txtNonManagerHours.Visible = True
            lblNonManagerHours.Visible = True
            chkContract.Visible = False
        Else
            txtNonManagerHours.Visible = False
            lblNonManagerHours.Visible = False
            chkContract.Visible = True
        End If
        txtNonManagerHours.Text = CStr(40)
    End Sub
```

This code mainly makes the appropriate form controls visible or invisible depending on the state of the check boxes chkContract and chkNonManager. Finally, we complete the design of the form by adding event handlers for btnClear and btnExit Click events:

```
    Private Sub btnClear_Click(ByVal sender As System.Object, ByVal e As _
        System.EventArgs) Handles btnClear.Click
        'Clear controls to their default state

        txtSSN.Text = ""
        txtLastName.Text = ""
        txtFirstName.Text = ""
```

```
        txtAge.Text = ""
        txtAddress.Text = ""
        txtRank.Text = ""

        chkContract.Checked = False
        txtRate.Text = ""
        txtHours.Text = ""
        lblCompensation.Text = ""

        chkNonManager.Visible = True
        chkNonManager.Checked = False
        txtNonManagerHours.Text = CStr(40)

        txtBonus.Text = ""
        txtSalary.Text = ""
        txtSSN.Focus()
    End Sub

    Private Sub btnExit_Click(ByVal sender As System.Object, ByVal e As _
        System.EventArgs) Handles btnExit.Click
        'Terminate the Project
        End
    End Sub
End Class
```

Note that the Windows Form Designer generated code for controls is not included here. Keep in mind that the windows form is a class that inherits from `System.Windows.Forms.Form` class; hence, the declarations for the Form are contained within a `Public Class...End Class` block structure.

4.6   MORE ON OBJECT ORIENTATION

This section presents additional OO concepts and syntax that would be beneficial in designing better applications. These topics include shared members, binding of objects, abstract methods, and classes, among others.

4.6.1   Shared Members

If a specific method in a class is repetitively required in various project modules, we can create a shared method using the `Shared` keyword. Then this shared method can be referenced directly using the class name without creating an object instance. The default scope of shared methods is `Public`. The following code shows one such shared method:

```
Public Class ComputeValues
    Shared Function FindSquare(ByVal intNumber As Integer) _
    As Integer
        Return intNumber ^ 2
    End Function
End Class
```

Client Code

The client code for the preceding method is as follows:

```
Dim intSqrdNumber As Integer
Dim intNo As Integer = 5
intSqrdNumber = ComputeValues.FindSqaure(intNo)
```

Many such shared methods can be placed in a common class module for easy reference. Also, shared methods can be overloaded increasing flexibility in design. Similar to shared methods, shared variables can also be defined. The default scope of shared variables is `Private` unlike shared methods where it is `Public`. The shared variable is common across all instances of the class. If the scope of the shared variable is changed to `Public`, then it is available to all code within the application. Following are two example declarations of shared variables:

```
Public Class SomeClass
    Private Shared intNumber As Integer
    Public Shared intAnotherNumber As Integer
End Class
```

4.6.2 Instantiation of Objects

An object can be instantiated in the following two ways (there is no difference in terms of performance between the two):

```
1.    Dim objNew As AClass
      objNew = New AClass()

2.    Dim objNew As New AClass()
```

However, since variables can have block-level scope, if an object variable is required at the block level, the first method is preferable. The binding method of both methods is known as early binding. Since `Option Strict On` is the default setting in VB.NET, all objects are early bound unless `Option Strict Off` is set that would allow the use of late binding. An example of late binding is:

```
Dim objNew As Object
objNew = New AClass()
```

While both binding methods have advantages, late binding is not recommended. Early binding performs better under most conditions than late binding.

4.6.3 More on Abstraction

In the lab, a public method called `Compensation` was used in the `Employee` class definition. This is an `Overridable` method, and the subclasses had their own implementation of the method. Basically, the `Compensation` method had no code. For such methods where method definitions were not provided, there is a better alternative using the `MustOverride` keyword:

```
Public MustOverride Function Compensation() As Long
```

If `MustOverride` is used as shown, then the subclasses *must* have an implementation of the method, and method definition in the parent class is not allowed. Note also the missing `End Function`. Such methods are knows as *abstract methods*. Similarly, we can create an *abstract base class* that provides only interfaces and no implementation using the `MustInherit` keyword. Consider the following declaration of an abstract base class:

```
Public MustInherit Class SomeClass
      Public MustOverride Sub SomeMethod()
      Public MustOverride Function SomeFunction() As Long
End Class
```

Such base classes are useful in creating higher level frameworks for a system. If `MustInherit` is used, then the project *must* have a subclass that inherits from the parent `SomeClass` with implementations for both `SomeMethod` and `SomeFunction` methods. The keyword `NotInheritable` does the opposite of `MustInherit`, preventing inheritance:

```
Public NotInheritable Class SomeClass
      --- Class definition ---
End Class
```

No subclass of class `SomeClass` can be created using `Inherits` keyword.

4.6.4   `MyBase` and `MyClass`

What if, in the subclass definition, a method of the parent class needs to be invoked when the method is overridden in the subclass? In general, if, for some reason, an element in the parent class needs to be invoked from the subclass, the `MyBase` keyword provides a way. However, `MyBase` refers only to the immediate parent of the current subclass—that is, one level up:

```
Public Class SuperClass
      --- Code ---

      Public Overridable Sub SomeMethod()
            --- Method definition ---
      End Sub
End Class

Public Class SubClass
      Inherits SuperClass

      Public Sub SubClassMethod()
            MyBase.SomeMethod()
            --- More code ---
      End Sub

      Public Overrides Sub SomeMethod()
            --- Method definition ---
      End Sub

End Class
```

In the preceding code segment, `SubClassMethod` invokes `SomeMethod` of the `SuperClass`, using the `MyBase` keyword. In the absence of the `MyBase` keyword,

SubClassMethod would invoke SomeMethod of the subclass. SuperClass elements with Public, Friend, and Protected scope can be invoked with the MyBase keyword.

Because of the flexibilities provided by Overridable, Overrides, Overloads, and other syntax in VB.NET, sometimes it becomes difficult to invoke a specific method. Consider a scenario in which the code in a superclass invokes a method from a subclass created from the superclass, as illustrated in the following code:

```
Public Class SuperClass
    Public Sub SomeMethod()
        Call Compute()
        --- other code ---
    End Sub
    Public Overridable Sub Compute()
        --- Method definition ---
    End Sub
End Class

Public Class SubClass()
    Inherits SuperClass

    Public Overrides Sub Compute()
        --- Different definition of method ---
    End Sub
End Class
```

Client Code

When the client code

```
Dim objNew As New SubClass()
Call objNew.SomeMethod()
```

makes a call to the SomeMethod of SuperClass, SomeMethod calls the Compute method. But since objNew is an instance of SubClass, the Compute method in the SubClass will be invoked rather than the Compute method of the SuperClass, even though SomeMethod is present in SuperClass. Methods in VB.NET are *virtual*, meaning that if an object is of type SubClass, only the SubClass implementation of the method will be invoked and not the SuperClass implementation of the method. But if the SuperClass method needs to be invoked, the MyClass keyword must be used. Thus, the preceding SuperClass method SomeMethod should be defined as follows:

```
Public Sub SomeMethod()
    Call MyClass.Compute()
    --- other code ---
End Sub
```

Because of the MyClass keyword, when Call objNew.SomeMethod () statement is executed, SomeMethod will invoke Compute method defined in its class.

SUGGESTED HOME ASSIGNMENTS

1. Design a class module to compute the GPA for students given the letter grades for five courses. Design a form to instantiate this class. Raise events whenever necessary.
2. Modify the design of the `ContractEmployee` subclass of the lab to include a constructor method. The constructor method should accept hours worked and rate per hours as input parameters. Also modify the form code accordingly.
3. Make the `Employee` class an abstract base class and redesign the lab accordingly.

TEST YOURSELF

1. What are objects? Give examples of three objects.
2. Discuss the advantages of OOP.
3. What are the three main OOP concepts?
4. Is VB.NET a true object-oriented language? If so, how?
5. Are Visual Basic controls objects? Explain.
6. What is the function of `Set` and `Get` statements in the `Public Property` structure?
7. How is a class object instantiated? Give examples.
8. Explain `WithEvents` keyword. Where is it used?
9. If the `Get` structure is missing in a `Public Property` structure, what does it mean?
10. Does VB.Net support inheritance? If so, how?
11. Explain what a constructor method is.
12. Where is the `RaiseEvent` statement written?
13. Where should the procedure associated with the `RaiseEvent` statement be written?
14. What is the function of `Overloads` statement?
15. Explain the purpose of `MyBase` and `MyClass` keywords.
16. Explain `Overrides` and `Overridable` keywords.
17. What is the purpose of `Inherits` statement?
18. Why does the following statement appear above all code in the form module of the lab exercise?

    ```
    Private WithEvents objCoEmployee As ContractEmployee
    ```

19. What is the difference between the preceding statement and the following statement?

    ```
    objCoEmployee = New ContractEmployee()
    ```

20. How and when are objects destroyed?

Directories, Files, Paths, and Sequential File Access

CHAPTER OBJECTIVES

After completing this chapter, students should understand and be able to use

- The Path Class
- The Directory Class
- The File Class
- The DirectoryInfo Class
- The FileInfo Class
- The SaveAs dialog
- The Open dialog
- The StreamReader Class
- The StreamWriter Class

5.1   AIMS OF CHAPTER

The objective of this chapter is, first, to discuss and demonstrate how VB.NET handles directories, files, and paths, and, second, to discuss and show how VB.NET handles files sequentially. The chapter will discuss in detail the Directory, File, DirectoryInfo, FileInfo, and Path classes, and some of the more applicable methods of the Stream group of classes for handling sequential access. In doing so, the concepts of sequential access are discussed. The chapter also introduces the SaveAs and the Open dialog forms and shows how to apply them to enhance the interface of VB.NET programs.

The next chapter will expand on this material and discuss how to apply the FileStream class to the creation of binary and random access files, and the application of encryption and serialization through them.

A set of forms is developed in the lab part of the chapter to provide hands-on experience with the classes discussed in the chapter.

5.2   PATHS, DIRECTORIES, AND FILES

Windows, and indeed any other operating system, saves and manages data in Files. These computer files are the equivalent of their paper namesake. They are places identified by a name in which data can be stored. These files are grouped together into larger clusters where several files can be held together, usually because they have something in common. These clusters are called Directories. Directories can also be clustered together into higher order directories. For example, in the Figure 5.1, Explorer shows that WINNT is a directory. This directory contains many other directories, including one called Classes. The latter directory contains two files: dajava and xmldso. The address of a directory or of a file is called its Path. In Figure 5.1, the path is "C:\WINNT\java\classes". The path typically contains the letter code of the drive, in this case the "C" drive, and the hierarchy of directories, in this case "WINNT\java\classes". Had the path belonged to a file, it would also have contained the filename and its extension, such as "C:\WINNT\java\classes\dajava.ZIP", where "dajava.ZIP" is the filename and "ZIP" its extension.

As an analogy, if you are unfamiliar with the terms directory, file, and path, think of the directory as room with filing cabinets inside it, of a subdirectory as the actual filing cabinets inside that room, and of files as the folders that are inside these cabinets. The drive (being the "A:" drive for a diskette, the "C:" drive usually for the hard drive, and so on) in this analogy is the name of the building in which the room, equivalent to a directory in Windows, is located. A path in this analogy is the address of a given folder or of a cabinet. Just as a path in the analogy would normally contain the building name, the room number, the cabinet name, and possibly the folder ID, the path in Windows contains the drive, the directory, subdirectories, and possibly also the filename. The file contains records with data. In the analogy, the folder (a.k.a. file) contains

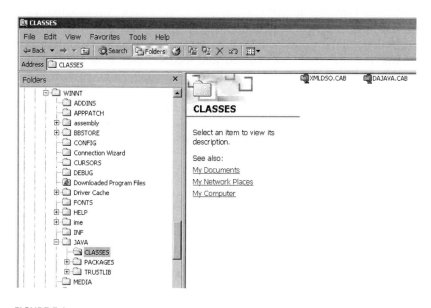

FIGURE 5.1

sheets of paper that are equivalent to records, with words, numbers, and pictures on them. These words, numbers, and pictures are equivalent to the data in the file.

VB.NET has dedicated classes for handling directories and the files within them. These classes, and many others we will discuss in this chapter, reside in the `System.IO` namespace, which is dedicated to Input and Output (IO) operations. The classes are the `Directory` and `DirectoryInfo` classes, which handle directories, the `File` and `FileInfo` classes, which handle files, and the `Path` class, which conveniently shows the elements of a path. Because the methods of these two classes are defined as shared there is no need for the `New` operator to create an instance when accessing their methods.

5.2.1 The Directory Class

The `Directory` class contains methods that provide information about directories: whether a specific directory exists, when it was created, what its root director is, and so on. This class also provides many methods for managing directories: creating directories, deleting them, moving them, and so on. And, the class contains methods that can set the properties of a directory: changing the date and time when it was created, the registration of when it was last accessed, and so on. The methods (interestingly, this class has no properties, although some of the methods would seem to be properties at first glance) can be placed into several groups. All the methods of this class reside in the System.IO namespace. However, being *shared* classes, it is enough to just add the namespace before the name of each of these methods to activate it.

The first group of methods retrieves information about a directory at a given path. All these methods start with the word "Get" with the exception of the `Exists` method. The `Exists` method receives as a parameter a string with the path name and returns either a `True` or a `False` value, depending on whether the directory exists. The `GetCurrentDirectory` method returns the path of the current directory (i.e., the active directory) as a string. The `GetCreationTime` returns a date value with the data and time when the directory was created. The `GetDirectoryRoot` method returns the name of the root directory as a string. The `GetLastAccessTime` method returns a date value of when the directory was last accessed, and the `GetLastWriteTime` method returns the date when it was last updated. The `GetDirectories` method returns a *collection* with the names of the subdirectories (i.e., the names of the directories included within this directory). This collection can then be read with a `For Each` loop to access all the subdirectories within it. The code demonstrates these methods. Run the following application in the lab to get a good hands-on feeling for how this works:

```
Dim strPath As String

If Not IO.Directory.Exists(strPath) Then
    strPath = System.IO.Directory.GetCurrentDirectory()
End If

Console.WriteLine("Creation Time    " & _
    System.IO.Directory.GetCreationTime(strPath))
Console.WriteLine("Current Directory " & _
    System.IO.Directory.GetCurrentDirectory)
Console.WriteLine("Directory Root    " & _
    System.IO.Directory.GetDirectoryRoot(strPath))
```

```
Console.WriteLine("Last Access Time  " & _
    System.IO.Directory.GetLastAccessTime(strPath))
Console.WriteLine("Last Write Time   " & _
    System.IO.Directory.GetLastWriteTime(strPath))

Dim strContains As String() = _
    System.IO.Directory.GetDirectories(strPath)
Dim strDir As String
For Each strDir In strContains
    Console.WriteLine(" The Path contains this directory " & _
        strfile)
Next
```

The second group of methods changes this information about a directory at a given path. All these methods start with the word "Set". The SetCreationTime receives a date value with the data and time that will replace the current date and time in which the directory was created. The setLastAccessTime method receives a date value with the data and time that will replace the date and time of when the directory was last accessed, and the SetLastWriteTime method of when it was last updated. The GetCurrentDirectory method sets the parameter it receives, a path, as the current directory. In the following code the path of a directory and a date and time value are accessed from textboxes and are used to set the creation, last access, and last update time of a directory and to make it the current directory:

```
Dim strPath As String = txtInput.Text
Dim datCreate As Date

If IsDate(txtDateCreated.Text) Then
    datCreate = CDate(txtDateCreated.Text)
    If System.IO.Directory.Exists(strPath) Then
        System.IO.Directory.SetCreationTime _
                (strPath, datCreate)
        System.IO.Directory.SetLastAccessTime _
                (strPath, datCreate)
        System.IO.Directory.SetLastWriteTime _
                (strPath, datCreate)
        System.IO.Directory.SetCurrentDirectory(strPath)
    Else
        MessageBox.Show("Path is inappropriate")
    End If
Else
    MessageBox.Show("Date is incorrect")
End If
```

The third group of methods moves and deletes the directory. The Move method moves a directory from one path to another, and the Delete method deletes it. The latter method can either delete an empty directory or, optionally, also delete all that it contains. In the following code, a directory is moved from one path to another, proving that it exists in the first path and does not exist in the second (both paths are given in textboxes):

```
If System.IO.Directory.Exists(txtInput.Text) Then
    If Not System.IO.Directory.Exists(txtMoveTo.Text) Then
        System.IO.Directory.Move(txtInput.Text, txtMoveTo.Text)
    Else
        MessageBox.Show("Destination path already exists")
    End If
Else
    MessageBox.Show("Source path does not exist")
End If
```

In the case of the `Delete` method, the indicator of whether to delete the directory and all its subdirectories and files is set based on the value of a check box. The optional second parameter of the method specifies when set to `True` that the content of the directory should also be deleted. A directory cannot be deleted if it contains files or subdirectories, unless this parameter is set to `True`. The following code is illustrative:

```
If System.IO.Directory.Exists(txtInput.Text) Then
    If chkDelete.Checked Then
        System.IO.Directory.Delete(txtInput.Text, True)
    Else
        System.IO.Directory.Delete(txtInput.Text)
    End If
Else
    MessageBox.Show("Source path does not exist")
End If
```

5.2.2   The File Class

The `File` class contains methods that provide information about files, sets this information, and other methods that perform operations on the file, such as moving, copying, and deleting it. The first group of methods provides information about the file. As in the case of the `Directory` class, the `Exists` method returns a `True` value if the file exists and a `False` value if it does not. The `GetCreationTime` method returns the creation date and time of the file as a date value, while the `GetLastAccessTime` method returns its last access date and time, and the `GetLastWriteTime` method when it was last updated. The `File` class also returns an `Enum` named `GetAttributes` with the attributes of the file, among them whether it is archived, compressed, hidden, read only, or temporary. The value of the `Enum` needs to read in conjunction with the `GetAttributes` method. In the following code example, the details of a file whose path is provided in a textbox are shown in the Output window, provided that exist such details:

```
Dim strPath As String = txtInput.Text

If System.IO.File.Exists(strPath) Then
    Console.WriteLine("Create on          " & _
        System.IO.File.GetCreationTime(strPath))
    Console.WriteLine("Last accessed on    " & _
        System.IO.File.GetLastAccessTime(strPath))
```

```
Console.WriteLine("Last updated on      " & _
        System.IO.File.GetLastWriteTime(strPath))

' Examine the file attributes Enum.
' Beware of bugs this is how it should be done.
If System.IO.File.GetAttributes(strPath) And _
       System.IO.FileAttributes.Archive Then
       Console.WriteLine("File is archived     ")
Else
       Console.WriteLine("File is not archived     ")
End If
If System.IO.File.GetAttributes(strPath) And _
       IO.FileAttributes.ReadOnly Then
       Console.WriteLine("File is readonly    ")
Else
       Console.WriteLine("File is not readonly      ")
End If
Else
    MessageBox.Show("Source file does not exist")
End If
```

Programming Note: Methods in the `Directory` and the `File` classes are *shared*. This means that the methods can be used without being instantiated with the `New` keyword.

As with the `Directory` method, there are the equivalent methods that set these values also in the `File` class. These methods have the same names and parameters and return the same values: `SetCreationTime`, `SetLastAccessTime`, and `SetLastWriteTime`. In addition, there is also the `SetAttributes` method that is used to set the `Enum` values of the file. Each `Enum` value must be set individually. The default `Enum` value of a file is `Normal`. The code is as follows:

```
System.IO.File.SetAttributes _
        (strPath, IO.FileAttributes.Archive)
System.IO.File.SetAttributes _
        (strPath, IO.FileAttributes.Hidden)
```

VB.NET guides the code as you enter it (Figure 5.2). There is no need to memorize the list of `Enum` values.

The third set of methods performs operations on the file, such as copying it, moving it, and deleting it with the appropriately named methods: `Copy`, `Move`, and `Delete`. The `Copy` and the `Move` methods receive two parameters, the origin path and the destination path. The `Delete` method receives only one parameter, the path of the file that is to be deleted. In the examples of code that follow, the origin and the destination paths are provided in textboxes. The code verifies that the origin path exists and that the destination path does not. This operation is done within a Try Block so that any IO exceptions will be caught by the code rather than result in a runtime error. The `IOException` is an error exception that resides in the `System.IO` namespace and relates to any kind of IO error. Adding it to the Try Block will catch every error

```
System.IO.File.SetAttributes(strpath, | )
```

SetAttributes (path As String, **fileAttributes As System.IO.FileAttributes**)
fileAttributes:
   The desired System.IO.FileAttributes, such as Hidden, ReadOnly, Normal, and Archive .

FIGURE 5.2
IO File Attributes.

that relates to any input or output device or operation. Without it, any IO error will result in a runtime error message. Here is the code:

```
Try
    If System.IO.File.Exists(txtInput.Text) Then
        If Not System.IO.File.Exists(txtCopyFile.Text) Then
            System.IO.File.Move(txtInput.Text, txtCopyFile.Text)
        Else
            MessageBox.Show("Destination file already exists")
        End If
    Else
        MessageBox.Show("Source file does not exist")
    End If
Catch err As System.IO.IOException
    MessageBox.Show("unexpected IO error")
End Try
```

The same operation can be done with a combination of a `Copy` and a `Delete` method:

```
Try
    If System.IO.File.Exists(txtInput.Text) Then
        If Not System.IO.File.Exists(txtMoveFile.Text) Then
            System.IO.File.Copy(txtInput.Text, txtMoveFile.Text)
            System.IO.File.Delete(txtInput.Text)
        Else
            MessageBox.Show("Destination file already exists")
        End If
    Else
        MessageBox.Show("Source file does not exist")
    End If
Catch err As System.IO.IOException
    MessageBox.Show("unexpected IO error")
End Try
```

The other methods in this class deal with handling files as arrays of bytes. These will not be covered in this chapter.

5.2.3   The Path Class

Both the `File` and the `Directory` class handle paths. Although a path can conveniently be thought of as a string and broken down into its parts with string operators and functions, it is useful to have a set of dedicated methods that break it down into its components. That is, precisely what the `Path` class does. The `GetDirectoryName` method returns a string with the directory name. The `GetExtension` method returns a string with the file extension; this might be "txt" for text files or "doc" for Word files. The `GetFileName` method will return a string with the filename including its extension, while `GetFileNameWithoutExtension` will return a string with the filename excluding its extension. The `GetFullPath` will return the full path of the file, and the `HasExtension` will return a `True` or `False` value depending on whether the file has an extension. The `DirectorySeparatorChar`, `PathSeparator`, and `VolumeSeparatorChar` all return a single appropriate separator character. The following code example demonstrates this:

```
Dim strpath As String = "C:\Myfiles\MyExample\MyFile.txt"
IO.Path.GetDirectoryName(strPath)

Console.WriteLine("Extension is " & _
                System.IO.Path.GetExtension(strPath))
Console.WriteLine("File Name is " & _
                System.IO.Path.GetFileName(strPath))
Console.WriteLine("Without extension it is " & _
                System.IO.Path.GetFileNameWithoutExtension(strPath))
Console.WriteLine("Full path is " & _
                System.IO.Path.GetFullPath(strPath))
Console.WriteLine("It has an extension " & _
                System.IO.Path.HasExtension(strPath))
Console.WriteLine("The directory separator is " & _
                 System.IO.Path.DirectorySeparatorChar)
Console.WriteLine("The path separator is " & _
                System.IO.Path.PathSeparator)
Console.WriteLine("The volume separator is " & _
                System.IO.Path.VolumeSeparatorChar)
```

The Output window will show

```
Extension is .txt
File Name is MyFile.txt
Without extension it is MyFile
Full path is C:\Myfiles\MyExample\MyFile.txt
It has an extension True
The directory separator is \
The path separator is ;
The volume separator is :
```

5.2.4   The DirectoryInfo and FileInfo Classes

A more efficient pair of classes that handles directories and files is the `DirectoryInfo` and `FileInfo` classes. These two classes are more efficient because unlike the `Directory` and the `File` classes, they do not return `Strings`. (See discussion in Chapter 2 about why the `String` data type is not the most efficient way of handling string data.) However, these two classes require a `New` operator to be instantiated before they can be used, because their methods are not shared. The method names and functionality are essentially the same, as the following code shows:

```
Try
    Dim myDirectory As IO.DirectoryInfo
    myDirectory = New IO.DirectoryInfo(txtNewPath.Text)

    Console.WriteLine("The Current Path is " & txtNewPath.Text)

    If myDirectory.Exists Then
       Console.WriteLine("This directory was created on " & _
       myDirectory.CreationTime.ToString)

       Console.WriteLine("Its root directory is " & _
       myDirectory.Root().ToString)

       Console.WriteLine("The File extension is " & _
       myDirectory.Extension().ToString)

       Dim myfiles As IO.FileInfo
       For Each myfiles In myDirectory.GetFiles()
            Console.WriteLine (myfiles.ToString)
       Next

       Dim myDirs As IO.DirectoryInfo
       For Each myDirs In myDirectory.GetDirectories()
            Console.WriteLine("Its sub-directories are " & _
       myDirs.ToString)
       Next
    End If
Catch ioerror As Exception
    Console.WriteLine("Got an Error ")
Finally
    Console.WriteLine("Completed ")
End Try
```

The two classes also enable other operations on files and directories in a manner that is equivalent to the `Directory` and `File` classes. In the next example of code, we demonstrate the `Delete` method of the `DirectoryInfo` method. In the process, we also take advantage of the ability of the Try block not only to catch errors, but to throw (create) them as well. The path of the directory is set according to the text of a textbox. Note that this value can be only assigned after the object has been instantiated with the `New` keyword. Note also that `expPath` is declared as an `Exception`. An `Exception` can be set to contain a message that will be available in the Catch section of a Try Block. The

Exception is thrown in the code when it is recognized that there is no reason to continue with the rest of the code in the block. Throwing the exception with the Throw statement is somewhat equivalent to the Exit statement elsewhere in VB.NET: Both cause an immediate exit of the current code and the continuation of the code execution after that block. The difference is that the Throw statement can also pass a message with the value that is assigned to the exception. The Catch statements are then executed one at a time until the appropriate Catch is found, the same as a Select Case statement works of the three Catches in the following code, the middle one will be the one to catch this exception when it is thrown:

```
Dim myDirectory As IO.DirectoryInfo
Dim expPath As Exception

myDirectory = New IO.DirectoryInfo(txtNewPath.Text)

Try
    If Not myDirectory.Exists Then
        ' This is s neat way to overcome the need for goto
        expPath = New Exception("Sorry directory does not exist")
        Throw expPath
    Else
        myDirectory.Delete()
    End If

Catch ioErr As System.IO.IOException
    MsgBox(ioErr.Message)
Catch exppath
    ' we can catch the Throw exceptions this way, by name
    MsgBox(expPath.Message)
Catch otherErr As Exception  ' Or generally this way
    otherErr = expPath          ' and then assign the message
                                ' explicitly
    MsgBox(otherErr.Message)
End Try
```

Programming Note: It is always better to detect an IO error explicitly with an If statement by examining the methods of the Directory, File, DirectoryInfo and FileInfo classes, rather than relying on catching them in the Try Block. It is much more efficient that way and avoids the need to activate system resources. Having said that, we can still assert that using the Throw statement to leave a section of code within the Try Block is a good, efficient, and readable way of handling nonsystem errors.

5.3 DIRECTORY AND FILE DIALOGS

Handling the user interface of directories and files requires of course a more complex dialog, and a standardized one across applications at that. VB.NET provides these standardized Windows interfaces through dedicated classes: OpenFileDialog and SaveFileDialog.

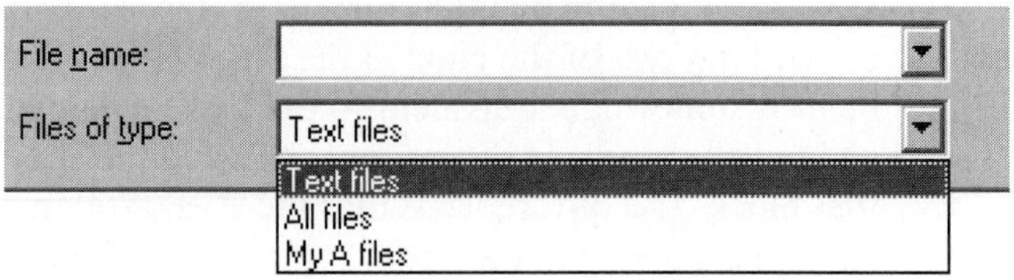

File name:	
Files of type:	Text files

Text files
All files
My A files

FIGURE 5.3
The Open File Dialog Filter.

5.3.1   The `OpenFileDialog` Class

The `OpenFileDialog` opens the standardized Open dialog. This class contains many methods and properties. Among the most important of these are the `ShowDialog` method that opens the standard Windows Open dialog, the `Filter` property that specifies which filename patterns will be displayed, the `Title` property that sets the caption on the top of the dialog box, and the `FileName` property that contains the name of the chosen file. By setting the filename pattern, the `Filter` can limit the display to only certain file extensions, such as "*.txt" and "*.doc", but also to limit the pattern by any other criteria.

A new instance the `OpenFileDialog` class must be created first:

```
Dim myOpen As OpenFileDialog = New OpenFileDialog()
```

And then the properties that set the content of the display can be set. The filter is set by specifying pairs of text, where the first text value in each pair is the filter title and the second is the actual filter. The text values must be separated by a vertical line. The filter is written using the asterisks to specify that a string of any characters at any length will be accepted for this filter value. For example, if only files with a "txt" extension should be displayed in the dialog (i.e., only filenames that end with the four-character letter suffix of ".txt" should be filtered into to the display), the filter should be set to the string `"Text files |*.txt"`, where the `Text files` part specifies the value to be displayed in the Dialog window and the `*.txt` part specifies the actual filter. In this case, the filter will cause only files with the suffix of ".txt" to be displayed. Note that this filtering can be applied to any pattern. The filter in Figure 5.3 will display three lines in under the section of "Files of type" in the Open dialog window display.

```
myOpen.Filter = _
        "Text files |*.txt|All files |*.*|My A files |*A*.*"
```

The `Title` property can be set to change the caption. The Open Dialog window is displayed with the `ShowDialog` method:

```
myOpen.Title = "My Open Dialog"
myNewPath = myOpen.ShowDialog
```

Figure 5.4 shows what will be displayed.

Once the user chooses a filename by double-clicking it or by clicking it once and then clicking the Open button, the `FileName` property will contain the name of the chosen file:

```
Dim strFile As String
strFile = myOpen.FileName
```

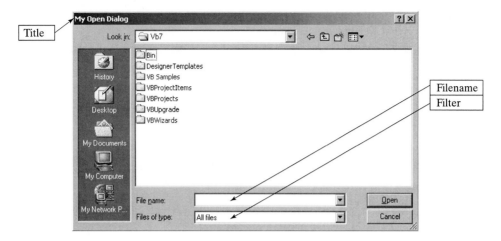

FIGURE 5.4
The Open Dialog Window.

Of course these properties can be set and read both before and after the Open Dialog window is shown. This can be a convenient way, for example, of setting the default filename before the window is displayed:

```
myOpen.Title = "My Open Dialog"
myOpen.FileName = "my suggested name"
myOpen.Filter = "Text files |*.txt|All files |*.*"
myNewPath = myOpen.ShowDialog
```

5.3.2   The `SaveFileDialog` Class

The `SaveFileDialog` opens the standardized Save dialog (Figure 5.5). Among the most important of its methods and properties are the `ShowDialog` method that opens the

FIGURE 5.5
The Save As Dialog Window.

standard Windows Save dialog, and the same `Filter`, `Title` and `FileName` properties as in the `OpenFileDialog` class. Additionally, the `CheckFileExists` property specifies whether a dedicated message box with a warning will appear if the user tries to save the file to an existing filename. The `SaveFileDialog` class is used in the same way as `OpenFileDialog`. A new instance of the class must be created first:

```
Dim mySaveAs As SaveFileDialog = New SaveFileDialog()
Dim strFile As String

    ' This will enable the selection of non existent files
mySaveAs.CheckFileExists = False
    ' Set the filter
mySaveAs.Filter = _
    "Text files |*.txt|All files |*.* | Word Files | *.doc"
    ' Display the dialog
myNewPath = mySaveAs.ShowDialog
    ' Read the selected filename
strFile = mySaveAs.FileName
```

5.4   STREAMS AND THE SEQUENTIAL ACCESS METHOD

The classes we discussed up until now in the chapter deal with managing the directories and files. Accessing the content of the files, the actual data they hold, is done through another set of classes dealing with the stream of data. In this chapter, we will discuss two of these classes that are used for sequential file access the `StreamWriter` and the `StreamReader`.

Accessing files in VB.NET can be done in three primary ways: sequential access, binary access, and direct access. Sequential access reads and writes the data to and from the file one record at a time in sequence, and in sequence only. This is somewhat like playing an old tape recorder. Songs, think of the tape as a file and of the songs as records in this file, must be accessed in the sequence in which they were added to the tape. Even moving fast forward actually involved accessing all the songs in sequence up to the requested position. It is impossible to go directly to a certain song. One must literally roll the tape to get there. The same applies to sequential access. Getting to a certain record requires reading through all the preceding records. The exception to this analogy is that, unlike a tape where the tape can be rolled backwards to access a preceding song, the sequential access only moves forward. The direct access method on the other hand, in more in tune with a CD player. One can go directly to a certain song without accessing all the preceding songs. The location of the song on the CD can be a key through which it is accessed directly, literally skipping over any preceding records. The binary access method is even more powerful. With this access method, it is possible to go directly to any byte on the file through its location. It would be like accessing a specific musical note on the CD, regardless of the song it is part of or whether it belongs to a song at all. Another good example of the application of a sequential access method is printing a report. When a report is printed, it is printed one line or page at a time in sequence. There is no way to skip forward while printing. Nor is there any way to revisit a page after it has been printed. Once printed, a line or a page is not accessible again to the program.

The sequential access method deals with reading the contents of a file sequentially; that is, one line or record after another beginning with the first record and ending with the last. Records in the sequential access method can be read in only in this one direction. Reading a previous record is only possible by closing the file and opening it up again at the beginning. There is another aspect to files, *exclusiveness*. To clarify this term let us look at another example of a sequential access method, a roll of kitchen paper towel. The roll must be opened before it can be used. But it can only be opened if no one else is holding it exclusively. In an analogous manner, a file must be opened before it can be read and this opening process must check that the file is available. Paper-towel sheets are then accessed one at a time and in the sequence in which they appear in the roll. You cannot get to sheet number 10 without going through sheets 1 through 9. In an analogous manner, records in a sequential access method are also read in sequence. Reading record 10 requires reading through records 1 through 9. There is no way to skip directly to record 10; nor is there a way to go back from record 10 and reread record 3. (Skipping is possible with the random access method that will be discussed in the next chapter.) Reading record 3 after reading record 10 requires closing the file; in an analogous manner, this means rolling back the paper towel and opening it again at the beginning. And, just as a roll of paper towel can be made exclusive, (i.e., not available to others until the current user finishes), so, too, can a file be made exclusive. It is impossible for other users get to a sheet, analogous to reading a record if the paper-towel roll is being held exclusively by another user. That is why when a user is done with a paper-towel roll others should be notified. This, in an analogous manner, is the same as closing a file in the sequential access method.

In the code examples and the lab, we will use Notepad files to demonstrate the sequential access method. Notepad files have a .txt extension, marking them as text files in Windows. Notepad files are usually read through the Notepad program or through other word processors. These programs do not exactly apply the sequential access method, because the user can scroll back and forth within the file. In a truly sequential access method, that privilege does not exist: Lines must be read forward and in sequence only. Figure 5.6 demonstrates sequential access. A file is opened. The

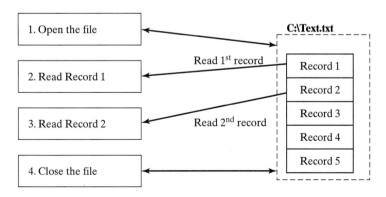

FIGURE 5.6
Sequential Access.

records are then read in the sequence in which they appear in the file with that done, the file is closed.

Reading the content of a file sequentially can be done in many ways. Perhaps the easiest way is with the StreamReader class. A StreamReader object must first be instantiated. The constructor (the New method) receives one parameter: the path where the file, known now as a *stream*, is located. The instantiation opens the file to sequential access. Actually, being an object-oriented language, this command equates the new object and the file, making the object one and the same from the program's point of view as the file itself is. The file is now a stream of data within this object. With the file now open, records or bytes can be read in sequence from the beginning of the file to its end. Records, which in a Notepad file are lines, are read with the ReadLine method. Single bytes are read with the ReadByte method. The remainder of the file can read with the ReadToEnd method. Once the program is done with the file, it should be closed with the Close method to make it available to other applications. Note that when a file is read one byte at a time, also control characters are read. These control characters, like vbCrLf, which specifies a new line, specify among other things when a new record begins. There is no access to these control characters when the whole record is read because in that case they are used to determine where the current record ends and where the new one begins.

The next example of code demonstrates how this is done. A new instance of the class is initiated, and if the filename that was entered in a textbox exists, then the next line in the file is read through the ReadLine method. This is done over and over again, controlled by a While loop until an empty line is read, meaning that the end of the file has been reached. Each line as it is read is added to a textbox as a new line. The vbCrLf literal is a new line control character also in a textbox. It causes the textbox to start a new line. The Close method disconnects the stream object from the file. Here is the code:

```
Dim myStream As IO.StreamReader
Dim strLine As String

If IO.File.Exists(txtMyFile.Text) Then
    myStream = New IO.StreamReader(txtMyFile.Text)
    strLine = myStream.ReadLine
    While strLine <> Nothing
        'myStream.Read() ' reads the next character
        'myStream.ReadToEnd() ' reads to the end of the stream
        txtLines.Text &= strLine & vbCrLf
        strLine = myStream.ReadLine
    End While
    myStream.Close()
Else
    MessageBox.Show("File does not exist")
End If
```

Programming Note: Always close a stream when you are finished using it. Keeping it open uses up system resources and, depending on how the file is opened, may prohibit other applications from accessing it.

Writing sequentially to a file is done with the `StreamWriter` class. This class is the mirror image of the `StreamReader` class. Again, a file must be opened first by instantiating an object with the file at a specified path. And, with this done, records or bytes can be written to the file with the `WriteLine` and the `WriteByte` methods, respectively. Being a sequential access method, records and bytes are added to the file in the order that they are written. When writing to the file is completed, the file should be closed. Again, this is done with the `Close` method.

The code that follows demonstrates how to write sequentially to a file. A new instance of the class, the object `myStream`, is declared. If the filename that was entered in a textbox exists, then the new stream object is initiated and connected to it. A new line is then written to the file through the stream with the `WriteLine` method. *This line will write over whatever was in the file beforehand.* If the filename that was entered in a textbox does not exist, the code throws an `ArgumentException` exception. Since there is no Try Block to catch the exception, it will result in a runtime error which will display the message that is passed as a parameter to the exception. The code is as follows:

```
Dim myStream As IO.StreamWriter
Dim strLine As String

If IO.File.Exists(txtMyFile.Text) Then
    myStream = New IO.StreamWriter(txtMyFile.Text)
    ' This will replace existing content of the file
    myStream.WriteLine(txtNewLine.Text)
    myStream.Close()
Else
    ' this will open a system error message box
    Throw New ArgumentException("File does not exist")
End If
```

If the new line is to be added to the end of the file, rather than replacing the content of the file, the stream needs to be opened for *append*. This is done by adding a second parameter to the constructor when the object is initiated. By default, this parameter is `False`, meaning no append. No append means that whatever is written through the stream will write over what was there beforehand. By setting this parameter to `True`, the stream will append the new line (i.e., add it to the end of the file without erasing what is already there):

```
myStream = New IO.StreamWriter(txtMyFile.Text, True)
```

The `StreamWriter` class also supports adding one character at a time to a file, rather than a whole line. This is done with the `Write` method:

```
myStream.Write("A")
```

5.4.1 A Quick Word on Buffers

In the background, `StreamWriter` objects actually write to a stream buffer, which in turn writes to an Encoder buffer. These buffers can be accurately thought of as work areas. In the stream buffer the system handles the data in a more efficient manner than had it been written to the file with each write method. Although it is more efficient to work with buffers, occasionally it is necessary to force VB.NET to write a buffer as is to the file. This might happen, for example, before handling an error in the Catch section of a Try Block. Forcing the stream buffer to be written to the encoder is done with the `Flush` method:

```
mystream.Flush
```

Whether a stream buffer is used at all can be set with its `AutoFlush` property (setting it to `False` will eliminate the use of the stream buffer):

```
myStream.AutoFlush = True
```

LAB 5.1: DIRECTORY AND FILE ACCESS

Lab Objectives:

Review the Directory, File, and Path Classes, along with their methods and properties.

Application Overview

The lab builds a form that analyzes paths, files, and directories and handles move, copy, and delete operations on them. All the Buttons perform operations on the textbox on the top right-hand side of the form. The Analyze Path, Analyze File, and Analyze Directory Buttons demonstrate the methods and properties that their respective classes provide for gaining information about the path, file, or directory that is displayed in the textbox. The analyzed details are presented in the List Box just below it. The Copy File Button copies the file to the path that is specified in the textbox next to it. The Move File and Move Directory Buttons likewise move the file or directory to the path in the textbox next to them. The Delete Directory and Delete File delete it; the check box next to the Delete Directory Button indicates that all the subdirectories and files in the directory should also be deleted. The Set Dates of Directory sets the appropriate dates in the directory according to the date that is specified in the TextBox next to it, providing the TextBox has a valid data and time combination.

Part 1: Build the Form

Add a new project and solution, name them **prjChapter5**, making the project handle a Windows Form. Name the form **frmChapter5a**. Add the Buttons, textboxes, and check box as shown in Figure 5.7. Objects starting with "btn" are Buttons, those starting with "txt" are TextBoxes, those starting with "lst" are List Boxes, and those starting with "chk" and check boxes. Write the appropriate string in the text properties of each object to correspond to what appears in Figure 5.7.

Part 2: Adding the Path Code

When btnAnalyze is clicked, the information about the path is displayed in the List Box. The code used is as follows:

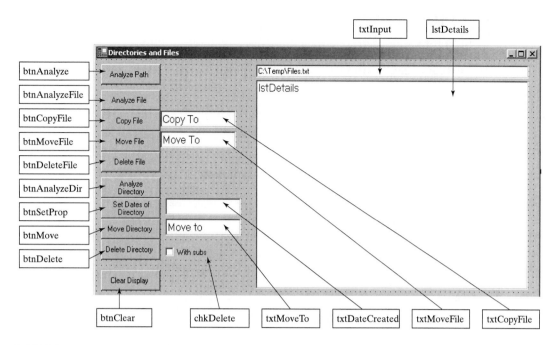

FIGURE 5.7

```
Private Sub btnAnalyze_Click(ByVal sender As System.Object, _
             ByVal e As System.EventArgs) Handles btnAnalyze.Click
   Dim strPath As String = txtInput.Text

   lstDetails.Items.Add("Details of the path " & strPath)
   lstDetails.Items.Add("Directory is " & _
             System.IO.Path.GetDirectoryName(strPath))
   lstDetails.Items.Add("Extension is " & _
             System.IO.Path.GetExtension(strPath))
   lstDetails.Items.Add("File Name is " & _
             System.IO.Path.GetFileName(strPath))
   lstDetails.Items.Add("Without extension it is " & _
             System.IO.Path.GetFileNameWithoutExtension(strPath))
   lstDetails.Items.Add("Full path is " & _
             System.IO.Path.GetFullPath(strPath))
   lstDetails.Items.Add("It has an extension " & _
             System.IO.Path.HasExtension(strPath))
   lstDetails.Items.Add("The directory separator is " & _
             System.IO.Path.DirectorySeparatorChar)
   lstDetails.Items.Add("The path separator is " & _
             System.IO.Path.PathSeparator)
   lstDetails.Items.Add("The volume separator is " & _
             System.IO.Path.VolumeSeparatorChar)
   lstDetails.Items.Add("")

End Sub
```

Part 3: Adding the File Code

The file information is presented in the same way in the textbox:

```
Private Sub btnAnalyzeFile_Click(ByVal sender As System.Object, _
    ByVal e As System.EventArgs) Handles btnAnalyzeFile.Click

Dim strPath As String = txtInput.Text

If System.IO.File.Exists(strPath) Then
    lstDetails.Items.Add("Details of the file " & strPath)
    lstDetails.Items.Add("Create on            " & _
        System.IO.File.GetCreationTime(strPath))
    lstDetails.Items.Add("Last accessed on     " & _
        System.IO.File.GetLastAccessTime(strPath))
    lstDetails.Items.Add("Last updated on      " & _
        System.IO.File.GetLastWriteTime(strPath))

    ' get the file attributes Enum
    System.IO.File.GetAttributes(strPath)
    ' read the fileattributes Enum
    lstDetails.Items.Add("File is archived     " & _
        System.IO.FileAttributes.Archive)
    lstDetails.Items.Add("File is compressed   " & _
        System.IO.FileAttributes.Compressed)
    lstDetails.Items.Add("File is hidden       " & _
        System.IO.FileAttributes.Hidden)
    lstDetails.Items.Add("File is readonly     " & _
        System.IO.FileAttributes.ReadOnly)
    lstDetails.Items.Add("File is temporary    " & _
        System.IO.FileAttributes.Temporary)

    ' examine the file attributes Enum
    ' beware of bugs this is how it should be done
    If System.IO.File.GetAttributes(strPath) And _
        System.IO.FileAttributes.Archive Then
        lstDetails.Items.Add("File is archived     ")
    Else
        lstDetails.Items.Add("File is not archived    ")
    End If
    If System.IO.File.GetAttributes(strPath) And _
        IO.FileAttributes.ReadOnly Then
        lstDetails.Items.Add("File is readonly    ")
    Else
        lstDetails.Items.Add("File is not readonly     ")
    End If
Else
    MessageBox.Show("Source file does not exist")
End If
End Sub
```

The file is copied, moved, and deleted with the use of the appropriate methods. In this case, the code is inside a Try block so that errors can be caught in the code:

```vb
Private Sub btnCopyFile_Click(ByVal sender As System.Object, _
        ByVal e As System.EventArgs) Handles btnCopyFile.Click

    Try
        If System.IO.File.Exists(txtInput.Text) Then
            If Not System.IO.File.Exists(txtCopyFile.Text) Then
                System.IO.File.Copy(txtInput.Text, _
                                    txtCopyFile.Text)
                lstDetails.Items.Add("File copied  ")
            Else
                MessageBox.Show("Destination file already exists")
            End If
        Else
            MessageBox.Show("Source file does not exist")
        End If
    Catch err As System.IO.IOException
        MessageBox.Show("unexpected IO error")
    End Try

End Sub

Private Sub btnMoveFile_Click(ByVal sender As System.Object, _
        ByVal e As System.EventArgs) Handles btnMoveFile.Click

    Try
        If System.IO.File.Exists(txtInput.Text) Then
            If Not System.IO.File.Exists(txtMoveFile.Text) Then
                System.IO.File.Move(txtInput.Text, _
                                    txtMoveFile.Text)
                lstDetails.Items.Add("File moved  ")
            Else
                MessageBox.Show("Destination file already exists")
            End If
        Else
            MessageBox.Show("Source file does not exist")
        End If
    Catch err As System.IO.IOException
        MessageBox.Show("unexpected IO error")
    End Try

End Sub

Private Sub btnDeleteFile_Click(ByVal sender As System.Object, _
        ByVal e As System.EventArgs) Handles btnDeleteFile.Click

    Try
        If System.IO.File.Exists(txtInput.Text) Then
            System.IO.File.Delete(txtInput.Text)
            lstDetails.Items.Add("File deleted  ")
        Else
            MessageBox.Show("Source file does not exist")
        End If
    Catch err As System.IO.IOException
        MessageBox.Show("unexpected IO error")
    End Try

End Sub
```

Part 4: Adding the Directory Code

The directory information is presented in the same way in the textbox:

```
Private Sub btnAnalyzeDir_Click(ByVal sender As System.Object, _
        ByVal e As System.EventArgs) Handles btnAnalyzeDir.Click

    Dim strPath As String = txtInput.Text

    If strPath = Nothing Or _
        (Not System.IO.Directory.Exists(strPath)) Then
        strPath = System.IO.Directory.GetCurrentDirectory()
        lstDetails.Items.Add _
                ("Directory does not exist. Replaced by " & strPath)
    End If

    lstDetails.Items.Add("Details of the directory " & strPath)
    lstDetails.Items.Add("Creation Time      " & _
            System.IO.Directory.GetCreationTime(strPath))
    lstDetails.Items.Add("Current Directory " & _
            System.IO.Directory.GetCurrentDirectory)
    lstDetails.Items.Add("Directory Root      " & _
            System.IO.Directory.GetDirectoryRoot(strPath))
    lstDetails.Items.Add("Last Access Time  " & _
            System.IO.Directory.GetLastAccessTime(strPath))
    lstDetails.Items.Add("Last Write Time    " & _
            System.IO.Directory.GetLastWriteTime(strPath))

    Dim strContains As String() = _
            System.IO.Directory.GetDirectories(strPath)
    Dim strfile As String

    For Each strfile In strContains
        lstDetails.Items.Add _
                ("   The Path contains this directory " & strfile)
    Next
End Sub
```

The directory is updated, moved, and deleted using the appropriate methods. In this case, the code is inside a Try Block so that errors can be caught in the code:

```
Private Sub btnSetProp_Click(ByVal sender As System.Object, _
        ByVal e As System.EventArgs) Handles btnSetProp.Click
    Dim strPath As String = txtInput.Text
    Dim datCreate As Date

    If IsDate(txtDateCreated.Text) Then
        datCreate = CDate(txtDateCreated.Text)
        If System.IO.Directory.Exists(strPath) Then
            System.IO.Directory.SetCreationTime _
                        (strPath, datCreate)
```

```
                    System.IO.Directory.SetLastAccessTime _
                                (strPath, datCreate)
                    System.IO.Directory.SetLastWriteTime _
                                (strPath, datCreate)
                    System.IO.Directory.SetCurrentDirectory(strPath)
            Else
                MessageBox.Show("Path is inappropriate")
            End If
        Else
            MessageBox.Show("Date is incorrect")
        End If
    End Sub


    Private Sub btnMove_Click(ByVal sender As System.Object, _
            ByVal e As System.EventArgs) Handles btnMove.Click

        If System.IO.Directory.Exists(txtInput.Text) Then
            If Not System.IO.Directory.Exists(txtMoveTo.Text) Then
                System.IO.Directory.Move(txtInput.Text, txtMoveTo.Text)
            Else
                MessageBox.Show("Destination path already exists")
            End If
        Else
            MessageBox.Show("Source path does not exist")
        End If
    End Sub


    Private Sub btnDelete_Click(ByVal sender As System.Object, _
            ByVal e As System.EventArgs) Handles btnDelete.Click

        If System.IO.Directory.Exists(txtInput.Text) Then
            If chkDelete.Checked Then
                System.IO.Directory.Delete(txtInput.Text, True)
            Else
                System.IO.Directory.Delete(txtInput.Text)
            End If
        Else
            MessageBox.Show("Source path does not exist")
        End If
    End Sub
```

Part 5: The Last Touch

The List Box is cleared with the last Button in the form:

```
    Private Sub btnClear_Click(ByVal sender As System.Object, _
            ByVal e As System.EventArgs) Handles btnClear.Click
        lstDetails.Items.Clear()
    End Sub
```

To make the date in the txtDateCreated textbox contain a default valid date, set the value of its Text property to Today. Today is a reserved keyword, it is a function that returns today's date. Since this must be done when the form is initializing (i.e., before it is being displayed), the code needs to be added in the New subroutine that is usually hidden in the topmost Region section of the code:

```
#Region " Windows Form Designer generated code "
    Public Sub New()
        MyBase.New()

        'This call is required by the Windows Form Designer.
        InitializeComponent()

        'Add any initialization after the InitializeComponent() call
        txtDateCreated.Text = CStr(Today())
    End Sub
```

Part 6: Application Demo

Figure 5.8 shows what the application will look like when it is run. Analyze the path. Analyze the file (Figure 5.9).
And copy the file, with an error message (Figure 5.10).

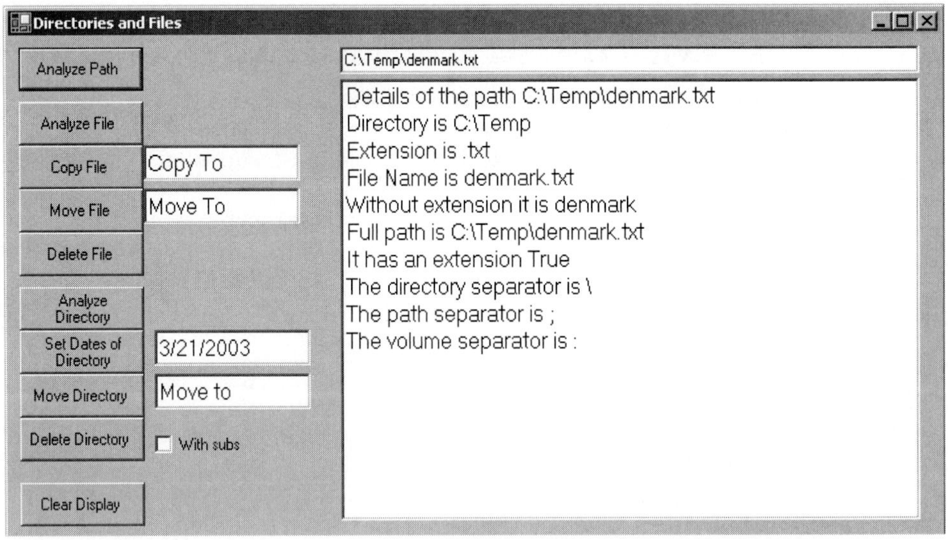

FIGURE 5.8
"Result of "Analyze Path"."

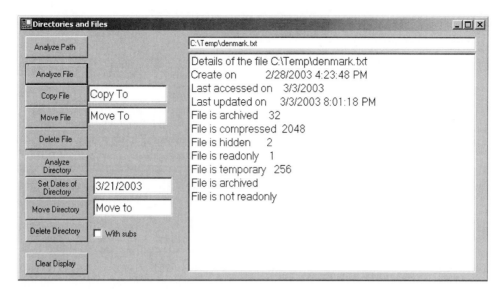

FIGURE 5.9
"Result of "Analyze File"."

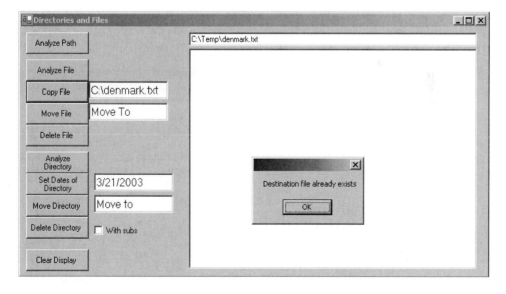

FIGURE 5.10
"Error message when destination file exists".

LAB 5.2: THE SEQUENTIAL ACCESS METHOD

Lab Objectives:

1. Review the `StreamReader` and `StreamWriter` classes.

2. Review the `OpenFileDialog` and the `SaveFileDialog` dialogs.

Application Overview

The lab reads a text file sequentially, adds lines to it, and replaces its content. The file details are given in a textbox or in the standard Windows dialogs. The preview of the application shown next handles part of William Shakespeare's *Hamlet, Prince of Denmark*, Act I, Scene III.

We will start by running the application and clicking on the Save As dialog (Figure 5.11). This will create a file even if one does not yet exist.

This will open the Save As dialog where we will choose "C:\Temp" as the directory and "Denmark.txt" as the file. (See Figure 5.12.)

We will proceed at this stage to add the words from the play. We will enter the first line into the textbox at the Button of the form and click on Replace File with Line as in Figure 5.13. We will then proceed to add the other lines one at a time by entering each into the textbox at the bottom of the form and clicking Append Line Button.

When we are done, if we click the Read File Button, Figure 5.14 shows what will be displayed.

Clicking on the Clear Display Button will clear the poem from the textbox. If we want to open it again, all we need to do it click the Open File Dialog Button (Figure 5.15) and there select the appropriate directory and file.

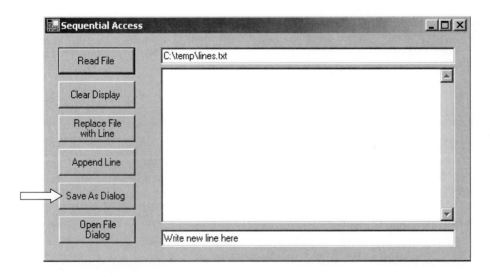

FIGURE 5.11
"The Sequential Access Method Lab".

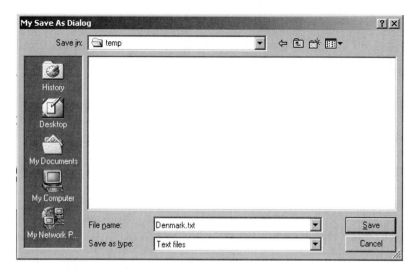

FIGURE 5.12
The My Open Dialog Window.

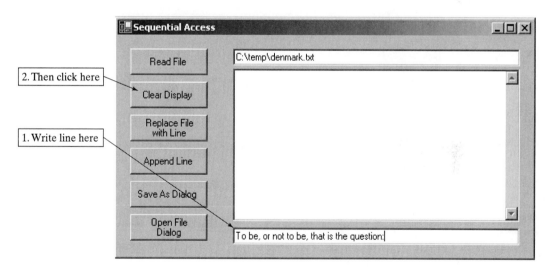

FIGURE 5.13
Adding a line to the file with the lab project.

Part 1: Build the Form

Add a new project and solution, name them **prjChapter5b**, making the project handle a Windows Form. Name the form **frmSequentialAccess**. Add the Buttons, textboxes, and check box as shown. In Figure 5.16, objects starting with "btn" are Buttons, those starting with "txt" are textboxes, and the one starting with "lst" is a List Box. Write the appropriate string in the text properties of each object to correspond to the figure.

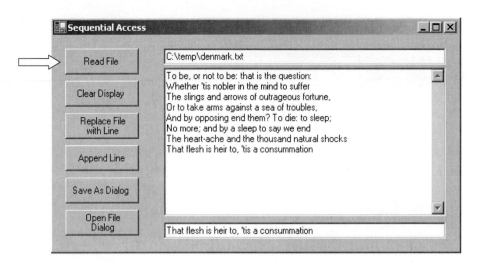

FIGURE 5.14
Displaying all the lines in the file.

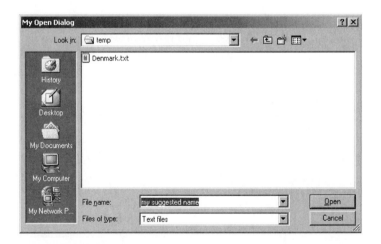

FIGURE 5.15
The My Open Dialog Window.

Make txtLines multilined and with a vertical scrollbar by setting the properties by the same name accordingly.

Part 2: Add the Code Part 1

Reading, replacing, and appending to the file is done as discussed earlier with the following code:

```
Private Sub btnRead_Click(ByVal sender As System.Object, _
        ByVal e As System.EventArgs) Handles btnRead.Click
```

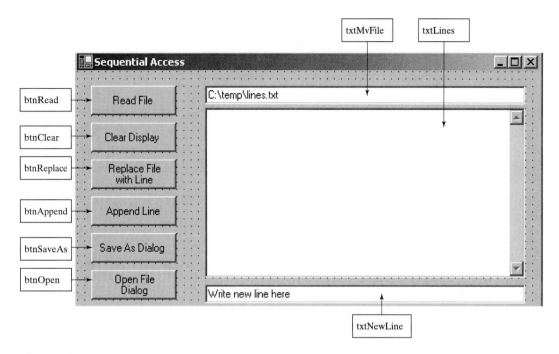

FIGURE 5.16
The Sequential Access Lab.

```
        Dim myStream As IO.StreamReader
        Dim strLine As String

        If IO.File.Exists(txtMyFile.Text) Then
            myStream = New IO.StreamReader(txtMyFile.Text)
            strLine = myStream.ReadLine
            While strLine <> Nothing
                txtLines.Text &= strLine & vbCrLf
                strLine = myStream.ReadLine
            End While
            myStream.Close()
        Else
            MessageBox.Show("File does not exist")
        End If
    End Sub

    Private Sub btnReplace_Click(ByVal sender As System.Object, _
            ByVal e As System.EventArgs) Handles btnReplace.Click

        Dim myStream As IO.StreamWriter
        Dim strLine As String

        If IO.File.Exists(txtMyFile.Text) Then
            myStream = New IO.StreamWriter(txtMyFile.Text)
            ' This will replace existing content of the file
            myStream.WriteLine(txtNewLine.Text)
```

```
            myStream.Close()
        Else
            ' this will open a system error message box
            Throw New ArgumentException("File does not exist")
        End If

    End Sub
    Private Sub btnAppend_Click(ByVal sender As System.Object, _
            ByVal e As System.EventArgs) Handles btnAppend.Click

        Dim myStream As IO.StreamWriter
        Dim strLine As String

        If IO.File.Exists(txtMyFile.Text) Then
            myStream = New IO.StreamWriter(txtMyFile.Text, True)
            ' This will append to the existing content of the file
            myStream.WriteLine(txtNewLine.Text)
            myStream.Close()
        Else
            MessageBox.Show("File does not exist")
        End If

    End Sub
```

Part 3: Add the Code Part 2

The two dialogs are also added as discussed earlier:

```
        Private Sub btnSaveAs_Click(ByVal sender As System.Object, _
                ByVal e As System.EventArgs) Handles btnSaveAs.Click
            Dim mySaveAs As SaveFileDialog = New SaveFileDialog()
            Dim myNewPath As DialogResult
            Dim myStream As IO.StreamWriter
            Dim strFile As String

    ' This will enable the selection of non existent files
            mySaveAs.CheckFileExists = False

            mySaveAs.Title = "My Save As Dialog"
            mySaveAs.Filter = _
                "Text files |*.txt|All files |*.* | Word Files | *.doc"
            myNewPath = mySaveAs.ShowDialog

            strFile = mySaveAs.FileName
            If strFile = Nothing Then
                MessageBox.Show("Invalid file", "Save As Caption", _
                            MessageBoxButtons.OK)
            Else
                myStream = New IO.StreamWriter(strFile)
                myStream.Write(txtLines.Text)
                myStream.Close()
            End If
        End Sub
```

```
Private Sub btnOpen_Click(ByVal sender As System.Object, _
        ByVal e As System.EventArgs) Handles btnOpen.Click
    Dim myOpen As OpenFileDialog = New OpenFileDialog()
    Dim myNewPath As DialogResult
    Dim myStream As IO.StreamReader
    Dim strFile As String

    myOpen.Title = "My Open Dialog"
    myOpen.FileName = "my suggested name"
    myOpen.Filter = _
            "Text files |*.txt|All files |*.*|My A files |*A*.*"
    myNewPath = myOpen.ShowDialog

    strFile = myOpen.FileName
    If strFile = Nothing Then
        MessageBox.Show("Invalid file", "Open Caption", _
                MessageBoxButtons.OK)
    Else
        myStream = New IO.StreamReader(strFile)
        txtLines.Text = myStream.ReadToEnd()
        txtMyFile.Text = myOpen.FileName
        myStream.Close()
    End If
End Sub
```

SUGGESTED HOME ASSIGNMENTS

1. Build a new form that will read a file sequentially, the filename will be entered in a textbox. The application will then create a new file in the same directory for each individual word in the file. Name each directory to match each individual word in the file. A report of what files were created should appear in a multilined textbox in the same form.
2. Build a new form that will read all the filenames in a directory and report the longest filename in a textbox on the same form. The directory name will be entered on the same form.
3. Build a new form that will add a new file to an existing directory. The directory name will be entered in the form, as will the filename. In the new file, write its name.

TEST YOURSELF

1. Discuss the importance of adding a Try Block when accessing a file.
2. When would you prefer the Directory class and when the DirectoryInfo class?
3. What is a file and what is a directory?
4. What will the following command do (two answers, depending on the whether the file exists)?

```
Console.WriteLine("Create on        " & _
    System.IO.File.GetCreationTime(strPath))
```

5. How do you check if a file exists?
6. What is the Enum in the File class?
7. Using only String functions, write the equivalent of IO.Path.GetExtension and IO.Path.GetFileNameWithoutExtension.

8. Write a filter for an OpenFileDialog that will accept only Excel (xls) and Word (doc) extensions.
9. What is a sequential access method?
10. What is a stream?
11. Why and when should streams be closed?
12. What does this code do?

```
Throw New ArgumentException("File does not exist")
```

13. What does the Flush method do? Why would it be necessary?
14. Discuss the importance of the Path class.
15. What would be the advantage of reading a file one byte at a time rather than one record at a time?
16. What is vbCrLf, and where is it used?
17. Are the data presented in a List Box an example of sequential access? Why or why not?
18. The sequential access method is simple, what are its limitations?
19. Describe three applications where a sequential access method is needed.
20. Describe three applications where a sequential access method is not relevant.

C H A P T E R   6

The Binary Access Method

CHAPTER OBJECTIVES

After completing this chapter, students should be able to

1. Understand and use the `FileStream` class
2. Use the binary access method
3. Apply the binary access method to achieve

   - Encryption and
   - The random access method

4. Make objects persistent through *serialization*

6.1　AIMS OF CHAPTER

In the last chapter, we discussed both directory and file management through VB.NET and the sequential access method. In this chapter, we will expand on file access and discuss the binary access method and what can be done with it. In what follows, we examine the binary access method and how it leads to encryption and the direct (random) access method. In addition, the chapter will cover *serialization: how objects can be made persistent through file access*. Finally, a set of forms is developed to provide hands-on experience with the classes discussed.

6.2　INTRODUCTION TO BINARY ACCESS

The binary access method reads and writes the data in a file as bytes that can be accessed at any offset (position in the file) and at any length. Thus, the primary limitation of sequential access method, reading and writing records and bytes only in sequence from the first to the last, does not apply here. In contrast to the sequential access method, the binary access method accesses just bytes, rather than bytes or records, and it accesses them randomly. Random access means that the data can be read and written in any order and in any sequence. The binary access method provides three important tools. First, it enables encryption and compression by virtue of allowing the program to access the data one byte at a time and in any sequence. Second, it provides a method for making an object persistent. Third, it is an excellent way of creating and handling single-user records as though through a database, but without actually implementing one.

Let us look at these topics one at a time, starting with encryption and compression. A picture, for example, can be stored as a set of five number combinations: the x-coordinate, the y-coordinate, and three numbers for the density of the three RGB basic colors (red, green, and blue). Each element in the set will represent one pixel, which is one dot in the screen. Typically, most pixels will have the same color as the previous pixel. Just look at this page as though it was a picture. Almost all the white pixels are preceded by other white pixels, and the same applies to many of the black ones, and to many of the gray ones in the screen shots. This principle also applies to many pictures; there are blocks of color in the picture in which the color of one dot is the same as the color in the preceding dot. If we could read the picture 5 bytes at a time, corresponding to reading the set of numbers representing one pixel at a time, we could compress the picture considerably by replacing a group of continuous pixels of the same color with an alternative representation that would state that from coordinate (x_1, y_1) to coordinate (x_2, y_2) all the pixels have the same color. This would be analogous in Excel to replacing a formula that adds the values of many consecutive cells in a spreadsheet by using the + sign and stating the (x, y) coordinates of each, with the Excel Sum function. (And so, instead of writing "=A1+A2+A3+A4+A5...+A100", we could write "=SUM(A1:A100)".) This type of pattern-matching algorithm is at the core of the Fractal compression method. This type of compression is only workable because the data can be read as a set of numbers, bytes, rather than as the type of data they actually are. This compression method also results in an encryption; the data no longer show the same pattern as they would have without the compression. The same type of compression can be done with text too. We will demonstrate an encryption method in this chapter.

The second technique that is made available with the binary access method is making objects persistent. Being persistent means that an object—and recall that an object can contain numerous data in the form of many properties—can be stored and re-created from this stored copy. Imagine an object that is an instantiation of a special kind of Employee class, such as the one we discussed in Chapter 4. That specific class may hold information about the employee utilizing several hundred properties. Storing that data in a file by copying the value of each property into a record and then reconstructing the object by reading the file and assigning the value of each property from its corresponding record requires a lot of long complex code. Worse still, adding another property or removing an existing one will require rewriting the code. However, being able to store the object as is by making it persistent and reconstructing it as is from its stored copy is much easier and requires much less coding. In this manner, an application can easily and simply store the data in its objects from one execution of the application to the next.

The third technique that is made available with the binary access method is the creation of a direct access method. With a direct access method, records can be stored and accessed on the basis of their key. In the last chapter, we saw a sequential access method lab in which each line in a Notepad file was treated as one record. In the case of a small Notepad file, such access makes sense, but suppose that the application needs to access only certain lines from a very large file. In such a case, reading the file sequentially would require too much time and possibly too much memory also. Suppose that that file contains a whole book. In a sequential file, there would be no mechanism to index the lines, stating, for example, where Chapter 6 begins. Getting to Chapter 6 would require reading through all the preceding lines. In this book, that would mean reading over 391000 characters in over 8800 lines to get to this line. On the other hand, with a direct access method, we could add an index that would state the line numbers on which Chapters 6 and 7 start and then go directly to the line in the file where Chapter 6 starts and read the lines from there until the line before the one where Chapter 7 starts. Adding keys and allowing direct access through these keys is a feature that the direct access method enables because it can utilize the binary access method. We will build a slightly easier application in the lab of this chapter.

6.2.1 The Binary Access Class

The binary access method uses the `FileStream` class. This class is more powerful than the previous `Stream` classes we covered. The typical sequence of code in a binary access method is that (1) the file is opened when it is instantiated with the `FileStream` object, (2) data are read or written to the file through the methods of the `FileStream` object, and (3) optionally, when the access to the file can be closed, the `Close` method releases the connection of the object to the file.

Determining the parameters with which the file will be opened is done through the parameters passed to the constructor of the `FileStream` class when a new `FileStream` object is instantiated. The constructor receives at least two parameters: The first parameter is the path that identifies the file, as in other `Stream` objects. There is no limitation on the extension or content of this file. The second parameter is the file access mode. This parameter specifies in what mode the file will be opened—that is, whether it will replace, create, add to, or open an existing file. There are six file access modes:

`IO.FileMode.Append`	This opens an existing file and appends the new data to its end. If the file does not exist, it will be created.
`IO.FileMode.Create`	This creates a new file. If the file already exists, it is overwritten.
`IO.FileMode.CreateNew`	This method also creates a new file. But if the file already exists, an `IOException` exception is thrown.
`IO.FileMode.Open`	This opens an existing file. If the file does not exist, an `IOException` exception is thrown.
`IO.FileMode.OpenOrCreate`	This opens an existing file. If the file does not exist, it is created.
`IO.FileMode.Truncate`	This opens an existing file but deletes its data.

The third parameter is optional. It specifies the file access mode. There are three modes:

`IO.FileAccess.Read`	This allows only reading the data.
`IO.FileAccess.ReadWrite`	This is the default. It allows both reading and writing data.
`IO.FileAccess.Write`	This allows only writing data.

The last parameter, which is also optional, specifies the *locking mechanism*. Locking limits access to the file by other applications while it is being held by this application. The four available modes are as follows:

`IO.FileShare.None`	This places a lock on the file. No other application can share access to the file with the current application. Any requests to open the file by other applications will be denied.
`IO.FileShare.Read`	This, too, places a lock on the file, but allows other applications to read it although not to update it.
`IO.FileShare.ReadWrite`	This allows other applications to read and to update the file.
`IO.FileShare.Write`	This allows other applications to update the file.

6.2.2 Binary Access Reading

Accessing a file in the binary access method requires opening it first. A file is opened when a `FileStream` object is instantiated, connecting it to a file. Opening the file connects it to the object and enables operations on it. In the code example that follows, a new `FileStream` object is instantiated, connecting it to a file name that appears in the textbox txtMyFile. The file is opened in such a way that it is shared with other applications that wish to read it, but not with those that wish to update it (write to it). If the file does not exist, an exception will be thrown, because the second parameter says `Open` rather than `OpenOrCreate`. Here is the code:

```
Dim myStream2 As IO.FileStream

myStream2 = New IO.FileStream(txtMyFile.Text, _
                        IO.FileMode.Open, _
                        IO.FileAccess.ReadWrite, _
                        IO.FileShare.Read)
```

Once a file has been opened, it can be accessed, but only as bytes. The `FileStream` class does not allow working with `Strings` the way the `Streams` discussed in the last chapter did. To accommodate this limitation, we will declare an array of `Bytes` and a `Byte` variable. Data will be read and written in the form of bytes into these variables:

```
Dim byteArray(1000) As Byte
Dim byteSample As Byte
```

There are two methods for reading bytes in the binary access method: `Read` and `ReadByte`. The `Read` method reads a group of consecutive bytes into an array of bytes.

This method has three parameters: (1) the name of the array of bytes into which the data will be read, (2) the offset in the file from where the bytes will be read, and (3) the number of bytes that will be read. In the following code 20 bytes starting from position 10 in the file—corresponding to the 11th byte because the first byte is in position 0—are read into the byte array just defined:

```
myStream2.Read(byteArray, 10, 20)
```

The `ReadByte` method, on the other hand, reads only a single byte. The position of the current byte that will be read—its offset—is given by the `Position` property. This value is automatically incremented by one after each activation of the `ReadByte` method. Consequently, the next activation of the `ReadByte` method will read the next byte in the file, creating sequential access. The `Position` property can be set in the code, which allows reading any byte in the file and not necessarily the next one in sequence. Thus, bytes can also be read in a nonsequential manner as in the following code:

```
myStream2.Position = 10
Console.WriteLine("The current position is " & _
        myStream2.Position)
Console.WriteLine("The byte at that position is " & _
        myStream2.ReadByte)

Console.WriteLine("The new position is " & _
        myStream2.Position)
Console.WriteLine("The byte at that position is " & _
        myStream2.ReadByte)

myStream2.Position = 10
Console.WriteLine("The byte in the original position was " & _
        myStream2.ReadByte)
```

When the preceding code, the `Output` window will correspondingly show

```
The current position is 10
The byte at that position is 108
The new position is 11
The byte at that position is 105
The byte in the original position was 108
```

Note that the value read from the file, because bytes are numbers, is always a number between 0 and 255. Regardless of what is read, a string or even a picture, the `Read` and `ReadByte` methods retrieve only those byte values. This requires additional code to translate the byte values into an appropriate data type for the program. One way of doing so in the case of data that contain a string is to translate the byte value back into its corresponding character value. This is done with the `Chr` function, which returns the character represented by a specific numeric value from 0 through 255:

```
myStream2.ReadByte(byteSample)
txtID.Text = Chr(byteSample)
```

Of course, this works both ways. When a string value needs to be stored in a byte format, as will inevitably be the case with the binary access method, each character in the string must be translated into its corresponding byte value. This is done with the AscW function, which returns the byte value—a number between 0 and 255—that represents a specific character:

```
byteSample = AscW("D")
```

6.2.3   Binary Access Writing

Writing to a binary file is also done with two methods: the Write and the WriteByte methods. The WriteByte method writes a byte to the current position in the file. As with the ReadByte method, this position can be read or set with the Position property. The Write method writes an array of bytes from an array into a specific offset in the file. The offset from where to start writing these bytes is provided by the second parameter. The number of bytes to be written is provided by the third parameter. In the following code, for example, 20 bytes starting from position 10 in the file are written from a byte array:

```
myStream2.Write(byteArray, 10, 20)
```

A single byte is written with the WriteByte method, which has only one parameter: the byte that will be written. The offset must be set separately with the Position property. Thus, the code equivalent to the preceding line of code will require setting the offset with the Position property and then writing the bytes in order, one at a time:

```
Dim J As Integer

' Set the starting position in the file.
myStream2.Position = 10
For J = 0 To 19
    ' Write each byte in turn
    myStream2.WriteByte(byteArray(J))
Next
```

6.2.4   A Quick Word on Synchronization

There are two ways of handling buffers with the FileStream class. The data can be handled in a *synchronous IO manner* or in an *asynchronous IO manner*. By default, FileStream is synchronous. In the synchronous mode, the Stream buffer is kept identical with the file itself. This means that any changes made to the buffer are written immediately to the file each time they occur. The result is a high volume of IO traffic to the file and back. In the asynchronous mode, the Stream buffer may be changed without these changes taking effect immediately in the file. This makes for much faster applications because it allows for less IO accesses to the file, but at the cost of synchronization.

This property can be set when the FileStream object is instantiated by adding two more parameters—the size of the buffer in bytes and an indicator that the Stream is asynchronous:

```
myStream2 = New IO.FileStream(txtMyFile.Text, _
                              IO.FileMode.Open, _
                              IO.FileAccess.ReadWrite, _
                              IO.FileShare.Read, _
                              100, _
                              True)
```

Because the `FileStream` class accesses data one byte at a time and because it can access the bytes randomly (i.e., also in a nonsequential manner) it is especially suited to handle encryption, read to and write from direct (random) access files, and make objects persistent. These applications are discussed next.

6.3 ENCRYPTION THROUGH THE `FileStream` CLASS

Encryption involves changing a message through a transformation function so that without the de-encryption formula, its contents are meaningless. There are many complicated techniques to encrypt data. Perhaps the simplest way is to switch letters. Something like changing each "a" into a "b", each "b" into a "c", and so on. More complex methods might consider the location of the letter in the file, or change each letter into a different letter or combination of letters each time. In a nutshell, many of these encryptions techniques read a letter or maybe more (i.e., one byte or more) at a time and replace each letter with another letter or a combination of letters. The binary access method is especially suited for the application of such algorithms.

In what is perhaps the simplest of these algorithms, the value of each byte is replaced with another value that is directly derived from it, such as adding 1 to the value of each byte. Recall that bytes contain a number between 0 and 255, and that each number corresponds to a specific character. Adding 1 to the byte value that represents a certain letter will make the byte value correspond to another letter. For example, adding 1 to the byte value of the letter "a" will change its byte value to correspond with the letter "b". Such an algorithm would change every "a" into a "b", every "b" into a "c", and so on. De-encrypting consists of undoing the encryption—in this case, subtracting 1 from the current byte value of each letter.

The following code demonstrates encrypting a file in the manner just described:

```
Dim myStream As IO.FileStream
Dim I As Integer
Dim byteValue As Byte, intCalc As Integer

Try
    myStream = New IO.FileStream(txtPath.Text, _
                                 IO.FileMode.Open, _
                                 IO.FileAccess.ReadWrite, _
                                 IO.FileShare.None)

    For I = 0 To myStream.Length - 1
        intCalc = CInt(myStream.ReadByte())
        intCalc += 1
        If intCalc > 255 Then intCalc -= 255
```

```
                    ' each write and read advances the position by 1
                myStream.Position -= 1
                myStream.WriteByte(CByte(intCalc))
        Next
        myStream.Close()
    Catch
        MessageBox.Show("Problems writing the file", _
                        "IO Message", _
                        MessageBoxButtons.AbortRetryIgnore, _
                        MessageBoxIcon.Error)
    End Try
```

The file is opened with a FileStream object for both reading and writing. The file is not shared with any other application. During the encryption process, there is no reason to share the file. The file is then read one byte at a time in a For Loop. The number of bytes to be read is limited in the loop by the value of the Length property of the file. This property specifies the number of bytes in the file. The loop goes until this length minus one. The loop is limited to this length minus one, because the position of the first byte is zero. In the loop, the value of each byte is incremented. This is handled in an integer variable to avoid an overflow exception in the byte variable. If the value after being incremented is more than a byte can hold, the modulus of the number is taken. Thus, if the new value is 256, which is more than a byte can hold, it is changed into 0. This avoids an overflow exception. Reading the byte advances the position of the next byte to be read in the file. This can be seen in the value of the Position property. Consequently, it is necessary to bring this position one byte back before writing the modified byte's value with the WriteByte method.

Decoding the encrypted file will take the opposite operation, subtracting 1 from the value of each byte. Again, a modulus is necessary to avoid placing a value smaller than 0 in the byte. The code is as follows:

```
    Try
        myStream = New IO.FileStream(txtPath.Text, _
                                     IO.FileMode.Open, _
                                     IO.FileAccess.ReadWrite, _
                                     IO.FileShare.None)

        For I = 0 To myStream.Length - 1
            intCalc = CInt(myStream.ReadByte())
            intCalc -= 1
            If intCalc < 0 Then intCalc += 255
            myStream.Position -= 1
            myStream.WriteByte(CByte(intCalc))
        Next
        myStream.Close()
    Catch
        MessageBox.Show("Problems writing the file", _
                        "IO Message", _
                        MessageBoxButtons.AbortRetryIgnore, _
                        MessageBoxIcon.Error)
    End Try
```

6.4   SERIALIZATION (CREATING PERSISTENT OBJECTS)

One of the great advantages of the `FileStream` class is that it can also store and retrieve objects. This is extremely important because otherwise objects could not be persistent, meaning that their values could not be passed from one running of the program to another. Objects, as we saw in the previous chapters, can be created and manipulated in the code. Taking that a step further, it is also necessary on occasion to store the current state of an object or objects and retrieve them later, possibly even by other applications. The process of converting the state of an object to a stream of bytes, and in doing so making it possible to store it to a binary file, is called *serialization*. The process of reading it back from the file into a program is called *deserialization*. Through these mechanisms, objects can be made *persistent*; that is, an object can retain its state even after the program that accessed it is no longer running.

Handling serialization in VB.NET is simple. (The alternative would be to specifically write each variable in the object to a file, manage the file's content, and build some mechanism that would know how to reconstruct the values of the variables in the object correctly.) To serialize an object, it must first be made *serializable*. This is done by adding the `<Serializable()>` attribute to the class declaration:

```
<Serializable()> Public Class Book
    Public strBookName As String
    Public ISBN As String
    Public intPages As Integer
    Public dblPrice As Double
    Public strAuthor As String
    Public strPublisher As String

    Public Sub New(ByVal prmName As String, _
                   ByVal prmISBN As String, _
                   ByVal prmPages As Integer, _
                   ByVal prmPrice As Double, _
                   ByVal prmAuthor As String, _
                   ByVal prmPublisher As String)
        strBookName = prmName
        ISBN = prmISBN
        intPages = prmPages
        dblPrice = prmPrice
        strAuthor = prmAuthor
        strPublisher = prmPublisher
    End Sub

End Class
```

It is also convenient at this stage to import the appropriate namespace for easier coding:

```
Imports System.Runtime.Serialization
```

With this background done, making an object persistent requires no more than opening a binary file, as we did already, with

```
Dim myStream As FileStream
Dim strPath As String = txtPath.Text

myStream = New FileStream(strPath, _
                          FileMode.Open, _
                          FileAccess.Write)
```

and writing the object to the binary file through a *binary formatter*,

```
Dim myBinary As New Formatters.Binary.BinaryFormatter()

myBinary.Serialize(myStream, myBooks)
myStream.Close()
```

The following demonstrates the whole process of creating a persistent object and serializing it. In this case, we will dimension and then serialize an array named `My Books`.

```
Private Sub btnSerialize_Click( _
            ByVal sender As System.Object, _
            ByVal e As System.EventArgs) _
            Handles btnSerialize.Click

    Dim myStream As FileStream
    Dim strPath As String = txtPath.Text
    Dim myBooks() As Book

    ReDim Preserve myBooks(2)
    myBooks(0) = New Book("Book 1", "1", 100, _
                          100, "One", "Publisher 1")
    myBooks(1) = New Book("Book 2", "2", 200, _
                          20, "Two", "Publisher 2")

    Dim myBinary As New Formatters.Binary.BinaryFormatter()

    myStream = New FileStream(strPath, _
                    FileMode.Open, _
                    FileAccess.Write)

    myBinary.Serialize(myStream, myBooks)
    myStream.Close()
    myBooks(0) = Nothing
    myBooks(1) = Nothing
```

In the code, an object array is declared, the class of which is the class we just defined. Two object-elements in the array are created by redimensioning the array and instantiating the objects. The objects are set to `Nothing` after they are serialized to demonstrate later when these persistent objects are deserialized that their respective object states have been retrieved.

Once a persistent object has been serialized, deserializing it requires no more than opening the binary file and reading the persistent object with the `Deserialize` method of the `BinaryFormatter`:

```
myStream = New FileStream(strPath, _
                          FileMode.Open, _
                          FileAccess.Read, _
                          FileShare.ReadWrite)
myBooks = myBinary.Deserialize(myStream)
myStream.Close()
End Sub
```

That is all it takes to make an object persistent. The file containing the object can be viewed with Notepad, although, obviously, the contents will be hard to read. (See Figure 6.1.)

FIGURE 6.1
Contents in the Notepad file are difficult to read.

6.5   THE DIRECT (RANDOM) ACCESS METHOD

Another useful application of the `FileStream` class is the creation of a random access method. This access method is also known as the direct access method because records can be accessed with it directly, meaning that the key of the record will determine where the record is in the file, which allows the record to be read and updated directly. In the direct access method, records are read and updated in any given order, by specifying the offset of the record.

In order to understand the direct access method, it is necessary to compare it with the sequential access method. Sequential access reads records or bytes one at a time in the order in which they appear in the file, much like reading a good book one page at a time without skipping. This is fine when the data are like a book. Often, however, records need to be accessed according to their identifying key, rather than in sequence. Think about a library as an example of this. If searching for a book would require a sequential retrieval of all the preceding books, nothing would get done. Locating a book in a sequential manner would require going through all the aisles and shelves that happen to be placed before the aisle and shelf where the desired book is located, rather than going directly to the appropriate aisle and shelf. That is not practical. A library would work better if it had a method where the key of the book, say its ISBN or its title, could direct the librarian directly to the aisle and shelf where the book is located.

That in a nutshell is what the direct access method does. Each record has a key. That key determines where in the file (in our analogy, the library) the record (in our analogy, the book) should be located. In the simplest of applications of this method, the location would be a direct function of the key value: a "hash" function. Handling the

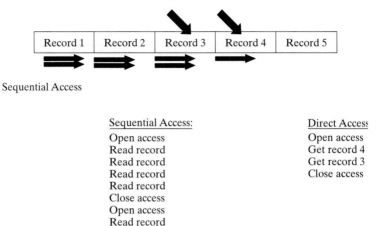

FIGURE 6.2
Comparison of direct and sequential access methods.

file in this manner does not preclude sequential access. On the contrary, a direct access file can also support sequential reading, as in a library. We will demonstrate this in the lab at the end of the chapter.

Figure 6.2 demonstrates the difference between the sequential and the direct access methods. When record number 4 is read in a sequential access method, records 1 through 3 must be read first. If record number 3 needs to be read next, the file must be closed and reopened first, and records 1 through 2 must be read again before record number 3 can be read. Of course, with only five records, this makes little difference. However, when record number 40,000 out of 50,000 needs to be accessed, it does. In the direct access method, on the other hand, finding the location of a record is like asking a librarian to find the location of a record. With this location address in hand, accessing the record directly without the need to read through all the preceding records is possible. This difference is much like that between a tape-recorder (with sequential access to songs on the tape) and a CD player where songs can be accessed directly by specifying their track number.

The direct access method can be applied to both fixed-length and variable-length records. When applied to fixed-length records, the key of the record translates into a record number. The offset of that record number (i.e., how many bytes it is away from the beginning of the file) can then be calculated by multiplying the record number by the standard length of the records in the file. Note that the beginning and end of each record is determined through a calculation. There is no indicator in the file to specify when a new record begins. It is the responsibility of the program to calculate this correctly. Handling variable-length records is much more complex and will not be discussed here. Suffice it to say that if variable-length records need to be accessed directly, either a database should be used or the data should be stored as objects.

6.5.1   Issues about the Design of a Random Access Method File

Because a direct access method file can grow in size as new records are added to it, there is a need to store information about the file somewhere. A most obvious place to store such information is in the file itself in its first record. In the example of the application of the direct access method that we will build next, the first record will contain, in its first five bytes, the number of records currently held in the file. As records will be added, this value will be updated.

Another important issue with random access method files is that records are not physically deleted. In other words, when a record is deleted, its place in the file is not eliminated (what might be called a "physical delete"; rather, an indicator is set in the record specifying that it has been deleted and that the application program reading it should treat it as such (we call this a "logical delete"). The code needs to know how to handle this situation.

Also, since the `FileStream` object itself works only with bytes and byte arrays, the code must be written to handle input and output as bytes. Bytes, as a reminder, contain a numeric value from 0 to 255. Casting the byte values into their appropriate corresponding values is therefore a necessity. Last, but not least, a `FileStream` object will allow reading and writing beyond the supposed end of file. Remember that the end of the file is a calculated value that the application program is superimposing on the binary access method. As far as the binary access method is concerned (i.e., the `FileStream` object), the application program is reading and writing bytes into a file, with no practical limitation whatsoever on adding bytes to the end of the file or even reading from an offset that is beyond the current length of the file. This can be quite dangerous because it means that a program can access memory it might not have permission to access, although the .NET framework supposedly examines this.

> **Programming Note:** Since it is possible to read bytes beyond the current allocation of a file with the `FileStream` object, the application program should examine the `Length` property explicitly to avoid that unintended activity.

6.5.2   Locating a Record with the Random Access Method

Assuming for simplicity that all the records are fixed length, applying the random access method to locate a given record requires instantiating a `FileStream` object, which will open the file, and then reading bytes from the calculated offset at the given length of the record. However, there is an extra layer of complexity involved because a `FileStream` object reads and writes only bytes and arrays of bytes. If the record contains any other data type, which one can safely assume that it might, then the data must be converted to a byte array first, which can be somewhat of a nuisance with the limited casting ability of byte arrays.

> **Programming Note:** It is better to handle a direct access method application with an array of persistent objects. That will avoid the need to cast byte arrays into other data types and provide the whole functionality that objects allow.

In the following code, the path of the file is provided in a textbox named txtPath:

```
Dim myStream As IO.FileStream
myStream = New IO.FileStream(txtPath.Text, _
                            IO.FileMode.Open)
```

With the file open, the offset of the record needs to be calculated. We shall assume at this stage that each record is 25 bytes long and that the key we are looking for is entered in another textbox that is named txtID. We will also assume that, earlier on, it was verified that the value entered in the textbox is numeric. (The entire code will be developed in the lab.) Accordingly, the offset will be 25 times the numeric value entered in the textbox. The code which verifies that this offset is still inside the existing file, using the Length property of the FileStream object, is

```
Dim I As Integer
Dim byteRecord (25) As Byte

If myStream.Length < CInt (txtID.Text) * 25 Then
      MessageBox.Show ("No such friend")
Else
```

If all is well, then the offset in the file is set with the Position property and the next 25 bytes are read with the Read method. The data from the file are read into a byte array. This cannot be changed, so the data must be cast 1 byte at a time into the equivalent character with the Chr function, as in the following code:

```
myStream.Position = CInt(txtID.Text) * 25
myStream.Read(byteRecord, 0, 25)

txtID.Text = Nothing
For I = 0 To 4
   txtID.Text &= Chr(byteRecord(I))
Next
txtName.Text = Nothing
For I = 5 To 24
    txtName.Text &= Chr(byteRecord(I))
Next
End If
myStream.Close()
```

6.5.3   Adding a New Record with the Random Access Method

Adding a new record to the file requires reading the first record in the file. This first record, as previously discussed, contains the number of records currently in the file. If there is no record (i.e., if the length of the file is zero), a new file is created. If the file exists, it is updated with the new number of records. The new record is then created by copying a Char array into the Byte array, translating each character into its corresponding byte value with the AscW function. This function returns the ASCII byte value of a character.[11] Following is the relevant code:

```
Dim myStream As IO.FileStream
Dim I As Integer
Dim byteRecord(25) As Byte
Dim chrRecord(25) As Char
Dim intKey As Integer
Dim strCalc As String

Try
    myStream = New IO.FileStream(txtPath.Text, _
                                IO.FileMode.OpenOrCreate, _
                                IO.FileAccess.ReadWrite, _
                                IO.FileShare.None)

    If myStream.Length = 0 Then
        ' If the file is empty, initialize a new table
        ' The next available key is kept in the initial 5 bytes
        chrRecord = "1" & Space(24)
        For I = 0 To 24
            byteRecord(I) = AscW(chrRecord(I))
        Next
        strCalc = "00001"
    Else
    ' If the exists then
    '     Read the first record. This is the control record.
    '     It contains the current size of the table

        myStream.Read(byteRecord, 0, 25)
        strCalc = Chr(byteRecord(0)) & _
                     Chr(byteRecord(1)) & _
                     Chr(byteRecord(2)) & _
                     Chr(byteRecord(3)) & _
                     Chr(byteRecord(4))
        If Not IsNumeric(strCalc) Then strCalc = "1"
        If CDbl(strCalc) > 99998 Then strCalc = "1"
    End If
```

Having either created a new control record (the first record in the file where the length of the file is kept) or updated the existing one, the control record needs to be written

---

[11]If **Option Strict** is **On**, then the assignment statement

```
chrRecord = "1" & Space(24)
```

will not work. It is necessary in that case to handle the characters explicitly:

```
Dim I As Integer
chrRecord(0) = CChar("1")
For I = 1 To 25
    chrRecord(I) = CChar(" ")
Next
```

back to the file with its updated content. The work area record—the array of characters—is translated into the array of bytes and is written to the beginning of the file with
the following code:

```
' Update key record
intKey = CInt(strCalc)
intKey = intKey + 1
strCalc = intKey
chrRecord = strCalc.ToCharArray & Space(24)
For I = 0 To 24
    byteRecord(I) = AscW(chrRecord(I))
Next

myStream.Position = 0
myStream.Write(byteRecord, 0, 25)
```

Now the new record can be created. The data are arranged as characters into the character array. This is necessary so that the same field of data will also be in the same position in file. Additional spaces are added to buffer the data to the correct length in the
character array. With that done, the character array is cast into the byte array with the
AscW function. This process highlights the advantage that persistent object arrays create. In a persistent object array, all this is done in the background as an abstract
process, without all this manual handling of the bytes. Here is the code:

```
' Update form
txtID.Text = CStr(intKey)

' Build output record
Dim intLength(2) As Integer
intLength(0) = txtID.Text.Length
If intLength(0) > 5 Then intLength(0) = 5
intLength(1) = txtName.Text.Length

chrRecord = txtID.Text.ToCharArray(0, intLength(0)) & _
            Space(5 - intLength(0)) & _
            txtName.Text.ToCharArray(0, intLength(1)) & _
            Space(20 - intLength(1))

' Translate output record to a byte array
For I = 0 To 25
    byteRecord(I) = AscW(chrRecord(I))
Next

' Add new record to its position in the file
myStream.Position = intKey * 25
myStream.Write(byteRecord, 0, 25)
myStream.Close()
Catch
    MessageBox.Show("Problems writing the file", _
                    "IO Message", _
                    MessageBoxButtons.AbortRetryIgnore, _
                    MessageBoxIcon.Error)
End Try
```

6.5.4   Deleting a Record with the Random Access Method

Deleting a record is much the same as updating it, since the record is not actually deleted, but only marked as such. In this case, the delete operation is carried out by writing the letter "D" into the first character of the record. Physically deleting the record would require rearranging the file and rebuilding the function that translates a records key to its location. The following code is used:

```vb
Dim myStream As IO.FileStream
Dim I As Integer
Dim byteRecord(25) As Byte
Dim chrRecord(25) As Char
Dim intKey As Integer
Try
    myStream = New IO.FileStream(txtPath.Text, _
                                 IO.FileMode.OpenOrCreate, _
                                 IO.FileAccess.ReadWrite, _
                                 IO.FileShare.None)

    If myStream.Length = 0 Or _
        Not IsNumeric(txtID.Text) Or _
        CInt(txtID.Text) <= 0 Then
        MessageBox.Show("No file found")
    Else
        If myStream.Length < CInt(txtID.Text) * 25 Then
            MessageBox.Show("No such friend")
        Else
            intKey = CInt(txtID.Text)
            myStream.Position = intKey * 25
            myStream.Read(byteRecord, 0, 25)

            ' Mark record as deleted in its ID
            txtID.Text = "D"
            Dim intLength As Integer
            intLength = txtName.Text.Length
            If intLength > 20 Then intLength = 20

            chrRecord = "D     " & _
                        txtName.Text.ToCharArray _
                            (0, intLength) _
                        Space(20 - intLength)

            ' Translate output record to a byte array
            For I = 0 To 24
                byteRecord(I) = AscW(chrRecord(I))
            Next
            ' Add new record to its position in the file
            myStream.Position = intKey * 25
            myStream.Write(byteRecord, 0, 25)
            myStream.Close()
        End If
```

```
            End If
            myStream.Close()
        Catch
            MessageBox.Show("Problems writing the file", _
                            "IO Message", _
                            MessageBoxButtons.AbortRetryIgnore, _
                            MessageBoxIcon.Error)
        End Try
```

6.5.5   Reading the Next Record with the Random Access Method

Reading the next record requires calculating where the next record begins. This is more than the position of the current record plus its length, because the next record may have been deleted. Consequently, reading the next record must examine whether that record has not been logically deleted. The rest of the code is the same as with locating a record:

```
myStream = New IO.FileStream(txtPath.Text, _
                            IO.FileMode.OpenOrCreate, _
                            IO.FileAccess.ReadWrite, _
                            IO.FileShare.None)

If myStream.Length = 0 Or _
    CInt(txtID.Text) <= 0 Then
    MessageBox.Show("No file found")
Else
    If myStream.Length < CInt(txtID.Text) * 25 Then
        MessageBox.Show("No such friend")
    Else
        intKey = CInt(txtID.Text)
        intKey += 1 ' move to next friend
        myStream.Position = intKey * 25

        byteRecord.Initialize()
        byteRecord(0) = AscW("D")
        While Chr(byteRecord(0)) = "D"
                        ' record has been deleted
            myStream.Read(byteRecord, 0, 25)
            If Chr(byteRecord(0)) = "D" Then
                        ' deleted record
                intKey += 1 ' move to next friend
                If myStream.Length > intKey * 25 Then
                    myStream.Position = intKey * 25
                    myStream.Read(byteRecord, 0, 25)
                Else
                    byteRecord(0) = AscW("N")
                    byteRecord(1) = AscW("o")
                    byteRecord(2) = AscW("n")
```

```
                            byteRecord(3) = AscW("e")
                            byteRecord(4) = AscW(".")
                    End If
                End If
            End While
        End If
    End If
```

LAB 6: EXERCISING THE BINARY ACCESS METHOD

Lab Objectives:

1. Exercise encryption
2. Make an object persistent
3. Build a random access method

Application Overview

The lab has three parts. In the first part, a file is encrypted and de-encrypted. For user interface convenience, the file can also be read and written to through the form. In the second part of the lab, an object array is created, made persistent, and emptied with one command button, and then recreated from its persistent copy with a second command button. The last part of the lab creates a direct access method application in which the names of friends, their address, and their telephone numbers are added, retrieved, updated, and deleted.

Application Demo, Part 1

To demonstrate the application, we will read a Notepad file (the one we created in Chapter 5), encrypt it, read it again, de-encrypt it, and read it once more. First, we read the file. (See Figure 6.3.)

You can also write a poem directly into the multilined textbox and write it into the file with the Write Button. Next, we will encrypt it and read it again. Note how the text of the Encrypt Button changes to De-encrypt. Read the file back into the textbox

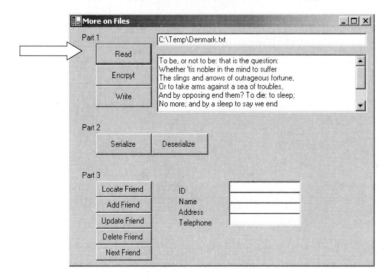

FIGURE 6.3
Reading a Notepad file.

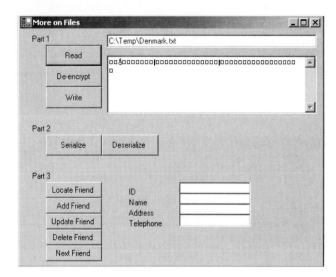

FIGURE 6.4
Contents in textbox are unreadable.

with the Read Button. See how the data have changed; note especially that the content is no longer multilined, because the end-of-line characters were also encrypted. The contents are clearly unreadable, as shown in Figure 6.4.

But, de-encrypting it and reading it once more will restore the file's contents, including the end-of-line characters (Figure 6.5).

Application Demo Part 3

We will add several friends by entering their data and clicking on Add Friend. The ID will be generated automatically. (See Figure 6.6.) With this done, locating a friend involves entering the ID and clicking the Locate Friend Button. In Figure 6.7, friend ID 3 was read. Should we want to update this friend, all we need to do is change the fields and click Update Friend. The change will be kept in the file. Deleting a friend currently

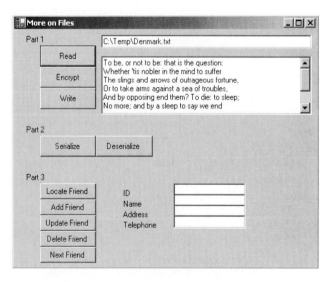

FIGURE 6.5
De-encrypted contents.

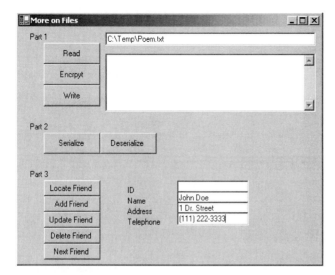

FIGURE 6.6
Automatically generated ID.

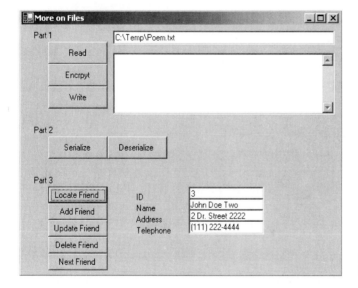

FIGURE 6.7
Locating a friend through an ID.

being displayed is accomplished by clicking the Delete Friend Button. The Next Friend Button will read the file sequentially.

Part 1: Building the Form

Add a new project and solution, name them **prjChapter6**, making the project handle a Windows Form. Name the form **frmChapter6**. Add the Buttons, textboxes, and check box as shown in Figure 6.8. Objects starting with "btn" are Buttons, and those starting with "txt" are textboxes. The textbox txtPoem is multilined and has a vertical scrollbar. Write the appropriate string in the text properties of each object to correspond to the example in the figure.

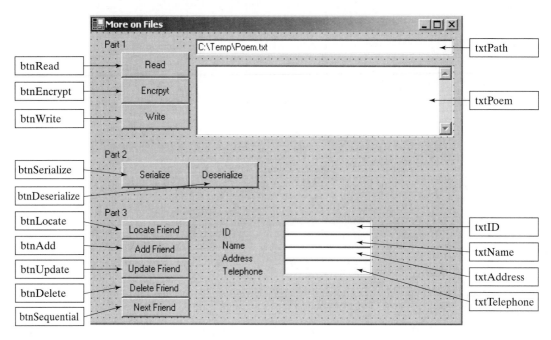

FIGURE 6.8
Lab 6

Part 2.1: Adding the Code for Encryption

The Encrypt Button encrypts the data in the file identified by the path in txtPath. For user convenience, the Read Button reads the file and displays its contents in the multi-lined txtPoem textbox, and the Write Button writes the contents of the txtPoem textbox into the file identified by the path in txtPath. Reading and writing the file was covered in the previous chapter. Therefore, there is nothing new in the following code:

```
Private Sub btnRead_Click(ByVal sender As System.Object, _
            ByVal e As System.EventArgs)_
            Handles btnRead.Click
    Dim myStream As IO.StreamReader

    Try
        myStream = New IO.StreamReader(txtPath.Text)
        txtPoem.Text = myStream.ReadToEnd
        myStream.Close()
    Catch
        MessageBox.Show("Problems reading the file", _
                "IO Message", _
                MessageBoxButtons.AbortRetryIgnore, _
                MessageBoxIcon.Error)
    End Try
End Sub
```

```vbnet
Private Sub btnWrite_Click(ByVal sender As System.Object, _
            ByVal e As System.EventArgs) _
            Handles btnWrite.Click
    Dim myStream As IO.StreamWriter

    Try
        myStream = New IO.StreamWriter(txtPath.Text)
        myStream.WriteLine(txtPoem.Text)
        myStream.Close()
    Catch
        MessageBox.Show("Problems writing the file", _
                    "IO Message", _
                    MessageBoxButtons.AbortRetryIgnore, _
                    MessageBoxIcon.Error)
    End Try
End Sub
```

The encryption is completed by reading the file byte by byte and adding modulus 100 to the value of each byte:

```vbnet
Private Sub btnEncrypt_Click(ByVal sender As System.Object, _
            ByVal e As System.EventArgs) _
            Handles btnEncrypt.Click

    Static bolEncrypt As Boolean = True
    Dim myStream As IO.FileStream
    Dim I As Integer
    Dim byteValue As Byte, intCalc As Integer

    Try
        myStream = New IO.FileStream(txtPath.Text, _
                            IO.FileMode.Open, _
                            IO.FileAccess.ReadWrite, _
                            IO.FileShare.None)

        If bolEncrypt Then
            btnEncrypt.Text = "De-encrypt"
            bolEncrypt = False

            myStream.Position = 0
            For I = 0 To myStream.Length - 1
                intCalc = CInt(myStream.ReadByte())
                intCalc -= 100
                If intCalc < 0 Then intCalc += 255
                myStream.Position -= 1
                myStream.WriteByte(CByte(intCalc))
            Next
        Else
            btnEncrypt.Text = "Encrypt"
            bolEncrypt = True

            myStream.Position = 0
            For I = 0 To myStream.Length - 1
```

```
                        intCalc = CInt(myStream.ReadByte())
                        intCalc += 100
                        If intCalc > 255 Then intCalc -= 255
               ' Each write and read advance the position by 1
                        myStream.Position -= 1
                        myStream.WriteByte(CByte(intCalc))
                Next

            End If

            myStream.Close()
        Catch
            MessageBox.Show("Problems writing the file", _
                        "IO Message", _
                        MessageBoxButtons.AbortRetryIgnore, _
                        MessageBoxIcon.Error)
        End Try
    End Sub
```

Part 2.2: Adding the Code for Serialization

To get serialization to work, import the `Serialization` library first. Add the `Imports` statement at the top of the code:

```
Imports System.Runtime.Serialization   ' Add this
Imports System.IO                       ' And this

Public Class Form1
```

Now we can add a serializable class to the form. The new class is made serializable by adding the keyword `<Serializable()>` in front of the class statement. The new class, named `Book`, contains six public variables and a constructor that sets values into those variables:

```
<Serializable()> Public Class Book
    Public strBookName As String
    Public ISBN As String
    Public intPages As Integer
    Public dblPrice As Double
    Public strAuthor As String
    Public strPublisher As String

    Public Sub New(ByVal prmName As String, _
                ByVal prmISBN As String, _
                ByVal prmPages As Integer, _
                ByVal prmPrice As Double, _
                ByVal prmAuthor As String, _
                ByVal prmPublisher As String)

        strBookName = prmName
        ISBN = prmISBN
```

```
            intPages = prmPages
            dblPrice = prmPrice
            strAuthor = prmAuthor
            strPublisher = prmPublisher
      End Sub
End Class
```

The next sections of code handle the Serializable and Deserializable Buttons. An array with two objects of the new Book class is defined and instantiated. The contents of the two new objects are written to the Output window. The objects are then added to the file with the BinaryFormatter, making then persistent objects. If the application is stopped at this stage and restarted, the Deserializable Button will reconstruct the state of the objects. That is what making an object persistent means. Here is the code:

```
Private Sub btnSerialize_Click(ByVal sender As System.Object, _
                ByVal e As System.EventArgs) _
                Handles btnSerialize.Click

      Dim myStream As FileStream
      Dim strPath As String
      Dim myBooks() As Book

      ReDim Preserve myBooks(2)
      myBooks(0) = New Book("Book 1", "1", _
                100, 100, "One", "Publisher 1")

      myBooks(1) = New Book("Book 2", "2", _
                200, 20, "Two", "Publisher 2")

      Console.WriteLine("This is what is passed to Serialization")
      Console.WriteLine(myBooks(0).ISBN)
      Console.WriteLine(myBooks(0).dblPrice)
      Console.WriteLine(myBooks(1).ISBN)
      Console.WriteLine(myBooks(1).dblPrice)

      Dim myBinary As New Formatters.Binary.BinaryFormatter()

      Try
            strPath = txtPath.Text
            myStream = New FileStream(strPath, _
                                FileMode.Open, _
                                FileAccess.Write)

            myBinary.Serialize(myStream, myBooks)
            myStream.Close()
            myBooks(0) = Nothing
            myBooks(1) = Nothing
      Catch
            MessageBox.Show("Opps")
      End Try

End Sub
```

```vbnet
Private Sub btnDeserialize_Click _
            (ByVal sender As System.Object, _
             ByVal e As System.EventArgs) _
             Handles btnDeserialize.Click
    Dim myStream As FileStream
    Dim strPath As String = txtPath.Text
    Dim myBooks() As Book
    Dim myBinary As New Formatters.Binary.BinaryFormatter()   '

    ReDim myBooks(2)

    Try
        strPath = txtPath.Text
        myStream = New FileStream(strPath, FileMode.Open,_
                    FileAccess.Read, FileShare.ReadWrite)
        myBooks = myBinary.Deserialize(myStream)
        myStream.Close()

        Console.WriteLine _
            ("This is what is returned from Deserialization")
        Console.WriteLine(myBooks(0).ISBN)
        Console.WriteLine(myBooks(0).dblPrice)
        Console.WriteLine(myBooks(1).ISBN)
        Console.WriteLine(myBooks(1).dblPrice)

    Catch
        MessageBox.Show("Opps")
    End Try

End Sub
```

Part 2.3: Adding a Direct Access Method

The entire code handling the file access is written as follows (all code included was explained earlier in the chapter):

```vbnet
Private Sub btnLocate_Click(ByVal sender As System.Object, _
                ByVal e As System.EventArgs) _
                Handles btnLocate.Click

    Dim myStream As IO.FileStream
    Dim I As Integer
    Dim byteRecord(99) As Byte
    Dim chrRecord(99) As Char
    Dim intKey As Integer
    Dim strCalc As String

    Try
        myStream = New IO.FileStream(txtPath.Text, _
                            IO.FileMode.OpenOrCreate, _
                            IO.FileAccess.ReadWrite, _
                            IO.FileShare.None)
```

```vb
        If Not IsNumeric(txtID.Text) Then txtID.Text = "0"
        If myStream.Length = 0 Or _
            CInt(txtID.Text) <= 0 Then
            MessageBox.Show("No file found")
        Else
            If myStream.Length < CInt(txtID.Text) * 100 Then
                MessageBox.Show("No such friend")
            Else
                intKey = CInt(txtID.Text)
                myStream.Position = intKey * 100
                myStream.Read(byteRecord, 0, 100)

                txtID.Text = Nothing
                For I = 0 To 4
                    txtID.Text &= Chr(byteRecord(I))
                Next

                txtName.Text = Nothing
                For I = 5 To 34
                    txtName.Text &= Chr(byteRecord(I))
                Next

                txtAddress.Text = Nothing
                For I = 35 To 69
                    txtAddress.Text &= Chr(byteRecord(I))
                Next

                txtTelephone.Text = Nothing
                For I = 70 To 99
                    txtTelephone.Text &= Chr(byteRecord(I))
                Next

            End If
        End If
        myStream.Close()
    Catch
        MessageBox.Show("Problems writing the file", _
                        "IO Message", _
                        MessageBoxButtons.AbortRetryIgnore, _
                        MessageBoxIcon.Error)
    End Try
End Sub

Private Sub btnSequential_Click _
            (ByVal sender As System.Object, _
            ByVal e As System.EventArgs) _
            Handles btnSequential.Click

    Dim myStream As IO.FileStream
    Dim I As Integer
    Dim byteRecord(99) As Byte
    Dim chrRecord(99) As Char
```

```
Dim intKey As Integer
Dim strCalc As String

Try
    myStream = New IO.FileStream(txtPath.Text, _
                                IO.FileMode.OpenOrCreate, _
                                IO.FileAccess.ReadWrite, _
                                IO.FileShare.None)

    If Not IsNumeric(txtID.Text) Then txtID.Text = "0"
    If myStream.Length = 0 Or _
        CInt(txtID.Text) <= 0 Then
        MessageBox.Show("No file found")
    Else
        If myStream.Length < CInt(txtID.Text) * 100 Then
            MessageBox.Show("No such friend")
        Else
            intKey = CInt(txtID.Text)
            intKey += 1 ' move to next friend
            myStream.Position = intKey * 100

            byteRecord.Initialize()
            byteRecord(0) = AscW("D")
            While Chr(byteRecord(0)) = "D"
                ' record has been deleted
                myStream.Read(byteRecord, 0, 100)
                If Chr(byteRecord(0)) = "D" Then
                    ' deleted record
                    intKey += 1 ' move to next friend
                    If myStream.Length > intKey * 100 Then
                        myStream.Position = intKey * 100
                        myStream.Read(byteRecord, 0, 100)
                    Else
                        byteRecord(0) = AscW("N")
                        byteRecord(1) = AscW("o")
                        byteRecord(2) = AscW("n")
                        byteRecord(3) = AscW("e")
                        byteRecord(4) = AscW(".")
                    End If
                End If
            End While

            txtID.Text = Nothing
            For I = 0 To 4
                txtID.Text &= Chr(byteRecord(I))
            Next

            txtName.Text = Nothing
            For I = 5 To 34
                txtName.Text &= Chr(byteRecord(I))
            Next

            txtAddress.Text = Nothing
```

```vb
            For I = 35 To 69
                txtAddress.Text &= Chr(byteRecord(I))
            Next

            txtTelephone.Text = Nothing
            For I = 70 To 99
                txtTelephone.Text &= Chr(byteRecord(I))
            Next
        End If
    End If
    myStream.Close()
Catch
    MessageBox.Show("Problems writing the file", _
                "IO Message", _
                MessageBoxButtons.AbortRetryIgnore, _
                MessageBoxIcon.Error)
End Try
End Sub

Private Sub btnUpdate_Click _
            (ByVal sender As System.Object, _
             ByVal e As System.EventArgs) _
             Handles btnUpdate.Click

Dim myStream As IO.FileStream
Dim I As Integer
Dim byteRecord(99) As Byte
Dim chrRecord(99) As Char
Dim intKey As Integer
Dim strCalc As String

Try
    myStream = New IO.FileStream(txtPath.Text, _
                                IO.FileMode.OpenOrCreate, _
                                IO.FileAccess.ReadWrite, _
                                IO.FileShare.None)

    If myStream.Length = 0 Or _
        Not IsNumeric(txtID.Text) Or _
        CInt(txtID.Text) <= 0 Then
        MessageBox.Show("No file found")
    Else
        If myStream.Length < CInt(txtID.Text) * 100 Then
            MessageBox.Show("No such friend")
        Else
            intKey = CInt(txtID.Text)
            myStream.Position = intKey * 100
            myStream.Read(byteRecord, 0, 100)

            ' Build output record.
            Dim intLength(4) As Integer
            intLength(0) = txtID.Text.Length
            If intLength(0) > 5 Then intLength(0) = 5
```

```
                      intLength(1) = txtName.Text.Length
                      If intLength(1) > 30 Then intLength(1) = 30
                      intLength(2) = txtAddress.Text.Length
                      If intLength(2) > 35 Then intLength(2) = 35
                      intLength(3) = txtTelephone.Text.Length
                      If intLength(3) > 30 Then intLength(3) = 30

                      chrRecord = txtID.Text.ToCharArray _
                              (0, intLength(0)) & _
                                Space(5 - intLength(0)) & _
                                txtName.Text.ToCharArray _
                              (0, intLength(1)) & _
                                Space(30 - intLength(1)) & _
                                txtAddress.Text.ToCharArray _
                              (0, intLength(2)) & _
                                Space(35 - intLength(2)) & _
                                txtTelephone.Text.ToCharArray _
                              (0, intLength(3)) & _
                                Space(30 - intLength(3))

                      ' Translate output record to a byte array.
                      For I = 0 To 99
                          byteRecord(I) = AscW(chrRecord(I))
                      Next

                      ' Add new record to its position in the file.
                      myStream.Position = intKey * 100
                      myStream.Write(byteRecord, 0, 100)
                      myStream.Close()

                  End If
              End If
              myStream.Close()
          Catch
              MessageBox.Show("Problems writing the file", _
                          "IO Message", _
                          MessageBoxButtons.AbortRetryIgnore, _
                          MessageBoxIcon.Error)
          End Try
      End Sub

      Private Sub btnDelete_Click _
                      (ByVal sender As System.Object, _
                       ByVal e As System.EventArgs) _
                       Handles btnDelete.Click

          Dim myStream As IO.FileStream
          Dim I As Integer
          Dim byteRecord(99) As Byte
          Dim chrRecord(99) As Char
          Dim intKey As Integer
          Dim strCalc As String
```

```
Try
    myStream = New IO.FileStream(txtPath.Text, _
                                 IO.FileMode.OpenOrCreate, _
                                 IO.FileAccess.ReadWrite, _
                                 IO.FileShare.None)

If myStream.Length = 0 Or _
    Not IsNumeric(txtID.Text) Or _
    CInt(txtID.Text) <= 0 Then
    MessageBox.Show("No file found")
Else
    If myStream.Length < CInt(txtID.Text) * 100 Then
        MessageBox.Show("No such friend")
    Else
        intKey = CInt(txtID.Text)
        myStream.Position = intKey * 100
        myStream.Read(byteRecord, 0, 100)

        ' Mark record as deleted in its ID.
        txtID.Text = "Del"

        ' Build output record.
        Dim intLength(4) As Integer
        intLength(0) = txtID.Text.Length
        If intLength(0) > 5 Then intLength(0) = 5
        intLength(1) = txtName.Text.Length
        If intLength(1) > 30 Then intLength(1) = 30
        intLength(2) = txtAddress.Text.Length
        If intLength(2) > 35 Then intLength(2) = 35
        intLength(3) = txtTelephone.Text.Length
        If intLength(3) > 30 Then intLength(3) = 30

        chrRecord = txtID.Text.ToCharArray _
                    (0, intLength(0)) & _
                      Space(5 - intLength(0)) & _
                      txtName.Text.ToCharArray _
                    (0, intLength(1)) & _
                      Space(30 - intLength(1)) & _
                      txtAddress.Text.ToCharArray _
                    (0, intLength(2)) & _
                      Space(35 - intLength(2)) & _
                      txtTelephone.Text.ToCharArray _
                    (0, intLength(3)) & _
                      Space(30 - intLength(3))

        ' Translate output record to a byte array.
        For I = 0 To 99
            byteRecord(I) = AscW(chrRecord(I))
        Next

        ' Add new record to its position in the file.
        myStream.Position = intKey * 100
```

```vb
                    myStream.Write(byteRecord, 0, 100)
                    myStream.Close()

                End If
            End If
            myStream.Close()
        Catch
            MessageBox.Show("Problems writing the file", _
                            "IO Message", _
                            MessageBoxButtons.AbortRetryIgnore, _
                            MessageBoxIcon.Error)
        End Try
    End Sub

    Private Sub btnAdd_Click _
                (ByVal sender As System.Object, _
                 ByVal e As System.EventArgs) _
                 Handles btnAdd.Click

        Dim myStream As IO.FileStream
        Dim I As Integer
        Dim byteRecord(99) As Byte
        Dim chrRecord(99) As Char
        Dim intKey As Integer
        Dim strCalc As String

        Try
            myStream = New IO.FileStream(txtPath.Text, _
                                IO.FileMode.OpenOrCreate, _
                                IO.FileAccess.ReadWrite, _
                                IO.FileShare.None)

            If myStream.Length = 0 Then
                ' If the file is empty, this is a new file.
                ' Initialize the file.
                ' The next available key is kept in the initial 5 bytes.
                chrRecord = "1" & Space(99)
                For I = 0 To 99
                    byteRecord(I) = AscW(chrRecord(I))
                Next
                strCalc = "00001"
            Else
                ' Read first record. This record is the control record.
                ' It contains the current size of the table.
                myStream.Read(byteRecord, 0, 100)
                strCalc = Chr(byteRecord(0)) & _
                          Chr(byteRecord(1)) & _
                          Chr(byteRecord(2)) & _
                          Chr(byteRecord(3)) & _
                          Chr(byteRecord(4))
                If Not IsNumeric(strCalc) Then strCalc = "1"
                If CDbl(strCalc) > 99998 Then strCalc = "1"
            End If
```

```vb
    ' Update key record
    intKey = CInt(strCalc)
    intKey = intKey + 1
    strCalc = intKey
    chrRecord = strCalc.ToCharArray & Space(99)
    For I = 0 To 99
        byteRecord(I) = AscW(chrRecord(I))
    Next
    myStream.Position = 0
    myStream.Write(byteRecord, 0, 100)

    ' Update form.
    txtID.Text = CStr(intKey)

    ' Build output record.
    Dim intLength(4) As Integer
    intLength(0) = txtID.Text.Length
    If intLength(0) > 5 Then intLength(0) = 5
    intLength(1) = txtName.Text.Length
    If intLength(1) > 30 Then intLength(1) = 30
    intLength(2) = txtAddress.Text.Length
    If intLength(2) > 35 Then intLength(2) = 35
    intLength(3) = txtTelephone.Text.Length
    If intLength(3) > 30 Then intLength(3) = 30

    chrRecord = txtID.Text.ToCharArray(0, intLength(0)) & _
                Space(5 - intLength(0)) & _
                txtName.Text.ToCharArray(0, intLength(1)) & _
                Space(30 - intLength(1)) & _
                txtAddress.Text.ToCharArray(0, intLength(2)) & _
                Space(35 - intLength(2)) & _
                txtTelephone.Text.ToCharArray(0, intLength(3)) & _
                Space(30 - intLength(3))

    ' Translate output record to a byte array.
    For I = 0 To 99
        byteRecord(I) = AscW(chrRecord(I))
    Next

    ' Add new record to its position in the file.
    myStream.Position = intKey * 100
    myStream.Write(byteRecord, 0, 100)
    myStream.Close()
Catch
    MessageBox.Show("Problems writing the file", _
                "IO Message", _
                MessageBoxButtons.AbortRetryIgnore, _
                MessageBoxIcon.Error)
End Try
End Sub
```

SUGGESTED HOME ASSIGNMENTS

1. Build a new form with a Button that will encrypt a file by adding 10 to every even-numbered byte and 25 to each odd-numbered byte. Add another Button that will de-encrypt the code.
2. Build a new form with three Buttons and a textbox. The first Button will read a file whose address is given in the textbox. If the file does not exist, an error message should appear in a message box. The file should be read to its end and its content stored in a persistent object. Do this by assigning the content of the file to a variable that is defined in that object. You will also have to define the class that that object will instantiate. The second Button will make the object persistent. The third Button will reconstruct the file from the deserialized object.

TEST YOURSELF

1. Compare and contrast the `FileStream` and the `StreamReader` classes.
2. When would it be appropriate not to read data with the `FileStream` class?
3. What is offset, and what is position? Are they the same?
4. What is the `Position` property? What function does it serve?
5. What do the `Chr` and `AscW` functions do? Why are they necessary in the binary access method?
6. Write code that will do the same as the following line of code, but will use the `ReadByte` method:

   ```
   myStream2.Read(byteArray, 10, 20)
   ```

7. Suggest a more complex encryption method than the one discussed in the chapter.
8. Why is the binary access method good for encryption algorithms?
9. If a three-line file is encrypted, how many lines will it contain?
10. What is the `Length` property of the file?
11. What is serialization? What are the advantages of it?
12. What is `<Serializable()>`?
13. Why make an object persistent rather than storing its values in a file?
14. What is a binary formatter?
15. What is the random access method?
16. What are the advantages of using a direct access method?
17. How does a program know when a new record begins in a direct access method file?
18. How are records deleted in a direct access method file?
19. How could a direct access method be implemented when only a sequential access method is available?
20. How could a sequential access method be implemented with a direct access method?

CHAPTER 7

Graphics and Animation

CHAPTER OBJECTIVES

After completing this chapter, students should be able to:

1. Understand `System.Drawing.Graphics` and some of the major objects such as the following:

   - `Ellipse`
   - `Icon`
   - `Polygon`
   - `Arc`
   - `Line`
   - `Pie`

2. Understand the concept of color and how it is applied in VB.NET with

   - The `Color` collection
   - `FromArgb`
   - `Pen`
   - `Brush`

3. Be able to use simple animation with a timer

7.1   AIMS OF CHAPTER

This chapter introduces the `System.Drawing.Graphics` class, which handles the subclasses with which graphics are applied in VB.NET. Through this `Graphics` object, shapes such as lines, polygons, circles, and ellipses are drawn. As will be demonstrated in the application-building lab, `Graphics` also allow the building of diagrams to display information in a more readable manner. The chapter also discusses the `Pen` and `Brush` subclasses and how their color can be set using explicit color names and the `FromArgb` method. Lastly, the chapter will introduce animation and its application with the `Timer` and the `PictureBox` controls.

The application-building lab reviews generating and displaying random numbers as a line chart, a bar chart, and a pie chart. The pie chart displays both arcs and slices.

7.2   THE `System.Drawing.Graphics`

7.2.1   Overview of Graphics in VB.NET

Graphics in VB.NET deals with drawing lines, polygons (triangles, rectangles, pentagons, etc.), circles, ellipses, arcs, and many other geometrical shapes. It also includes the ability to present text in special fonts. All this functionality is handled in VB.NET through the subclasses in the `System.Drawing.Graphics` class. This class is automatically included in a form through the default command

```
Inherits System.Windows.Forms.Form
```

Adding graphics to a form, however, requires instantiating a `Graphics` object. In this case, we named it grpGraphics:

```
' Add a graphics Object
Dim grpGraphics As System.Drawing.Graphics
grpGraphics = Me.CreateGraphics
```

A `Graphics` object can be instantiated on a form, as in the preceding code, or on any control such as a picture box or Button, as in the following code:

```
grpGraphics = Button1.CreateGraphics
```

The graphic shapes will be drawn accordingly on the surface of the object in which the `Graphics` object was instantiated. In the case of the preceding code, all the graphics will be drawn on the Button.

In addition, depending on the graphic shape that will be drawn and whether only its outlines will be drawn or the shape will be filled, either a `Pen` or a `Brush` object must also be instantiated. A `Pen` object is used to draw the outer line of the shape, its circumference; a `Brush` object is used to fills in the shape. The next section discusses several of the most popular shapes.

7.2.2   Polygons and Points

Polygons, graphically speaking, are any closed shape connecting points on a plane. These include triangles, connecting three points; rectangles, connecting four points; pentagons, connecting five points; and so on. To make things simple, all polygons in VB.NET can be defined in the same way. First, the points that will specify the nodes of the polygon should be specified in a `Point` array. The `Point` data type, as its name implies, handles graphic points by specifying their *x*- and *y*-coordinates in pixels on the plane that is the surface of the form or the control.

The dimension of the array should correspond to the number of nodes that define the polygon. So, if we wish to draw a triangle, as in the following code, an array of points with three entries should be defined:

```
Dim pntPoint(2) As System.Drawing.Point
```

Then, the *x*- and *y*-coordinates of each point in pixels from the top left corner of the form should be entered. Note that an array of dimension 3 starts at entry 0:

```
pntPoint(0).X = 0   ' in pixels from top left
pntPoint(0).Y = 0
pntPoint(1).X = 100
pntPoint(1).Y = 100
pntPoint(2).X = 0
pntPoint(2).Y = 100
```

Having defined the nodes of the polygon, we need to define either a pen or a brush, to mark the outline of the polygon or fill the polygon, respectively. In this case, we will instantiate a pen, specifying its color as dark blue and its width as 1 (Width is an optional parameter whose default value is 1):

```
' Add a pen in dark blue
Dim penDraw As New System.Drawing.Pen _
    (System.Drawing.Color.DarkBlue,1)
```

Once a Pen has been declared, its color and width can be changed by instantiating a new pen object and setting the color and width:

```
penDraw = New Pen(Color.Green, 4)
```

A polygon is drawn with the DrawPolygon method, which receives two parameters—a Pen object and the array of points that define its nodes:

```
grpGraphics.DrawPolygon(penDraw, pntPoint)
```

As the Point array contains three points, the resulting polygon will be a triangle:

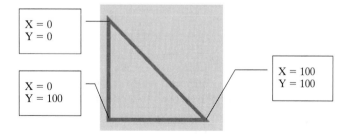

Note that the way the *x*- and *y*-coordinates are set is a bit misleading. Typically, when a grid is laid on a plane, the *x*-coordinates increase as one moves to the right and the *y*-coordinates increase as one moves up. In VB.NET, however, the *y*-coordinates increase as one moves down on the plane created by the surface of the form or the control. The origin—point (0,0)—is the top left corner of the surface of the form or the control in which the Graphics object was instantiated.

Had we wanted to fill in the polygon, we would have used a brush. In the following code, the brush color is crimson:

```
' Draw a triangle
Dim bshBrush As System.Drawing.Brush
bshBrush = New SolidBrush(Color.Crimson)

grpGraphics.FillPolygon(bshBrush, pntPoint)
```

This method can be used with any polygon. However, in the special case of a rectangle, VB.NET also allows its drawing with a dedicated method called DrawRectangle:

```
grpGraphics.DrawRectangle(penDraw, 200, 200, 300, 100)
```

Here, the five parameters are the pen, the *x*-coordinate at the top left of the rectangle, the *y*-coordinate at the top left of the rectangle, its width, and its height. The preceding code is shorthand for drawing a rectangle. The longhand code would appear as follows:

```
Dim rctRectangle As Rectangle
rctRectangle.X = 400
rctRectangle.Y = 400
rctRectangle.Height = 400
rctRectangle.Width = 400
grpGraphics.DrawRectangle(penDraw, rctRectangle)
```

First, a Rectangle object is declared, and then its X, Y, Height, and Width properties are assigned explicitly before it is passed as a parameter to the DrawRectangle method.

As before, if we wish to fill the shape rather than just draw it, we need to use a Brush object and a FillRectangle method. The following code shows two equivalent ways in which this can be done:

```
grpGraphics.FillRectangle(bshBrush, rctRectangle)
```

```
grpGraphics.FillRectangle(bshBrush, 10, 20, 30, 40)
```

7.2.3 Lines

A line connects two points. Lines are drawn with the DrawLine method. Drawing a line requires specifying the color and width of the line with the Pen object and stating the X and Y coordinates of the two points. As with a polygon, the latter can be done with pairs of numbers or with Point objects:

```
           ' Pen      from(X,Y) to(X,Y)
grpGraphics.DrawLine(penDraw, 20, 200, 30, 300)
```

It can also be done with a Pen object:

```
Dim pntPoint(2) As System.Drawing.Point
pntPoint(0).X = 20   ' in pixels from top left
pntPoint(0).Y = 200
```

```
pntPoint(1).X = 30
pntPoint(1).Y = 300

grpGraphics.DrawLine(penDraw, pntPoint(0), pntPoint(1))
```

7.2.4   Ellipses and Circles

Ellipses and circles are additional shapes that are handled by the `Graphics` object. Graphically, circles are ellipses that happen to have only one center. As so, in keeping with the object-oriented philosophy of VB.NET, ellipses and circles are handled by the same set of methods in VB.NET. To specify an ellipse or a circle, VB.NET requires specifying the rectangle in which the ellipse or the circle is enclosed.[12] An ellipse is enclosed by a rectangle, a circle by a square. This is a very convenient way of specifying the outline of the ellipse or circle, because it allows placing shapes near each other without complicated algebraic calculations of the appropriate centers and radiuses. Ellipses and circles are drawn by means of the same two methods—`DrawEllipse` to draw its outline and `FillEllipse` to fill it in: After the last line in the first paragraph, please add, "The following code contains some preparatory steps. First, a `Graphics` object is dimensioned. Through this object the ellipses will be drawn. Then, to handle the outline color of the ellipses a `Pen` object is dimensioned, and to handle the fill color a `Brush` object is dimensioned."

```
' Add a graphics Object
Dim grpGraphics As System.Drawing.Graphics
grpGraphics = Me.CreateGraphics

' Add a violet pen and a crimson brush
Dim penDraw As New System.Drawing.Pen _
    (System.Drawing.Color.BlueViolet)
Dim brhDraw As System.Drawing.Brush
bshBrush = New SolidBrush(Color.Crimson)
```

Since ellipses and circles are enclosed in a rectangle, the properties of the rectangle must be specified—in this case, as with the rectangle methods, its top left *x*-coordinate, its top left *y*-coordinate, its width, and its height. These properties can be specified in shorthand:

```
' Then, draw the outlines
grpGraphics.DrawEllipse(penDraw,30, 150, 30, 60)
```

Alternatively, the properties can be specified in longhand by defining a `Rectangle` object and assigning its properties explicitly. Note that in this case the shape will be an ellipse, because the height and width are not equal, meaning that the shape is enclosed by a rectangle. As before, the shape is filled with a brush:

---

[12]This is a marked departure from VB6 where it was required to use the linear algebra notation in which a circle was defined by its center and radius. Ellipses were defined by the midpoint between the two centers, the radius, and its "aspect" (i.e., how much the circle defined by the center and radius was to be squashed into an ellipse).

```
Dim rctRectangle As Rectangle
rctRectangle.X = 40
rctRectangle.Y = 40
rctRectangle.Height = 40
rctRectangle.Width = 80
grpGraphics.FillEllipse(bshBrush, rctRectangle)
```

The ellipse will look like this:

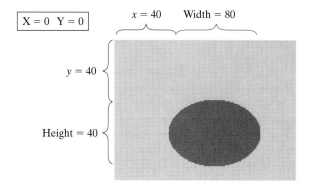

7.2.5   Arcs and Pies

An arc is a section of the circumference of an ellipse or of a circle. A pie is a filled-in portion of an ellipse or a circle. Arcs are drawn with the DrawArc method, pies are drawn with FillPie method and the DrawPie method. As with other shapes, a Graphics object must be instantiated first. In the case of DrawArc method, a Pen should also be declared. The following code below defines a red pen with a width of 4:

```
' Add a graphics Object
Dim grpGraphics As System.Drawing.Graphics
grpGraphics = Me.CreateGraphics

' Add a green pen of width 4
Dim penDraw As New System.Drawing.Pen _
        (System.Drawing.Color.Green, 4)
```

Next, an arc is drawn with the DrawArc method. DrawArc receives six parameters. The first four parameters specify the rectangle that encompasses the circle or ellipse that the arc belongs to. As with the DrawEllipse method, these parameters specify the X and Y coordinates of the top left point of the rectangle, its Width and its Height. The other two parameters specify the angle in degrees from where the arc will start clockwise from the rightmost point of the shape, and its sweep also in degrees and clockwise.[13] The following code draws four arcs in different colors and in increasing width:

---

[13]This is in stark contrast to VB6 and math textbooks, where arcs and slices are specified in radians and built counterclockwise.

```
'                                   X, Y, Width, Height, start, sweep
grpGraphics.DrawArc(penDraw, 300, 80, 150,    150,     0,     90)

' Pen color and width are changed and new arcs are drawn
penDraw = New Pen(Color.Blue, 8)
grpGraphics.DrawArc(penDraw, 300, 80, 150, 150, 90, 90)

penDraw = New Pen(Color.Red, 12)
grpGraphics.DrawArc(penDraw, 300, 80, 150, 150, 180, 90)

penDraw = New Pen(Color.HotPink, 16)
grpGraphics.DrawArc(penDraw, 300, 80, 150, 150, 270, 90)
```

The result of the code is the following drawing:

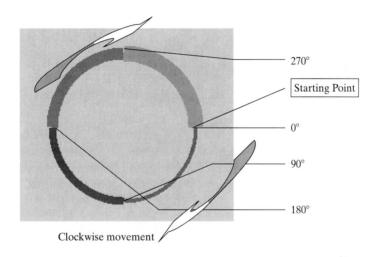

Clockwise movement

In the drawing, a green arc starts at degree 0 and covers a sweep of 90 degrees, ending at degree 90, calculated clockwise. Next, a blue arc with a width of 8 is drawn, starting at 90 degrees and extending for 90 degrees to end at 180 degrees. This is followed by a red arc of width 12 that starts at 180 degrees and extends 90 degrees to end at 270 degrees, where a pink arc with a width of 16 starts and sweeps 90 degrees to complete the circle.

Filling in an arc makes it a pie. This is done with the `FillPie` method and, as was the case with filling in a polygon, with a `Brush` rather than a `Pen`. The following code uses a `Rectangle` object to specify the location and size of the rectangle that contains the ellipse or circle that the arc belongs to:[14]

```
Dim rctR As Rectangle
With rctR
```

---

[14]The `With` block is a shorthand technique in VB. Everything starting with a period inside the block is treated as though it started with the object name specified at the `With` statement. For example, `.X = 600` means the same as `rctR.X = 600`.

```
        .X = 600
        .Y = 100
        .Height = 200
        .Width = 200
    End With
    Dim bshBrush As Brush
    bshBrush = New SolidBrush(Color.Cyan)
    grpGraphics.FillPie(bshBrush, rctR, 270, 45)
```

Then a pie starting at 270 degrees (a straight angle directed vertically upwards) and sweeping 45 degrees (an eighth of a circle) clockwise is drawn:

7.2.6 Bezier

Another neat shape provided by VB.NET is the Bezier, which is a rounded line connecting four points. These shapes are very convenient when it comes to drawing waves or rounded corners. Beziers are drawn with the DrawBezier method. In shorthand, this method has nine parameters: a Pen and four pairs of X and Y coordinates. The code is as follows:

```
' Add a graphics Object
Dim grpGraphics As System.Drawing.Graphics
grpGraphics = Me.CreateGraphics

' Add a violet pen
Dim penDraw As New System.Drawing.Pen _
    (System.Drawing.Color.BlueViolet)

grpGraphics.DrawBezier(penDraw, _
    100, 100, 150, 250,    _
    350, 310, 400, 400)
```

In longhand, the method has only five parameters: a Pen and four Points. This is demonstrated in the following code, in which a Point array with four entries is defined and then values are assigned to its X and Y properties:

```
Dim pntBezier(4) As Point
pntBezier(0).X = 500
pntBezier(0).Y = 100
pntBezier(1).X = 500
pntBezier(1).Y = 200
pntBezier(2).X = 600
```

```
pntBezier(2).Y = 200
pntBezier(3).X = 600
pntBezier(3).Y = 100

penDraw = New Pen(Color.Red, 5)

grpGraphics.DrawBezier (penDraw, pntBezier(0), _
    pntBezier(1), pntBezier(2), pntBezier(3))
```

After changing the color and width of the pen, the Bezier is drawn. If another Bezier is drawn, the code would be similar to the following:

```
pntBezier(0).X = 520
pntBezier(0).Y = 110
pntBezier(1).X = 520
pntBezier(1).Y = 40
pntBezier(2).X = 580
pntBezier(2).Y = 40
pntBezier(3).X = 580
pntBezier(3).Y = 110

penDraw = New Pen(Color.Green, 3)

grpGraphics.DrawBezier (penDraw, pntBezier(0), _
    pntBezier(1), pntBezier(2), pntBezier(3))
```

The result would then be the following drawing:

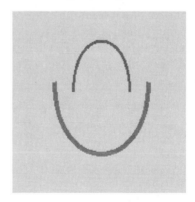

7.2.7   Special Fonts and Icons

The Graphics object also supports writing text with special backgrounds and fonts on the surface of a form or control. This is done by declaring a Font object and assigning its font name, size, and style:

```
Dim grpGraphics As System.Drawing.Graphics
grpGraphics = Me.CreateGraphics

Dim fntFont As Font
'                    font name, size, style
fntFont = New Font("Impact", 50, FontStyle.Italic)
```

The background is then set through the `Brush` object. In this case, it is assigned a .bmp file as the background with the `TextureBrush` method. The .bmp file assigned here is one of the default wallpaper screens that comes with Windows 2000 and NT:

```
Dim bshBrush As Brush

bshBrush = New TextureBrush(System.Drawing.Image.FromFile( _
                ("C:\winnt\greenstone.bmp")))
```

Now the text can be written with the desired font and background with the `DrawString` method. The method has five parameters: the text, font, brush, and the X and Y coordinates of the top left pixel where the text will be written. The code is as follows:

```
grpGraphics.DrawString("Hello", fntFont, bshBrush, 90, 90)
```

The result will be the following drawing:

7.2.8   Color

Up to this point in the chapter, we set the color property of a pen or brush with one of the scores of preassigned values in the Color collection. VB.NET lets us also define our own colors, which can come in very handy when random colors need to be generated in diagrams, as we shall see in the application building lab. The value of a color is kept in a Color type variable, where its color can be assigned out of the existing colors in the Color collection:

```
Dim clrColor As System.Drawing.Color
clrColor = Color.Tan
clrColor = Color.Yellow
```

Building colors dynamically is done with the `FromArgb` method.[15] The method has three parameters, integer values ranging from 0 to 255 that contain the amount of each of the three basic colors—red, green, and blue—that will constitute the new color. All the colors the human eye can see are combinations of these three basic colors; the human eye has receptors for only these basic colors. (In addition, the human eye also has a separate night-vision system that sees in black and white.) VB.NET takes advantage of this to let us program colors dynamically. The following code generates a random color and assigns it to the Color object:[16]

---

[15]This method is equivalent to the RBG function in VB6.
[16]RND is a function that returns a random value between 0 and 1. Multiplying it by 255 and assigning the value to an integer will result in an integer between 0 and 255. RND is equivalent in its purpose to the Random class that was introduced earlier in the book.

```
Dim red, green, blue As Integer

red = Rnd(0) * 255
green = Rnd(0) * 255
blue = Rnd(0) * 255
clrColor = Color.FromArgb(red, green, blue)
```

The new color can then be used as any other color:

```
Dim bshMsg As Brush
Dim penChart As Pen

System.Drawing.Pen(clrColor)
bshMsg = New SolidBrush(clrColor)
```

7.2.9 Animation

Animation, moving pictures, is achieved in VB.NET the same way it is done in the movies: Pictures are changed fast enough that the human eye cannot tell that a picture has changed. So long as the pictures change faster than 20 times a second, which is approximately the rate at which the human eye samples the world, the illusion of movement can be achieved. An easy way of doing so in VB.NET is through a `Timer` that controls a `PictureBox`.

To demonstrate how this is done, let's draw a few controls: a Button, a horizontal scroll bar, and three picture boxes placed exactly one on top of the other. The `Image` property of the picture boxes should be set to read the icons in the "C:/Program Files/Microsoft Visual Studio.NET/Common7/Graphics/icons" directory. The icons added are TRFFC10A, TRFFC10B, and TRFFC10C. Also, add a `Timer`, and name it tmrLights (see Figure 7.1).

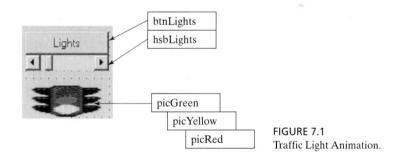

FIGURE 7.1
Traffic Light Animation.

To demonstrate animation, add the following code:

```
If tmrLights.Enabled = True Then
    tmrLights.Enabled = False
Else
    tmrLights.Enabled = True
End If
```

Double-click the Button, and in the code window add code to turn the timer on and off.

Now double-click the timer and the code will cause the pictures to appear in order, with the red light taking longer:

```
Static intLight As Integer = 0
picGreen.Visible = False
picYellow.Visible = False
picRed.Visible = False

Select Case intLight
    Case 0
        picGreen.Visible = True
    Case 1
        picYellow.Visible = True
    Case Else
        picRed.Visible = True
End Select

intLight += 1
If intLight = 5 Then intLight = 0
```

Last, add the code behind the horizontal scroll bar to control the speed of the timer. Also, set the Minimum property of the scroll bar to 1. The code will change the interval of the timer whenever the bar on the scroll bar is moved. That way, the speed at which the lights change can be controlled. The relevant code is

```
tmrLights.Interval = hscLights.Value * 10
```

Now run the application and try it out.

LAB 7: GRAPHICS

Lab Objectives:

Exercise graphics by building a set of charts that display data graphically. We will discuss

- Graphics, Brush, Pen, Font, and Rectangle
- Color and FromArgb
- Clear
- DrawString
- DrawRectangle and FillRectangle
- DrawLine
- DrawArc and FillPie
- Timer and RND

Application Overview

This application generates 20 random numbers and then displays them in a line chart, bar chart, or a pie chart, depending on the Button clicked. New random numbers are generated when the Random Numbers Button is clicked. The application also contains a timer that automatically activates the generation of random numbers by raising the Click event on the Random Numbers Button.

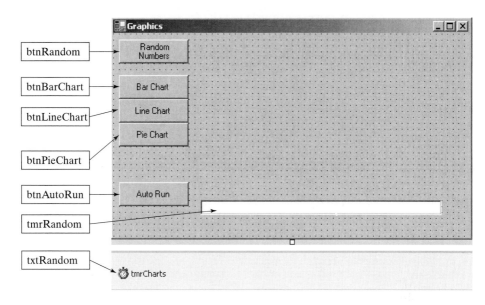

FIGURE 7.2
Lab 7.

Part 1: Building the Form

Create a new form and name it frmChapter7a. Change its caption to "Graphic" with the `Text` property. Then add the Buttons, textbox, and timer as shown in Figure 7.2, and name them accordingly. Make the `Enabled` property of txtRandom `False`. This will prevent users from changing the values displayed there. Make the three chart-generating Buttons not visible by changing their `Visible` property to `False`.

Part 2: Adding the Nongraphic Code

When the form is displayed for the first time, only the Random Numbers and Auto Run Buttons are visible. When Random Numbers is clicked, 20 random numbers are generated and presented in the textbox. Only then will the other three Buttons become visible. If the Random Numbers Button is clicked again, a new set of 20 random numbers will be generated, presented in the textbox, and then the last chart will be redrawn. The next code handles those activities.

In the `Public` class section, we will define three new variables—an array that will hold the 20 random numbers, an integer to hold their total, and a string that will contain the name of the last chart drawn:

```
Public Class frmCharts
    Dim intRandom(20) As Integer ' The random numbers
    Dim intTot As Integer        ' Sum of random numbers
    Dim strLast As String        ' Last chart drawn
```

Now we will add the code behind the Random Numbers Button. The code generates 20 random numbers in a loop, assigning them to the array, summarizing them in intTot, and concatenating them to the textbox. Note that the first random number is assigned to the textbox. This clears the previous text that might have been there from previous clicks of the Button. Having generated the numbers for the charts, the other three Buttons are now made visible, and, depending on the last chart that was displayed—the value is stored in strLast—the subroutines in charge of the Click event of that chart is called. The code is as follows:

```
Private Sub btnRandom_Click( _
        ByVal sender As System.Object, _
        ByVal e As System.EventArgs) _
        Handles btnRandom.Click

    Dim I As Integer
    Dim myRandom As New Random()

    txtRandom.Text = ""
    txtRandom.Enabled = False
    intTot = 0
    For I = 0 To 19
        intRandom(I) = CInt(myRandom.Next(I) * 10)
        intTot = intTot + intRandom(I)
        If I <> 0 Then txtRandom.Text = txtRandom.Text & ","
        txtRandom.Text = txtRandom.Text & CStr(intRandom(I))
    Next

    btnBarChart.Visible = True
    btnLineChart.Visible = True
    btnPieChart.Visible = True

    Select Case strLast
        Case Is = "Bar"
            Call btnBarChart_Click(Me, e)
        Case Is = "Line"
            Call btnLineChart_Click(Me, e)
        Case Is = "Pie"
            Call btnPieChart_Click(Me, e)
        Case Else
    End Select
End Sub
```

Now we are ready to add the code for the charts. First, we will add the code that handles the bar chart. As shown in Figure 7.3, that display contains a grid, title, and a dynamically generated set of rectangles which create the bars. The first 10 bars are outlined; the last 10 bars are filled.

The code first sets the value of strLast so that Random Numbers will "know" which subroutine to call and then generates 20 random colors:

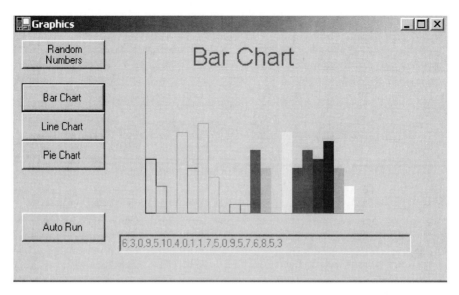

FIGURE 7.3
Bar chart.

```
Private Sub btnBarChart_Click( _
        ByVal sender As System.Object, _
        ByVal e As System.EventArgs) _
        Handles btnBarChart.Click

    Dim bshMsg As Brush
    Dim fntMsg As Font
    Dim grpChart As Graphics
    Dim penChart As Pen
    Dim clrColor(20) As System.Drawing.Color
    Dim red, green, blue As Integer
    Dim I As Integer

    strLast = "Bar"
    ' Generate 20 colors
    For I = 0 To 19
        red = Rnd(I) * 255
        green = Rnd(I) * 255
        blue = Rnd(I) * 255
        clrColor(I) = Color.FromArgb(red, green, blue)
    Next
```

Next, with the Clear method, the form is cleared of any previous graphics. Then the header, where it says "Bar Chart" on the form and the grid are drawn. Here is the code:

```
' Clear graphics
grpChart = Me.CreateGraphics
grpChart.Clear(System.Drawing.Color.LightGray)
```

```
' Add Header
bshMsg = New SolidBrush(Color.DarkGreen)
fntMsg = New Font("Arial", 20, FontStyle.Regular)
grpChart.DrawString("Bar Chart", fntMsg, bshMsg, 200, 10)

' Draw Grid in Forest Green
penChart = New System.Drawing.Pen(Color.ForestGreen)
grpChart.DrawLine(penChart, 150, 20, 150, 200)
grpChart.DrawLine(penChart, 150, 200, 400, 200)
```

The actual chart is then drawn as rectangles with the following code:

```
' Draw Chart as Rectangles
Dim pntRect As System.Drawing.Rectangle
pntRect = New System.Drawing.Rectangle()

Dim X As Integer = 150  ' X at the grid origin
Dim Y As Integer = 200  ' Y at the grid origin
For I = 0 To 19
    ' Rectangle position: X and Y at upper left
    pntRect.X = X + I * 12
    pntRect.Y = Y - intRandom(I) * 10

    ' Rectangle size: Width is always 12, but
    ' height is calculated based on the current
    ' random number.
    pntRect.Height = intRandom(I) * 10
    pntRect.Width = 12

    ' Draw the rectangle, making the first 10
    ' only outlined and the last 10 filled.
    If I < 10 Then
        ' Each bar in a different color
        penChart = New System.Drawing.Pen(clrColor(I))
        ' Draw bar
        grpChart.DrawRectangle (penChart, pntRect)
    Else
        ' Each bar in a different color
        bshMsg = New SolidBrush(clrColor(I))
        ' Draw bar
        grpChart.FillRectangle(bshMsg, pntRect)
    End If
    Next
End Sub
```

The code that handles the line chart (Figure 7.4) begins the same way as the code that handles the bar chart:

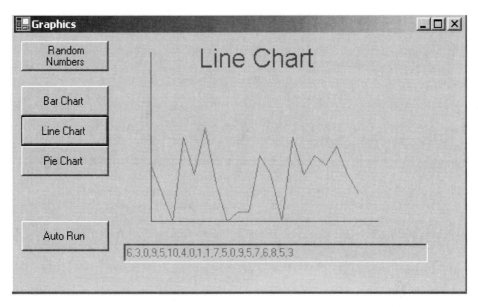

FIGURE 7.4
Line chart.

```
Private Sub btnLineChart_Click(_
        ByVal sender As System.Object, _
        ByVal e As System.EventArgs) _
        Handles btnLineChart.Click
    Dim bshMsg As Brush
    Dim fntMsg As Font
    Dim grpChart As Graphics
    Dim penChart As Pen
    Dim red, green, blue As Integer
    Dim clrColor As System.Drawing.Color = Color.Teal
    Dim I As Integer

    strLast = "Line"
    ' Header
    bshMsg = New SolidBrush(Color.DarkGreen)
    fntMsg = New Font("Arial", 20, FontStyle.Regular)
    grpChart = Me.CreateGraphics
    grpChart.Clear(System.Drawing.Color.LightGray)
    grpChart.DrawString("Line Chart", fntMsg, bshMsg, 200, 10)

    ' Draw Grid
    penChart = New System.Drawing.Pen(Color.ForestGreen)
    grpChart.DrawLine(penChart, 150, 20, 150, 200)
    grpChart.DrawLine(penChart, 150, 200, 400, 200)
```

Where the code differs is in the drawing of the actual chart. In the case of a line chart, the code simply connects the current segment to where the last segment ended. The first segment begins at the origin of the grid. The end of each segment is calculated so that x is advanced a fixed amount from the previous x, while the new y is calculated from the current random number:

```
' Draw Chart
Dim X As Integer = 150  ' X at the grid origin
Dim Y As Integer = 200  ' Y at the grid origin

' Draw Chart in different color than grid
penChart = New System.Drawing.Pen(Color.DarkGoldenrod)
' Build segments.
' 20 points have 19 segments connecting them
For I = 0 To 18
        ' A line connects a two points: a starting
        ' point and an ending point.
        ' The starting point is the current X
        ' and a Y that is derived from the current
        ' random number.
        ' The ending point is the current X
        ' advanced by 12 pixels and a Y that is
        ' derived from the next random number.

        grpChart.DrawLine(penChart, _
                X, Y - intRandom(I) * 10, _
                X + 12, Y - intRandom(I + 1) * 10)

        ' Advance current X
        X = X + 12
    Next
End Sub
```

The pie chart starts the same way, except that no grid is drawn:

```
Private Sub btnPieChart_Click( _
        ByVal sender As System.Object, _
        ByVal e As System.EventArgs) _
        Handles btnPieChart.Click

    Dim bshMsg As Brush
    Dim fntMsg As Font
    Dim grpChart As Graphics
    Dim penChart As Pen
    Dim red, green, blue As Integer
    Dim clrColor(20) As System.Drawing.Color
    Dim I As Integer
    Dim intAngle, intSweep As Integer
    Dim rctPie As System.Drawing.Rectangle

    strLast = "Pie"

    ' Having generated the 20 colors randomly,
    ' we will explicitly add colors by name in the pie chart,
```

```
' just to show how it can be done.
clrColor(0) = Color.AliceBlue
clrColor(1) = Color.Beige
clrColor(2) = Color.Crimson
clrColor(3) = Color.DarkBlue
clrColor(4) = Color.DodgerBlue
clrColor(5) = Color.Firebrick
clrColor(6) = Color.Gainsboro
clrColor(7) = Color.Honeydew
clrColor(8) = Color.IndianRed
clrColor(9) = Color.Khaki
clrColor(10) = Color.Lavender
clrColor(11) = Color.Magenta
clrColor(12) = Color.Maroon
clrColor(13) = Color.NavajoWhite
clrColor(14) = Color.OldLace
clrColor(15) = Color.PaleGoldenrod
clrColor(16) = Color.RosyBrown
clrColor(17) = Color.SaddleBrown
clrColor(18) = Color.Tan
clrColor(19) = Color.Yellow

' Build Header
bshMsg = New SolidBrush(Color.DarkGreen)
fntMsg = New Font("Arial", 20, FontStyle.Regular)
grpChart = Me.CreateGraphics
grpChart.Clear(System.Drawing.Color.LightGray)
grpChart.DrawString("Pie Chart", fntMsg, bshMsg, 200, 10)
```

The first 10 random numbers are drawn with an arc, showing only the outline of the segment of the circle they represent. These 10 segments are drawn with the DrawArc method, which receives as parameters numbers for the X, Y, Width, and Height of the rectangle that encompasses the circle. The next 10 random numbers are drawn with the FillPie method, and this time the parameters of the rectangle that encompasses the circle are passed as a Rectangle object. Before each segment is drawn, a new color, whether for the Pen or for the Brush, is generated. Here is the relevant code:

```
' Set Rectangle details
Dim X As Integer = 200  ' X at top left
Dim Y As Integer = 50   ' Y at top left
rctPie = New System.Drawing.Rectangle()
rctPie.X = X        ' upper left X
rctPie.Y = Y        ' upper left Y
rctPie.Height = 150
rctPie.Width = 150

penChart = New _
    System.Drawing.Pen(Color.ForestGreen)
penChart.Width = 2
```

```
' Draw the segments
For I = 0 To 19
        ' Sweep of segment will be its ratio to
        ' the total and remembering the whole
        ' circle has 360 degrees.
    intSweep = intRandom(I) / intTot * 360

    If I < 10 Then
        penChart.Color = clrColor(I)
        grpChart.DrawArc(penChart, _
                X, Y, 150, 150, intAngle, intSweep)
    Else
        bshMsg = New SolidBrush(clrColor(I))
        grpChart.FillPie _
            (bshMsg, rctPie, intAngle, intSweep)
    End If
    intAngle = intAngle + intSweep
    Next

End Sub
```

The result is as seen in Figure 7.5.

Now let's add the "Auto Run" functionality. When this Button is clicked, the timer is activated. The timer then calls the subroutine that handles the Click event on the Random Numbers Button in order to generate a new chart:

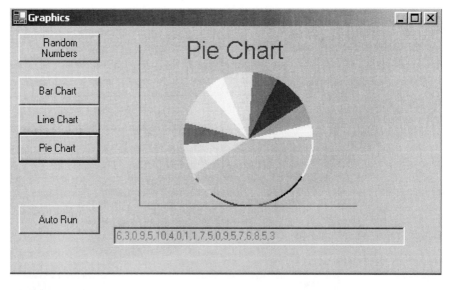

FIGURE 7.5
Pie chart.

```
Private Sub btnAutoRun_Click( _
        ByVal sender As System.Object, _
        ByVal e As System.EventArgs) _
        Handles btnAutoRun.Click

    If tmrRandom.Enabled = True Then
        tmrRandom.Enabled = False
    Else
        tmrRandom.Enabled = True
    End If
End Sub
```

The "Auto Run" turns the timer on and off. The timer just calls the subroutine that generates new random numbers:

```
Private Sub tmrCharts_Tick(ByVal sender As System.Object, _
                ByVal e As System.EventArgs) Handles tmrCharts.Tick
    Call btnRandom_Click(Me, e)
End Sub
```

SUGGESTED HOME ASSIGNMENTS

1. Build a new form that will generate and display 10 random numbers in a pie chart, as done in the lab, but will fill the pie chart anticlockwise rather than clockwise.
2. Build a form and add a Button to it. When the Button is clicked, a small brown ball (generate this as a circle) will start rolling (do this with a timer) along the inside perimeter of the Button. When the button is pressed again, turn the ball red and start rolling it in the opposite direction. When the Button is clicked a third time, stop the ball, make it purple, and place it in the center of the Button.
3. Build a new form. Add a set of three overlapping picture boxes with traffic lights in them, as we did above, and a Button that will control whether the lights change every 5 seconds or remain the same. Add another Button that will draw a large rectangle on the form. Add another Button that will add a small red square inside the rectangle. Make the square much smaller than the rectangle. Now, make the square move about erratically inside the rectangle, but only when the current "light" icon in the traffic lights picture boxes is green.

TEST YOURSELF

1. How would you draw a parallelogram ⬭ in VB.NET with the methods we have covered?
2. How would you draw a moving square on the surface of a picture box?
3. Compare and contrast a Pen and a Brush.
4. What is the Point object?
5. What is the advantage of passing a parameter with a Rectangle?
6. How do you change the color and width of a Pen?
7. How could you dynamically change the shape a DrawPolygon method creates so that it will create a triangle or a rectangle without need to change the code? (*Hint*: Remember the Point object.)
8. Is the triangle drawn with the following command pointing up or down?

```
.DrawPolygon (penD, 20, 0, 18, 10, 22, 10)
```

9. Explain how a circle is drawn.
10. How would you draw a triangle so that its three sides are in different colors?
11. Why does `.DrawRectangle` have either two or five parameters?
12. What is a Bezier?
13. What is the advantage of adding text with a `.DrawString` method when text can be added with large font anyway?
14. Explain how color is handled in VB.NET.
15. What color will `color.FromArgb(255,0,0)` return?
16. Explain how animation works.
17. What is the advantage of connecting a timer to picture boxes?
18. Show how a Button can toggle a timer on and off.
19. How would you generate random numbers between 1 and 30?
20. How would you generate random numbers between 20 and 30?

C H A P T E R   8

Multithreading

CHAPTER OBJECTIVES

After completing this chapter, students should

1. Understand the concept of, and need for, multithreading
2. Be able in utilize

- Threading
- Prioritization
- Making threads sleep
- Joining threads
- `Abort` and `Suspend`

3. Understand

- Atomicity
- Deadlock
- How `SyncLock` works

8.1   AIMS OF CHAPTER

This chapter discusses the concepts of *multitasking* and *multithreading* and how multi-threading is done in VB.NET. In doing so, the chapter introduces *time slicing, prioritization*, and coordinating threads. The chapter discusses when multithreading should be applied and the risks of doing so. The chapter discusses some of the dangers, especially in handling shared data, involved in multithreading and how *synchronization* can solve some of these.

The lab at the end of the chapter demonstrates multithreading in the context of a user interface with exceedingly long functionality, and how multithreading can applied in this case to run that long functionality without locking the form.

8.2   MULTITASKING AND MULTITHREADING

Multitasking is the ability of a computer to run more than one task or program at a time, or at least in what seems to be at the same time. Multitasking enables a computer to run a word processor, email, and a host of other programs at the same time while giving the impression that each is running all by itself and all the time. If you are running Windows NT, then you are probably familiar with the task bar at the bottom of the screen and with the Task Manager (you open it by keying alt+cntl+del and choosing Task Manager) that show the tasks that are currently running on the computer. Multitasking is a powerful and, in today's computerized world, a necessary characteristic of a computer. In reality, however, only one task at a time can run on each CPU. It is the incredible speed of the CPU and the multitasking mechanisms that are built into the operating system that make it seem as though many tasks are running simultaneously.

Multitasking works at the operating system level: It is a feature of Windows. Multithreading does the same thing, but at a program level. Thus, while multitasking will allow many tasks to run simultaneously under Windows, multithreading will allow many elements of the same task (what we call *threads*) to run simultaneously. That is, multithreading can be thought of as multitasking at a program (task) level. For example, Word (a task under Windows) may print a document (one thread) while at the same time the user is typing in another document (second thread). That Word is not "stuck" while printing is an example of multithreading: *two or more program-level activities running at the same time*. It is a powerful and necessary tool.

Actually, VB.NET itself applies multithreading all the time. Any program running in VB.NET has at least two threads: (1) *main*, which is the current Sub Main of the application, and (2) the VB.NET garbage collection task that is continuously running in the background at low priority.

In this chapter, we will discuss multithreading and how to apply it with VB.NET. The ability to run more than one activity at a time in one program, multithreading, is not as simple as it may seem. True, VB.NET provides excellent tools that make it relatively easy to create and manage threads, but having many threads run simultaneously raises many difficulties in coordinating among the threads. This need to coordinate among parallel threads raises unique problems that are much harder to debug than in single-thread tasks. Because of the need to coordinate among the threads—accessing shared data and splitting processing time—and because many things go on in the background beyond the control or even notice of the task itself, multithreading can create very subtle bugs that seem to occur randomly. We will discuss some of these throughout the chapter.

Multithreading should be used when there is a good reason to have several activities of the same program running in parallel and at the same time. Saving a document in Word while allowing the user to continue editing another document is one good example of such a need. In general, many of these cases deal with user-interface functions that take an extraordinary long period of time to complete and where it is inconceivable to have the application locked until that operation completed. Another set of cases where it makes sense to have multithreading is when the functionality that the program performs naturally divide up into separate and unrelated functions, such as saving the document while editing another document. But, although necessary in many cases, multithreading should not be applied blindly. Handling multithreading requires a substantial processing overhead by the program and it makes the programming that much harder because of the need to coordinate among the threads.

8.2.1   Declaring a Thread

Multithreading deals with starting a new *method* and running it independently of the current method as a new thread. (Remember that functions and subroutines are also methods.) That new thread will keep on running until the procedure where it was created ends, until it is forced to stop with Abort or Suspend methods, or until it ends itself. While it is running, it will be an independent unit of running code—what we call a thread. Before getting into a discussion of the details of multithreading, let us create a small multithreaded application and get a hands-on feeling for how it works with a form. Since multithreading requires a different mind-set than other programming aspects of VB.NET, getting that hands-on understanding is very helpful.

We will assume that the form is named frmMultiThreading. Since the functionality needed for multithreading appears in the System. Threading library, adding this library will allow *intelliSense* to guide with the syntax. Being an imported library, it must be imported before any other code is executed. Hence, it must be added before the Public class statement of the form. Let us add that first:

```
Imports System.Threading   ' Must be added before any other code

Public Class frmMultiThreading
    Inherits System.Windows.Forms.Form
```

The thread itself needs to be a method in a class other than the class (in this case, the class of our form) in which it is going to be started. Logically, this is necessary because the thread will be running independently of the class in which it was started. Accordingly, we will define a new class and within it a method that will be the thread:

```
Public Class SampleThreadClass
    Public Sub SampleThreadMethod()
        Console.WriteLine("I am a thread. I am alive!")
    End Sub
End Class
```

Note that the method, and not the class, is made into a thread. For now, the thread will just announce its existence. We will make it more complex once the basic mechanism of how to get multithreading to work is clear.

Now that the class and method for the thread are ready, we can start the thread from our form with a Button. Starting the thread requires three steps. First, shown in Step 1 in the code that follows, the class within which the method is declared needs to be instantiated. It is named myThreadClass in the example. With this done, and sequence of commands is important here, a new instance of ThreadStart can be declared. This is shown in Step 2. The new ThreadStart object must refer to a method within the class that was defined in Step 1. The **AddressOf** keyword is added automatically by *intelliSense*. Note that the method is within the instantiated class of Step 1. With that ready, a thread itself can at last be defined as a new instance of a thread object. That is Step 3. Now the thread can be started with the Start method. It is important to note that because `ThreadStart` can have no parameters, all threads must be subroutines with no parameters. Data cannot be passed back and forth to threads the way they can with subroutines and functions. Passing data requires other mechanisms. The steps are coded (with comments) as follows:

```
Private Sub btnThread1_Click(ByVal sender As System.Object, _
                             ByVal e As System.EventArgs) _
                      Handles btnThread1.Click

    ' Step 1:
    ' Instantiate the class within which the method
    ' that will be threaded resides.
    Dim myTheadClass As New SampleThreadClass()

    ' Step 2:
    ' Start a new thread with the method that will be
    ' threaded within the instance of the class created
    ' in this subroutine. Note that the method name is
    ' within the object declared in this subroutine.
    Dim myThreadMethod As New ThreadStart(AddressOf _
                             myTheadClass.SampleThreadMethod)

    ' Step3:
    ' With that ready, the new thread can be created
    ' applying to the method we just instantiated.
    Dim myThread As New Thread(myThreadMethod)

    ' Step4:
    ' Start the new thread
    myThread.Start()

End Sub
```

There is an important caveat here. The `Start` method, despite its implied functionality, does not actually start the thread. What the `Start` method does is indicate to the operating system that there is a new thread and that this new thread can be started whenever the operating system is ready. This is very different from activating methods that we saw in previous chapters. There, when a method was activated, it ran immediately. Here, on the other hand, when a thread is started, there will be a gap in time that is beyond the control of the programmer until the thread starts. That is because control is given to a thread by the operating system, rather than by the program that created it.

8.2.2 Running the Thread

VB.NET provides a special window called the `Thread` window to allow for better debugging of threaded applications. If we were to place a breakpoint on the `Console.WriteLine` command and run the application, then, when the application would stop on the breakpoint, we could track all the threads currently running (except for the garbage collection, which is run automatically by VB.NET). To enhance the demonstration, we will use the `Name` property of the thread to identify the threads. Just before the `myThread.Start()` command we will add a thread name in the `Name` property. The `Name` property gives the thread a name that will identify it. Without

FIGURE 8.1
The Thread window.

giving it a name, the thread's name will be <no name>, which a very inconvenient way to distinguish among many threads. In the following code example we will name the thread "Test Thread Number 1." As with other objects, the name of the Thread object should be a meaningful name.

```
myThread.Name = "Test Thread Number 1"
```

With this done anywhere in the application, the following property can be used to identify the name of the thread:

```
Console.WriteLine("I am " & Thread.CurrentThread.Name)
```

When the application stops at the breakpoint, the Thread window will look like Figure 8.1. The ID column is an internal number that the operating system gives the thread. The Name column is the programmer-assigned name of the task. This is where the name we just specified will appear. We will discuss the Priority and Suspend columns next.

8.2.3 Time Slicing and Thread Priority

In the example we just created, the functionality was deliberately oversimplified. The thread really does nothing that would require a thread. Typically, we create threads for a function that takes a long time to complete. For example, if the thread were to constantly display the time, as does the code

```
Public Sub SampleThreadMethod()
    Dim I As Integer
    For I = 1 To 100000
        Console.WriteLine("Time is " & Hour(Now) _
                          & ":" & Minute(Now) &":" _
                          & Second(Now))
    Next
End Sub
```

then it would be more in nature of what we would expect a thread to do—that is, a time-consuming operation running in the background parallel to the form itself, which in this case would be the main thread.

We could also set the `Priority` property of the thread to reflect the fact that it is a less important thread than the form itself:

```
mythread.Priority = ThreadPriority.Lowest
```

Thread priority specifies how important that thread is relative to the other threads. Recall that the CPU executes only one command at a time and therefore only runs one thread at a time. The impression that many threads are running in parallel to each other is created by the operating system by giving a bit of CPU processing time to each thread in turn. The operating system determines what thread gets how much time, based on this property. There are five levels of priority to choose from:

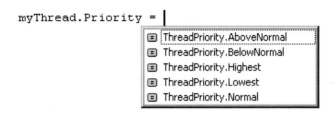

The operating system will distribute CPU time among the threads. This process is called *time slicing*. Without this process, a thread that does not want to surrender processing time by going to sleep (we will discuss this later) might continue running forever. In such a case, other threads might be *starved*. A starved thread is one that gets no processing time at all. The operating system prevents thread starvation by periodically taking away the processing from one thread and passing it to another based on the priority of each thread. This is done regardless of whether the thread agrees.

To demonstrate this process, we will add another thread to the code we just created (the new lines are shown in boldface):

```
Imports System.Threading   ' Must be added before any other code
Public Class frmMultiThreading

    Inherits System.Windows.Forms.Form
    Private Sub btnThread1_Click(ByVal sender As System.Object, _
                    ByVal e As System.EventArgs) _
                    Handles btnThread1.Click
        Dim myTheadClass As New SampleThreadClass()
        Dim myThreadMethod As New ThreadStart _
                (AddressOf myTheadClass.SampleThreadMethod)
        Dim myThreadMethod2 As New ThreadStart _
                (AddressOf myTheadClass.SampleThreadMethod2)
        Dim myThread As New Thread(myThreadMethod)
        Dim myThread2 As New Thread(myThreadMethod2)

        ' Start the new thread
        myThread.Name = "Test Thread Number 1"
        myThread.Priority = ThreadPriority.Normal
        myThread.Start()
```

```vb
            myThread2.Name = "Test Thread Number 2"
            myThread2.Priority = ThreadPriority.Highest
            myThread2.Start()
        End Sub

    Public Class SampleThreadClass
        Public Sub SampleThreadMethod()
            Dim I As Integer
            For I = 1 To 1000
                Console.WriteLine("Time is " & Hour(Now)_
                            & ":" & Minute(Now) &":" &_
                            Second(Now))
            Next
        End Sub
        Public Sub SampleThreadMethod2()
            Dim I As Integer
            For I = 1 To 1000
                Console.WriteLine("I is " & I)
            Next
        End Sub
    End Class
End Class
```

In the preceding code, a second thread is added and run parallel to the first one. The first thread runs a method that shows the time in a loop. The second thread runs a method that counts in a loop. Normally, based on the programming concepts we have learned up to now, we would expect each loop to run until its completion. But that is not what happens. Time slicing intervenes and, even though the logic of the loops is such that execution should continue inside a loop until it is completed, execution will stop in the middle of a loop and be passed to another thread until it is time for the first thread to get processing time. At that stage, processing will continue in the first thread from the point it stopped at as though nothing ever happened.

If we run the application, the Output window will show how the processing was split between the two threads:

```
Time is 15:49:44    Time is 15:49:44    I is 63            I is 84
Time is 15:49:44    Time is 15:49:44    I is 64            I is 85
Time is 15:49:44    Time is 15:49:44    Time is 15:49:45   I is 86
Time is 15:49:44    Time is 15:49:44    Time is 15:49:45   I is 88
Time is 15:49:44    Time is 15:49:44    Time is 15:49:45   I is 89
I is 1              Time is 15:49:44    Time is 15:49:45   I is 90
I is 2              Time is 15:49:44    Time is 15:49:45   I is 91
I is 3              Time is 15:49:44    Time is 15:49:45   I is 92
I is 4              Time is 15:49:44    Time is 15:49:45   I is 93
I is 5              Time is 15:49:44    Time is 15:49:45   I is 94
I is 6              Time is 15:49:44    Time is 15:49:45   I is 96
I is 7              Time is 15:49:44    Time is 15:49:45   Time is 15:49:45
I is 8              Time is 15:49:44    Time is 15:49:45   Time is 15:49:45
I is 9              Time is 15:49:44    Time is 15:49:45   Time is 15:49:45
```

```
I is 10           Time is 15:49:44    Time is 15:49:45    Time is 15:49:45
I is 11           Time is 15:49:44    Time is 15:49:45    Time is 15:49:45
I is 12           I is 33             Time is 15:49:45    Time is 15:49:45
I is 13           I is 34             Time is 15:49:45    Time is 15:49:45
I is 14           I is 35             Time is 15:49:45    Time is 15:49:45
I is 15           I is 36             Time is 15:49:45    Time is 15:49:45
I is 16           I is 37             Time is 15:49:45    Time is 15:49:45
I is 17           I is 38             Time is 15:49:45    Time is 15:49:45
I is 18           I is 39             Time is 15:49:45    Time is 15:49:45
I is 19           I is 40             Time is 15:49:45    Time is 15:49:45
I is 20           I is 41             Time is 15:49:45    Time is 15:49:45
I is 21           I is 42             Time is 15:49:45    Time is 15:49:45
I is 22           I is 43             Time is 15:49:45    Time is 15:49:45
I is 23           I is 44             I is 65             Time is 15:49:45
I is 24           I is 45             I is 66             Time is 15:49:45
I is 25           I is 46             I is 67             Time is 15:49:45
I is 26           I is 47             I is 68             Time is 15:49:45
I is 27           I is 48             I is 69             Time is 15:49:45
I is 28           I is 49             I is 70             Time is 15:49:45
I is 29           I is 50             I is 71             Time is 15:49:45
I is 30           I is 51             I is 72             Time is 15:49:45
I is 31           I is 52             I is 73             Time is 15:49:45
I is 32           I is 53             I is 74             Time is 15:49:45
Time is 15:49:44  I is 54             I is 75             Time is 15:49:45
Time is 15:49:44  I is 55             I is 76             I is 97
Time is 15:49:44  I is 56             I is 77             I is 98
Time is 15:49:44  I is 57             I is 78             I is 99
Time is 15:49:44  I is 58             I is 79             I is 100
Time is 15:49:44  I is 59             I is 80             I is 101
Time is 15:49:44  I is 60             I is 81             I is 102
Time is 15:49:44  I is 61             I is 82             I is 103
Time is 15:49:44  I is 62             I is 83
```

Changing the priority of any one of the threads will change the number of lines each of the threads displays in the Output window before losing control to the other thread.

8.2.4   Coordinating Threads

Giving priority to threads enables an overall distribution of average processing time among the threads. Occasionally, it is also necessary to actually stop a thread until another thread completes processing. In the preceding example, this may happen if the main thread, btnThread1_Click, must wait until a computation being run by thread 1 is completed. In such cases, the two threads are said to be *joined*. Making one thread wait for the other is done with the Join method. Note that what is happening is that the first thread is creating another, and then the first thread is waiting until the other completes execution. A thread can wait for another thread that it created. The following mechanism will not work with threads that it did not create:

```
myThread.Join()
```

Consequently, in the following sample code, when the main thread, btnThread1-_Click, gets to the Join command, it will wait until myThread finishes running:

```
Private Sub btnThread1_Click(ByVal sender As System.Object, _
                        ByVal e As System.EventArgs) _
                        Handles btnThread1.Click
    Dim myTheadClass As New SampleThreadClass()
    Dim myThreadMethod As New ThreadStart _
            (AddressOf myTheadClass.SampleThreadMethod)
    Dim myThread As New Thread(myThreadMethod)

    ' Start the new thread
    myThread.Name = "Test Thread Number 1"
    myThread.Start()

    ' Wait until the thread ends.
    myThread.Join()
End Sub
```

Alternatively, the Join method can be used to force the thread to wait either until the thread it created finishes or for a specific period of time, whichever is shorter. The parameter of the method in this case specifies how many milliseconds to wait:

```
' Wait until the thread ends or for two seconds
myThread.Join(2000)
```

8.2.5 Sleeping Threads

When a thread is waiting for another, it is said to be *blocked*. Another way of blocking a thread is forcing it to *sleep* for a given period number of milliseconds. In the following code example, thread 2 will not start running until thread 1 has run for 2 seconds, because the main thread that creates both thread 1 and thread 2 will sleep for 2 seconds after creating thread 1 and before creating thread 2:

```
' Start the new thread
myThread.Name = "Test Thread Number 1"
myThread.Priority = ThreadPriority.Normal
myThread.Start()

Thread.Sleep(2000)

myThread2.Name = "Test Thread Number 2"
myThread2.Priority = ThreadPriority.Highest
myThread2.Start()
```

Note that the sleep method belongs to the Thread class. It is not a method of a specific thread. Wherever it is written in the code, that thread will sleep for the designated period of time.

The output window will show this sleeping period very clearly, with the output from thread 1 appearing for more than 2 seconds before thread 2 starts printing its output. The lengthy period of time shows one of the inevitable problems with threading:

One can force when a thread will sleep, but it is up to the operating system to resume the sleeping thread, which may take longer than what the parameter says. The output will be as follows:

```
Time is 17:16:9  I is 23        Time is 17:16:9  I is 62                  I is 69
Time is 17:16:9  I is 24        Time is 17:16:9  I is 63                  I is 70
Time is 17:16:9  I is 25        Time is 17:16:9  I is 64                  I is 71
Time is 17:16:9  I is 26        I is 33          Time is 17:16:10  I is 72
Time is 17:16:9  I is 27        I is 34          Time is 17:16:10  I is 73
Time is 17:16:9  I is 28        I is 35          Time is 17:16:10  I is 74
Time is 17:16:9  I is 29        I is 36          Time is 17:16:10  I is 75
Time is 17:16:9  I is 30        I is 37          Time is 17:16:10  I is 76
Time is 17:16:9  I is 31        I is 38          Time is 17:16:10  I is 77
Time is 17:16:9  I is 32        I is 39          Time is 17:16:10  I is 78
I is 1           Time is 17:16:9  I is 40        Time is 17:16:10  I is 79
I is 2           Time is 17:16:9  I is 41        Time is 17:16:10  I is 80
I is 3           Time is 17:16:9  I is 42        Time is 17:16:10  I is 81
I is 4           Time is 17:16:9  I is 43        Time is 17:16:10  I is 82
I is 5           Time is 17:16:9  I is 44        Time is 17:16:10  I is 83
I is 6           Time is 17:16:9  I is 45        Time is 17:16:10  I is 84
I is 7           Time is 17:16:9  I is 46        Time is 17:16:10  I is 85
I is 8           Time is 17:16:9  I is 47        Time is 17:16:10  I is 86
I is 9           Time is 17:16:9  I is 48        Time is 17:16:10  I is 87
I is 10          Time is 17:16:9  I is 49        Time is 17:16:10  I is 88
I is 11          Time is 17:16:9  I is 50        Time is 17:16:10  I is 89
I is 12          Time is 17:16:9  I is 51        Time is 17:16:10  I is 90
I is 13          Time is 17:16:9  I is 52        Time is 17:16:10  I is 91
I is 14          Time is 17:16:9  I is 53        Time is 17:16:10  I is 92
I is 15          Time is 17:16:9  I is 54        Time is 17:16:10  I is 93
I is 16          Time is 17:16:9  I is 55        Time is 17:16:10  I is 94
I is 17          Time is 17:16:9  I is 56        Time is 17:16:10  I is 95
I is 18          Time is 17:16:9  I is 57        Time is 17:16:10  I is 96
I is 19          Time is 17:16:9  I is 58        I is 65
I is 20          Time is 17:16:9  I is 59        I is 66
I is 21          Time is 17:16:9  I is 60        I is 67
I is 22          Time is 17:16:9  I is 61        I is 68
```

When the Sleep method's parameter is zero, however, it does not mean sleep for zero milliseconds. Rather, in this case, it means relinquish the remainder of the time in the thread's time slot to the other threads—for example, changing the method of thread 2 in the preceding example so that the thread will relinquish all its remaining time in the time slot after it prints one line in the Output window (boldface code):

```
Public Sub SampleThreadMethod2()
    Dim I As Integer
    For I = 1 To 1000
        Console.WriteLine("I is " & I)
        Thread.Sleep(0)
    Next
End Sub
```

This change will result in output like this in the Output window:

```
Time is 18:14:11    Time is 18:14:11    Time is 18:14:11    Time is 18:14:12
Time is 18:14:11    Time is 18:14:11    Time is 18:14:11    Time is 18:14:12
Time is 18:14:11    Time is 18:14:11    Time is 18:14:11    Time is 18:14:12
I is 131            Time is 18:14:11    Time is 18:14:11    Time is 18:14:12
Time is 18:14:11    Time is 18:14:11    Time is 18:14:11    Time is 18:14:12
Time is 18:14:11    Time is 18:14:11    Time is 18:14:11    Time is 18:14:12
Time is 18:14:11    Time is 18:14:11    Time is 18:14:11    Time is 18:14:12
Time is 18:14:11    Time is 18:14:11    Time is 18:14:11    Time is 18:14:12
Time is 18:14:11    Time is 18:14:11    Time is 18:14:12    Time is 18:14:12
Time is 18:14:11    Time is 18:14:11    Time is 18:14:12    Time is 18:14:12
Time is 18:14:11    Time is 18:14:11    Time is 18:14:12    I is 135
Time is 18:14:11    Time is 18:14:11    Time is 18:14:12    Time is 18:14:12
Time is 18:14:11    Time is 18:14:11    Time is 18:14:12    Time is 18:14:12
Time is 18:14:11    Time is 18:14:11    Time is 18:14:12    Time is 18:14:12
Time is 18:14:11    Time is 18:14:11    I is 134            Time is 18:14:12
Time is 18:14:11    Time is 18:14:11    Time is 18:14:12    Time is 18:14:12
Time is 18:14:11    Time is 18:14:11    Time is 18:14:12    Time is 18:14:12
Time is 18:14:11    Time is 18:14:11    Time is 18:14:12    Time is 18:14:12
Time is 18:14:11    Time is 18:14:11    Time is 18:14:12    Time is 18:14:12
Time is 18:14:11    I is 133            Time is 18:14:12    Time is 18:14:12
Time is 18:14:11    Time is 18:14:11    Time is 18:14:12    Time is 18:14:12
Time is 18:14:11    Time is 18:14:11    Time is 18:14:12    Time is 18:14:12
Time is 18:14:11    Time is 18:14:11    Time is 18:14:12    Time is 18:14:12
Time is 18:14:11    Time is 18:14:11    Time is 18:14:12    Time is 18:14:12
Time is 18:14:11    Time is 18:14:11    Time is 18:14:12    Time is 18:14:12
Time is 18:14:11    Time is 18:14:11    Time is 18:14:12    I is 136
Time is 18:14:11    Time is 18:14:11    Time is 18:14:12    Time is 18:14:12
I is 132            Time is 18:14:11    Time is 18:14:12    Time is 18:14:12
Time is 18:14:11    Time is 18:14:11    Time is 18:14:12    Time is 18:14:12
Time is 18:14:11    Time is 18:14:11    Time is 18:14:12
Time is 18:14:11    Time is 18:14:11    Time is 18:14:12
Time is 18:14:11    Time is 18:14:11    Time is 18:14:12
```

Note that the change causes the thread to behave as though there is no loop at all. That is one of the peculiar aspects of programming with multi-threading.

Programming Note: The Sleep method can be used also in applications that do not apply multithreading to make a program stop for a designated period of time before it continues execution. Such a break can be useful when the user interface requires a delayed presentation of information.

The sleep method can also make the thread sleep forever, a kind of Sleeping Beauty syndrome. This is done when the Sleep parameter specifies timeout.infinite. And, just as with the Sleeping Beauty, there is an exception to that that can wake up the thread. That exception is called ThreadInterruptedException.[17] It may not be as romantic, and it may take longer to awaken the sleeping thread, because it is the operating system that must first notice that the thread is awake and then assign it CPU time, but it works. Here is an example of how this can be done: The thread method prints a line in the Output window and goes to sleep indefinitely, but it can catch an interrupt exception. The thread method is started as a thread in the Button1_Click subroutine and is then awoken with an interrupt. Note that when the thread method is awakened, it is awakened in the code within the Catch block:

```
Public Class SampleThreadClass
    Public Sub SampleThreadMethod3()
        Dim I As Integer
        Try
            Console.WriteLine("I am about to sleep " & _
                    Thread.CurrentThread.Name)
            Thread.Sleep(Timeout.Infinite)
        Catch WakeUp As ThreadInterruptedException
            Console.WriteLine("I am awake again " & _
                    Thread.CurrentThread.Name)
        End Try
    End Sub
End Class

Private Sub Button1_Click(ByVal sender As System.Object, _
                            ByVal e As System.EventArgs)_
                            Handles Button1.Click
    Dim myTheadClass As New SampleThreadClass()
    Dim myThreadMethod3 As New ThreadStart _
            (AddressOf myTheadClass.SampleThreadMethod3)
    Dim myThread3 As New Thread(myThreadMethod3)

    ' Start the new thread
    myThread3.Name = "Test Thread Number 3"
    myThread3.Start()
    Thread.Sleep(2000)
    myThread3.Interrupt()
End Sub
```

To summarize, the Sleep method has one of three parameters:

Thread.Sleep (n)	Suspend the thread for *n* milliseconds.
Thread.Sleep (0)	Suspend the thread until the next time slice.
Thread.Sleep (Timeout.Infinite)	Suspend the thread until it is awoken with an outside exception.

---

[17]An interrupt is an operating system intervention call that overrides everything else the computer is doing at that time. It is like a cellular phone going off in the middle of a discussion. Everybody stops what they are doing and pays attention to the ringing cellular phone and handles it. Only after the exception has been handled does the operating system return CPU time to the other threads.

8.2.6   Aborting a Thread

Once running, a thread can be aborted by the thread that started it. In the preceding code example, the Button1_Click subroutine, after starting the thread myThread3, can then abort it (i.e., force it to abort) with the Abort or the Suspend method:

```
myThread3.Name = "Test Thread Number 3"
myThread3.Start()
myThread3.Abort()
```

The Abort method kills the thread by throwing a ThreadAbortException. The thread cannot be resurrected after that. It is dead.

The Suspend method, on the other hand, just suspends the thread. When the thread is suspended it can be resumed with the Resume method. When the thread is suspended, the suspended number in the Threads window is increased to 1. The Resume method decreases the suspend number in the Threads window to 0, marking that the thread can run again. A nonsuspended thread that is resumed results in a runtime error. It is not recommended to use either Abort or Suspend because there is no guaranty that the thread will complete whatever it is doing correctly.

In the following code example, a new thread is started with one of the methods we built before:

```
Private Sub Button2_Click(ByVal sender As System.Object, _
                          ByVal e As System.EventArgs) _
                Handles Button2.Click

    Dim myTheadClass As New SampleThreadClass()
    Dim myThreadMethod As New ThreadStart(AddressOf _
            myTheadClass.SampleThreadMethod)
    Dim myThread4 As New Thread(myThreadMethod)
    ' Start the new thread
    myThread4.Name = "Test Thread Number 3"
    myThread4.Start()
```

After the Start method, the Threads window (Figure 8.2) will show that the thread is active and not suspended. (The third thread in the window is a left over from when a

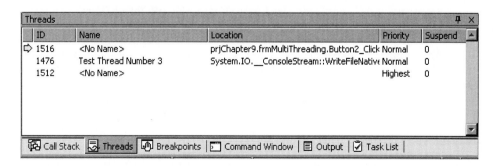

FIGURE 8.2
Thread window showing that Test Thread Number 3 is active.

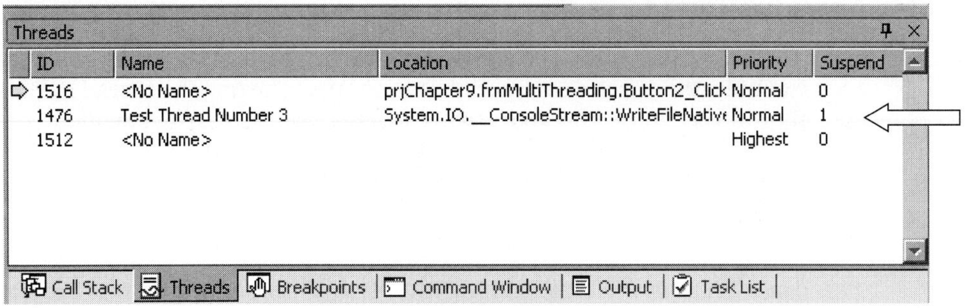

FIGURE 8.3
Thread Window Showing that Test Thread Number 3 is suspended.

previous thread was aborted with the `Abort` method. We did not restart VB.NET to show the danger of the `Abort` method.)

When the thread is then suspended, the `Threads` window will show a value greater than zero in the Suspend column (Figure 8.3):

```
myThread4.Suspend()
```

The thread will stay suspended until it is resumed:

```
    myThread4.Resume()
End Sub
```

Figure 8.4 summarizes these methods. The Father thread starts a Son thread, assigning it its priority. Both threads run parallel to each other at this stage. When the Father thread issues a `Join` command, the Father thread will go into a waiting mode until the Son finishes running. When the Son finishes running, the Father will resume. When the Father later on issues a `Sleep` command, the Father thread will be deactivated for the period of time in milliseconds specified in the `Sleep` command.

8.3   SHARING DATA AMONG THREADS AND SYNCHRONIZATION

The big issue with threads is *synchronizing* among many threads that handle shared data. Many of these issues are the same issues that a database management system (DBMS), such as Oracle or SQL Server, handles automatically when coordinating among transactions and will be discussed in detail in those chapters. Suffice it to say that two of the major problems involved are (1) overriding and ignoring another thread's changes in the shared data and (2) deadlocks. Whenever threads share data, these two issues should be a major concern and are a most likely source of the worst kind of bugs, the undetectable nondeterministic ones that change the data in manners that cannot be recreated easily because there are so many elements that need to interact with each other in just a certain manner for the bug to arise. For example, a bug that

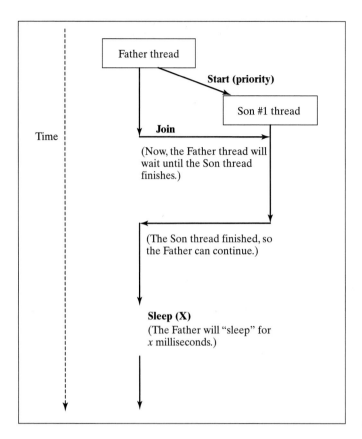

FIGURE 8.4
"Example of the `Start` `Join` and `Sleep` Methods."

is created when thread 1 overrides the data that thread 2 wrote without thread 2 being aware of it, is the kind of bug that is very hard to recreate because recreating it requires running the two thread again and at exactly the same time sequence. Of course, when the bug is created by the interaction of three of more threads, which is more likely, recreating the exact scenario may be practically impossible. Think of tracking and recreating the sequence of events that leads to a bug when thread 1 overrides the data changes made by thread 2 while thread 2 is overriding the changes made to the data by thread 3, which itself is overriding other changes made to the data by thread 2 and by thread 1, etc. That is not a nice clean bug, by any account.

These synchronization problems are made worse by the inability of threaded methods to handle parameters and return values. *A threaded method must be a subroutine with no parameters.* As a result, data can be passed and can be shared with a threaded method only through other means, such as `Public` variables in `Modules`. This places the onus of synchronization fully on the programmer.

A DBMS handles all that tracking of independent threads, which are named *transactions* in a database world, automatically making all the necessary coordination totally transparent to the transactions involved. This in itself is a good reason to use a

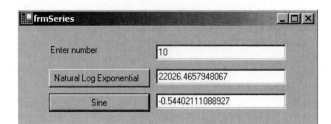

FIGURE 8.5
Demonstrating multithreading.

DBMS when there is a need to coordinate threads, rather than go through the very complex synchronization and deadlock handling that will be discussed in this part of the chapter.

To illustrate how complex these synchronization problems can be, the next example demonstrates a small part of the problem of coordinating threads. The example also gives a hands-on feeling of how threading can help make user interfaces better. Suppose that a form has two Buttons and three textboxes. The first Button computes the natural logarithm exponent of a number given in the first textbox and presents the solution in the second textbox. The second Button computes the sine of the number in the first textbox and presents the solution in the third textbox. Both the natural logarithm exponent and the sine of a number are computed from an infinite series; therefore, once started, both algorithms should continue forever.[18] The longer the series is run, the more accurate the solution will be. We will build this application in the lab later in the chapter. The application will look like Figure 8.5.

Because both series involve an awfully long calculation, actually an endless one, it is inconceivable that the form should get "stuck" until the calculation is completed. What should happen is that as each part of the mathematical function is calculated, the new estimate of the function should be displayed in the form. In other words, two threads should be running in the background calculating and updating the results constantly, but without locking the form. Note that this is precisely the type of functionality that justifies using threads, as we discussed earlier. Since the two generated values are independent of each other, threading should pose no synchronization problem.

But we can create an artificial synchronization problem. Note that both expressions require calculating the factorial of a number. Correctly, we should write the code so that each activation of the factorial function will be independent of any other concurrent activation. Note that myExp does not return a value. What it does is place the calculated expression in a Public variable named dblCalcExp. The input parameter to the subroutine, intInput, is also a Public variable. That is necessary because a

---

[18]A quick reminder:
The natural logarithm exponent of x is exp $(x) = 1 + x + x^2/2! + x^3/3! + \cdots$.
The Sine of x is $\mathrm{Sin}(x) = x - x^3/x! + x^5/5! - x^7/7! \ldots$, where $a!$ is the factorial of a.

threaded method cannot receive or return values. Values are shared through `Public` variables:

```
Public Sub myExp()
    Dim I As Integer
    For I = 0 To 100
        dblCalcExp = dblCalcExp + _
                intInput ^ I / myFactCopy.myFact(I)
    Next
End Sub

Public Function myFact(ByVal X As Integer) As Double
    Dim I As Integer
    Dim dblCalc As Double = 1

    For I = 1 To X
        dblCalc = dblCalc * I
    Next
    Return (dblCalc)
End Function
```

But then we can artificially create a synchronization problem by making `dblCalc` a `Public` variable in the class in which the function `myFact` resides. This is a deliberately simple problem; in reality, synchronization problems are much more complex. Nonetheless, the same principle holds: uncoordinated access to shared data causes bugs. The following code is illustrative:

```
Module Module1
    Public intInput As Integer
    Public dblCalc As Double
    Public Class myFunctions
        Public Function myFact(ByVal X As Integer) As Double
            Dim I As Integer
            dblCalc = 1
            For I = 1 To X
                dblCalc = dblCalc * I

            ' And to make concurrency problems more evident
            ' we will force the thread to sleep so that the
            ' probability of a collision of threads is higher.
                Thread.Sleep(2000)
            Next
            Return (dblCalc)
        End Function
    End Class
End Module
```

Now we have a problem. The two threads, one calculating the exponent and the other the sine, use the same factorial function. This alone would not be a problem if the data were private. Functions with private data are *threadable*, meaning that the same function can be activated from many threads concurrently without causing any problem. But that is not the case, once we make the data public. As it stands, if two threads were to activate the function concurrently, there would be an unavoidable concurrency problem, because each would override the value that the other thread placed and is referencing in dblCalc. Actually, in the code, we are forcing the function to sleep many times while the factorial is being calculated, thus increasing the likelihood of one thread interfering with the other.

8.3.1 Synchronization

What needs to be done to avoid synchronization errors is to force VB.NET to let each thread complete the loop in the factorial function without any interruptions. This property of having a section of code run with a guarantee that no interruptions will occur while it is being executed is called *atomicity*. Atomicity in VB.NET is forced with the SyncLock statement. Everything within the SyncLock block is guaranteed to run without interruptions. It is imperative to be careful with this statement, because too many locks, or locks on too large a section of code, can deteriorate the performance of the application.

> **Programming Note:** A word of caution: If the code within a SyncLock is forced to sleep, then the block will nonetheless remain locked, which can make the entire application "freeze."

The SyncLock block locks a whole object; it cannot be used to lock a single variable. Since synchronization cannot be forced on a variable, but only on an object within the current method, some modifications to the code are needed. First, a method-specific copy of the factorial function, named myFactCopy, is created. It is this object that is then locked with the SyncLock statement. The Sleep command is retained in the example to force the method to run slow enough that, without synchronization, there would be bugs caused by shared data:

```
Public Sub myExp()
    Dim I As Integer
    Dim myFactCopy As New myFunctions()
    SyncLock (myFactCopy)
        For I = 0 To 100
            dblCalcExp = dblCalcExp + _
                intInput ^ I / myFactCopy.myFact(I)
            Thread.Sleep(2000)
        Next
    End SyncLock
End Sub
```

Of course, the same must be done for all the subroutines that use that shared data:

```
Public Sub mySine()
    Dim I As Integer
    Dim myFactCopy As New myFunctions()
```

```
SyncLock (myFactCopy)
    For I = 0 To 100
        dblCalcExp = dblCalcExp + _
            (-1) ^ (I + 1) * intInput ^ (I * 2 - 1) _
            / myFact(I * 2 - 1)
        Thread.Sleep(2000)
    Next
End SyncLock
End Sub
```

This is all that is needed. Now all the code within the block is atomic: It will run without interruptions. The latter is necessary because all the threads accessing the shared data must lock the same object for SyncLock to work. Thus,

```
SyncLock (Me)
```

would not provide a good solution because the shared data may still be accessed through other methods.

8.3.2   Deadlocks

The almost inevitable result of synchronization is the possibility of the creation of deadlocks. A deadlock is created when two or more threads are waiting indefinitely for each other, but none can move to release the resource the other thread is waiting for because they themselves are waiting. For example, imagine that thread 1 is currently holding a lock on object A and is requesting another lock on object B. At the same time, thread 2 is already holding object B and is requesting another lock on object A. Thread 1 has no choice but to wait until thread 2 finishes, because it cannot get a lock on object B as long as thread 2 has a lock on it. The trouble is that thread 1 will have to wait indefinitely, because thread 2 cannot release its lock on object B. To do so, thread 2 must finish running. But, thread 2 must wait until thread 1, which is itself waiting, finishes because thread 2 cannot get a lock on object A as long as thread 1 has a lock on it.

Such a case may happen when thread 1 is attempting to copy data from file 1 to file 2, while thread 2 is attempting to copy data from file 2 to file 1. It is imperative that both files be locked during this process, or else there will be no synchronization and the shared data (i.e., the files) will get corrupted. In such a case, the following sequence of events will lead to a deadlock: Thread 1 issues a lock on file 1. But before it has time to issue a lock on file 2, thread 2 issues a lock on file 2. Now each thread holds one of the resources and is waiting for the other. Thread 1 holds file 1 and is waiting for thread 2 to release file 2. Thread 2 holds file 2 and is waiting for thread 1 to release file 1. But thread 1 is going to wait forever because thread 2 cannot move; it is waiting for thread 1. So thread 2 will also wait forever because thread 1 is not moving.

Of course, deadlocks can occur when there are more than just two threads involved. But it is the same principle over again. A thread is holding a needed resource that is blocking another thread, but the first thread cannot release its resource because it is waiting for the other thread to release its resource, which the other thread cannot do because it is waiting for the first thread to release its resource.

TABLE 8.1 How thread status changes as a result of multithreading methods.

Another Thread Calls on This Thread	Resulting Status in This Thread
`Thread.Start`	Unchanged (until this thread responds)
`Thread.Sleep`	`WaitSleepJoin`
`Thread.Suspend`	`SuspendRequested`
`Thread.Resume`	`Running`
`Thread.Interrupt`	`Running`
`Thread.Abort`	`AbortRequested`
This Thread	
Responds to the `Thread.Start` and starts running.	`Running`
Calls `Monitor.Wait` on another object.	`WaitSleepJoin`
Calls `Thread.Join` on another thread.	`WaitSleepJoin`
Responds to a `Thread.Suspend` request.	`Suspended`
Responds to a `Thread.Abort`.	`Aborted`

There is no way to resolve a deadlock from within any of the threads involved. Once a thread is waiting, it is stuck. It cannot drive in reverse, as a matter of speech, and release its locks. An outside thread must do so. That is not easy, because any changes made to shared data must be undone correctly first. A DBMS will handle that. Doing it manually is anything but recommended.

8.4 STATES OF A THREAD

A thread can be in one of several states. The property `ThreadState` specifies the state of the thread. When a thread is created, it is in a state called `Unstarted`. At this stage, another thread must start it with the `Start` method so that it can run. Until the thread responds, its state remains `Unstarted`. Once it responds, its state changes to `Running`. At this stage, the status of the thread can keep on changing, depending on what actions other threads take about it and how it responds. Table 8.1 summarizes these statuses.

LAB 8: EXERCISING MULTITHREADING

Lab Objectives:
Exercise multithreading

Application Overview

This lab contains a form that calculates the natural logarithm exponent and the sine of a number that is entered in a textbox. Since the natural logarithm exponent and the sine are both the result of an infinite series, they are calculated in the background with

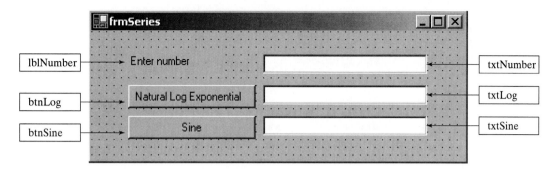

FIGURE 8.6
Lab 8.

threads and are updated on the form on a regular basis without having the form locked indefinitely while the calculation is taking place.

Part 1: Build the Form

Add a new project and solution, and name them **prjChapter8**, making the project handle a Windows Form. Name the form **frmSeries**. Add the Buttons and textboxes as shown in Figure 8.6. Objects starting with "btn" are Buttons, and those starting with "txt" are textboxes. Write the appropriate string in the text properties of each object to correspond to the figure.

Part 2.1: Adding the Code for the Threaded Methods

The threaded methods will appear in a separate module because they are not part of the internal functionality of the form itself. Add a new module to the project. (Point to the project in the Solution Explorer, then click the right mouse button on Add, and in the pop-up menu that will open, click Add Module.) In the module, add the following code, with three Public variables at the top of the code that will be used to pass values to and from the form:

```
Imports System.Threading

Module Module1
    Public intInput As Integer
    Public dblCalcExp As Double
    Public dblCalcSine As Double

    Dim dblCalc As Double


    Public Class myFunctions

        Public Sub myExp()
            Dim I As Integer
            Dim myFactCopy As New myFunctions()
            SyncLock (myFactCopy)
                For I = 0 To 100
                    dblCalcExp = dblCalcExp + _
```

```
                              intInput ^ I / myFactCopy.myFact(I)
                        Thread.Sleep(2000)
                  Next
            End SyncLock
      End Sub

      Public Sub mySine()
            Dim I As Integer
            Dim myFactCopy As New myFunctions()
            SyncLock (myFactCopy)
                  For I = 1 To 100
                        dblCalcSine = dblCalcSine + (-1) ^ (I + 1) _
                              * intInput ^ (I * 2 - 1) / _
                              myFactCopy.myFact(I * 2 - 1)
                        Thread.Sleep(2000)
                  Next
            End SyncLock
      End Sub

      Public Function myFact(ByVal X As Integer) As Double
            Dim I As Integer
            dblCalc = 1
            For I = 1 To X
                  dblCalc = dblCalc * I
            Next
            Return (dblCalc)
      End Function
   End Class

End Module
```

Part 2.2: Adding the Code for the Form

The two Buttons will create threads of the methods in the class described in Part 2.1. The values from the module are copied automatically onto the form from the module with the help of a timer. Note the Imports command and where it appears in the code:

```
Imports System.Threading

Public Class frmSeries
Inherits System.Windows.Forms.Form

      Private Sub btnLog_Click(ByVal sender As System.Object, _
                        ByVal e As System.EventArgs) _
                        Handles btnLog.Click

            Dim myTheadClass As New myFunctions()
            Dim myThreadMethod As New ThreadStart _
                        (AddressOf myTheadClass.myExp)
            Dim myThread As New Thread(myThreadMethod)

            ' Start the new thread
```

```
        If IsNumeric(txtNumber.Text) And Int(txtNumber.Text) > 0 Then
            intInput = Int(txtNumber.Text)
        End If

        myThread.Name = "Exp(X)"
        myThread.Start()
        tmrSeries.Enabled = True

    End Sub

    Private Sub btnSine_Click(ByVal sender As System.Object, _
                              ByVal e As System.EventArgs) _
                              Handles btnSine.Click

        Dim myTheadClass As New myFunctions()
        Dim myThreadMethod As New ThreadStart _
                    (AddressOf myTheadClass.mySine)
        Dim myThread As New Thread(myThreadMethod)

        ' Start the new thread
        myThread.Name = "sin(X)"
        myThread.Start()
    End Sub

    Private Sub tmrSeries_Tick(ByVal sender As System.Object, _
                               ByVal e As System.EventArgs) _
                               Handles tmrSeries.Tick
        txtLog.Text = dblCalcExp
        txtSine.Text = dblCalcSine
    End Sub

End Class
```

SUGGESTED HOME ASSIGNMENT

Build a new form that will generate a counter and display it in a textbox. The counter should wake up every 2 seconds and increment itself by 1. Do this with a threaded method. Do not do this with a timer control. The value from the counter should be displayed in a textbox. At the same time, the form should constantly display the current time. Displaying the time should be handled with a separate threaded method that will wake up every half second to update the time shown on the form. The time should be displayed in a second textbox. Both threaded methods should be turned on and off with a click of a Button (in another part of the form). The latter part of the exercise requires using a shared variable that will indicate to the threaded methods whether to continue execution or to return their time slice with Sleep (0). Do not use Suspend.

TEST YOURSELF

1. What is multithreading? How does it differ from multitasking?
2. Give three examples of multitasking in common applications that you use on a regular basis.
3. When is it unwise to apply multitasking?
4. Explain the sequence of commands that is necessary to get a thread started.

5. What does the Start method do?
6. What is *time slicing*? Why is it needed?
7. How can a thread be starved?
8. What is Join? When is it used?
9. What will Thread.Sleep (0) do?
10. What does Resume do?
11. Discuss the uses of Sleep.
12. Why is shared data a problem with threads?
13. What is a deadlock?
14. What is *synchronization*?
15. How can *synchronization* create deadlocks?
16. How does *synchronization* solve the shared data problem?
17. What is *atomicity*? Where is it needed? Why does it help?
18. What is SyncLock? What is its purpose?
19. How can parameters be passed to a threaded method?
20. What does the following command do?

    SyncLock (myFactCopy)

C H A P T E R   9

Overview of Database Programming

CHAPTER OBJECTIVES

After completing this chapter, students should

1. Possess a knowledge of database concepts
2. Be able to apply database concepts to how VB.NET accesses a database
3. Understand how to connect a database to VB.NET
   - Through SQL Server
   - Through Access
4. Discuss the details of the `Connection` class
5. Be able to apply the Data Adapter classes to fill Data Sets and, through them, Data Controls

9.1   AIMS OF CHAPTER

This chapter is an overview of database concepts and how databases are handled in VB.NET. It also deals with accessing a database through dedicated controls. The next chapters will delve into specific parts of the .NET framework that handles database access, based on the overview given in this chapter.

The first part of the chapter discusses the essentials of database systems that are necessary to understand how ADO.NET connects to them and how in later chapters the `DataSet` object applies them. The second part of the chapter demonstrates connecting databases to VB.NET, discusses database access through the data controls, and explains the overall structure of ADO.NET. This is done while discussing the `Connection` class.

The lab at the end of the chapter demonstrates data controls.

9.2   DATABASES

A database management system (DBMS), sometimes called a database engine, is a software package that manages, controls, and coordinates data. A single DBMS typically handles many databases, each database being a set of logically related data structures and their data. In a relational DBMS, such as Access, Oracle, or SQL Server, a database is a set of logically related tables, such as tables dealing with "Friends," "Addresses," and "Pets."

The defining attribute of a DBMS is that the data it manages are totally hidden from the application programs and any access to the data and to the data definition is done only through the DBMS and its predefined interface. Because the data in a DBMS are kept separate from the application programs, the DBMS can control and coordinate the application programs' access to the data. In relational databases, discussed next, this interface is the Structured Query Language, or as it is better known, SQL (pronounced "see-qual").

There are many advantages to using a DBMS in comparison with the nondatabase files. In nondatabase files, each topic is kept in a separate file, but without cross-referencing and without coordinated access. Consequently, when data are added or changed, the application program must itself check that the new data do not contradict existing data ("data integrity" in database terminology). For example, if a client's address has changed, the new address will have to be updated in all the files that contain it. If the address is not changed accordingly, this will result in an "update anomaly," whereby the data in one file contain one address and the data in another file contain a contradicting second address. A DBMS can overcome such problems by defining Referential Integrity Constraints, discussed later. Another problem with nondatabase files is that the application program can access the data directly, without a coordinating mechanism. As a result, one program can erroneously erase what another application program is doing. A DBMS can overcome such problems through a Concurrency Control Mechanism (Figure 9.1) that regulates and coordinates application program manipulation of the data.

Other major limitations in the nondatabase files are the need to keep copies of the same data, such as address, in more than one file, because of a lack of a central repository (data dictionary) that specifies what data are kept where and in what format and because of a lack of data independence. As a rule, a DBMS provides both a data repository and data independence. Data independence means that if the data structure of a table changes (which would occur, for instance, when a field that was an Integer data type became a Double data type or when a new field is added to a table) or if an index is added or dropped, then the application programs referencing the changed table or index do not need to be changed or recompiled, unless they directly access the data that have been changed and must access the data in their new format. These advantages of using a DBMS, and many others, are the direct result of allowing the application programs access to the data only through a controlled interface, as is diagrammatically shown in Figure 9.2.

9.2.1   Tables, Tuples (rows), and Attributes (columns)

DBMS's are classified by the way they present the data. The first-generation DBMS's, such as IMS/DB and IDMS, were navigational databases; they presented

DBMS

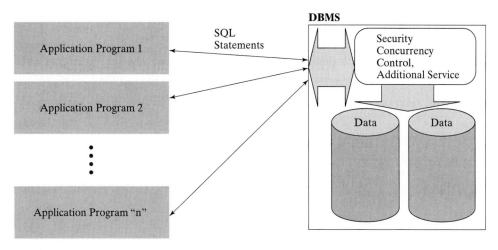

FIGURE 9.1
Coordinating and managing data access through the SQL interface.

Relation/Table

Column/Attribute

Friends : Table

	ID	FirstName	LastName	Date of Birth	Salary	Spouse	Golf	Baseball	Tennis	Gender	Telephone	CarType
+	1	Mickey	Bruce	1/1/1920	$790,000	Mo	✓	✓	☐	Male	(111) cal-lme1	Minivan
+	2	Mo	Bruce	1/2/1925	$800,000	Mickey	☐	☐	✓	Female		Minivan
+	3	Kent	Bruce	4/4/1938	$70,000		☐	☐	☐	Androgynous	(222) 333-3333	Minivan
+	4	Fred	Foley	5/5/1990	$70,000	Wilma	✓	✓	✓	Male	(555) 999-8888	Motorcycle
+	5	Barney	Ruben	8/8/1988	$70,000	Betty	✓	☐	☐	Male	(444) 444-4444	Snow Plow
+	6	Betty	Ruben	9/9/1899	$70,000	Barney	☐	☐	✓	Female	(444) 444-4444	Snow Plow
+	7	Pam	Foley	8/8/1877	$70,000		☐	☐	☐	Female		Motorcycle
+	8	Bill	Ruben	8/8/1878	$70,000		☐	☐	☐	Male		4WD
+	9	Al	Duke	7/7/1888	$70,000		☐	☐	☐	Male		Motorcycle
+	10	George	Duke	1/1/1911	$70,000	Jane	☐	☐	☐	Male		Motorcycle
+	11	Julia	Duke	1/2/1912	$70,000	George	☐	☐	☐	Male		4WD
+	12	Judy	Duke	1/3/1212	$70,000		☐	☐	☐	Male		4WD
+	13	Estel	Duke	1/4/1444	$70,000		☐	☐	☐	Male		Motorcycle
+	14	Brit	Crow	5/5/1955	$70,000		☐	☐	☐	Androgynous		Minivan
+	15	Rossanne	Duke	6/6/1966	$70,000		☐	☐	☐	Female		4WD
+	16	Sammy	Man	5/5/1955	$70,000	Sam	☐	☐	☐	Male		4WD
+	17	Sam	Man	6/6/1988	$780,000	Sammy	☐	☐	☐	Female		4WD
+	18	Tom	Lion	8/8/1955	$70,000		✓	☐	☐	Male		Snow Plow
+	19	Charles	Lion	9/9/1956	$70,000		✓	☐	☐	Male		Motorcycle
+	20	Paul	Crow	4/4/1944	$70,000		☐	☐	☐	Male		Minivan
+	21	Tim	Crow		$70,000		☐	☐	☐	Male		Minivan
+	22	Tom	Crow		$70,000		☐	☐	☐	Male		Minivan
+	23	Wilma	Foley	4/4/1956	$70,000	Fred	☐	☐	☐	Female		Motorcycle
*	(imber)				$70,000							

Tuple/Row

Item

FIGURE 9.2
The table of Friends as shown in Access.

data in a hierarchy or in a network structure, respectively, using pointers to connect the records. This was not a very convenient way to handle data. In 1980, the first relational database was created at IBM, practically replacing the first-generation DBMS. All relational databases trace their ancestry to this first relational DBMS, named "System R" after the mathematical relational theory it was based on.

In relational databases, the data are presented in the form of interrelated `Tables`, although the data may not be actually stored in that format (as is the case with Access). In database terminology, a table is also known as a `Relation` (not to be mixed up with a `Relationship`, which will be discussed later). Each table is a collection of data on a particular subject, much as each sheet in a spreadsheet deals with a particular subject. Also like a spreadsheet, each table is made of rows and columns. Each row, called a `Tuple` in database terminology, represents one instance of the subject the table deals with. Each column, called an `Attribute` in database terminology, contains one data element about the particular subject. In the sample Friends.mdb ("mdb" is the suffix used to identify Access databases) Access database that comes with the CD, for example, the "Friends" table, Figure 9.2, contains data about friends. The data in the table are organized in rows, one for each friend, and columns, one for each data item about each friend. Presenting the data in the form of interrelated tables is one of the major advantages of a relational database. Tables are the most intuitive and easiest way to view data dealing with text, numbers, and dates.

In order to start Access, click on the 📋 icon to start Access 2002. Once in Access, in order to open a table, make sure that in the Database Window (the window Access starts with) the current object is set to Tables, and then double-click on the Friends table or click once and then click on the Open icon. Doing so will open a datasheet view of the table. The datasheet view is shown in Figure 9.3. The data in the datasheet have been sorted according to "ID" (by clicking on the "ID" column and then on the 📊 icon to sort it in ascending order).

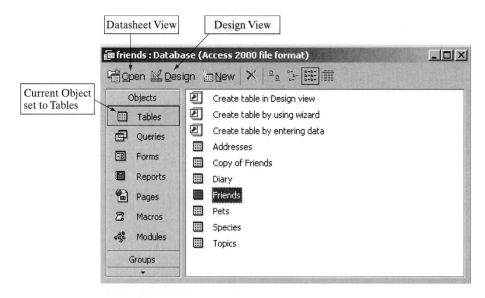

FIGURE 9.3
The Database window in Access showing the Friends database.

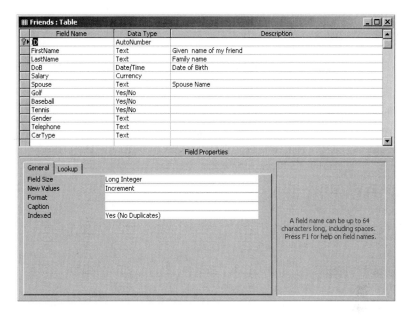

FIGURE 9.4
The Design View window in Access showing the schema (data structure) of the
Friends table with details of the ID data item.

The actual structure of the table, the fields it contains, and the data type and other
properties of each field are shown in Access by clicking on the Design View icon
(See Figure 9.4.) The design of the table supports all the data types that Visual Basic
supports. In addition, Access supports many other properties, such as an initial value,
masks, and validation rules. We will not deal with these topics in this book.

9.2.2 Example of Tables, Tuples (rows) and Attributes (columns)

Let's look at the table of Friends and add a column to it that will contain the friend's
primary email address. The email address will be another column in the table that is
another attribute of a friend. Adding the column requires being in the Design mode,
as in the diagram above. First add a row in the window, as shown below with the
arrow. Make its name "email" and its Data Type a Text. Text is equivalent to a String
data type in VB.NET. You can also add a Description as a comment. The tab below
where it says General will allow us to specify more details about the data type. We will
ignore those.

Saving the changes will add that column to the table.

9.2.3 Indexes and Keys

Relational DBMS's also support Indexes. An index provides access to rows in a table
based on a Key that is composed of one or more columns. A database index, much like
an index in an encyclopedia, is a separate file that enables faster retrieval of data. And,

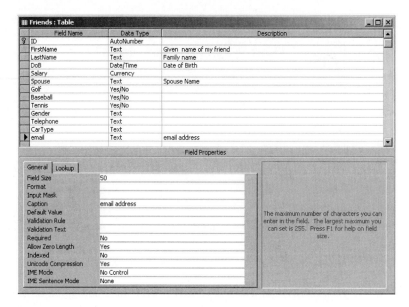

FIGURE 9.5
The Design View window in Access showing the schema (data structure) of the
Friends table with details of the email data item.

ID	FirstName	LastName	Date of Birth	Salary	Spouse	Golf	Baseball	Tennis	Gender	Telephone	CarType	email address
1	Mickey	Bruce	1/1/1920	$790,000	Mo	☑	☑	☐	Male	(111) cal-lme1	Minivan	
2	Mo	Bruce	1/2/1925	$800,000	Mickey	☐	☐	☑	Female		Minivan	
3	Kent	Bruce	4/4/1938	$70,000		☐	☐	☐	Androgynous	(222) 333-3333	Minivan	
4	Fred	Foley	5/5/1990	$70,000	Wilma	☑	☑	☑	Male	(555) 999-8888	Motorcycle	
5	Barney	Ruben	8/6/1988	$70,000	Betty	☑	☐	☐	Male	(444) 444-4444	Snow Plow	
6	Betty	Ruben	9/9/1899	$70,000	Barney	☐	☐	☑	Female	(444) 444-4444	Snow Plow	
7	Pam	Foley	8/8/1877	$70,000		☐	☐	☐	Female		Motorcycle	
8	Bill	Ruben	8/8/1878	$70,000		☐	☐	☐	Male		4WD	
9	Al	Duke	7/7/1888	$70,000		☐	☐	☐	Male		Motorcycle	
10	George	Duke	1/1/1911	$70,000	Jane	☐	☐	☐	Male		Motorcycle	
11	Julia	Duke	1/2/1912	$70,000	George	☐	☐	☐	Male		4WD	
12	Judy	Duke	1/3/1212	$70,000		☐	☐	☐	Male		4WD	
13	Estel	Duke	1/4/1444	$70,000		☐	☐	☐	Male		Motorcycle	
14	Brit	Crow	5/5/1955	$70,000		☐	☐	☐	Androgynous		Minivan	
15	Rossanne	Duke	6/6/1966	$70,000		☐	☐	☐	Female		4WD	
16	Sammy	Man	5/5/1955	$70,000	Sam	☐	☐	☐	Male		4WD	
17	Sam	Man	6/6/1988	$780,000	Sammy	☐	☐	☐	Female		4WD	
18	Tom	Lion	8/8/1955	$70,000		☑	☐	☐	Male		Snow Plow	
19	Charles	Lion	9/9/1956	$70,000		☑	☐	☐	Male		Motorcycle	
20	Paul	Crow	4/4/1944	$70,000		☐	☐	☐	Male		Minivan	
21	Tim	Crow		$70,000		☐	☐	☐	Male		Minivan	
22	Tom	Crow		$70,000		☐	☐	☐	Male		Minivan	
23	Wilma	Foley	4/4/1956	$70,000	Fred	☐	☐	☐	Female		Motorcycle	

Record: 1 of 23

FIGURE 9.6
The Datasheet View of the Friends table reflecting the updated schema in Access.

just as in an encyclopedia, there can be many indexes on each table. Also, each index can be made out of many fields (columns), such as, in the case of an encyclopedia, last-name, first-name and article-title. In addition, in a DBMS, an index can, although it need not be, also be used to ensure uniqueness of values, such as not allowing the same Friend ID to appear more than once in the "Friends" table. The management and use of indexes, but not their definition, is handled automatically by the DBMS. The application programs have no access to the indexes and cannot force the DBMS to decide when and if to use an index.

When the key (1) is unique (i.e., no two rows in the table have the same key), (2) is minimal (i.e., no field can be taken out of the key and still have it remain unique), and (3) cannot contain Null values, the index is said to be a Candidate Key. For example, an index of nationality and passport-number on a table of travelers is likely to be a Candidate Key, because no two travelers (rows in the table) will have the same combination of nationality and passport-number, while neither nationality nor passport-number alone will provide a unique key.

There can be many Candidate Keys in a table. One of these is chosen as the Primary Key, at which stage all the other Candidate Keys are called Alternate Keys. There can be only one primary key in a table. The Primary Key is marked in Access and in SQL Server with a special key icon, ▧ . Apart from performance considerations where in some DBMS's the Primary Key is faster because the data in the table are sorted in the order of the Primary Key, a Primary Key and an Alternate Key behave the same. The Indexes window in Access can be opened when you are in the Design window by clicking the indexes icon, ▧ . In Figure 9.7, for example, the "PrimaryKey" index is the ID. This index is unique. There are four more indexes. The DoB index indexes the date of birth; the Given Name index indexes the first name and within it the last name. The Last Name index indexes the last name and within it the first name, and the email index indexes the email addresses.

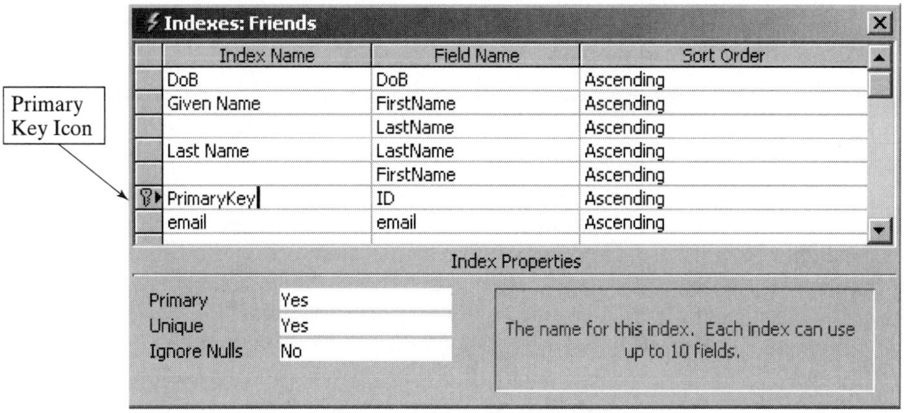

FIGURE 9.7
The Indexes window of the Friends table in Access.

Poets

First Name	Last Name	Baseball team (**FK**)
William	Kethe	Braves
Lord	Byron	Phillies
Charles	Dickens	Tigers
Michael	Drayton	Null
James	Shirley	Null
John	Dryden	Braves
John	Milton	Pilots

Teams (Primary Table)

Baseball team	City
Braves	Atlanta
Phillies	Philadelphia
Mets	New York
Indians	Cleveland
Tigers	Detroit
Yankees	New York
Pilots	Seattle

Figure 9.8
Example of a Foreign Key (FK).

9.2.4 Relationships

An additional use of indexes is to allow the definition of `Foreign Keys`. A Foreign Key is a value of one or more columns in one table that must exist in another table (known as the `Primary Table`) or be null. In Figure 9.8, the combination of "Last Name" and "First Name" is the `Primary Key` of the "Poets" table, while "Baseball team" is the `Primary Key` of the "Teams" table. The `Primary Keys` are marked, as customary, with an underline. In order to guarantee that each "Baseball team" in "Poets" exists as a "Baseball team" in "Teams," "Baseball team" in "Poets" should be defined as a `Foreign Key` on "Baseball team" in "Teams." In that way, if a baseball team is specified in the table of "Poets," the DBMS will check that the entered value indeed exists in the "Teams" table before allowing the change. A Foreign Key need not be unique; often it has double entries in order to allow for a one-to-many relationship.

> **Programming Note:** A Foreign Key can be used in association with a Primary Key or any other unique index.

In the Friends database, there are many Foreign Keys. You can see these in the Relationship window as lines connecting the tables. In the example in Figure 9.9 we see the Foreign Key relationship between Pets and Species, where a Species in the table of Pets is a Foreign Key on the Species in the table of Species. This means that no pet can have a species that is not already defined in the table of Species.

The `Foreign Keys` define the `Referential Integrity` constraints among the tables of a database. There are several types of referential integrity constraints:

1. *Nonenforced*: The Foreign Key relationship is defined, but not enforced.
2. *Enforced*: The Foreign Key relationship is defined and enforced. No value can be added or changed in the Foreign Key if the new value does not already exist in the primary (referenced) table. Likewise, a value cannot be deleted or changed in the primary table if it exists in the Foreign Key. Referential integrity is enforced by checking the box where it says Enforce Referential Integrity. When enforced, as in Figure 9.9, no pet can have a species value that is

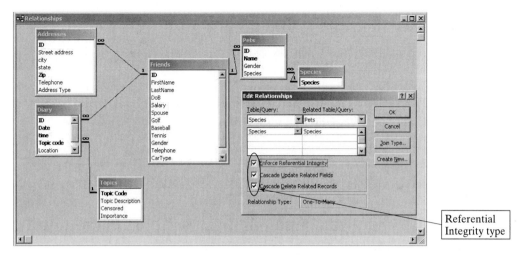

FIGURE 9.9
The Relationships window of the Friends database with an inset Edit Relationship window in Access.

not already defined in the Species table. It also means that a species in the Species table cannot be changed or deleted if it is referenced by the Pets table, unless cascading update and cascading delete are specified, respectively.

3. *Cascading Update*: The Foreign key relationship is defined and enforced. No value can be added or changed in the Foreign Key if the new value does not already exist in the primary table. Likewise, a value cannot be deleted from the primary table if it exists in Foreign Key. But a value can be changed (updated) in the primary table, in which case the new value will be automatically assigned also to the Foreign Key. For example, in the referential integrity constraint between Pets and Species, any change in the species in the Species table will carry over to the Pets table. That means, for example, that if the species value of "dog" in the Species table changes to K9, then all the dogs in the Pets table will also have a species name of K9.

4. *Cascading Delete*: The Foreign key relationship is defined and enforced. No value can be added or changed in the Foreign Key if the new value does not already exist in the primary table. Likewise, a value cannot be changed in the primary table if it exists in Foreign Key. But the value can be deleted from the primary table. In the latter case, all the rows that contained the deleted value in the Foreign Key will be deleted too. That means, for example, that if the species value of "dog" in the Species table is deleted, then all the pets who are dogs in the Pets table will also be deleted.

5. *Cascading Update and Cascading Delete*: The Foreign key relationship is defined and enforced. No value can be added to the Foreign Key if the value does not already exist in the primary table, but if a value is deleted or changed in the primary table, the change will also take effect in the referencing table, changing the Foreign Keys and deleting the rows where the value has been changed, respectively.

9.3   AN OVERVIEW OF ADO.NET

ADO.NET, or ActiveX Data Objects™ of .NET, handles all connectivity to outside data sources such as databases through the ODBC (an industry standard based on Windows that applies an Application Programming Interface, or API, to access databases through SQL) or through other dedicated channels. Connectivity is performed through OLE (Object Linking and Embedding is an industry standard that allows objects to link and to contain other objects) in classes that reside in the System.Data.OleDb namespace. Connectivity to SQL Server 2000 is also available through specifically dedicated equivalently named classes in the System.Data.SqlClient namespace. Using these especially dedicated classes is much faster than using the OLE-based classes in the System.Data.OleDb namespace. The classes in the System.Data.SqlClient start with the Sql prefix rather than the OleDb prefix that is used by the classes in the System.Data.OleDb namespace. Using the SQL Server dedicated classes just requires in most cases replacing the class prefix. We will use both namespaces in this book. Another important namespace for ADO is the Data namespace. This namespace contains the DataSet class that we will use extensively in the next chapters. Before doing any database connectivity, it is advisable to import these namespaces explicitly. Doing so saves the need to type the namespace name before the name of each class. *These commands must be added before the class statement that is the first executable command in the object*, as in the following cod

```
Imports System.Data.OleDb
imports System.Data.SqlClient
Imports System.Data

Public Class frmFriends
```

Accessing data from a database can be conveniently thought of as a three-tier process (Figure 9.10): (1) establishing a connection to the Data Source, (2) executing SQL commands through that connection, and, when applicable, (3) handling the data that is returned from those SQL commands. In the uppermost tier, an actual connection is established with the database. This is done with the appropriately named OleDbConnection or SqlConnection class. The former will work with any database that has an OLE DB connectivity. The latter is used for creating a connection to SQL Server 7 and higher. Once this connection is established, an SQL command (see the appendix on SQL syntax) can be executed on the database. SQL commands are handled through the OleDbCommand class, the OleDataAdapter class, or their SQL Server equivalent. These classes must specify the connection being used. The data returned as a result of an SQL command, assuming that the SQL statement does in fact return data, are handled by the third tier, either through a DataSet object or a Data Reader object. A DataSet is a local copy of the database held by the VB.NET application on which all database functionality can be done. A Data Reader is a local copy of the database held by the VB.NET application on which only read-forward without update can be done.

A key feature of ADO.NET is that it works in a *disconnected mode*. This means that after the data are copied from the Data Source to a Data Set, the Data Set is not connected anymore to that Data Source. Any changes made to the Data Source after it has been copied will be transparent to the Data Set and any changes made to the Data

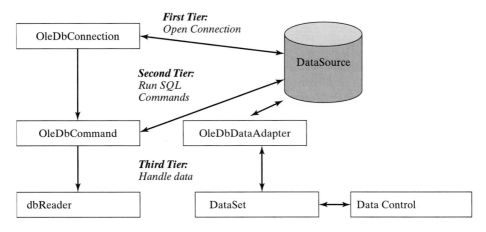

FIGURE 9.10
The three tiers of accessing data in ADO.NET.

Set will not be reflected in the Data Source, unless an explicit command to do so is executed. This method is the Update method of the Data Adapter.

Possibly the simplest way of handling this data in the third tier is with the OleDbDataReader, which is a read-forward only and without update capability copy of the data, or with a Data Control. We will discuss the Data Grid control in this chapter. More complex manipulation of the data is completed with the DataSet, which is a local disconnected copy of the database portion. We will discuss the DataSet object in detail in later chapters. In this chapter, we will use the Dataset only as a means of passing on the data from the Data Adapter to a Data Control, such as the Data Grid.

9.3.1   The .NET Data Providers

The types of Data Sources that .NET knows how to work with are called Data Providers. These databases have OLE that enable them to work with .NET. The Provider name in .NET is the type of database that is being used: SQL Server, Oracle, Access, and so on. (See Table 9.1.) All these connections are *managed connections*, meaning that the CLR manages all aspects of the classes (see Chapter 1 for a brief discussion on CLR). Being a managed connection means that the .NET architecture will provide much of the service in connecting to these databases.

TABLE 9.1   "ADO.NET providers"

Provider (Database Type)	Provider name in .NET	Namespace
SQL Server	SQLOLEDB	System.Data.SqlClient
Oracle	MSDAORA	System.Data.OleDb
Access 2000 and Access 2002	Microsoft.Jet.OLEDB.4.0	System.Data.OleDb
Access 97	Microsoft.Jet.OLEDB.3.5	System.Data.OleDb

TABLE 9.2   "Major ADO.NET Data objects"

Class	Class name in `System.Data.OleDb`	Class name in `System.Data.SqlClient`
Connection	`OleDbConnection`	`SqlConnection`
DataAdapter	`OleDbDataReader`	`SqlDataReader`
Command	`OleDbCommand`	`SqlCommand`
DataReader	`OleDbDataReader`	`SqlDataReader`
DataSet Resides in `System.Data`	`DataSet`	`DataSet`

9.3.2   .NET Data Objects

To enable the functionality shown in Table 9.1, the .NET architecture provides a set of dedicated classes that handle all the necessary functionality. There are five major classes involved in this data access through .NET. These classes (Table 9.2) are conveniently grouped into what is called a *connected layer* and a *disconnected layer*. The *connected layer* works with a database and hence its name. This layer, the top two tiers in the diagram, is in charge of establishing a connection with the Data Source and sending it SQL commands. Both functionalities work with the Data Source—hence their name: the connected layer. The *connected layer* contains the Connection, DataAdapter, and Command classes. (The actual name of the class will depend on whether it is in the `System.Data.SqlClient` namespace or the `System.Data.OleDb` namespace.) Despite this name, the data, once read, are disconnected from the database. The data themselves are handled in the *disconnected layer* that consists of the DataSet and the DataReader classes. The data in these two latter classes are handled in a disconnected manner, meaning that the DataSet and DataReader objects do not work at all with the Data Source. Moreover, the DataSet can be used even when no database is involved.

In a nutshell, the Connection class establishes a connection to the database, opens the connections, closes the connection, and handles transactions. The Command class handles SQL commands through the connection to a database that is established with a Connection object. The DataAdapter copies data back and forth from the database to a local copy. The DataReader, as its name implies, reads the data sequentially. A DataSet object can be thought of as a local copy of a database in the current application. We will discuss the DataSet extensively in the next chapters.

9.4   CONNECTING VB.NET TO SQL SERVER DATABASES

9.4.1   Preparatory Steps, Linking VB.NET to an SQL Server Data Source

This section assumes that there is a running instance of SQL Server that is connected to the PC on which VB.NET is running. If you do not have SQL Server, skip to the next section where connectivity through Access 2002 is discussed. However, be aware that there are things that can be done with SQL Server that cannot be done with Access 2002.

FIGURE 9.11
Server Explorer window.

Toggle tabs

FIGURE 9.12
Choosing Server Explorer in the
View menu.

Before adding the connection objects to a VB.NET project, it is advisable to add the Server Explorer window. This window (Figure 9.11) helps manage the connection to databases. This window is located in a tabbed control with the toolbox. Point the cursor onto the Server Explorer icon, just above the toolbox icon, and this window will open.

Alternatively, you can add this window by choosing the Server Explorer in the View menu (Figure 9.12). The resulting window will show all the currently open data sources and server connections. The Server Explorer window is tabbed together with the toolbox.

The current Server Explorer window contains no connections. We will add a connection to a Server, namely, an SQL Server database, and another connection in the next section to a Data Connection (a local ODBC database), namely, an Access database.

To add a new server, click Servers in the Server Explorer window with the right mouse button, and then click Add Server. (See Figure 9.13.) In the window that will open, enter the Windows name of the computer where the Server is. The computer name will obviously be different from what appears in the example. This will add the connection automatically to the Server Explorer, provided that the DBMS is running. Expand the display by clicking the ⊞ icons to explode the display and show the tables.

We will take advantage of this interface to demonstrate some of the database features discussed earlier in the chapter. We will add two tables together with their primary

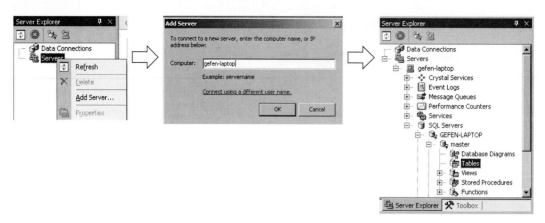

FIGURE 9.13
Adding a server.

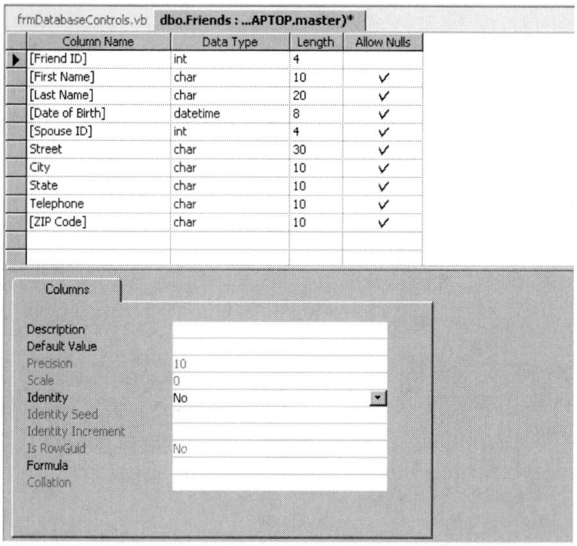

FIGURE 9.14
Adding a table to the SQL
Server database through
VB.NET.

keys and then specify the referential integrity constraint. Adding a new table to the database through VB.NET just requires clicking with the right mouse button on Tables and selecting "New Table" after selecting the database. In the window that will open, we will create the first table of the example we will use throughout the next chapters. Enter the data as shown in Figure 9.14.

We will save the table by clicking the tab of the table with the right mouse button and selecting "Save Table" as in Figure 9.15.

In the window that will open (Figure 9.16), name the table Friends and click OK.

Next, we will add a Primary Key to the table by clicking (with the right mouse button) the gray box near the [Friend ID] row and selecting the option "Set Primary

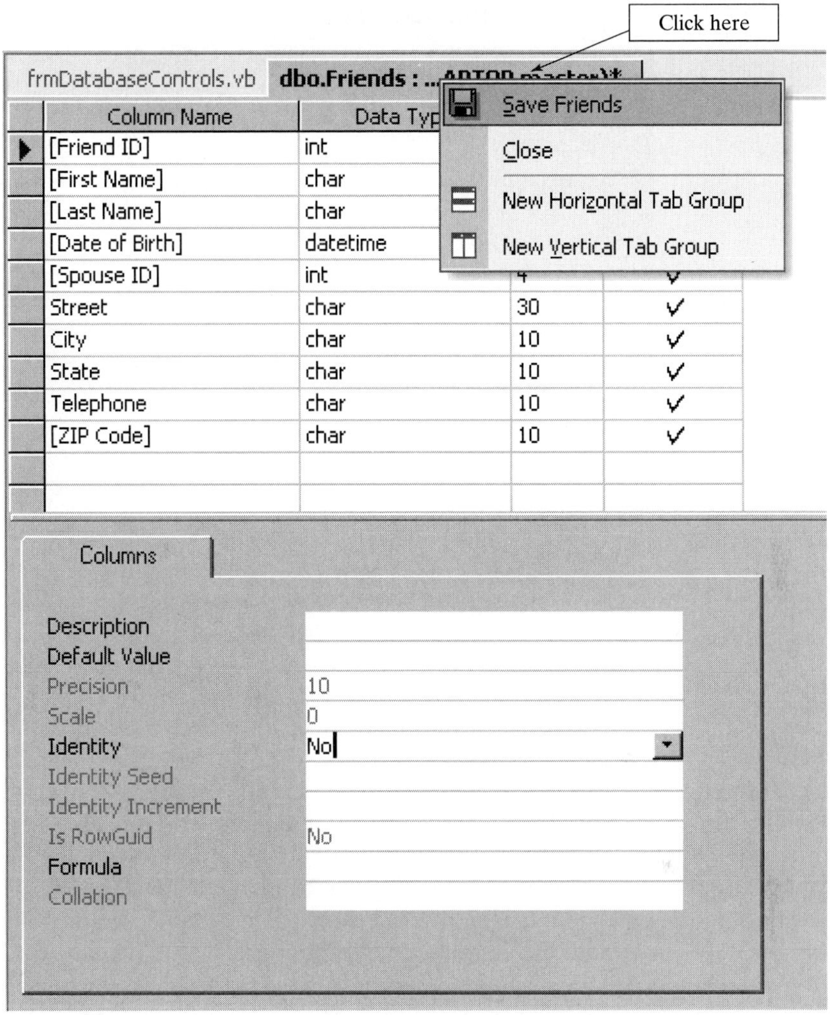

Click here

	Column Name	Data Typ			
▶	[Friend ID]	int			
	[First Name]	char			
	[Last Name]	char			
	[Date of Birth]	datetime			
	[Spouse ID]	int	4	✓	
	Street	char	30	✓	
	City	char	10	✓	
	State	char	10	✓	
	Telephone	char	10	✓	
	[ZIP Code]	char	10	✓	

frmDatabaseControls.vb   **dbo.Friends : ...ABTOP master)***

Save Friends

Close

New Horizontal Tab Group

New Vertical Tab Group

Columns

Description	
Default Value	
Precision	10
Scale	0
Identity	No
Identity Seed	
Identity Increment	
Is RowGuid	No
Formula	
Collation	

FIGURE 9.15
Saving the table.

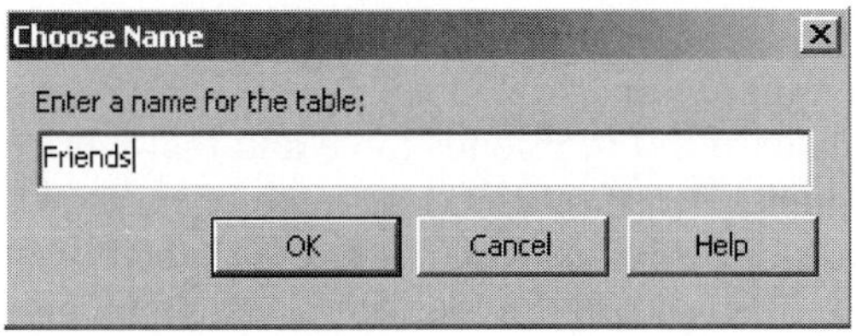

Choose Name   ✕

Enter a name for the table:

Friends

OK	Cancel	Help

FIGURE 9.16
Choosing a name.

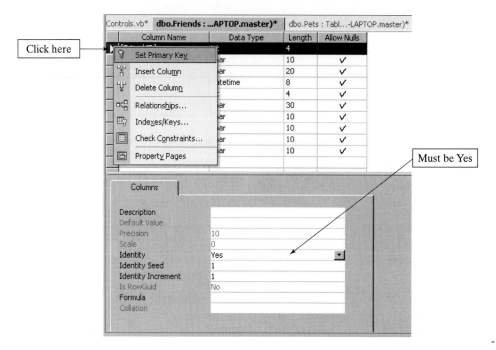

FIGURE 9.17
Setting the Primary Key.

Key" in the popup menu that will appear. This will add a little yellow key icon to the column. The yellow key indicates that this column is now the primary key. You must make sure the Identity of the Friend ID field is "Yes" before making the field into the primary key, otherwise the primary key will not be a unique key (Figure 9.17). A quick glance at the Server Explorer window will show the new table and its fields. The new table has been added into the database in SQL Server.

We will proceed to add another table, Pets, in the same way, as shown in Figure 9.18. In this case, however, the Primary Key is composed of two fields. Click the right mouse button as you move the mouse down to paint both boxes in the gray column, and then proceed as before. Save the table, naming it Pets.

The last thing that needs to be done is to add the Relationships. Click the gray column with the right mouse button, as you did before to create a primary key. Then, in the popup menu, select "Relationships". (See Figure 9.19.) In the window that will open, click New and then add the fields as shown below in Figure 9.19. This will create a referential integrity constraint in the data, meaning that a pet cannot be added if the Friend ID does not already exist in the Friends table and that a Friend ID in the Pets table cannot be changed unless the new Friend ID already exists in the Friends table. The checks at the bottom of the window indicate that the relationship has cascading update and cascading delete. Cascading update in this example will mean that if the Friend ID in Friends is changed that change will automatically carry over, or cascade, to the Pets table. Cascading delete in this case will mean that if a friend is deleted, so will the pets tied to that friend.

atabaseControls.vb* | dbo.Friends : Ta...-LAPTOP.master)* | **dbo.Table1 : ...APTOP.master)*** ◀ ▷ ✕

Column Name	Data Type	Length	Allow Nulls
[Pet Name]	char	10	
[Friend ID]	int	4	
Species	char	10	✓
Age	int	4	✓

Columns

Description	
Default Value	
Precision	0
Scale	0
Identity	No
Identity Seed	
Identity Increment	
Is RowGuid	No
Formula	
Collation	<database default>

FIGURE 9.18
Creating the Pets table.

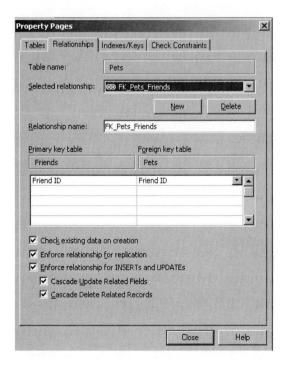

FIGURE 9.19
Specifying a Foreign Key relationship through the Property Pages window.

As a footnote, you can click the Indexes/Keys tab at the top of the window to verify that the primary key has been added properly (Figure 9.20). Additional indexes can be added by clicking the "New" button and then selecting the columns and sort order and whether the index is unique. A unique index will not allow duplicate values in the columns it relates to.

With the tables, indexes, and relationship in place, we will create the database diagram. Adding a diagram requires right-clicking Database Diagrams and selecting New Diagram. (See Figure 9.21.) In the window that will open, add both tables.

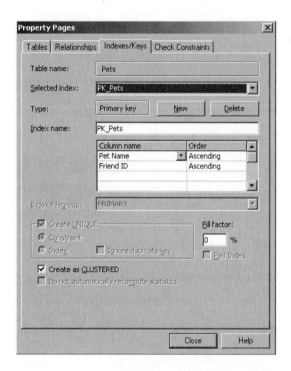

FIGURE 9.20
The Indexes/Keys tab.

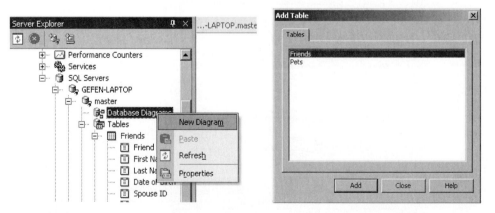

FIGURE 9.21
Adding a Diagram to an existing SQL Server database.

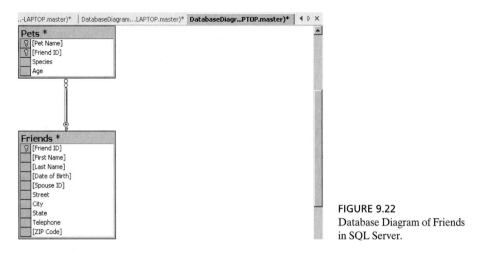

FIGURE 9.22
Database Diagram of Friends
in SQL Server.

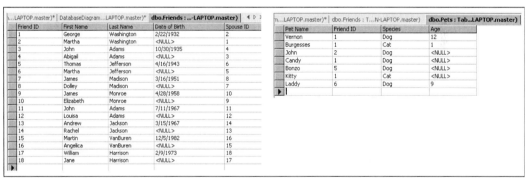

FIGURE 9.23
Adding data to the tables through VB.NET.

This will place both tables in the window and automatically draw the database diagram based on the information added earlier as seen in Figure 9.22. SQL Server knows how to specify the relationship between the two tables based on the relationships information entered before.

At this stage, add data to both tables by double-clicking the table name in the Server Explorer window. Accidentally, these friends have famous names (Figure 9.23). We will use the data in the next few chapters.

9.5   CONNECTING VB.NET TO AN ACCESS DATABASE

9.5.1   Preparatory Steps, Linking VB.NET to an Access Data Source

Adding a connection to a Data Connection is much the same, except that these connections are done through the ODBC and its wizard interface. We will connect to the Friends Access database, which comes with the book CD. To add a new data connection, right-click Data Connections in the Server Explorer, and, in the popup menu, select Add Connection, as shown in Figure 9.24.

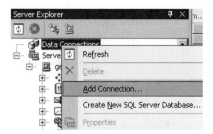

FIGURE 9.24
Adding a Connection to an existing
Access database.

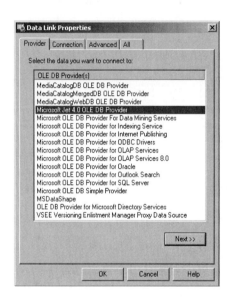

FIGURE 9.25
Specifying the Access 2002 Provider with the
DataLink Properties window.

This will open up the Data Link Properties Wizard. Choose the first tab, named Provider. The Provider property contains the name of the OLE DB data provider. Among these OLE DB are the following:

- SQLOLEDB – OLE DB of Microsoft SQL Server
- Microsoft.Jet.OLEDB.4.0 – OLE DB of Access 2000 and Access 2002
- Microsoft.Jet.OLEDB.3.51 – OLE DB of Access 97
- MSDAORA – OLE DB of Oracle

In this case, choose Jet 4.0 and then in the Connection tab enter the path to the database. It is worthwhile testing the connection at this stage. The wizard will open up at the Connection tab. Click the Provider tab to its left, and the window in Figure 9.25 will open. Select Jet 4.0.

Then, either click the Next button or the Connection tab. Both do the same thing. In the Connection window, see Figure 9.26 click the three dots and enter the location of the Friends database. It is advisable to make a copy of the database on the hard drive, because the database on the CD cannot be updated. This will add a connection to Access in the Server Explorer.

The Data Connection will show the tables and views (stored queries) in the database (Figure 9.27). Access does not support stored procedures so none will appear

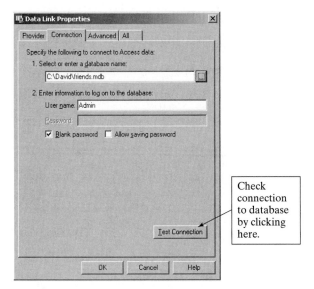

Check
connection
to database
by clicking
here.

FIGURE 9.26
Specifying the Access 2002 Connection
with the DataLink Properties window.

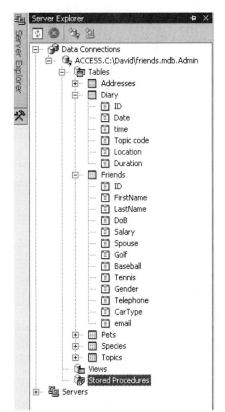

FIGURE 9.27
Friends database content as shown in the Server Explorer window.

ID	FirstName	LastName	DoB	Salary	Spouse	Golf	Baseball
1	Mickey	Bruce	1/1/1920	790000	Mo	1	1
2	Mo	Bruce	1/2/1925	800000	Mickey	0	0
3	Kent	Bruce	4/4/1938	70000	<NULL>	0	0
4	Fred	Foley	5/5/1990	70000	Wilma	1	1
5	Barney	Ruben	8/8/1988	70000	Betty	1	0
6	Betty	Ruben	9/9/1899	70000	Barney	0	0
7	Pam	Foley	8/8/1877	70000	<NULL>	0	0
8	Bill	Ruben	8/8/1878	70000	<NULL>	0	0
9	Al	Duke	7/7/1888	70000	<NULL>	0	0
10	George	Duke	1/1/1911	70000	Jane	0	0
11	Julia	Duke	1/2/1912	70000	George	0	0
12	Judy	Duke	1/3/1212	70000	<NULL>	0	0
13	Estel	Duke	1/4/1444	70000	<NULL>	0	0
14	Brit	Crow	5/5/1955	70000	<NULL>	0	0
15	Rossanne	Duke	6/6/1966	70000	<NULL>	0	0
16	Sammy	Man	5/5/1955	70000	Sam	0	0
17	Sam	Man	6/6/1988	780000	Sammy	0	0
18	Tom	Lion	8/8/1955	70000	<NULL>	1	0
19	Charles	Lion	9/9/1956	70000	<NULL>	1	0
20	Paul	Crow	4/4/1944	70000	<NULL>	0	0
21	Tim	Crow	<NULL>	70000	<NULL>	0	0
22	Tom	Crow	<NULL>	70000	<NULL>	0	0
23	Wilma	Foley	4/4/1956	70000	Fred	0	0

FIGURE 9.28
Data View of the Friends table.

here. In contrast to SQL Server, Tables and Diagrams cannot be added to Access through the Data Connection.

But, as before double-clicking a table will open it and allow updating its data, as in Figure 9.28.

9.6   ACCESS A DATABASE WITH DATA CONTROLS (RATHER THAN SERVER EXPLORER)

The first thing that must be done when accessing a database, or any other data source for that matter, through an application is to establish a connection to it. This is done by the OleDbConnection or, in the case of SQL Server, the SqlConnection objects. There are basically two ways of adding these objects to the project: as a data control with the help of a wizard or explicitly in the code. Because this object has many parameters, we will add it through the controls in this chapter and examine its parameters and then show in the next chapters how this can be done in the code without the aid of data controls.

Connecting the data source to a VB.NET application requires no more than a drag and drop of the "Tables" in the Server Explorer onto the form (Figure 9.29). This will automatically create the three objects at the bottom of the page. Dropping an individual table will create a connectivity to that table alone.

The three objects that are generated as a result are an SqlConnection to the SQL Server database and two SqlDataAdapters. There are two Data Adapters because there are two tables. One Data Adapter for each table.

Clicking the SqlConnection1 object once with the left mouse button will result in that object's properties being shown in the Properties window. The most important of these properties, and actually the only one that must be set, is the ConnectionString property. The generated properties of the SqlConnection specify in a series of subparameters the

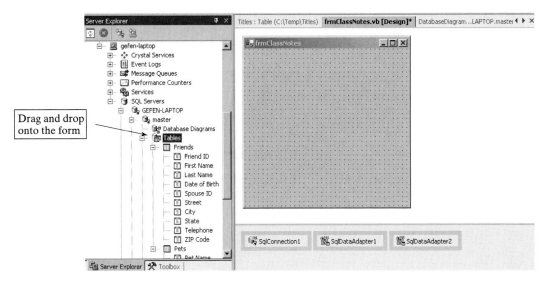

FIGURE 9.29
Connecting an existing data source to a form.

name of the server, the database, and security information. The subparameters are separated by semicolons. These will be discussed later in this chapter.

The Data Adapters already have SQL statements. These were generated automatically through the drag and drop. The `SelectCommand.CommandText` property of `SqlDataAdapter1`, for example, states,

```
SELECT [Friend ID], [First Name], [Last Name], [Date of Birth],
[Spouse ID], Street, City, State, Telephone, [ZIP Code] FROM Friends
```

And the Insert command states

```
INSERT INTO Friends([First Name], [Last Name], [Date of Birth],
[Spouse ID], Street, City, State, Telephone, [ZIP Code]) VALUES
(@Param1, @Param2, @Param3, @Param4, @Street, @City, @State, @Tele-
phone, @Param5); SELECT [Friend ID], [First Name], [Last Name], [Date
of Birth], [Spouse ID], Street, City, State, Telephone, [ZIP Code]
FROM Friends WHERE ([Friend ID] = @@IDENTITY)
```

The next thing that needs to be added is a DataSet so that the data in the Sql-DataAdapter can be read. Right-click SqlDataAdapter1, and choose Generate Dataset (Figure 9.30).

The will open up the Generate Dataset wizard (Figure 9.31), where a new dataset will be created for the purpose of reading the Friends table.

As a result, a new dataset will be created. Double-click it in the Solution Explorer window to display its contents as shown in Figure 9.32.

With this done, the dataset needs to be filled with the data in the DataAdapter, and then this dataset needs to be bound to a specific Data Control, such as a Data Grid or a textbox, where the data will appear.

FIGURE 9.30
Generating a Dataset through an existing Data Adapter.

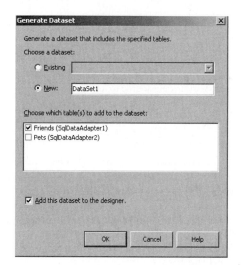

FIGURE 9.31
The Generate Dataset wizard.

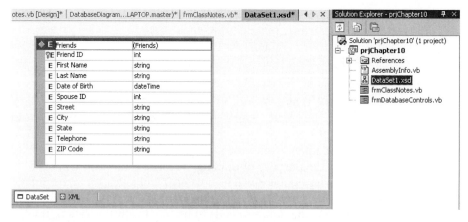

FIGURE 9.32
Dataset content generated through the Solution Explorer.

9.6.1 A Short Demo

Let us demonstrate this with a short application. Draw the form in Figure 9.33 containing a Data Grid and four Buttons. Name them as shown in the figure. The controls in the work area below the form should already be there as a result of dragging and dropping the SQL Server and Access databases onto the form as done in the previous pages.

To add the hidden controls, open the toolbox on the data tab (Figure 9.34). By default, it will be on the Windows forms tab.

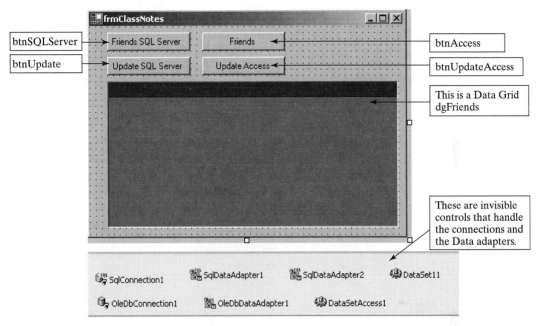

FIGURE 9.33
A Demo application connecting to SQL Server and Access.

FIGURE 9.34
The Data tab of the Toolbox.

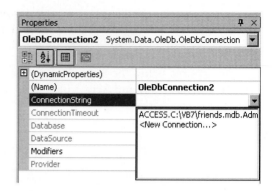

FIGURE 9.35
Generating a new or choosing an existing Connection String through the Properties window.

FIGURE 9.36
Data Adapter Configuration wizard.

Drag and drop an OleDbConnection object from the toolbox to the form. Then, in the Properties window, click the `ConnectionString` property. This will open a pull-down menu with the list of already established connections. Either choose the appropriate connection, shown in Figure 9.35 to connect to the Friends Access database, or click < `New Connection. . . `>, to open the wizard we already saw in the Solution Explorer.

After choosing the Friends Access database, drag and drop an OleDBDataAdapter control to the form. This will automatically open the Data Adapter Configuration wizard as shown in Figure 9.36. Click Next.

In the window that will open, (Figure 9.37) choose the connection we just established. Click Next.

In the next window, (Figure 9.38) choose to access the data through SQL. (Actually, you have no choice there.) Click Next.

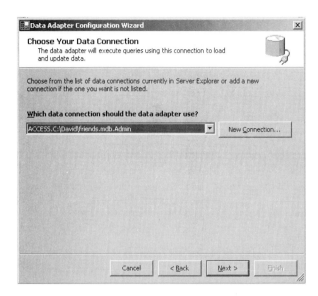

FIGURE 9.37
Specifying the Connection in the Data
Adapter Configuration wizard.

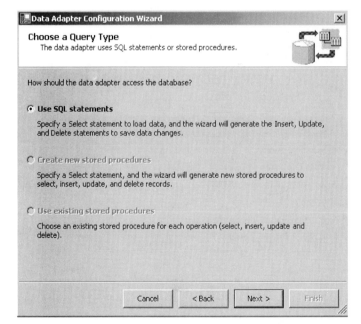

FIGURE 9.38
Specifying the Query Type in the Data
Adapter Configuration wizard.

In the next window (Figure 9.39), we will need to enter the SQL statements. Conveniently, there is a tool called the Query Builder. We will discuss it in more detail in the next chapters. For now, just click the Query Builder button.

The Query Builder will generate the SQL statements. In the Query Builder, choose the Friends table by either double-clicking it or clicking it once and then clicking the Add button as shown in Figure 9.40. After you choose the table, click Close.

FIGURE 9.39
The SQL Statements window of the Data Adapter Configuration wizard.

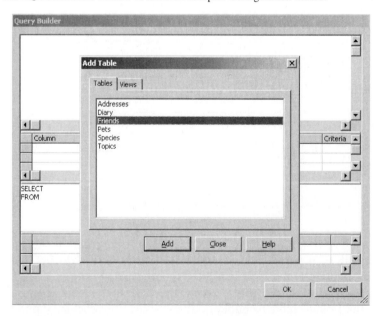

FIGURE 9.40
Generating the SQL statement with a Query By Example (QBE) window in the
Data Adapter Configuration wizard. Part 1: Selecting the tables and views.

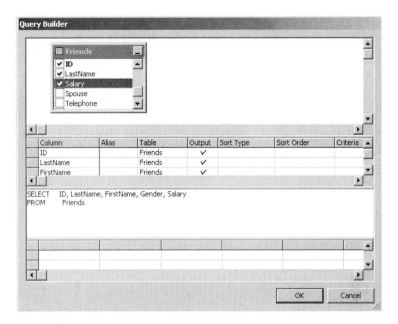

FIGURE 9.41
Generating the SQL statement with a Query By Example (QBE) window in the
Data Adapter Configuration wizard. Part 2: Selecting columns.

Next, just click the columns to add: ID, LastName, FirstName, Gender, and
Salary. Replace from "Click the Okay button." to end of line 3 with "As the parameters
of the QBE are set in figure 9.41, the SQL statement will be automatically generated in
the third window pane of the QBE window. In this case, the SQL statement that will be
generated will select all the columns, and will show data for those columns from all the
rows in the Friends table. That data (selected columns and rows) will eventually be
available in the Data Set once it is generated. Clicking on the OK button in figure 9.41
will move the generated the SQL statement back to the SQL Statement window of the
Data Adapter Configuration wizard." This will generate the SQL statement that will
select all the columns, and all the rows in the Friends table to the Data Set then will
eventually be generated.

The SQL statement will be copied into the Data Adapter wizard see Figure
9.42. We could have written the SQL ourselves, but with a Query Builder to build it
and guaranty its correct syntax, that is the recommended way of doing it. What's
more, as we shall see in the next chapters, the Query Builder can build quite complex
commands and run then as a matter of testing that the command does what we expect it to do.

Click Next to see what the wizard will generate. In this case, the wizard will generate all the SQL commands that the Data Adapter will need and a table mapping.
Click Finish. (See Figure 9.43.)

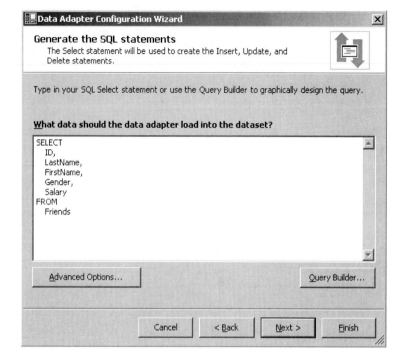

FIGURE 9.42
The SQL statement that was generated from the QBE is shown in the SQL Statements window of the Data Adapter Configuration wizard.

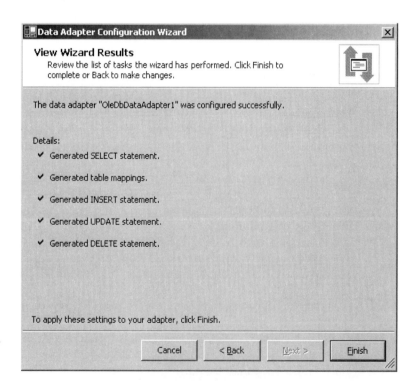

FIGURE 9.43
The View Wizard Results window of the Data Adapter Configuration wizard.

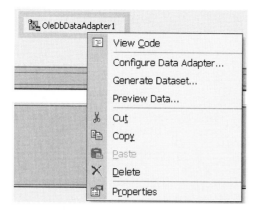

FIGURE 9.44
Activating the Generate Dataset wizard.

Generate Dataset

Generate a dataset that includes the specified tables.

Choose a dataset:

○ Existing [▼]

● New: DataSetAccess

Choose which table(s) to add to the dataset:

☑ Friends (OleDbDataAdapter3)

☑ Add this dataset to the designer.

OK   Cancel   Help

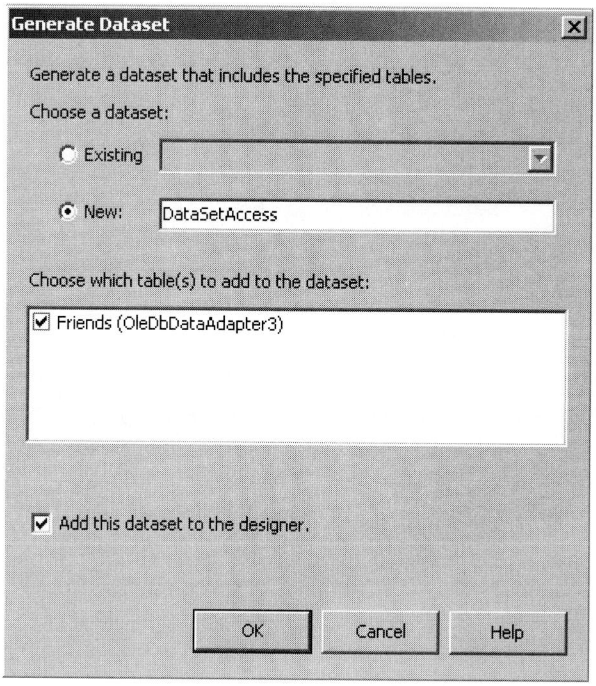

FIGURE 9.45
Specifying dataset name in the
Generate Dataset wizard.

With this done, the Connection and the Data Adapter are ready, but not yet the Data Set. To generate the Data Set, click the DataAdpater control with the right mouse button and choose Generate Dataset as in Figure 9.44.

In the wizard that will open, choose to create a new Data Set and name it DataSetAccess (Figure 9.45). Then, click OK.

This will add an XSD file to the project as seen in Figure 9.46.

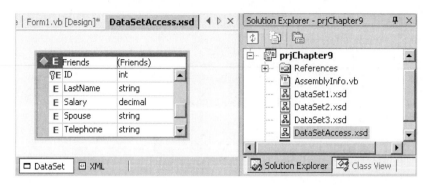

FIGURE 9.46
Viewing the xsd files that were created by the Generate Dataset wizard.

Repeat this process with the SQL Server Connection and Data Adapter controls. The following code will handle the Click events on the four buttons:

```
Private Sub btnFriends_Click(ByVal sender As System.Object, _
                ByVal e As System.EventArgs) _
                Handles btnSQLServer.Click

    DataSet11.Clear()
    SqlDataAdapter1.Fill(DataSet11)
    dgFriends.SetDataBinding(DataSet11, _
            DataSet11.Friends.ToString)
End Sub

Private Sub btnAccess_Click(ByVal sender As System.Object, _
                ByVal e As System.EventArgs) _
                Handles btnAccess.Click
    DataSetAccess1.Clear()
    '                                        from how-many
    OleDbDataAdapter1.Fill(DataSetAccess1, 1,   200, _
                                        "Friends")
    dgFriends.SetDataBinding(DataSetAccess1, _
                        DataSetAccess1.Friends.ToString)
End Sub

Private Sub btnUpdate_Click(ByVal sender As System.Object, _
                ByVal e As System.EventArgs) _
                Handles btnUpdate.Click

    If DataSet11.HasChanges Then
        SqlDataAdapter1.Update(DataSet11)
    End If
End Sub

Private Sub btnUpdateAccess_Click( _
                ByVal sender As System.Object, _
```

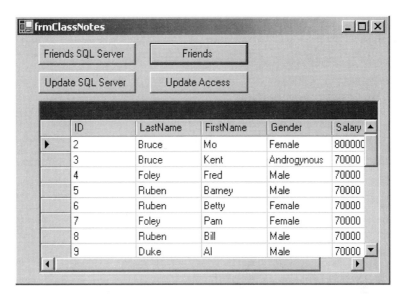

FIGURE 9.47
Viewing the Access Friends database through the Demo application.

```
                ByVal e As System.EventArgs) _
                Handles btnUpdateAccess.Click
    If DataSetAccess1.HasChanges Then
        OleDbDataAdapter1.Update(DataSetAccess1)
    End If
End Sub
```

In the first command, the `Fill` method is used to fill the dataset with data from the SQL Server database. In the second command, the now filled dataset is bound to a data grid control. The `SetDataBinding` method has two parameters: the name of the dataset and the name of the table within it from where the data definitions will be taken. The name of the table can be entered directly as a string, as in `btnAccess_Click`, or as a property of the dataset, as in `btnFriends_Click`. Note that the `Fill` method can be set to specify from what record number to begin filling the dataset, the first record being number 0, and how many records to write to it. But, when these options are used, the name of the table must also be added as a parameter. This is demonstrated in the second subroutine.

Run the application. Clicking Friends will show the data in the Friends table in the Access database (Figure 9.47). Changes may be made to the data in the Data Grid. These changes will be copied to the Access database when the Update Access buttons clicked.

Clicking the Friends SQL Server button will show the data in the Friends table in the SQL Server database (Figure 9.48). Again, the data in the Data Grid may be updated. To carry those changes in the data to the database, click the Update SQL Server button.

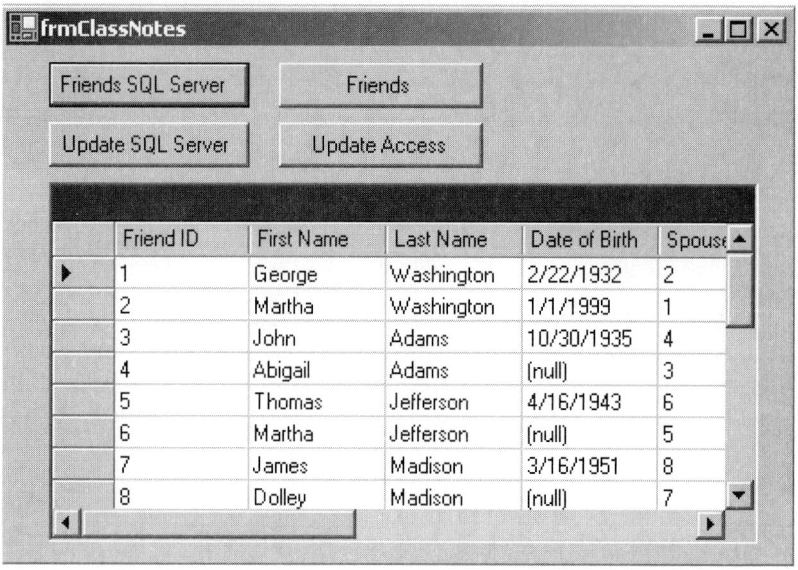

FIGURE 9.48
Viewing the SQL Server Friends database through the Demo application.

9.6.2 A Review of What Just Happened

So, what has ADO.NET been doing? First, we created a connection to the database through an SqlConnection object and read the data through an SqlDataAdapter object. The parameters, including the SQL statements were all generated automatically by the wizards. The connection was done automatically and in the background because we used controls rather than writing the code explicitly. At this stage, the Data Adapter has the data, but the data cannot be displayed. Displaying the data requires placing it in a DataSet object. This object is our local copy of the portion of the database that we read with the Data Adapter.

The Fill method copies the data in the Data Adapter into a DataSet object. This DataSet object can then be read and updated through a variety of means, including a Data Grid control. Any changes made to the DataSet are tested on this local copy of the database, *but no changes are made to the actual database because the dataset is disconnected from it.* Forcing the changes that were made on the data in the Dataset into the database itself requires another Data Adapter method, namely, the Update method. Exactly the same technique works with the Access database, except that the object types start with "OleDb" rather than "Sql".

A very important point to remember is that all database access in ADO.NET is done in a disconnected mode. The Connection layer objects—SqlConnection, OleDb-Connection, SqlDataAdapter, OleDbDataAdapter, SqlCommand, and OleDbCommand—connect to the database only for the duration of the one SQL statement that is executed and disconnect from it thereafter. Any data retrieved are handled without any connection to the database until the Update method is executed, when again a one-time connection is established with the database.

Thus, in the preceding application, a connection was established with the databases so that the data could be read. But once the data had been retrieved that connection was severed automatically. All changes made in the database after that point are transparent to the application and vice versa. When the dataset is updated back to the database, the connection is reestablished, but only for as long as it takes to update the data. That done, the connection is severed again.

9.7   A CLOSER LOOK AT THE CONNECTION CLASS PROPERTIES

The only property that can be changed in the Connection classes' objects, apart from Modifiers, is their `ConnectionString`. This one property contains as subparameters all the information needed to establish and manage the connection to the database. These parameters can be set only when the object is not currently connected to the database. The following list details some of the most important the subparameters of this property (subparameters can be set only as subparameters of the `ConnectionString` property; they cannot be set independently).

- `Connect Timeout` or `Connection Timeout`
  - This subparameter specifies how long in seconds the application will be allowed to wait for the resources (tables, indexes, etc.) that the SQL statement requires. If the resource is not made available to the transaction within the time period specified in the subparameter, the transaction is rollbacked: it is aborted, all its changes undone, and an error exception is raised. Timeout is the preferred way in which databases handle suspected deadlocks.[19] By default, the connect timeout is 15 seconds. Setting the connect timeout to 0 will not limit the time an application waits for a resource and may, as a result, choke the database.

- `Data Source` or `Server` or `Address` or `Network Address`
  - Is the name of the Server, in the case of Server Connections, or of the path where the database is, in the case of Data Connections. This subparameter must be specified. It has no default value.

---

[19]When concurrency control conflicts occur, such as when two transactions try to update the same record, the DBMS lets the later transaction wait for the resource (record, index, or any other database resource) until the transaction that is currently holding the resource releases it. This may not always work because it is possible that the transaction that is currently locking the resource is itself waiting for a resource that is being locked by a transaction waiting for the resource it itself is holding. Suppose, for example, that transaction T1 is locking record R1 while waiting for the right to issue a lock (an exclusive access) to record R2 to become available, while at the same time transaction T2 that owns the lock on R2 is waiting for the lock on R1 to be released. This situation, in which two transactions are waiting for each other and neither can complete its execution because of the other transaction, is called a *deadlock*. Deadlocks can, of course, involve more than two transactions. For example, transaction T1 may be locking record R1 while waiting for record R2, that is being locked by transaction T2, to be released. At the same time, transaction T2 is not able to complete its own processing and so release R2, because it is waiting for the lock on record R3 to be removed. But the lock on record R3 cannot be removed because transaction T3 that owns it is waiting for the lock on record R1, currently held by transaction R1, to be released. As a result, T1 is waiting for T2, T2 is waiting for T3, and T3 is waiting for T1, and none can complete their execution.

- `Initial Catalog` or `Database`
  - In the case of a Server where many database may be handled, this is the name of the database that is being connected.
- `Integrated Security` or `Trusted_Connection`
  - This optional subparameter of the SqlConnection class specifies whether the connection should be secured. By default, it is not. When its value is SSPI or Yes, the connection is secure.
- `Packet Size`
  - The packet size in bytes that will be used when communicating with SQL Server.
- `User ID`
  - The user ID for logging into the database.
- `Password`
  - The password of the preceding user ID for logging into the database.
- `Persist Security Info`
  - When a connection is established to an SQL Server database, the database returns an updated Connection String. This subparameter specifies whether sensitive information, such as the password, should be included in this returned Connection String. By default, the value is `False`.

There are also a host of database-specific subparameters. In the case of SQL Server, for example, there are additional parameters for handling pooling. Pooling allows several connections to be managed together as one pool. This can greatly improve database performance. SQL Server will decide what connections to pool together based on the Connection String. Basically, one pool is created for each unique combination of connection strings. If two connections are made and both have the same connection string parameter, then one pool will be created to handle both, unless the subparameters that follow prohibit it. But if two connections are made with different connection string parameters, then two pools will be created to handle them. Connections will then be removed from the pool when their time has expired (the `Connection Lifetime` subparameter). The following list details some of the most important subparameters that help manage the pooling:

- `Pooling`
  - When set to `True`, the default value, connections will be pooled for improved performance.
- `Max Pool Size`
  - Specifies the maximum number of connections allowed in a pool. By default, the value is 100.
- `Min Pool Size`
  - Specifies the minimum number of connections allowed in a pool. By default, the value is 0.
- `Connection Lifetime`
  - This subparameter specifies how long in seconds a connection can be open in a pool. The default value of 0 specifies the maximum allowed time. If a connection has no pool, it will wait until a new pool that can handle it is available.

- `Connection Reset`
  - When a connection is removed from the pool, the connection to the database is automatically reset. Setting the this subparameter to "false" will avoid that. This avoids the need for another roundtrip from the application to the server.

9.8   SOME CONNECTION CLASS METHODS

The methods in the Connection class handle all the functionality necessary for creating and maintaining the connection to the database. We will discuss these methods as each becomes applicable to its chapter. Note that all these methods are run within a Try Block. This is essential because that way exceptions can be caught and displayed.

Opening a connection is done with the `Open` method. This method has no parameters:

```
Dim myConnection As New SqlClient.SqlConnection()
Try
    myConnection.ConnectionString = "data source=GEFEN-LAPTOP;" & _
                                    "initial catalog=master;" & _
                                    "integrated security=SSPI;" & _
                                    "persist security info=True;" & _
                                    "workstation id=GEFEN-LAPTOP;" & _
                                    "packet size=4096"
    myConnection.Open()
Catch e1 As Exception
    ' It is imperative to use Try and Catch
    ' because the error message will get lost otherwise
    Console.WriteLine(e1.Message)
End Try
```

Closing a connection is done with the `Close` method or the `Dispose` method:

```
myConnection.Close()
myConnection.Dispose()
```

It is important to close connections when they are no longer needed because that releases database resources, such as allowing the pool to add new connections, and releases memory. The `Close` method will wait for any transactions running under the connection to complete. The `Dispose` method will destroy the connection without waiting; avoid the latter method.

LAB 9: EXERCISING THE DATA ADAPTER AND DATA BINDING

Lab Objectives:
1. Review establishing a connection to a database through a Connection object.
2. Exercise applying a Data Adapter and a DataSet.
3. Review binding a control to a DataSet.

4. Look at how to add SQL to a Data Adapter.
5. Look at the Query Builder.
6. Catch database exceptions.

Application Overview

The lab contains a form with a Data Grid control that displays data from the Friends Access database, depending on which buttons have been clicked. The "List Friends" button will display the first 10 records in the Friends table (Figure 9.49). The "Read Next 10 Friends" will, as its name says, read the next 10 records and then the next after those and so on.

When a cell in the gray column is then clicked, the corresponding ID will be copied to the textbox in Figure 9.50.

If at this stage, the Show Pets of Friends button is clicked, then all the pets of that friend will be shown as in Figure 9.51.

Part 1: Build the Form

Add a new project and solution, name them **prjChapter9**, making the project handle a Windows Form. Name the form **frmDatabaseControls**. Add the buttons and textboxes as shown in Figure 9.52. Objects starting with "btn" are buttons, those starting with "txt" are textboxes, and those starting with "dg" are Data Grids. The data Grid will be bound dynamically in the code. Write the appropriate string in the Text properties of each object to correspond to what appears below.

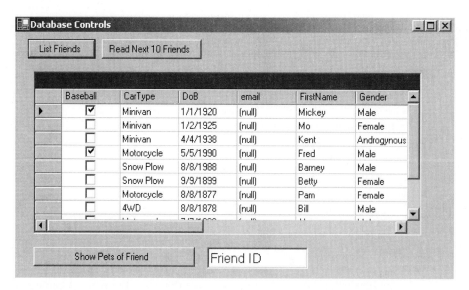

FIGURE 9.49
Lab 9: Displaying the Access Friends table.

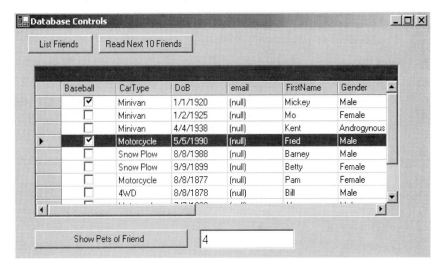

FIGURE 9.50
Lab 9: Selecting a friend.

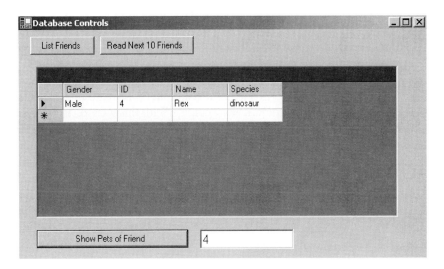

FIGURE 9.51
Lab 9: Displaying the pets of the selected friend.

Part 2.1: Adding the OleDb Controls

At this stage, it is assumed that the database has been connected to VB.NET. If not, go back to the section in the chapter that explains how to connect an Access database to the IDE. Open the Data tab in the toolbox, and drag and drop an OleDbConnection control onto the form. This control will place itself beneath the form and name itself

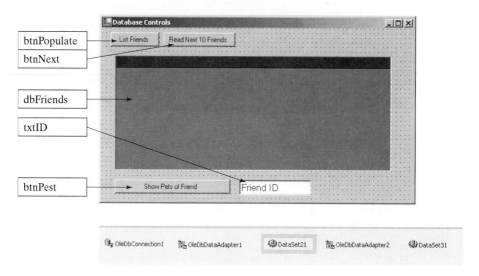

FIGURE 9.52
Lab 9.

OleDbConnection1. Right-click it while pointing at this control. In the Properties window, click the `ConnectionString` property and choose < New Connection...>. This will open the wizard we saw earlier in the chapter. Connect this control to the Friends Access database.

Next, drag and drop an `OleDbDataAdapter` control onto the form. This control will place itself beneath the form and name itself OleDbDataAdapter1. A Data Adapter wizard (Figure 9.53) will automatically open up. With this wizard, as we saw earlier, connect the control to the OleDbConnection1 control we just created and in the appropriate window enter the SQL command "Select * From Friends".

Repeat this operation once more with another OleDbDataAdapter, except that this time make the SQL statement "Select * From Pets". (See Figure 9.54.)

Now, right-click each Data Adapter in turn, and choose Generate Dataset as in Figure 9.55. Name the Data Set of the first Data Adapter Dataset2 and of the second one Dataset3. Recall that we already have one Data Set from earlier in the chapter.

Part 2.2: A Detour

Right-click the OleDbDataAdapter control, and choose Preview Data as in Figure 9.56 The window that will open will let you access the data in the database when you click the Fill Dataset button. (See Figure 9.57.)

Part 2.3: Adding the Code for btnPopulate

Clicking this button will populate the Data Grid with the first 10 rows from Friends. The next section of code will handle that:

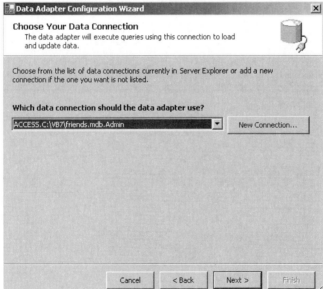

FIGURE 9.53
Data Adapter Configuration wizard.

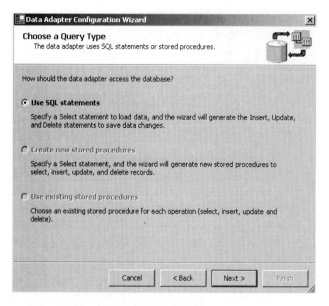

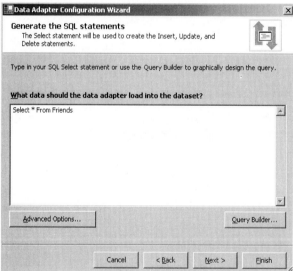

FIGURE 9.54

Entering the SQL statement directly in the Data Adapter Configuration wizard.

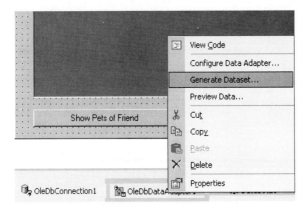

FIGURE 9.55
Generating the dataset.

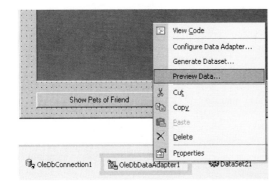

Figure 9.56
Running a preview of the data in the Data
Adapter.

```
Public Class Form1

    Inherits System.Windows.Forms.Form
' Add this line here
Dim dblRowNumber As Double    ' Add this declaration here

Private Sub btnPopulate_Click(ByVal sender As System.Object, _
        ByVal e As System.EventArgs) Handles btnPopulate.Click

    ' Populate the Data Grid from the beginning of the Friends Table
    Try
        ' Clear the Data Set
        DataSet21.Clear()

        ' Copy the first 10 records into the Data Set
        '                              From Length
        OleDbDataAdapter1.Fill(DataSet21, 0, 10, "Friends")

        ' Bind the Data Grid to the Data Set so that the grid will
        ' show the contents of the Data Set
        dgFriends.SetDataBinding(DataSet21, "Friends")

        ' Mark that the Friends have been
        ' displayed from record number 0 onwards
```

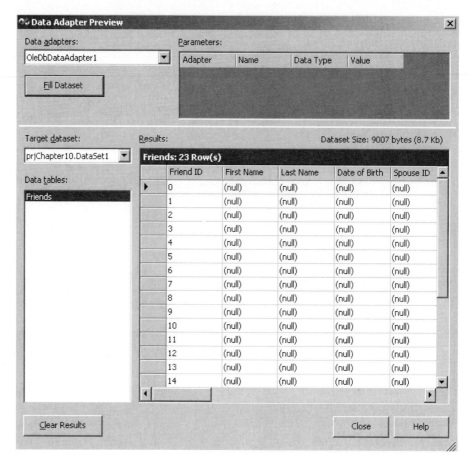

FIGURE 9.57
The previewed data in the Data Adapter.

```
        dblRowNumber = 0
    Catch err1 As Exception
        MessageBox.Show(err1.Message)
    End Try
End Sub
```

Part 2.4: Adding the Code for btnNext

Clicking this button will show the next 10 rows of code:

```
Private Sub btnNext_Click(ByVal sender As System.Object, _
        ByVal e As System.EventArgs) Handles btnNext.Click
    ' Show the next 10 friends

    ' Clear the current display in the Data Grid
    DataSet21.Clear()
```

```
' Mark that the Data Set will be populated from where
' the last Fill method ended off.
dblRowNumber += 10

' Fill 10 rows into the Data Set
OleDbDataAdapter1.Fill(DataSet21, dblRowNumber, 10, "Friends")

' Bind the Data Grid to the Data Set to show its content
dgFriends.SetDataBinding(DataSet21, "Friends")

End Sub
```

Part 2.5: Adding the Code for the Data Grid

Clicking the right gray column of the Data Grid will copy the ID from that row to the textbox, as in the following code:

```
Private Sub dgTitles_Click(ByVal sender As System.Object, _
        ByVal e As System.EventArgs) Handles dgFriends.Click
    ' The ID is copied from the clicked row in the Data Grid to
    ' the textbox

    ' Here the item number in the row is six because of the way
    ' the Query Builder built the SQL. Make sure what column it is
    ' with your application before copying the column number.
    ' Remember the first column is indexed 0.
    txtID.Text = _
            dgFriends.Item(dgFriends.CurrentCell.RowNumber, 7)
End Sub
```

Part 2.6: Adding more Code for btnPets

Clicking this button will replace the display in the Data Grid with the list of pets of the friend whose ID appears in the textbox. The code is as follows:

```
Private Sub btnPets_Click(ByVal sender As System.Object, _
        ByVal e As System.EventArgs) Handles btnPets.Click
    ' Clicking here will show all the pets of the friend whose
    ' ID appears in the textbox

    Try

        If txtID.Text <> "" Then
            DataSet31.Clear()

            ' Change the Select SQL so that only rows
            ' belonging to the specific friend will be chosen
            ' Be sure to work here with Data Adapter 2
            OleDbDataAdapter2.SelectCommand.CommandText = _
            " Select * from Pets " & _
            " Where ID = " & _
            txtID.Text
```

```
' Fill rows into the Data Set
' Be sure to work here with Data Adapter 2
OleDbDataAdapter2.Fill(DataSet31, "Pets")

' Bind the Data Grid to the Data Set to show its content
dgFriends.SetDataBinding(DataSet31, "Pets")

    End If
Catch e1 As Exception
    MessageBox.Show(e1.ToString)
End Try

End Sub
End Class
```

SUGGESTED HOME ASSIGNMENTS

1. Build a new form that will show all the Friends in a Data Grid. The data come from the Friends Access database. When a gray row in the Data Grid is clicked, replace the current content of the Data Grid with Addresses of that friend.
2. Add a Button and another Data Grid to the preceding form. When the button is clicked, show in the new Data Grid all the Diary entries of that friend.
3. Add another button that, when clicked, will replace the content of the Data Grid, which had the friends in it, with a list of all the friends who have the same species of pet as the first pet this friend has.

TEST YOURSELF

1. What is a database? What is its purpose?
2. How are data accessed from a relational database?
3. What is data integrity? How is it enforced? What is referential integrity?
4. Discuss what data independence is and how a DBMS manages it.
5. Discuss what keys and indexes are.
6. Discuss the need for foreign keys.
7. Discuss the three-tier access to data in a database.
8. What does it mean to say that ADO.NET works in a *disconnected* mode?
9. Discuss the process in which a Server and a Data Connection are connected to VB.NET.
10. Discuss how Data Controls are connected to a DBMS.
11. What happens when a Table is dragged and dropped from Server Explorer to a form?
12. Discuss two ways to create DataSets.
13. What is the Connection String? How is it set and what is its purpose.
14. Discuss the `Fill` and `Update` Methods and how they are related.
15. Does the `Fill` method work the same way with Access as it does with SQL Server?
16. What is the purpose of the DataSet object, what is it, and when is it needed?
17. Discuss the Connect Timeout, when is it set, and for what purpose.
18. Discuss what a Try Block should be used for in accessing a database.
19. Discuss what is Pooling.
20. Discuss what deadlocks are.

CHAPTER 10

The Connected Layer Command and DataReader Classes

CHAPTER OBJECTIVES

After completing this chapter, students should have an understanding of the following topics

1. The Command Object
   - Properties and Methods
   - Passing Parameters
   - Running SQL Select Commands
2. The DataReader Object
3. Managing Transactions
4. Activating Stored Procedures

10.1 AIMS OF CHAPTER

In the last chapter, we introduced the ADO connectivity diagram and discussed the first tier and its Connection classes. The Command objects SQLCommand and OleDbCommand are at the center of this chapter. These classes, residing in the second tier, handle the SQL commands that are passed to the Data Source once the connection has been established. The Command objects handle two categories of SQL commands: those that execute queries and those that execute non-query SQL statements. Queries are Select SQL statements and return a value or values when they are executed. Non-query SQL statements include commands such as Insert, Update, and Delete that change the values of the data, and Create, Alter, and Drop that change the data schema.

The chapter also introduces the `SQLDataReader` and the `OleDbDataReader`. These two classes are used to display the results of an SQL query run with the Connection classes, when the data are to be displayed with in a read-only and forward-only move. Passing parameters through the `Parameter` class to SQL commands is also demonstrated as are transactions, stored procedures, and nonquery SQL statements.

The lab at the end of the chapter demonstrates the DataReader classes in both Access and SQL Server and passing parameters to SQL statements.

10.2 A QUICK REVIEW OF ESSENTIAL SQL WITH THE QUERY BUILDER IN THE SERVER EXPLORER

Throughout this chapter, we will write and review quite a bit of SQL. This section is a quick review of the some of the most essential commands in SQL. (A detailed listing of SQL appears in the appendix.) The overview uses the Friends database that comes with the accompanying CD. The SQL commands will be generated and run through the Server Explorer that we saw already in Chapter 9. Through the Server Explorer, the Query Builder can also be opened. We will use Query Builder to generate SQL code, and we will also see its results in Chapter 11.

Before we discuss the Query Builder, let us take a quick look at the data and its display. Retrieving the data from a table can be done through the Server Explorer. See Figure 10.1. Figure 10.2 shows the table that will be displayed. Notice the icons at the top of the IDE. We will need these to open different related windows.

Open the Results pane, SQL pane, Grid pane, and Diagram pane. The IDE will look like Figure 10.3 as a result. This is the same as the Query Builder we shall discuss in Chapter 11. At this stage, we will make do with a review of the Select SQL command alone.

The SQL command can be entered directly in the SQL pane or generated through the Diagram pane (to select columns) and Grid pane (to add the details of the `Where`, `Group By`, `Having`, and `Sort By` clauses). Items selected in the Diagram pane will

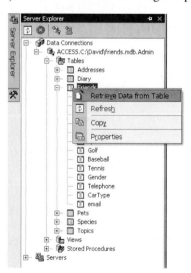

FIGURE 10.1
Using the Server Explorer to retrieve data.

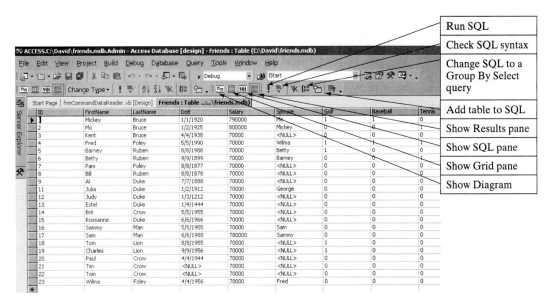

FIGURE 10.2
Contents of the Friends table as shown through the Server Explorer.

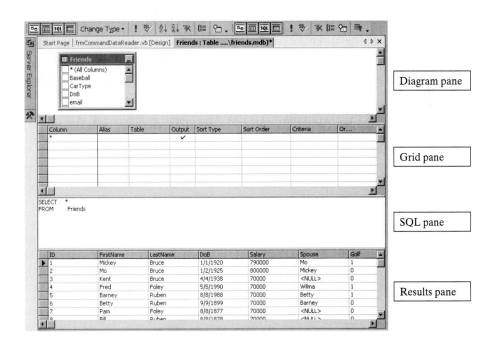

FIGURE 10.3
The Query Builder.

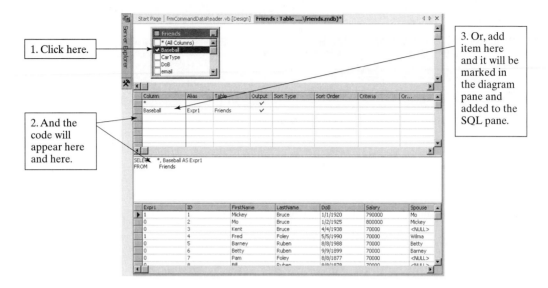

FIGURE 10.4
Selecting a data item in the Query Builder.

automatically appear in the Grid pane and the SQL pane. In Figure 10.4, for example the data item *Basketball* was selected in the Diagram pane and as a result is automatically added to the Grid and SQL panes. Likewise, items marked in the Grid pane will automatically be marked in the Diagram pane and appear in the SQL pane. *Changes made to the SQL statement in the SQL pane will only be carried over to the Diagram and Grid panes when the Verify SQL, ⚗ , or Run Query, ！ , buttons are clicked* (or the equivalent options chosen from the popup menu that will open when you right mouse click on the SQL pane). The Run Query will show the results of the query in the Result pane.

10.2.1 The SQL Select Command

Selecting rows and columns from a table is done with the Select command. In this case, we will select all the rows and all the columns from the table of Friends:

```
Select * From Friends
```

In the IDE, it will look like Figure 10.5 after Run Query has been clicked.

Limiting what columns will be chosen is done by selecting the specific columns in the Diagram or Grid windows or writing the column name in the SQL pane (Figure 10.6). The order in which the columns are chosen in the Diagram pane and that corresponds to their order in the Grid pane and in the Select statement will determine their order in the output.

Limiting the rows is done with the Where clause, as in Figure 10.7, where only male friends are shown. The criteria can be entered in the Criteria column of the Grid pane or directly in the SQL pane. The gender does not appear in the Result pane, because the column gender has been unselected in the Diagram pane.

Adding the keyword Distinct to the SQL command will show only rows with distinct values. In the case in Figure 10.8, only one occurrence of every combination of

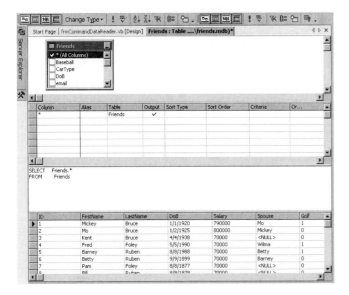

FIGURE 10.5
Selecting all the data items in the
Query Builder.

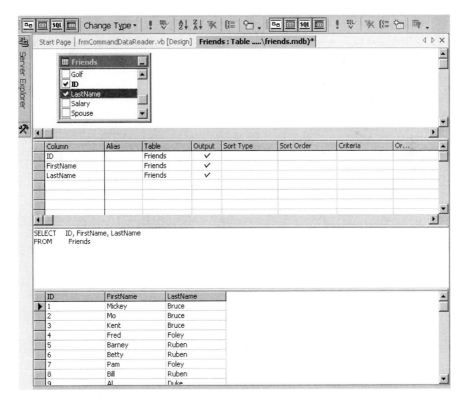

FIGURE 10.6
Selecting specific data items in the Query Builder.

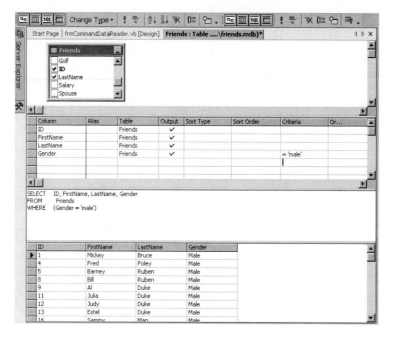

FIGURE 10.7
Adding a Criterion in the Grid pane.

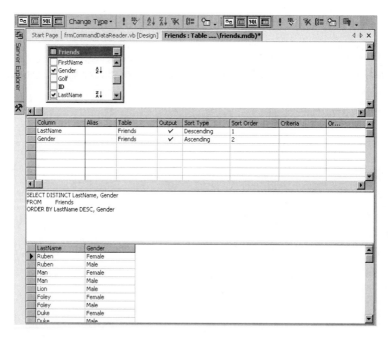

FIGURE 10.8
Specifying Sort Type and Sort Order in the Grid pane.

last name and gender will be shown. Ordering the output is done with the Order By keyword. This can be added in the Sort Type and Sort Order columns of the Grid pane or in the SQL statement. The order of the column names in the SQL statement determines their order in the output. The output can be sorted in ascending order, by default, or in descending order. Descending order is marked in the SQL statement with the DESC keyword. The order is also shown in the Diagram pane with the ↕ and ↕ icons.

Additional options, including Group By, Having, Inner Join, and Outer Join, as well as the Insert, Update, and Delete SQL commands will be discussed in Chapter 11.

10.3 AN OVERVIEW OF THE COMMAND OBJECT AND THE DATAREADER

The Command objects SQLCommand and OleDbCommand handle the SQL commands that are passed to the Data Source once the connection in tier 1 has been established. SQLCommand handles SQL commands passed to SQL Server. OleDbCommand handle SQL commands passed to any other Data Source.

10.3.1 Some Basic Command Class Properties and Methods

The most important properties, and indeed in many cases the only ones that must be set in a Command object, are the CommandText property, where the SQL statement or stored procedure name appears as a string, and the Connection property that specifies the name of the object that is the Connection object to the Data Source to which the SQL command or stored procedure call is being sent. By setting the Connection property to an object name, the same SQL statement or the same stored procedure name can be activated in different databases. The next example shows how this is done with Access. A Connection object and a Command object are declared and instantiated (the latter with the New keyword). The ConnectionString property is set and the connection opened. Next, the SQL command is assigned to the CommandText Property of the Command object and the Command object is connected to the Connection object. With that done, the SQL command can be executed. In this case, being a non-query (an SQL statement that does not return a value), it is executed with the ExecuteNon-Query method on the Friends Access database. The non-query will delete one line from the table of Friends. The ConnectionString of the Connection object is set to the corresponding value in an OleDbConnection object that supposedly is already connected to the database. (The appendix discusses SQL syntax in detail.) The code is as follows:

```
Dim myConnection2 As New OleDb.OleDbConnection()
Dim myCommand2 As New OleDb.OleDbCommand()
Try
    ' Assign Connection String from a Connection control
    ' where supposedly the wizard already built them.
    ' It is imperative to use Try and Catch
    ' Connection String.
    myConnection2.ConnectionString = _
        OleDbConnection1.ConnectionString

    ' Open the connection
    myConnection2.Open()
```

```
    ' Build the SQL command and assign it to the
    ' Command Text property of the Command object.
    myCommand2.CommandText = "Delete FROM Friends "
                            "    Where ID = '1' ; "

    ' Tie the Command object to the specific Connection object.
    myCommand2.Connection = myConnection2

    ' And, execute the Command object as a nonquery,
    ' meaning that no returned values are expected.
    myCommand2.ExecuteNonQuery()

Catch e1 As Exception
    ' It is imperative to use Try and Catch
    ' because the error message will get lost otherwise.
    Console.WriteLine(e1.Message)
Finally
    ' Always close a Connection when you are done.
    myConnection2.Close()
End Try
```

The same task in SQL Server will be performed almost identically, assuming that the same table exists in the SQL Server database, too, except for the classes of the Connection and Command objects and the ConnectionString property itself. Here is the code:

```
Dim myConnection As New SqlClient.SqlConnection()
Dim myCommand As New SqlClient.SqlCommand()
Try
    ' Build the Connection String.
    myConnection.ConnectionString = _
                            "data source=GEFEN-LAPTOP;" & _
                            "initial catalog=master;" & _
                            "integrated security=SSPI;" & -
                            "persist security info=True;" & _
                            "workstation id=GEFEN-LAPTOP;" & _
                            "packet size=4096"

    ' Open the connection
    myConnection.Open()

    ' Build the SQL command and assign it to the
    ' Command Text property of the Command object.
    myCommand.CommandText = "Delete FROM Friends "
                            "    Where Friend_ID = '1' ; "

    ' Tie the Command object to the specific Connection object.
    myCommand.Connection = myConnection

    ' And, execute the Command object as a nonquery,
    ' meaning that no returned values are expected.
    myCommand.ExecuteNonQuery()
```

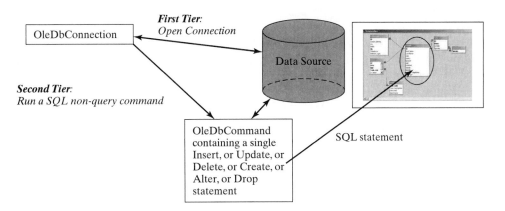

First Tier:
Open Connection

OleDbConnection

Data Source

Second Tier:
Run a SQL non-query command

OleDbCommand
containing a single
Insert, or Update, or
Delete, or Create, or
Alter, or Drop
statement

SQL statement

FIGURE 10.9
Managing non-queries in ADO.NET.

```
Catch e1 As Exception
    ' It is imperative to use Try and Catch
    ' because the error message will get lost otherwise.
    Console.WriteLine(e1.Message)
Finally
    ' Always close a Connection when you are done.
    myConnection2.Close()
End Try
```

Figure 10.9 shows this process. It is the same whether run on Access or SQL Server. The Connection object establishes a connection to the Data Source. With this connection, a non-query SQL statement is executed through the Command object on the data or schema in the Data Source.

10.3.2 Some Basic DataReader Properties and Method

The preceding examples executed a non-query SQL statement. Executing a query SQL statement requires some minor changes. First, the returned value of the SQL statement, usually a view in the structure of a table, must be assigned into an appropriate data structure. In the last chapter the view was assigned to a data bound control through a DataSet that was filled through a DataAdapter object. Alternatively, the data can be assigned to a DataReader through a Command object. We do the latter in this chapter. We will examine DataSets in detail later in the book. A DataReader is an object that stores a table and allows a sequential forward reading through its Read method. Data can only be read and can only be read forward in this object. The Read method advances the cursor—the pointer in the view—to the next row, making the data in the columns of that row available with a group of Get methods, such as GetString, which returns the String value of the data in a given column.

How to use the DataReader is shown in Figure 10.10. The code declares and instantiates a Connection and a Command object as before, this time adapted to SQL Server, but the same exact technique works with the OleDb classes. A DataReader is also declared.

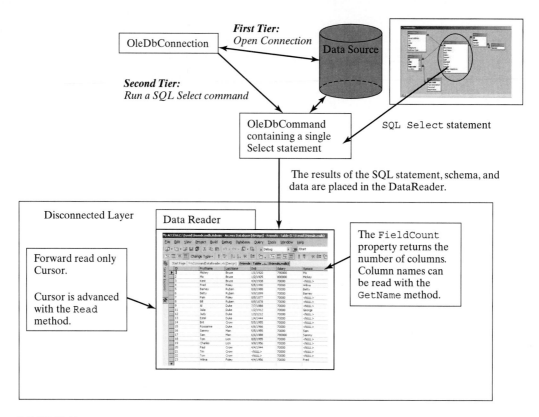

FIGURE 10.10
Managing Select queries with a Data Reader object.

Make note to declare the DataReader without parentheses. Adding the parentheses to the SqlDataReader class will make the myReader object into an object array.

Since the SQL statement that is assigned to the CommandText property is a Select statement, the ExecuteReader method is used to retrieve the view and assign it to the DataReader. When retrieving data with the ExecuteReader method, it is possible to state how the data will be read. By default, the entire view is read into the DataReader. This is equivalent to adding the parameter CommandBehavior.Default, which reads all the data returned from the SQL statement as rows in a view and also creates the schema of that view. A slightly better way of reading the data is with the CommandBehavior.Sequential-Access parameter, as done in the example. This option reads the data as a stream and allows the cutting up of that stream according to the data fields within it with the Get methods—more on those in a moment. The other parameters include CommandBehavior-.SingleRow, which returns only one row rather than all the rows in the view, and CommandBehavior.SingleResult, which returns only one field. The method can be activated to return only the view schema with the CommandBehavior.SchemaOnly parameter or only the primary key information with the CommandBehavior.KeyInfo parameter. In the code example, the CommandBehavior.SequentialAccess parameter is applied and, consequently, each time the Read method of the DataReader is activated, the cursor moves to the next row in the view. The Read method is a function and returns a True value if the end of the file has not yet been reached or a False value if it has.

Once the end of the file is reached or after an error has occurred, the Command, Connection, and DataReader are closed with the Close method. *Once data are read into a DataReader, no new data can be read into it until it is closed.*

Here is the code:

```
' Dimension the Connection Object
Dim myConnection As New SqlClient.SqlConnection()

' Dimension the Command Object
Dim myCommand As New SqlClient.SqlCommand()

' Dimension the Data Reader Object
Dim myReader As SqlClient.SqlDataReader 'No () in SQLDataReader

Try
    ' Build the Connection String
    myConnection.ConnectionString = _
                            "data source=GEFEN-LAPTOP;" & _
                            "initial catalog=master;" & _
                            "integrated security=SSPI;" & _
                            "persist security info=True;" & _
                            "workstation id=GEFEN-LAPTOP;" & _
                            "packet size=4096"
    ' Open the connection
    myConnection.Open()

    ' Build the SQL command and assign it to the
    ' Command Text property of the Command object.
    myCommand.CommandText = _
            "SELECT  [First Name], [Last Name] FROM Friends; "
    ' Tie the Command object to the specific Connection object.
    myCommand.Connection = myConnection

    ' Execute the SQL Command, and place its result in the Data
    ' Reader.
    myReader = _
        myCommand.ExecuteReader(CommandBehavior.SequentialAccess)

    ' Read the next line in the Data Reader.
    ' The first time the method is activated, the first row
    ' is returned.
    ' When there are no more rows to be read, the method
    ' returns the value False.
    Do While myReader.Read

        ' Add the items in the row that are accessed with the
        ' Get methods. In this case, the items are accessed
        ' as strings with the GetString method.
        ' It is imperative that the items be read in their
        ' order in the row. Items too can only be read forward.
        lstReader.Items.Add(myReader.GetString(0) & " " & _
                        myReader.GetString(1))

    Loop
```

```
Catch e1 As Exception
    ' Show any error message.
    Console.WriteLine(e1.Message)
Finally
    ' When done, close the Data Reader, Command, and Connection.
    myReader.Close()
    myCommand.Close()
    myConnection.Close()
End Try
```

When a row is read with the Read method of the DataReader, the data in the columns can be read in several ways. The GetString() method will return a String value of the data in column that is indexed in the method. So if the code says myReader.GetString(1) then the data in the second column (remember everything in VB.NET is indexed with 0 being the first entry) will be returned in a String format. Any of the multiple other Get methods can be used to retrieve the data cast into other data types that are supported by VB.NET or by SQL, such as GetBoolean, GetByte, GetDouble, Get Float (for Single precision floating point), and so on. Alternatively, the Item property can be used to retrieve the data of the item at a given column number, or the GetValue method can be used to retrieve the data in its native format (i.e., in its format as stored in the Data Source).

The GetName method will return the column name. The total number of columns is registered in the FieldCount property. FieldCount has no index. One important caveat: *Once a column has been read*, *only the columns that appear after it in the same row can be read*, just as only rows after the current row can be read with the Next method. Thus, while the command

```
lstReader.Items.Add(myReader.GetString(0) & " " & _
                    myReader.GetString(1))
```

is perfectly valid, the command

```
lstReader.Items.Add(myReader.GetString(1) & " " & _
                    myReader.GetString(0))
```

is not (bold font added for emphasis).

10.4   A LOOK AT SOME MORE PROPERTIES AND METHODS[20]

10.4.1   Command Timeout Property

The CommandTimeout property determines how long in seconds the DBMS will allow the SQL statement to wait until it can be executed. Occasionally, an SQL command cannot execute immediately, because resources that it requires are being held by other applications. These resources may be tables, rows in a table, or indexes that the SQL statement accesses. If these resources are held by another application, the SQL command will have to wait its turn. But, since allowing transactions to wait until the SQL command can be executed may cause extensive deadlocks in the database (see previous

---

[20]VB.NET also supports some future use properties that are not yet included in SQL Server, such as the Depth property of the DataReader and XMLReader. These topics are not included in the book.

chapter), the DBMS must limit the amount of time the transaction waits. This limit is set in two places: in the connection, as shown in the previous chapter, and in the SQL statement itself with this property. By default, the value of this property is 30 seconds. The property can be read and set in the code:

```
Dim intInterval As Integer = 30
myCommand.CommandTimeout = intInterval
intInterval = myCommand.CommandTimeout
```

10.4.2 Command Type Property

The CommandType property determines whether the string in the CommandText is an SQL statement, a call to a stored procedure, or a direct access to a whole table. Stored procedures are discussed in the next chapter. Direct access to a whole table is like writing an SQL statement of Select * From <table name>. The Direct Access option circumvents the standard SQL interface mandated in all ISO-compliant DBMSs and is not supported by SQL Server. The default value of this property is a SQL statement.

It is imperative that SQL statements be executed only when this parameter is set to Text and that stored procedures be called only when it is set to StoredProcedure. In the case of an SQL statement, the code will be

```
myCommand.CommandType = CommandType.Text
myCommand.CommandText = _
            "SELECT  [First Name], [Last Name] FROM Friends; "
```

and, in the case of a stored procedure,

```
myCommand.CommandType = CommandType.StoredProcedure
myCommand.CommandText = "myProcedure1"
```

10.4.3 Other Command Properties

The UpdatedRowSource property will be discussed in the context of DataSets. The Transaction property is discussed in Section 10.8. The Parameters property is discussed toward the end of this chapter and in the next.

10.4.4 Some Other Command Methods

We have already seen the ExecuteReader and ExextureNonQuery methods. Another method of this group is ExecuteScalar. This method returns a single value, as in the SQL statement.

```
Select Count(ID) From Friends.
```

It is more efficient to execute the SQL statement with the ExectureScalar method when the SQL query returns a single. The data can be read in this case directly into a variable. This method has no parameters:

```
' Define and instantiate the Connection and Command objects.
Dim myConnection As New SqlClient.SqlConnection()
Dim myCommand As New SqlClient.SqlCommand()
' This is where the result of the SQL statement will be placed.
Dim intResult As Integer
```

```
Try
   ' Build the Connection String
   myConnection.ConnectionString = _
                        "data source=GEFEN-LAPTOP;" & _
                        "initial catalog=master;" & _
                        "integrated security=SSPI;" & -
                        "persist security info=True;" & _
                        "workstation id=GEFEN-LAPTOP;" & _
                        "packet size=4096"

   ' Open the connection.
   myConnection.Open()

   ' Build the SQL command and assign it to the
   ' Command Text property of the Command object.
   myCommand.CommandText = "SELECT  Count(*) FROM Friends; "

   ' Tie the Command object to the specific Connection object.
   myCommand.Connection = myConnection

   ' And, execute the Command object as a scalar query.
   intResult = myCommand.ExecuteScalar
   ' Show the result in a List Box.
   lstReader.Items.Add("There are " & intResult & " friends.")
Catch e1 As Exception
   ' It is imperative to use Try and Catch
   ' because the error message will get lost otherwise
    Console.WriteLine(e1.Message)
Finally
   ' Always close a Connection when you are done.
   myConnection.Close()
End Try
```

The Cancel method cancels a command if it is currently running. It does nothing otherwise. The ResetCommandTimeout method resets the CommandTimeout property to its default. Here is the relevant code:

```
myCommand.Cancel()
myCommand.ResetCommandTimeout()
```

The Prepare method of the Command object makes the DBMS *precompile* the SQL statement at that point in time. Precompile is a process in which the DBMS analyzes the SQL statement based on the existing meta-data (such as what indexes each table has, how "good" each index is, how many rows there are in each table, and so on) to determine the most efficient access path for it when it will be eventually executed. This access path will contain, for example, which indexes to apply and in what order to join tables. Determining the access path is the absolute prerogative of the DBMS. The application programs have absolutely no say in the process and indeed should not because that is one of the basic background services that a relational database supplies. Every SQL statement must be precompiled either before it is run or during execution. When it is precompiled prior to execution, it is said that the SQL statement went through *early binding*. When the most efficient path is resolved during runtime (i.e., at the last possible moment), it is said that the SQL statement went through *late binding*. Early binding occurs when the application program is compiled. Any subsequent change to the SQL statements during runtime, such as when the SQL statement is built dynamically in a string variable and only then passed to the Command object, will automatically result in a late binding, even if the SQL had been previously precompiled in early binding. Nonetheless, even when late binding is used, it is convenient occasionally to compile the SQL statement before it is actually executed, for example to take advantage of a lull in the processing of the transaction. This is done with the `Prepare` method:

```
myCommand.Prepare()
```

10.5   THE XML READER

XML, or Extensible Markup Language, is a complementary language to HTML. It handles things that HTML does not. XML is a structured cross-platform method of describing data by inserting tags, describing data type and additional information, and separating the user interface from the data. Each data item is encapsulated within special tags in XML. XML describes the data structure, supplementing the display of data handled by HTML. Being a central part of the .NET Architecture, SQL Server can pass the results of an SQL query back to the application program also in XML format. Since the objective of the book is VB.NET and not XML, we will not go any deeper into the syntax of XML; suffice it to say that VB.NET provides the tools to read and edit XML. Primary among these is the XMLReader, which can be connected to an SQL Command object just as the DataReader is. This section demonstrates this and explains some of the properties and methods of the XMLReader class.

An XMLReader resides in the XML Namespace and must be declared:

```
' Define XML Reader
Dim myXMLReader As Xml.XmlReader
```

Once it is declared, the XML Reader can receive the result of an SQL statement that is executed in a Command object, except that SQL Server must be told to return the data in XML format by adding the "FOR XML AUTO" suffix to the SQL statement, as in the following code:

```
' Define and instantiate the Connection and Command objects.
Dim myConnection As New SqlClient.SqlConnection()
Dim myCommand As New SqlClient.SqlCommand()

' Set the Connection String (code is abridged here)
' and open the connection.
myConnection.ConnectionString = ...
myConnection.Open()

' Tie the Command object to the Connection object.
myCommand.Connection = myConnection

' Build the SQL statement, requesting XML format.
myCommand.CommandText = "SELECT  * FROM Friends FOR XML AUTO"
```

The Command object must be executed accordingly to handle an XML SQL result:

```
' Retrieve result of SQL statement into an XML Reader
myXMLReader = myCommand.ExecuteXmlReader
```

With that done, the XMLReader contains the view that is the result of the SQL query and can be read. Since the Read method does not return an end-of-file value, it must be examined explicitly with the EOF property in a Do While statement:

```
' Read next line in XML format
myXMLReader.Read()
Do While Not myXMLReader.EOF
```

The AttributeCount property will then contain the number of attributes, (columns in the SQL view) in the XML row that has been just read. This property can be used to control a For loop that reads through the items. The loop's limit is AttributeCount - 1 because the first item is indexed 0. The items are read with the Item property. The next row in the XMLReader is read with the Read method. The code is written as follows:

```
    For I = 0 To myXMLReader.AttributeCount - 1
        lstReader.Items.Add(myXMLReader.Item(I))
    Next
    myXMLReader.Read()
Loop
```

10.5.1 Some Other XMLReader Methods

As with the DataReader, the Close method closes the XML Reader and makes it possible to open it again with new data. The Skip method, skips one row in the XML-Reader data. The GetAttribute(I) method retrieves the value of the indexed item in the row. Thus, myXMLReader.GetAttribute(0) is the same as myXMLReader.Item(0), both return the value of the first item.

10.6 READING THE DATABASE SCHEMA

The DataReader can also be applied to reading the schema (the internal data structure of a view or table) with the GetSchemaTable method. In the next example of code, the DataReader is filled with the Schema Only information of the SQL statements. Figure 10.11 demonstrates the process involved.

The code to access this schema is as follows:

```
' Define and instantiate a Connection object.
' and a Command object
Dim myConnection3 As New SqlClient.SqlConnection()
Dim myCommand3 As New SqlClient.SqlCommand()

' Define a Data Reader object.
Dim myReader3 As SqlClient.SqlDataReader 'check there is no ()

Dim I As Integer

Dim strData(7) As String.
```

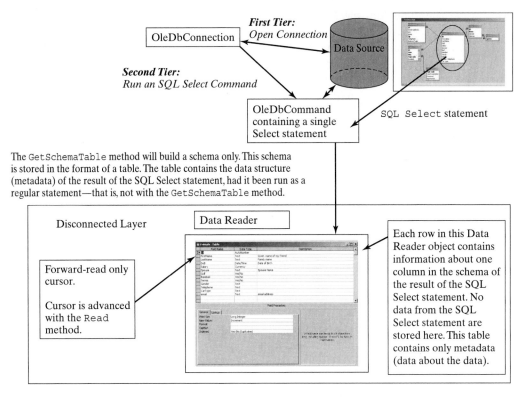

The GetSchemaTable method will build a schema only. This schema is stored in the format of a table. The table contains the data structure (metadata) of the result of the SQL Select statement, had it been run as a regular statement—that is, not with the GetSchemaTable method.

FIGURE 10.11
Reading table schema with a Data Reader object.

```
Try
    ' Build the Connection String.
    myConnection3.ConnectionString = _
                            "data source=GEFEN-LAPTOP;" & _
                            "initial catalog=master;" & _
                            "integrated security=SSPI;" & _
                            "persist security info=True;" & _
                            "workstation id=GEFEN-LAPTOP;" & _
                            "packet size=4096"

    ' Open the connection.
    myConnection3.Open()

    ' Build the SQL command, and assign it to the
    ' Command Text property of the Command object.
    myCommand3.CommandText = "SELECT  * FROM Friends; "

    ' Tie the Command object to the specific Connection object.
    myCommand3.Connection = myConnection3

    ' And, execute the Command object to read only the schema.
    myReader3 = _
        myCommand3.ExecuteReader(CommandBehavior.SchemaOnly)
```

The data from the DataReader are then copied into a string array, showing the table name, number of rows, and the column headers in the schema. This is demonstrated in two ways, with the `Item` property and with the `Caption` property. The concatenation of these string entries in the array is presented in a List Box separated by tabs. The tabs are inserted by placing `Chr(9)`, which is the character value of a tab, between them with the assistance of the `Join` method of the String class. Following is the code:

```
' The TableName property returns the table name.
strData(0) = myReader3.GetSchemaTable().TableName

' The Count property returns the number of rows in the table.
strData(1) = myReader3.GetSchemaTable().Rows.Count

' Access the name of the first column.
strData(2) = _
        myReader3.GetSchemaTable().Columns.Item(0).ToString

' Access the name of the subsequent columns.
strData(3) = _
        myReader3.GetSchemaTable().Columns.Item(1).ToString
strData(4) = _
        myReader3.GetSchemaTable().Columns.Item(2).ToString
strData(5) = _
        myReader3.GetSchemaTable().Columns.Item(3).ToString

' It is the same whether you write ToString or Caption.
strData(6) = _
        myReader3.GetSchemaTable().Columns.Item(4).Caption

' Add the preceding information to the List Box, separated by
' tabs.
lstReader.Items.Add(Join(strData, Chr(9)))

' Close the Data Reader so we can reopen it again
' with other data.
myReader3.Close()
```

A more practical application of the DataReader reading the schema is to examine the names of the columns in the table and their data type. The following code does just that, showing the sequence of the columns, their name, and their length:

```
' Reread the schema.
myReader3 = _
        myCommand3.ExecuteReader(CommandBehavior.SchemaOnly)

' Define Data Table and Data Row.
Dim dtbSchema As DataTable
Dim myRow As DataRow
Dim strName As String
```

```
' Read schema into the DataTable.
 dtbSchema = myReader3.GetSchemaTable()

' Print header information in the List Box.
 lstReader.Items.Add("Sequence" & Chr(9) & _
                        "Column Name" & Chr(9) & "Length")

' Read all the rows in the schema, each row corresponding
' to the details of one column.

' Data Rows are read with a For Each that reads through the
' Collection of Data Rows in the Data Table.
 For Each myRow In dtbSchema.Rows
     strName = myRow(0)
     strName = strName.PadRight(20)

     ' Chr(9) is the same as inserting a tab with vbTab.
     lstReader.Items.Add(myRow(1) & Chr(9) & Chr(9) & _
                            strName & Chr(9) & myRow(2))
 Next

Catch e1 As Exception
    Console.WriteLine(e1.Message)
Finally
    ' Always close a Connection when you are done.
    myConnection3.Close()
End Try
```

Of course, knowing what appears in each column of the schema is helpful, and that is what we got in the previous lines of code. Reading the table schema requires a special object, one of the DataTable class. Each row in that table also requires a special object, one of the DataRow class. The DataTable is filled with the GetSchemaTable method, and the rows in the table are then read one at a time with a For Each loop. We will discuss the DataTable and DataRow classes in Chapter 13.

10.6.1 Running Example

We will build an application to examine this code in the lab at the end of this chapter. This is what the output will look like. The Data Table we created contains the schema of the table that would have been created had we run the SQL statement to read the data. For convenience, we will call the Data Table we just created the Schema Data Table. There is no actual data from the database in the Schema Data Table; it only contains metadata (data about the structure of the tables).

The column titles in the Schema Data Table (Figure 10.12) appear in the top two lines. The Data Rows contain information about the columns in the table that would have been created had we run the SQL statement to read the data. By reading the Data Rows in the Schema Data Table we can display information about that schema.

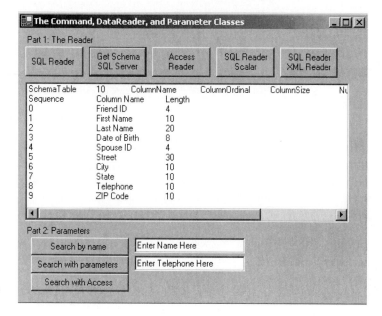

FIGURE 10.12
Showing the metadata of the Friends table.

10.7 PASSING PARAMETERS TO A COMMAND OBJECT

Last chapter introduced an initial ADO diagram. It is now time to expand this diagram and add to it the Parameter objects from the SQLParameter and the OleDbParameter classes. The diagram will be further expanded in the next chapters. Parameters are values that are passed to SQL statements or to Stored Procedures (these too are handled by the Data Source) and serve the same theoretical purpose that parameters passed to a subroutine or a function serve: to pass values that may change among different activations of the SQL statement or of the stored procedure. Parameters are part of the second tier.

In the diagram in Figure 10.13, we made a slight change compared with what we did the previous chapter. Although the Data Adapter classes seem as though they access the Data Source directly, and indeed it seems so when working with the wizards, in effect

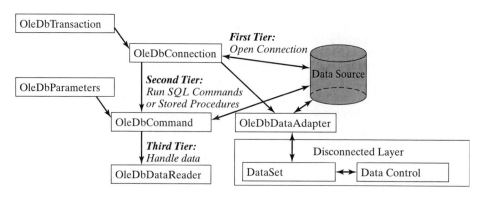

FIGURE 10.13
Adding Parameters and Transactions to the three tier ADO.NET diagram.

the Data Adapter access the Data Source through SQL statements. These SQL statements are embedded within Command objects that are part of the properties of the Data Adapter object. We shall explore this in detail in the next few chapters, when we write the Data Adapter code explicitly.

10.7.1 What are Parameters?

SQL statements often need to be built dynamically. In other words, there is a need for some kind of mechanism that will allow at least part of the SQL statement to change from one execution of the SQL command to another. Such a case may happen for example with an SQL statement that is used to read all the rows in a table of friends where the first name or the last name of the friend contain within them a sequence of letters, a string, that is entered in a textbox. There are several ways to handle such a need. The obvious way of handling such a case, albeit the least effective, is to rebuild the SQL statement each time a new value is entered in the textbox based on the value that was entered. This is what happens in the code example that follows, where txtName is the name of the textbox:

```
' Build the SQL command, and assign the values in its
' Where clause from a textbox.
myCommand.CommandText = _
    "SELECT  [First Name], [Last Name],[Telephone] " & _
    " FROM Friends " & _
    " Where [First Name] = '" & txtName.Text & "' Or " & _
    "       [Last Name]  = '" & txtName.Text & "'
    " Order by [First Name], [Last Name] ; "
```

> **Programming Note:** Wherever SQL syntax expects a single-space character, many additional spaces can be inserted. The additional spaces are ignored. Nonetheless, it improves the readability of the text accordingly to insert spaces wherever doing so may align the elements of the SQL statement in a more readable manner, as shown in the example.

> **Programming Note:** It is always a good idea when splitting an SQL command on several lines (itself a good idea because it saves the need to scroll left and right in order to read the entire statement) to add a space before the first word on each row. SQL ignores unnecessary spaces, but when a space is required by SQL syntax and is missing from the string, the DBMS returns a runtime error. It is easy to avoid at least some of these runtime errors by inserting such a space.

This process, however, is rather bulky from a programming point of view because it is as though a new subroutine were written for each combination of parameters that it can accept. Worse still, doing so detracts from the ability of the DBMS to optimize the SQL statement and calculate its optimal path in the data. When the SQL statement of the Command object is different in each execution of the Command object, each execution requires a new precompilation at runtime, *late binding*, of the SQL statement because the DBMS cannot be prepared in advance.

Avoiding these pitfalls is easily done with the application of parameters to the SQL statements. Parameters passed to an SQL statement, and the same applies to stored procedures, serve the same purpose as parameters passed to a subroutine or to a function. Parameters pass values that are inserted into the SQL statement. These parameters are objects that instantiate the SQLParameter or the OleDbParameter classes. Because only the parameters change from one execution of the Command object (or stored procedure) to another, the DBMS can compile the optimal access path for the SQL statement only once. Moreover, this can be done in advance with *early binding* and so increase runtime efficiency and make late binding (i.e., during runtime itself) unnecessary.

10.7.2   Specifying Parameters in the SQL Statements

The SQLClient Namespace classes behave differently here from the OleDb Namespace Classes. Parameters in SQL statements that are passed to SQL Server are inserted into the SQL statements as a parameter name with an @ prefix, as shown later, where only rows with a matching value to the parameters are selected. (Specifically, the matching is done between the value of [First Name] and the parameter @Name, or between [Last Name] and the parameter @Name, or between [Telephone] and the parameter @Tele.) The square brackets [ ] encapsulate the name of an attribute (column in a table) that contains a space in its column name. Note that the same parameter can be used many times, as is the case with @Name. Parameter names must begin with a @ and must be an integral part of the SQL statement.

That way, exactly the same SQL statement is executed, regardless of the parameter values passed to it. *The order of the parameters in the SQL statement passed to SQL Server is immaterial. The order of the parameters in the SQL statement passed to other providers, such as Access, matters.* The parameters are identified by their name, as in the following code:

```
' Define and instantiate an SQL command.
Dim myCommand As New SqlClient.SqlCommand()

' Build the SQL command.
' Parameters are included in the text itself with a @ prefix.
myCommand.CommandText = _
          "SELECT  [First Name], [Last Name], Telephone " & _
          " FROM Friends " & _
          " Where [First Name] = @Name Or " & _
          "       [Last Name] = @Name Or " & _
          "       [Telephone] = @Tele   " & _
          " Order by [First Name], [Last Name] ; "
```

Parameters can be passed to any SQL statement, not only Select statements:

```
myCommand.CommandText = _
          "Update Friends Set Telephone = @Tele " & _
          " Where [First Name] = @Name Or " & _
          "       [Last Name] = @Name ; "
```

```
myCommand.CommandText = _
        "Delete From Friends " & _
        " Where [First Name] = @Name Or " & _
        "            [Last Name] = @Name ; "
```

.NET handles other DBMS Providers, such as Oracle and Access differently. When a parameter is inserted into an SQL command that is passed to a different provider (i.e., with the classes in OleDb Namespace), the parameters cannot be named and each must be specified in the SQL command with a "?" character. Needless to say, the order of the parameters in these SQL statements is crucial in this case because the parameters are identified by their sequence in the command rather than by a unique name. Here, too, parameters can be passed to any SQL statement, not only Select statements—and, here, too, the parameter must be embedded in the SQL statement:

```
' Define and instantiate an SQL command object.
Dim myCommand2 As New OleDb.OleDbCommand()

' Define the SQL statement.
' Pass parameters to the SQL statement with ? characters.
myCommand2.CommandText = _
            "SELECT * FROM Titles " & _
            " Where Title = ? Or [Year Published] = ?"
```

10.7.3 Building the Parameters in the VB Code

The parameters in the SQL statement must be matched by parameters in the `Parameter` collection of the Command objects. This is a collection because there can be any number of Parameter objects included within the Command object. For example, when the Data Adapter wizard built this SQL command for handling an Update in one of the previous examples, the SQL statement was

```
UPDATE Friends SET Baseball = ?, CarType = ?, DoB = ?, email = ?,
FirstName = ?, Gender = ?, Golf = ?, LastName = ?, Salary = ?, Spouse
= ?, Telephone = ?, Tennis = ? WHERE (ID = ?) AND (Baseball = ?) AND
(CarType = ? OR ? IS NULL AND CarType IS NULL) AND (DoB = ? OR ? IS NULL
AND DoB IS NULL) AND (FirstName = ?) AND (Gender = ? OR ? IS NULL AND
Gender IS NULL) AND (Golf = ?) AND (LastName = ?) AND (Salary = ? OR ?
IS NULL AND Salary IS NULL) AND (Spouse = ? OR ? IS NULL AND Spouse IS
NULL) AND (Telephone = ? OR ? IS NULL AND Telephone IS NULL) AND (Ten-
nis = ?) AND (email = ? OR ? IS NULL AND email IS NULL)
```

When the Data Adapter wizard built the collection of matching parameters, that is what it did. You can open this window by right clicking the Data Adapter object and then expanding its display of the `UpdateCommand` property. In this expanded view, click the `Parameters` property to open the adjacent window with the Parameter Collection Editor. The Parameter Collection Editor shows the matching parameter in the `Parameter` collection of every parameter in the preceding SQL command. There is exactly the same number of parameters in the collection as there is in the SQL statement, their order is

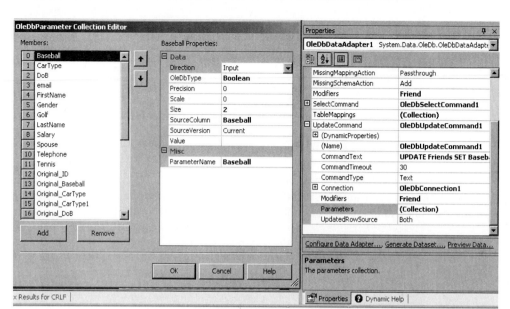

FIGURE 10.14
Opening the Parameter Collection Editor through the Properties window

also exactly the same, and so is their data type. The Properties window and the Parameter Collection Editor that is opened through it are shown in Figure 10.14.

The parameters are passed by the VB code to the SQL statements or to the stored procedures either by explicitly instantiating a Parameter object and adding it to the Parameter collection of the Command object or by implicitly creating a parameter by adding it to the collection in the Command object without instantiating it beforehand. Explicitly instantiating a Parameter object requires declaring it, instantiating it, setting its relevant properties, and adding it to the Command object. At a minimum, the `ParameterName` and `Value` properties must be set. If casting may be an issue, it is recommended to set the `DbType` property, too.[21] This property specifies the data type of

---

[21]The data types supported by SQLClient and by OleDb are equivalent, but named differently. Some of these names are as follows (not all the other data types in ADO are currently supported):

DbType in SQLClient	DbType in OleDb (equivalent in many cases to VB.NET data types)
Bit	Boolean
DateTime	DBTimeStamp
Decimal	Decimal
Float	Double
Real	Single
SmallInt	SmallInt (equivalent to Int16)
Int	Int (equivalent to Int32 and to Integer)
String	VarWChar

the parameter. *It is imperative that the* `ParameterName` *be a String and that it start with an @ sign.* The code is as follows:

```
' Declare and instantiate a Command object.
Dim myCommand As New SqlClient.SqlCommand()

' Declare and instantiate a Parameter object.
Dim prmName As SqlClient.SqlParameter
prmName = New SqlClient.SqlParameter()

' Set the properties of this parameter object.
prmName.ParameterName = "@Name"
prmName.DbType = DbType.String
prmName.Value = txtName.Text

' Add the Parameter object to the Parameter
' Collection of the Command object.
myCommand.Parameters.Add(prmName)
```

To avoid misunderstandings, the DbType "String" as set here is not a String data type as defined in VB.NET. It is a variable length string data type that is not supported anymore by VB.NET. This string can contain up to 4000 characters, and its length is determined according to the length of the text it contains. If a larger string size is needed the `Size` property should be set accordingly to the maximum string size. The data type `DbType.StringFixedLength` is closer in concept to the String data type in VB.NET (although it is not the same because it is not handled as an object in the parameter).

Of course, many Parameters may be added to one Command, because the Command object handles them as a collection. The order in which the Parameters are added to the Command is not important in SQL Server, but is crucial with other providers (i.e., DBMS). In practical terms, this means that when the SQLClient classes are used, the order of the parameters is immaterial because the parameters are identified by their name, while when the OleDb classes are used the order in which the parameters are added to the Command is crucial because that it was identifies each parameter. The `ParameterName` property identifies the parameter and enables matching it to its corresponding parameter in the SQL Statement. In OleDB the order in which Parameters are added to the Command determines the order in which they will appear in the SQL statement.

Additional properties of the Parameter class that are used with DataSets and with stored procedures include `Direction`, which specifies whether the parameter is an input to the SQL statement or stored procedure (the default), is output, or is both:

```
prmName.Direction = ParameterDirection.Input
prmName.Direction = ParameterDirection.InputOutput
prmName.Direction = ParameterDirection.Output
```

Parameters may be declared and instantiated explicitly before being added to the Command object:

```
' Declare and instantiate a Parameter object.
Dim prmTele As SqlClient.SqlParameter
prmTele = New SqlClient.SqlParameter()
```

```
' Set the properties of this parameter object.
prmTele.ParameterName = "@Tele"
prmTele.Value = txtTelephone.Text

' Add the Parameter object to the Parameter
' Collection of the Command object.
myCommand.Parameters.Add(prmTele)
```

Alternatively, parameters can be declared implicitly in the Add method of the Command object. The Add method can be overloaded in several ways. The next example contains the parameter name, its data type, and length, and the Value property of the Add method specifies the value that will be passed to the parameter in the SQL statement. If the SQL statement is being executed by SQL Server, then all the references to the parameter name within the SQL statement will receive this value. The code is as follows:

```
' Add the Parameter object to the Parameter Collection of the
' Command object, by implicitly declaring it with its properties.
myCommand.Parameters.Add("@Tele", SqlDbType.Char, 10).Value = _
                        txtTelephone.Text

myCommand.Parameters.Add("@Name", SqlDbType.Char, 20).Value = _
                        txtName.Text.Trim
```

Parameters work almost the same as with OleDb classes, except that the parameters are assigned to the SQL statement according to their sequence. This means that the first "?" in the SQL statement will be replaced with the first parameter that is added to the Parameter collection of the Command with the Add method, that the second "?" in the SQL statement will be replaced with the second parameter that is added with the Add method, and so on. Obviously, each parameter in this case relates to only one "?" in the SQL statement. The ParameterName property is applicable only within the VB.NET code; it is immaterial to the SQL statement, but contributes to the readability of the code:

```
' Declare and instantiate the Command object.
Dim myCommand2 As New OleDb.OleDbCommand()

' Assign the SQL command to the Command object.
' Parameters are stated as ? characters.
myCommand2.CommandText = "SELECT * FROM Titles " & _
                    " Where Title = ? Or [Year Published] = ?"

' Declare and instantiate the first Parameter.
Dim prmName As New OleDb.OleDbParameter()
' Assign its name property.
prmName.ParameterName = "@Name"
' Assign its value property
prmName.Value = txtName.Text
' Specify in the appropriate property that the parameter is
' input only to the SQL statement, meaning that the SQL
' statement will not return a value through this parameter.
```

```
prmName.Direction = ParameterDirection.Input
' And add it to the Parameters Collection of the above Command.
myCommand2.Parameters.Add(prmName)

' Do the same with the second Parameter.
Dim prmTele As New OleDb.OleDbParameter()
prmTele.ParameterName = "@Tele"
prmTele.Value = txtTelephone.Text
prmTele.Direction = ParameterDirection.Input
myCommand2.Parameters.Add(prmTele)
```

An even more efficient way of handling SQL statements in general, and this goes also for parameters, is with a stored procedure.

10.8   MANAGING TRANSACTIONS

A transaction is an indivisible complete unit of activity on a database or any other data source. By default, all activity by VB.NET on a database is performed through transactions. A new transaction is started, for example, when an event on a control or a form is fired. VB.NET will handle each interaction with the user as one transaction. In other words, each click on a button control, function, or Enter key on the keyboard is treated as a single transaction. As a transaction, the entire set of related calls to the DBMS can either succeed completely or fail completely. Either all the SQL commands succeed, or all fail; there is no option of only some SQL commands in the transaction succeeding. Transactions are never half done activities, a transaction cannot do only part of its activity. Transactions are crucial when working with a database because it is the grouping of SQL statements into one transaction that signals to the DBMS that all these SQL statements must either complete successfully or must all be undone in a process called *rollback*. The result of a rollback is that all the changes a transaction did in the database are undone and the database reverts to its previous state, as though the transaction never occurred.

Although not recommended unless there is a good reason, transactions can be managed manually in VB.NET, circumventing the automatic handling provided by VB.NET. Transactions are handled manually through the application of SqlTransaction or OleDbTransaction objects. Such cases may be justified when a transaction needs to span several interactions with the user. In such a case, a transaction would be started when the user enters data in one form, but not committed until data from a later form is processed. This may happen, for example, when data spanning two or three forms are being collected, but the data are processed only when all the data have been entered. As a result, if data from a later form are erroneous, the changes made by the first form in this sequence should be undone with the rollback command. Enabling this command requires an override of the default transaction management mechanism of ADO.NET. Another case where such an override may be necessary is when a single interaction with the user needs to be handled as a set on unrelated transactions in which some transactions are allowed to commit even if others rollback. The example we will work on in the next section handles just such a case.

10.8.1 Creating a Transaction

A Transaction object is created as any other object is:

```
' Declare a Transaction object
Dim myTransaction As SqlClient.SqlTransaction
```

Before we handle the rest of the code with the Transaction object, let us just add the necessary additional code dealing with the Connection object and the Command object. *A transaction is run within a Connection.* This is a requirement, because a single transaction can contain several SQL commands and, as such, cannot be part of any single Command object. The code is as follows:

```
' Declare and instantiate a Connection and a Command object.
Dim myConnection As New SqlClient.SqlConnection()
Dim myCommand As New SqlClient.SqlCommand()

Try
    ' Assign the Connection String parameter from a control.
    myConnection.ConnectionString = _
        SQLConnection1.ConnectionString

    ' Open the Connection.
    myConnection.Open()

    ' Tie the Command object to the specific Connection object.
    myCommand.Connection = myConnection
```

> **Programming Note:** Unless the operations of one form must be broken down to independent transactions, it is not recommended to explicitly define and use transactions.

10.8.2 Isolation Level

Once defined, the transaction is started with the `BeginTransaction` method of the Connection object. This method can be overridden with four types of parameters. It can receive no parameters at all, or only an *isolation level*, or only a transaction name, or both an isolation level and a transaction name. It is recommended to always give a transaction a name. That way, it can be tracked, and when more than one transaction is run simultaneously, each can be handled explicitly and with less chance of a glitch (bug) within the program. It is also recommended to always specify the isolation level; relying on defaults is a bad habit—defaults may change from one release of a language or software package to the next, as indeed happened with VB.NET. *Isolation level tells the DBMS how to handle concurrency control among the many transactions running simultaneously on the same data.*

One of the great advantages of a DBMS is that the data in the database are available to many users concurrently. Providing the data simultaneously to many users requires that the DBMS guarantee that no user or transaction interfere with another.

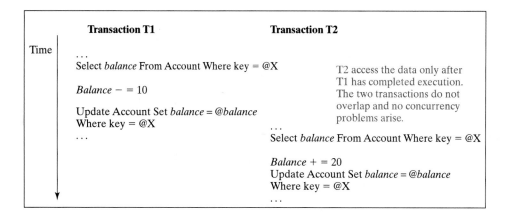

FIGURE 10.15
No concurrency control problems.

Managing this is called *concurrency control*. Handling concurrency control is an essential and crucial aspect of any multiuser DBMS. Concurrency control involves separating the section of the database that each transaction is handling from all the other concurrent transactions. When concurrency control is not managed correctly, one transaction may override changes made by another transaction without either transaction realizing that data have been lost from the database and that the data are no longer consistent. There are three types of problems that can happen when concurrency control is not handled correctly: *Lost Update, Temporary Update*, and *Incorrect Summary*.

The lost update problem occurs when two transactions update the same data item concurrently. If there is no concurrency control, one transaction may complete successfully, but have the changes that it made to the database overwritten by the other transaction. Suppose, for example, that there are two transactions: transaction T1 in which Barney withdraws $10 from a shared account that currently holds $100 and transaction T2 in which Betty deposits $20 into the same account. In most cases, the two transactions will not interfere with each other. T1 will read the balance, update it, and commit its changes and only then will T2 read and update the database. The balance when both transactions commit will be a correct $110. (See Figure 10.15.)

Now, suppose that there is no concurrency control and that T2 starts executing before T1 completes its execution. In this case, T2 will read the current balance in the database ($100) after T1 read it (at point "A"), but before T1 updated it. T2 will then update the database (at point "B") with a new balance ($120). But then T1 (at point "C") will register its own update to the database, making the balance $90 and completely erasing the update done by T2. This is the *lost update* problem. (See Figure 10.16.)

The *temporary update* problem occurs when, again, two transactions attempt to update the same data item concurrently, but one transaction is forced to rollback after the second transaction had already read the data that the now aborted transaction

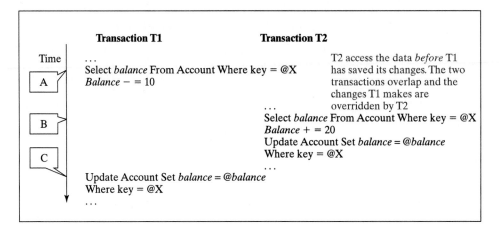

FIGURE 10.16
The lost update problem.

updated. Such cases can happen when the *Isolation Level* is not set appropriately. In Figure 10.17, this could occur when the isolation level of the database connection of T2 is set to ReadUncommitted (allow the transaction to read also uncommitted data of other transactions). Using the same example as above, suppose that T1 read the balance and updated it correctly (point "A"), but is then forced to abort because of some error such as division by zero (point "C"). However, this occurs after T2 had already read and updated the data (point "B"). Specifically, T2 would read the balance after

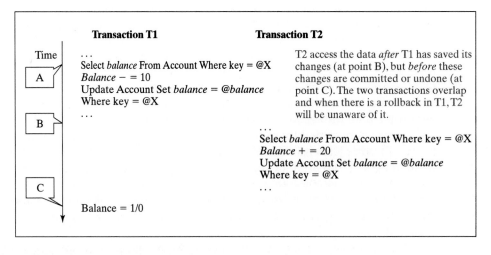

FIGURE 10.17
The temporary update problem.

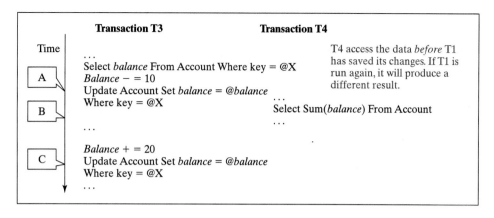

FIGURE 10.18
The incorrect summary problem.

T1 updated its original $100 to $90. T2 will update the balance to $110. If T1 aborts, the balance updated by T2 based on the changes made by T1 will be $110 rather than $120.

The third concurrency control problem is the *incorrect summary* problem (Figure 10.18). This problem is also known as a *Dirty Read* or *Phantom Data*. The problem occurs when one transaction is allowed to read the data while the data are still being updated by another transaction. Suppose, for example, that while transaction T3 is updating the data in Barney and Betty's account (point "A"), transaction T4 is summarizing all the accounts. If T4 reads the data (point "B") before T3 has finished updating the data (point "C"), then T4 will show an incorrect summary of the data.

10.8.3 Setting the Isolation Level

.NET supports several levels of concurrency control. In descending degrees of providing isolation, the main ones are as follows:

- `IsolationLevel.Serializable`—The transaction locks the data it has read and prevents all other transactions from accessing it. This will provide strong concurrency control, but will prevent transactions from running concurrently on the same data.

- `IsolationLevel.RepeatableRead`—The transaction will read and update only data that have neither been read nor updated by other transactions and will not allow other transactions to read or to update that data. This isolation level will guaranty a *Repeatable Read*, meaning that if the same Select statement is run twice within the transaction it is guaranteed that exactly the same result will be returned. Lost Update, Temporary Update, and Incorrect Summary problems will not occur with this isolation level.

- `IsolationLevel.ReadCommitted`—The transaction will read and update only data that have been committed. It will not read or update data that are being handled by other transactions until the other transactions complete execution.

Lost Update and Temporary Update problems will not occur with this isolation level, but Repeatable Read is not guaranteed, so Incorrect Summary problems may occur.

- `IsolationLevel.ReadUncommitted`—Allows the transaction to read and update data at any time regardless of other transactions handling the same data. This isolation level should be avoided when data can be updated in the database. It is applicable in a data-warehouse when it is known that the data are not updateable.

- `IsolationLevel.Chaos`—Allows the transaction to read the data at any time, regardless of locks placed by other transactions. This isolation level should be avoided.

Typically, transactions have either a `RepeatableRead` or a `ReadCommitted` isolation level, depending on whether repeatable read is essential. The higher the degree of the isolation level, the more likely a transaction is to lock the data more than necessary and hence to cause other transactions to wait unnecessarily until it completes its execution.

We will create the transaction with a `RepeatableRead` isolation level and give it a name. *This Transaction object must now be connected to the Command object so that the SQL statements it contains will be executed within the boundaries of the transaction.* The code is

```
' Begin the transaction in the Connection object, and monitor it
' through the Transaction object.
' Here the transaction object is tied to the Connection object,
' its isolation level is set, and it is given a name.
myTransaction = _
          myConnection.BeginTransaction _
                (IsolationLevel.RepeatableRead, _
                "myTransaction")

' Tie the Transaction object to a specific Command object. As a
' result, the Command object will be handled through this
' Transaction object. This operation will tie this Command object
' to all the other Commands that will be tied to this Transaction
' object. All these commands, being part of one transaction, will
' either all succeed or all fail as one unit.
myCommand.Transaction = myTransaction
```

With the Transaction object ready and the Command object tied to it, we can execute SQL statements inside the transaction. In this case, we are running a nonquery SQL statement to drop a table and its data from the database schema and create a new copy of it. The Drop command is run inside a separate Try Block, so that if the table does not exist, execution will not jump to the Catch of the outer Try Block and, in doing so, skip the next set of statements that create a new table. Here is the code:

```
' Do this inside another Try block so we can catch errors.
Try
    ' Assign a Drop SQL statement to the Command object.
```

```
    myCommand.CommandText = "Drop Table myTable; "
        ' And, execute the SQL statement.
    myCommand.ExecuteNonQuery()
Catch
End Try

    ' Assign a new SQL statement to the Command object.
    ' It does not matter if the different SQL statements are
    ' passed to the Data Source through one Command object or
    ' through many. All these SQL commands, by virtue of their
    ' Command object or objects being tied to the same Transaction
    ' object, will be run as one unit. As one transaction, either
    ' all the SQL statements will succeed or all will be undone
    ' when the DBMS will rollback the one transaction.
    myCommand.CommandText = _
            Create Table myTable (Name Char(20));"
    myCommand.ExecuteNonQuery()
```

At this stage, it might make sense to force the changes onto the database. In database terminology, this is called *Commit*. Because we are running on SQL Server, there are two degrees of commit: Save and Commit. Save, handled by a method by the same name, allows the creation of a temporary *save point* to which the transaction can revert without undoing everything it has done since it started or since the last time it committed with the Commit method. This is a convenient way of setting named milestones within the transaction and reverting back to those milestones by name when an error occurs. Save points must be given a name. The Save method is supported only by SQL Server:

```
    ' Save Points work only with SQL Server.
    myTransaction.Save("mySavePoint1")
```

We can now insert some rows into the table:

```
    Dim I As Integer
    For I = 0 To 10
        ' The Insert SQL command inserts one row into a table.
        myCommand.CommandText = _
                "Insert Into myTable Values ('" & CStr(I) & "');"
        ' After building the Insert SQL command, run it.
        myCommand.ExecuteNonQuery()
    Next
```

The delete and update SQL commands work the same way. We will delete a row just to demonstrate how also the Delete and Update SQL statements are run with the same ExecuteNon-Query method:

```
    ' The Delete SQL command deletes rows from a table.
    myCommand.CommandText =  _
            "Delete from myTable Where Name = '991' ;"
```

```
' After building the SQL command, run it.
myCommand.ExecuteNonQuery()

' The Update SQL command updates the values of columns in rows
' in the table.
myCommand.CommandText = _
        "Update myTable Set Name = '22' Where Name = '2' ;"
' After building the SQL command, run it.
myCommand.ExecuteNonQuery()
```

The Commit method will force the changes into the database. Once the commit has been executed, the changes are durable, meaning that they are guaranteed to remain so in the database until another SQL statement explicitly changes them. The command to use is

```
myTransaction.Commit()
```

Had we done a Rollback instead of a commit at this stage, all the changes done by this transaction since the last commit statement would have been undone. If there was no previous commit statement, then all the changes since this transaction began will be undone. The command is

```
myTransaction.Rollback()
```

If we want to roll back only until the previous *Save Point* (recall that this works only with SQL Server), we can add the name of the save point to the rollback. In that case, only changes since the named save point will be undone. Changes made prior to the save point will not be lost. Here is the command:

```
myTransaction.Rollback("mySavePoint1")
```

10.8.4 Transactions in the OleDb Namespace

With the exception of creating Save Points, the classes in the OleDb Namespace behave the same.

10.9   A BRIEF LOOK AT STORED PROCEDURES

A stored procedure is like a subroutine that is stored in the database and activated just as SQL statements are. In its simplest form, a stored procedure is an SQL statement. The following code demonstrates creating and then running a stored procedure, with and without parameters:

```
' Declare and instantiate Connection and Command objects.
Dim myConnection As New SqlClient.SqlConnection()
Dim myCommand As New SqlClient.SqlCommand()

' Declare a Data Reader.
Dim myReader As SqlClient.SqlDataReader
```

```
Try
      ' Set the Connection String and open the Connection.
      myConnection.ConnectionString = _
            SqlConnection1.ConnectionString
            myConnection.Open()
            ' Tie the connection to the Command object.
            myCommand.Connection = myConnection
```

Note that the example is run on SQL Server. Except for the class prefix being OleDb and the connection string, it runs the same with the OleDb Namespace classes. Access, however, does not support these classes.

Before creating the stored procedures, we will make sure none exist with that name. This is done in a separate Try Block so that, should an error occur—and it will— if the stored procedures do not exist, the error will be caught and ignored rather than stop the entire process, which is what will happen if the error is caught by the outer Try Block:

```
Try
      ' Handle errors in this block separately.

      ' Build SQL statements that will drop the two stored
      ' procedures and execute them.
       myCommand.CommandType = CommandType.Text
       myCommand.CommandText = "Drop Procedure myProcedure1;"
       myCommand.ExecuteNonQuery()
       myCommand.CommandText = "Drop Procedure myProcedure2;"
       myCommand.ExecuteNonQuery()
Catch
End Try
```

Building a stored procedure is almost the same as any other SQL statement. It is run with an ExecuteNon-Query method and its CommandType property is Text. Recall that everything an application does with a relational database once the connection to it has been established is done through SQL commands. Creating a stored procedure is no exception, and the following code cannot run on Access:

```
' Build a stored procedure.
myCommand.CommandType = CommandType.Text

' The following SQL statement will build a stored procedure
' when it is executed:.
myCommand.CommandText = _
                "Create Procedure myProcedure1  AS " & _
                "    Select * From Friends  ;        "

' Execute the SQL statement to build the stored procedure.
myCommand.ExecuteNonQuery()
```

Calling the stored procedure is slightly different from executing a regular SQL command. The `CommandType` property of the Command object must be set to `StoredProcedure`. Otherwise, its result can be read as with any other SQL statement. The code is as follows:

```
' Setting the Command object to calling the stored procedure.
myCommand.CommandType = CommandType.StoredProcedure
myCommand.CommandText = "myProcedure1"

' Call the stored procedure, and place the results
' in a Data Reader.
myReader = _
      myCommand.ExecuteReader _
      (CommandBehavior.SequentialAccess)
' Once in a Data Reader, the data are treated the same.
' The Data Reader is in the disconnected layer.
While myReader.Read
   ' Here we will print the data in the Output window.
   Console.Writeline _
           (myReader.GetValue(0).ToString.PadRight(15) & _
           " " & _
            myReader.GetValue(1).ToString.PadRight(15) & _
           " " & _
           myReader.GetValue(2).ToString.PadLeft(15))
End While

' Close the Data Reader when done.
myReader.Close()
```

Like any SQL statement, a stored procedure can receive parameters. These are specified just as they would be with an SQL statement:

```
' Build a stored procedure with a parameter.
myCommand.CommandType = CommandType.Text
myCommand.CommandText = _
      "Create Procedure myProcedure2 " & _
      " @name varChar(10) AS " & _
      "    Select * From Friends        " & _
      "       Where [First Name] = @name  ; "
myCommand.ExecuteNonQuery()
```

The stored procedure is called just as an SQL statement with parameters would be, again with the exception that the `CommandType` property must be `StoredProcedure`:

```
' Call it with a parameter.
myCommand.CommandType = CommandType.StoredProcedure
myCommand.CommandText = "myProcedure2"
myCommand.Parameters.Add _
            ("@name", SqlDbType.Char, 20).Value = "George"
myReader = _
```

```
        myCommand.ExecuteReader _
            (CommandBehavior.SequentialAccess)
    While myReader.Read
        Console.Writeline _
            (myReader.GetValue(0).ToString.PadRight(15))
    End While
    myReader.Close()

Catch e1 As Exception
    MessageBox.Show(e1.Message)
End Try
```

LAB 10: THE COMMAND, DATAREADER, AND PARAMETERS CLASSES

Lab Objectives:
1. Practice the Command and DataReader Classes in SQL Server.
2. Practice the Command and DataReader Classes in Access.
3. Practice scalar reading with the Command and DataReader Classes in SQL Server.
4. Look briefly at the XMLReader
5. Pass Parameters to SQL Server
6. Pass Parameters to Access

Application Overview

The lab contains two sections. In the first section, a series of SQL Select statements are executed with Command objects and the resulting view is read with DataReaders and displayed in a List Box. This section accesses SQL Server and Access. The second part of the lab places Parameters in SQL Select statements that limit the selection of the rows that will be displayed. This section also accesses both SQL Server and Access.

If you do not have SQL Server, skip the sections dealing with it; some of the functionality cannot be reproduced with Access.

Part 1: Build the Form

Add a new project and solution, name them **prjChapter10**, making the project handle a Windows Form. Name the form **frmCommandDataReader**. Add the Buttons, textboxes, labels, and List Box as shown in Figure 10.19. Objects starting with "btn" are buttons; those starting with "txt" are textboxes. Labels start with "lbl", List Boxes with "lst". Write the appropriate strings in the Text properties of each object to correspond to what appears in Figure 10.19.

Part 1: Adding the Code for the SQL Server, btnReader

Reading the view that is returned from the SQL statement is done with a Data Reader. The Data Reader is executed to provide a sequential access of the data. Following is the code:

```
Private Sub btnReader_Click(ByVal sender As System.Object, _
            ByVal e As System.EventArgs) Handles btnReader.Click
```

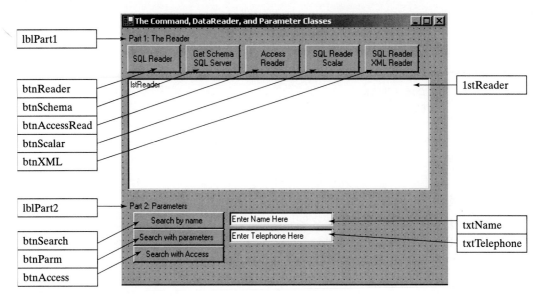

FIGURE 10.19
Lab 10.

```
Dim myConnection As New SqlClient.SqlConnection()
Dim myCommand As New SqlClient.SqlCommand()
Dim myReader As SqlClient.SqlDataReader  ' make sure there are no ()
Try
    ' The connection string will be different on other computers.
    ' To build a connection string on your machine, drag and drop a
    ' SQL Connection control on the form and let the wizard guide you
    ' through building this string. Then, copy it into the code. The
    ' parameters are machine and server dependent.
    myConnection.ConnectionString = _
     "data source=GEFEN-LAPTOP;initial catalog=master;integrated" & _
     " security=SSPI;persist security info=True;" & _
     "workstation id=GEFEN-LAPTOP;packet size=4096"

    ' Open the connection.
    myConnection.Open()

    ' Built the SQL command.
    myCommand.CommandText = _
          "SELECT  [First Name], [Last Name] FROM Friends; "

    ' Tie the SQL Command object to the Connection object.
    myCommand.Connection = myConnection

    ' Set the SQL Command object's properties.
    myCommand.CommandTimeout = 30

    ' Execute the SQL command placing the results in a Data Reader.
    myReader = _
          myCommand.ExecuteReader(CommandBehavior.SequentialAccess)
```

```
            ' Read through the Data Reader and add the items of each
            ' row to the List Box.
            Do While myReader.Read
                lstReader.Items.Add(myReader.GetString(0) & " " & _
                                    myReader.GetString(1))
            Loop

        Catch e1 As Exception
            ' It is imperative to use Try and Catch
            ' because the error message will get lost otherwise.
            Console.WriteLine(e1.Message)
        Finally
            ' Close the Connection when done.
            myConnection.Close()
        End Try
    End Sub
```

Figure 10.20 shows what the Button will produce when it is clicked.

Part 2.1: Reading the SQL Server Schema, btnSchema

This time, the Data Reader reads only the Schema:

```
Private Sub btnSQLSchema_Click(ByVal sender As System.Object, _
    ByVal e As System.EventArgs) Handles btnSQLSchema.Click

        Dim myConnection3 As New SqlClient.SqlConnection()
        Dim myCommand3 As New SqlClient.SqlCommand()
        Dim myReader3 As SqlClient.SqlDataReader  ' make sure there are no ()
        Dim I As Integer
```

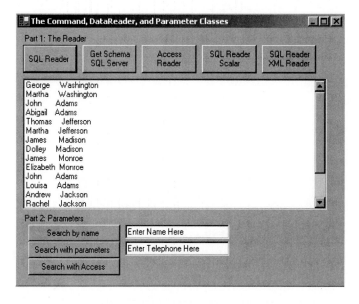

FIGURE 10.20
Showing the SQL Server Friends data with the SQL Reader button.

```
        Try
            ' See comment in Part 2.1.
            myConnection3.ConnectionString = _
            "data source=GEFEN-LAPTOP;initial catalog=master;integrated" & _
            " security=SSPI;persist security info=True;" & _
            "workstation id=GEFEN-LAPTOP;packet size=4096"

            ' Open the connection.
            myConnection3.Open()

            ' Build the SQL command.
            myCommand3.CommandText = "SELECT  * FROM Friends; "

            ' Tie the SQL Command object to the Connection object.
            myCommand3.Connection = myConnection3

            ' Execute the SQL Command but only to read the schema.
            ' Tie results of the SQL Command will be placed in a Data Reader.
            myReader3 = myCommand3.ExecuteReader(CommandBehavior.SchemaOnly)

            Dim dtbSchema As DataTable
            Dim myRow As DataRow
            Dim strName As String

            ' Read the schema into a Data Table.
            dtbSchema = myReader3.GetSchemaTable()

            ' Place header information in the List Box.
            lstReader.Items.Add("Sequence" & Chr(9) &  _
                                    "Column Name" & Chr(9) & "Length")

            ' Read the rows in the Data Table with a For Each loop on all
            ' the rows in its Rows collection.
            For Each myRow In dtbSchema.Rows
                strName = myRow(0)
                strName = strName.PadRight(20)

                ' Chr(9) is the same as vbTab
                lstReader.Items.Add(myRow(1) & Chr(9) & Chr(9) & _
                                    strName & Chr(9) & myRow(2))
            Next
        Catch e1 As Exception
            Console.WriteLine(e1.Message)
        Finally
            ' Close the Connection when done.
            myConnection3.Close()
        End Try
    End Sub
```

Figure 10.21 shows what the Button will produce when it is clicked.

Part 2.3: Reading with the OleDb, btnAccessRead

This section demonstrates reading data sequentially through an SQL statement with the Data Reader, as in Part 2.1, except that it is done here with the classes in the OleDb Namespace:

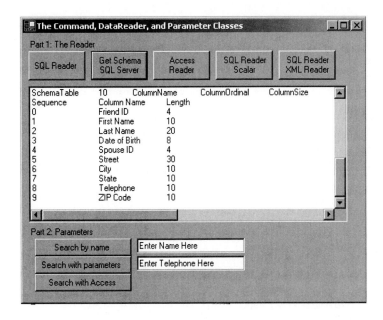

FIGURE 10.21
Showing the SQL Server Friends
table schema with the Get Schema
SQL Server button.

```
Private Sub btnAccessReader_Click(ByVal sender As System.Object, _
        ByVal e As System.EventArgs) Handles btnAccessReader.Click

    ' Declare and instantiate Connection and Command Objects.
    Dim myConnection2 As New OleDb.OleDbConnection()
    Dim myCommand2 As New OleDb.OleDbCommand()

    ' Declare Data Reader.
    Dim myReader2 As OleDb.OleDbDataReader   ' make sure there are no ()

    Try
        ' Assign parameters to connect to the Access database.
        ' The path on your machine may be different.
        myConnection2.ConnectionString = _
            "Provider=Microsoft.Jet.OLEDB.4.0;" & _
            "Persist Security Info=False;" & _
            "User ID=Admin;" & _
            "Data Source=C:\Friends.mdb;"

        ' Open the connection.
        myConnection2.Open()

        ' Build SQL command.
        myCommand2.CommandText = _
            "SELECT ID, FirstName, LastName FROM Friends; "

        ' Tie Command object to the connection just established.
        myCommand2.Connection = myConnection2

        ' Execute SQL Command, and place the results in the Data Reader.
        myReader2 = _
            myCommand2.ExecuteReader(CommandBehavior.SequentialAccess)
```

```vb
Dim I As Integer
' Read the data in the Data Reader, one row at a time.
' The Read method will return False when it reaches the
' end of the file.
Do While myReader2.Read
    ' Add first three items in the current row of the Data Reader
    ' to the List Box.
    lstReader.Items.Add( _
        myReader2.GetValue(0).ToString & " " & _
        myReader2.GetValue(1).ToString & " " & _
        myReader2.GetValue(2).ToString)

    ' Show only first 100 rows.
    I = I + 1
    If I > 100 Then Exit Do
Loop
myReader2.Close()
Catch e1 As Exception
    ' It is imperative to use Try and Catch
    ' because the error message will get lost otherwise.
    Console.WriteLine(e1.Message)
Finally
    myConnection2.Close()
End Try
```

Figure 10.22 shows what the button will produce when it is clicked.

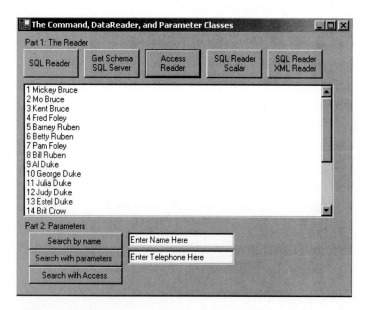

FIGURE 10.22
Showing the Access Friends data
with the Access Reader button.

Part 2.4: Reading Scalar Data, btnScalar

The result returned from an SQL statement can also be only a single value, a scalar, in which case the data can be read without a Data Reader:

```
Private Sub btnScalar_Click(ByVal sender As System.Object, _
        ByVal e As System.EventArgs) Handles btnScalar.Click

    Dim myConnection As New SqlClient.SqlConnection()
    Dim myCommand As New SqlClient.SqlCommand()

    Try
        ' See comment in Part 2.1.
        myConnection.ConnectionString = _
        "data source=GEFEN-LAPTOP;initial catalog=master;integrated" & _
        " security=SSPI;persist security info=True;" & _
        "workstation id=GEFEN-LAPTOP;packet size=4096"

        ' Open the connection.
        myConnection.Open()

        ' Build the SQL command.
        myCommand.CommandText = "SELECT  Count(*) FROM Friends; "

        ' Tie the SQL Command object to the Connection object.
        myCommand.Connection = myConnection

        ' Execute the SQL Command, but only to read a single value.
        ' There will only be a single value because the SQL statement
        ' is Count(*).
        Dim intResult As Integer
        intResult = myCommand.ExecuteScalar ' no parameters
        lstReader.Items.Add("There are " & CStr(intResult) & " friends.")

    Catch e1 As Exception
        Console.WriteLine(e1.Message)
    Finally
        ' Close the Connection when done.
        myConnection.Close()
    End Try
End Sub
```

Figure 10.23 shows what the Button will produce when it is clicked.

Part 2.5: The XML Reader, btnXML

In working with SQL Server, the SQL statement can return its view also in XML format:

```
Private Sub btnXML_Click(ByVal sender As System.Object, _
        ByVal e As System.EventArgs) Handles btnXML.Click

    Dim myConnection As New SqlClient.SqlConnection()
    Dim myCommand As New SqlClient.SqlCommand()
```

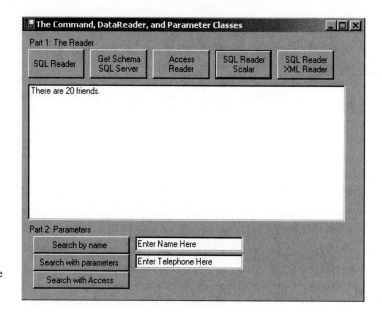

FIGURE 10.23
Showing the number of rows in the
SQL Server Friends table with the
SQL Reader Scalar button.

```
Dim myXMLReader As Xml.XmlReader
Dim I As Integer

Try
    ' See comment in Part 2.1.
    myConnection.ConnectionString = _
     "data source=GEFEN-LAPTOP;initial catalog=master;integrated" & _
     " security=SSPI;persist security info=True;" & _
     "workstation id=GEFEN-LAPTOP;packet size=4096"

    ' Open the connection.
    myConnection.Open()

    ' Build the SQL command.
    ' This only works with SQL Server.
    myCommand.CommandText = "SELECT  * FROM Friends FOR XML AUTO"

    'Tie the SQL Command object to the Connection object.
    myCommand.Connection = myConnection

    ' Read the results of the SQL statement into an XML Reader.
    myXMLReader = myCommand.ExecuteXmlReader

    'Do While myXMLReader read a value
    myXMLReader.Read()
    Do While Not myXMLReader.EOF
        lstReader.Items.Add(" Attribute Count " & _
                    myXMLReader.AttributeCount)

        For I = 0 To myXMLReader.AttributeCount - 1
            lstReader.Items.Add(myXMLReader.Item(I))
```

```
                    '    This will do the same thing.                    '
                    ' lstReader.Items.Add(myXMLReader.GetAttribute(I))
                Next
                lstReader.Items.Add("")
                myXMLReader.Read()
            Loop
        Catch e1 As Exception
            Console.WriteLine(e1.Message)
        Finally
            ' Close the Connection, Command, and XML reader when done.
            myXMLReader.Close()
            myCommand.Cancel()
            myConnection.Close()
        End Try
    End Sub
```

Figure 10.24 shows what the Button will produce when it is clicked.

Part 3.1: Building SQL Dynamically, btnSearch

Parameters can be inserted into an SQL statement by rewriting the statement anew each time. The parameters are read from the two textboxes:

```
Private Sub btnSearch_Click(ByVal sender As System.Object, _
        ByVal e As System.EventArgs) Handles btnSearch.Click

    Dim myConnection As New SqlClient.SqlConnection()
    Dim myCommand As New SqlClient.SqlCommand()
    Dim myReader As SqlClient.SqlDataReader   ' make sure there are no ()
```

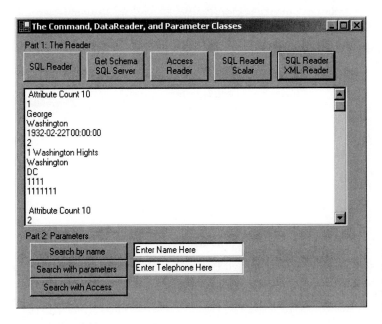

FIGURE 10.24

Showing the SQL Server Friends data using the XML Reader with the SQL Reader XML Reader button.

```
Try
    lstReader.Items.Clear()
    ' See comment in Part 2.1.
    myConnection.ConnectionString = _
     "data source=GEFEN-LAPTOP;initial catalog=master;integrated" & _
     " security=SSPI;persist security info=True;" & _
     "workstation id=GEFEN-LAPTOP;packet size=4096"

    ' Open the connection.
    myConnection.Open()

    ' Build the SQL command.
    ' The wildcard character % in SQL Server
    ' is the same as * in Access and other DBMS.
    myCommand.CommandText = _
            "SELECT  [First Name], [Last Name], [Telephone] " & _
            " FROM Friends " & _
            " Where [First Name] like '%" & _
                    txtName.Text & "%' Or " & _
            "       [Last Name] Like '%" & _
                    txtName.Text & "%'  or " & _
            "       [Telephone] like '%" & _
                    txtTelephone.Text & "%' " & _
            " Order by [First Name], [Last Name] ; "

    ' Tie the SQL Command object to the Connection object.
    myCommand.Connection = myConnection

    ' Execute the SQL Command to place the results in the Data
    ' Reader.
        myReader = _
          myCommand.ExecuteReader(CommandBehavior.SequentialAccess)

    ' Read Data Reader one row at a time.
    Do While myReader.Read
        ' Place results in the List Box.
        lstReader.Items.Add(myReader.GetString(0) & " " & _
                            myReader.GetString(1) & " " & _
                            myReader.GetValue(2).ToString)
    Loop
Catch e1 As Exception
    Console.WriteLine(e1.Message)
Finally
    myConnection.Close()
End Try
End Sub
```

Part 3.2: A Better Way, Adding Parameters, btnParm

A better way of passing parameters is through Parameter objects. The parameters are
declared implicitly in this example (the chapter discusses declaring these explicitly,
too):

```vb
Private Sub btnParm_Click(ByVal sender As System.Object, _
        ByVal e As System.EventArgs) Handles btnParm.Click

    Dim myConnection As New SqlClient.SqlConnection()
    Dim myCommand As New SqlClient.SqlCommand()
    Dim myReader As SqlClient.SqlDataReader  ' make sure there are no ()

    Try
        ' See comment in Part 2.1.
        myConnection.ConnectionString = _
          "data source=GEFEN-LAPTOP;initial catalog=master;integrated" & _
          " security=SSPI;persist security info=True;" & _
          "workstation id=GEFEN-LAPTOP;packet size=4096"

        ' Open the connection.
        myConnection.Open()

        ' Build the SQL command.
        ' The wildcard character % in SQL Server
        ' is the same as * in Access and other DBMS.
        ' Parameters must be marked with "?" in the OleDb namespace
        ' Parameters must be named in SQL Server
        myCommand.CommandText = _
                    "SELECT  [First Name], [Last Name], Telephone " & _
                    " FROM Friends " & _
                    " Where [First Name] = @Name Or " & _
                    "       [Last Name] = @Name Or " & _
                    "       [Telephone] = @Tele    " & _
                    " Order by [First Name], [Last Name] ; "
        ' Add parameter values from the textboxes to the Parameter
        ' collection of the Command object.
        myCommand.Parameters.Add _
              ("@Tele", SqlDbType.Char, 10).Value = txtTelephone.Text
        myCommand.Parameters.Add _
              ("@Name", SqlDbType.Char, 20).Value = txtName.Text.Trim

        ' Tie the SQL Command object to the Connection object.
        myCommand.Connection = myConnection

        ' Execute the SQL Command, and place results in the Data Reader.
        myReader = _
              myCommand.ExecuteReader(CommandBehavior.SequentialAccess)

        ' Clear the List Box by clearing its Items collection.
        lstReader.Items.Clear()

        ' Read the Data Reader one row at a time.
        Do While myReader.Read
        ' Add items of current row to List Box.
        lstReader.Items.Add( _
                myReader.GetValue(0).ToString.PadRight(15) & " " & _
                myReader.GetValue(1).ToString.PadRight(15) & " " & _
                myReader.GetValue(2).ToString.PadLeft(15))
```

```
            Loop
      Catch e1 As Exception
            Console.WriteLine(e1.Message)
      Finally
            myConnection.Close()
      End Try
End Sub
```

Figure 10.25 shows what the Button will produce when it is clicked.

Part 3.3: Parameters with OleDb, btnAccess

Parameters are passed with the "?" wildcard character in the OleDb Namespace. Here is how it is done:

```
Private Sub btnAccess_Click(ByVal sender As System.Object, _
        ByVal e As System.EventArgs) Handles btnAccess.Click

    ' Declare and instantiate Connection and Command objects.
    Dim myConnection2 As New OleDb.OleDbConnection()
    Dim myCommand2 As New OleDb.OleDbCommand()

    ' Declare Data Reader.
    Dim myReader2 As OleDb.OleDbDataReader    ' make sure there are no ()
```

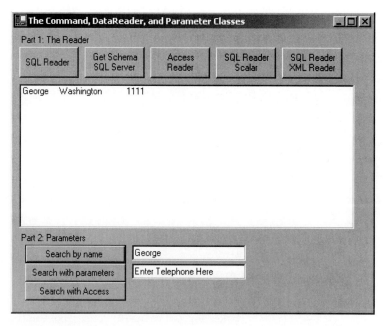

FIGURE 10.25
Searching the table with SQL parameters.

```vb
Try
    ' Clear List Box with the Clear method of its Items collection.
    lstReader.Items.Clear()
    ' Assign Connection String to Connection object
    myConnection2.ConnectionString = _
        "Provider=Microsoft.Jet.OLEDB.4.0; " & _
        "Persist Security Info=False;" & _
        "User ID=Admin;" & _
        "Data Source=C:\Friends.mdb;"

    ' Open the connection.
    myConnection2.Open()

    ' Built the SQL command.
    ' Parameters are marked with a ? character.
    myCommand2.CommandText = _
        "SELECT ID, FirstName, LastName FROM Friends " & _
        " Where FirstName = ? Or " & _
        "       LastName = ? Or " & _
        "       Telephone = ? "

    ' Tie the SQL Command object to the Connection object.
    myCommand2.Connection = myConnection2

    ' Declare and instantiate parameter of First Name.
    Dim prmFName As New OleDb.OleDbParameter()
    ' Assign its name and value properties.
    prmFName.ParameterName = "@FName"
    prmFName.Value = txtName.Text
    ' Add it to the Parameter collection of the Command object.
    myCommand2.Parameters.Add(prmFName)

    ' Declare and instantiate parameter of Last Name.
    Dim prmLName As New OleDb.OleDbParameter()
    ' Assign its name and value properties
    prmLName.ParameterName = "@LName"
    prmLName.Value = txtName.Text
    ' Add it to the Parameter collection of the Command object.
    myCommand2.Parameters.Add(prmLName)

    ' Declare and instantiate parameter of Telephone.
    Dim prmTele As New OleDb.OleDbParameter()
    ' Assign its name and value properties.
    prmTele.ParameterName = "@Tele"
    prmTele.Value = txtTelephone.Text
    ' Add it to the Parameter collection of the Command object.
    myCommand2.Parameters.Add(prmTele)

    ' Tie the SQL Command object to the Connection object.
    myCommand2.Connection = myConnection2

    ' Execute the SQL Command and place results in the Data Reader.
    myReader2 = _
```

```
myCommand2.ExecuteReader(CommandBehavior.SequentialAccess)

' Read row in the Data Reader.
Do While myReader2.Read

    ' Add the items of the current row to the List Box.
    lstReader.Items.Add( _
        myReader2.GetValue(0).ToString.PadRight(15) & " " & _
        myReader2.GetValue(1).ToString.PadRight(15) & " " & _
        myReader2.GetValue(2).ToString.PadLeft(15))
Loop
Catch e1 As Exception
    ' It is imperative to use Try and Catch
    ' because the error message will get lost otherwise.
    Console.WriteLine(e1.Message)
Finally
    myConnection2.Close()
End Try
End Sub
```

SUGGESTED HOME ASSIGNMENTS

1. Build a new form that will receive as a parameter the name of a friend and will return all that friend's pets from the Friends database. The list of pets should be presented in a List Box.
2. Build a new form that will receive as a parameter a year and will return the number of friends born that year from the Friends database.
3. Build a new form that will receive as a parameter a year and will return the pet names that contain the letter "A" that belong to friends born that year from the Friends database.

TEST YOURSELF

1. Discuss how Command objects are tied to Data Reader objects.
2. Compare and contrast the Data Reader and the XML Reader.
3. What is the primary objective of a Data Reader?
4. Discuss how the output from a Select statement can be read in any other way except a Data Reader.
5. How are Connection objects tied to Command objects, and why is this necessary?
6. What is the purpose of the CommandText and Connection properties of the Command objects?
7. What is the advantage of using parameters in SQL statements?
8. Discuss the limitation of a DataReader reading the data only sequentially.
9. What does this code do?

```
Dim myReader As SqlClient.SqlDataReader
If myReader Then
End If
```

10. Discuss the GetString() method of a DataReader.

11. What is wrong with this?

```
myReader.GetString(1) & myReader.GetString(0)
```

12. What do you think are the advantages of having a timeout parameter in both the Command objects and the Connection objects?

13. What is the `CommandType` property of the Command objects?

14. Discuss when `ExecuteScalar` is appropriate.

15. What is `Prepare`? Why is it needed?

16. Discuss early and late binding.

17. Discuss what parameters are in the context of the Command objects.

18. When does the order of the parameters matter?

19. Compare and contrast passing parameters to an OleDbCommand versus to an SQL-Command.

20. Discuss some of the central properties of the Parameter class.

More on the Connected Layer

CHAPTER OBJECTIVES

After completing this chapter, students should be able to

1. Apply the `Data Form Wizard`
2. Understand additional `DataAdapter` Properties

- `SelectCommand`
- `InsertCommand`
- `UpdateCommand`
- `DeleteCommand`

3. Understand the methods employed by the `Data Form Wizard`
4. Read XSD diagrams
5. Work with the Query Builder Window

- Building `Select` Queries
- Building `Group By` Queries
- Building Action Queries

11.1 AIMS OF CHAPTER

Having covered some of the basic aspects of database connectivity and the Connected Layer last chapter, this chapter introduces some of the automated tools related to this layer that are included in VB.NET, namely, the `Query Builder` and the `Data Form Wizard`. The Query Builder is an SQL generating wizard that, through a QBE (*Query By Example*) interface, makes building SQL commands much easier. The Data Form Wizard creates forms that access databases and other data sources. Through the Data Form Wizard, additional aspects of the Connection Layer will be briefly introduced, including XSD diagrams and action queries. *Action queries*, also known as *nonquery SQL statements*, consist of all the non-Select SQL statements, such as `Update`, `Delete`, and `Insert`, as well as Data Definition Language statements such as `Create` and `Drop`. The chapter also discuses additional features of the Connection Layer, looking in more depth at the Data Adapter object.

The labs demonstrate building an application with the wizards, modifying the generated SQL statements with the Query Builder, passing parameters to the SQL statement, and modifying the code in the generated forms. The lab contains both Access and SQL Server Data Form Wizards.

11.2   THE DATA FORM WIZARD

The Data Form Wizard is a neat, easy, and quick way to generate forms that access a database. In this section, we will see how to run the wizard and examine the output it creates. To start the wizard, click the File Menu and choose Add New Item, type ctrl+shift+A, or right-click the project in the Solution Explorer, and from there, choose Add and then Add New Item from the popup menus. In the window that opens, choose Data Form Wizard (Figure 11.1).

This will start the wizard. Click Next, and in the form that opens, you will be asked if you want the form that will be created to use an existing dataset or to create a new one. A `Dataset`, as we will discuss extensively in the next chapter, is a local copy of the database. If there is no previously defined dataset, obviously you will have to choose to add a new one, as is done later. When a new dataset is added you must add the name it will be given. In this case, we will follow the naming convention in the documentation and name the dataset myDataset. (See Figure 11.2.) You may name it anything you wish. There are no checks on the name of this object, just as there are no checks on the names of any other object. It is suggested by some that datasets start with a "ds" prefix.

The wizard will now request you to enter the database details. In this case, we will enter the information that will enable the wizard to utilize an existing connection string and connect to the database we created in Chapter 9 with SQL Server (Figure 11.3).

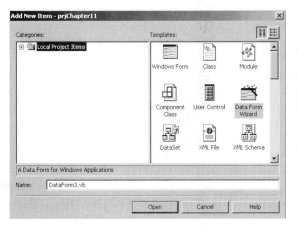

FIGURE 11.1
Starting the wizard.

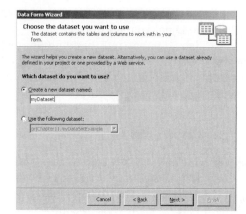

FIGURE 11.2
Naming the dataset.

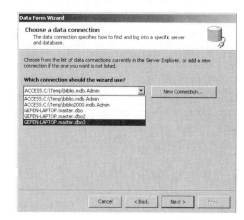

FIGURE 11.3
Choosing the Data Connection.

A new connection string can be created by clicking on the New Connection Button. Doing so will open the Data Link Properties window that we discussed in the previous chapters. Then click the Next Button. You may need to enter the login information at this stage. If your SQL Server is running on a laptop, make sure that it is running, and choose [local] as the Server name (Figure 11.4).

This will bring up the list of tables and views (stored predefined SQL statements) that the database contains. (See Figure 11.5.) We will choose Friends and Pets either by double-clicking on each or by clicking once and then on the ☒ Button to select the tables. The unselect Button, ☒ , will deselect a table or view. Having done that, click the Next Button.

At this stage, since we included more than one table, we need to specify how the tables are related to each other. Had we specified only one table, this form would not have popped up. If we skip the form by clicking the Next Button, the form that will be generated by the wizard will handle only one table. When we specify the relationships, we must give each one a name and specify what tables and what columns in each table are involved. There can be many relationships added at this stage. *But, the wizard can generate a form that can handle only one relationship.* To add a relationship, give it a

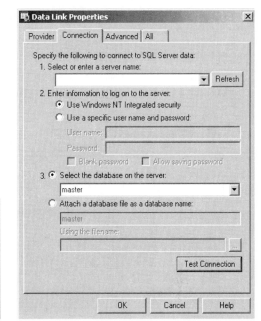

FIGURE 11.4
Specifying the Connection parameters.

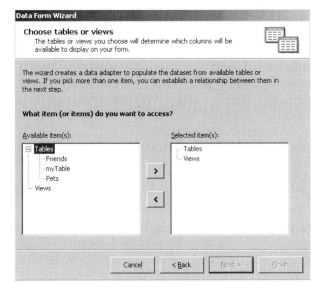

FIGURE 11.5
Choosing the tables and views from where the data will be selected.

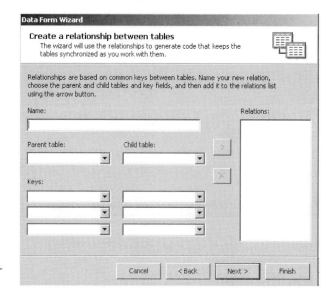

FIGURE 11.6
Naming the relationship and specifying its tables and Foreign Key.

name. The name must not contain spaces. In the example in Figure 11.6, the relationship name is PetOwners. Then, specify the Parent table and the Child table. The difference between a Parent and a Child table is that the cardinality of the relationship is 1:*n*,
where one parent can have many children, but each child only has one parent. In the
example that follows, the Parent tables being Friends means that each friend can have
any number of pets, but each pet is owned by only one friend. The keys based on which
tables will be joined (matched) must also be specified. When all this is done, click on
the ⟩ Button to add the relationship. (See Figure 11.6.) The list of relationships will
appear in the box on the right–hand side of the form. After adding a relationship in this
manner, the TextBoxes on the left-hand side will be cleared and you can either enter
another relationship—there is no limit to the number of relationships entered—or
click the Next button to continue with the form specifications.

Clicking Next will produce the next form in the wizard, in which the columns that
will be displayed are chosen. (See Figure 11.7.) Select the columns by checking them
and then click on the Next button. This will open the last panel in the wizard, in which
we will be asked what type of form we wish to create.

In this panel (see Figure 11.8) we can then choose to show the data either in a
grid or one row at a time. We will choose a grid in this example and click Finish. That
will generate the form and all its code. Generating the form may take some time. The
wizard must generate the Data Set objects you can see this as it is being done in the Solution Explorer window.

Running the form will now show all the friends (the Parent table) in the upper
grid and all the pets (the Child table) of the friend whose row is being highlighted in
the lower grid. *Had we chosen only one table earlier in the "Choose Tables or Views"
section of the wizard, then only the upper grid would have been generated.*

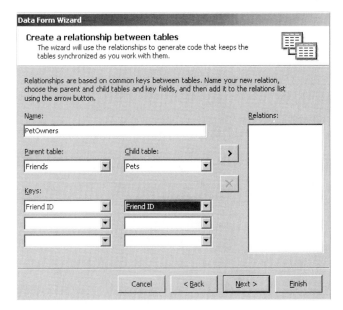

FIGURE 11.6
(*Continued*)

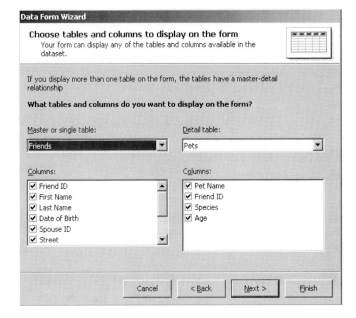

FIGURE 11.7
Selecting the columns in each of
the tables.

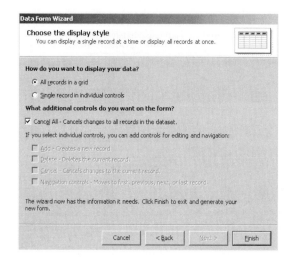

FIGURE 11.8
Choosing display style.

Adding, deleting, and updating rows is done as in Access or SQL Server. Change the values of a row, and the update will take place once you leave the row. Add a row at the end of the grid, and it will be added to the dataset. Highlight a row and click the Delete key on the keyboard, and it will be deleted. All the changes are immediately made in the dataset, whether they occurred in the grid of the Parent of the Child tables. *These changes, however, will not be carried over to the database unless the Update Button is clicked* (Figure 11.9). The form has a Connection control, a Dataset control, and two Data Adapter controls, one each for each of the tables. These controls are placed below

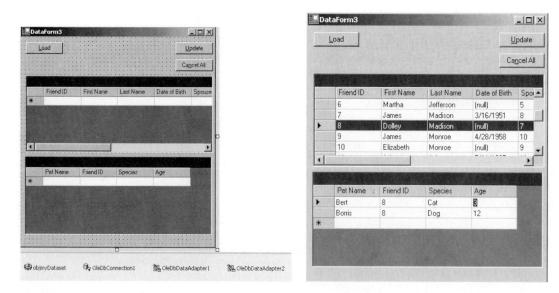

FIGURE 11.9
The form the Data Form wizard creates, in the design mode (left) and running (right).

FIGURE 11.10
The two-table XSD as generated by the
Data Form wizard.

the form. The reason is that the Connection, Dataset, and Data Adapter controls are
invisible at runtime and so are not placed on the form itself.

The wizard also generates an XSD, or XML Schema Reference diagram. The
XSD is equivalent to an Entity Relationship diagram that you may have come across in
a database analysis and design class. The diagram can be displayed by double-clicking
the myDataset.xsd in the Solution Explorer window.

The entities (the two tables in Figure 11.10) are shown as rectangles with a large
E in the top left corner. Each row in these rectangles contains the name and data type
of the selected columns in the table in the order in which they appear in the actual
table. Key fields are marked, as in SQL Server and Access, with a yellow key icon. The
relationship is marked with a diamond connecting the related entities. The circle, ,
and crow's foot, , symbols specify the cardinality in the standard Entity Relationship
notation, with a circle being the 1 and the crow's foot being the many. In this case, each
friend, connected with a circle to the Relationship, can have many pets, connected to
the Relationship with a crow's foot. Right-clicking the diamond in the XSD will open a
popup menu with an option to edit the relationship (Figure 11.11).

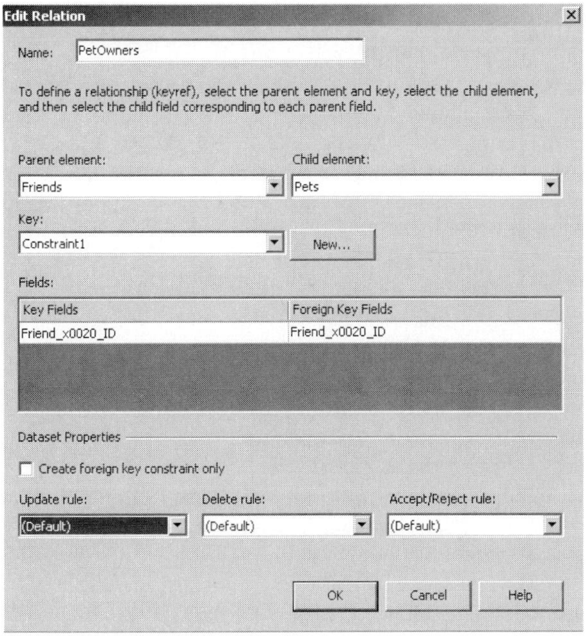

FIGURE 11.11
The Edit Relationship window of the
XML display.

The Update and Delete rules can be set here in the same way they can in the database itself (see Chapter 9), to allow cascading updates and deletes, which will cause updates and deletes in the Parent table to be carried over to the Child table. Alternatively, the set null, set default, or no rule at all can be applied, in which case the connected column in Child table will be set to null, to the default value of its data type or column (see discussion in Chapter 13), or not affected at all, respectively, when the connected field in the Parent is changed or deleted.

The Relationship can be deleted through the appropriate option in the same popup menu, although at this stage that would not be a good idea. An option in the same popup menu can also present the XML code of the XSD:

```xml
<?xml version="1.0" encoding="utf-8"?>
<xs:schema id="myDataset" targetNamespace="http://www.tempuri.org/
myDataset.xsd"
xmlns:mstns="http://www.tempuri.org/myDataset.xsd"
xmlns="http://www.tempuri.org/myDataset.xsd"
xmlns:xs="http://www.w3.org/2001/XMLSchema" xmlns:msdata="urn:
schemas-microsoft-com:xml-msdata" attributeFormDefault="qualified"
elementFormDefault="qualified">
        <xs:element name="myDataset" msdata:IsDataSet="true">
        <xs:complexType>
        <xs:choice maxOccurs="unbounded">
          <xs:element name="Friends">
           <xs:complexType>
            <xs:sequence>
             <xs:element name="Friend_x0020_ID" msdata:
                    ReadOnly="true" msdata:AutoIncrement
                    ="true" type="xs:int" />
             <xs:element name="First_x0020_Name" type="xs:string"
                    minOccurs="0" />
             <xs:element name="Last_x0020_Name" type="xs:string"
                    minOccurs="0" />
             <xs:element name="Date_x0020_of_x0020_Birth"
                    type="xs:dateTime" minOccurs="0" />
             <xs:element name="Spouse_x0020_ID" type="xs:int"
                    minOccurs="0" />
             <xs:element name="Street"
                    type="xs:string" minOccurs="0" />
             <xs:element name="City"
                    type="xs:string" minOccurs="0" />
             <xs:element name="State"
                    type="xs:string" minOccurs="0" />
             <xs:element name="Telephone"
                    type="xs:string" minOccurs="0" />
             <xs:element name="ZIP_x0020_Code"
                    type="xs:string" minOccurs="0" />
            </xs:sequence>
           </xs:complexType>
          </xs:element>
```

```xml
            <xs:element name="Pets">
              <xs:complexType>
                <xs:sequence>
                  <xs:element name="Pet_x0020_Name"
                        type="xs:string" />
                  <xs:element name="Friend_x0020_ID" type="xs:int" />
                  <xs:element name="Species"
                        type="xs:string" minOccurs="0" />
                  <xs:element name="Age"
                        type="xs:int" minOccurs="0" />
                </xs:sequence>
              </xs:complexType>
            </xs:element>
          </xs:choice>
        </xs:complexType>
        <xs:unique name="Constraint1"
              msdata:PrimaryKey="true">
          <xs:selector xpath=".//mstns:Friends" />
          <xs:field xpath="mstns:Friend_x0020_ID" />
        </xs:unique>
        <xs:unique name="Pets_Constraint1"
              msdata:ConstraintName="Constraint1"
              msdata:PrimaryKey="true">
          <xs:selector xpath=".//mstns:Pets" />
          <xs:field xpath="mstns:Pet_x0020_Name" />
          <xs:field xpath="mstns:Friend_x0020_ID" />
        </xs:unique>
        <xs:keyref name="PetOwners" refer="Constraint1">
          <xs:selector xpath=".//mstns:Pets" />
          <xs:field xpath="mstns:Friend_x0020_ID" />
        </xs:keyref>
      </xs:element>
</xs:schema>
```

Additional features can now be added to the form. In fact, using the wizard to generate the initial form and then modifying it can make programming much faster, easier, and standardized.

11.2.1 A Quick Review, This Time with Access and a Single Record Display with Controls

The Data Form wizard works just the same with Access, except for the standard difference in Data Link Properties windows. (See Chapter 9.) In this example, we will connect to the Friends.mdb Access database, include a single table, and present it. The Friends database is included in the CD. Its data diagram is given in Figure 11.12.

Many of the steps are identical to what we did with SQL Server. First, we will add a form with the Data Form wizard to the project. In the Solution window, right-click the Project, and select Add (Figure 11.13). Then we select Add New Item.

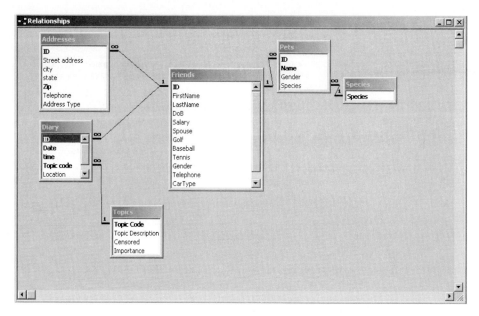

FIGURE 11.12
Data diagram of Friends database as shown in the Relationship window of Access.

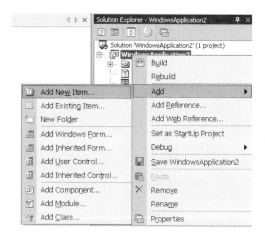

FIGURE 11.13
Adding a form.

In the window that will open, select Data Form wizard and change the name of the object to DataForm2.vb. Then, click Open. (See Figure 11.14.)

The Data Form wizard will open (Figure 11.15).
Click Next, name the dataset myDataset2, and click Next again, as shown in Figure 11.16. In the next window, connect the Data Set to one of the connections we have already established with the database (Figure 11.17). If you do not have such a connection, click New Connection and look in Chapter 9 for information on how to connect to Access.

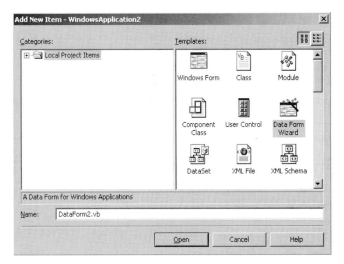

FIGURE 11.14
Activating the Data Form wizard.

In the ensuing window, select the Friends table. Tables are selected by clicking the table name and then the right-pointing arrow, as in Figure 11.18. This will move the table to the right-hand side panel. Deselecting a table is done by clicking it in the right panel and then clicking on the left-pointing arrow. This will move the table back to the left panel. Views, stored queries, can also be selected in this manner. After you select the Friends table, click Next, and choose all the columns (see Figure 11.19). Click Next.

There will be no relationship to add here because there is only one table. Select all the columns for display and a single-row presentation (see Figure 11.20).

FIGURE 11.15
Data Form wizard.

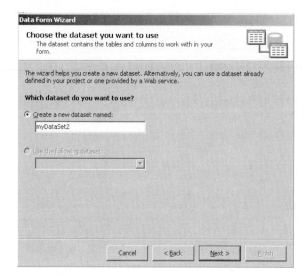

FIGURE 11.16
Choosing or creating the dataset
for the wizard.

The resulting form will look like Figure 11.21. The Load Button fills the dataset with data from the table. The four navigation Buttons with arrows on them navigate through the dataset. The Add and Delete Buttons add a new row or delete the current row, respectively. Any changes made to the data in the textboxes are automatically updated in the dataset, because these textboxes are *bound controls*. A bound control shows the value in the object it is bound to and automatically updates that value when the value in the bound control is changed. In this case, the textboxes are bound to a Data Column and so show and update the value in the appropriate Item in the current

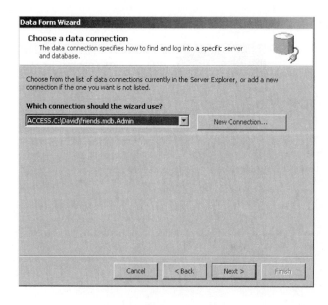

FIGURE 11.17
Choosing the Connection object
for the wizard.

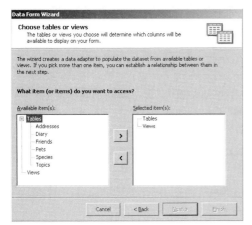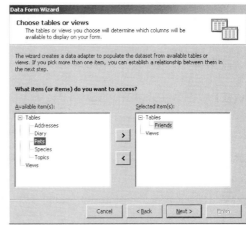

FIGURE 11.18
Selecting the tables and views for the wizard.

FIGURE 11.19
Choosing the columns.

Data Row. The Cancel Button cancels any changes made to the row currently being displayed. The changes made on the form are all done on the data in the dataset, not in the Data Source (database), because the dataset is *disconnected* from the database, meaning that changes made to it are not carried over to the database unless forced to. The changes are carried over to the Data Source when the Update Button is clicked. The Cancel All Button undoes these changes in the dataset, unless they have been committed to the Data Source already with the Update Button.

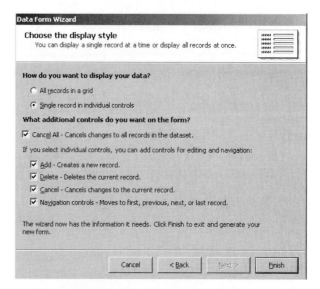

FIGURE 11.20
Choosing the display mode.

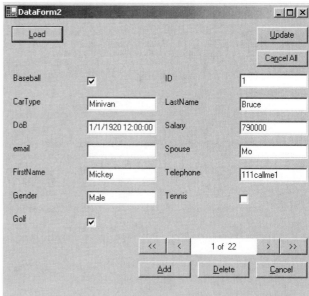

FIGURE 11.21
The form as generated by the Data Form wizard.

11.2.2 A Look at the Generated Controls

- The `OleDbConnection` object is the same as we saw in Chapters 9 and 10. Its `ConnectionString` property contains the database details as generated through the wizard.

- The `Dataset` contains the data structure and content. When it is generated, the result is an XSD diagram. The XSD diagram is tied to the Dataset through the `Namespace` property of the Dataset. The XSD diagram, as we saw already, specifies the tables involved, the columns in each, the keys of the tables, and the relationships among the tables.

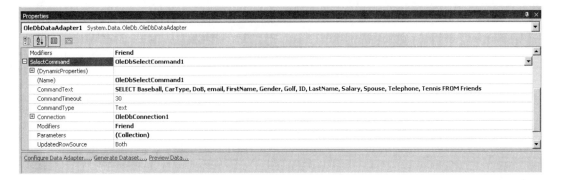

FIGURE 11.22
The Properties window showing the `CommandText` property of the `Select` Command as it was generated by the wizard.

- The `OleDbDataAdapter` has specific sets of properties for Select, Insert, Update, and Delete. For each of these SQL statements, the Properties window shows the appropriate properties, including the `Connection`, the `Timeout`, the `CommandType`, and the actual SQL statement in the `CommandText` property. Figure 11.22 shows the SQL command as it was generated by the wizard. That is the way Data Adapter objects handle data from a database, with a separate SQL statement with its own SQL related properties for each SQL command. This allows the setting of different connections and timeout properties for each SQL statement. *The SQL statements are properties of the Command objects that are incorporated into the Data Adapter. It is only through these SQL statements that the database is accessed.*

The SQL statements themselves are worth a close look, especially at their parameters that allow for updating or deletion, based on any combination of the columns:

- INSERT INTO Friends(Baseball, CarType, DoB, FirstName, Gender, Golf, LastName, Salary, Spouse, Telephone, Tennis) VALUES (?, ?, ?, ?, ?, ?, ?, ?, ?, ?, ?)
- DELETE FROM Friends WHERE (ID = ?) AND (Baseball = ?) AND (CarType = ? OR ? IS NULL AND CarType IS NULL) AND (DoB = ? OR ? IS NULL AND DoB IS NULL) AND (FirstName = ?) AND (Gender = ? OR ? IS NULL AND Gender IS NULL) AND (Golf = ?) AND (LastName = ?) AND (Salary = ? OR ? IS NULL AND Salary IS NULL) AND (Spouse = ? OR ? IS NULL AND Spouse IS NULL) AND (Telephone = ? OR ? IS NULL AND Telephone IS NULL) AND (Tennis = ?)
- UPDATE Friends SET Baseball = ?, CarType = ?, DoB = ?, FirstName = ?, Gender = ?, Golf = ?, LastName = ?, Salary = ?, Spouse = ?, Telephone = ?, Tennis = ? WHERE (ID = ?) AND (Baseball = ?) AND (CarType = ? OR ? IS NULL AND CarType IS NULL) AND (DoB = ? OR ? IS NULL AND DoB IS NULL) AND (FirstName = ?) AND (Gender = ? OR ? IS NULL AND Gender IS NULL) AND (Golf = ?) AND (LastName = ?) AND (Salary = ? OR ? IS NULL AND Salary IS NULL) AND (Spouse = ? OR ? IS NULL AND Spouse IS NULL) AND (Telephone = ? OR ? IS NULL AND Telephone IS NULL) AND (Tennis = ?)

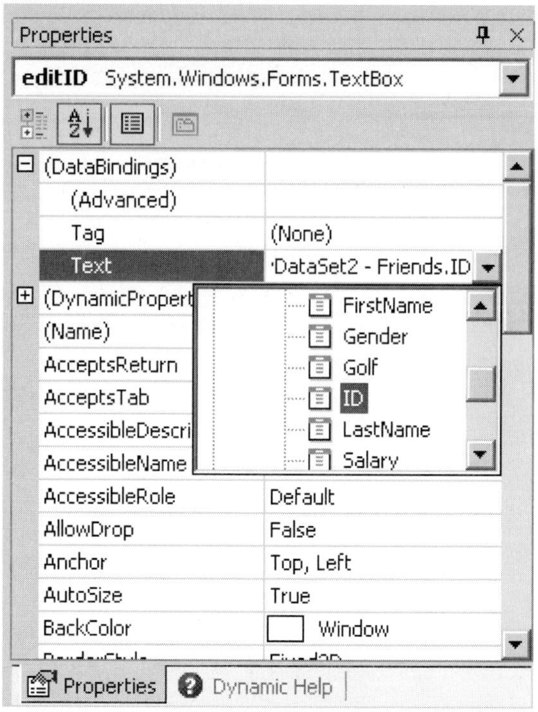

FIGURE 11.23
Property window showing binding details
of a data bound textbox control.

- SELECT Baseball, CarType, DoB, FirstName, Gender, Golf, ID, Last-Name, Salary, Spouse, Telephone, Tennis FROM Friends

Each of the textboxes is bound to its corresponding column in the cluster of properties that is specified under the rubric property of (DataBindings). See Figure 11.23 for details of how this data binding is registered in the Property window of one of the data bound textboxes.

The code behind the Buttons will be discussed next.

11.2.3 A Look at the Generated Controls

The Load Button activates a method named LoadDataSet. This method is defined within the form as a public method. This method creates a new Dataset object that is the mirror image of the Dataset control that appears on the form. In VB.NET terms, the new Dataset object is defined as an object of the class of the Dataset control and is instantiated. This allows it to inherit all the properties of the Dataset control. The connection to the database is opened again with the Connection object and the new dataset is filled from the Data Adapter object. The data are then copied to the original Dataset control. The data are copied from the new Dataset object to the Dataset control by emptying the Dataset control with the Clear method and then merging the data in the new Dataset object into it with the Merge method. This elaborate process allows VB.NET to *repopulate* the Dataset control (that is the database term from placing data in it) without rebinding the Bound Controls, the TextBoxes, in the form. In a simplified nutshell this is what the code does (excluding the Try blocks and subroutine statements):

```
Dim objDataSetTemp As prjChapter11.objmyDataSet2
objDataSetTemp = New prjChapter11.objmyDataSet2()

objDataSetTemp.EnforceConstraints = False
Me.OleDbConnection1.Open()
Me.OleDbDataAdapter1.Fill(objDataSetTemp)

obyMyDataSet2.Clear()
obyMyDataSet2.Merge(objDataSetTemp)
```

The Add Button ends the current editing in the row being displayed so that the entered values will not override what is being displayed and then adds the data entered in a new row:

```
Me.BindingContext(objmyDataSet2, _
               "Friends").EndCurrentEdit()
Me.BindingContext(objmyDataSet2, "Friends").AddNew()
```

The Delete Button removes the current row from the dataset and resets the position in the dataset so that the next row, if one exists, will now be displayed:

```
If (Me.BindingContext(objmyDataSetTitles, _
        "Friends").Count > 0) Then
      Me.BindingContext(objmyDataSetTitles, _
          " Friends").RemoveAt _
          (Me.BindingContext(objmyDataSetTitles,
          "Friends").Position)
      Me.objmyDataSetTitles_PositionChanged()
End If
```

The Cancel Button simply cancels the current editing done on the row being displayed. This row is identified through the `Position` property and then redisplays the data from the dataset:

```
Me.BindingContext(objmyDataSetTitles, _
            "Friends").CancelCurrentEdit()
Me.objmyDataSetTitles_PositionChanged()
```

All the Navigation Buttons change the Position property and redisplay the data. In the following case, it is with the ⏵ Button:

```
Me.BindingContext(objmyDataSetTitles, _
               "Friends").Position = _
        (Me.BindingContext(objmyDataSetTitles, _
               "Friends").Position + 1)
Me.objmyDataSetTitles_PositionChanged()
```

The Update button is where the changes in the Dataset object, our local copy of the Data Source (database, in this case), are actually carried over to the Data Source. All the changes up to now were done only on the local copy of the Data Source that we kept in the `Dataset` object. These changes were until now totally invisible to any other transaction accessing the database. Forcing these changes from the `Dataset` object to the Data Source is done here. If changes were made to the data in the Dataset, as shown in the ChangedRows property, then the connection to the Data Source is reopened and the changes carried over with the Update method of the DataAdatpter. The DataAdapter does a great service here. It knows when to apply an Update SQL command, when an Insert SQL command, and when a Delete SQL command. These commands will be generated in the background for each affected row, based on the InsertCommand, DeleteCommand, and UpdateCommand properties of the DataAdapter. There is no need to write individual SQL statements in the code to handle this update process, and there is no need to go through the rows of the Dataset and choose which ones need to be updated. All that is done automatically by this powerful method:

```
If (Not (ChangedRows) Is Nothing) Then
    Me.OleDbConnection1.Open()
    OleDbDataAdapter1.Update(ChangedRows)
End If
Me.objmyDataSetTitles_PositionChanged()
```

If we wish to undo all the changes made to the Dataset, the Clear All Button will handle that with a single activation of the RejectChanges method.

11.3   THE QUERY BUILDER WINDOW

11.3.1   Prep Stages

Up until now, we coded the SQL statements directly into the code. A neat way to avoid typos while doing so is to take advantage of the Query Builder. The Query Builder is activated when a Command Control is copied into the form. First drop and drag an SQLConnection control from the toolbox onto the form. Click the ConnectionString property in the Properties Window and then <New Connection>.

This will open the Build Link Properties wizard. (See Chapter 9 for details on how to connect to a database with this wizard.) Here is a brief review: Choose the appropriate provider from the Provider Tab. (See Figure 11.25.) Then, in the Connection Tab, enter the User ID and password required by your database and the database name. Depending on the installation, you may also need to enter the Server name. (In the example that follows, the DBMS is on a laptop.) Then test the connection by clicking on the Button with that name. The same process should be followed with other providers. A special case is Access. (See Chapter 9 on how to connect to it.)

11.3.2   Select Queries

Now the SqlConnection or the OleDbConnection control can be dragged and dropped on the form. Set the Connection property of the control to the existing connection that you just established. Do this by selecting Existing in the right-hand side of the property, as shown in Figure 11.26.

At last, the Query Builder can be opened by clicking the three dots in the CommandText property. The Query Builder opens with a window named Add Table in front of it. This is where tables and views (results or previously stored queries) can be added to the Query By Example (QBE) interface of the Query Builder. These tables and queries will appear in the From clause of the SQL statement that will be generated.

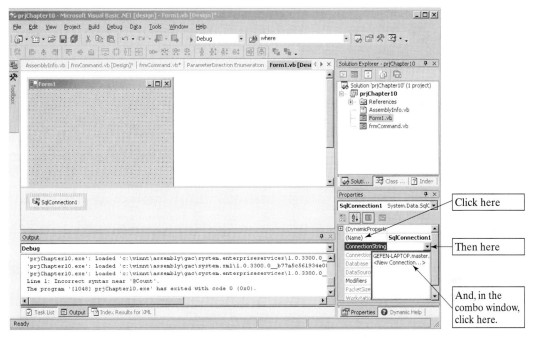

FIGURE 11.24
Creating an SQL Connection by dropping an sqlConnection control on the form.

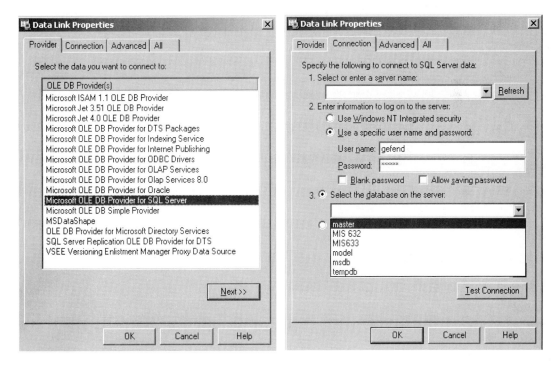

FIGURE 11.25
Specifying the Provider (left diagram) and then its Connection parameters (right diagram) for the wizard.

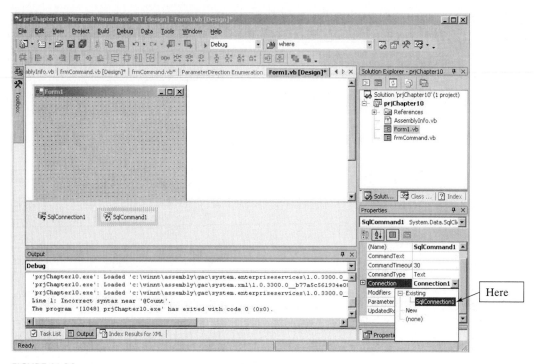

FIGURE 11.26
Connecting the SQLCommand object to the existing Connection object.

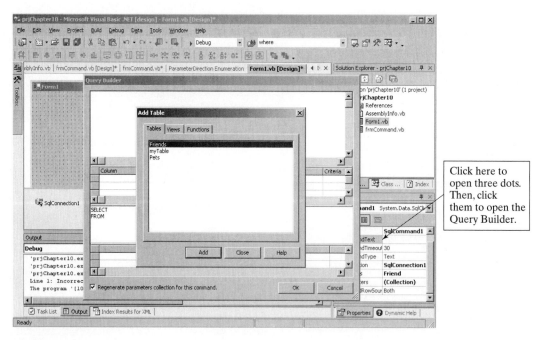

FIGURE 11.27
Opening the Query Builder through the Command object.

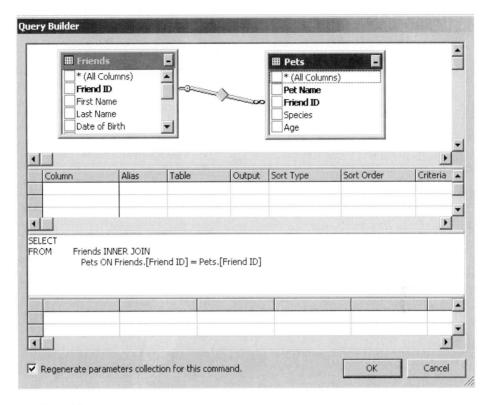

FIGURE 11.28
Query Builder showing the two selected tables and the relationship between them. The relationship is copied automatically from the database schema where that relationship was previously defined.

In this example, we will choose Friends and Pets by double-clicking each, or by clicking once and then clicking the Add Button. After the Close Button is clicked, the window will look like Figure 11.28.

Notice that the two tables are already connected in the upper portion of the window. That is because the relationship was defined when we built the database in Chapter 9. The second section of the window contains the list of columns that will be retrieved with the SQL statement, their sorting order, and any limiting criteria. The third portion contains the generated SQL statement. The bottom portion will contain the results of the SQL statement when it is run.

Clicking on the diamond between the two tables will open up a Properties window (Figure 11.29), showing the type of join between the two tables. By default the join type is an *Inner Join*, which only presents rows from both tables that are matched by equivalent values in the other table. The two check boxes at the bottom of the window will change the join to an *Outer Join*, where all the values from one table will be shown, but only matched ones from the other table will be shown. For example, had we chosen to display "All rows from friends", then even friends without pets would have been selected.

Close the window.

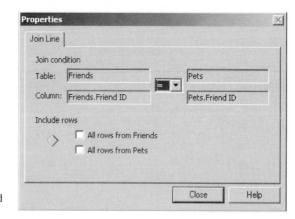

FIGURE 11.29
Properties window of the relationship (the diamond in figure 11-28) between the tables.

Now, clicking the check boxes near the field names in the top portion of the window of each table will include the clicked fields in the output of the SQL statement. The SQL statement will be automatically regenerated to show these changes as in Figure 11.30.

Sorting the output from the query is done by specifying the order in which the fields will be sorted, in the Sort Order column, and the sort type. Doing so will add

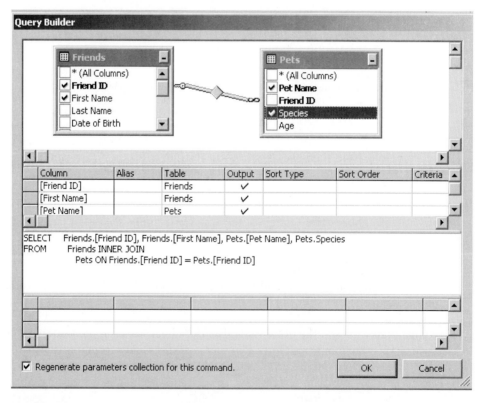

FIGURE 11.30
Automatically regenerated SQL statement.

an icon next to the field name in the table indicating the direction of the sort. Unclicking the Output column will remove the field from the output, but leave it in the second portion of the window for sort and selection criteria reasons. (See how this is done with the Species column of the Pets table.) The Alias column allows the giving of an alias caption to the field name. This caption is the name of the field as it will be returned from the SQL statement. Finally, the Criteria columns indicate which rows will be selected from the database. Based on these Criteria, the `Where` criteria of the SQL statement will be created by the wizard. Fields included in the Criteria are marked in the top portion of the window with the icon of a filter. (See the City and Species columns in the diagram.) The Criteria are built in such a way that all rules in the same column of the window relate to each other with an And operator, while all rules in other columns relate with an Or operator. In the next example, the Where clause of the SQL says

```
"(Friends.City = 'NYC') OR (Friends.City = 'Philadelphia') AND
(Pets.Species = 'dog')"
```

The "Or" is because "NYC" is in a different column of Criteria than the other two rules. The "And" is because "Philadelphia" and "dog" are in the same column of the Criteria (Figure 11.31).

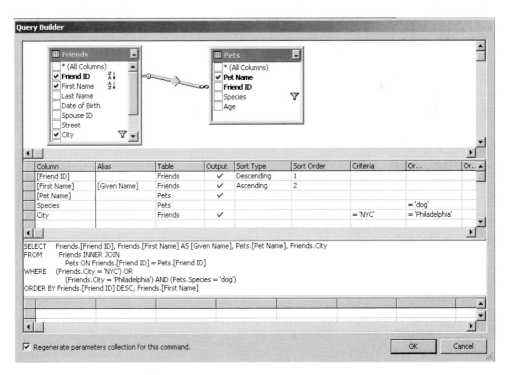

FIGURE 11.31
Adding Criteria, Sort Type, and Sort Order. Note the `And` and `Or` operators in the SQL statement.

The verified SQL statement can now be copied into the code or run within the code as though it were a Command object.

To run the query, right-click the QBE, and in the menu that will open, select the "Run" option. The result of the query will be shown in the bottom part of the window.

11.3.3 Group By Select Queries

Group By queries show aggregate results. In their simplest form, Group By queries show aggregate data for all the selected rows in the table or in the view of joined tables. Aggregate data can deal with the Count of how many rows answer a certain criteria or the Max or Min value of a given filed among rows that satisfy a criteria. To change the Query Builder mode so that it can handle Group By queries, right-click while pointing at the top portion or at the SQL statement portion of the window, and select "Group By" from the popup menu. Doing so will add a new column named "Group By" to the second section of the window.

The "Group By" column has several options. The "Min", "Max", and "Count" are aggregate functions that return a single value each containing the smallest value of that column, the largest, and the total number of values, respectively. These values relate to all the data. However, adding a Group By option in another column allows these aggregate values to be calculated for each value in the "Group By" column. For example, the QBE in Figure 11.32 will show how many friends there are all together who live in

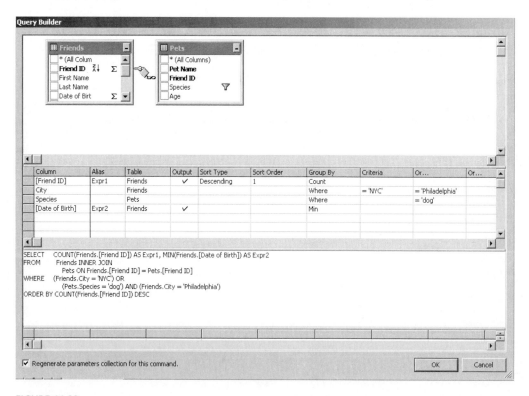

FIGURE 11.32
Adding aggregate functions, minimum and count, through the Group By option.

New York City and have a pet (they must have a pet to be included in the `Where` criterion of the SQL statement because the Join will enforce the selections of only rows in Friends that are matched with Pets) or who live in Philadelphia and have a dog. When only some of the rows need to be included in the aggregate function, the `Where` option limits which rows are included from the original data.

Adding City once more to the second portion of the QBE window will add it with a `Group By` option and will result in displaying the preceding values per each City value.

Programming Note: The `Having` clause in the SQL statement limits the groups that will be displayed based on the Group By, while the `Where` clause limits the rows that will be retrieved. When only certain values should be retrieved from the database, apply the Where clause.

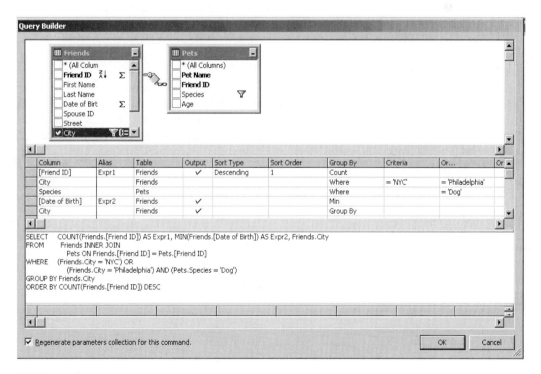

FIGURE 11.33
Adding subcategories with the Group By option.

11.3.4 Action Queries

Action queries are SQL statements that are nonqueries. These include the SQL statements Insert, Update, and Delete. These commands are called *Action Queries* because they change the database. Changing the QBE of the Query Builder to handle Action Queries is done again by right-clicking while pointing at the Query Builder window and then choosing the appropriate option in the popup menu. In this case (Figure 11.34), the choice is among Insert From, Insert Into, Update, Delete, and Make Table. The Update option changes the value of a column or columns based on specified Criteria. The Delete option removes the rows based on these Criteria. The Where criteria of both these options is set in exactly the same manner as it is with a Select query. The Insert Into option adds rows to a table from values specified in the query. The Insert From option insert into a new table the results of a Select query. The Make Table runs a Select query and inserts the rows of the resulting view into a new table. When running a Make Table or an Insert From query, you will be asked to enter the name of the appropriate target table. With the Make Table option the table will be created automatically based on the results of the Select statement and include the columns names and data types of the result of the Select query.

The examples that follow run action queries. This time it is done on an Access 2002 database. From a Query Builder point of view, there is no difference who the provider (DBMS) is. It will work the same with SQL Server, Oracle, Access 2002, and many other DBMS, as long as only standard ANSI SQL is written. The first example is of an Update statement (Figure 11.35).

You can also copy the field name by clicking the pull-down menu in the column where it says Column in the second portion of the window. This can be quite useful when you need to have the same column several times in the SQL. Or you can just type it in, as shown in Figure 11.36, where the updated value is derived from the existing value.

Delete works the same way, just change the query type to Delete in the popup menu (Figure 11.37) that appears when the right mouse button is clicked while pointing at the window.

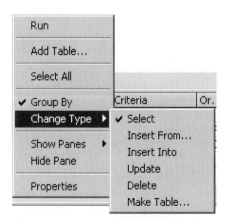

FIGURE 11.34
Changing the query type in the Query Builder.

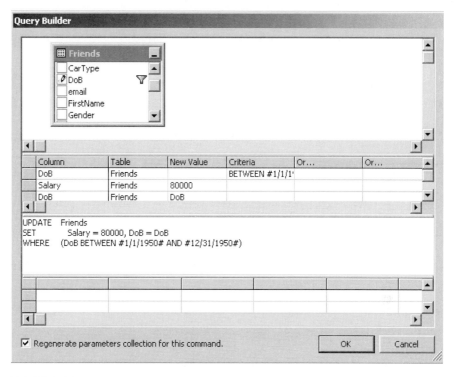

FIGURE 11.35
The Update query type.

Then write the Delete query as shown in Figure 11.38.

An Insert Action Query requires only the values that will be inserted. There is no Where clause with an Insert SQL statement (Figure 11.39).

The Insert From option creates a new table that contains the result from a Select statement. You can either select which columns will be included from the original table, just as you would with any other Select statement, or you can click on the (All Columns) option in the tables at the top section of the window to indicate that all the columns are to be copied (Figure 11.40). Including all the columns is denoted in SQL with an asterisk, rather than naming all the columns explicitly. The Where clause works exactly the same with Action Queries as with Select Queries. The query in Figure 11.40, however, will not run, because it will create duplicate values in the Pets table.

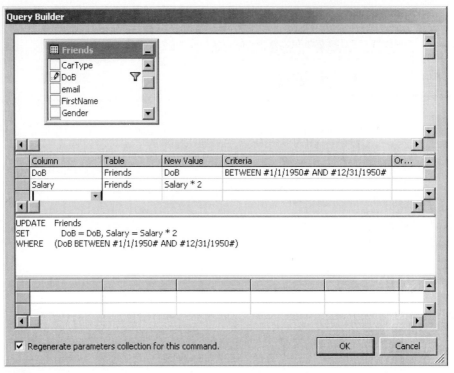

FIGURE 11.36
Setting the New Value of Salary as a function.

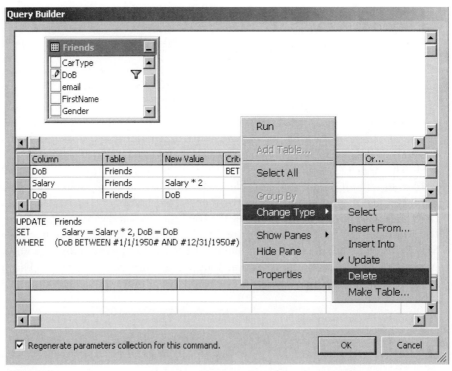

FIGURE 11.37
Changing the query type to Delete.

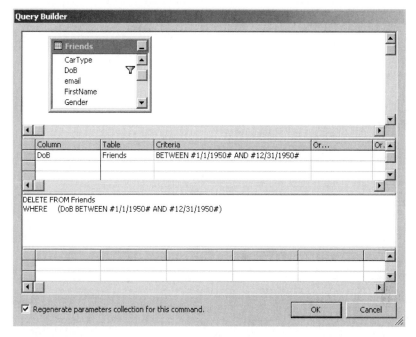

FIGURE 11.38
The Delete query type.

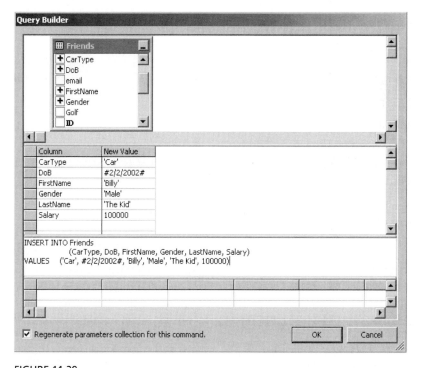

FIGURE 11.39
The Insert query type.

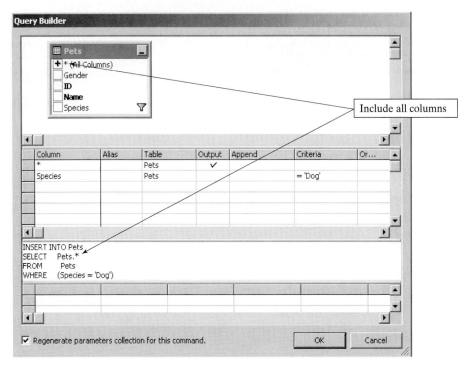

FIGURE 11.40
Inserting the result of a `Select` query.

LAB 11.1: EXERCISING THE DATA FORM WIZARD

Lab Objectives:
1. Practice the Data Form wizard in Access
2. Examine the code generated by the Data Form wizard

Application Overview

Having demonstrated the Wizard with SQL Server, we will demonstrate and explain it with Access in the lab.

Part 1: Build the First Form

Add a new project and solution. Name both **prjDataWizard**, making the project handle a Windows Form. Open the Data Form wizard, naming the new form **frmFriends**. To open the wizard, right-click while pointing at the project name in the Solution Explorer, and in the popup menu, select Add New Item. Name the form **frmFriends** (Figure 11.41).

Click on the Open Button. The wizard will open. Click Next. In the next screen, name the Dataset **dsFriends** as in Figure 11.42.

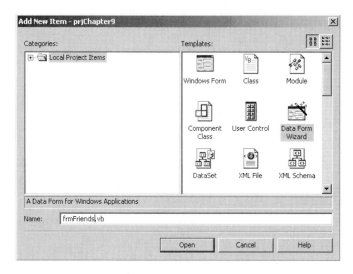

FIGURE 11.41
Starting the Data Form wizard.

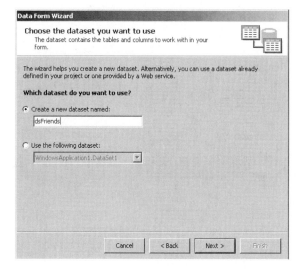

FIGURE 11.42
Choosing the dataset for the Data Form wizard.

In the ensuing screen, connect the new form to Friends.mdb. The Provider is Jet 4.0, and the Database Name should be the path where the database is located. Then select to display data from the tables of Friends and Pets.

Specify how the two tables are related, and then click on the arrow as in Figure 11.44.

Click Next. In the window that will open, select the columns as shown in Figure 11.45.

Click Next in the next window, (see Figure 11.46) and generate the form, showing all the records in a grid.

Figure 11.47 shows what the form will look like after it is generated. As you click on a row in the top grid, the pets of the friends in the top grid will appear in the bottom grid.

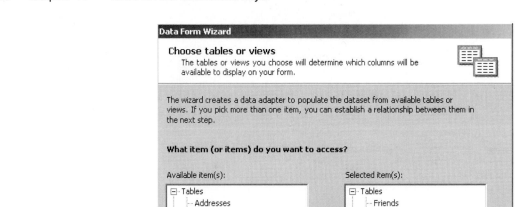

FIGURE 11.43
Choosing the tables for the Data
Form wizard.

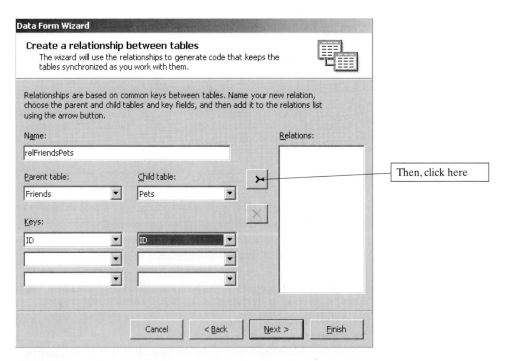

FIGURE 11.44
Specifying the relationship among the chosen tables for the Data Form wizard.

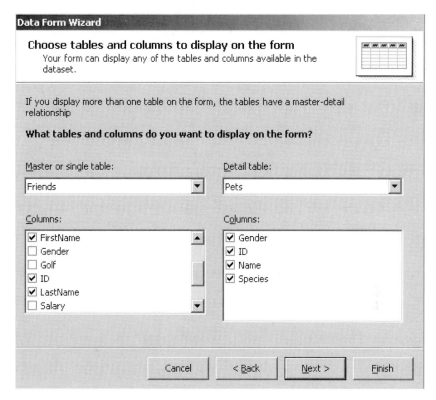

FIGURE 11.45
Specifying the columns to be displayed for the Data Form wizard.

Part 2: A Look at the Details

Double-clicking the XSD line in the Solution Explorer will reveal the diagram in Figure 11.48. The XSD shows two tables. That is because we included two tables through the wizard.

The code itself is also much as the code in SQL Server was for a single-row display:

- The Connection, Command, and Dataset objects are as before.
    - The Connection object contains the connection details based on what was entered to the wizard.
    - The Command object contains the SQL statements for Select, Update, Insert, and Delete. These last three will be used automatically when the Update button is clicked.
    - The Dataset object is tied to the XSD diagram.
- The Load button creates a new dataset that inherits from the Dataset control, opens the Dataset object, disables its data constraints, fills it from Data Adapter, and then reinstates the data constraints. In a nutshell, the code is

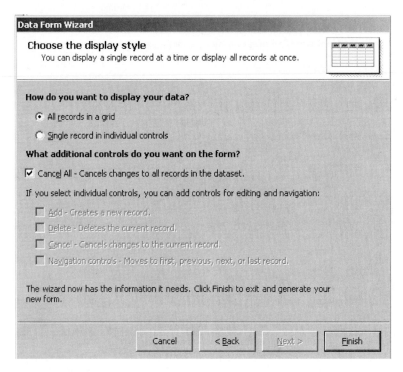

FIGURE 11.46
Specifying display style for the Data Form wizard.

```
Dim objDataSetTemp As prjDataWizard.dsFriends
objDataSetTemp = New prjDataWizard.dsFriends()
Me.OleDbConnection1.Open()
Me.OleDbDataAdapter1.Fill(dataSet)
dataSet.EnforceConstraints = True
Me.OleDbConnection1.Close()
dataSet.EnforceConstraints = False
```

- Any changes made on the Grid are automatically carried over to the dataset, because the grid is bound to it.
- The Update button then updates the Data Source (the database) and accepts all the changes to the dataset. The changes are accepted to the dataset only after they are made to the Data Source because it is possible that the data source may reject these changes due to the activity of other transactions that may have changed the contents of the database since the data were copied into the Grid. The code is as follows:

```
Me.UpdateDataSource(objDataSetChanges)
objdsTitles.Merge(objDataSetChanges)
objdsTitles.AcceptChanges()
```

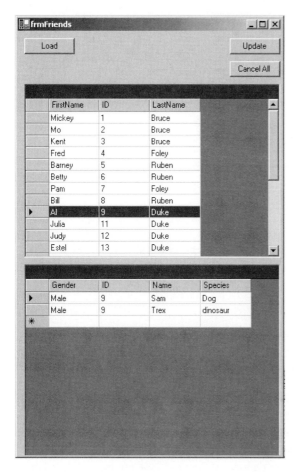

FIGURE 11.47
The form generated by the Data Form wizard.

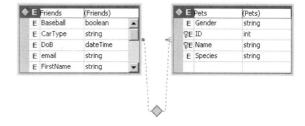

FIGURE 11.48
The XSD as generated by the Data Form wizard.

- The Cancel All Button simply rejects all the changes made to the dataset:

```
Me.objdsTitles.RejectChanges()
```

Part 3: Make This the Startup Form

Make this form the startup form by changing the Properties of the Project. Right-click the Project in the Solution Explorer window, and in the popup menu select Properties. In the ensuing window, select this form as the startup object (Figure 11.49).

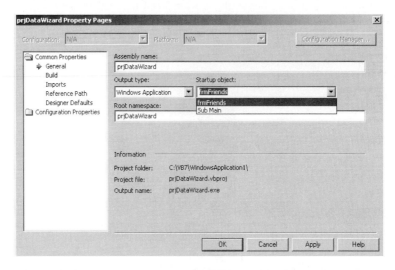

FIGURE 11.49
Changing the Startup object in the Project Property window.

LAB 11.2: EXERCISING THE DATA FORM WIZARD WITH PARAMETERS IN SQL SERVER

Lab Objectives:

1. Practice the Data Form wizard in SQL Server
2. Add code to the forms created by the Data Form wizard
3. Pass parameters to a form generated by the wizard (this must be done in SQL Server; Access cannot handle VB.NET parameters)

Application Overview

The lab will display the friends from the SQL Server Friends database we built in Chapter 9. A Button will be added to the automatically generated form that will then open a form with all the pets of the friends. The latter form, shown in Figure 11.50, will also be generated by the wizard and modified.

Part 1: Build the Friends Form

In the current **prjDataWizard** Project, open the Data Form wizard, naming the new form **frmFriends**. Open the wizard as before. Name the dataset **dsFriends**, and connect it to the SQL Server database either with an existing connection or with a new one. (See discussions earlier in this chapter and in Chapter 9.) Select the Friends table and all its columns, and generate a Single Record form.

Now add a Module to the Project by right-clicking the Project in the Solution Explorer window and selecting Add and then Add Module from the popup menu. The module will contain data that will be passed from one form to the other. Name the module **modFriend**. In the module, declare a Public variable:

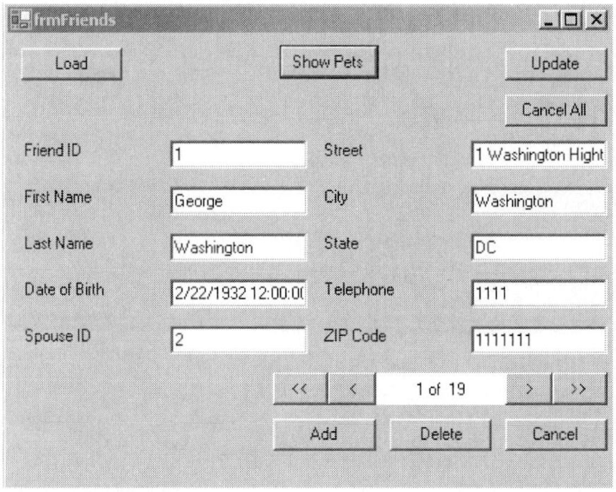

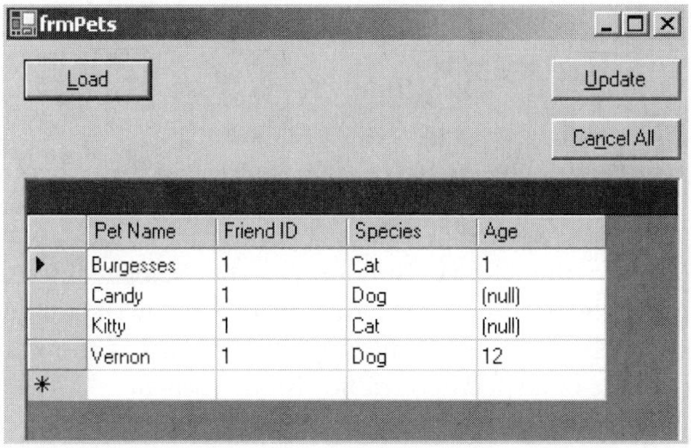

FIGURE 11.50
Running Lab 11.2.

```
Module modFriend
      Public intFriendID As Integer
End Module
```

Part 2: Build the Pets Form

In the current **prjDataWizard** Project, open a new Data Form Wizard again, naming the new form **frmPets**. Connect it to the same SQL Server database, but to the Pets table. Display all the columns in the table. Make this form a grid.

At this stage, we need to add a parameter to the Select statement of the Data Adapter. Click the OldDbDataAdapter1 object once (in this example the connection to SQL Server is made through an ODBC), and then explode the display of the SelectCommand property to expose the CommandText property. Click it, and then click the icon of three dots that will appear inside it the CommandText property. See Figure 11.51.

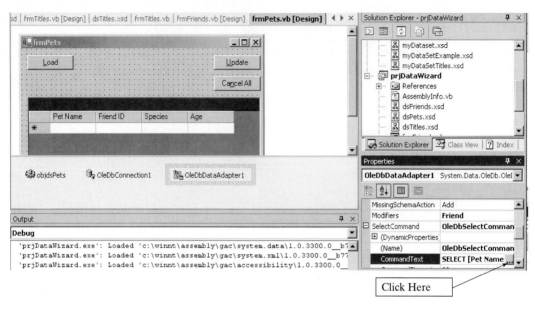

FIGURE 11.51
Showing the automatically generated `Select` SQL statement of the Data Adapter.

This will open up the Query Builder for the Select statement of the Data Adapter. See Figure 11.52. In the Criteria of [Friend ID], write a question mark character, "?". VB.NET will correct the syntax to "= ?". This is the parameter that will make sure that only pets of a specified friend will be shown.

We can actually check the parameter at this stage by looking at the `Parameter` property of the `SelectCommand`. Scroll down in the Properties window, and click the `Parameters` property within the `SelectCommand`. This will highlight the line and add a three-dot icon to it. Click the three dots icon to reveal the Parameter Collection Editor. This shows what parameters the specific SQL statement has. In this case, we can see that the SQL statement has one parameter named Friend_ID and that it is an Integer. See Figure 11.53.

Close the window. Next, double-click the gray background of frmPets. This will create the subroutine that will handle the Load event of the form. This event is raised (started) each time the form is loaded; that is, after it is created, but before it is displayed. In this subroutine, add the following code:

```
Private Sub frmPets_Load(ByVal sender As System.Object, _
             ByVal e As System.EventArgs) Handles MyBase.Load
    'Add This to place a value in the SQL command.

    Dim prmValue As New OleDb.OleDbParameter()
    prmValue.DbType = DbType.Int16
    prmValue.Value = modFriend.intFriendID
    OleDbDataAdapter1.SelectCommand.Parameters.Item(0) = prmValue

    Call btnLoad_Click(Me, e)
End Sub
```

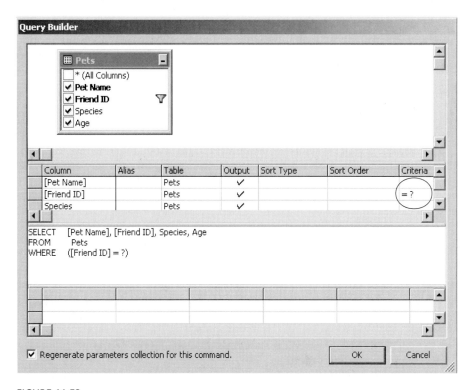

FIGURE 11.52
Manually changing the automatically generated `Select` SQL statement of the Data Adapter, adding a parameter.

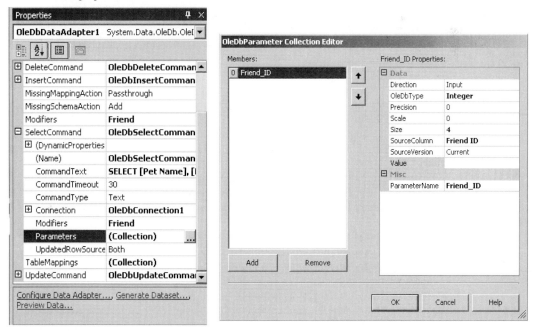

FIGURE 11.53
The `Parameters` Collection that will be generated as a result of changing the `Select` Statement.

This code defines a `Parameter` object, assigns it the value of the `Public` variable in the module, and then assigns the `Parameter` object as the first item in the `Parameters` collection of the `Select Command` of the Data Adapter. The code then calls the generated Button that loads the data into the grid.

Part 3: Connect the Forms

Add a Button to frmFriends. Name it btnPets. Make its `Text` property Show Pets. This Button will open the Pets form and show the pets of the current friend. To do so, add the following code, which assigns the Friend ID to the module and shows the pets form:

```
modFriend.intFriendID = CInt(editFriend_ID.Text)

Dim frmPets As New frmPets()
frmPets.Show()
```

SUGGESTED HOME ASSIGNMENTS

1. Make a replica of Friends.mdb in SQL Server. With the Data Form wizard, build two forms. The first will show the list of friends in a grid. When a friend is clicked, the second form will open showing only the list of diary entries relating to that friend. The list of entries will also be shown in a grid. When a grid line in the second form is clicked, all the friends of that diary meeting should be presented in the first form. There may be many friends in each diary meeting.
2. Add to each of the forms a Button that will display all the friends in the first form and all the pets in the second form.

TEST YOURSELF

1. Discuss the advantages of generating a prototype application with the Data Form wizard.
2. Discuss the advantages of building SQL with the Query Builder, as opposed to writing the SQL code.
3. What is XSD?
4. Why and when are diamonds included in an XSD?
5. When would you edit an XSD relationship, or would you?
6. What are the two types of forms that the Data Form wizard generates?
7. What are Group By queries?
   The next set of SQL questions relate to the Friends Access Database that come with the CD.
8. With the Query Builder, analyze and display how many friends there are by Car Type.
9. With the Query Builder, analyze and display how many diary entries there are on VB.
10. With the Query Builder, analyze and display how many diary entries there are for each friend.
11. With the Query Builder, analyze and display who is the most met friend.
12. With the Query Builder, analyze and display who is the most met friend by gender.
13. With the Query Builder, analyze and display how many pets there are all together and how many by species.
14. With the Query Builder, analyze and display the youngest and the oldest friend.
15. With the Query Builder, analyze and display how many friends there are in each city.

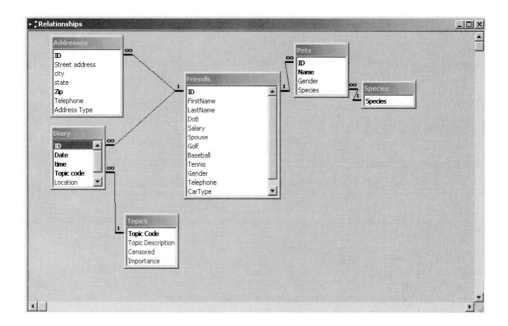

16. With the Query Builder, analyze and display all the diary meetings about Visual Basic.
17. With the Query Builder, analyze and display all the friends who have "A" in their name or the name of their pet.
18. With the Query Builder, analyze and display all the pets of the friends born 20 or more years ago.
19. With the Query Builder, analyze and display how many friends there are in each state.
20. With the Query Builder, analyze and display the oldest friend in each state.

C H A P T E R   1 2

The Disconnected Layer

CHAPTER OBJECTIVES

After completing this chapter, students should possess

1. An understanding of the overall picture of ADO.NET
2. An appreciation of what classes are at play in the disconnected layer and how they relate to each other

- `DataSet`
- `DataTable`
- `DataColumn`
- `DataRow`
- `DataRelation`
- `Constraint`
- `DataView`

3. The knowledge or how to apply the collections in the disconnected layer
4. The ability to built a dataset as local copy of the database

- Manipulate it
- Commit its changes to the database
- Manage the dataset

12.1   AIMS OF CHAPTER

In previous chapters, we introduced ADO connectivity and discussed its first tier, the Connection classes, and the second tier, the Command classes. We also discussed the Data Reader classes and touched on the Data Adapter classes as they are automatically constructed through the Data wizard. Those classes compose the connected layer—the objects that are connected to an external data source, most commonly a database.

In this chapter, we will discuss the *disconnected layer*—the objects that compose to create a local disconnected copy of the database in the application. These classes are the `DataSet` and its related classes: the `DataTable`, `DataColumn`, `DataRow`, `DataView`, `DataRelation`, and `Constraint`. We will discuss these in detail and demonstrate them. In doing so, we will access data from a database to construct a single table dataset. This dataset will be manipulated while disconnected from the database. The manipulations on this dataset will be updated back to the database through a specially constructed Data Adapter object. The lab at the end of the chapter will demonstrate some of these options in both Access and SQL Server.

12.2   AN OVERVIEW OF THE DATA SET CLASS AND ITS RELATED CLASSES

12.2.1 An Overview of the Disconnected Classes

The classes discussed up to now were mostly those in charge of activities relating to the connection to and manipulation of a connected Data Source, in this case a database. Objects of the Connection classes (objects in plural because there is one for SQL Server and another for OleDb) established the connection to the Data Source, in our case a database; objects of the Command classes handled the individual SQL statements that were passed to it; when a Command object returned a value or values, objects of the Data Reader classes held these results and made accessing them easy. We also discussed the Data Adapter classes as created by the Data File wizard. A Data Adapter object contains four SQL statements and so makes manipulating a database possible even without explicit Command objects. All these classes are part of the *connected* layer of ADO.NET. The layer is called the connected layer because objects that instantiate classes in this layer are intended to work with a Data Source while having an established active thread (connection) to it. These classes actively connect to the Data Source.

In contrast, classes in the *disconnected layer* handle data in the Data Set or Data Reader, where there in no longer an active connection to the Data Source from where these data were copied. And so, while the connected layer works with the Data Source directly, and hence its name, the disconnected layer works with data that have already been read from the Data Source and placed in a Data Set or Data Reader. In a Data Set and a Data Reader, the data are handled independently and without relation to their original Data Source, hence, its name the *disconnected* layer. An overview of the connected and the disconnected layers of ADO.NET are shown in Figure 12.1.

Once the data have been copied to a Data Set object or data control, the data can be manipulated (read, updated, deleted, or added) in the Data Set or data control, regardless of the Data Source. The disconnected layer is built around the Data Set. The `Dataset` class can be thought of as a private single-user relational database with all the functionality of such a database. The Data Set is made up of a collection of interrelated tables, where each table is made up of columns and rows and where each table may

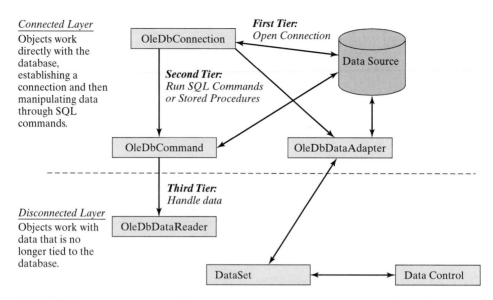

FIGURE 12.1
Overview of the connected and the disconnected layers of ADO.NET.

have a relation with any other table.[22] Various constraints on the tables can also be added. These constraints deal with uniqueness and foreign key relationships. The uniqueness constraint deals with guarantying that a combination of one or more columns uniquely identifies each row in the table. Foreign key relationships are discussed in Chapter 9.

Having said that, the Dataset is not exactly a fully functional database as it lacks some of the basic and most fundamental functionalities of a DBMS such as allowing many concurrent transactions to execute on the data simultaneously. It does, however, have a lot of convenient database functionality that make accessing and updating the data easy.

The Data Set is a locally held disconnected copy of a database or of part of it. Typically, a Data Set is populated (Fill in VB.NET terminology) through a Data Adapter, which, in turn, applies SQL commands to access a database that is identified with a Connection object. But the Data Set is disconnected, meaning that any changes made to its data or to its schema (the database structure) will be totally unrelated to the database from which the data were taken. By the same token, any changes made to the data in the database after the Data Set was filled will be totally invisible to the Data Set. That is what we mean when we say that the database and the Data Set are *disconnected* in .NET terms. (This is not exactly the same as disconnected in database

---

[22]It is convenient to think of the collections in .NET as arrays of same-type objects, with the exception that these objects can be referenced not only by their index number in the collection, but also by their name.

terms.)[23] Changes made to the Data Set can be updated into the database through the Data Adapter in the *connected* layer with its `Update` method. Only classes in the connected layer can be connected to a Data Source such as a database.

An instantiated `Dataset` object can be thought of as a package of interrelated tables that are mostly, but still optionally, with the ability to be later on reconnected to the Data Source they were derived from through a Data Adapter object. These tables are managed in the Data Set by `DataTable` objects. Each of these objects roughly corresponds to a table in a relational database. Each Data Table object is a member in the `Tables` collection of the Data Set. Conceptually, this means that a Data Set has a collection of tables within it, just as a relational database contains tables within it. This also means that all the tables in a Data Set can read with a `For Each loop`. Note that data reside in these tables, which, in turn, reside in a Data Set. The data are not directly accessible through the Data Set. Rather, accessing and updating the data is done either through a bound control, as we saw in the previous chapters, or through `DataTable` objects, which we will do in this chapter.

In the case when the Data Set is filled by the Data Adapter, it will typically contain one table only. This table will contain the result of the Select command in the Data Adapter. Recall, that the Data Adapter has four SQL statements embedded within it. A connection to the Data Source must be established before the Data Adapter can issue the Select SQL statement. The processes that take place as a result of the Data Adapter `Fill` method and the classes in the disconnected layer that will be affected by it are shown in Figure 12.2

Each `DataTable` object contains a collection of `Columns` that corresponds to the `DataColumn` class and a collection of `Rows` that corresponds to the `DataRow` class. The columns and their properties constitute the schema of the table. The rows contain the actual data stored in the table. As a result of the `Fill` method of the Data Adapter, the result of the SQL statement will be held in a `DataTable`. The schema of the table, its columns, will be defined based on the SQL statement and be registered in a collection of `Columns` that corresponds to the `DataColumn` class. The actual data will be kept in a collection of `Rows`. All changes made to this data will change the Data Row and the Data Table inside the Data Set only; the Data Source will not be changed yet because no SQL statement is issued by these changes.

---

[23]To avoid misunderstandings, it should be made clear that the term *disconnected* has two meanings in this context. In .NET, it describes a group of classes that handle data without directly accessing a Data Source. In database terminology, however, the term means working with a database with an *optimistic concurrency control* method—a method in which potential conflicts between transactions, such as one transaction accidentally overriding changes made by another, are checked only when a transaction completes its execution and requests the DBMS to commit its changes. Alternatively, in a *conservative concurrency control* method, the DBMS places locks in the data or examines timestamps in the data so that no transaction can manipulate rows that are currently being manipulated by another transaction. The current .NET architecture only works with the optimistic concurrency control method. It is impossible to lock the data that a transaction accesses or to examine its timestamps to avoid overlap with other transactions. In practical terms, this means that when the data that were changed in the Data Set are written back to the database with the Data Adapter `Update` method, it is possible that the operation will fail because the data had been changed by another transaction since they were read by this transaction. A Try Block is essential therefore in every data accessing section of code in VB.NET to catch such database-generated errors and handle them accordingly.

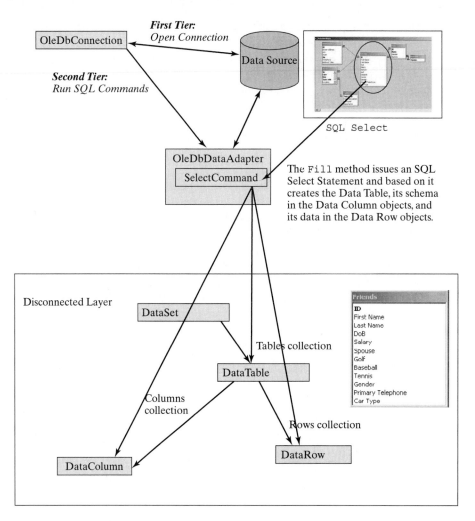

FIGURE 12.2
The Fill method of the Data Adapter and its related classes.

When and if the changes made to the Data Set need to be updated back to the Data Source, the Update method of the Data Adapter needs to be activated. This method will scan all the Data Rows in the Data Table, and for each one that was changed, it will issue an Insert, Update, or Delete SQL statement, depending on the changes made to that row. Only through this Data Adapter method in the *connected* layer can these changes be carried back to the Data Source itself. As before, a connection to the Data Source must be established before the Data Adapter can issue the SQL statements. Note how, in Figure 12.3, the Update method updates only data from the Data Row objects. Changes made to the other objects, such as the Data Columns and Data Tables are ignored.

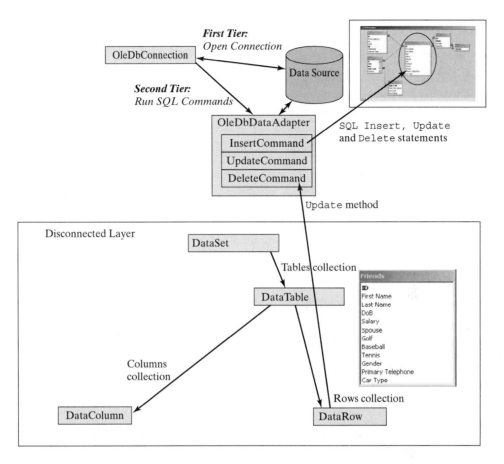

FIGURE 12.3
The Update method of the Data Adapter and its related classes.

12.2.2 An Overview of the Classes in the Data Table

Within the Data Set object, there is the Data Table, which contains Data Columns and Data Rows. The processes that take place as a result of the Data Adapter Update method and the classes in the disconnected layer that will be affected by it are shown in Figure 12.3. Within each Data Row, the data are referenced and updated as part of an Item collection. The index of an Item in the collection corresponds to the index of the column in the table. For example, a Data Table representing a table with three columns will have three objects in its Columns collection. There will also be three Item objects in each of the rows of that table. The first item in the row will relate to the first column, the second item to the second column, and so on. Constraints on the content of these columns are recorded with objects in the Constraint class. There are two types of constraints on the data in a Data Table: foreign key constraints and uniqueness constraints. Constraints are managed as a collection in the DataTable. Views are supported with a DataView object. This object is contained in the DataTable object.

The relationships between any two tables in a Data Set can be mapped with an object of the `DataRelation` class, which corresponds to a *foreign key* in a relational database. An object of this class will specify the columns in the parent table and the related columns in the child (dependent) table.[24] The column in the parent table and the columns in the child table are managed as two separate collections, `ParentColumn` and `ChildColumns`, respectively. The `DataRelation` objects are managed as a collection in the `DataSet` object. When a relation is added through a `DataRelation` object a new `Constraint` object is automatically added to the Data Tables involved. This constraint also contains the *foreign key* rule that specifies what needs to be done when the value of the parent column changes and what needs to be done when a value that does not exist in the parent column is placed in a child column.

The Data Relation and Constraint rules relate to columns. These columns are handled as collections in the `DataRelation` object and in the `Constraint` object. The `DataRelation` class has two column collections. These collections are called `ChildColumns`, relating to the columns in the dependent table, and `ParentColumns`, relating to the primary table. Both these collections are related to the `DataColumn` class.

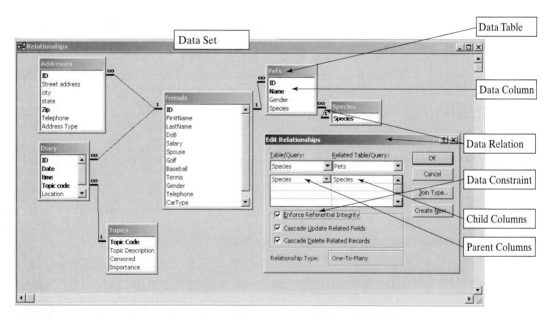

FIGURE 12.4
Relationship window as shown in Access with overlay of matching ADO.NET classes.

---

[24]For example, in the Friends and Pets database that we created in Chapter 9, a row in the Pets table cannot be added unless the value of the [Friend ID] column in that row already exists in the Friends table. This constraint is managed with a foreign key. The foreign key will establish the constraint between the [Friend ID] column in the parent table, being Friends, and the [Friend ID] column in the child table, being Pets. The same foreign key relationship an be seen in the Friends Access database. A Pet cannot be added if its Species does not exist in the Species table.

The Constraint class has either one or two collections of columns, depending on the type of constraint. When the constraint enforces uniqueness there is one collection of columns, named Columns. When the constraint enforces a foreign key there are two collections of columns, named Columns, for the parent column, and RelatedColumns, for the child columns. These collections are composed of objects of the DataColumn class.

It is convenient to relate to the objects within a Data Set by comparing them with their equivalent database counterparts. Figure 12.4 shows the Relationships window in Access 2002 of the Friends database that comes with the CD. The window shows the whole database with all its schema. Think of this whole diagram as the Data Set. Each table in the database corresponds to one Data Table in ADO. Each column in each table in the database corresponds to one Data Column object in ADO. Each foreign key relationship (foreign key relationships are the lines that connect the tables in the figure) corresponds to one Data Relation object, and within each of these foreign keys, if the key is enforced, each constraint in the database corresponds to a Data Constraint object in ADO.

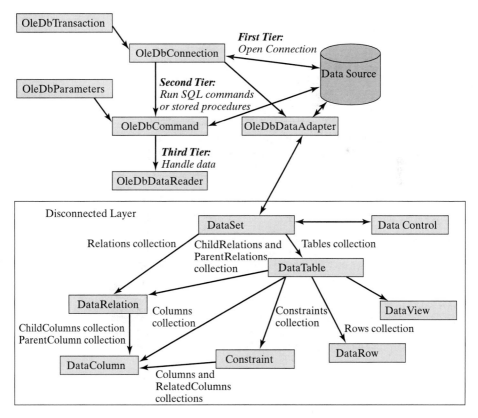

FIGURE 12.5
Expanded view of ADO.NET with listing of the disconnected classes and the collections that connect among them.

It will be convenient at this stage to expand the ADO model we saw in the previous chapters with the disconnected layer classes. We will use these additional ADO disconnected layer classes throughout this chapter.

12.2.3 An Example

The ADO.NET diagram in Figure 12.5 can seem a bit complex, but it really is quite manageable. Figure 12.6 is the XSD of the database we created in Chapter 9 with SQL Server. The Entities have been moved around a bit in the diagram to make reading easier. The entire XSD represents a Data Set object that can manipulate the data in both tables. The Data Set contains two tables in the `Tables Collection`. Each table in turn contains many `DataColumns` that are grouped into a `Columns Collection`. The relationship between the two tables is handled with the `DataRelation` object. This object, too, is part of a collection in the Data Set. The diagram also shows the `Columns` collection of Data Table (1) and the `Constraints` collection of Data Table (0). The `Columns` collection of Data Table (0) and the `Constraints` collection of Data Table (1) also exist, but are not drawn in the figure. The Unique and Foreign Key constraints in Data Table (0) are both collections containing Columns.

Alternatively, Figure 12.7 shows part of the Friends Access database.

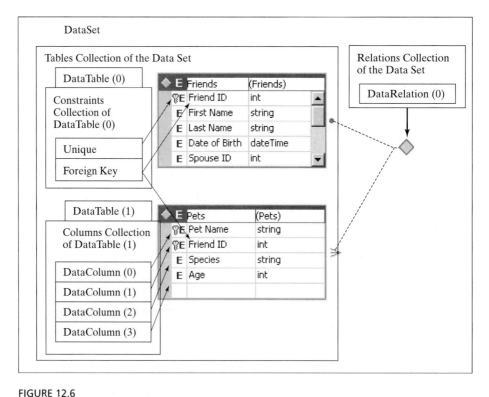

FIGURE 12.6
XSD representation of the SQL Server relationship between the Friends and the Pets tables with overlay of matching ADO.NET classes, collections, and properties.

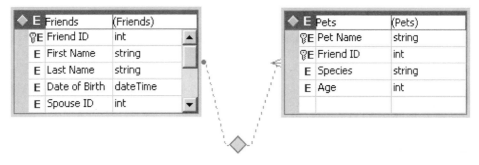

FIGURE 12.7
XSD representation of the Access relationship between the Friends and Pets tables.

12.2.4 A Look at Some of the Disconnected Layer Hierarchy of Class Methods

The overall functionality of the disconnected layer is quite large. To make sure that we do not lose track of where everything fits in, we will look at this functionality in sections and in perspective. Before we begin, though, let's take a look at the overall separation of responsibility among the classes by mapping some of the most important methods of each class.

Figure 12.8 shows what are probably the most important methods of the disconnected layer. The diagram excludes the Constraint, DataRelation, and DataView classes. Typically, Constraints and Data Relations will be set in the database itself and just copied as-is into the Data Set by the Data Adapter. We will deal with these classes in the next chapter.

The responsibility of the Data Adapter is to fill the Data Set with content, data and schema, from the database, or any other Data Source, and to update the database or Data Source with the changes made to the data in the Data Set. Only changes in the data can be updated back to the Data Source. Schema changes cannot be updated from the Data Set back to the Data Source because the Data Adapter does not support the SQL statements that are necessary for modifying the schema of the database. Changes to the Data Source schema, such as adding a column or a table, can be done in VB.NET only through Command objects.

The data that are read are placed in a Data Set with the Data Adapter's Fill method. (As we shall see later, a Data Set can be dimensioned and used to handle data even without reading the data from a database, but that is not the main objective of a Data Set.) When changes made to the data in the Data Set need to be updated back into the Data Source, such as the actual database, the operation is done wholly with the Update method of the Data Adapter. Remember, .NET works in a disconnected mode with the database, so any changes made to the Data Set are totally transparent to the database until they are updated explicitly into the database with the Update method. As noted in the previous chapters, *the Dataset is in the disconnected layer, and so changes made to it have no effect on the database until the Data Adapter forces them explicitly with the Update method.*

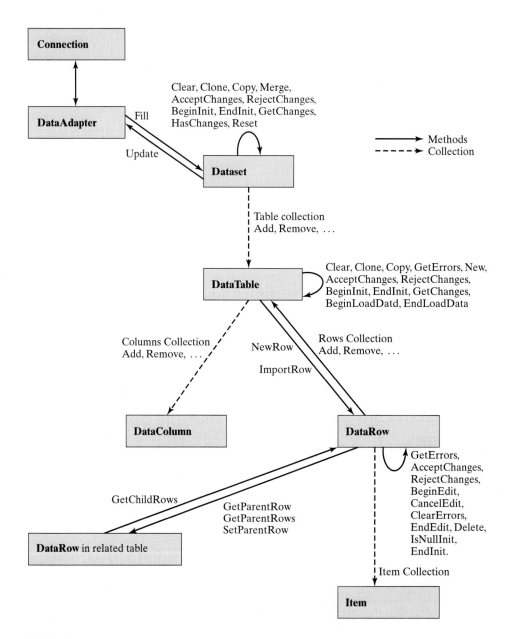

FIGURE 12.8
Methods and collections of the Dataset and its related classes.

The Data Set itself has a number of methods that handle the data and their schema. Typically, these methods will be applicable only once the data are filled into the Data Set, although, as we shall see in the next chapter, a Data Set can manipulate data regardless of the existence of a database. The Data set methods include `Copy`, which copies one Data Set into another; `Merge`, which merges two Data Sets into one; `Clone`, which copies the data structure of one Data Set into another Data Set without copying the actual data; `AcceptChanges`, which accepts all the changes made to all the objects in the Data Set, including all its Data Tables and Data Relations, in one operation; and so on. We shall examine these methods in detail later in the chapter.

The tables in the Data Set (remember, there can be many of these because the Data Set is conceptually the same as a single-user relational database) are related to the Data Set through its `Table` collection. This collection enables access to individual tables either by name or by their index in the collection. Tables can also be added and removed with appropriately named methods of this collection. It is through this `Table` collection that `DataTable` objects are tied to the Data Set.

Each `DataTable` has methods that handle operations on that specific table. The name and functionality of many of these methods is identical to those of the Data Set, with the exception that the Data Table methods apply only to their specific table while the same-named methods in the Data Set relate to the entire Data Set and all its tables. For example, the `Copy` method of the Data Set class will copy the entire Data Set, including all its tables and what is within them, their rows, columns, etc. On the other hand, the `Copy` method of a Data Table will copy the entire table, including all its rows and columns, but not other tables.

The same principle also applies to the classes that are below the `DataTable` class in the .NET hierarchy, `DataRow`, `DataColumn`, and so on. Collections are used to access these classes and to add and remove objects from them, while methods apply to the entire object and hence relate to all occurrences of the objects below it in the hierarchy. The `DataRow` and the `DataColumn` objects of a `DataTable` object are managed through the `Rows` and the `Columns` collections of the `DataTable`. We will examine these methods in detail when we discuss the methods of each class.

12.3   A SIMPLE EXAMPLE OF THE DATASET AND DATATABLE CLASSES

A convenient way of examining the methods and properties of the ADO classes is to get a hands-on feeling with the code. The form we will build will read and update data from the Titles table in the Biblio database. (This is one of the sample databases that comes with Access. If you do not have it, skip to the next section and see example with the Friends database.) We will build it in sections. Note that the code will be identical with any other provider, except that with SQL Server the Connection and Data Adapter classes will come from the `SQLClient` namespace. *The Lab at the end of this chapter builds an expanded version of this form and application with SQL Server. If you wish to examine the code in SQL Server, refer to the lab.* The accompanying code CD has this lab in both Access and SQL Server. The current section deals with the Biblio database.[25] The next section replicates it with the Friends database.

---

[25]Biblio is a database that used to come with Access. When you open the database with Access 2002 you will be asked to convert it to Access 2002 format. If you do not have Biblio, use the Friends database.

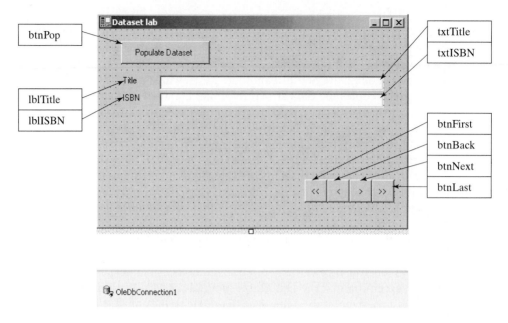

FIGURE 12.9
Demonstrating the Dataset and DataTable classes.

Add a new form. Name it frmDataset. Add the Buttons, labels, and text boxes as in Figure 12.9. Make the `Enabled` property of the four navigation Buttons, those with arrows on them, `False`. Then add an OleDbConnection control (make sure to add a control from the toolbox, rather than dimension an object in the code). Connect the control to the database with its `ConnectionString` property. If a connection does not already exist, create one by choosing <new connection . . .> in the property. This will open up the connection wizard that will automatically build the connection string to handle Biblio.mdb with Jet 4. (You will need to open the Biblio database with Access 2002 first. Doing so will translate the database from an Access 97 format to an Access 2002 format. Jet 4 works only with the Access 2000 and Access 2002 format.) Creating the connection string with the wizard is convenient shorthand that will save a lot of coding when building the connection object.

Alternatively, the example can be run with SQL Server on the Friends and Pets database. If you are connecting to the Friends and Pets database, replace any reference to Title and ISBN with Name and ID, respectively, throughout the code. For example, txtTitle will become txtName. Note that the [Friend ID] is the first column in Friends and that [First Name] is the second. Also, throughout make sure to work with the `SQLClient` namespace.

12.3.1   Populating the Data Set

Add this code to the top of the form class:

```
Public Class frmDataset
    Inherits System.Windows.Forms.Form
```

```
' Add these lines here
Dim myConnection As New OleDb.OleDbConnection()
Dim myDataAdapter As OleDb.OleDbDataAdapter
Dim myDataset As DataSet
Dim myDataTable As New Data.DataTable()
Dim intPosition As Integer
```

The objects mentioned in the code are the objects that we need shared throughout the methods in the form.

With that done, we can add the code that will demonstrate the Data Set and its related class. Double-click btnPop, and in the subroutine that will be automatically generated add this code. This is probably the simplest application of a Data Set. We will read one table only, and an untyped one at that. (We will discuss typed and untyped Data Sets later in the chapter.) The code instantiates a new instance of the Data Adapter object that we previously dimensioned. This Data Adapter is necessary because only through it will we be able to access the database and copy data into the Data Set. The Data Adapter at this stage will only support a Select SQL statement, because the data will only be displayed at this stage. This SQL statement is necessary for the Fill method through which the data will be copied into the Data Set. Later we will add the other SQL statements that will enable the Update method too.

Since only one SQL statement is used in the Data Adapter, it is instantiated with the SQL statement as one parameter and the Connection object as the other. Later we will change this situation when we add more SQL statements to the Data Adapter. The code is as follows:

```
Private Sub btnPop_Click(ByVal sender As _
    System.Object, ByVal e As System.EventArgs) _
    Handles btnPop.Click

    Dim strSelect As String

    Try
        ' Save on long typing and just copy
        ' the connection string from the control.
        ' And, open the connection.
        myConnection.ConnectionString = _
            OleDbConnection1.ConnectionString
        myConnection.Open()

        ' Build the SQL statement
        ' and place it in the Data Adapter.
        ' The Data Adapter has two parameters:
        ' the SQL statement and the connection object.
        strSelect = "Select Title, ISBN from Titles"
        myDataAdapter = New _
            OleDb.OleDbDataAdapter(strSelect, _
            myConnection)
```

```
' Working with an untyped dataset and a single
' table. The variable intSize will contain the
' number of rows in the dataset.
Dim intSize As Integer
myDataset = New DataSet()
intSize = myDataAdapter.Fill(myDataset)

' With the Dataset filled, we can look at its
' first table by assigning it to a DataTable
' object.
myDataTable = myDataset.Tables(0)

' Working with an untyped dataset and a single
' table
txtTitle.Text = _
    myDataTable.Rows(0).Item(0).ToString
txtISBN.Text = _
    myDataTable.Rows(0).Item(1).ToString

' Make the navigation Buttons enabled, now that
' navigation makes sense.
btnFirst.Enabled = True
btnLast.Enabled = True
btnNext.Enabled = True
btnBack.Enabled = True

Catch e1 As Exception
    MessageBox.Show(e1.Message)
End Try
End Sub
```

The data values are assigned from the first and second items in the first row in the Rows collection of the Data Table. The values are cast into a string with the ToString method. The variable intSize will contain the number of rows in the table.

The preceding code used the Data Set object as though it were an *untyped* Data Set. The code referenced the table and the items by their index, rather than by their names. Untyped Data Set objects are referenced by their index number in the collection they belong to. The first Data Table object, in this case it is the only table, is indexed 0. Had there been another Data Table, the second Data Table would have been indexed 1. In the same way, the first item in the row is indexed 0 and the second is indexed 1.

A Data Table is a member in the Tables collection. Because of that, we can use a For Each loop to loop through the Data Tables in the Data Set. We can indeed do that in this case, too (although it really makes little sense with only one table):

```
' Alternative code 1
Dim myTable As DataTable
For Each myTable In myDataset.Tables
    txtTitle.Text = myTable.Rows(0).Item(0).ToString
Next
```

Alternatively, since there is only one data table involved, we can skip the definition of the Data Set altogether (the next sections of navigation code, however, will need to be redone, too):

```
' Alternative code 2
intSize = myDataAdapter.Fill(myDataTable)
```

12.3.2 Navigation

With the Data Set populated, we can add the code to navigate through it. The navigation is handled in the code example by keeping track of the current row number with an integer named `intPosition`. The number of rows in the table is given by the `Rows.Count` property. We rely on `intPosition` rather than on `intSize` because the number of rows in the table can change after it is loaded when rows are added or deleted.

Navigating to the next row in the table, which translates as the next Data Row member in the `Rows` collection of the specific Data Table, requires advancing `intPosition` by 1, provided that the end of the collection has not yet been reached. The Try Block is there because later we will enable deleting rows from the table. In such a case, it is possible that we will try to read a deleted row. The `Catch` clause will handle these cases:

```
Private Sub btnNext_Click(ByVal sender As System.Object, _
          ByVal e As _ System.EventArgs) Handles btnNext.Click
    ' Navigate to next row
    Try
       If intPosition < myDataset.Tables(0).Rows.Count - 1 _
       Then
         intPosition += 1

         ' See later paragraph about adding code here.

         txtTitle.Text = _
           myDataset.Tables(0).Rows(intPosition).Item(0).ToString
         txtISBN.Text = _
           myDataset.Tables(0).Rows(intPosition).Item(1).ToString
       End If

    Catch ' when reading rows that were deleted
         txtTitle.Text = ""
         txtISBN.Text = ""
    End Try
End Sub
```

A better way of handling deleted rows when navigating is to add this section of code after incrementing `intPosition`. The code examines whether the `RowState` property of the current row indicates that the row has been deleted. The `RowState` property uses Enums to indicate the status of a Data Row. A Data Row can be `Added`, `Deleted`, `Detached` (not tied to any Data Table), `Modified`, or `Unchanged`. It is better to handle the deleted rows this way than with the Catch of the Try Block. Here is the code:

```
    Do While myDataset.Tables(0).Rows(intPosition).RowState = _
            DataRowState.Deleted = True And _
        (intPosition < myDataset.Tables(0).Rows.Count - 1)

        intPosition += 1

Loop
```

The same logic applies to the other navigation Buttons. Moving to the previous row involves subtracting 1 from `intPosition` so long as the new value is still within range. Moving to the first row involves setting `intPosition` to 0. Moving to the last row involves setting `intPosition` to the size of the collection. The code is as follows:

```
Private Sub btnBack_Click(ByVal sender As System.Object, _
            ByVal e As System.EventArgs) Handles btnBack.Click
    ' Navigate to previous row.

    Try
        If intPosition > 0 Then
            intPosition -= 1
            txtTitle.Text = _
              myDataset.Tables(0).Rows(intPosition).Item(0).ToString
            txtISBN.Text = _
              myDataset.Tables(0).Rows(intPosition).Item(1).ToString
        End If
    Catch ' when reading back to first rows that were deleted
        txtTitle.Text = ""
        txtISBN.Text = ""
    End Try
End Sub

Private Sub btnLast_Click(ByVal sender As System.Object, _
            ByVal e As System.EventArgs) Handles btnLast.Click
    ' Navigate to last row.

    Try
        intPosition = myDataset.Tables(0).Rows.Count - 1
        txtTitle.Text = _
          myDataset.Tables(0).Rows(intPosition).Item(0).ToString
        txtISBN.Text = _
          myDataset.Tables(0).Rows(intPosition).Item(1).ToString
    Catch ' when reading rows that were deleted
        txtTitle.Text = ""
        txtISBN.Text = ""
    End Try
End Sub

Private Sub btnFirst_Click(ByVal sender As System.Object, _
            ByVal e As System.EventArgs) Handles btnFirst.Click
    ' Navigate to first row

    Try
        intPosition = 0
```

```
    txtTitle.Text = _
     myDataset.Tables(0).Rows(intPosition).Item(0).ToString
    txtISBN.Text = _
     myDataset.Tables(0).Rows(intPosition).Item(1).ToString
  Catch
    txtTitle.Text = ""
    txtISBN.Text = ""
  End Try
End Sub
```

12.3.3 Typed and Untyped Data Sets

The preceding code referenced the Tables, the Rows, and the Item collections through the respective index of each. Referencing objects in a collection in this way is handling the Data Set as an *untyped* Data Set, because it does not bring into account the explicit typing of the objects. Objects in a collection can also be read according to their name. In this case, each Data Table can be read based on its table name and each item based on the column name it relates to. Referencing objects in a collection in this way is handling the Data Set as a *typed* Data Set:

```
txtTitle.Text = _
myDataset.Tables("Titles").Rows(intPosition).Item("Title").ToString

txtISBN.Text = _
myDataset.Tables("Titles").Rows(intPosition).Item("ISBN").ToString
```

12.3.4 A Look at the XML

With the dataset populated, we can also look at the XML. XML is the language with which .NET communicates with Data Sources. We will not spend much time on XML; it is a whole language in its own right. The XML can be written to a file with the appropriate method:

```
myDataset.WriteXmlSchema("C:\a.txt")
```

The XML of our Data Set is

```
<?xml version="1.0" standalone="yes"?>
<xs:schema        id="NewDataSet"        xmlns=""
    xmlns:xs="http://www.w3.org/2001/XMLSchema"
xmlns:msdata="urn:schemas-microsoft-com:xml-msdata">
    <xs:element name="NewDataSet" msdata:IsDataSet="true">
     <xs:complexType>
      <xs:choice maxOccurs="unbounded">
       <xs:element name="Table">
        <xs:complexType>
         <xs:sequence>
          <xs:element name="Title" type="xs:string"
             minOccurs="0" />
          <xs:element name="ISBN" type="xs:string"
```

```
                    minOccurs="0"/>
               </xs:sequence>
             </xs:complexType>
            </xs:element>
          </xs:choice>
        </xs:complexType>
      </xs:element>
    </xs:schema>
```

12.3.5 Manipulating the Data Set

Data Rows are added with the appropriately named method of the Rows collection. You may wish to add a Button named btnAdd to the form to handle this operation. Adding a row involves creating a new instance of a row in the Rows collection with the NewRow method, setting the values of its items, and then tying the new row to the collection with the Add method:

```
Private Sub btnAdd_Click(ByVal sender As System.Object, _
        ByVal e As System.EventArgs) Handles btnAdd.Click

    ' The Data Row is the object we will add to the
    ' Rows collection.
    Dim myRow As DataRow

    ' We begin by setting the schema of this Data Row
    ' to match the Rows collection data structure.
    myRow = myDataset.Tables(0).NewRow

    ' We set its values
    myRow.Item(0) = txtTitle.Text
    myRow.Item(1) = txtISBN.Text

    ' And add it to the Rows collection.
    myDataset.Tables(0).Rows.Add(myRow)

End Sub
```

Deleting a row just requires deleting it from the Rows collection:

```
Private Sub btnDelete_Click(ByVal sender As System.Object, _
        ByVal e As System.EventArgs) Handles btnDelete.Click

    ' Deleting a row means removing it from the
    ' Rows collection
    myDataset.Tables(0).Rows(intPosition).Delete()

    ' And repositioning the displayed data to the next
    ' row in the Rows collection
    If intPosition < myDataset.Tables(0).Rows.Count - 1 Then
        intPosition += 1
    Else
        intPosition = myDataset.Tables(0).Rows.Count - 1
    End If
```

```
txtTitle.Text = _
  myDataset.Tables(0).Rows(intPosition).Item(0).ToString
txtISBN.Text = _
  myDataset.Tables(0).Rows(intPosition).Item(1).ToString
```

End Sub

After the row is deleted, the code advances to the next row in the collection and displays it. You may wish to add a Button named btnDelete to the form to handle this operation.

Updating a row just requires setting the new values into the row items. You may wish to add a Button named btnUpdate to the form to handle that:

```
Private Sub btnUpdate_Click(ByVal sender As System.Object, _
    ByVal e As System.EventArgs) Handles btnUpdate.Click

  ' Updating just means setting the values in the
  ' appropriate Item of the current row
  myDataset.Tables(0).Rows(intPosition).Item(0) = _
      txtTitle.Text
  myDataset.Tables(0).Rows(intPosition).Item(1) = _
      txtISBN.Text
```

End Sub

All the changes—adding, deleting, and updating rows—are registered in the Data Row involved, in the Data Table, and in the Data Set. Each of these objects has an AcceptChanges and a RejectChanges method. That can commit or undo, respectively, the changes to the Data Set. The changes will be pending until this is done. The existence of pending changes is registered in the HasChanges method (yes, this is a method, not a property), which will return the value True if there are any pending changes. Once changes have been accepted, the HasChanges method will return the value False. Note that this is the case even if the changes have not yet been committed to the database.

Rejecting all the changes at a Data Row level will undo all the changes to that row only. Rejecting all the changes at a Data Table level will undo all the changes to all the rows but only those rows in that specific table. Rejecting all the changes at a Data Set level will undo all the changes. The code is

```
myDataset.Tables(0).RejectChanges()
myDataset.Tables(0).AcceptChanges()
```

The same applies to clearing a Data Table or a Data Set. Clear will empty only its object:

```
myDataset.Clear()
```

12.3.6 Applying a Filter to the Data Set

A filter enables the selection of rows from a Data Table according to specific criteria. Conveniently, these criteria are equivalent to the Where clause in an SQL statement. A filter is applied with the RowFilter method. The rows that are selected with it can then be read through the Default View of the Data Table. The `DefaultView` contains an `Item` collection. Reading the items in this collection is done in an equivalent manner as reading the items in the `Item` collection of a Data Row. In the code that follows, a filter selects only those rows in which the Title contains, somewhere inside it, a string with a value that is entered in a textbox named txtFilter (see the appendix for a detailed discussion of the `Like` keyword in SQL):

```
myDataTable.DefaultView.RowFilter = _
    "Title Like '%" &txtFilter.Text &"%'"

Dim I As Integer
For I = 0 To myDataTable.DefaultView.Count - 1
    Console.WriteLine(myDataTable.DefaultView(I).Item(0))
Next
```

12.4 SOME CHANGES TO ALLOW THE DATASET TO BE COPIED INTO A DATABASE

12.4.1 Changing the Data Adapter

To copy the changes made in the Data Set into the database requires that some changes be made to the Data Adapter. The Data Adapter we built earlier has only a Select SQL statement. That is all we needed to retrieve the data. However, now that we need to update changes back to the database, we must add Update, Delete, and Insert SQL commends to the Data Adapter. Accordingly, we need to build the appropriate SQL statements and tie them to the appropriate properties of the Data Adapter. Since the form we built only handles two columns and since one of these is the ISBN, which we will assume cannot be updated because it is the primary key, these statements are relatively simple:

```
Try
    ' The other SQL commands
    Dim strSelect As String = "Select Title, ISBN from Titles"
    Dim strUpdate As String = _
        "Update Titles set Title = @Title Where ISBN = @ISBN"
    Dim strDelete As String = "Delete from Titles Where ISBN = @ISBN"
    Dim strInsert As String = _
        "Insert into Titles values " & _
        "(@Title, Null, @ISBN, 1, Null, Null, Null, Null)"
```

What must be accounted for, however, is that these statements need to work with SQL parameters, because the values passed to these SQL statements will change depending on the row that is affected by the SQL statement. (Note that the example here applies explicit parameter names, rather than the "?" wildcard. According to the VB.NET documentation this should work only with SQL Server, but it works very well also with OleDb connecting to an Access database.) The SQL statements will be assigned to Command objects. We will assign the Connection object to the Command objects at this stage. After the Command objects are instantiated, we will tie the parameters to them. In this case, we are creating the parameters through the `Add` method of the `Parameters` collection. The `Add` method can receive several combinations of arguments. In the following code specifies the name of the parameter, its data type, its length, and the column name it applies to:

```
' Define the Command objects
Dim sqlUpdate, sqlDelete, sqlInsert, sqlSelect As _
        OleDb.OleDbCommand

' Tie the Command objects to the Data Adapter
sqlUpdate = New OleDb.OleDbCommand(strUpdate, myConnection)
sqlDelete = New OleDb.OleDbCommand(strDelete, myConnection)
sqlInsert = New OleDb.OleDbCommand(strInsert, myConnection)
sqlSelect = New OleDb.OleDbCommand(strSelect, myConnection)

' Add the parameters of the SQL Commands
'       parameter
'       name      , data type                  ,length, column name
sqlUpdate.Parameters.Add _
        ("@Title", Data.OleDb.OleDbType.Char, 255, "Title")
sqlUpdate.Parameters.Add _
        ("@ISBN", Data.OleDb.OleDbType.Char, 20, "ISBN")
sqlDelete.Parameters.Add _
        ("@ISBN", Data.OleDb.OleDbType.Char, 20, "ISBN")
sqlInsert.Parameters.Add _
        ("@Title", Data.OleDb.OleDbType.Char, 255, "Title")
sqlInsert.Parameters.Add _
        ("@ISBN", Data.OleDb.OleDbType.Char, 20, "ISBN")
```

These Command objects will be assigned to the appropriate properties of the Data Adapter, and the data can then be accessed:

```
'This replaces
' myDataAdapter = _
'     New OleDb.OleDbDataAdapter(strSelect, myConnection)
myDataAdapter = New OleDb.OleDbDataAdapter()
myDataAdapter.SelectCommand = sqlSelect
myDataAdapter.UpdateCommand = sqlUpdate
myDataAdapter.DeleteCommand = sqlDelete
myDataAdapter.InsertCommand = sqlInsert

' This says activate the Fill method of this Data Adapter
' object with its Select Command object to read the data
' in the Titles tables. The data will be read into myDataset
' and the number of records will be placed in intSize.
intSize = myDataAdapter.Fill(myDataset, "Titles")
```

12.4.2 Updating the Database from the Data Set

With the Data Adapter rebuilt to support all four of its SQL commands, changes made to the Data Set can be updated into the database. The code creates a new Data Set and then copies only the changed rows into it. This is necessary because we do not want to update the database with all the rows in the Data Set. The GetChanges method copies only those Data Rows that have been changed. This method can receive an argument limiting the operation only to added rows, only to deleted rows, only to modified rows, or only to unchanged rows. The new Data Set is then updated into the database with the Update method of the Data Adapter. It is permissible to Fill one Data Set with the Data Adapter and then to Update the database with another. The code is as follows:

```
Try
    Dim myNewDataset As DataSet
    'Only pass the changed rows to the data adapter
        myNewDataset = myDataset.GetChanges()
        If Not myNewDataset.HasErrors Then
            myDataAdapter.Update(myNewDataset, "Titles")
        End If
    End If
Catch e1 As Exception
    MessageBox.Show(e1.Message)
End Try
```

12.5   ANOTHER ACCESS DATABASE, FRIENDS

This section replicates the previous one, but with the Friends database that is supplied with the CD. The overall functionality is the same. Here, we demonstrate the application as it is run. The application assumes that Friends is on drive D and that the drive allows updates.

Part 1: Build the Form

In this section, we will build the complete form, accessing the Friends database. We will create a new Form and name it frmFriends. In addition to the controls shown in Figure 12.10, we add an OleDbConnection control, name it OleDbFriends, and, through the wizard that will open when you choose <New Connection ...> in its ConnectionString property, tie that control to the Friends database. In the Data Link Properties window that will open, you should choose Jet 4 in the first tab as the Provider, because this is an Access 2002 database.

Part 2: Adding the Declarations Section Objects

In this section, we will add the objects that will be referenced in all the classes:

```
' Objects used throughout the form
Dim myConnection As New OleDb.OleDbConnection()
Dim myDataAdapter As OleDb.OleDbDataAdapter
Dim myDataset As DataSet
Dim myDataTable As New Data.DataTable()
Dim intPosition As Integer
Dim myBackup As DataTable
```

Part 3: The Populate Dataset Button

In this section, we will write the complete code as it was developed in the preceding sections. Among the minor changes we shall make for this application, we will read

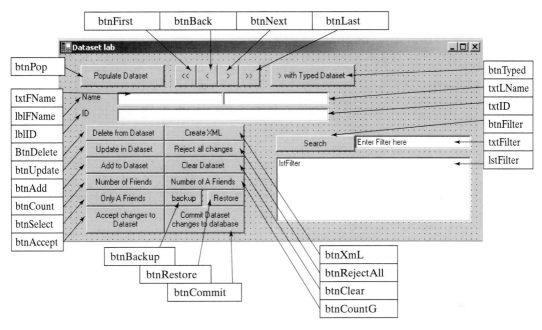

FIGURE 12.10
Demonstrating the Dataset and its related class through the Access Friends database.

three columns from the database, rather than two. The SQL statements and the parameters have been changed accordingly. Here is the code:

```
Private Sub btnPop_Click(ByVal sender As System.Object, _
        ByVal e As System.EventArgs) Handles btnPop.Click

Try
   ' Save on long typing and just copy the connection
   ' string from the control
   ' And, open the connection
   Try
        myConnection.Close() ' in case it is being reopened
   Catch
   End Try
   myConnection.ConnectionString = OleDbFriends.ConnectionString
   myConnection.Open()

   ' Build the SQL statements
   ' Add semicolon at the end of each statement
   Dim strSelect As String = _
        "Select ID, FirstName, LastName from Friends;"
   Dim strUpdate As String = _
        "Update Friends set FirstName= @FName, " &_
        " LastName = @LName  Where ID = @ID;"
```

```vb
Dim strDelete As String = _
    "Delete from Friends Where ID = @ID;"
Dim strInsert As String = _
    "Insert into Friends values (@ID, @FName, @LName , " &_
    "Null, 70000, Null, Null, Null, Null, Null, Null, Null);"

' Define the Command objects
Dim sqlUpdate, sqlDelete, sqlInsert, sqlSelect As _
        OleDb.OleDbCommand

' Instantiate the SQL statements to the Data Adapter
sqlUpdate = New OleDb.OleDbCommand(strUpdate, myConnection)
sqlDelete = New OleDb.OleDbCommand(strDelete, myConnection)
sqlInsert = New OleDb.OleDbCommand(strInsert, myConnection)
sqlSelect = New OleDb.OleDbCommand(strSelect, myConnection)
 myDataAdapter = New OleDb.OleDbDataAdapter()

' Tie the SQL commands to the Data Adapter
myDataAdapter.SelectCommand = sqlSelect
myDataAdapter.UpdateCommand = sqlUpdate
myDataAdapter.DeleteCommand = sqlDelete
myDataAdapter.InsertCommand = sqlInsert

 ' MUST add parameters in the same order as they appear
 'in the SQL statement
sqlUpdate.Parameters.Add( _
        "@FName", Data.OleDb.OleDbType.Char, 20, "FirstName")
sqlUpdate.Parameters.Add( _
        "@LName", Data.OleDb.OleDbType.Char, 20, "LastName")
sqlUpdate.Parameters.Add( _
        "@ID", Data.OleDb.OleDbType.Integer, 4, "ID")

sqlInsert.Parameters.Add( _
        "@ID", Data.OleDb.OleDbType.Integer, 4, "ID")
sqlInsert.Parameters.Add( _
        "@LName", Data.OleDb.OleDbType.Char, 20, "LastName")
sqlInsert.Parameters.Add( _
        "@FName", Data.OleDb.OleDbType.Char, 20, "FirstName")

sqlDelete.Parameters.Add( _
        "@ID", Data.OleDb.OleDbType.Integer, 4, "ID")

' Working with an untyped dataset and a single table
Dim intSize As Integer
myDataset = New DataSet()

' In this case because there is only one table in the
' dataset we can read directly into the DataTable
intSize = myDataAdapter.Fill(myDataset, "Friends")

' With the Dataset filled, we can look at its
' first table by assigning it to a DataTable object.
myDataTable = myDataset.Tables(0)
Dim myTable As DataTable
```

```
    For Each myTable In myDataset.Tables
        txtID.Text = myTable.Rows(0).Item(0).ToString
        txtFName.Text = myTable.Rows(0).Item(1).ToString
        txtLName.Text = myTable.Rows(0).Item(2).ToString
    Next

    ' Make the navigation buttons enabled, now that
    ' navigation makes sense.
    btnFirst.Enabled = True
    btnLast.Enabled = True
    btnNext.Enabled = True
    btnBack.Enabled = True

  Catch e1 As Exception
    MessageBox.Show(e1.Message)
  End Try
End Sub
```

Part 4: The Navigation Buttons

The navigation buttons are much as they were in the previous application, except that they handle three columns:

```
Private Sub btnNext_Click(ByVal sender As System.Object, _
    ByVal e As System.EventArgs) Handles btnNext.Click

' Navigate to next row
  Try
    If intPosition < myDataset.Tables(0).Rows.Count - 1 Then
        intPosition += 1
        txtID.Text = _
            myDataset.Tables(0).Rows(intPosition).Item(0).ToString
        txtFName.Text = _
            myDataset.Tables(0).Rows(intPosition).Item(1).ToString
        txtLName.Text = _
            myDataset.Tables(0).Rows(intPosition).Item(2).ToString
    End If
  Catch ' when reading rows that were deleted
    txtFName.Text = ""
    txtLName.Text = ""
    txtID.Text = ""
  End Try
End Sub

Private Sub btnBack_Click(ByVal sender As System.Object, _
        ByVal e As System.EventArgs) Handles btnBack.Click
' Navigate to previous row
  Try
    If intPosition > 0 Then
        intPosition -= 1
        txtID.Text = _
```

```
                          myDataset.Tables(0).Rows(intPosition).Item(0).ToString
              txtFName.Text = _
                          myDataset.Tables(0).Rows(intPosition).Item(1).ToString
              txtLName.Text = _
                          myDataset.Tables(0).Rows(intPosition).Item(2).ToString
        End If
     Catch ' when reading back to first rows that were deleted
        txtFName.Text = ""
        txtLName.Text = ""
        txtID.Text = ""
     End Try
  End Sub

  Private Sub btnLast_Click(ByVal sender As System.Object, _
          ByVal e As System.EventArgs) Handles btnLast.Click
  ' Navigate to last row
     Try
        intPosition = myDataset.Tables(0).Rows.Count - 1
        txtID.Text = _
                  myDataset.Tables(0).Rows(intPosition).Item(0).ToString
        txtFName.Text = _
                  myDataset.Tables(0).Rows(intPosition).Item(1).ToString
        txtLName.Text = _
                  myDataset.Tables(0).Rows(intPosition).Item(2).ToString
     Catch ' when reading rows that were deleted
        txtFName.Text = ""
        txtLName.Text = ""
        txtID.Text = ""
     End Try
  End Sub

  Private Sub btnFirst_Click(ByVal sender As System.Object, _
        ByVal e As System.EventArgs) Handles btnFirst.Click
     Try
        ' Navigate to first row
        intPosition = 0
        txtID.Text = _
                  myDataset.Tables(0).Rows(intPosition).Item(0).ToString
        txtFName.Text = _
                  myDataset.Tables(0).Rows(intPosition).Item(1).ToString
        txtLName.Text = _
                  myDataset.Tables(0).Rows(intPosition).Item(2).ToString
     Catch
        txtFName.Text = ""
        txtLName.Text = ""
        txtID.Text = ""
     End Try
  End Sub

  Private Sub btnTyped_Click(ByVal sender As System.Object, _
      ByVal e As System.EventArgs) Handles btnTyped.Click
```

```
' Navigate to next row
   If intPosition <myDataset.Tables("Friends").Rows.Count - 1 Then
        intPosition += 1
     Do While _
           myDataset.Tables("Friends").Rows(intPosition).RowState = _
           DataRowState.Deleted And _
           (intPosition < myDataset.Tables("Friends").Rows.Count - 1)
          intPosition += 1
     Loop

     txtID.Text = _
     myDataset.Tables("Friends").Rows(intPosition).Item("ID").ToString
     txtFName.Text = _
     myDataset.Tables("Friends").Rows(intPosition).Item("FirstName")
     txtLName.Text = _
     myDataset.Tables("Friends").Rows(intPosition).Item("LastName")
   End If
End Sub
```

Part 5: Try It Out

Run the application and click on Populate Dataset. Figure 12.11 shows what happens.
Navigating to next with the > arrow will bring the next friend. See Figure 12.12.
The other navigation buttons will move to the next, previous, last, and first records in
the table.

Part 6: Updating the Dataset

After the dataset has been populated, the current record can be deleted from it with
the Delete button, or it can be updated with the Update button. Adding a New row is
done with the Add to Dataset button:

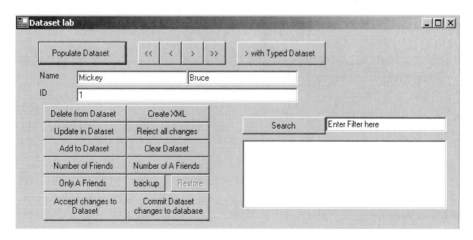

FIGURE 12.11
Demonstrating the Dataset and its related class with Access. Populating the Dataset.

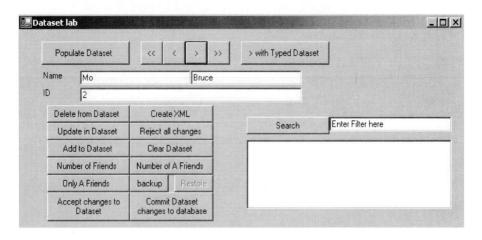

FIGURE 12.12
Demonstrating the Dataset and its related class with Access. Navigating to next record.

```vb
Private Sub btnDelete_Click(ByVal sender As System.Object, _
    ByVal e As System.EventArgs) Handles btnDelete.Click

  ' Delete current row, as identified with intPosition, with
  ' the Delete method of the Rows collection.
  myDataset.Tables(0).Rows(intPosition).Delete()
  Try
    ' Then navigate forward one row.
    If intPosition < myDataset.Tables(0).Rows.Count - 1 Then
        intPosition += 1
    Else
        intPosition = myDataset.Tables(0).Rows.Count - 1
    End If
    txtID.Text = _
            myDataset.Tables(0).Rows(intPosition).Item(0).ToString
    txtFName.Text = _
            myDataset.Tables(0).Rows(intPosition).Item(1).ToString
    txtLName.Text = _
            myDataset.Tables(0).Rows(intPosition).Item(2).ToString
  Catch
    txtFName.Text = ""
    txtLName.Text = ""
    txtID.Text = ""
  End Try
End Sub

Private Sub btnUpdate_Click(ByVal sender As System.Object, _
            ByVal e As System.EventArgs) Handles btnUpdate.Click

  ' Update current row, as identified with intPosition, by
```

```
           ' setting its values to those in the textboxes
           myDataset.Tables(0).Rows(intPosition).Item(0) = txtID.Text
           myDataset.Tables(0).Rows(intPosition).Item(1) = txtFName.Text
           myDataset.Tables(0).Rows(intPosition).Item(2) = txtLName.Text
       End Sub

       Private Sub btnAdd_Click(ByVal sender As System.Object, _
                   ByVal e As System.EventArgs) Handles btnAdd.Click
           Dim myRow As DataRow

           ' Insert is done by defining a Row in the structure of the rows in
           ' the Rows collection
           myRow = myDataset.Tables(0).NewRow

           ' setting its values
           myRow.Item(0) = txtID.Text
           myRow.Item(1) = txtFName.Text
           myRow.Item(2) = txtLName.Text

           ' and adding it to the Rows collection.
           myDataset.Tables(0).Rows.Add(myRow)
       End Sub
```

Let us try the application out. After populating the dataset, navigate to the 10th record and delete it. See Figure 12.13. Record 11 will be displayed automatically. We will update this record, then navigate back one record and insert a new record.

If we scroll through the dataset, we will see the modified values. To copy them to the database, we will click on the Commit Dataset button. The database will show the changed values. (See Figure 12.14.)

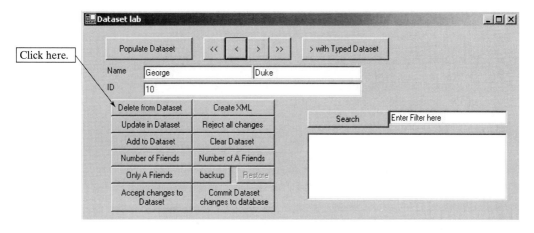

FIGURE 12.13
Demonstrating the Dataset and its related class with Access. Deleting current record.

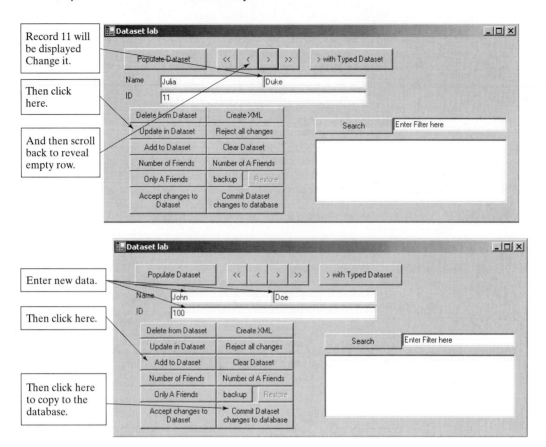

FIGURE 12.13
(*Continued*)

Part 7: Count and Select

Clicking the Number of Friends Button will activate the `Compute` method that we will apply to compute the number of friends. The display should show 23. The code is

```
Private Sub btnCount_Click(ByVal sender As System.Object, _
        ByVal e As System.EventArgs) Handles btnCount.Click
    txtFName.Text = "There are " & _
        CStr(myDataset.Tables(0).Compute( _
        "Count(ID)", "ID is not Null")) & _
        " Friends"
    txtID.Text = ""
End Sub
```

The equivalent of a Select SQL command can be run directly on the dataset. This will happen when the Only A Friends button is clicked. This button will select only

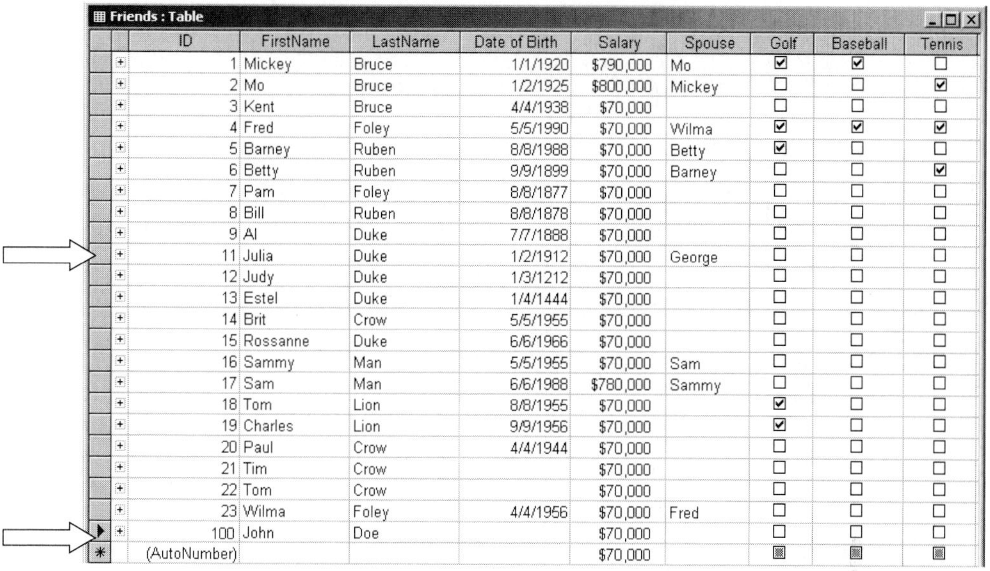

Friends : Table

ID	FirstName	LastName	Date of Birth	Salary	Spouse	Golf	Baseball	Tennis
1	Mickey	Bruce	1/1/1920	$790,000	Mo	☑	☑	☐
2	Mo	Bruce	1/2/1925	$800,000	Mickey	☐	☐	☑
3	Kent	Bruce	4/4/1938	$70,000		☐	☐	☐
4	Fred	Foley	5/5/1990	$70,000	Wilma	☑	☑	☑
5	Barney	Ruben	8/8/1988	$70,000	Betty	☑	☐	☐
6	Betty	Ruben	9/9/1899	$70,000	Barney	☐	☐	☑
7	Pam	Foley	8/8/1877	$70,000		☐	☐	☐
8	Bill	Ruben	8/8/1878	$70,000		☐	☐	☐
9	Al	Duke	7/7/1888	$70,000		☐	☐	☐
11	Julia	Duke	1/2/1912	$70,000	George	☐	☐	☐
12	Judy	Duke	1/3/1212	$70,000		☐	☐	☐
13	Estel	Duke	1/4/1444	$70,000		☐	☐	☐
14	Brit	Crow	5/5/1955	$70,000		☐	☐	☐
15	Rossanne	Duke	6/6/1966	$70,000		☐	☐	☐
16	Sammy	Man	5/5/1955	$70,000	Sam	☐	☐	☐
17	Sam	Man	6/6/1988	$780,000	Sammy	☐	☐	☐
18	Tom	Lion	8/8/1955	$70,000		☑	☐	☐
19	Charles	Lion	9/9/1956	$70,000		☑	☐	☐
20	Paul	Crow	4/4/1944	$70,000		☐	☐	☐
21	Tim	Crow		$70,000		☐	☐	☐
22	Tom	Crow		$70,000		☐	☐	☐
23	Wilma	Foley	4/4/1956	$70,000	Fred	☐	☐	☐
100	John	Doe		$70,000		☐	☐	☐
(AutoNumber)				$70,000		■	■	■

FIGURE 12.14
Result of deleting the current record shown in Access.

friends with the letter *A* in their first name and retain just these names in the dataset. Subsequent navigation will show only these friends. The code is as follows:

```
Private Sub btnSelect_Click(ByVal sender As System.Object, _
        ByVal e As System.EventArgs) Handles btnSelect.Click

  Dim myNewDataRows() As Data.DataRow
  Dim mySingleRow As Data.DataRow
  Dim myColumn As Data.DataColumn
  Dim myTable As DataTable

  myTable = myDataset.Tables(0).Copy
  myDataset.Tables(0).Clear()

  ' By doing this the rows in the array will belong to Friends
  myNewDataRows = myTable.Select("FirstName like '*A*'", "ID DESC")
  Console.WriteLine(" We have " & myNewDataRows.Length & " rows")

  '        myDataset.Tables(0).Rows.Clear()
  For Each mySingleRow In myNewDataRows
      ' must do this
      mySingleRow.EndEdit()

      ' We must import the row because it belongs to another table
      ' only rows that do not belong to another table can be added
      myDataset.Tables(0).ImportRow(mySingleRow)
  Next
  myDataset.Tables(0).AcceptChanges()
End Sub
```

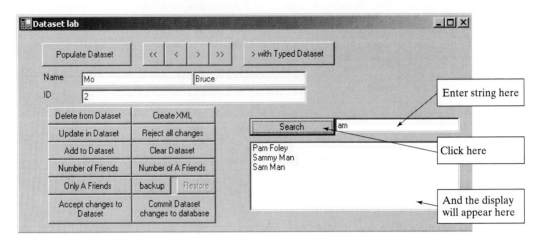

FIGURE 12.15
Demonstrating the Dataset and its related class with Access. The Search option.

Part 8: Filters

The Search button also analyzes the dataset, but this time with a filter. The filter creates a `DefaultView` into which it places the results of the equivalent of a `Where` clause of an SQL statement. In this case, the SQL statement is looking for all the friends that contain the string in the textbox near this button in their first name. The syntax of the `Like` clause in SQL is explained in the appendix. The names are placed in the list box. See Figure 12.15. Here is the code:

```
Private Sub btnFilter_Click(ByVal sender As System.Object, _
        ByVal e As System.EventArgs) Handles btnFilter.Click
    lstFilter.Items.Clear()
    myDataTable.DefaultView.RowFilter = _
        "FirstName Like '%" & txtFilter.Text & "%'"
    Dim I As Integer
    For I = 0 To myDataTable.DefaultView.Count - 1
        lstFilter.Items.Add( _
            myDataTable.DefaultView(I).Item(1).ToString & " " &_
            myDataTable.DefaultView(I).Item(2).ToString)
    Next
End Sub
```

12.6 ADDITIONAL DATA SET METHODS AND PROPERTIES

The preceding code applied several Data Set properties and methods. Here is a listing, in alphabetical order, of additional useful properties and methods:[26]

---

[26]Some methods, such as `BeginInit` and `EndInit`, are intended for the .NET Framework infrastructure only. They should not be used directly in application code and, as such, are not discussed here.

12.6.1 Additional Properties

- The `CaseSensitive` property specifies whether string comparisons will be case sensitive or not. By default, this property is set to `False`, meaning, for example, that the string "a" is counted the same as the string "A".
- The `DataSetName` property is the name of the Data Set.
- The `EnforceConstraints` property determines whether the constraints in the `Constraints` collection will be enforced. By default, this property is set to `True`. In loading a Data Set from a database, it is advisable to set it off and so improve performance. It can be assumed that the constraints were managed correctly in the database. Rechecking each one is a waste. The Data Form wizard also sets this property to `False` before it loads the Data Set.
- The `HasErrors` property returns a `True` value if there are errors in the Data Set or a `False` value otherwise. This property should be checked before the `Update` method of a Data Adapter is activated.
- The `Relations` property contains the `Relations` collection.
- The `Tables` property contains the `Tables` collection.

12.6.2 Additional Methods

- The `Clear` method deletes all the data from the Data Set, but leaves the schema intact. In other words, all the Data Rows are deleted, but the Data Tables, Data Columns, Constraints, and Data Relations remain. The code is

```
myDataset.clear()
```

- The `Clone` method makes a copy of the Data Set schema. It copies the Data Tables, Data Columns, Constraints, and Data Relations, but does not copy the Data Rows. The code is

```
myNewDataSet = myDataset.clone()
```

- The `Copy` method makes a copy of the Data Set schema and its data. The following code copies the Data Tables, Data Columns, Constraints, Data Relations, and the Data Rows:

```
myNewDataSet = myDataset.copy()
```

- The `Merge` method combines two Data Sets into one. It merges the Data Set in the argument into the first Data Set. If the second argument is set to `True`, then changes made to the data in the first Data Set will be retained. If the schema of the two Data Sets are not identical, a third argument can be specified to dictate what action should be taken. The missing schema in the receiving Data Set can be added with the following code, or it can be ignored:

```
myDataset.Merge(myNewDataset)
'Retain original data
myDataset.Merge(myNewDataset, True)
```

```
'Retain original data and adjust schema
myDataset.Merge _
        (myNewDataset, True, MissingSchemaAction.Add)
```

- The Reset method resets the Data Set to its original data:

```
myDataset.Reset()
```

12.7 ADDITIONAL DATA TABLE METHODS AND PROPERTIES

Many of the Data Set properties and methods apply also to the Data Table class. Here is a listing, in alphabetical order, of additional useful Data Table properties and methods:

12.7.1 Additional Properties

- The CaseSensitive property, as in the Data Set class, specifies whether string comparisons will be case sensitive or not. By default, this property is set to False.
- The ChildRelations property contains a read-only collection of the child relations part of the Data Relations of the Data Set that apply to this Data Table.
- The Columns property contains the collection of Data Columns in the Data Table.
- The Constraints property contains a read-only collection of Constraints that apply to this Data Table.
- The DataSet property contains the read-only name of the Data Set that owns this Data Table.
- The HasErrors property, as in the Data Set class, specifies whether any row in the Data Table has an error.
- The MinimumCapacity property specifies the default number of rows that will be allocated to a new empty table. By default, its value will be 25. Setting the minimum capacity to a larger number will improve performance, because allocating memory before a table is being filled is faster than allocating memory while it is being filled:

```
mytable.MinimumCapacity = 200
```

- The ParentRelations property contains a read-only collection of the parent relations part of the Data Relations of the Data Set that apply to this Data Table.
- The Rows property contains the collection of Data Rows belonging to this Data Table.
- The TableName property contains the name of the table.

12.7.2 Additional Methods

- The AcceptChanges, RejectChanges, Clear, Clone, Copy, GetChanges, and RejectChanges perform the same operation on a Data Table as they do on a Data Set:

```
myDataset.Tables(0).Clear()
```

- The Compute method is where the equivalents of aggregate functions (Count, Sum, etc.) of an SQL Select statement are executed on the rows of a Data Table. This method has two arguments. The first is the aggregate function, such as "Count (ISBN)". The second argument is the limiting condition, such as "ISBN is not Null". The code is

```
txtTitle.Text = "There are " & _
                CStr(myDataset.Tables(0).Compute _
                ("Count(ISBN)", "ISBN is not Null")) & _
                " Titles"
```

The preceding statement is equivalent to an SQL statement, except that it is run on the Data Table, rather than on the database. The SQL statement is

```
Select "Count(ISBN)"
   From Titles
   Where ISBN is not Null
```

- The GetErrors method returns an array of that contains the Data Rows in the Data Table with errors.
- The ImportRow method allows adding a row from another table as a row in this table. Rows in other tables cannot be added to a table with the Add method, because a Data Row can belong to only one Data Table.
- The Select method returns an array of Data Rows that satisfy a given condition. This method is conceptually equivalent to the Where clause of an SQL statement. Its syntax is also equivalent to the Where clause of an SQL statement. *When the method is performed on a Data Set that was filled from a database, it is imperative to add the EndEdit method as shown in the following code*:

```
Dim myNewDataRows() As Data.DataRow
Dim mySingleRow As Data.DataRow

myNewDataRows = myDataset.Tables(0).Select _
        ("Title like '*Access*'", "ISBN DESC")
For Each mySingleRow In myNewDataRows

    ' MUST DO THIS
    mySingleRow.EndEdit()

    Console.WriteLine(mySingleRow.Item(0).ToString)
Next
```

LAB 12.1: THE DATASET

Lab Objectives:
Exercise working with a single-table database-related Data Set:

- Populating
- Navigating
- Manipulating data
- Filtering

- Selecting
- Committing changes back to the database

Application Overview

This lab contains a form that reads the data in the SQL Server Friends and Pets database that we built in Chapter 9. The data in the Friends table are read into a Data Set when the Populate Button is clicked. The Navigation Buttons to the right of the Populate Button navigate through the Data Set. The data are shown in two textboxes that are placed just under these Buttons. Operations on the Data Set are performed by methods that are activated through Buttons that appear beneath the textboxes. The Buttons deal with updating, deleting, and adding rows to the Data Set, creating an XML, clearing the Data Set, and accepting and rejecting all changes made to it, demonstrating the Compute method by counting the number of friends, demonstrating the Select method to identify only friends with "G" in their name, and committing the changes back to the database. On the right-hand side of the form is a List Box that shows filtered values in the Data Set based on values entered to the textbox just above it. The filtered values are extracted with a view.

The accompanying CD has this lab in both Access and SQL Server. The Access version works with the Biblio database. When running the lab with Access, the Biblio database must be changed from an Access 97 database to an Access 2002 database. This is done by opening the Biblio database in Access 2002 and okaying its change to an Access 2002 database. The Access version also deals with the Friends database as built in the preceding sections.

Part 1: Build the Form

Add a new project and solution, and name the project **prjChapter12**, making the project handle a Windows Form. Name the form **frmDataset**. Add the Buttons, List Box, labels, and textboxes as shown in Figure 12.16. Objects starting with "btn" are Buttons, those starting with "txt" are textboxes, those starting with "lbl" are labels, and the one starting with "lst" is a List Box.

Now add an SQL Connection control to the form and set its ConnectionString property to the Friends and Pets database. Leave its name SqlConnection1.

Part 2: Adding the Code for Populating and Navigating the Data Set

In the Declarations section of code, where code that is common to all the methods is written, beneath the Inherits statement, add these lines (The Public Class and the Inherits statements will already appear in the code):

```
Public Class frmDataSet
    Inherits System.Windows.Forms.Form

    ' Add these lines here
    Dim myConnection As New SqlClient.SqlConnection()
    Dim myDataAdapter As SqlClient.SqlDataAdapter
    Dim myDataset As DataSet
    Dim myDataTable As New Data.DataTable()
    Dim intPosition As Integer
    Dim myBackup As DataTable
```

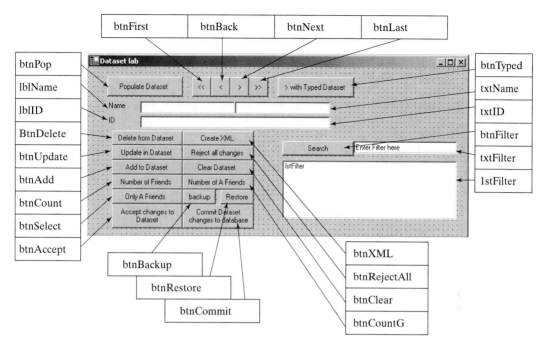

FIGURE 12.16
Lab 12.1.

Click each of the command Buttons in turn, and add the following code to each (this is the same code as we added in the chapter):

```
Private Sub btnPop_Click(ByVal sender As System.Object, _
        ByVal e As System.EventArgs) Handles btnPop.Click

    Try
        ' Save on long typing and just copy the connection
        ' string from the control
        ' And, open the connection
        Try
            myConnection.Close() ' in case it is being reopened
        Catch
        End Try
        myConnection.ConnectionString =
            SqlConnection1.ConnectionString
        myConnection.Open()

        ' Build the SQL statement
        ' and place it in the Data Adapter
        ' The Data Adapter has two parameters:
        ' the SQL statement and the connection object

        ' The other SQL commands
        Dim strSelect As String = _
            "Select [First Name], [Friend ID] from Friends"
```

```vbnet
        Dim strUpdate As String = _
          "Update Friends set [First Name] = @FN Where
                             [Friend ID] = @ID"
        Dim strDelete As String = _
          "Delete from Friends Where [Friend ID] = @ID"
        Dim strInsert As String = _
          "Insert into Friends ([First Name]) values (@FN)"
        Dim sqlUpdate, sqlDelete, sqlInsert, sqlSelect As _
              SqlClient.SqlCommand

        sqlUpdate = New SqlClient.SqlCommand(strUpdate, myConnection)
        sqlDelete = New SqlClient.SqlCommand(strDelete, myConnection)
        sqlInsert = New SqlClient.SqlCommand(strInsert, myConnection)
        sqlSelect = New SqlClient.SqlCommand(strSelect, myConnection)

        myDataAdapter = New SqlClient.SqlDataAdapter()
        myDataAdapter.SelectCommand = sqlSelect
        myDataAdapter.UpdateCommand = sqlUpdate
        myDataAdapter.DeleteCommand = sqlDelete
        myDataAdapter.InsertCommand = sqlInsert

        sqlUpdate.Parameters.Add _
              ("@FN", Data.SqlDbType.Char, 10, "First Name")
        sqlUpdate.Parameters.Add _
              ("@ID", Data.SqlDbType.Int, 4, "Friend ID")
        sqlDelete.Parameters.Add _
              ("@ID", Data.SqlDbType.Int, 4, "Friend ID")
        sqlInsert.Parameters.Add _
              ("@FN", Data.SqlDbType.Char, 10, "First Name")

        Dim intSize As Integer
        myDataset = New DataSet()

        intSize = myDataAdapter.Fill(myDataset, "Friends")

        ' With the Dataset filled, we can look at its
        ' first table by assigning it to a DataTable
        ' object.
        myDataTable = myDataset.Tables(0)

        ' Working with an untyped dataset and a single table
        txtName.Text = myDataTable.Rows(0).Item(0).ToString
        txtID.Text = myDataTable.Rows(0).Item(1).ToString

        ' Make the navigation Buttons enabled, now that
        ' navigation makes sense.
        btnFirst.Enabled = True
        btnLast.Enabled = True
        btnNext.Enabled = True
        btnBack.Enabled = True
        btnTyped.Enabled = True

    Catch e1 As Exception
        MessageBox.Show(e1.Message)
    End Try
End Sub
```

```
Private Sub btnNext_Click(ByVal sender As System.Object, _
        ByVal e As System.EventArgs) Handles btnNext.Click
    ' Navigate to next row
    Try
        If intPosition < myDataset.Tables(0).Rows.Count - 1 Then
            intPosition += 1
            txtName.Text = _
                myDataset.Tables(0).Rows(intPosition).Item(0).ToString
            txtID.Text = _
                myDataset.Tables(0).Rows(intPosition).Item(1).ToString
        End If
    Catch ' when reading rows that were deleted
        txtName.Text = ""
        txtID.Text = ""
    End Try
End Sub

Private Sub btnBack_Click(ByVal sender As System.Object, _
        ByVal e As System.EventArgs) Handles btnBack.Click
    ' Navigate to previous row
    Try
        If intPosition > 0 Then
            intPosition -= 1
            txtName.Text = _
                myDataset.Tables(0).Rows(intPosition).Item(0).ToString
            txtID.Text = _
                myDataset.Tables(0).Rows(intPosition).Item(1).ToString
        End If
    Catch ' when reading back to first rows that were deleted
        txtName.Text = ""
        txtID.Text = ""
    End Try
End Sub

Private Sub btnLast_Click(ByVal sender As System.Object, _
        ByVal e As System.EventArgs) Handles btnLast.Click
    ' Navigate to last row
    Try
        intPosition = myDataset.Tables(0).Rows.Count - 1
        txtName.Text = _
            myDataset.Tables(0).Rows(intPosition).Item(0).ToString
        txtID.Text = _
            myDataset.Tables(0).Rows(intPosition).Item(1).ToString
    Catch ' when reading rows that were deleted
        txtName.Text = ""
        txtID.Text = ""
    End Try
End Sub

Private Sub btnFirst_Click(ByVal sender As System.Object, _
        ByVal e As System.EventArgs) Handles btnFirst.Click
```

```
        Try
            ' Navigate to first row
            intPosition = 0
            txtName.Text = _
              myDataset.Tables(0).Rows(intPosition).Item(0).ToString
            txtID.Text = _
              myDataset.Tables(0).Rows(intPosition).Item(1).ToString
        Catch
            txtName.Text = ""
            txtID.Text = ""
        End Try
    End Sub


    Private Sub btnTyped_Click(ByVal sender As System.Object, _
            ByVal e As System.EventArgs) Handles btnTyped.Click
        ' Navigate to next row
        If intPosition < myDataset.Tables("Friends").Rows.Count - 1 Then
            intPosition += 1

            txtName.Text = _
myDataset.Tables("Friends").Rows(intPosition).Item("First Name").ToString

            txtID.Text = _
myDataset.Tables("Friends").Rows(intPosition).Item("Friend ID").ToString

        End If
    End Sub
```

Part 3: Adding the Code for Manipulating the Data Set

The code for manipulating the data set is as follows:

```
    Private Sub btnDelete_Click(ByVal sender As System.Object, _
            ByVal e As System.EventArgs) Handles btnDelete.Click
        myDataset.Tables(0).Rows(intPosition).Delete()
        Try
            If intPosition < myDataset.Tables(0).Rows.Count - 1 Then
                intPosition += 1
            Else
                intPosition = myDataset.Tables(0).Rows.Count - 1
            End If
            txtName.Text = _
                myDataset.Tables(0).Rows(intPosition).Item(0).ToString
            txtID.Text = _
                myDataset.Tables(0).Rows(intPosition).Item(1).ToString
        Catch
            txtName.Text = ""
            txtID.Text = ""
        End Try
    End Sub
```

```vb
Private Sub btnUpdate_Click(ByVal sender As System.Object, _
        ByVal e As System.EventArgs) Handles btnUpdate.Click

    If txtName.Text.Length > 10 Then
        MessageBox.Show("name is more than 10 characters long")
    Else
        myDataset.Tables(0).Rows(intPosition).Item(0) = txtName.Text
    End If
End Sub

Private Sub btnAdd_Click(ByVal sender As System.Object, _
        ByVal e As System.EventArgs) Handles btnAdd.Click
    Dim myRow As DataRow

    myRow = myDataset.Tables(0).NewRow
    myRow.Item(0) = txtName.Text
    myRow.Item(1) = txtID.Text
    myDataset.Tables(0).Rows.Add(myRow)
End Sub
```

Part 4: Other Operations on the Data Set

Most of the other operations on the data set are one line long. Here are all of them:

```vb
Private Sub btnRejectAll_Click(ByVal sender As System.Object, _
        ByVal e As System.EventArgs) Handles btnRejectAll.Click
    myDataset.Tables(0).RejectChanges()
End Sub

Private Sub btnClear_Click(ByVal sender As System.Object, _
        ByVal e As System.EventArgs) Handles btnClear.Click
    myDataset.Clear()
End Sub

Private Sub btnAccept_Click(ByVal sender As System.Object, _
        ByVal e As System.EventArgs) Handles Button1.Click
    myDataset.Tables(0).AcceptChanges()
End Sub

Private Sub btnCommit_Click(ByVal sender As System.Object, _
        ByVal e As System.EventArgs) Handles btnCommit.Click
    Try
        ' Be careful AcceptChanges will turn HasChanges off
        If myDataset.HasChanges() Then

            Dim myNewDataset As DataSet
            'only pass the changed rows to the data adapter
            ' can limit here to only added deleted modified or
            ' unchanged
            myNewDataset = myDataset.GetChanges()

            If Not myNewDataset.HasErrors Then
                myDataAdapter.Update(myNewDataset, "Friends")
            End If
        End If
```

```vbnet
        Catch e1 As Exception
            MessageBox.Show(e1.Message)
        End Try
    End Sub

    Private Sub btnXML_Click(ByVal sender As System.Object, _
            ByVal e As System.EventArgs) Handles btnXML.Click
        myDataset.WriteXmlSchema("C:\a.txt")
    End Sub

    Private Sub btnCount_Click(ByVal sender As System.Object, _
            ByVal e As System.EventArgs) Handles btnCount.Click

        txtName.Text = "There are " &_
            CStr(myDataset.Tables(0).Compute _
                ("Count([Friend ID])", "[Friend ID] is not Null")) &_
                " Friends"
        txtID.Text = ""
    End Sub

    Private Sub btnCountVB_Click(ByVal sender As System.Object, _
            ByVal e As System.EventArgs) Handles btnCountVB.Click

        txtName.Text = "There are " &_
                CStr(myDataset.Tables(0).Compute _
                    ("Count([Friend ID])", "[First Name]
                        like '*G*'") &_
                    " First names with G")
        txtID.Text = ""
    End Sub

    Private Sub btnSelect_Click(ByVal sender As System.Object, _
            ByVal e As System.EventArgs) Handles btnSelect.Click

        Dim myNewDataRows() As Data.DataRow
        Dim mySingleRow As Data.DataRow
        Dim myColumn As Data.DataColumn
        Dim myTable As DataTable

        myTable = myDataset.Tables(0).Copy
        myDataset.Tables(0).Clear()

        ' by doing this the rows in the array will belong to Titles
        myNewDataRows = myTable.Select _
            ("[First Name] like '*G*'", "[Friend ID] DESC")
        For Each mySingleRow In myNewDataRows
            ' must do this
            mySingleRow.EndEdit()
            Console.WriteLine(mySingleRow.Item(0).ToString)

            ' we must import the row because it belongs to another table
            ' only rows that do not belong to another table can be added
            myDataset.Tables(0).ImportRow(mySingleRow)
        Next
        myDataset.Tables(0).AcceptChanges()
    End Sub
```

Part 5: Adding the Filter

The results of the filter are read through the Default View:

```
Private Sub btnFilter_Click(ByVal sender As System.Object, _
        ByVal e As System.EventArgs) Handles btnFilter.Click

    lstFilter.Items.Clear()
    myDataTable.DefaultView.RowFilter = _
        "[First Name] Like '%" & txtFilter.Text &"%'"
    Dim I As Integer
    For I = 0 To myDataTable.DefaultView.Count - 1
        lstFilter.Items.Add(myDataTable.DefaultView(I).Item(0).ToString)
        Console.WriteLine(myDataTable.DefaultView(I).Item(0))
    Next
End Sub
```

Part 6: Adding the Filter

Add a backup option with the following code:

```
Private Sub btnBackup_Click(ByVal sender As System.Object, _
        ByVal e As System.EventArgs) Handles btnBackup.Click
    myBackup = myDataset.Tables(0).Copy
    myBackup.AcceptChanges()
    btnRestore.Enabled = True
End Sub

Private Sub btnRestore_Click(ByVal sender As System.Object, _
        ByVal e As System.EventArgs) Handles btnRestore.Click
    ' Being a table from a database, the Copy method will not work
    ' The error message being Property 'Item' is 'ReadOnly'

    myDataset.Tables(0).AcceptChanges()
    Dim myRow As DataRow
    For Each myRow In myBackup.Rows
        myDataset.Tables(0).ImportRow(myRow)
    Next
End Sub

End Class
```

SUGGESTED HOME ASSIGNMENTS

1. Build a new form that will perform the operations shown earlier on the Pets table of the Friends and Pets SQL Server database.
2. Build a new form that will complete the operations shown earlier on the Diary table of the Friends Access database.

TEST YOURSELF

1. Discuss the major differences between the connected layer and the disconnected layers.
2. Explain the logic of how a Data Adapter accesses a database.
3. Discuss the separation of responsibilities between the Data Set class and the Data Table class.
4. Discuss the types of constraints that can be added to a Data Set and when you would apply each.
5. Explain why a Data Adapter cannot change the Data Source schema.
6. Discuss the objective of the `Item` collection.
7. Discuss the collections of `Columns` in .NET and what each is in charge of.
8. Discuss the objective and usage of the `Tables` collection.
9. Discuss the conceptual equivalences of an array and a collection.
10. Discuss when reading a Data Set in untyped manner may be best.
11. Discuss what you can do with the `Count` property of the `Rows` collection.
12. What is `RowState`?
13. What happens when a deleted row is read?
14. Why do you think rows are added to a table through the `Rows` collection, rather than through a Data Table method?
15. Suggest what might have happened if a program accepted changes at a Data Row level only?
16. Discuss what is a filter and why and when you would apply it.
17. How is a `Filter` method different from a `Select` method?
18. Discuss the `Compute` method and when it would be a good idea to apply it.
19. What is `Merge`?
20. What is `MinimumCapacity`?

Multitable Data Sets

OBJECTIVES

After completing this chapter, students should be able to

1. Apply objects

- `DataRelation` objects
- `Constraint` objects

2. Build a Data Set without a Data Source

- Defining the Data Set
- Adding tables, columns, rows, relations, and views to it
- Defining its relations and constraints

13.1 AIMS OF CHAPTER

This chapter continues the review of the disconnected layer of the ADO.NET architecture. The chapter examines multitable Data Sets, how `Constraint` and `DataRelation` objects assist in establishing foreign key relationships, and how `Constraint` objects can handle uniqueness constraints. This is first demonstrated with Data Tables that are copied from a database and later with Data Tables that are built into the application itself together with their related Data Columns—that is, without their schema being filled from a database. The advantages of working with such a disconnected Data Set, serving as a standalone database, are discussed and demonstrated.

The initial set of labs reviews the concepts discussed in the chapter. The last lab in the chapter builds a relatively large application where a standalone library database is built, demonstrating a disconnected multitable Data Set application.

13.2   MULTITABLE DATA SETS

13.2.1   The Objective

The single-table Data Set, introduced in Chapter 12, may be among the most common applications of Data Sets. But inherent in its simplicity is the fact that *a Select SQL command returns at most a single view*, which is presented in ADO.NET as a single multicolumn multirow Data Table.[27] As a result, a Data Set that is connected to a relational database with a single Data Adapter or a single Command object will contain at most a single Data Table. Usually, that is all that is needed, but occasionally there is an advantage to working with a Data Set that handles more than one Data Table at a time. We saw an example of such a case in Chapter 11, where the Data Form wizard presented data from two related tables together, effectively circumventing the one Data Table per Data Set limitation. The Data Form wizard did this by creating a separate Data Table and a separate Data Adapter for each table of interest in the database, by employing a dedicated set of SQL statement for each, and then connecting the two Data Tables with a Data Relation object.

It is, of course, necessary to work with several Data Tables concurrently in other situations. In fact, most transactions do much more than just present the data of one table or query or of two related tables, which is what the Data Form wizard does. Take, for example, an application that handles a transfer of funds from a checking account to a savings account. Such a transaction will probably need to access and update at least four tables in the same transaction. It will need to access the client table to check client details and authorization. It will also need to access the banking account table to check whether funds can be withdrawn and then to actually withdraw these funds from the account. It will need to access the savings table to add a new record. And, it will need to register the transaction in a dedicated transactions table. Working with all these tables concurrently requires a mechanism that will guarantee that all the data integrity constraints, such as foreign key rules, will be enforced correctly and at the appropriate time.

In a pre-.NET configuration, working with several tables concurrently would not have been a concern of the application program. All data integrity constraints, including cascading update and delete, would have been checked and handled by the DBMS whenever an SQL statement changed data. This check would have been totally transparent to the application program and would have occurred at the most appropriate moment through the DBMS. In a .NET configuration, that is not the case. Because the Data Set is disconnected, the constraints on these four tables must be enforced at the Data Set level. The application program cannot rely on the DBMS to handle these functions until the data are updated back into the database through the Data Adapter. Waiting for the DBMS in this manner to check uniqueness and foreign key constraint may result in postponing the checks until it is too late. The DBMS will catch the errors but at the last possible moment, after extensive processing may have already taken place. Moreover, the DBMS will generate only general error messages rather than produce specific error messages tied to specific user input and specific rows in the tables. Working directly with the database, as done in the pre-.NET era, would have guaranteed

---

[27]In database terminology, a View is the result of a Select SQL statement.

that all the constraints on the data were held—and at the most appropriate moment. However, that is not an option with .NET, wherein the data are manipulated in a disconnected Data Set until the last moment.

Because of this, a .NET application needs to handle all the data constraints itself. The Data Form wizard that we saw in Chapter 11 and discussed in Chapter 12 is a good example of handling such constraints. The wizard copied appropriate sections of the database schema and data into Data Tables, Data Columns, and Data Rows *and* also copied the database constraints into Constraint and Data Relation objects. It is through these Constraint and Data Relation objects that the foreign key and uniqueness rules are checked and applied whenever data are changed in the Data Set in the same manner as they would have been handled by the DBMS.

In this chapter, we will discuss how to manage these objects through VB.NET code and how to specify how the Data Tables relate to each other. The chapter also discusses building Data Sets that are not derived from a database.

13.2.2   The Need for Data Sets as Standalone Databases

Why, then, should we want to have a Data Set as a standalone database if, in doing so, we need to add all this DBMS functionality to our code and handle it manually when it could have been handled automatically by the DBMS? The answer to that is twofold. On the one hand, it is necessary because .NET works with databases in a disconnected mode, so the application program has no alternative but to make up for this missing functionality when the processing involves more than accessing one or two tables, as we have done up to now. Had the application program not done so, the cost of having transactions (think of these as grouped-together SQL statements that represent one inseparable unit of work) such as those that handle the Update method of the Data Adapter would have been too high because they might fail more often.

But there is another reason why we should want to have a Data Set as a standalone database. The DBMS does many things in addition to managing the constraints. First and foremost, a DBMS is there to allow many transactions to access the same data concurrently without interfering with each other. This is called *concurrency control*. Concurrency control is a very expensive process to support and requires constant monitoring of all the transactions and all the resources (tables, indexes, rows, etc.) in the database. If we can avoid it, which would be the case with standalone databases that only have one transaction running at a time, so much the better.

Another reason for having a Data Set as a standalone database is that a Data Set is primarily an object. Objects can be made persistent and can enjoy all the benefits of inheritance. As an object, a Data Set can be the base of inheritance of other Data Sets, allowing the creation of many independent instances of the database. This may be very helpful when a work process, such as managing the design of a bridge, requires some basic functionality and basic data structure, but still differs from one bridge to another. In such cases, it would be helpful if a standard basic bridge database could be created as a Data Set and then inherited and modified in inherited instantiated copies of the object for the specific requirements of new bridges. A side benefit of this would also be that, by having the database as an object, it would be possible to manage version control with it. Daily copies can be created and kept, while current changes would be made on another copy. Should there be a need to revert to a previous copy, handling the design as a set of inherited objects would allow it.

13.2.3 Handling Many Tables Copied from a Database by a Single Data Set

In the previous chapters, a Data Set typically had one Data Table. That single Data Table had its schema defined and its data filled through a Data Adapter object. When several Data Tables are filled in this manner, it is sometimes advantageous to include all the Data Tables in one Data Set. Doing so, as previously discussed, allows the inclusion of Data Relation and Constraint objects. We will handle all this in sections. First, two Data Tables from two Data Sets will be merged into one Data Set in the code example. In the code, two new Data Sets are instantiated, and each is filled from a dedicated Data Adapter. The two Data Sets are then merged. The code is as follows:

```
Dim myDataset1, myDataset2 As DataSet
Dim intSize As Integer
Try

    ' Built dataset with both tables
    myDataset1 = New DataSet()
    myDataset2 = New DataSet()
    intSize = SqlDataAdapter1.Fill(myDataset1)
    intSize = SqlDataAdapter2.Fill(myDataset2)
    myDataset1.Merge(myDataset2)
```

We will assume that both Data Adapters are controls and that the form which contains them also has a Data Connection object. The object SqlDataAdapter1 fills the first Data Adapter with the schema and all the rows of the Friends table in the Friends and Pets database, while SqlDataAdapter2 fills the first Data Adapter with the schema and all the rows of the Pets table in the Friends and Pets database. The two Data Sets are then merged into the first Data Set. With that done, the Data Set myDataset1 will contain two Data Tables, one from each of the Data Adapters.

The two Data Tables can be read as members in the Tables collection of the Data Set, with the name of each table given by the TableName property. Since each Data Table itself contains a collection of Columns, that part of the schema of each table can also be shown by looping through each of the Column members in the Columns collection. The column name is given by the ColumnName property. In the next section of code, we will display the table names in a List Box named lstPets and the names of all the columns in each of the tables, padded on the left to make the presentation balanced:

```
' Search through the collections to show all
'the tables, their columns and data
Dim myTable As DataTable
Dim myRows As DataRow
Dim myCol As DataColumn
Dim I, intTableNumber As Integer
Dim strRow, strColumns As String

intTableNumber = 0
For Each myTable In myDataset1.Tables
    'list of tables from the collection
    lstPets.Items.Add("Table " & _
            myDataset1.Tables(intTableNumber).TableName)
```

```
'list of columns within each table
strColumns = ""
For Each myCol In myTable.Columns
    strColumns = strColumns & myCol.ColumnName.PadLeft(12)
Next
lstPets.Items.Add(strColumns)
```

The rows (i.e., the actual data) in each table can be accessed through the Rows collection of each Data Table. Notice that the actual data reside in the Items collection of each Data Row. The number of items in each row will obviously be the same as the number of columns in each table. This is because all relational database schemas must conform with the 1NF (First Normal Form) rule, which says that each and every row in a table must have exactly the same number of columns and that all items in a column must have exactly the same data type. Consequently, a loop from zero to the number of columns in the Data Table, which is the value of the Count property of the collection of Columns in the Data Table, will have the same number of items in it as the number of items in the Data Row collection. We will take advantage of that to loop through the data and display them, too. The code is as follows:

```
'built one List Box item for each row in the table
' more or less matching the columns
strRow = ""
For Each myRows In myTable.Rows
    For I = 0 To myTable.Columns.Count - 1
        strRow &= myRows.Item(I).ToString.PadLeft(12)
    Next
    lstPets.Items.Add(strRow)
    strRow = ""
Next

intTableNumber += 1
Next
```

13.3   APPLYING DATA RELATIONS AND CONSTRAINTS

13.3.1   Adding a Data Relation and its Constraints

Because the Data Set we have just created is disconnected from the actual database, the constraints on the data that would have been handled automatically by the database had the Data Set been connected must now be handled explicitly by the VB.NET code. Handling the constraints at a Data Set level, which would not have been the case with pre-.NET applications, is necessary because otherwise any unsatisfied constraint that the database may have on the data would have caused the Update method of the Data Adapter to fail. As previously discussed, leaving the constraint and foreign key relationships to be checked by the DBMS would make it too late to handle each error in the data by the VB.NET application on a record-by-record basis. Moreover, leaving the checking to that late stage would enable the VB.NET application at most to provide a general error saying that all the modifications to the data were rejected. That is why it is necessary to add Data Relation and Constraint objects to a Data Set.

The following code adds such a Data Relation and its constraints:

```
Dim myRelation As DataRelation
Dim myParentCol, myChildCol As DataColumn

myParentCol = New DataColumn()
myChildCol = New DataColumn()
myParentCol = myDataset1.Tables("Friends").Columns("Friend ID")
myChildCol = myDataset1.Tables("Pets").Columns("Friend ID")
```

Note that the Data Relation matches the foreign key constraint already in place in the Friends and Pets database. (We put that foreign key constraint there in Chapter 9.) A foreign key relationship consists at a minimum of a column in the Parent table and a column in the Child table. Both these columns are instances of the Data Column class and both need to be set to the appropriate column in each of their respective tables. The Data Relation object specifies how the Parent and the Child columns are related.

With the two Data Column objects created, instantiated, and set, the Data Relation object that connects the two can be added. A Data Relation is instantiated with either three or four parameters. The first parameter is its name. A Data Relation must have a name. It must also have a Parent column and a Child column. The Parent column and the Child column can be arrays. The last, and optional, parameter specifies whether Constraint objects will be created automatically in each of the two tables to enforce the foreign key that is specified in the Data Relation object. The `True` value will create appropriate Constraints objects:

```
myRelation = New DataRelation _
    ("Friends and their Pets", myParentCol, myChildCol, True)
```

Now the Data Relation needs to be added to the Data Set as another member in its `Relations` collection:

```
myDataset1.Relations.Add(myRelation)
```

We can now view the constraint that was just created through the Data Relation. This Constraint object is a member of the `Constraints` collection of the Data Table. Constraints can be referenced either with a `For Next` Loop or through an index. In the following code, the two constraints that were created through the Data Relation are read:

```
Dim myConstraint As Constraint
For Each myConstraint In myDataset1.Tables(0).Constraints
        lstPets.Items.Add(" Constraint name is " & _
            myConstraint.ConstraintName & _
            " Table is " & myConstraint.Table.TableName)
Next

lstPets.Items.Add(" Constraint name is " & _
        myDataset1.Tables(1).Constraints(0).ConstraintName & _
```

```
" Table is " & _
myDataset1.Tables(1).Constraints(0).Table.TableName)
```

In this code, the first Constraint, which is in the first Data Table, is referenced with a `For Next` Loop. The second Constraint, which is in the second Data Table, is referenced through its index. For each constraint, its name and its table name are placed in a List Box called lstPets.

We can read the specific Child Data Rows of each Parent Data Row through the `GetChildRows` collection of the Data Relation. As with other collections, the Child Data Rows can be read with a `For Each` loop or through an index. The entire Data Row is retrieved through this collection, not only its Data Columns in the Data Relation. In other words, as the color matching shows in the screenshots in Figure 13.1, through the `GetChildRows` collection of each individual Data Row in the parent table, all related Data Rows and all their columns in the child table can be retrieved.

The following code shows how the retrieval can be done in VB.NET:

```
myRelation = myDataset1.Relations(0)
Dim myParentRow As DataRow

For Each myParentRow In myDataset1.Tables("Friends").Rows
    For Each myChildRow In myParentRow.GetChildRows(myRelation)
        lstPets.Items.Add(myChildRow.Item(0).ToString.PadLeft(20))
    Next
Next
```

In the preceding code, two `For Each` Loops are applied. In the outer loop, all the Parent Data Rows in the Parent Data Table are read. For each one of these Parent Data Rows, all the related Child Data Rows belonging to it are read. These Child Data Rows are Data Rows in the Child Data Table. Identifying which Child Data Rows belong to each Parent Data Row is done through the Data Relation.

The Constraints—in this case those created automatically by the Data Relation object—can also be read through their appropriate collection. There are two types of constraints that are supported by the Constraint class: `UniqueConstraint` and `ForeignKeyConstraint`. The `TypeOf` function returns an indication of what type of constraint a given constraint is.

The Constraint object will have different content, depending on its type. When the Constraint object deals with enforcing a unique constraint, the Data Columns involved

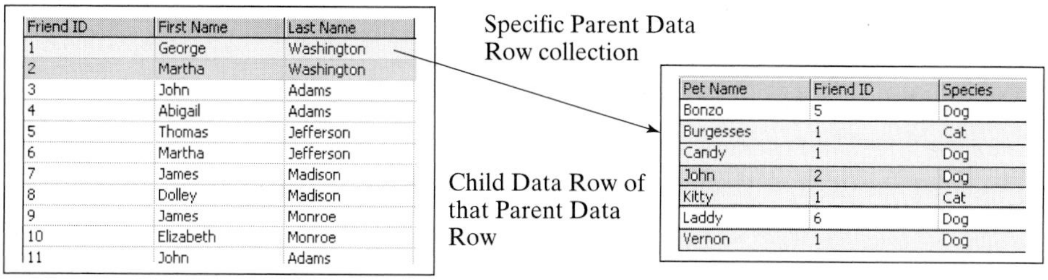

Friend ID	First Name	Last Name
1	George	Washington
2	Martha	Washington
3	John	Adams
4	Abigail	Adams
5	Thomas	Jefferson
6	Martha	Jefferson
7	James	Madison
8	Dolley	Madison
9	James	Monroe
10	Elizabeth	Monroe
11	John	Adams

Specific Parent Data Row collection

Child Data Row of that Parent Data Row

Pet Name	Friend ID	Species
Bonzo	5	Dog
Burgesses	1	Cat
Candy	1	Dog
John	2	Dog
Kitty	1	Cat
Laddy	6	Dog
Vernon	1	Dog

FIGURE 13.1
Parent Data Row and their Child Data Row.

are managed with a single collection of Data Columns within the Constraint object. A `UniqueConstraint` object is created and set with the Constraint object. The Data Columns in this `UniqueConstraint` object are then retrieved with a `For Each` loop. The code is as follows:

```
For Each myTable In mydataset1.Tables
    For Each myConstraint In myTable.Constraints
        lstDetails.Items.Add("    Constraint " & _
                        myConstraint.ConstraintName & _
                        " is ",& _
                        myConstraint.GetType.ToString)

        If TypeOf myConstraint Is UniqueConstraint Then

            Dim myUniqueConstraint As UniqueConstraint
            myUniqueConstraint = _
                Ctype(myConstraint, UniqueConstraint)

            Dim myColumn As DataColumn
            For Each myColumn In myUniqueConstraint.Columns
                lstDetails.Items.Add("        Unique Column " & _
                            myColumn.ColumnName)
            Next
        End If
```

When the Constraint object is a `ForeignKeyConstraint`, meaning that it deals with enforcing a foreign key constraint, it contains two Data Column collections. The `Columns` collection contains the columns in the parent table, and the `RelatedColumns` collection contains the columns in the child table. The Data Columns in both of these collections can also be retrieved with a `For Each` loop, as in the following code:

```
If TypeOf myConstraint Is ForeignKeyConstraint Then
    Dim myForeignKeyConstraint As ForeignKeyConstraint
    myForeignKeyConstraint = _
        CType(myConstraint, ForeignKeyConstraint)

    Dim myColumn As DataColumn
    For Each myColumn In myForeignKeyConstraint.Columns
        lstDetails.Items.Add("        Parent Column " & _
                    myColumn.ColumnName)
    Next

    For Each myColumn In _
            myForeignKeyConstraint.RelatedColumns

        lstDetails.Items.Add("        Child Column " & _
            myForeignKeyConstraint.RelatedTable.ToString & _
            "." & _
            myColumn.ColumnName)
    Next
```

The actual foreign key rules on how to handle Delete and Update changes in the parent table are given by the `DeleteRule` and the `UpdateRule` properties. The `DeleteRule` and the `UpdateRule` properties contain one of several values:

Cascade	This option means cascading delete or cascading update, depending on whether it applies to the `DeleteRule` or the `UpdateRule` property.
	When applied to a `DeleteRule`, the matching rows in the child table will be automatically deleted when related rows are deleted from the parent table.
	When applied to an `UpdateRule`, the matching rows in the child table will be automatically updated to the new value as set in their matching rows in the parent table.
None	This option means that no action will be taken on the corresponding rows in the Child Data Row when changes are made to the Parent Data Rows.
	When applied to a `DeleteRule`, the matching rows in the child table will be left as-is, even when their related rows are deleted from the parent table.
	When applied to an `UpdateRule`, the matching rows in the child table will remain as-is, even when a new value is set in their matching rows in the parent table.
SetDefault	This option means that when changes are made to the Parent Data Rows, the value of the items in corresponding columns in the Child Data Rows will be set to their defined default values.
	When applied to a `DeleteRule`, the items of the Related columns of the child table that match the deleted rows in the parent table will be set to the default value of the column. This default value can be explicitly set in the schema of the database or the Date Set. Unless an explicit default value is given, the default value will be the default value of the data type. For example, items with a numeric data type in the Related columns of affected child Data Rows will be set to zero.
	When applied to an `UpdateRule`, the same applies. The items in Related columns of the child table that match the updated Data Rows in the parent table will be set to their default value.
SetNull	This option means that when changes are made to the Parent Data Rows, the value of the items in corresponding columns in the Child Data Rows will be set to Null.
	This option works almost the same as the previous option, except that the items of the Related columns of the child table that match the deleted or updated rows in the parent table will be set to Null rather than to a default value.

The `DeleteRule` and the `UpdateRule` properties can be set or read in the code. In the following code, their content is added to a list box:

```
          lstDetails.Items.Add("        Delete Rule is " & _
                  myForeignKeyConstraint.DeleteRule.ToString)
          lstDetails.Items.Add("        Update Rule is " & _
                  myForeignKeyConstraint.UpdateRule.ToString)
      End If
    Next
  Next
```

The type of foreign key rule can also be part of an `If` statement or an assignment statement. In such cases, it is necessary to compare its value or assign it from an appropriate Enum, named `Rule`. There are four `Rule` values: `Cascade`, `None`, `SetDefault`, and `SetNull`. These rule values apply to both Delete Rules and Update Rules. The code is

```
If myForeignKeyConstraint.DeleteRule = Rule.None Then
    myForeignKeyConstraint.DeleteRule = Rule.SetDefault
End If
If myForeignKeyConstraint.UpdateRule = Rule.None Then
    myForeignKeyConstraint.UpdateRule = Rule.SetDefault
End If
```

13.4 BUILDING A DATA SET WITHOUT A DATA ADAPTER

As we have seen them up to now, Data Sets have dealt with a local copy of an external database, with both schema and data being copied from the database with the Data Adapter `Fill` method. That is a primary objective of a Data Set; however, a Data Set and its schema can be created also independently of any database. Although, in such cases, the Data Set would be an internal unshared application-specific database, there are several good reasons for creating one. An internal unshared application-specific database is still precisely that—a fully operational database with all the auxiliary services a database provides.

A Data Set manages not only data, but also metadata, namely, the database schema that contains the Data Relation and the Constraint objects. Thus, while it is possible to store the *data* just as well in an array of dedicated Structures, as we shall show, the same does not apply to the *schema*. When data are stored in an array of dedicated Structures, all the metadata checks, uniqueness, and foreign key relations must be coded into every instance of adding or changing data. That would have required, for example, adding methods that would check whether a specific Friend_ID value exists in the Friends array each time a new Pet is added or its Friend_ID changed. That would also require methods to handle cascading update and cascading delete every time a Friend_ID value is changed or deleted, respectively, in the Friends array. Adding such unnecessary code is hardly a good idea. Coding these relationships involves writing unnecessary, redundant code:

```
Structure FriendsDataSet
    Public Friend_ID As Integer
```

```
    Public First_Name As String
    Public Last_Name As String
    Public Date_Of_Birth As Date
    Public Spouse_ID As Integer
End Structure

Structure PetsDataSet
    Public Friend_ID As Integer
    Public Pet_Name As String
    Public Gender As String
    Public Species As string
End Structure

Dim Friends() As FriendsDataSet
Dim Pets() As PetsDataSet
```

A Data Set, on the other hand, avoids unnecessary, redundant code and writes the code where it functionally belongs, in the data schema. Moreover, defining these data as a Data Set also lets us take full advantage of the many dedicated methods a Data Set and its related classes have, including the `Compute, Filter,` and `Select` methods that we discussed last chapter. Had we stuck with an array of Structures, adding these methods would have been unavailable or would have required writing dedicated methods to support them.

There is another advantage to a Data Set. When an object is made persistent, that object and what it includes are stored. Other objects, even those related to it, are left intact. (See discussion on persistent objects in Chapter 6.) So long as the object, such as a Structure array, has a simple data structure, that will work okay. But once the data begin to be interrelated, which is what we do when we add Data Relation objects, it is better to store all the data-related objects as one object and to do so in one operation. Grouping all the data into one object, a Data Set, enables precisely that. When a Data Set is made persistent, all the objects it contains are made persistent and stored at the same time. Think of it as storing and then retrieving a built jigsaw puzzle as one unit, which is analogous to handling the data with a Data Set, as opposed to breaking it up and reconstructing it each time it is stored and retrieved, which is analogous to handling the data with Structures and specifically written methods.

13.4.1 The Data Column Constructor

A Data Table, being a table, needs columns to map its data. These Data Column objects must be defined and instantiated before they can be added to a Data Table. There are several ways to instantiate a Data Column, depending on the parameters passed to the constructor method. The constructor method can receive one of five sets of parameters:

- It can receive no parameters at all, in which case its properties should be set in the code before it can be added to the `Columns` collection of a Data Table. It is highly recommended in that case to assign the column name with the `ColumnName` property in the code:

```
Dim myColumnA As New DataColumn
myColumnA.ColumnName = "AnnualIncome"
```

- It can receive one parameter with the column name:

```
Dim myColumnA As New DataColumn("AnnualIncome")
```

- It can receive two parameters; the first with the column name, the second with the data type of the items that will eventually be in that column once Data Rows are added to the Data Table. The data type is one of the data types discussed in Chapter 2. These include Boolean, String, Integer, and so on. A convenient way of specifying the data type is with the GetType function. This function returns the data type of an object:

```
Dim myColumnA As New _
        DataColumn("AnnualIncome", GetType(Integer))
```

- It can receive three parameters, the first two the same as in the previous item and the third containing an expression, called a *derived attribute* in database terminology. The objective of a creating a derived attribute is to dynamically and automatically calculate a value based on the value of other columns. *A good example of a derived attribute is a column named Age that is calculated automatically* based on another column containing Date of Birth. Rather than explicitly recalculating the value of the Age column each time a new row is added to the table and each time the Data of Birth is changed, adding the *expression* parameter will make these calculations part of the schema, and so the calculation will be done automatically and documented in the schema. (Here is another reason to have a Data Set rather than a Structure.) Another example of an expression is an Actual Price column that is calculated automatically based on the Price-before-tax and Sales-tax-rate columns. The following example demonstrates another case, calculating monthly income on the basis of the annual income column just defined:

```
Dim myColumnB As New DataColumn _
                    ("MonthlyIncome", _
                    GetType(Integer), _
                    "AnnualIncome / 12")
```

A small caveat here is that the expression is evaluated during runtime, so any typo will be caught only when the code is executed. In the following code, the expression is written as a String literal (it can also be a string variable):

```
myTable2.Columns.Add(myColumnA)
myTable2.Columns.Add(myColumnB)

Dim myDataRow As DataRow
myDataRow = myTable2.NewRow()
myDataRow.Item(0) = 120000
myTable2.Rows.Add(myDataRow)

Console.WriteLine("Annual Income is  " & _
            myDataRow.Item(0).ToString)
```

```
Console.WriteLine("Monthly Income is " & _
                myDataRow.Item(1).ToString)
```

- The Data Column constructor can receive four parameters: the foregoing three and MappingType, which specifies how the WriteXML method we saw in Chapter 12 will write this column to an XML document. The MappingType Enum can have one of four values: Attribute, Element, Hidden, or SimpleContent. Attribute writes the column as an attribute in XML, Element as an element. Hidden will map the column to an internal hidden structure, while Simple Content will write it as text. The code is

```
Dim myColumnB As New DataColumn _
            ("MonthlyIncome", _
            GetType(Integer), _
            "AnnualIncome / 12", _
            MappingType.Attribute)
```

13.4.2 AutoNumbers

Occasionally, it is necessary to add an autoincrementing column to a database. This column, for example, could be an artificial Primary Key that is basically a nonrepeating numeric value. Typically, such column values, known sometimes in database terminology as autonumber, are generated when there is no obvious collection of columns that provides a unique key for the table. For example, a table containing only the names of people would require such a Primary Key because names may be repeated.

Setting a Data column to be such an autonumber requires setting its AutoIncrement property to True, meaning that, with every new row, the value of this item will be automatically incremented. It is convenient to specify explicitly what the increment step will be with the AutoIncrementStep property, to make it read only, with the ReadOnly property, and to clarify that its values are unique with the Unique property. Usually, the increment step is set to 1. By doing so, the item in that column in the first Data Row will be 0, in the second it will be 1, in the third 2, and so on, automatically creating a unique key. The code is

```
Dim mycolumnC As New DataColumn("PK")
myTable2.Columns.Add(mycolumnC)

mycolumnC.AutoIncrement = True
mycolumnC.AutoIncrementStep = 1
mycolumnC.ReadOnly = True
mycolumnC.Unique = True
```

13.4.3 Building the Data Set

A Data Set, whether with or without a Data Source, is composed first and foremost of a collection of Data Tables, themselves made up of Data Columns and Data Rows. When building a Data Set without a Data Source, such as a Data Set that is unrelated to a Data Adapter, one can either work with a single Data Table, in which case dimensioning a

Data Set can be skipped, or with a collection of interrelated Data Tables, in which case it is necessary to dimension a Data Set to hold all the objects together. In this example, we will define a single table Data Set.

Our Data Set will be named `myPersonalDS` and will contain one Data Table named `myFriendsTable`. The constructors of both objects can receive either no parameter or one parameter with the typed object name. In this case, we will give only the Data Table a typed name, thereby allowing reference to the Data Table by its name and not only by its index in the `Tables` collection of the Data Set (see Chapter 12 on typed reference):

```
Dim myPersonalDS As New DataSet()
Dim myFriendsTable As New DataTable("myFriends")
```

We can now proceed to add columns to the Data Table. First, we will dimension and instantiate four columns. In this case, the constructor has only one parameter, with the column name:

```
Dim colFirstName As New DataColumn("First Name")
Dim colLastName As New DataColumn("Last Name")
Dim colAddress As New DataColumn("Address")
Dim colTelephone As New DataColumn("Telephone")
```

The other Data Column properties can be set at this stage. Just to clarify that it can be done also by setting the property explicitly, the `ColumnName` property will also be set. The other properties being set are the Data Type, Default Value, and its maximum length. The Data Type is set with the `GetType` function:

```
colFirstName.DataType = Type.GetType("System.String")
colFirstName.MaxLength = 30
colFirstName.DefaultValue = "John"
colFirstName.ColumnName = "First Name"

colLastName.DataType = Type.GetType("System.String")
colLastName.MaxLength = 30
colAddress.DataType = Type.GetType("System.String")
colAddress.MaxLength = 100
colTelephone.DataType = Type.GetType("System.String")
colTelephone.MaxLength = 14
```

With the Data Column objects ready, they can be added to the `Tables` collection of the appropriate Data Table:

```
myFriendsTable.Columns.Add(colFirstName)
myFriendsTable.Columns.Add(colLastName)
myFriendsTable.Columns.Add(colAddress)
myFriendsTable.Columns.Add(colTelephone)
```

Finally, data can be added to the table, by adding instantiated and set Data Rows to the `Rows` collection. In the following code, because we previously assigned a name to each column with its ColumnName property, we take advantage of typing to reference each item by its column name, rather than by its index:

```
' Add rows.
Dim myRow As DataRow ' make sure there are no ()
Dim I As Integer
For I = 0 To 9
    myRow = myFriendsTable.NewRow()
    myRow("First Name") = "Friend " & CStr(I)
    myRow("Last Name") = "Family " & CStr(I * 10)
    myRow("Address") = "Street " & CStr(I * 9)
    myRow("Telephone") = _
        CStr(I).PadLeft(3, "0") & " " & _
        CStr(I).PadLeft(7, "0")

    myFriendsTable.Rows.Add(myRow)
Next
myFriendsTable.AcceptChanges()
```

We can also add the Data Table to a Data Set, although this is can be skipped when only one Data Table exists:

```
myPersonalDS.Tables.Add(myFriendsTable)
```

Programming Note: Data Tables can also be added to Data Sets that are filled from a Data Source, but these changes to the schema cannot be updated back to the Data Source through the Data Adapter. The Data Adapter does not support the necessary SQL statements.

13.4.4 Manipulating the Data in a Data Set without a Data Source

The Data rows can be manipulated as done in Chapter 12. Rows are added with the NewRow method, deleted with the Delete method, and updated by setting their item values:

```
' Lost friend number 9
myFriendsTable.Rows(9).Delete()

' Changed friend 5
myFriendsTable.Rows(5)("First Name") = "Amigo"
myFriendsTable.Rows(5)("Last Name") = "Pal"
myFriendsTable.Rows(5)("Address") = "Home"
myFriendsTable.Rows(5)("Telephone") = "111 222-3333"

' Made friends again 9
myRow = myFriendsTable.NewRow
myRow.Item(0) = "John "
myRow.Item(1) = "Doe "
myFriendsTable.Rows.Add(myRow)
```

13.4.5 Adding a View of Changed Data Rows

An important property of the Data Row class is `DataRowState`. This property contains information about whether the Data Row has been added, deleted (yes, deleted Data Rows *can* be read), or modified and whether it is unchanged or is detached (not currently connected to a Data Table). We can do that, even read deleted rows, by applying a Data View. A view can be thought of as a window through which real data in a table can be examined. The view, just as a window in the real world, does not contain any data. It just filters them. And, just as a window can be painted to allow only certain colors through, so too a view can be set to show only certain types of rows. The following code reads only deleted rows through a Data View:

```
Dim myFriendsView As New DataView(myFriendsTable)
' Show all deleted rows.
For I = 0 To myFriendsView.Count - 1
    If Not myFriendsView(I).Row.RowState = _
                DataRowState.Deleted Then
        myRow = myFriendsView(I).Row
        lstView.Items.Add( _
                    myRow.Item("First Name").padright(15) & _
                    myRow.Item("Last Name").padright(15))
    End If
Next
```

Alternatively, we can add a filter to the Data View and show only added, deleted, unchanged, or modified rows (with the `ModifiedCurrent` property). When working with the filter, we can also retrieve all the current rows in the Data Table (with the `CurrentRows` Enum value), the original value of modified rows (with the `ModifiedOriginal` Enum value), or the original rows as read from the Data Source (with the `OriginalRows` Enum value). The following code filters only the added rows through a Data View and then only the original values of rows that were changed:

```
' RowStateFilter will make view show only Added rows.
myFriendsView.RowStateFilter = DataViewRowState.Added

lstView.Items.Add("Only added rows")
For I = 0 To myFriendsView.Count - 1
    myRow = myFriendsView(I).Row
    lstView.Items.Add(myRow.Item("First Name").padright(15) & _
            myRow.Item("Last Name").padright(15))
Next
' Display original values of modified rows.
myFriendsView.RowStateFilter = DataViewRowState.ModifiedCurrent
lstView.Items.Add("")
lstView.Items.Add("Modified values ")
For I = 0 To myFriendsView.Count - 1
    If Not myFriendsView(I).Row.RowState = DataRowState.Deleted Then
        myRow = myFriendsView(I).Row
```

```
lstView.Items.Add(myRow.Item("First Name").padright(15) & _
                        myRow.Item("Last Name").padright(15))
    End If
Next
```

13.5   ADDITIONAL DATA ROW METHODS AND PROPERTIES

We have already seen the `AcceptChanges` and the `RejectChanges` methods in the Data Set and Data Table classes. The same two methods also apply to the Data Row class, except that Accept Changes and Reject Changes relate to an individual row in the table—that is, to a single Data Row object. Another needed method is the `IsNull` method. As in other instances when the method was applied, here, too, it returns a `True` or `False` value, depending on whether the object it relates to (in this case, a Data Row) is null.

Occasionally, it may be necessary to specify that one or more Data Rows have an error. This may happen, for example, when a large of number of rows is affected by an single operation and it is beneficial to let the whole process complete and then handle the erroneous rows one at a time. We saw already in Chapter 12 how the `HasErrors` method of a Data Set returns a `True` value when there are errors. The same works also with the Data Row. We can also manually set a Data Row to be in error, and hence let `HasErrors` detect it, with the `RowError` property. This property can be set to a string value with the error message, in which case the `HasErrors` property will detect that the row has an error, or to the literal `Nothing`, in which case the `HasErrors` property will detect that the row is error free:

```
myRow.RowError = "I am in error, oops"
If myRow.HasErrors = True Then
    Console.WriteLine("This Row has an error of " & _
        myRow.RowError)
End If

myRow.RowError = Nothing
If myRow.HasErrors = True Then
    ' this line will not be executed
    Console.WriteLine("This Row has an error of " & _
        myRow.RowError)
Else
    ' this line will be executed
    Console.WriteLine("This Row is no longer in error " & _
        myRow.RowError)
End If
```

LABS: OVERVIEW

The lab section of this chapter contains two parts:
1. Three small labs that summarize the material of the chapter. These labs directly deal with the code examples that appear throughout the chapter. The objective is to examine the complex material in sections, devoting a relatively small single lab to each topic.
2. A larger lab for general practice of the concepts covered in the chapter.

LAB 13.1

Lab Objectives:

Exercise working with a single-table database-filled Data Set:

- Copying Data Sets as created by a Data Adapter
- Merging the Data Sets
- Showing the content of the merged Data Set
- Building a Data Relation between the two Data Tables
- Reading the Data Rows through the Data Relation

Application Overview

The lab contains two Data Adapters that read the data in the Friends and Pets database that we built in Chapter 9. Each table is read by a different Data Adapter. The two Data Sets are then combined in the code, a Data Relation is added and the merged data are read through the Data Relation. This operation is broken down into two sections. The first section merges the Data Sets and reads them. The second section adds a Data Relation and reads the data through it.

Part 1: Build the Form

Add a new project and solution. Name the solution and project **prjChapter13**. Name the Windows form **frmMultiTables**. Add the Buttons and list box as shown in Figure 13.2. Objects starting with "btn" are Buttons; the one starting with "lst" is a list box. Write the appropriate string in the `Text` properties of each object to correspond to what appears in the figure. Make the `Enabled` property of btnRelations of `False`. The three controls below the form will be added in Part 2.

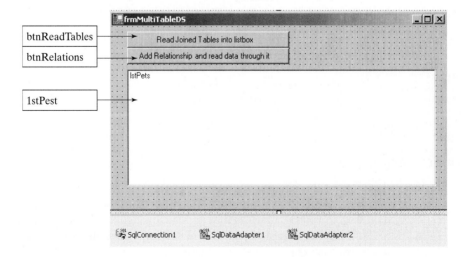

FIGURE 13.2

Part 2: Add the Data Controls

Next, add the data controls by copying an SQL Connection control from the toolbox onto the form and then either setting its `ConnectionString` property to the existing connection we established in previous chapters to the Friends and Pets SQL Server database or opening a new connection and following its instructions to open a new connection through the wizard as shown in Chapter 9. Then, copy an SQL Data Adapter control onto the form, set its connection string through the wizard that will automatically open to the SQL Connection control we just created, tell the wizard to use SQL statements, and then choose the Friends table and all its fields. The screen-shots in Figure 13.3 summarize the input given to the wizard. Your Connection name, in the second screenshot, may be different. This example is slightly different from those of previous chapters, where we created the controls by dropping the Tables from the Server Explorer.

Repeat the process with the Pets Table from the stage where an SQL Connection control is dropped on the form.

Part 3: Add the Code for btnReadTables

In the Declarations section, add the dimensioning of the objects that will be used by both Buttons:

```
Public Class frmMultiTableDS
    Inherits System.Windows.Forms.Form
    Dim myDataset1, myDataset2 As DataSet
    Dim myRelation As DataRelation
    Dim myParentCol, myChildCol As DataColumn
```

FIGURE 13.3
The Data Adapter Configuration wizard.

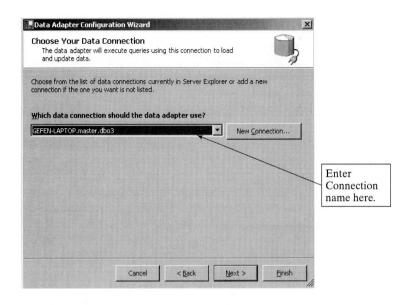

Enter Connection name here.

Choose SQL.

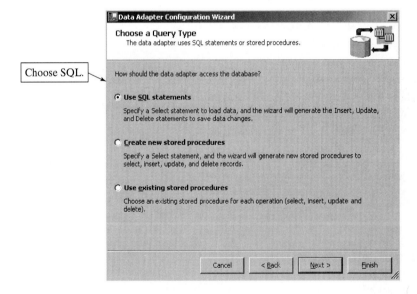

FIGURE 13.3
(*Continued*)

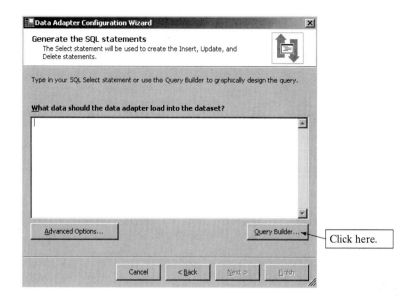

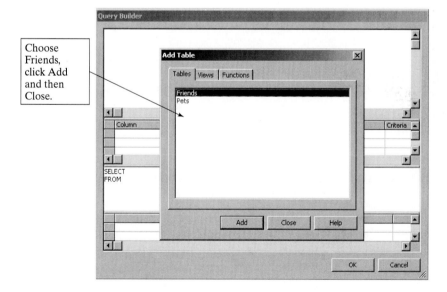

FIGURE 13.3
(*Continued*)

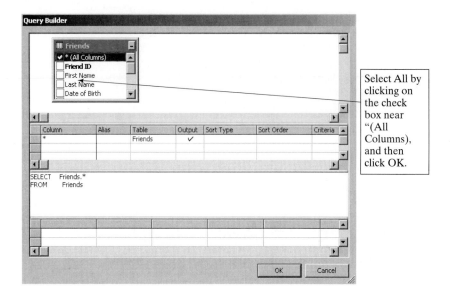

FIGURE 13.3
(*Continued*)

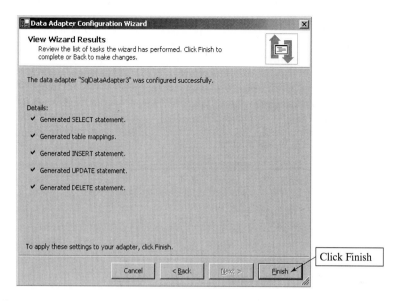

FIGURE 13.3
(*Continued*)

In the subroutine that handles the `Click` event on the Read Joined Tables Button, add the following code:

```
Private Sub btnReadTables_Click(ByVal sender As System.Object, _
        ByVal e As System.EventArgs) Handles btnReadTables.Click
    Dim strSelect As String
    Dim intSize As Integer
    Dim I, intTableNumber As Integer
    Dim strColumns As String
    Dim strRow As String

    Try
        Try
            ' clear datasets and list box in case Button
            ' clicked twice
            myDataset1.Dispose()
            myDataset2.Dispose()
            lstPets.Items.Clear()
        Catch
        End Try

        ' Built dataset with both tables
        myDataset1 = New DataSet()
        myDataset2 = New DataSet()
        intSize = SqlDataAdapter1.Fill(myDataset1)
```

```
                    intSize = SqlDataAdapter2.Fill(myDataset2)
                    myDataset1.Merge(myDataset2)

                    ' Search through the collections to show all
                    ' the tables, their columns and data
                    Dim myTable As DataTable
                    Dim myRows As DataRow
                    Dim myCol As DataColumn

                    intTableNumber = 0
                    For Each myTable In myDataset1.Tables
                        'list of tables from the collection
                        lstPets.Items.Add("Table " & _
                              myDataset1.Tables(intTableNumber).TableName)

                        'list of columns within each table
                        strColumns = ""
                        For Each myCol In myTable.Columns
                            strColumns = strColumns & _
                                myCol.ColumnName.PadLeft(12)
                        Next
                        lstPets.Items.Add(strColumns)

                        'built one List Box item for each row in the table
                        ' more or less matching the columns
                        strRow = ""
                        For Each myRows In myTable.Rows
                            For I = 0 To myTable.Columns.Count - 1
                                strRow &= myRows.Item(I).ToString.PadLeft(12)
                            Next
                            lstPets.Items.Add(strRow)
                            strRow = ""
                        Next

                        intTableNumber += 1
                    Next

                    btnRelations.Enabled = True

            Catch e1 As Exception
                MessageBox.Show(e1.Message)
            End Try
        End Sub
```

Clicking on the Button will display the contents of the two tables in the list box.

Part 4: Add the Code for btnRelations

Clicking this Button will show the data from both tables together. (See Figure 13.4.) That is, for each Friend, it will show a list of his or her Pets. This is done by reading the related rows in Pets through the Data Relation. The code is as follows:

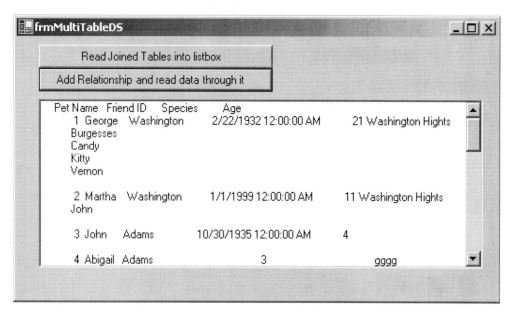

FIGURE 13.4
Lab 13.1 showing joined tables.

```vb
Private Sub btnRelations_Click(ByVal sender As System.Object, _
        ByVal e As System.EventArgs) Handles btnRelations.Click
    Dim strColumns, strRow As String
    Dim I As Integer

    Try
        ' Add relation between the two tables
        Try
            myParentCol = New DataColumn()
            myChildCol = New DataColumn()
            myParentCol = _
                    myDataset1.Tables("Friends").Columns("Friend ID")
            myChildCol = myDataset1.Tables("Pets").Columns("Friend ID")
            myRelation = New DataRelation("Friends and their Pets", _
                            myParentCol, myChildCol, True)
            myDataset1.Relations.Add(myRelation)
        Catch
            ' Ignore this error.
            ' It means that the relation already exists
        End Try

        Dim myTable As DataTable
        Dim myParentRow As DataRow
        Dim myCol As DataColumn
        Dim myChildRow As DataRow
```

```vbnet
                    ' Prepare list of columns in parent table
                    strColumns = ""
                    For Each myCol In myDataset1.Tables("Pets").Columns
                        strColumns = strColumns & myCol.ColumnName.PadLeft(12)
                    Next

                    lstPets.Items.Clear()
                    lstPets.Items.Add(strColumns)

                    ' Built one List Box item for each row in the table
                    ' more or less matching the columns
                    For Each myParentRow In myDataset1.Tables("Friends").Rows
                        strRow = ""
                        For I = 0 To myDataset1.Tables("Friends").Columns.
                                                            Count - 1
                            strRow &= myParentRow.Item(I).ToString.
                                                            PadLeft(12)
                        Next
                        lstPets.Items.Add(strRow)

                        strRow = ""
                        myRelation = myDataset1.Relations(0)
                        For Each myChildRow In myParentRow.
                                                    GetChildRows(myRelation)

                            lstPets.Items.Add(myChildRow.Item(0).ToString.
                                                            PadLeft(20))
                        Next

                        lstPets.Items.Add("")
                    Next

                    Dim myConstraint As Constraint
                    For Each myConstraint In
        myDataset1.Tables(0).Constraints
                        lstPets.Items.Add(" Constraint name is " & _
                                        myConstraint.ConstraintName & _
                            " Table is " & myConstraint.Table.TableName)
                    Next
                    lstPets.Items.Add(" Constraint name is " & _
                            myDataset1.Tables(1).Constraints(0).
                                            ConstraintName & _
                            " Table is " & _
                            myDataset1.Tables(1).Constraints(0).Table.
                                            TableName)

                    lstPets.Items.Add("")

                Catch e1 As Exception
                    MessageBox.Show(e1.Message)
                End Try
            End Sub
        End Class
```

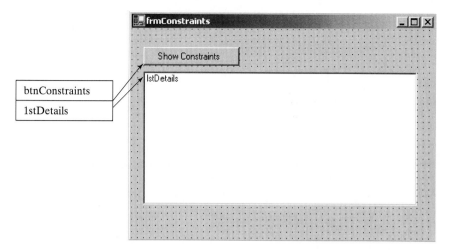

FIGURE 13.5
Lab 13.2.

LAB 13.2

Lab Objectives:
Examine the Data Relations and Constraints Objects in an existing Data Set.

Application Overview

The lab references a Data Adapter that was created by the Data File wizard and prints out the details of the Data Relation and Constraints objects it created.

Part 1: Build the Form

Add a new Windows form. Name the form **frmConstraints**. Add the Button and List Box as shown in Figure 13.5.

Part 2: Add a Data Form with the Wizard

Next, create a Data Form that accesses both the Friends and the Pets tables. Repeat the procedure in Chapter 11 to create a form named frmCreateDS, with a Data Set named myDataSet3 that will be related to two Data Adapters.

Here is a brief reminder how to create the form: Right mouse click on the project in the Solution Explorer. In the popup menu, select Add and then Add New Item. In the Add New Item window, select the Data Form wizard icon and name it frmCreadeDS; then click Open to start the Data Form Wizard. In the second form of the wizard, tell it to create a new Data Set and name it myDataSet3. Then choose the connection and select both tables from the database. Specify how the two tables are connected, as we did in Chapter 11. Choose to display all columns from both tables. And ask to create a form with "All records in a grid." This is how the form that is generated will look. (See Figure 13.6.)

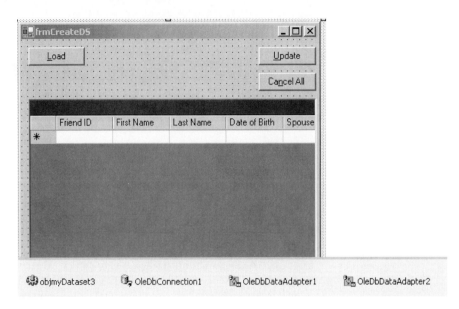

FIGURE 13.6
The automatically generated form.

Double-click the Load Button, and then change the code that was automatically generated so that the Load Button method is Friend, rather then Private. We will need to call this subroutine from the code we are about to write:

```
' Change this to Friend
Friend Sub btnLoad_Click(ByVal sender As System.Object, _
        ByVal e As System.EventArgs) Handles btnLoad.Click
```

Part 3: Add the Code

With the Data Set created, we can read its Data Relation and Constraint objects. Double-click on btnConstraints, and add the code that follows. We discussed this code earlier in the chapter. For each table, the code shows all the constraints. For each constraint, depending on its type, all the columns in its collections are shown. If the Constraint is a foreign key, the details of the update and delete rules are also shown. Here is the code:

```
Private Sub btnConstraints_Click(ByVal sender As System.Object, _
        ByVal e As System.EventArgs) Handles btnConstraints.Click

    ' Build the dataset with the wizard. That form is frmCreateDs.
    ' Then, make its Load method Friend so it can be referenced
    Dim frmCreateDScopy As New frmCreateDS()
    Call frmCreateDScopy.btnLoad_Click(Me, e)
    Dim mydataset1 = frmCreateDScopy.objmyDataset3
    Dim myConstraint As Data.Constraint
    Dim myTable As Data.DataTable

    lstDetails.Items.Clear()
```

```
For Each myTable In mydataset1.Tables
    lstDetails.Items.Add("List of constraints in table " & _
        myTable.TableName)
    For Each myConstraint In myTable.Constraints
        lstDetails.Items.Add("      Constraint " & _
                    myConstraint.ConstraintName & _
                    " is " & _
                    myConstraint.GetType.ToString)

        Dim myColumn As DataColumn
        If TypeOf myConstraint Is UniqueConstraint Then
            Dim myUniqueConstraint As UniqueConstraint
            myUniqueConstraint = _
                CType(myConstraint, UniqueConstraint)
            For Each myColumn In myUniqueConstraint.Columns
                lstDetails.Items.Add("      Unique Column " & _
                            myColumn.ColumnName)
            Next
        End If

        If TypeOf myConstraint Is ForeignKeyConstraint Then
            Dim myForeignKeyConstraint As ForeignKeyConstraint
            myForeignKeyConstraint = CType(myConstraint, _
                ForeignKeyConstraint)
' We add Tostring so we can see the meaning of the rule
' rather than "Rule" and a number, where the number is
' the Rule in the FK as set by XSD
' with 0 is "Null", 1 is "Cascade", 2 is "Set Null",
' and 3 is "Set Default"}

            If myForeignKeyConstraint.DeleteRule = _
                Rule.None Then
                myForeignKeyConstraint.DeleteRule = _
                    Rule.SetDefault
            End If
            If myForeignKeyConstraint.UpdateRule = _
                Rule.None Then
                myForeignKeyConstraint.UpdateRule = _
                Rule.SetDefault
            End If
            lstDetails.Items.Add("      Delete Rule is " & _
                myForeignKeyConstraint.DeleteRule.ToString)
            lstDetails.Items.Add("      Update Rule is " & _
                myForeignKeyConstraint.UpdateRule.ToString)

            For Each myColumn In myForeignKeyConstraint.Columns
                lstDetails.Items.Add("      Parent Column " & _
                    myColumn.ColumnName)
            Next

            For Each myColumn In _
                myForeignKeyConstraint.RelatedColumns
                lstDetails.Items.Add("      Child Column " & _
```

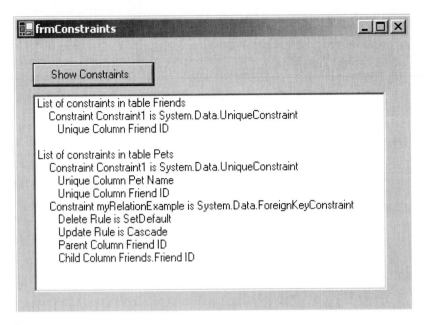

FIGURE 13.7
Showing the constraints in a generated Data base.

```
                                myForeignKeyConstraint.RelatedTable.ToString &_
                                "." & _
                                myColumn.ColumnName)
                    Next
                End If
            Next
            lstDetails.Items.Add("")
        Next
    End Sub
```

Running the application will affect the information from the Constraint objects, as shown in Figure 13.7.

REVIEW LAB 3

Lab Objectives:
1. Create a Data Set with a Data Table and its related Data Columns
2. Add Data Rows to the Data Table
3. Manipulate the Data Rows
4. Apply a Data View to display only the deleted rows, and only the added rows, and only the original values of the changed rows
5. Demonstrate adding expressions and autonumbers to Data Columns

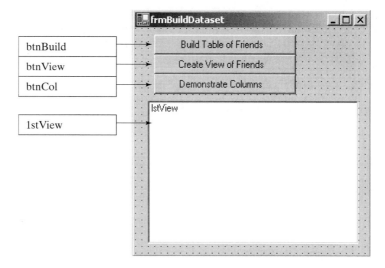

FIGURE 13.8
Lab 13.3.

Application Overview

The lab creates its own Data Set, builds its schema, and populates its with btnBuilt. It then manipulates the data in the Data Rows and shows different views of the rows with btnView. Expressions and autonumbers are demonstrated with btnCol.

Part 1: Build the Form

Add a new Windows form. Name the form **frmBuildDataSet**. Add the Buttons and list box as shown with their appropriate Text properties, as shown in Figure 13.8.
    Add the following code in the Declarations section:

```
Public Class frmBuildDataset
    Inherits System.Windows.Forms.Form

    Dim myPersonalDS As New DataSet()
    Dim myFriendsTable As New DataTable("myFriends")
```

We will need these objects throughout the class. Through the Dim statements, the Data Table is given a name; the Data Set is not.

Part 2: Add the Code for btnBuild

This code has been explained in the chapter:

```
Private Sub btnBuild_Click(ByVal sender As System.Object, _
        ByVal e As System.EventArgs) Handles btnBuild.Click

    Dim I As Integer
    ' Create columns.
    Dim colFirstName As New DataColumn("First Name")
```

```vbnet
        Dim colLastName As New DataColumn("Last Name")
        Dim colAddress As New DataColumn("Address")
        Dim colTelephone As New DataColumn("Telephone")

        colFirstName.DataType = Type.GetType("System.String")
        colFirstName.MaxLength = 30
        colFirstName.DefaultValue = "John"
        colFirstName.ColumnName = "First Name"

        colLastName.DataType = Type.GetType("System.String")
        colLastName.MaxLength = 30
        colAddress.DataType = Type.GetType("System.String")
        colAddress.MaxLength = 100
        colTelephone.DataType = Type.GetType("System.String")
        colTelephone.MaxLength = 14

        myFriendsTable.Columns.Add(colFirstName)
        myFriendsTable.Columns.Add(colLastName)
        myFriendsTable.Columns.Add(colAddress)
        myFriendsTable.Columns.Add(colTelephone)

        ' Add rows.
        Dim myRow As DataRow
        For I = 0 To 9
            myRow = myFriendsTable.NewRow()
            myRow("First Name") = "Friend " & CStr(I)
            myRow("Last Name") = "Family " & CStr(I * 10)
            myRow("Address") = "Street " & CStr(I * 9)
            myRow("Telephone") = CStr(I).PadLeft(3, "0") & " " & _
                    CStr(I).PadLeft(7, "0")
            myFriendsTable.Rows.Add(myRow)
        Next
        myFriendsTable.AcceptChanges()

        myPersonalDS.Tables.Add(myFriendsTable)   ' we can do this too
    End Sub
```

Part 3: Add the Code for btnView

This code, too, has been explained in the chapter:

```vbnet
    Private Sub btnView_Click(ByVal sender As System.Object, _
            ByVal e As System.EventArgs) Handles btnView.Click
        Dim I As Integer
        Dim myFriendsView As New DataView(myFriendsTable)
        Dim myRow As DataRow   ' make sure there are no ()

        ' Lost friend number 10
        myFriendsTable.Rows(9).Delete()

        ' Changed friend 6
        myFriendsTable.Rows(5)("First Name") = "Amigo"
```

```
myFriendsTable.Rows(5)("Last Name") = "Pal"
myFriendsTable.Rows(5)("Address") = "Home"
myFriendsTable.Rows(5)("Telephone") = "111 222-3333"


' Made friends again with 9
myRow = myFriendsTable.NewRow
myRow.Item(0) = "John "
myRow.Item(1) = "Doe "
myFriendsTable.Rows.Add(myRow)
' Show all rows.
lstView.Items.Clear()
lstView.Items.Add("Only added or modified rows")
' For Each myRow In myFriendsView will not work because there
' is no collection of rows in the view
For I = 0 To myFriendsView.Count - 1
    If Not myFriendsView(I).Row.RowState = _
           DataRowState.Deleted Then
        myRow = myFriendsView(I).Row
        lstView.Items.Add( _
                    myRow.Item("First Name").padright(15) & _
                    myRow.Item("Last Name").padright(15))
    End If
Next


' RowStateFilter will make view show only Added rows.
myFriendsView.RowStateFilter = DataViewRowState.Added

lstView.Items.Clear()
lstView.Items.Add("Only added rows")
For I = 0 To myFriendsView.Count - 1
    myRow = myFriendsView(I).Row
    lstView.Items.Add(myRow.Item("First Name").padright(15) & _
                myRow.Item("Last Name").padright(15))
Next


' Display original values of modified rows.
myFriendsView.RowStateFilter = DataViewRowState.ModifiedCurrent
lstView.Items.Add("")
lstView.Items.Add("Modified values ")
For I = 0 To myFriendsView.Count - 1
    If Not myFriendsView(I).Row.RowState = _
               DataRowState.Deleted Then
        myRow = myFriendsView(I).Row
        lstView.Items.Add( _
               myRow.Item("First Name").padright(15) & _
               myRow.Item("Last Name").padright(15))
    End If
Next
End Sub
```

Part 4: Add the Code for btnCol

The following code also has been explained in the chapter:

```vb
Private Sub btnCol_Click(ByVal sender As System.Object, _
        ByVal e As System.EventArgs) Handles btnCol.Click

    ' Define the Data Set and Data Table
    Dim myDataSet2 As New DataSet()
    Dim myTable2 As New DataTable()
    myDataSet2.Tables.Add(myTable2)

    ' Define the Columns and add them to the Data Table
    Dim myColumnA As New DataColumn( _
            "AnnualIncome", GetType(Integer))
    Dim myColumnB As New DataColumn( _
            "MonthlyIncome", GetType(Integer), _
            "AnnualIncome / 12", _
            MappingType.Attribute)
    Dim mycolumnC As New DataColumn("PK")

    myColumnA.ColumnName = "AnnualIncome"
    myTable2.Columns.Add(myColumnA)
    myTable2.Columns.Add(myColumnB)
    myTable2.Columns.Add(mycolumnC)

    mycolumnC.AutoIncrement = True
    mycolumnC.AutoIncrementStep = 1
    mycolumnC.ReadOnly = True
    mycolumnC.Unique = True

    ' Add data in a Data Row
    Dim myDataRow As DataRow
    myDataRow = myTable2.NewRow()
    myDataRow.Item(0) = 120000
    myTable2.Rows.Add(myDataRow)

    ' Show how the derived attribute works
    Console.WriteLine("Annual Income is  " & _
            myDataRow.Item(0).ToString)
    Console.WriteLine("Monthly Income is " & _
            myDataRow.Item(1).ToString)
    Console.WriteLine("PK  is " & myDataRow.Item(2).ToString)

    ' Add more data in a Data Row
    myDataRow = myTable2.NewRow()
    myDataRow.Item(0) = 120002
    myTable2.Rows.Add(myDataRow)

    Console.WriteLine("Annual Income is  " & _
            myDataRow.Item(0).ToString)
    Console.WriteLine("Monthly Income is " & _
            myDataRow.Item(1).ToString)
```

```
        Console.WriteLine("PK  is " & myDataRow.Item(2).ToString)

        myDataRow = myTable2.NewRow()
        myDataRow.Item(0) = 120004
        myTable2.Rows.Add(myDataRow)

        Console.WriteLine("Annual Income is  " & _
            myDataRow.Item(0).ToString)
        Console.WriteLine("Monthly Income is " & _
            myDataRow.Item(1).ToString)
        Console.WriteLine("PK  is " & myDataRow.Item(2).ToString)

    End Sub
End Class
```

GENERAL PRACTICE LAB: A LIBRARY APPLICATION WITH A DISCONNECTED DATA SET

Lab Objectives:
A general review of many of the issues of multitable Data Sets
  1. Creating a multitable, multirelation Data Set
  2. Adding Data Columns
  3. Specifying Data Relations and implementing foreign key rules through them
  4. Navigating through the data
  5. Manipulating the Data Rows

  - Adding Data Rows
  - Deleting Data Rows, including cascading delete
  - Updating Data Rows

  6. Applying the `Select` method to select only specific data from the tables
  7. Adding autonumbers to Data Columns

Application Overview

The application developed in this lab is a small standalone library system handled by one form. There are three parts to the form. The upper part deals with Patron management, which includes adding, deleting, and updating patrons, and navigating through the existing table of patrons with the arrow Buttons. In addition, each time a patron is shown, all that patron's activities (namely, what books were borrowed and when they were returned) are shown in the List Box. (See Figure 13.9.) To make the demonstration easy, the Auto Populate Button adds data to the Data Tables. Each patron and each book is automatically given an ID number, starting with 0. The examples that follow are based on the data shown in the figure.

The application also supports locating patrons by entering part of their name into the Patron Name textbox and clicking on the Locate Patron Button. In the example in Figure 13.10, the string "Ge" was entered into the textbox and when the Locate Patron Button was clicked, the list box displayed the list of names. The first name in the list box was also copied into the Patron Name textbox.

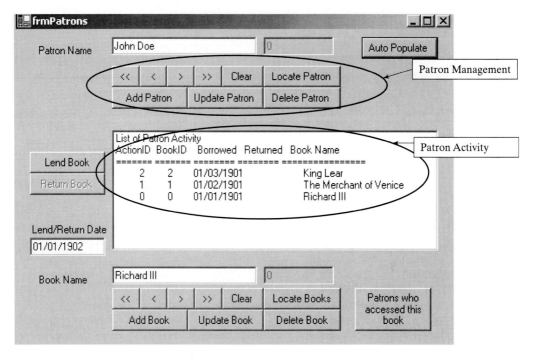

FIGURE 13.9
The Library application will initial data.

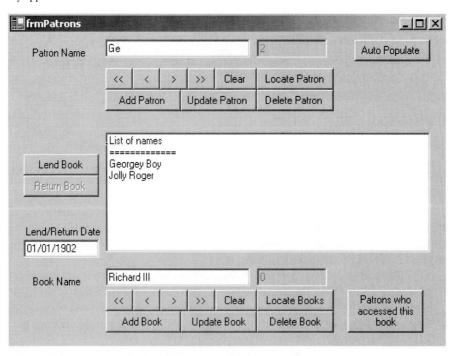

FIGURE 13.10
Search on patron name with the Locate Patrons button.

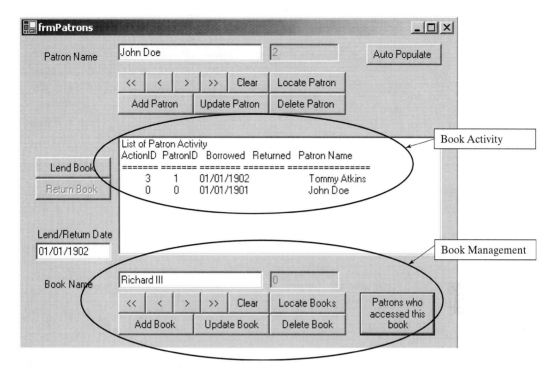

FIGURE 13.11
Sharing book activity of selectd patron.

The lower part of the form handles the books. Navigating is done with the arrow Buttons. Adding, updating, and deleting books are done with the appropriately named Buttons. Additionally, there is a Button with the title "Persons who accessed this book". Clicking on that Button will show all the activity on that book, namely, what patrons borrowed the book and when, if applicable, each returned it. The screenshot in Figure 13.11 shows the book activity of a book named Richard III.

The middle section of the form, apart from displaying patron activity, book activity, and patron names, also handles lending and returning books.

To lend a book to a patron, scroll to the appropriate patron in the top part of the form and to the appropriate book in the bottom part of the form. After changing the Lend/Return date in the textbox in the middle left part of the form, click the Lend Book Button. This will add an activity relating to the specific patron and book, marking that the book has been lent to that patron on the specified data. This activity will receive an automatically generated Activity ID. The books are virtual books, so the same book can be lent out simultaneously to many patrons.

In the center of the form is a list box where, as we just saw, patron activity and book activity are displayed. When an item (a line) in the list box is clicked, whether it is currently showing book activity or patron activity, the Returned Book Button becomes enabled. Clicking one of the three title lines in the list box will do nothing. Clicking the

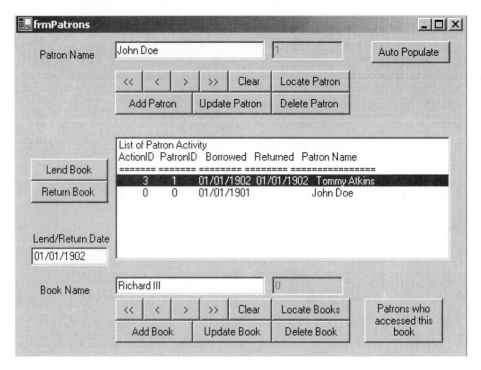

FIGURE 13.12
Returning a book with the Return Book button.

Return Book Button will update the activity in the clicked line with the date the book was returned. The date is taken from the Lend/Return textbox, provided that it is a valid date. Scrolling through the books or the patrons will show the updated return date. (See Figure 13.12.)

Part 1: Data Design

Three tables support the processes just described:

- Patrons
- Books
- Activity

The Patrons table contains a Patron Name, a string, and an automatically generated Patron ID. Patron ID is an Auto Increment Integer. The Books table also contains a string, this one containing the Book Name, and an automatically generated Book ID, which is also an Auto Increment Integer. Since the relationship between these two tables is a many-to-many relationship, meaning that each patron can borrow many books and each book can be borrowed by many patrons, the relationship between the two tables must be handled by a third table. That table is the Activity table. Activity contains an automatically generated Activity ID, which is an Auto Increment Integer, the Patron ID and Book ID, the date the book was borrowed, and the date it was returned.

The three Data Tables reside in a Data Set. We will first define (i.e., dimension) the Data Set and a few other necessary variables. Note that only the Data Set needs to be dimensioned in the Declarations section of the class. The Data Tables and Data Relations that will soon be added to the Data Set are included within it and as such will be recognized wherever the Data Set is recognized. The Data Set and variables are defined in the Declarations section to make them available to all the methods in the class (i.e., to all the subroutines in the form). The code is

```
Public Class frmPatrons
    Inherits System.Windows.Forms.Form

    ' The dataset of patrons, books, and activity
    Dim dsPatronBooks As New DataSet()

    ' Position in the Patrons Table
    Dim intPosition As Integer = 0

    ' Position in the Books Table
    Dim intBook As Integer = 0

    ' Position in the Activity Table
    Dim intActivityID As Integer
```

The Data Set itself, representing a standalone database, will be built when the form is loaded. The first table to be defined and instantiated is the Patrons table. The Data Table and its Data Columns are defined and instantiated. The Data Table is given a name at its instantiation. The code is as follows:

```
Private Sub frmPatrons_Load(ByVal sender As System.Object, _
            ByVal e As System.EventArgs) Handles MyBase.Load

    Try
        ' The table of patrons
        Dim colPatronName As New DataColumn()
        Dim colPatronID As New DataColumn()
        Dim tblPatrons As New DataTable("Patrons")
```

The appropriate properties are set in the Data Columns. Both Data Columns are given a Column Name, which will allow for *typed* referencing. The PatronID column is set as a unique read-only Auto Increment column. This will, in effect, make it an automatically generated Primary Key. Here is the code:

```
colPatronID.ColumnName = "PatronID"
colPatronID.DataType = GetType(Integer)
colPatronID.AutoIncrement = True
colPatronID.AutoIncrementStep = 1
colPatronID.ReadOnly = True
colPatronID.Unique = True

colPatronName.ColumnName = "PatronName"
colPatronName.DataType = GetType(String)
```

The Data Columns are then added to the `Columns` collection of the Data Table. With that, the first table is ready.

```
tblPatrons.Columns.Add(colPatronID)
tblPatrons.Columns.Add(colPatronName)
```

The same is done to define the Books table:

```
' The table of books
Dim colBookName As New DataColumn()
Dim colBookID As New DataColumn()
Dim tblBooks As New DataTable("Books")

colBookID.ColumnName = "BookID"
colBookID.DataType = GetType(Integer)
colBookID.AutoIncrement = True
colBookID.AutoIncrementStep = 1
colBookID.ReadOnly = True
colBookID.Unique = True

colBookName.ColumnName = "BookName"
colBookName.DataType = GetType(String)

tblBooks.Columns.Add(colBookID)
tblBooks.Columns.Add(colBookName)
```

The Activity table has five columns. Its primary key is a column named ActivityID, which is also a unique read-only auto-increment column. Note that, because *a Data Column cannot be assigned to more than one Data Table*, new Data Columns are defined for this Data Table, even though logically the column ActPatronID is the same as PatronID and ActBookID is the same as BookID. We also assign default values to the two dates in the table. The code runs as follows:

```
' The table of Activty
Dim colActivityID As New DataColumn()
Dim colActPatronID As New DataColumn()
Dim colActBookID As New DataColumn()
Dim colLendDate As New DataColumn()
Dim colReturnDate As New DataColumn()
Dim tblActivity As New DataTable("Activity")

colActivityID.ColumnName = "ActivityID"
colActivityID.DataType = GetType(Integer)
colActivityID.AutoIncrement = True
colActivityID.AutoIncrementStep = 1
colActivityID.ReadOnly = True
colActivityID.Unique = True

colActPatronID.ColumnName = "ActPatronID"
colActPatronID.DataType = GetType(Integer)
```

```
colActBookID.ColumnName = "ActBookID"
colActBookID.DataType = GetType(Integer)

colLendDate.ColumnName = "LendDate"
colLendDate.DataType = GetType(String)
colLendDate.DefaultValue = _
               Now.Month.ToString.PadLeft(2) & "/" & _
               Now.Day.ToString.PadLeft(2) & "/" & _
               Now.Year.ToString.PadLeft(4)

colReturnDate.ColumnName = "ReturnDate"
colReturnDate.DataType = GetType(String)
colReturnDate.DefaultValue = Nothing

tblActivity.Columns.Add(colActivityID)
tblActivity.Columns.Add(colActPatronID)
tblActivity.Columns.Add(colActBookID)
tblActivity.Columns.Add(colLendDate)
tblActivity.Columns.Add(colReturnDate)
```

The Data Tables are then added to the Data Set, which will then also allow the definition of Data Relations to map how the Data Tables relate to each other. It is through these Data Relations that the foreign keys will be mapped and the cascading delete made possible. The cascading delete will ensure that when a patron is deleted from the Patrons table, all the activity that patron did, as recorded in the Activity table, will automatically be deleted, too. This is possible because the Patrons table is defined as the Parent table in the Data Relation and the Activity table as the Child table. The same will be done with the Books table and its relation with the Activity table. When a book is deleted, all activity on that book will be deleted, too. Here is one more advantage of having a Data Set to manage the data rather than a array of Structures.

Two Data Relations are added to the Data Set. In this example, we will instantiate both relations with the same object, relActivity, which will be instantiated and added twice to the `Relations` Collection of the Data Set. The first time the object is instantiated, it is set to map the connection between the Patrons and the Activity tables. The second instantiation connects the Books table to the Activity table. Each instantiation has four parameters: the name of the relation as a string, the Parent column as a Data column, the Child column as a Data column, and a `True` value to create Constraint objects as well. The following is the code:

```
' Add tables to dataset
dsPatronBooks.Tables.Add(tblPatrons)
dsPatronBooks.Tables.Add(tblBooks)
dsPatronBooks.Tables.Add(tblActivity)

' Add relations
' These will automatically add cascading update and delete
' something an array or a structure cannot do.
Dim relPatronActivity As DataRelation
```

```
relPatronActivity = New DataRelation( _
 PatronActivity", _
 dsPatronBooks.Tables("Patrons").Columns("PatronID"), _
 dsPatronBooks.Tables("Activity").Columns("ActPatronID"), _
True)

dsPatronBooks.Relations.Add(relPatronActivity)

relPatronActivity = New DataRelation( _
  "BookActivity", _
 dsPatronBooks.Tables("Books").Columns("BookID"), _
 dsPatronBooks.Tables("Activity").Columns("ActBookID"), _
 True)

dsPatronBooks.Relations.Add(relPatronActivity)
```

Last, we will set an initial value for the date textbox:

```
txtDate.Text = Now.Month.ToString.PadLeft(2) & "/" & _
               Now.Day.ToString.PadLeft(2) & "/" & _
               Now.Year.ToString.PadLeft(4)

    Catch e1 As Exception
        MessageBox.Show(e1.Message)
    End Try
End Sub
```

Part 2: Build the Form

Add the controls to the form, and name it **frmPatrons**. Add the Buttons, textboxes, labels, and list box as shown with their appropriate Text properties. See details in Figure 13.13. Make the Enabled property of btnReturnBooks False. That will prevent returning a book that has not been lent out. Also make the Enabled property of txtPatronID and txtBookID False; neither can be updated.

Part 3: Handle the Patron Navigation Buttons

This is essentially the same algorithm as we saw already in Chapter 12. The variable intPosition keeps the current row number in the Patrons table. We navigate by changing its value and referencing the Data Row that is indexed by its value. After the items of each row are copied to their respective textboxes, the Show_Books subroutine is called to display all the books each patron has an activity with. The code is as follows:

```
Private Sub btnPatron1_Click(ByVal sender As System.Object, _
        ByVal e As System.EventArgs) Handles btnPatron1.Click
    Try
        ' Set the position
        ' And then read the items at that row position.
```

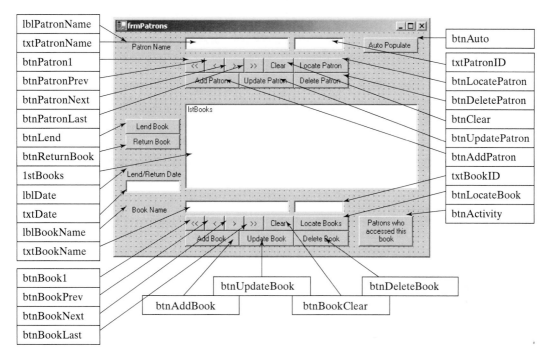

FIGURE 13.13
The Library application.

```
            intPosition = 0
            txtPatronName.Text = _
              dsPatronBooks.Tables("Patrons").Rows(intPosition).Item(1)
            txtPatronID.Text = _
              dsPatronBooks.Tables("Patrons").Rows(intPosition).Item(0)

        Call show_books()
    Catch
            txtPatronName.Text = ""
            txtPatronID.Text = ""
    End Try
End Sub

Private Sub btnPatronPrev_Click(ByVal sender As System.Object, _
        ByVal e As System.EventArgs) Handles btnPatronPrev.Click
    Try
        ' Set the position
        ' And then read the items at that row position.

        If intPosition > 0 Then intPosition -= 1

        txtPatronName.Text = _
          dsPatronBooks.Tables("Patrons").Rows(intPosition).Item(1)
```

```vbnet
            txtPatronID.Text = _
              dsPatronBooks.Tables("Patrons").Rows(intPosition).Item(0)

         Call show_books()
      Catch
         txtPatronName.Text = ""
         txtPatronID.Text = ""
      End Try
   End Sub

   Private Sub btnPatronNext_Click(ByVal sender As System.Object, _
         ByVal e As System.EventArgs) Handles btnPatronNext.Click
      Try
         ' Set the position
         ' And then read the items at that row position.
         If intPosition < _
              dsPatronBooks.Tables("Patrons").Rows.Count - 1 _
              Then intPosition += 1

         txtPatronName.Text = _
           dsPatronBooks.Tables("Patrons").Rows(intPosition).Item(1)
         txtPatronID.Text = _
           dsPatronBooks.Tables("Patrons").Rows(intPosition).Item(0)
         Call show_books()
      Catch
         txtPatronName.Text = ""
         txtPatronID.Text = ""
      End Try
   End Sub

   Private Sub btnPatronLast_Click(ByVal sender As System.Object, _
         ByVal e As System.EventArgs) Handles btnPatronLast.Click
      Try
         ' Set the position
         ' And then read the items at that row position.

         intPosition = _
           dsPatronBooks.Tables("Patrons").Rows.Count - 1

         txtPatronName.Text = _
           dsPatronBooks.Tables("Patrons").Rows(intPosition).Item(1)
         txtPatronID.Text = _
           dsPatronBooks.Tables("Patrons").Rows(intPosition).Item(0)
         Call show_books()
      Catch
         txtPatronName.Text = ""
         txtPatronID.Text = ""
      End Try
   End Sub
```

The Show_Books subroutine will display all the books the patron borrowed, the borrowing date, and the return date, if one exists. Displaying this information requires retrieving all the Data Rows in the Activity table that contain the Patron ID currently being displayed. The Select method is applied here to identify those rows. Then, for each one of those rows, we copy the items into a string variable that will soon be placed into the list box. The items are padded so that the display in the list box will have balance columns. The Book Name of each activity is then retrieved with a Select method on the Books table. In this Select, there is no need for a For Each loop, because we know that there is only one Book Name for every Book ID. Here is the code:

```
Private Sub show_books()
    Try
        Dim rowActions() As DataRow
        Dim rowBooks() As DataRow
        Dim rowAction, rowBook As DataRow
        Dim strLine, strLoan, strReturn As String
        Dim intBookID As Integer

        ' Make header lines in the List Box
        lstBooks.Items.Clear()
        lstBooks.Items.Add("List of Patron Activity ")
        lstBooks.Items.Add( _
            "ActionID  BookID    Borrowed    Returned    Book Name ")
        lstBooks.Items.Add( _
            "======= ======= ======== ======== =================")

        ' Select Data Rows from the Activity table
        rowActions = dsPatronBooks.Tables("Activity").Select( _
                "ActPatronID = " & CInt(txtPatronID.Text), _
                "ActivityID Desc")
        For Each rowAction In rowActions
            ' Get the data from the Activity table
            strLoan = rowAction.Item(3).ToString.PadLeft(18)
            If rowAction.Item(4).ToString.Length = 0 Then
                strReturn = rowAction.Item(4).ToString.PadLeft(20)
            Else
                strReturn = rowAction.Item(4).ToString.PadLeft(12)
            End If

            strLine = rowAction.Item(0).ToString.PadLeft(10) & _
                    rowAction.Item(2).ToString.PadLeft(10) & _
                    strLoan & strReturn

            ' get the data from the Books table
            intBookID = rowAction.Item("ActBookID")
            rowBooks = _
                dsPatronBooks.Tables("Books").Select("BookID = " & _
                intBookID)
            strLine &= "    " & rowBooks(0).Item("BookName")
```

```
                     ' Add the line to the List Box
                     lstBooks.Items.Add(strLine)

                     ' and display the first book's details in the TextBoxes
                     txtBookName.Text = rowBooks(0).Item("BookName")
                     txtBookID.Text = rowBooks(0).Item("BookID")
            Next
            Catch e1 As Exception
                 MessageBox.Show(e1.Message)
            End Try
      End Sub
```

Part 4: Handle the Patron Manipulation Buttons

These are essentially the same algorithms as we saw already in Chapter 12, except that the ID column is now filled automatically because of the way the Patron ID column was defined. Note that when a patron is deleted, all the activities of that patron in the Activity table are automatically deleted, too, thanks to the Data Relation. No additional code needs to be written, because this process is registered in the Data Set schema with the Data Relation object. The code is

```
      Private Sub btnAddPatron_Click(ByVal sender As System.Object, _
              ByVal e As System.EventArgs) Handles btnAddPatron.Click
          Dim rowPatron As DataRow
          rowPatron = dsPatronBooks.Tables("Patrons").NewRow
          rowPatron("PatronName") = txtPatronName.Text
          dsPatronBooks.Tables("Patrons").Rows.Add(rowPatron)
      End Sub

      Private Sub btnUpdatePatron_Click(ByVal sender As System.Object, _
              ByVal e As System.EventArgs) Handles btnUpdatePatron.Click
          dsPatronBooks.Tables("Patrons").Rows(intPosition).Item(1) = _
              txtPatronName.Text
          dsPatronBooks.Tables("Patrons").AcceptChanges()
      End Sub

      Private Sub btnDeletePatron_Click(ByVal sender As System.Object, _
              ByVal e As System.EventArgs) Handles btnDeletePatron.Click
          dsPatronBooks.Tables("Patrons").Rows(intPosition).Delete()
          dsPatronBooks.Tables("Patrons").AcceptChanges()
          Call btnPatronNext_Click(Me, e)
      End Sub
```

Part 5: Handle the Locate Patron Button

This Button shows all the patrons whose name contains the string that is currently in the Patron Name textbox. These patrons are identified with the Select method, this time applying the Like keyword and two asterisk placeholders. The result of the Select is placed in an array of Data Rows, and then, for each Data Row in the array, the Patron

Name item is added to the list box. The Patron Name and Patron ID of the first patron that satisfies the `Select` are also copied into the respective textboxes. The code is as follows:

```
Private Sub btnLocatePatron_Click(ByVal sender As System.Object, _
        ByVal e As System.EventArgs) Handles btnLocatePatron.Click

    Dim rowSelectRows() As DataRow
    Dim rowName As DataRow

    ' Prepare the Select method
    rowSelectRows = _
            dsPatronBooks.Tables("Patrons").Select( _
                "PatronName Like '*" & _
                txtPatronName.Text & "*'")

    txtPatronName.Text = rowSelectRows(0).Item(1)
    txtPatronID.Text = rowSelectRows(0).Item(0)

    ' show all the names in the List Box
    lstBooks.Items.Clear()
    lstBooks.Items.Add("List of names")
    lstBooks.Items.Add("=============")

    For Each rowName In rowSelectRows
        lstBooks.Items.Add(rowName.Item(1))
    Next
End Sub
```

Part 6: Handle the Book Navigation Buttons

The Book navigation Buttons apply the same algorithms as the Patron navigation Buttons:

```
Private Sub btnBook1_Click(ByVal sender As System.Object, _
    ByVal e As System.EventArgs) Handles btnBook1.Click
    Try
        ' Set the position
        ' And then read the items at that row position.

        intBook = 0
        txtBookName.Text = _
            dsPatronBooks.Tables("Books").Rows(intBook).Item(1)
        txtBookID.Text = _
            dsPatronBooks.Tables("Books").Rows(intBook).Item(0)
    Catch
        txtBookName.Text = ""
        txtBookID.Text = ""
    End Try
End Sub
```

```
Private Sub btnBookPrev_Click(ByVal sender As System.Object, _
        ByVal e As System.EventArgs) Handles btnBookPrev.Click
    Try
        ' Set the position
        ' And then read the items at that row position.

        If intBook > 0 Then intBook -= 1
        txtBookName.Text = _
          dsPatronBooks.Tables("Books").Rows(intBook).Item(1)
        txtBookID.Text = _
          dsPatronBooks.Tables("Books").Rows(intBook).Item(0)
    Catch
        txtBookName.Text = ""
        txtBookID.Text = ""
    End Try
End Sub

Private Sub btnBookNext_Click(ByVal sender As System.Object, _
        ByVal e As System.EventArgs) Handles btnBookNext.Click
    Try
        ' Set the position
        ' And then read the items at that row position.

        If intBook < dsPatronBooks.Tables("Books").Rows.Count - 1 _
            Then intBook += 1

        txtBookName.Text = _
          dsPatronBooks.Tables("Books").Rows(intBook).Item(1)
        txtBookID.Text = _
          dsPatronBooks.Tables("Books").Rows(intBook).Item(0)
    Catch
        txtBookName.Text = ""
        txtBookID.Text = ""
    End Try
End Sub

Private Sub btnBookLast_Click(ByVal sender As System.Object, _'
        ByVal e As System.EventArgs) Handles btnBookLast.Click

    Try
        ' Set the position
        ' And then read the items at that row position.

        intBook = dsPatronBooks.Tables("Books").Rows.Count - 1
        txtBookName.Text = _
          dsPatronBooks.Tables("Books").Rows(intBook).Item(1)
        txtBookID.Text = _
          dsPatronBooks.Tables("Books").Rows(intBook).Item(0)
    Catch
        txtBookName.Text = ""
        txtBookID.Text = ""
    End Try
End Sub
```

Part 7: Handle the Book Manipulation Buttons

The Book manipulation Buttons also apply the same algorithms as their Patron counterparts. Note that when a book is deleted, all the activities on that book in the Activity table are automatically deleted, too, thanks to the Data Relation object:

```
Private Sub btnAddBook_Click(ByVal sender As System.Object, _
        ByVal e As System.EventArgs) Handles btnAddBook.Click
    Dim rowBook As DataRow
    rowBook = dsPatronBooks.Tables("Books").NewRow
    rowBook("BookName") = txtBookName.Text
    dsPatronBooks.Tables("Books").Rows.Add(rowBook)
End Sub

Private Sub btnUpdateBook_Click(ByVal sender As System.Object, _
        ByVal e As System.EventArgs) Handles btnUpdateBook.Click
    dsPatronBooks.Tables("Books").Rows(intBook).Item(1) = _
        txtBookName.Text
    dsPatronBooks.Tables("Books").AcceptChanges()
End Sub

Private Sub btnDeleteBook_Click(ByVal sender As System.Object, _
        ByVal e As System.EventArgs) Handles btnDeleteBook.Click
    dsPatronBooks.Tables("Books").Rows(intBook).Delete()
    dsPatronBooks.Tables("books").AcceptChanges()
    Call btnBookNext_Click(Me, e)
End Sub
```

Part 8: Handle the Locate Books Button

This Button, as well, applies the same overall algorithm as its Patrons counterpart:

```
Private Sub btnLocateBooks_Click(ByVal sender As System.Object, _
    ByVal e As System.EventArgs) Handles btnLocateBooks.Click

    Dim rowSelectRows() As DataRow
    Dim rowName As DataRow

    rowSelectRows = _
        dsPatronBooks.Tables("Books").Select( _
            "BookName Like '*" & txtBookName.Text & "*'")

    txtBookName.Text = rowSelectRows(0).Item(1)
    txtBookID.Text = rowSelectRows(0).Item(0)

    ' show all the book names in the List Box
    lstBooks.Items.Clear()
    lstBooks.Items.Add("List of matching books")
    lstBooks.Items.Add("=====================")
    For Each rowName In rowSelectRows
        lstBooks.Items.Add(rowName.Item(1))
    Next
End Sub
```

Part 9: Handle the Patron Activity on a Book Button

This Button shows all the actions that all the patrons had on a particular book. It applies the same overall algorithm as Show_Books:

```
Private Sub btnActivity_Click(ByVal sender As System.Object, _
    ByVal e As System.EventArgs) Handles btnActivity.Click
    Dim rowActions() As DataRow
    Dim rowPatrons() As DataRow
    Dim rowAction, rowPatron As DataRow
    Dim strLine, strLoan, strReturn As String
    Dim intPatronID As Integer

    lstBooks.Items.Clear()
    lstBooks.Items.Add("List of Patron Activity ")
    lstBooks.Items.Add( _
        "ActionID  PatronID   Borrowed   Returned   Patron Name ")
    lstBooks.Items.Add( _
        "======= ======= ======== ======== ================")
    rowActions = dsPatronBooks.Tables("Activity").Select( _
            "ActBookID = " & CInt(txtBookID.Text), _
            "ActivityID Desc")

    For Each rowAction In rowActions
        strLoan = rowAction.Item(3).ToString.PadLeft(18)

        If rowAction.Item(4).ToString.Length = 0 Then
            strReturn = rowAction.Item(4).ToString.PadLeft(20)
        Else
            strReturn = rowAction.Item(4).ToString.PadLeft(12)
        End If

        strLine = rowAction.Item(0).ToString.PadLeft(10) & _
                  rowAction.Item(1).ToString.PadLeft(10) & _
                  strLoan & strReturn

        intPatronID = rowAction.Item("ActPatronID")
        rowPatrons = _
            dsPatronBooks.Tables("Patrons").Select( _
                "PatronID = " & intPatronID)
        strLine &= "    " & rowPatrons(0).Item("PatronName")

        lstBooks.Items.Add(strLine)

        txtPatronName.Text = rowPatrons(0).Item("PatronName")
        txtBookID.Text = rowPatrons(0).Item("PatronID")
    Next
End Sub
```

Part 10: Lending Books

To lend a book, we navigate to the patron and the book involved and click the Lend Book Button. The Button adds a row to the Activity table with the Patron ID, the Book

ID, and the date from txtDate. The value of the Activity ID and the Return Date columns are set automatically. The code runs thus:

```
Private Sub btnLend_Click(ByVal sender As System.Object, _
        ByVal e As System.EventArgs) Handles btnLend.Click
    Dim rowLend As DataRow

    If IsDate(txtDate.Text) Then
        ' If the date is valid, add new row to the Activity table

        rowLend = dsPatronBooks.Tables("Activity").NewRow
        rowLend("ActPatronID") = CInt(txtPatronID.Text)
        rowLend("ActBookID") = CInt(txtBookID.Text)
        rowLend("LendDate") = txtDate.Text

        dsPatronBooks.Tables("Activity").Rows.Add(rowLend)

        Call show_books()
    Else
        MessageBox.Show("Enter a valid date")
    End If
End Sub
```

Part 11: Returning a Book

Returning a book involves clicking the related lending activity in the list box, setting the return date in the appropriate textbox, and then setting the Return Date in the activity to this date by clicking on the Return Book Button.

When the List Box is clicked, the Activity ID, which is the first value in each line except the title lines in the List Box, is copied into the intActivityID variable and the Return Book Button is enabled. If a title line is clicked, the Cint function will raise an exception and the Return Book Button will not be enabled. Here is the code:

```
Private Sub lstBooks_SelectedIndexChanged( _
        ByVal sender As System.Object, _
        ByVal e As System.EventArgs) _
        Handles lstBooks.SelectedIndexChanged

    Try
        Dim strLine As String
        strLine = lstBooks.SelectedItem
        strLine = strLine.TrimStart
        strLine = strLine.Substring(0, strLine.IndexOf(" "))
        intActivityID = CInt(strLine)

        btnReturnBook.Enabled = True

    Catch
    End Try
End Sub
```

The Return Book Button itself updates the date of the Data Row in the Activity table that is identified by intActivityID:

```
Private Sub btnReturnBook_Click(ByVal sender As System.Object, _
        ByVal e As System.EventArgs) Handles btnReturnBook.Click
    Try
        Dim rowLend As DataRow
        If IsDate(txtDate.Text) Then
            dsPatronBooks.Tables("Activity").Rows( _
                intActivityID).Item("ReturnDate") = txtDate.Text
            Call show_books()
        Else
            MessageBox.Show("Enter a valid date")
        End If
        btnReturnBook.Enabled = False
    Catch
    End Try
End Sub
```

Part 12: The Auto Populate Button

The application also has an Auto Populate Button that adds test data to the Data Tables. In essence, what this Button does is to set the values in the textboxes and then call the appropriate subroutine to add the data to its Data Table. With the data added, the subroutine calls the subroutines that navigate to the beginning of the Patrons table and the Books table. Here is part of the code:

```
Private Sub btnAuto_Click(ByVal sender As System.Object, _
        ByVal e As System.EventArgs) Handles btnAuto.Click

    btnAuto.Enabled = False

    txtPatronName.Text = "John Doe"
    Call btnAddPatron_Click(Me, e)
    txtPatronName.Text = "Tommy Atkins"
    Call btnAddPatron_Click(Me, e)

    txtBookName.Text = "Richard III"
    Call btnAddBook_Click(Me, e)
    txtBookName.Text = "The Merchant of Venice"
    Call btnAddBook_Click(Me, e)

    txtDate.Text = "01/01/1901"
    txtBookID.Text = "0"
    txtPatronID.Text = "0"
    Call btnLend_Click(Me, e)

    Call btnPatron1_Click(Me, e)
    Call btnBook1_Click(Me, e)
End Sub
```

SUGGESTED HOME ASSIGNMENTS

1. Build an equivalent system to the library system we just developed, but on an SQL Server database.
2. Upgrade the library system we just built by adding another table named Sagas that will specify which other books, if any, are related to any specific book. For example, such a table may specify that the books Richard I, Richard II, and Richard III are all part of one saga called the Richards.

   - Add a new table, named Sagas. This table will contain two columns, Saga ID and Saga Name. Saga ID will be generated automatically as we did with Book ID and Patron ID. The data type of Saga Name is a string. The primary key of the new table is Saga ID.
   - Also add a new column to Books, named Saga ID. This column will contain the Saga ID in Sagas or nothing. If it contains a Saga ID, that Saga ID must already exist in the Sagas table. So, add a Data Relation to tie the two tables.
   - To upgrade the library system, add a new form that will navigate through the sagas and add, delete, and update them. Adding a saga involves adding a saga name. Updating a saga involves changing the saga name. Deleting a saga will not delete any of the books.
   - Add to the new form a List Box that will show for each saga a list of all the books of that saga.
   - Add navigation Buttons to this form and to the library form that will allow navigation from one form to the other. When opening the Saga form from the library form, the display in the Saga form should begin with the saga of the current book, if such a saga exists. Otherwise, show the first Saga and its books.
3. Add to the new Saga form another list box that will show the patron ID and name of every patron that borrowed at least one book of that Saga.

TEST YOURSELF

1. Discuss, with examples, when a Data Set is more appropriate than an array of Structures.
2. Discuss the relationship between Data Relation and Constraint objects in a Data Set.
3. Discuss what additional functionality a Data Set must handle because it is disconnected from the database.
4. Explain why the number of Data Columns in a Data Table must be the same as the number of items in the `Items` Collection of the Data Row object of the same Data Table.
5. What is `GetChildRows`?
6. Discuss what Constraints are and their types.
7. Why is there sometimes one collection of Columns in a Constraint object and sometimes two?
8. Discuss how metadata are handled in a Data Set.
9. Discuss the advantages of adding an expression in a Data Column.
10. Give three examples where you would add an expression to a table.
11. Discuss what `AutoIncrement` is and how to apply it.
12. Discuss the advantages of a Data View.
13. Discuss what a filter is and the advantages of it.
14. When is the `Select` method appropriate?

15. Discuss what Cascading Delete is and how it is declared in the schema.
16. Discuss the advantages of specifying Cascading Update in the schema.
17. What Data Column properties must be set and why?
18. Explain why navigation through the Data Rows of a Data Table is the same whether the Data Set schema was created by a Data Adapter or manually.
19. Explain the problem with changing a Data Set schema that was created by a Data Adapter.
20. Discuss what can be done with the `DataRowState` property.

A Review of Active Server Pages.NET

CHAPTER OBJECTIVES

After completing this chapter, students should understand

1. How Web pages work
2. How HTML Formats text using tags such as
   - `<Strong></Strong>`, `<Title></Title>`, etc
   - Learn about HTML Form Controls such as Text Boxes, Option Buttons, Submit and Reset Buttons, etc.
3. The `Page` class and its properties, methods, and events
4. ASP.NET basics including postback and code-behind programming model
5. HTML server controls
6. ASP server controls and validation controls

14.1 AIMS OF CHAPTER

This chapter focuses on Active Server Pages.NET (ASP.NET), the Web side of the .NET platform. More sophisticated than earlier versions of ASP, ASP.NET provides both rich user interfaces and solid structure to aid in Web application development. ASP.NET introduces server controls that are grouped into HTML server controls, Web form controls, validation controls, and rich user controls. Server controls provide access to server-side events, methods, and properties. Unlike earlier versions of ASP, ASP.NET pages are compiled and rendered on the client. Pages in ASP.NET can be designed in any of the .NET languages. Since the primary focus of this book is VB.NET, the same will be used for the design of ASP.NET pages in this and the next chapter. This chapter introduces the basics of ASP.NET and the server controls with examples. Although some of the Hyper Text Markup Language (HTML) tags are explained in this chapter, a basic understanding of how HTML tags work will be helpful.

Also, knowledge of structured query language (SQL) and a good knowledge of ADO.NET are required to understand this chapter.

14.2   WEBPAGES AND WEB SERVER

The Internet is a collection of thousands of smaller networks of computers. The language of the Web, HTML along with TCP/IP protocol, makes it possible for computers on different networks operating under different hardware, software, and operating systems to share information. This has revolutionized computing and has led to today's information superhighway. A Web browser is software used to display Web pages containing the HTML code. HTML itself is strictly text based. For most part, HTML makes use of *block tags* to display information in a formatted way.

It is important to understand what happens when a Web address is typed in the browser. Suppose a person sitting in his home in New York is browsing the Internet. He types `http://www.drexel.edu/` (Web address for Drexel University in Philadelphia) in the address area of the browser. The address is known as the Uniform Resource Locator or more popularly, URL. In this address, `www.drexel.edu` is referred to as the domain name. This domain name is immediately converted into its official Internet Protocol (IP) address using a Domain Name Services (DNS) server. The request (also known as *HTTP Request*)[28] to retrieve the Web page of Drexel University is routed through many switches and routers and eventually reaches the Web server physically located at the Drexel University in Philadelphia. The Web server responds (*HTTP Response*) by serving the file to the client computer in New York. An individual needs to know only the URL address of an organization to reach the organization's Web page. The Web server receives the request for a specific page and serves the page. If the file is not available, the client's browser shows an appropriate error message. Having looked at an oversimplified version of how Internet works, it is time to take a closer look at a simple Web page (Figure 14.1) and its code.

The example Web page shown consists of only two lines and a link to another Web page. Most of the tags in HTML will have a start tag and a corresponding end tag. Such pairs of tags are known as *block tags*. The page starts with a `<html>` tag and ends with a corresponding `</html>` tag. All the HTML code should be written between these two tags. Browsers are not case sensitive. They treat `<HTML>` and `<html>` the same way. Next, we have `<head>...</head>` block tag that encloses another block tag, `<title>...</title>`. The title for the Web page that appears on the title area of the browser is coded inside `<title>...</title>` tags. The information that appears in the browser window is written inside the `<body>...</body>` tags. A new paragraph can be written using the `<p>...</p>` tags. To provide a link to another page, `<a href = `"Address of the next page">`linked text</a>` is used. This is also known as the anchor tag. The text to be linked is provided between the anchor tags. Instead of text, an image can also be used to link to another page. The code is

---

[28]The request contains, among other information, the IP address of the Drexel University Web server and client IP address. Otherwise, the Web server would not know where to send the Web page.

FIGURE 14.1
Sample Web Page 1.

```
<html>
<head>
       <title>Sample Web Page!</title>
</head>
<body>
<P>This is a Sample Web Page!</P>
<P>
     Click <A href = "http://www.prenhall.com">here</A> to go to
the Prentice Hall Web site. </P>
</body>
</html>
```

The common HTML tags are given in Table 14.1. Note that this is not the complete set of HTML tags. There are many more tags to define additional formatting such

TABLE 14.1   Common HTML Tags.

Tag	What it does?
`<H1>..</H1>`	Heading Size Tag `<H1>` - Largest, `<H6>` - Smallest
` `	Line Break, hard return (NOT a block tag)
`<CENTER>..</CENTER>`	To center text, graphics, etc.
`<P>..</P>`	New Paragraph
`<B>..</B>`	Make text bold
`<I>..</I>`	Make text italic
`<U>..</U>`	Underline text
`<S>..</S>`	Strikethrough Text
`<HR>`	Horizontal Line (NOT a block tag)
`<SUB>..</SUB>`	Subscript
`<SUP>..</SUP>`	Superscript

as Table, Frame, and List etc. Many HTML tags also have additional attributes. For example, to add a background image to the Web page, the following code is used:

```
<body background="background.jpg">
```

Here, the background attribute of the body tag has been assigned an image name. Similarly, many other tags have other attributes. It is suggested that the student should refer to the numerous online resources to learn more about HTML tags. HTML editors such as FrontPage and Netscape Composer can also be used to develop Web pages. These editors provide WYSIWYG (What You See Is What You Get) features that aid even novice developers who know little about HTML tags to design professional looking Web pages. Though earlier versions of HTML did not have a lot of features, more recent versions of HTML have many neat features that make Web browsing more user friendly. For example, current HTML standards have *form controls*, which are presented next.

14.2.1 Form Controls

In order to design an interactive Web page, there should be a way for users to enter input into a Web page. Form controls are designed just for that. The current version of HTML supports the following form controls: Text Boxes, Option Buttons, Check Boxes, Text Area, Select Boxes, File Upload, and Command Buttons—Button, Submit, and Reset. All of these controls have properties, such as `Name`, `Size`, and `Value`, similar to the properties of the controls used in Visual Basic.NET. Figure 14.2 shows a Web page with more

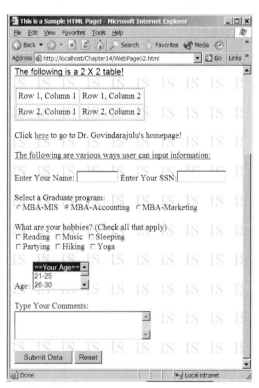

FIGURE 14.2
Sample Web page 2 with form controls.

HTML and Form controls. This page shows large and small fonts, different font types, a 2 × 2 Table, and all the different types of form controls that HTML supports. The Form controls, in general, are enclosed within `<Form ...>...</Form>` tags. This tag specifies what should happen after user enters data and clicks the Submit button. Specifically, the *action* and *method* attributes of the `Form` tag specify whether the data entered are sent as an attachment to a specified email address or sent to another page for processing.

The code for the page in Figure 14.2 is explained shortly in some detail. Comment lines enclosed within `<!-- ... -->` tags also offer additional explanation. The code is

```
<html>
<head> <!-- Heading Starts Here -->
<meta name="Author" content="Chittibabu Govindarajulu">
<meta name="keywords" content="Sample HTML, Forms, E-mail">
<meta name="description" content="Sample Webpage to explain HTML
capabilities">
<title>This is a Sample HTML Page!</title>
</head>    <!-- Heading is Complete -->
```

The preceding HTML code creates a title for the page. The `Meta` tags help search engines to locate a specific Web page on the Internet faster. Three `Meta` tags are shown—*Author*, *Keywords*, and *Description*:

```
<body background = "cisbgd.jpg">
<!-- Contents of the Page starts here -->

<h2>This is the Second Sample Page to<br>
   Demonstrate HTML & Form Controls!</h2><hr>

<!-- Different Font setting are illustrated here -->
<font size="+1">This is large font</font> <br>
<!-- <br> is the line break tag -->

<font size="-1">This is Small Font</font><br>
<font face="Arial" size="+1">This is Arial Font</font><br>
<font face="Times New Roman" size="1">This is Times New Roman
Font</font><br>
```

Next, the `<body>` tag's `background` attribute is set to an image so that the page will have a background. A formal title (not HTML `Title` tag) is then added with size setting to Heading 2 (`h2`). The tag `<hr>` produces a horizontal line below the title. Note that this is not a block tag—there is not an associated `</hr>` tag. The last few lines in the following code demonstrate HTML's capability to generate text of two different font sizes and font types:

```
<p>
<font face="Arial"><u>The following is a 2 X 2
table!</font></u></p>

<!-- Table definitions start here -->
<table cellspacing="2" cellpadding="5" border="1">
<!-- The above defines general table properties -->
```

```
<tr align="left">
    <td>Row 1, Column 1</td>
    <td>Row 1, Column 2</td>
</tr>
<!-- The above is code to generate a row with two columns -->

<tr align="left">
    <td>Row 2, Column 1</td>
    <td>Row 2, Column 2</td>
</tr>
<!-- This generates another row with 2 columns -->
</table>
```

A 2 × 2 table is presented next with a heading. The code shows that the definition of the first row is completed first before moving on to the next row. The column definitions are contained within each row definition. The overall table code is enclosed within `<table>...</table>` tags. The HTML Form control definitions start next. Note that all the Form controls *must* be enclosed within `<Form...>...</Form>` tags[29]. The Web page has been designed to forward user inputs to the email address: **Chitti@drexel.edu** by using `action` and `method` attributes of the `<Form>` tag. Here is the code:

```
<!-- User Inputs start here -->
<Form action="mailto:Chitti@drexel.edu" method="post">
<!-- Inputs are e-mailed to Chitti@drexel.edu -->

<p><u>The following are various ways user can Input
information:</u></p>
<p>
```

The following code creates a textbox, `txtStudentName`, that is 10 characters wide and can accept a maximum of 25 characters:

```
<!-- The following creates a textbox -->
Enter Your Name:
<Input type="text" name="txtStudentName" size="10"
maxlength="25">
<!-- The following creates a textbox with masked entry -->
Enter Your SSN:
<Input type="password" name="txtSSN" size="11"
maxlength="11"><br><br></p>
```

In this code, the `type` attribute of the `<Input>` tag is set to `Text` indicating that it is a textbox. If it is set to `Password`, as shown for the creation of the textbox `txtSSN`, the user entries in the textbox are masked. HTML Form controls also include hidden controls that are not visible on a Web page. They are declared by setting the `type` attribute of the `<Input>` tag to `hidden`. Hidden Form controls are used to carry values from one page to another.

---

[29]This is necessary so that all form control inputs are sent via the email. However, form controls linked to client script need not be placed inside <Form>...</Form> tags. Client script is defined in the next section.

Option buttons are defined next. To define an option button, the type feature of the `<Input>` tag is set to `Radio`. Option buttons in Visual Basic are placed inside a container so that they act as a single unit. In Web pages, however, option button controls are given the same name to act as a single unit. But, the `Value` property is assigned different values for different option buttons to identify which control was selected. In this example, all the option buttons are named `optClass`. To make an option button selected by default, type `Checked` in its definition as shown for option MBA-MIS. Option buttons are defined with the following code:

```
<!-- The following creates a set of Option buttons -->
<p>Select one of the following:<br>
<Input type="radio" Checked name="optClass" value="1"> MBA-MIS
   
<Input type="radio" name="optClass" value="2">
MBA-Accounting    
<Input type="radio" name="optClass" value="3">
MBA-Marketing</p>
```

The `type` attribute of the `<Input>` tag is set to `CheckBox` to create a check box. Each check box is assigned a unique `Name` and `Value`. The following code creates six check boxes:

```
<!-- The following creates six check boxes -->
<p>What are your hobbies? (Check all that apply)<br>
<Input type="checkbox" name="chkRead" Value="1"> Reading
   
<Input type="checkbox" name="chkMusic" value="1"> Music
   
<Input type="checkbox" name="chkSleep" value="1"> Sleeping <br>
<Input type="checkbox" name="chkParty" value="1"> Partying
   
<Input type="checkbox" name="chkHike" value="1">
Hiking    
<Input type="checkbox" name="chkYoga" value="1"> Yoga</p>
```

Select box Form control is similar to a list box control in Visual Basic. It does not have a textbox to enter user inputs. Users are allowed to select one or multiple items from a list. To create a select box, the `<Input>` tag is not used. Instead, a combination of `<Select>...</Select>` and `<Option>...</Option>` block tags are used. To make a list item selected by default, type `Selected` in the definition for that item:

```
<!- The following creates a select box for Age ->
<p>Age: <select name="Age" size="1">
<Option selected value="0">
<b>==Your Age==</Option>
<Option value="1">21-25</Option>
<Option value="2">26-30</Option>
<Option value="3">31-35</Option>
<Option value="4">36-40</Option>
```

```
<Option value="5">41-45</Option>
<Option value="6">Above 45</b></Option>
</select></p>
```

A text area control is defined with the use of the `<TextArea>....</TextArea>` tags, and the size of the text area is specified:

```
<!-- The following creates a Text Area -->
<p>Type Your Comments: <br>
<textarea cols="30" rows="3"
name="Comments"></textarea><br><br>
```

Finally, to submit the user inputs, a command button control of type `Submit` is required. To clear user inputs to the default state, a `Reset` command button control is used. For submitting data, an image can also be used instead of a `Submit` button. In addition to the `Submit` and `Reset` buttons, there is an additional generic command button control that can be used to activate events (similar to Visual Basic `Click` event) defined using client-side script. The syntax for `Submit` and `Reset` buttons is

```
<!-- The following creates a Submit button & a reset button -->
<Input type="submit" value="Submit Data">    <Input
type="Reset">
<!-- End of User Inputs -->
</Form>

</body>
</html>
```

Note the closing `</Form>`, `</body>`, and `</html>` tags.

Note that HTML Form controls do not have a Label control. The preceding example is meant to give the reader a bird's eye view of a Web page. There is more to HTML than what is presented here.

14.3   HOW FORM INPUTS ARE PROCESSED?

In the foregoing example, the form control inputs are sent to the specified email address as an attachment because of the following statement:

```
<Form action="mailto:Chitti@drexel.edu" method="post">
```

While this is useful, a better way is to send the inputs to another page for processing. In the traditional *Active Server Pages* (ASP) model,[30] it is the norm. For example, in

---

[30]Active server pages are developed, in general, using server-side VBScript and HTML. These pages have a .asp extension and are considered "dynamic" Web pages. The same page can produce different outputs for different inputs. A search results page in any site is an example of a dynamic page. The same page produces and displays different search results for different inputs.

the following statement, the inputs are sent to a page called `Process.asp` (ASP pages have `.asp` extension) for further processing:

```
<Form action="Process.asp" method="post">
```

The form inputs travel in Name = Value pairs separated by &. If John and 111-11-1111 were entered in the textboxes for name (`txtStudentName`) and SSN (`txtSSN`), respectively, `txtStudentName=John&txtSSN=111-11-1111` would be sent to the `Process.asp` page. If the method attribute is set to GET instead of POST, the form data would be passed to the next page as part of the URL:

http://localhost/Process.asp?txtStudentName John&txtSSN=111-11-1111.....

This `Process.asp` page would contain the code to process these inputs. The code in this page in most cases is a mix of VBScript and HTML. VBScript, a subset of Visual Basic, would contain the processing logic and HTML is used for rendering output. The .asp file itself resides on the Web server and executed by it when invoked. It is important to note that the code in .asp file is interpreted at runtime and not compiled. This is because the development of VBScript was an afterthought to meet the needs of the Internet. Most Visual Basic intrinsic functions can be used in VBScript. This scripting language also allows users to define their own subprograms and functions.

There are two flavors of VBScript: client-side VBScript and server-side VBScript. Since client-side VBScript is executed on the client's browser, it has limited functionality. Client-side VBScript is usually embedded into files with .htm or .html extension. In such files, form controls can be used without the `<Form>` tags. Because of this, the input values are processed by the script in the html file and executed by the client browser and not by the Web server. However, a typical use of client-side script is to validate the values entered in the form controls before passing it on to the server, thus reducing processing load on the Web server. Server-side VBScript is contained in files with .asp extension. Since the code is executed by the remote Web server, server-side script has more functionality such as connections to databases and their manipulation. Once the Web server completes the execution of the .asp page, *only* the results (mostly in HTML) are sent to the client. Thus, the client cannot see the processing logic contained in the file. The page is executed on the fly by the server and results are rendered on the client.

The Internet is considered "stateless." A Web server does not "remember" requests from specific clients. This is due to the use of HTTP (HyperText Transfer Protocol), which is connectionless by design. When a request for a file is received by the server, the file is served to the client and communications terminate. In other words, while it is possible to assess the average number of visitors to a specific site over a time unit, it is difficult to assess how many users are viewing the site's pages at any moment. This stateless nature of the Web makes it difficult to carry information contained in variables from one page to another. This is solved primarily by the use of cookies and session variables. Session variables are more resource intensive than cookies. A cookie is a piece of information stored on the client by the Web server. The cookies for a specific domain are sent along with the HTTP Request to the remote Web server. The Web server uses the information contained in cookies, alters them as necessary, and sends it back to the client along with the response (HTTP Response). Since the client sends the cookies to the server, information can be carried from one page to another; thus, "state" is maintained. Most Web servers commonly use cookies. If the Web server determines that cookies are not allowed by browsers (browsers allow the option of disallowing cookies to be set on the client), session variables are used. Actually, session variables also use a *SessionID* cookie to identify individual client sessions. All other information is stored in session variables. As mentioned earlier, session variables are resource intensive and hence are cleared from Web server's memory after a specified amount of time of inactivity or after session termination. The default time is 20 minutes, which can be altered. Session variables are specific to each client-server session, while cookies are not. Cookies are usually set to expire automatically after several weeks. However, a user can delete cookies from the system at any time.

ASP.NET architecture is completely different from the traditional asp model. It provides better state maintenance and handles some of the state maintenance on its own. The ASP.NET architecture is presented next.

14.4   INTRODUCTION TO ACTIVE SERVER PAGES.NET (ASP.NET)

ASP.NET is a unified Web development platform that provides the services necessary for building enterprise-class Web applications. A part of the .NET framework, ASP.NET is considered a revolution in Web application development. It offers a new programming model and a powerful infrastructure that allows the creation of a new breed of applications.

With ASP.NET, application development is more structured, and, unlike traditional ASP, the Web page and the page logic can reside in separate files. This is known as *code-behind* design (more later). Thus, Web application development is similar to windows application development. While it is still possible to create ASP.NET files using Notepad, Visual Studio.NET provides easy to use *graphical user interface* (GUI) tools for faster application development. These tools make debugging and editing easier. Since ASP.NET has been designed from scratch, there are many differences between traditional ASP and ASP.NET that will lead to compatibility issues. Converting ASP pages to ASP.NET pages is not as simple as renaming the file extension from `.asp` to `.aspx` (ASP.NET Web pages have `.aspx` extension). ASP.NET is not backward compatible. However, ASP.NET framework will not affect the functioning of the existing traditional ASP applications. They can run side by side. The `.asp` files will be executed by the script engine as usual and the `.aspx` files by the ASP.NET framework.

While it is not the aim of this book to compare ASP.NET with ASP, some comparisons are required to understand and appreciate the ASP.NET framework. Even though ASP has been successful in the world of Web development, a newer version would still be desirable for the following reasons:

- ASP-based pages are not compiled. ASP uses scripts (mainly VBScript), and the code is interpreted during runtime. This affects performance. Caching code in ASP does not help much.
- ASP lacks strongly typed variables. Only variable supported is `Variant`.
- ASP lacks structure to a Web page. The code and HTML are intermixed. The layout of the page and the code are almost inseparable in traditional ASP pages.

- Since different browsers display pages differently, programmers had to code ASP pages differently for different browsers.
- ASP does not have the capability to render Web pages to the different portable devices of today, such as palmtops and cellular phones.

ASP.NET benefits include the following:
- Compiled Web pages developed using any of the .NET-supported languages. This means better performance. All data types are supported.
- Code-behind architecture that separates page content and processing logic into different files.
- New server-based controls that provide rich interfaces and flexibility in coding.
- Rendering appropriate HTML for the server controls based on the client browser.
- An infrastructure to develop and deploy applications for the mobile devices.

14.4.1 Platform Requirements

In order to develop ASP.NET applications, Visual Basic.NET is required. The examples in this chapter and in chapters 15 and 16 were developed with Visual Studio.NET Professional edition. Since ASP.NET applications are Web applications, a Web server is required to run the applications developed in these chapters. The recommended Web server is Microsoft's Internet Information Server (IIS) 5.0 or higher. Other platform requirements are as follows:[31]

Processor:	Pentium II-class processor, 450 megahertz (MHz)
Operating System:	Microsoft Windows® XP Professional/Microsoft Windows 2000 Professional/Microsoft Windows 2000 Server/Microsoft Windows NT® 4.0 Workstation/Microsoft Windows NT 4.0 Server (Microsoft Windows Millennium Edition and Windows NT 4.0 Terminal Server are not supported)

14.4.2 Web Forms and Web Services

ASP.NET offers two models for developing applications: Web forms and Web services. Web forms enable developers to build powerful form-based Web pages. Using ASP.NET's server controls, Web pages can be designed rapidly from built-in reusable components. These server controls, as the name indicates, are programmed on the server and hence allow programmatic access to their properties, methods, and events. The code that runs on the server dynamically generates output suitable for the browser or client device. Visual Studio offers powerful *Rapid Application Development* (RAD) tools for designing and coding the Web form pages. These tools are part of the Visual Studio IDE (Integrated Development Environment) and they are a great help to design Web applications based on the code-behind model. Those who are new to Web application development will find that Web development is similar to Windows

---

[31]As given by Microsoft, `http://msdn.microsoft.com/vbasic/productinfo/sysreqs/default.asp`.

application development. Experienced developers of traditional ASP applications will find these tools a godsend even though it may take a little time getting used to the code-behind model (more on this model in Lab 14.1).

The Web services model allows remote access to server functionality. In an oversimplified way, Web services can be considered as subprograms or functions that perform a certain process and produce output when appropriate inputs are provided. But they reside on remote servers. Hence, it is possible for businesses to expose programmatic interfaces to their data and logic that can be used or manipulated by client or other server applications. The data exchange is XML based. As a result, applications written in any language can access XML Web services as long as they support XML standards. According to Microsoft "An XML Web service enables applications to exchange information between Web-based applications using standards like HTTP and XML messaging to move data across firewalls."

These models are possible through the ASP.NET structure, the .NET framework, and the .NET framework CLR (Common Language Runtime). This chapter and the next focus primarily on the Web forms model. The next section presents the Web forms code models.

14.4.3 Web Forms Code Models

The Web form pages, as mentioned earlier, contain server controls that can be programmed on the server side. There are two code models available to develop Web form pages. The first model is the traditional code inline model in which there is only one page. This page, with `.aspx` extension, contains the definitions of the server controls, the associated HTML, and the page logic. In the code-behind model, the page logic is placed in a separate file. (For Visual Basic.NET-based Web application, the file extension is .vb.) The Visual Studio IDE provides more support for the code-behind model, than the code-inline model. Before discussing the details of these models, it is necessary to understand the concept of round trips and the `Page` class.

14.4.4 Round Trips

When a client requests a Web page, the page is rendered on the client. After the client inputs information into the form controls, they are posted back to the server and the updated page after appropriate processing by the server is rendered back to the client. This is the postback architecture in ASP.NET. Thus, round trip is the trip the page makes from the client to the server and back.

14.4.5 The Page Class

Since ASP.NET is object based, a Web form page is actually a class derived from the `Page` class, which is contained in the `System.Web.UI` namespace. This page object represents the Web page and contains Web form controls. The object contains several properties, and some of them are listed in Table 14.2. The properties of the page object are helpful in identifying useful details such as client requests, responses to the clients, whether the page is displayed for the first time for that session, and validity of the page. The events associated with the page object are processed when invoked by the client

TABLE 14.2   Some Properties of the Page Object.

Property	Description
EnableViewState	True or False value of this property indicates whether the state of the server controls is maintained.
IsPostBack	Indicates whether the page is displayed for the first time (False) or not (True).
IsValid	True indicates that all the validation controls (covered later in this chapter) reported that the validation conditions have been met successfully. False indicates otherwise.
Request	Refers the request object.
Response	Refers the response object.
Session	Refers to the current session object.

request for a page. The Web form server controls also can invoke events contained in the page when their state changes. In addition to the events, the page object also contains methods. These methods serve useful purposes such as binding data to a server control, identifying the container for a specific server control, and finding whether a server control has child controls. The main events and few of the methods associated with the page object are presented in Table 14.3.

The difference between the Init and the Load events is that when the Init event executes, the server controls will have only default values and not the values entered by the client before the roundtrip. Only the Load event ensures that the controls contain values as entered by the user. In addition to the events in Table 14.3, there are other events such as PreRender and Error events. The Load event occurs every time the page is loaded in the postback architecture. This would make the code in the event execute for each postback. To avoid this, IsPostBack property of the page object comes in handy. When the page is accessed for the first time during a specific session, page object's IsPostBack property is False. During subsequent times that the page is

TABLE 14.3   Events/Methods of the Page Object

Event/Method	When Invoked?
Page_Init event	Invoked when the Web page is initialized.
Page_Load event	Invoked when the Web page is loaded.
Control event	Associated with server controls. Invoked when a control triggered the Web page to be reloaded.
Page_Unload event	Invoked when the Web page is unloaded from memory.
DataBind method	Binds a data source to a server control.
Equals method	Determines whether two objects are equal.
FindControl method	Helps to identify the container control for a specific server control.
HasControls method	Helps to determine whether a server control has child controls.

accessed (during the same session), the value becomes `True` automatically. This behavior of the `IsPostBack` property can be used in processing only required parts of the `Load` event code.

It is time to turn attention to the coding models of ASP.NET. In the code-behind model, there are two files: `.aspx` file for the user interface (UI) that contains all the server controls declarations and a .vb file for the code-behind page. These two files, act as a single unit when the application is run. The .vb file contains the class that defines the page logic. (It is imperative to note that this class inherits from the base `Page` class.) This class is compiled into a dynamic-link library (`.dll` file). The first time a client accesses the `.aspx` file (the Web page), which contains the UI elements, the ASP.NET framework compiles the file into another dynamic-link library. Note that the class generated by the `.aspx` file derives from the code-behind class. The `@Page` directives in the `.aspx` file link the page to the code-behind file. The second `.dll` file generates the output to the client. Thus, in the code-behind model, two pages act together, and they constitute an executable application.

In the code-inline model, there is only one Web forms page with the `.aspx` extension that contains both the UI elements and the page logic. However, the page logic in the file is not compiled into a class as in the code-behind model. In this model, the `.aspx` file derives from the `Page` class whereas the `.aspx` file in the code-behind model derives from the code-behind class (.vb file).

Functionally, both models are similar. Both use server controls and are compiled. In both models, clients access the `.aspx` file, and HTML output is streamed back to the client. Developers simply have a choice of selecting between two models. The code-inline model is simple and may be preferable to experienced ASP developers whereas the code-behind model is *similar* to Windows applications and is preferable to those who are new to Web application development. It is suggested that students follow the code-behind model as Visual Studio provides better support to it than the code inline model. While powerful IDE tools such as drag-and-drop support for non-visual elements (like data components) and IntelliSense are available to the code-behind model, very limited resources are available for the inline model. By default, when a new Web forms page is created, the IDE generates an `.aspx` page and a code-behind page. Lab 14.1 presents an application that demonstrates code for both the models.

ASP.NET offers the following five groups of server controls:

1. HTML server controls
2. Web form controls
3. validation controls
4. rich Web controls
5. user controls.

It is crucial to understand why we need server controls instead of simple HTML form controls. Server controls have several advantages that make them a vital element in the ASP.NET architecture:

- Server controls are compiled into objects with the page object.
- The ASP.NET architecture allows programmatic access to control properties, methods, and events. Thus, it is possible to access and manipulate the values of all the controls in the page.

- ASP.NET pages are truly event based, as is Windows programming.
- ASP.NET pages can generate HTML output appropriate to the browser, and they also have the ability to maintain control values (state) during roundtrips. These are done automatically without additional code.

14.5 HTML SERVER CONTROLS

HTML server controls are very similar to HTML controls with the exception of two additional attributes: `ID` and `runat = server`. These attributes make the regular HTML controls into server controls. HTML server controls were designed primarily to make it easier to upgrade the existing ASP Web applications to the ASP.NET infrastructure.

HTML server controls are defined within the `System.Web.UI.HtmlControls` namespace. This namespace contains specific classes for the HTML server controls, such as a textbox and a check box, and also a generic base class for the other HTML elements. The base class for all the HTML server controls is `System.Web.UI.HtmlControls.HtmlControl`. This class exposes several properties, methods, and events to other HTML controls. Each control also has specific additional properties and events. Table 14.4 shows some of the properties and methods of the base `HtmlControl` class.

The different HTML server controls, all of which can be programmatically accessed on the server, are as follows:

- **HtmlAnchor**—For the HTML anchor tag <a>
- **HtmlButton**—For HTML <button>
- **HtmlForm**—Allows access to <Form> on the server
- **HtmlGenericControl**—Allows access to tags that are not represented by a specific .NET framework, such as <div>, <body>, and <font>
- **HtmlImage**—For the <img> tag

TABLE 14.4 Few of the Base `HtmlControl` Class Properties and Methods

Property/Method	Description
`Attributes` property	Returns a collection of all the name/value pairs for the control.
`Disabled` property	Setting to `True` disables the control. Also, returns the Boolean value indicating whether control is disabled.
`EnableViewState` property	If set to `True`, maintains the viewstate (retains value) for the control after the current request is complete. A setting of `False` does not maintain viewstate.
`ID` property	Sets an identifier for the control.
`DataBind` method	Invokes data binding.
`HasControls` method	Returns `True` if the control has any child controls and `False` otherwise.

- **HtmlInputButton**—For the HTML `<input type = button>`, `<input type = submit>`, and `<input type= reset>` tags
- **HtmlInputCheckBox**—For the HTML `<input type = checkbox>` tag
- **HtmlInputFile**—For the HTML `<input type = file>` tag
- **HtmlInputHidden**—For the HTML `<input type = hidden>` tag
- **HtmlInputImage**—For the HTML `<input type = image>` tag
- **HtmlInputRadioButton**—For the HTML `<input type = radio>` tag
- **HtmlInputText**—For the HTML `<input type = text>` tag
- **HtmlSelect**—Represents the HTML `<select>` tag
- **HtmlTable**—For the HTML `<table>` tag
- **HtmlTableCell**—For the HTML `<td>` and `<th>` tags
- **HtmlTableRow**—For the HTML `<tr>` tag
- **HtmlTextArea**—Represents the HTML `<textarea>` tag

In a Web forms page that contains HTML server controls, clicking the Submit button triggers a round-trip to the server. The control values are posted to the server, the page is processed, and the updated page is sent back to the client. The main events for the HTML server controls are `ServerClick` and `ServerChange`. The `ServerClick` event is associated with the `HtmlAnchor`, `HtmlButton`, `HtmlInputButton`, and the `HtmlImage` controls. The `ServerChange` occurs for the `HtmlInputText`, `HtmlInputCheckBox`, `HtmlInputRadioButton`, `HtmlInputHidden`, `HtmlTextArea`, and `HtmlSelect` controls. While `ServerClick` triggers an immediate posting of form data to the server, the `ServerChange` events are handled in the order they occur, *only* when the page is posted by any of the other controls.

In the next lab section, the use of HTML server controls is demonstrated along with the code-behind and code-inline models of ASP.NET application. Although only a few HTML server controls are used in the lab application, it is a good start for a novice ASP.NET developer. The lab also demonstrates various other finer points of an ASP.NET application. For the Labs in this chapter and in Chapters 15 and 16 to work properly, a Web server (IIS) is required. When a Web server is installed, it creates a folder named *wwwroot* under the *inetpub* folder. The wwwroot folder is the default location for all Web applications. It should be noted that if the Web server is present on the same machine as Visual Basic.NET, the computer acts both as a client and a server. After the lab application is developed, running it from the Visual Studio/Visual Basic IDE opens the browser with the domain name *Localhost* (or the actual server name). Localhost represent the dummy local domain name. The application (named Mortgage) in Lab 14.1 is developed in a folder called Mortgage. Mortgage is a subfolder under Chapter14 folder. Chapter14 folder itself is a subfolder under wwwroot folder. Hence, the Web address of the Mortgage application would be as follows:

http://localhost/Chapter14/Mortgage/Mortgage.aspx

Note that `Mortgage.aspx` is the actual name of the Web page. It is not necessary to place applications under the default `wwwroot` folder. For simplicity, it is sufficient to say that it can be placed anywhere within the server.

Lab Exercises on CD

The lab exercises in Chapters 14, 15, and 16 are also available on CD. Since all these labs use the code-behind model, the following steps *must* be taken to make them work on student computers:

1. The labs for each chapter are contained within a folder of the chapter number. For example, Chapter 14's labs are under `chapter14` folder.
2. Copy the Chapter folders to the `wwwroot` folder.
3. Open `Control Panel`, and then open `Administrative Tools`. Select `Internet Services Manager` (in Windows 2000). From the left pane, expand the Computer Name. Expand the `Default Web Site` group. From the list, right-click the lab you want to run, and select `Properties` from the context menu. Click the `Create` button on the popup window. `Click Ok` to close the window and close `Internet Information Services` window. Now the application is setup correctly. This should be done for each lab application.
4. To run the application, type
   `http://localhost/ChapterNo/LabFolder/filename.ext` or
   `http://domain/ChapterNo/LabFolder/filename.ext`. For example, Lab 14.1 address would be `http://localhost/Chapter14/Mortgage/Mortgage.aspx`.

LAB 14.1: WEB FORMS WITH HTML SERVER CONTROLS

Lab Objectives:

The main lab objectives are as follows:
- Learn how to construct and code a Web forms page using code-behind and code-inline models of programming
- Learn about Visual Basic.NET IDE for developing ASP.NET applications
- Learn how HTML server controls work—specifically `HtmlInputText`, `HtmlInputButton`, and `HtmlGenericControl`
- Understand `ViewState` of controls
- Learn and Understand `@Page` directives

Application Overview:

This lab presents a simple application: the Mortgage Calculator. Three inputs are provided in `HtmlInputText` controls: `txtPrincipal`, `txtInterestRate`, and `txtYears`. An `HtmlInputButton` of type `Submit` is used for posting the form and an `HtmlGenericControl` for the `<div>` element is used for displaying the result.

Designing the Application—I (Code-Behind Model)

The code-behind model, as described earlier, consists of two files: an `.aspx` file for the UI elements and a .vb class file for the page logic. The VB.NET IDE provides great tools for the code-behind programming model. Open Visual Studio.NET and from the

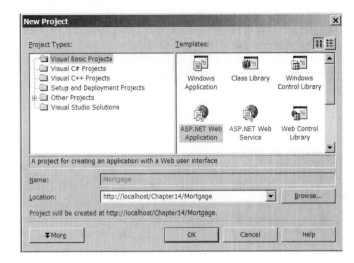

FIGURE 14.3
New project dialog box.

File menu, select `New` → `Project`. From the popup window, select `Visual Basic projects` and then `ASP.NET Web` application. In the Location textbox, type the name `Mortgage` as shown in Figure 14.3 at the end of URL, and click the `Ok` button.[32]

The IDE will show an empty Web form and from the toolbox on the left select the HTML tab to display HTML controls (Fig 14.4). VS.NET provides both a visual designer for the Web form, as well as a HTML code window. This is a neat feature. As controls are placed on the Web form to create the UI, HTML is generated automatically and editing the HTML reflects on the UI.

Rename the `WebForm1.aspx` in `Solution Explorer` window to `Mortgage.aspx`. Next, add the required controls to the Web form. As noted earlier, three textboxes, a submit button, and a `<div>` element for displaying output are required. The HTML toolbox provides all the necessary controls. Select and place the controls in the appropriate places on the Web form. Right-click on all the controls, and select `Run as Server Control` to make these controls HTML server controls. To place additional text on the Web form (such as a heading), code can be directly added in the HTML view by clicking on the HTML tab.

The completed Web page (with a sample calculation) is shown in Figure 14.5. In HTML view, add code wherever necessary in addition to the code generated by the IDE. The final code for the `Mortgage.aspx` page should be as follows:

```
<%@ Page Language="vb" AutoEventWireup="false"
Codebehind="Mortgage.aspx.vb" Inherits="Mortgage.WebForm1"
smartNavigation="true"%>
<!DOCTYPE HTML PUBLIC "-//W3C//DTD HTML 4.0 Transitional//EN">
<HTML>
```

---

[32]Again, installing IIS (Microsoft's Web server) will create a folder, wwwroot, under the folder Inetpub. The wwwroot folder is the default folder for storing Web applications. The ASP.NET application for the lab is stored in the Mortgage subfolder of the folder Chapter 14. Chapter 14 is a subfolder under the wwwroot folder.

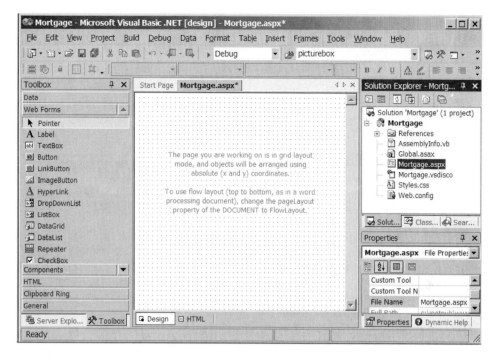

FIGURE 14.4
VS.NET IDE for ASP.NET.

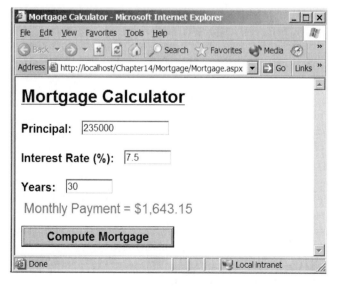

FIGURE 14.5
The Mortgage ASP.NET application.

```
<HEAD>
<title>Mortgage Calculator</title>
<meta content="True" name="vs_showGrid">
<meta content="Microsoft Visual Studio.NET 7.0" name="GENERATOR">
<meta content="Visual Basic 7.0" name="CODE_LANGUAGE">
<meta content="JavaScript" name="vs_defaultClientScript">
<meta content="http://schemas.microsoft.com/intellisense/ie5"
name="vs_targetSchema">
</HEAD>
<body MS_POSITIONING="GridLayout">
<h2><u><font face="Arial">Mortgage Calculator</font></u></h2>
<form id="Form1" method="post" runat="server">
    <P><h4><font face="Arial">Principal:  
    <INPUT type="text" size="14" id="txtPrincipal"
    runat="server"> </font></h4></P>
    <P><h4><font face="Arial">Interest Rate (%):  
    <INPUT id="txtInterestRate" type="text" size="5"
    runat="server"> </font></h4></P>
    <P><h4><font face="Arial">Years:  
    <INPUT id="txtYears" type="text" size="5" runat="server">
    </font></h4></P>
    <P><INPUT type="submit" value="Compute Mortgage"
    runat="server" id="btnSubmit" name="Submit1" style="FONT-
    WEIGHT : bold; FONT-SIZE: small; Z-INDEX: 101; LEFT: 15px;
    FONT-FAMILY: Arial; POSITION: absolute; TOP: 242px"></P>
    <DIV id="divResult" runat="server" style="DISPLAY: inline;
    FONT-WEIGHT: normal; FONT-SIZE: medium; Z-INDEX: 102; LEFT:
    15px; WIDTH: 313px; COLOR: red; FONT-FAMILY: Arial;
    POSITION: absolute; TOP: 193px; HEIGHT: 26px"
    ms_positioning="FlowLayout">Monthly Payment:</DIV>
</form>
</body>
</HTML>
```

Some key aspects of the preceding code are as follows:

- First of all, the page is designed using both design view and HTML view of the IDE. The controls were placed using the Design view, and some HTML code was added using HTML view. The page can be designed completely using the Design view alone. Both views are used to demonstrate that it could be done. When a Label HTML control is placed on the Web form in Design view, it creates a `<div>` HTML element. Using the Style builder dialog box available for the Style property of this control, different style elements were designed and ASP.NET automatically generated the code. The same was done for the HTML submit button. Note that there is no specific class available for the HTML label control; hence, HTMLGenericControl comes in handy here (more on this in the section title "Code-behind class file").

- The first line of code is the @Page directive, used to specify the page attributes, which affect how the page is created. These directives can also be using the

Properties window of the Web form. The `Language` attribute specifies the language used in the application. Any .NET-supported language can be used; in this application, it is VB.NET. `AutoEventWireup` specifies whether the page events such as `Load` and `Error` are automatically wired. A value of `False` (default) allows developers to override the page events. The `CodeBehind` attribute specifies the name of the code-behind file that contains the page logic. If the language used is VB, then the file extension would be .vb. Remember that in the code-behind programming model, there are two files. `Inherits` attribute specifies the name of the code-behind class the `.aspx` page inherits. `SmartNavigation` is a neat attribute that makes Web applications look like a traditional Windows application. The main identifying feature of a Web application while it is running is its 'flash' during page reloads. If the `SmartNavigation` is set to `True`, only parts of the page are updated and the rest of the page is unaffected. Basically, the Web page will not "flash," giving it the feel and look of a Windows application. It should be noted that this feature works only in Internet Explorer. The page properties can also be set using the Properties window.

- ASP.NET utilizes the `<Form>` tag for its postback architecture. In the preceding code, note that the `Action` attribute is missing in the `<Form>` tag. This is because the page is posted back to itself.[33] Thus, it is possible to access the server control's properties, call its methods, and react to the events it raises.

In addition to the Web form, the ASP.NET infrastructure creates many other files for the application as listed in `Solution Explorer`. The files associated with the lab application are as follows:

1. `Mortgage.aspx` and `Mortgage.aspx.vb`: For the code-behind model, as mentioned earlier, the first file contains the page UI and the second file the page logic (presented in the next section). The second file is visible in the `Solution Explorer` only when the *Show all files* tab icon is clicked.
2. `AssemblyInfo.vb`: A project information file that contains metadata about the assemblies such as name and version of the assembly.
3. `Web.config`: This file contains configuration data about the application.
4. `Global.asax`: An optional file for handling application-level events.
5. `Styles.css`: Cascading style sheets file to be used within the application.
6. `Mortgage.vsdisco`: An XML-based file that contains links (URLs) to resources providing discovery information for an XML Web service. Since the lab application is not a Web service, this file does not serve any useful purpose.

The Code-Behind Class File. Select the `Mortgage.aspx.vb` file in `Solution Explorer`, and then click the `View code` icon. VS.NET IDE automatically generates this class file when the Web form is designed with server controls. The file inherits from the `Page` class. The code is

---

[33]See Chapter 15 to learn how to pass form control data to a different page.

```
Public Class WebForm1
Inherits System.Web.UI.Page
     Protected WithEvents txtPrincipal As _
System.Web.UI.HtmlControls.HtmlInputText
     Protected WithEvents divResult As _
System.Web.UI.HtmlControls.HtmlGenericControl
     Protected WithEvents txtInterestRate As _
System.Web.UI.HtmlControls.HtmlInputText
     Protected WithEvents txtYears As _
System.Web.UI.HtmlControls.HtmlInputText
     Protected WithEvents btnSubmit As _
System.Web.UI.HtmlControls.HtmlInputButton
     Protected WithEvents Form1 As _
System.Web.UI.HtmlControls.HtmlForm
```

The declarations for all the server controls used in the `.aspx` page are generated automatically. Followed by this is the *Web Form Designer Generated code*. Note that since there is no specific class available for the HTML `<div>` element. This element, `divResult`, is declared as an `HtmlGenericControl`. In addition to this auto-generated code, page logic needs to be added for processing server control inputs. Since the `HtmlInputButton` control of type `Submit` is used, the page will be submitted when the button is clicked, thus initiating a postback. Add the following code for the `Page Load` event:

```
Private Sub Page_Load(ByVal sender As System.Object, ByVal e As _
System.EventArgs) Handles MyBase.Load
  'Put user code to initialize the page here
  If Not Page.IsPostBack Then
     divResult.Visible = False
  Else
     Dim sngPrincipal, sngInterest, sngPayment As Single
     Dim intYears As Integer

     sngPrincipal = CSng(txtPrincipal.Value)
     sngInterest = CSng(txtInterestRate.Value) / 1200
     intYears = CInt(txtYears.Value) * 12

     sngPayment = sngPrincipal * (sngInterest / (1 - (1 + _
     sngInterest) ^ -intYears))

     divResult.Visible = True
     divResult.InnerHtml = "Monthly Payment = " & _
     FormatCurrency(sngPayment)
  End If
End Sub
```

Instead of `Submit` type `HtmlInputButton`, `HtmlButton` control can also be used, but clicking on the button will not initiate a round-trip unless the `ServerClick` event is coded for the button control. For a good interface design, the results should be visible only after calculations are performed. Hence, in the `Load` event, `IsPostBack` property is checked to see whether the page is accessed for the first time. `IsPostBack` property value will be `True` if a postback occurred. The calculations are straightforward and `InnerHtml`[34] property of `divResult` is assigned the result of calculations after appropriate formatting. To run the application, press `F5`. This will open the application in the browser (Figure 14.5). Test the application by entering sample values and clicking the button. Note that this is a simple application; hence, invalid input values will crash it. *Validation* server controls presented later in the chapter can be used to check validity of inputs. Note that the server controls maintain their values after each postback. This is possible because the default value for `EnableViewState` attribute of the `@Page` directive is `True` and hence not explicitly shown in the code for `.aspx` page. Additionally, viewstate for an individual control can be turned on or off by setting the `EnableViewState` property of the control to `True` or `False`, respectively, using the Properties window. The default is `True`. ASP.NET uses a hidden form control to store the viewstate for the whole page. This can be viewed by selecting `Source` from the `View` menu of the Internet Explorer browser. When the page is posted back to the server, viewstate information is updated and stored back on the hidden control. For the example calculation shown in Figure 14.5, the part of the rendered HTML code is as follows (note the presence of a hidden form control, '`_VIEWSTATE`'):

```
..............................
<body MS_POSITIONING="GridLayout">
<h2><u><font face="Arial">Mortgage Calculator</font></u></h2>
<IFRAME ID=__hifSmartNav NAME=__hifSmartNav STYLE=display:none
src="IEsmartnav1"></IFRAME>
<form name="Form1" method="post" action="Mortgage.aspx"
id="Form1" __smartNavEnabled="true">
<input type="hidden" name="__VIEWSTATE"
value="dDwtODYyMjQyMTI0O3Q8O2w8aTwxPjs+O2w8dDw7bDxpPDk+O2z47bDx0PHA8bDxW
aXNpYmxlOz47bDxvPGY4+Ozs+Oz4+Oz4+Oz7Z3sk61T4GaNO0VONQFvd70gSnRA==" 
/>
..............................
```

The code-behind programming model is summarized as follows:

1. There are two main files. The `Mortage.aspx` is designed using the HTML view and Design view. This file contains the page UI, and it inherits from the class declared in `Mortage.aspx.vb` file.
2. The `Mortgage.aspx.vb` file contains the declarations of all the server controls used in the `.aspx` file and the page logic in the `Load` event. This file inherits from the `Page` class.
3. Both files are compiled at runtime, and the compiled .dll file for the `.aspx` file generates the HTML output to the client.
4. ASP.NET maintains page state across postbacks using a hidden control named `_VIEWSTATE`.

---

[34]`InnerHtml` property is a property of the `HtmlGenericControl` class and this property can be used to set or get the content between the opening and closing tags of the control, divResult, in the lab example.

Designing the Application – II (Code-Inline Model)   As discussed earlier, in this model there is only one file with `.aspx` extension. Both the UI and the page logic are contained in the same page. Hence, there is no separate class file that the `.aspx` file inherits, in direct contradistinction to the code-behind model. The `.aspx` file in this model inherits from the `Page` class. The code equivalent of the lab application based on this model is as follows:

```
<%@ Page Language="VB" SmartNavigation="true" %>
<script runat="Server">
      Sub Page_Load(obj As object, e As EventArgs)
         If Not Page.IsPostBack Then
             divResult.Visible = False
         Else
             Dim sngPrincipal, sngInterest, sngPayment As Single
             Dim intYears As Integer

             sngPrincipal = CSng(txtPrincipal.Value)
             sngInterest = CSng(txtInterestRate.Value) / 1200
             intYears = CInt(txtYears.Value) * 12

             sngPayment = sngPrincipal * (sngInterest _
      / (1 - (1 + sngInterest) ^ -intYears))

             divResult.Visible = True
             divResult.InnerHtml = "Monthly Payments = " & _
      FormatCurrency(sngPayment)
          End If
End Sub
      </script>

<html>
<body>
<h2><u><font face="Arial">Mortgage Calculator</font></u></h2>
<form id="Form1" method="post" runat="server">
<P><h4><font face="Arial">Principal:  <INPUT
type="text" size="14" id="txtPrincipal" runat="server">
</font></h4></P>
<P><h4><font face="Arial">Interest Rate (%):  <INPUT
id="txtInterestRate" type="text" size="5" runat="server">
</font></h4></P>
<P><h4><font face="Arial">Years:  <INPUT id="txtYears"
type="text" size="5" runat="server"></font></h4></P>
<P><INPUT type="Submit" value="Compute Mortgage" runat="server"
id="btnSubmit" name="Submit1" style="FONT-WEIGHT: bold; FONT-
SIZE: small; Z-INDEX: 101; LEFT: 15px; FONT-FAMILY: Arial;
POSITION: absolute; TOP: 242px"></P>
<DIV id="divResult" runat="server" style="DISPLAY: inline; FONT-
WEIGHT: normal; FONT-SIZE: medium; Z-INDEX: 102; LEFT: 15px;
WIDTH: 313px; COLOR: red; FONT-FAMILY: Arial; POSITION: absolute;
TOP: 193px; HEIGHT: 26px" ms_positioning="FlowLayout">Monthly
Payment:</DIV>
```

```
</form>
</body>
</html>
```

The code in this page is similar to the code in the code-behind model. Script tags are used in this code, and the @Page directive, for obvious reasons, does not have reference to the code-behind file and its class. Since, the code-behind model is the default model for VS.NET/VB.NET IDE, it is the recommended model. The remaining lab exercises in this chapter and Chapters 15 and 16 follow the code-behind model.

14.6   ASP.NET WEB FORM CONTROLS

All the Web form controls inherit from the `WebControl` class that exists in the `System.Web.UI.WebControls` namespace. Thus, all the controls that inherit from `WebControl` class have a common set of properties, events, and methods. Some of these are listed in Table 14.5. The need for another set of server controls in addition to ASP.NET framework's HTML server controls is clear, given the following considerations:

• Because of the differences in Web browsers, Web form controls automatically adjust their output depending on the target browser. HTML server controls render same output to all browsers.

• Web form controls simplify the process of creating interactive Web forms. Developers need not have knowledge of how HTML form controls work.

• Web form controls do not map directly to HTML tags. Hence, it allows developers to build new controls that automatically generate the UI.

• HTML server controls generate only one HTML element while several of the Web form controls generate more than one HTML element. For example, they

TABLE 14.5   Few of the `WebControl` Base Class Properties, Methods, and Events

Property/Method/Event	Description
`Attributes` property	Returns a collection of all the name/value pairs for the control.
`AccessKey` property	Sets or returns the keyboard shortcut key that moves the focus to the control.
`BackColor` property	Sets or returns the background color for the control.
`Enabled` property	`True` enables the control and `False` disables it. Also, returns the current state of the control.
`EnableViewState` property	Default value is `True`. Setting it to `False` disables viewstate of the control during subsequent page requests.
`ForeColor` property	Sets or returns the foreground color for the control.
`DataBind` method	Causes data binding to occur.
`HasControls` method	Returns a Boolean value indicating whether the control contains child controls.
`DataBinding` event	Invoked when the control is bound to a data source.

automatically add a label to the check box or radio button. This is very similar to Windows application development environment.

The Web form controls that inherit from the base `WebControl` class have their own properties and events. For example, the `CheckBox` Web form control has properties such as `AutoPostBack` and `Checked`. The `CheckedChanged` event is invoked when the check box is checked/unchecked. Lab 14.2 has examples of such specific events for Web form controls. The different Web form controls are briefly discussed in the next section.

14.6.1 Web Form Controls

There are several Web form controls, but only a few are discussed in this book, for brevity. These controls are similar to Windows form controls; hence, it is not difficult to understand the controls and their characteristics. The Web form controls are listed under the Web forms section of the toolbox. These can be easily placed on the form during design time by simple drag and drop and the HTML is automatically generated. However, the code for declaring each control is presented here for easy reference and to compare with HTML and HTML server controls. Also, the specific properties and events for each control are presented. Note that when the page is compiled, the controls in the page are compiled into objects. During runtime, appropriate equivalents of the Web form controls in the form of HTML form controls are rendered on the browser. For example, a `TextBox` Web form control will be rendered as a `<Input type="Text">` control. The control definitions in the following sections are taken from Lab 14.2.

14.6.2 Label Control

The label control is used to display text that cannot be modified by the client. Usually, labels are used to provide instructions for textboxes to clients. The ASP.NET code to create a label control is

```
<asp:label id="Label1" runat="server" Width="315px" Height="37px"
Font-Bold="True" Font-Size="Large" Font-Names="Arial" Font-Under-
line="True">New Mortgage Calculator</asp:label>
```

Note the `asp` prefix. All the Web form controls have the `asp` prefix and the control declaration end with the associated end tag as in `</asp:label>`. Labels do not have any specific events that can be raised. In addition to the design time addition of Web form controls, they also can be added during runtime. This is true in general for any server control. The following code adds a new Label control to a page:

```
Dim lblMessage As New Label()
Controls.Add(lblMessage)
lblMessage.Text = "This is a new Label"
```

After declaring an object of type `Label`, the new label control is added to the `Controls` collection[35] of the page using the `Add` method of the `Controls` collection. Then, the `text` property of the label is set to display an appropriate message.

---

[35]The page object's `Controls` property represents the collection of controls in the page.

14.6.3 TextBox Control

The purpose of a textbox control is to accept inputs. Unlike HTML controls, textbox control comes only in one flavor. There are no separate Web form controls that can render `<input type="Password">`, `<input type="Hidden">`, or `<textarea>` controls on the browser. Instead, the properties of the `TextBox` control can be altered to make it behave like the aforementioned controls. If the `TextMode` property is set to `SingleLine` (default value), it results in a regular textbox. If the property is set to `MultiLine`, multiple lines of input can be provided similar to a textarea control. Also, `Rows` and `Columns` properties determine number of rows and columns allowed in the control. This control has a `TextChanged` event that is invoked when the input text changes in the textbox. The code is

```
<asp:textbox id="txtInterestRate" runat="server" Width="73px"
Height="25px" Font-Bold="True" Font-Names="Arial"></asp:textbox>
```

14.6.4 CheckBox Control

This control allows users to check or uncheck a selection. The main event for the control is `CheckedChanged` event triggered when the `CheckBox` is checked or unchecked. The code is as follows:

```
<asp:checkbox id="chkTotalPmt" runat="server" Font-Names="Arial"
Font-Bold="True" Height="28px" Width="195px" Text="Show Total Pay-
ments"></asp:checkbox>
```

14.6.5 RadioButton Control

The `RadioButton` control allows users to select an item from a group of items. This control also has the `CheckedChanged` event as its main event:

```
<asp:RadioButton id="Male" runat="server" Font-Names="Arial"
Font-Bold="True" Height="28px" Width="131px" Text="Male" Group-
Name="Gender"></asp:RadioButton>
<asp:RadioButton id="Female" runat="server" Font-Names="Arial"
Font-Bold="True" Height="25px" Width="123px" Text="Female"
GroupName="Gender"></asp:RadioButton>
```

Note that the `RadioButton` controls belonging to the same group should have the same value for their `GroupName` attribute.

14.6.6 Button Control

The `Button` control can be used to submit the Web forms page along with user inputs in other controls. The `Button` control has an associated `Click` event that can be programmed on the server side. The code is

```
<asp:button id="btnCompute" AccessKey="M" runat="server"
Width="186px" Height="51px" Font-Bold="True" Font-Names="Arial"
Text="Compute Mortgage"></asp:button>
```

In addition to the `Button` control, `ImageButton` and `LinkButton` controls can also be used to submit the page. The function of the `AccessKey` attribute in the `Button` declaration is to provide a keyboard shortcut key to click the button. As in a Windows application, pressing the ALT key and the keyboard shortcut key clicks the button.

14.6.7 DropDownList Control

Similar to Windows DropDownList control, the Web form DropDownList control contains a list of items that the users can select from.

The items form a collection and contained in the Items property of the control. The Items property provides an icon that invokes the ListItem Collection Editor to provide list of items (Figure 14.6). The code to declare a DropDownList along with a list of choices is as follows:

```
<asp:dropdownlist id="ddlYears" runat="server" Width="117px"
Height="37px" Font-Bold="True" Font-Names="Arial">
        <asp:ListItem Value="10 Years">10 Years</asp:ListItem>
        <asp:ListItem Value="15 Years">15 Years</asp:ListItem>
        <asp:ListItem Value="20 Years">20 Years</asp:ListItem>
        <asp:ListItem Value="25 Years">25 Years</asp:ListItem>
        <asp:ListItem Value="30 Years" Selected="True">30
        Years</asp:ListItem>
</asp:dropdownlist>
```

The main event for the DropDownList is the SelectedIndexChanged event.

Another similar control is the ListBox control, except that it allows users to select multiple items from the list of choices.

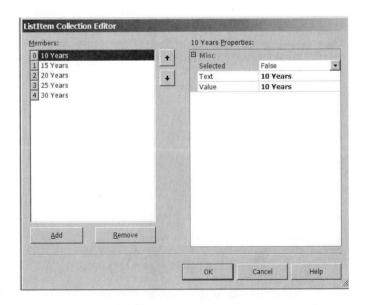

FIGURE 14.6
ListItem Collection Editor.

14.6.8   RadioButtonList Control

This is a new control provided by the ASP.NET framework and is not available in Windows forms. This control is similar to `DropDownList` and `ListBox` controls. The main event for this control is the `SelectedIndexChanged` event. This control also has a `ListItem collection Editor` to add items to the list. The list choices appear next to each other or one below another depending on whether the `RepeatDirection` property is set to `Horizontal` or `Vertical`. This control renders the `<input type="Radio">` control to the browser. The code is

```
<asp:RadioButtonList id="RadioButtonList1" runat="server"
Width="94px" Height="66px" Font-Bold="True" Font-Names="Arial">
    <asp:ListItem Value="Male"
    Selected="True">Male</asp:ListItem>
    <asp:ListItem Value="Female">Female</asp:ListItem>
</asp:RadioButtonList>
```

14.6.9   Other Controls

Only some of the Web form controls were presented so far. The purpose is to give a peek into how these controls are declared and to demonstrate how similar these controls are to the Windows forms controls. Several other Web form controls in the ASP.NET infrastructure are as follows:

- `LinkButton` control
- `ImageButton` control
- `Image` control
- `HyperLink` control
- `ListBox` control
- `CheckBoxList` control, and
- `Table` control

The next lab section demonstrates some of the Web form controls and their characteristics. This lab is similar to Lab 14.1 functionally, but uses Web form controls instead of HTML server controls.

LAB 14.2: WEB FORMS WITH WEB FORM SERVER CONTROLS

Lab Objectives:
The main lab objectives are as follows:
- Learn how to construct and code Web forms page using Web forms server controls
- Learn about server control events
- Learn more about postback

Application Overview:

This lab presents another version of the Mortgage Calculator application. Two `TextBox` controls—txtPrincipal and txtInterestRate—are used to accept inputs for principal and interest rate, respectively. A `DropDownList` control is used to select the mortgage period, and a `CheckBox` control is provided to indicate whether the user would like to know the total amount he or she would have paid at the end of mortgage period. The results will be displayed in three separate label controls: lblMonthPayment, lblYears and lblTotalPayment. Finally, a `Button` control is used to submit the page. Note that the code-behind model of programming is followed in this lab.

Designing the Application

Open Visual Studio.NET, and, from the `File` menu, select `New - > Project`. From the popup window, select `Visual Basic projects` and then `ASP.NET Web Application`. In the Location textbox, type the name ASPMortgage, and then click the `Ok` button. Rename the WebForm1.aspx to ASPMortgage.aspx. Drag and drop the controls and the final UI should be as shown in Figure 14.7.

The default appearance of the control can be modified as required by manipulating the `Style` property of each control. The code generated by the VS.NET IDE for the .aspx file is as follows:

```
<%@ Page Language="vb" AutoEventWireup="false"
Codebehind="ASPMortgage.aspx.vb" Inherits="ASPMortgage.WebForm1"
SmartNavigation="True"%>
<!DOCTYPE HTML PUBLIC "-//W3C//DTD HTML 4.0 Transitional//EN">
<HTML>
<HEAD>
<title>Mortgage Calculator</title>
```

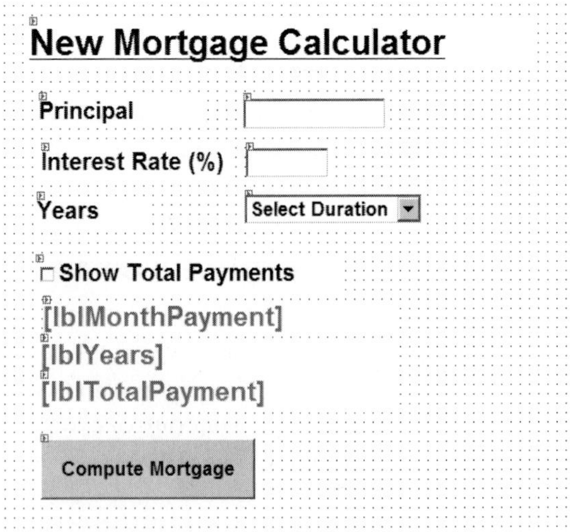

FIGURE 14.7
The Web form for ASPMortgage application (with Web Form Controls).

```
      <meta content="Microsoft Visual Studio.NET 7.0"
      name="GENERATOR">
      <meta content="Visual Basic 7.0" name="CODE_LANGUAGE">
      <meta content="JavaScript" name="vs_defaultClientScript">
      <meta
content="http://schemas.microsoft.com/intellisense/ie5"
name="vs_targetSchema">
</HEAD>
<body MS_POSITIONING="GridLayout">
<form id="Form1" method="post" runat="server">
<asp:label id="Label1" style="Z-INDEX: 101; LEFT: 30px; POSITION:
absolute; TOP: 22px" runat="server" Font-Underline="True" Font-
Names="Arial" Font-Size="Large" Font-Bold="True" Height="37px"
Width="315px">New Mortgage Calculator</asp:label>
<asp:label id="lblTotalPayment" style="Z-INDEX: 112; LEFT: 36px;
POSITION: absolute; TOP: 310px" runat="server" Font-Names="Arial"
Font-Size="Medium" Font-Bold="True" Height="18px" Width="310px"
ForeColor="Red"></asp:label>
<asp:label id="lblYears" style="Z-INDEX: 111; LEFT: 36px;
POSITION: absolute; TOP: 279px" runat="server" Font-Names="Arial"
Font-Size="Medium" Font-Bold="True" Height="18px" Width="310px"
ForeColor="Red"></asp:label>
<asp:textbox id="txtInterestRate" style="Z-INDEX: 106; LEFT:
179px; POSITION: absolute; TOP: 125px" runat="server" Font-
Names="Arial" Font-Bold="True" Height="25px"
Width="73px"></asp:textbox>
<asp:label id="Label2" style="Z-INDEX: 102; LEFT: 30px; POSITION:
absolute; TOP: 81px" runat="server" Font-Names="Arial" Font-
Bold="True" Height="28px" Width="138px">Principal</asp:label>
<asp:label id="Label3" style="Z-INDEX: 103; LEFT: 31px; POSITION:
absolute; TOP: 124px" runat="server" Font-Names="Arial" Font-
Bold="True" Height="29px" Width="141px">Interest Rate
(%)</asp:label>
<asp:label id="Label4" style="Z-INDEX: 104; LEFT: 31px; POSITION:
absolute; TOP: 168px" runat="server" Font-Names="Arial" Font-
Bold="True" Height="30px" Width="135px">Years</asp:label>
<asp:textbox id="txtPrincipal" style="Z-INDEX: 105; LEFT: 179px;
POSITION: absolute; TOP: 84px" runat="server" Font-Names="Arial"
Font-Bold="True" Height="26px" Width="125px"></asp:textbox>
<asp:dropdownlist id="ddlYears" style="Z-INDEX: 107; LEFT: 182px;
POSITION: absolute; TOP: 167px" runat="server" Font-Names="Arial"
Font-Bold="True" Height="37px" Width="117px">
  <asp:ListItem Value="0" Selected="True">Select
  Duration</asp:ListItem>
  <asp:ListItem Value="10 Years">10 Years</asp:ListItem>
  <asp:ListItem Value="15 Years">15 Years</asp:ListItem>
  <asp:ListItem Value="20 Years">20 Years</asp:ListItem>
  <asp:ListItem Value="25 Years">25 Years</asp:ListItem>
  <asp:ListItem Value="30 Years">30 Years</asp:ListItem>
</asp:dropdownlist>
<asp:checkbox id="chkTotalPmt" style="Z-INDEX: 108; LEFT: 33px;
```

```
POSITION: absolute; TOP: 210px" runat="server" Font-Names="Arial"
Font-Bold="True" Height="28px" Width="195px" AutoPostBack="True"
Text="Show Total Payments"></asp:checkbox>
<asp:label id="lblMonthPayment" style="Z-INDEX: 110; LEFT: 38px;
POSITION: absolute; TOP: 247px" runat="server" Font-Names="Arial"
Font-Size="Medium" Font-Bold="True" Height="8px" Width="308px"
ForeColor="Red"></asp:label>
<asp:button id="btnCompute" style="Z-INDEX: 109; LEFT: 36px;
POSITION: absolute; TOP: 349px" accessKey="M" runat="server"
Font-Names="Arial" Font-Bold="True" Height="51px" Width="186px"
Text="Compute Mortgage"></asp:button>
</form>
</body>
</HTML>
```

This code is generated automatically as, and when, new controls are placed on the form. Hence, the order in which the control declarations appear on the page may not necessarily be same as the order in which controls appear on the UI.

Controls other than the controls that submit the page (such as `Button` and `LinkButton` controls) can also initiate a round-trip. For example, in the preceding `CheckBox` declaration code, the `AutoPostBack` property is set to `True`, and if the `CheckBox` status changes during runtime, the page will be posted immediately. More details about postback are discussed later in this lab.

To demonstrate the events associated with the `CheckBox`, `DropDownList`, and `Button` controls, double-click each one of them to add the appropriate code. Following is the completed code for the code-behind file:

```
Public Class WebForm1
  Inherits System.Web.UI.Page
    Protected WithEvents Label1 As System.Web.UI.WebControls.Label
    Protected WithEvents Label2 As System.Web.UI.WebControls.Label
    Protected WithEvents Label3 As System.Web.UI.WebControls.Label
    Protected WithEvents Label4 As System.Web.UI.WebControls.Label
    Protected WithEvents txtInterestRate As _
    System.Web.UI.WebControls.TextBox
    Protected WithEvents txtPrincipal As _
    System.Web.UI.WebControls.TextBox
    Protected WithEvents ddlYears As _
    System.Web.UI.WebControls.DropDownList
    Protected WithEvents btnCompute As _
    System.Web.UI.WebControls.Button
    Protected WithEvents lblMonthPayment As _
    System.Web.UI.WebControls.Label
    Protected WithEvents lblYears As System.Web.UI.WebControls.Label
    Protected WithEvents lblTotalPayment As _
    System.Web.UI.WebControls.Label
    Protected WithEvents chkTotalPmt As _
    System.Web.UI.WebControls.CheckBox
```

```vb
#Region " Web Form Designer Generated Code "

    ............

#End Region

Private Sub Page_Load(ByVal sender As System.Object, ByVal e As _
System.EventArgs) Handles MyBase.Load
    'Put user code to initialize the page here
    If Not Page.IsPostBack Then
        lblMonthPayment.Text = ""
        lblTotalPayment.Text = ""
        lblYears.Text = ""
    End If
End Sub

Private Sub ddlYears_SelectedIndexChanged(ByVal sender As _
System.Object, ByVal e As System.EventArgs) Handles _
ddlYears.SelectedIndexChanged
    'Display Period Selected
    lblYears.Text = "Loan Duration " + ddlYears.SelectedItem.Text
End Sub

Private Sub btnCompute_Click(ByVal sender As System.Object, ByVal _
e As System.EventArgs) Handles btnCompute.Click

    'Compute Mortgage and Display Results
    Dim sngPrincipal, sngInterest, sngPayment As Single
    Dim intYears As Integer

    sngPrincipal = CSng(txtPrincipal.Text)
    sngInterest = CSng(txtInterestRate.Text) / 1200
    Select Case ddlYears.SelectedItem.Text
        Case "10 Years"
            intYears = 10
        Case "15 Years"
            intYears = 15
        Case "20 Years"
            intYears = 20
        Case "25 Years"
            intYears = 25
        Case "30 Years"
            intYears = 30
    End Select

    intYears = intYears * 12

    sngPayment = sngPrincipal * (sngInterest _
    / (1 - (1 + sngInterest) ^ -intYears))

    lblMonthPayment.Text = "Monthly Payments = " & _
    FormatCurrency(sngPayment)

    lblTotalPayment.Text = "Total Payments " & _
    FormatCurrency(sngPayment * intYears)
```

```
          'Display/Hide Total Payment
          lblTotalPayment.Visible = chkTotalPmt.Checked
     End Sub

     Private Sub chkTotalPmt_CheckedChanged(ByVal sender As _
     System.Object, ByVal e As System.EventArgs) Handles _
     chkTotalPmt.CheckedChanged
          'Show/Hide Total Payment Result
          lblTotalPayment.Visible = chkTotalPmt.Checked
     End Sub
End Class
```

The page `Load` event clears all the output from the three labels. There are three other events that need brief discussion:

- First, when the button is clicked, the page is submitted and the `Click` event is invoked. This event code computes the monthly and total payments (through the use of a `Select Case` structure) based on the inputs provided. Then, the results are assigned to the labels—`lblMonthPayment` and `lblTotalPayment`. This event is straightforward, occurring as the result of a button click.

- The code in the second event `SelectedIndexChanged` stores the mortgage period in the label, `lblYears`. This event does not occur immediately after the `DropDownList` selection changes, and it is invoked only when the page is submitted by a control such as the Button control. After the page submission, the server events are executed in the order they are invoked. For example, in the lab, suppose the user changes the mortgage period in the `DropDownList` from 30 years (default) to 15 years. Since `SelectedIndexChanged` event is associated with the control, it should be triggered immediately. However, this does not happen since no postback had occurred. Once the Button (or any other control that triggers a postback) is clicked, postback occurs and `SelectedIndexChanged` and `Click` events occur in that order. If, for some reason, `SelectedIndexChanged` needs to be triggered as soon as the selection changes, the `AutoPostback` property of the control should be set to `True`.

- For demonstration purposes, the `CheckBox` is setup with its `AutoPostBack` property set to True. Once the `CheckBox` is checked or unchecked, postback occurs at once and the `CheckedChanged` event is executed. Note, however, that if there are any pending events to be executed, they are executed before the `CheckedChanged` event. This `CheckBox` event makes the label, `lblTotalPayment`, visible or invisible based on `CheckBox`'s current state.

Build and run the application by pressing F5. While Lab 14.1 and 14.2 presented how HTML and Web form server controls work, the code is not perfect. What if alphanumeric inputs are provided in the textboxes? This would make the application crash. In Web applications, crashes should not be allowed, since these applications may be accessed by thousands of customers. ASP.NET provides a set of Validation server controls to check the validity of inputs.

14.7   VALIDATION CONTROLS

When user inputs are provided in form controls, they need to be checked for validity. Since these inputs may be used for database manipulation, inputs should be in an acceptable format to preserve data validity and integrity. Additionally, in a strongly typed language such as Visual Basic.NET, input data should be of correct type. Invalid data constitute one of the known reasons for application crashes, and in a Web setting, such crashes are highly undesirable, since thousands of customers may be accessing the Web application. Traditionally, inputs are validated using client-side script such as JavaScript or VBScript (mostly JavaScript), and in other instances validation is done on the server-side. ASP.NET framework has simplified input validation by providing a set of controls. For example, if a `TextBox` control needs to be validated, appropriate validation control or controls can be added to the form, and their properties can be set to link to the `TextBox` control. It is as simple as that. When validation controls are added to a Web form, input values entered in the control to be validated are passed to the validation control automatically. The validation controls check the values, and if they are invalid, the `IsValid` property of the validation control is set to `False`. Even if one validation control's `IsValid` property has a value of `False`, the `IsValid` property of the Web page itself becomes `False`. Then the page is sent back to the client with appropriate validation errors.

The validation controls automatically generate client-side script based on the client's browser type. Currently, however, the client-side validation works only if the browser supports Dynamic HTML (DHTML). The advantage of client-side validation is that errors are detected immediately, and the page will not be posted back to the server in case of an error. As an added security measure, server-side validation is also performed. This is a safeguard against "spoofed" values from hackers. There are six validation controls currently available, all of which inherit from the base `BaseValidator` class that is part of the `System.Web.UI.WebControls.BaseValidator` namespace. The following are the most commonly used properties of the `BaseValidator` class:

- `ControlToValidate` property: Sets or returns the name of the control to be validated.
- `EnableClientScript` property: As the name indicates, a value of `True` enables client script and `False` disables it. The default value is `True`.
- `ErrorMessage` property: Contains the text of the error message.

The `BaseValidator` class also has a `Validate` method to perform validation on the assigned server control. The various validation controls are as follows.

- `RequiredFieldValidator`: Checks the control to see whether the control is empty.
- `RangeValidator`: Checks whether the value in the control falls within the assigned minimum and maximum values. If the control has no value, validation is *not* performed.
- `CompareValidator`: Checks whether the value in one control matches the value in another control or a specified value.

- `RegularExpressionValidator`: Checks to see whether the value in a control is in a given format.
- `CustomValidator`: Checks control values using user-defined functions.
- `ValidationSummary`: This control displays all the validation errors in a summary format.

More than one validation control can be used to validate a single control. For example, suppose a textbox control needs to be validated. Suppose the values allowed are 10,000 to 1,000,000. Intuitively, it is obvious that `RangeValidator` is the control that should be used. If any value beyond the allowable range is entered in the textbox, the `RangeValidator` does its job and the `IsValid` property of the page becomes `False`. Also, an appropriate error message is displayed. However, if there is no value to check (i.e., if nothing is entered in the textbox), the `RangeValidator` does nothing. In this situation, `RequiredFieldValidator` control is also required to make sure inputs are entered in the textbox.

When validation controls are dragged and dropped at appropriate places on the Web form, preferably close to the controls they intend to validate, the IDE automatically generates the code for the validation controls based on their property settings. However, in the following sections, ASP.NET code to declare these controls is presented along with important characteristics of each control.

14.7.1 `RequiredFieldValidator` Control

As mentioned earlier, this control checks whether a specific control contains values. The main properties of this control are `ControlToValidate`, `ErrorMessage`, and `Display`. The first two properties are self-explanatory. The `Display` property determines the display behavior of the validation control. The values for this property are `Static`, `Dynamic`, and `None`. `Static` value indicates that the validation control is part of the page and the layout of the page does not change when error messages are displayed. `Dynamic` indicates that the validation controls become part of the page only when validation fails. Hence, page layout is altered when error messages are displayed. A value of `None` indicates that error messages are not displayed. This value is used when `ValidationSummary` control displays all validation errors. The code is

```
<asp:RequiredFieldValidator id="ReqdFldValdtrtxtPrincipal"
runat="server" Width="178px" Height="4px" Font-Bold="True" Font-
Size="XX-Small" Font-Names="Arial" ErrorMessage="Enter amount for
principal" ControlToValidate="txtPrincipal"> </asp:RequiredField-
Validator>
```

14.7.2 `RangeValidator` Control

This validator checks whether the values in the control falls within the specified range. The main properties of this control are `ControlToValidate`, `MaximumValue`, `MinimumValue`, and `Type`. `Type` indicates the data type of the value to be checked. The code is

```
<asp:rangevalidator id="RngValdtrtxtPrincipal" runat="server"
Font-Names="Arial" Font-Size="XX-Small" Font-Bold="True"
Height="17px" Width="188px" ControlToValidate="txtPrincipal"
ErrorMessage="Amount should be between 10,000 and 1,000,000"
Type="Integer" MaximumValue="1000000"
MinimumValue="10000"></asp:rangevalidator>
```

14.7.3 CompareValidator Control

The main properties of this control are ControlToValidate, ControlToCompare, ValueToCompare, ErrorMessage, and Display. A typical use of the control is to compare the password entered in one textbox with the password entered in the second (confirm password) textbox. Instead of comparing two controls, this validation control can also check the value of the control with a specified value given in the ValueToCompare property.

```
<asp:CompareValidator id="CmprValdtrtxtPassword"
ControlToCompare="txtPassword" ControlToValidate="txtConfirmPasswd"
ErrorMessage="Passwords does not match!"></asp:CompareValidator>
```

14.7.4 RegularExpressionValidator Control

This validation control checks whether the input values are in the specified format. If not, the validation fails. The properties to be noted for this control are ControlToValidate, ValidationExpression, and ErrorMessage. ValidationExpression property describes the format of the value to be checked. This control is useful in checking values such as telephone numbers and social security numbers. The code is

```
<asp:regularexpressionvalidator id="RegExpValdtrtxtInterestRate"
runat="server" Font-Names="Arial" Font-Size="XX-Small" Font-
Bold="True" Height="12px" Width="172px" ControlToValidate="txtIn-
terestRate" ErrorMessage="Enter interest rate in 00.00 format"
ValidationExpression="[0-9]{2}.[0-9]{2}"> </asp:regularexpression-
validator>
```

In this declaration, the ValidationExpression is [0-9]{2}.[0-9]{2}. [0-9] means any digit between 0 and 9. {2} indicates that two digits are required. The period (.) means that a period is expected. Similarly, after the period, two digits are required. Thus, values of 12.50, 08.95, or 06.50 are acceptable, while 12.735, 8.9, or 03.5 are not.

14.7.5 CustomValidator Control

This control makes use of a user-defined function to check the value of the control to be validated. If a client-side function is used, ClientValidationFunction property is assigned the function name. But if a server-side validation is performed, ServerValidate event must be coded. Thus, the important properties of this control are

`ControlToValidate`, `ClientValidationFunction`, and `ErrorMessage`. Lab 14.3 contains an example of this control with the `ServerValidate` event. The code is

```
<asp:customvalidator id="CstmVldtrddlYears" runat="server" Font-
Names="Arial" Font-Size="XX-Small" Font-Bold="True" Height="12px"
Width="131px" ControlToValidate="ddlYears" ErrorMessage="Select
mortgage duration"></asp:customvalidator>
```

14.7.6 `ValidationSummary` Control

This control is used to provide a summary of all the validation error messages. This control can be used instead of displaying validation error messages in individual validation controls. It is a matter of design preference. The main properties of this control are `HeaderText`, `DisplayMode`, `ShowSummary`, and `ShowSummaryBox`. `HeaderText` gives a title at the top of the validation summary. `DisplayMode` can be `List`, `BulletList`, or `SingleParagraph`, thus indicating how the summary is displayed. The default is `BulletList`. `ShowSummary` indicates whether the validation summary is displayed inline. The default value is `True`. `ShowSummaryBox` indicates whether the validation summary is displayed in a popup message box. The default is `False`. Here is the code:

```
<asp:validationsummary id="vldnsummaryWebform" runat="server"
HeaderText="Please correct the following errors">
</asp:validationsummary>
```

In Lab 14.3, Lab 14.2 was modified to include several validation controls. Except for `ValidationSummary` and `CompareValidator` controls, the use of all validation controls are demonstrated.

LAB 14.3: THE MORTGAGE APPLICATION (LAB 14.2) WITH VALIDATION CONTROLS

Lab Objectives:
The main lab objectives are as follows:
- Learn how to construct and code validation controls
- Learn about `ServerValidate` event for `CustomValidator` control

Application Overview

This lab uses the same application in Lab 14.2, but with validation controls. For the `TextBox` control, `txtPrincipal`, two validation controls—`RequiredFieldValidator` and `RangeValidator`—will be added. Similarly, `RequiredFieldValidator` and `RegularExpressionValidator` controls will be added to the `TextBox` control, `txtInterestRate`. Finally, for the `DropDownList`, `ddlYears`, a `CustomValidator` control is used.

Designing the Application

Open Visual Studio.NET, and select `New` → `Project` from the `File` menu. From the popup window, select `Visual Basic Projects` and then `ASP.NET Web Application`.

TABLE 14.6   Validation Controls for Lab 14.3 and Their Properties

Validation Control	Property Settings	
	Property	**Value**
RequiredFieldValidator	ID ControlToValidate ErrorMessage	ReqdFldValdtrtxtPrincipal txtPrincipal Enter amount for principal
RangeValidator	ID ControlToValidate ErrorMessage MaximumValue MinimumValue Type	RngValdtrtxtPrincipal txtPrincipal Amount should be between 10,000 and 1,000,000 1000000 10000 Integer
RequiredFieldValidator	ID ControlToValidate ErrorMessage	ReqdFldValdtrtxtInterestRate txtInterestRate Enter interest rate
RegularExpressionValidator	ID ControlToValidate ErrorMessage ValidationExpression	RegExpValdtrtxtInterestRate txtInterestRate Enter interest rate in 00.00 format [0-9]{2}.[0-9]{2}
CustomValidator	ID ControlToValidate ErrorMessage	CstmVldtrddlYears ddlYears Select mortgage duration

In the Location textbox, type the name `ValidASPMortgage`. Instead of redesigning the application from scratch, we can add the Web form from Lab 14.2 and modify it as necessary. First, delete the default Web form `WebForm1.aspx` from the `Solution Explorer`. Then, from the menu, select `Project` → `Add Existing Item`. From the popup menu, select the `ASPMortgage.aspx` file after locating it. (The code-behind class file `ASPMortgage.aspx.vb` will be added automatically.) Once the `.aspx` file is added to the project, rename it to `ValidASPMortgage.aspx`. Add the validation controls to the UI at the right of the respective controls. Table 14.6 shows the property settings for all the validation controls to link them to the controls to be validated. After adding controls and setting the properties, the UI should look like Figure 14.8. The following controls will be used:

- `txtPrincipal (TextBox)`—`RequiredFieldValidator` and `RangeValidator`
- `txtInterestRate (TextBox)`—`RequiredFieldValidator` and `RegularExpressionValidator`
- `ddlYears (DropDownList)`—`CustomValidator`

The code for the `.aspx` file is similar to that for `ASPMortgage.aspx` file, with one main change—the code for validation controls has been added:

```
<%@ Page Language="vb" AutoEventWireup="false"
Codebehind="ValidASPMortgage.aspx.vb"
```

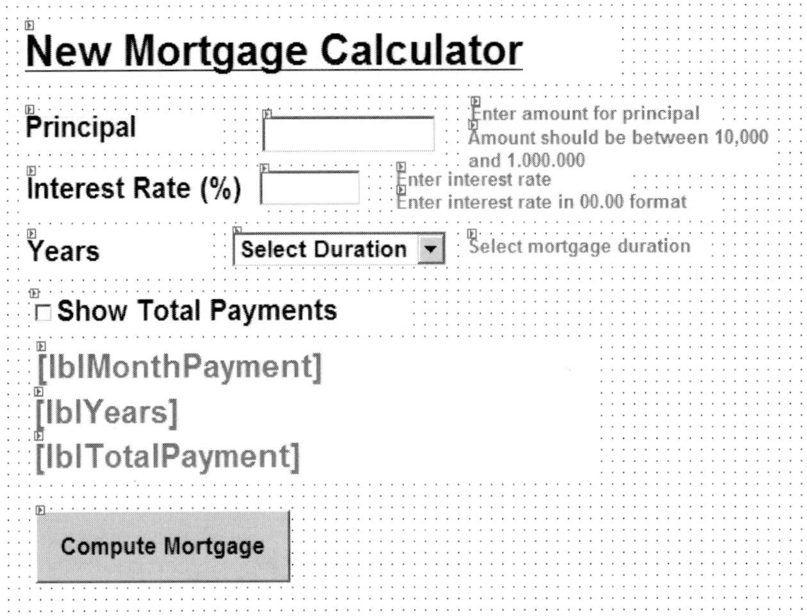

FIGURE 14.8
The UI for ValidASPMortgage.aspx file.

```
Inherits="ValidASPMortgage.WebForm1" SmartNavigation="True"%>
<!DOCTYPE HTML PUBLIC "-//W3C//DTD HTML 4.0 Transitional//EN">
<HTML>
<HEAD>
<title>Mortgage Calculator</title>
      <meta content="Microsoft Visual Studio.NET 7.0"
      name="GENERATOR">
      <meta content="Visual Basic 7.0" name="CODE_LANGUAGE">
      <meta content="JavaScript" name="vs_defaultClientScript">
      <meta
content="http://schemas.microsoft.com/intellisense/ie5"
name="vs_targetSchema">
</HEAD>
<body MS_POSITIONING="GridLayout">
<form id="Form1" method="post" runat="server">
<asp:label id="Label1" style="Z-INDEX: 101; LEFT: 30px; POSITION:
absolute; TOP: 22px" runat="server" Font-Underline="True" Font-
Names="Arial" Font-Size="Large" Font-Bold="True" Height="37px"
Width="315px">New Mortgage Calculator</asp:label>
<asp:label id="lblTotalPayment" style="Z-INDEX: 112; LEFT: 36px;
POSITION: absolute; TOP: 310px" runat="server" Font-Names="Arial"
Font-Size="Medium" Font-Bold="True" Height="18px" Width="310px"
ForeColor="Red"></asp:label>
<asp:label id="lblYears" style="Z-INDEX: 111; LEFT: 36px;
POSITION: absolute; TOP: 279px" runat="server" Font-Names="Arial"
```

```
Font-Size="Medium" Font-Bold="True" Height="18px" Width="310px"
ForeColor="Red"></asp:label>
<asp:textbox id="txtInterestRate" style="Z-INDEX: 106; LEFT:
179px; POSITION: absolute; TOP: 125px" runat="server" Font-
Names="Arial" Font-Bold="True" Height="25px"
Width="73px"></asp:textbox>
<asp:label id="Label2" style="Z-INDEX: 102; LEFT: 30px; POSITION:
absolute; TOP: 81px" runat="server" Font-Names="Arial" Font-
Bold="True" Height="28px" Width="138px">Principal</asp:label>
<asp:label id="Label3" style="Z-INDEX: 103; LEFT: 31px; POSITION:
absolute; TOP: 124px" runat="server" Font-Names="Arial" Font-
Bold="True" Height="29px" Width="141px">Interest Rate
(%)</asp:label>
<asp:label id="Label4" style="Z-INDEX: 104; LEFT: 31px; POSITION:
absolute; TOP: 168px" runat="server" Font-Names="Arial" Font-
Bold="True" Height="30px" Width="135px">Years</asp:label>
<asp:textbox id="txtPrincipal" style="Z-INDEX: 105; LEFT: 179px;
POSITION: absolute; TOP: 84px" runat="server" Font-Names="Arial"
Font-Bold="True" Height="26px" Width="125px"></asp:textbox>
<asp:dropdownlist id="ddlYears" style="Z-INDEX: 107; LEFT: 182px;
POSITION: absolute; TOP: 167px" runat="server" Font-Names="Arial"
Font-Bold="True" Height="37px" Width="117px">
  <asp:ListItem Value="Select Duration" Selected="True">Select
  Duration</asp:ListItem>
  <asp:ListItem Value="10 Years">10 Years</asp:ListItem>
  <asp:ListItem Value="15 Years">15 Years</asp:ListItem>
  <asp:ListItem Value="20 Years">20 Years</asp:ListItem>
  <asp:ListItem Value="25 Years">25 Years</asp:ListItem>
  <asp:ListItem Value="30 Years" 30 Years</asp:ListItem>
</asp:dropdownlist>
<asp:checkbox id="chkTotalPmt" style="Z-INDEX: 108; LEFT: 33px;
POSITION: absolute; TOP: 210px" runat="server" Font-Names="Arial"
Font-Bold="True" Height="28px" Width="195px" AutoPostBack="True"
Text="Show Total Payments"></asp:checkbox>
<asp:label id="lblMonthPayment" style="Z-INDEX: 110; LEFT: 38px;
POSITION: absolute; TOP: 247px" runat="server" Font-Names="Arial"
Font-Size="Medium" Font-Bold="True" Height="8px" Width="308px"
ForeColor="Red"></asp:label>
<asp:button id="btnCompute" style="Z-INDEX: 109; LEFT: 36px;
POSITION: absolute; TOP: 349px" accessKey="M" runat="server" Font-
Names="Arial" Font-Bold="True" Height="51px" Width="186px"
Text="Compute Mortgage"></asp:button>
<asp:requiredfieldvalidator id="ReqdFldValdtrtxtPrincipal"
style="Z-INDEX: 113; LEFT: 312px; POSITION: absolute; TOP: 79px"
runat="server" Font-Names="Arial" Font-Size="XX-Small" Font-
Bold="True" Height="4px" Width="178px"
ControlToValidate="txtPrincipal" ErrorMessage="Enter amount for
principal"></asp:requiredfieldvalidator>
<asp:rangevalidator id="RngValdtrtxtPrincipal" style="Z-INDEX:
114; LEFT: 312px; POSITION: absolute; TOP: 91px" runat="server"
Font-Names="Arial" Font-Size="XX-Small" Font-Bold="True"
```

```
Height="17px" Width="188px" ControlToValidate="txtPrincipal"
ErrorMessage="Amount should be between 10,000 and 1,000,000"
Type="Integer" MaximumValue="1000000"
MinimumValue="10000"></asp:rangevalidator>
<asp:regularexpressionvalidator id="RegExpValdtrtxtInterestRate"
style="Z-INDEX: 115; LEFT: 261px; POSITION: absolute; TOP: 139px"
runat="server" Font-Names="Arial" Font-Size="XX-Small" Font-
Bold="True" Height="12px" Width="172px"
ControlToValidate="txtInterestRate" ErrorMessage="Enter interest
rate in 00.00 format" ValidationExpression="[0-9]{2}.[0-9]{2}">
</asp:regularexpressionvalidator>
<asp:requiredfieldvalidator id="ReqdFldValdtrtxtInterestRate"
style="Z-INDEX: 116; LEFT: 261px; POSITION: absolute; TOP: 126px"
runat="server" Font-Names="Arial" Font-Size="XX-Small" Font-
Bold="True" Height="8px" Width="95px"
ControlToValidate="txtInterestRate" ErrorMessage="Enter interest
rate"></asp:requiredfieldvalidator>
<asp:customvalidator id="CstmVldtrddlYears" style="Z-INDEX: 117;
LEFT: 321px; POSITION: absolute; TOP: 171px" runat="server" Font-
Names="Arial" Font-Size="XX-Small" Font-Bold="True" Height="12px"
Width="131px" ControlToValidate="ddlYears" ErrorMessage="Select
mortgage duration"></asp:customvalidator>
</form>
</body>
</HTML>
```

The code for the `ValidASPMortgage.aspx.vb` file is the same as that for the `ASPMortgage.aspx.vb` file, with a few changes. First, the `ServerValidate` event for the `CustomValidator` control has to be coded. The code is

```
Private Sub CstmVldtrddlYears_ServerValidate(ByVal source As _
System.Object, ByVal args As _
System.Web.UI.WebControls.ServerValidateEventArgs) Handles _
CstmVldtrddlYears.ServerValidate
      'Validate DropdownList Control input
      If args.Value = "Select Duration" Then
            args.IsValid = False
      Else
            args.IsValid = True
      End If
End Sub
```

This event accepts two parameters: `Source` and `args`. `Source` is the control that invoked this event. In this case, it is the `CustomValidator` control, `CstmVldtrddl-lYears`. The `value` property of the parameter `args` contains the value of the control `ddlYears`. This value is used to check whether mortgage duration input was provided. If the `IsValid` property of the args parameter returns `False`, the validation test fails. Secondly, the `Click` event of the `Button` control is modified slightly to check whether the `IsValid` property of the page is `True`. It will be `True` if all the validation checks were successful. The check for page validity is not required if `CustomValidator` is not used. In the absence of the `CustomValidator`, if one of the other validations fails, the `IsValid` property of the page will be `False` immediately. Since the validation function for `CustomValidator` is coded on the server side, the function needs to be executed first and only after that the `IsValid` property of the page gets its final value. Hence, it must be checked before computations are performed in the `Click` event of `btnCompute`. Here is the relevant code:

```
Private Sub btnCompute_Click(ByVal sender As System.Object, ByVal e _
As System.EventArgs) Handles btnCompute.Click
        'Check Page Validity before computations
        If Page.IsValid Then
                …Computations performed here…
        End If
End Sub
```

Run the Web application and test it. When invalid values are provided in the textboxes or the dropdown list control, appropriate error messages appear at the specified locations. Figures 14.9a and 14.9b show such situations. In Figure 14.9a, the `RangeValidator` gives an error message since 1000 is an invalid value for principal. For the `txtInterestRate` textbox, `RequiredFieldValidator` gives an error message indicating that a value is required for interest rate. In Figure 14.9b, the textboxes have valid inputs, but the `dropdownlist` control has no mortgage duration selected. Hence, the `CustomValidator`'s `servervalidate` event fires and the validation test fails, giving an appropriate error message.

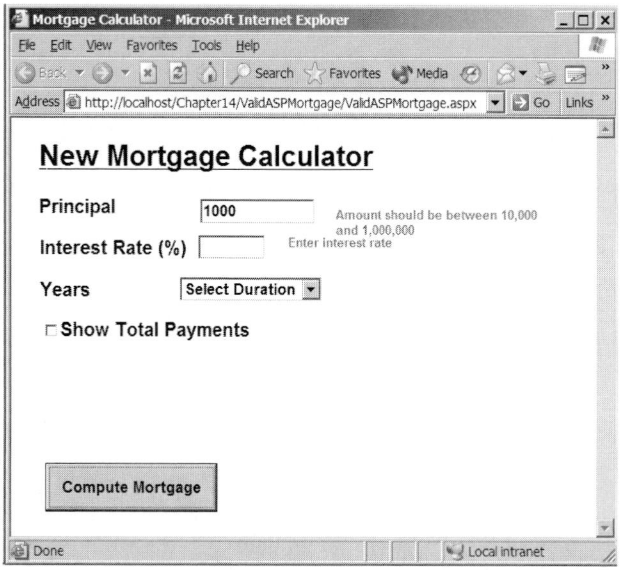

FIGURE 14.9A
Validation controls at work.

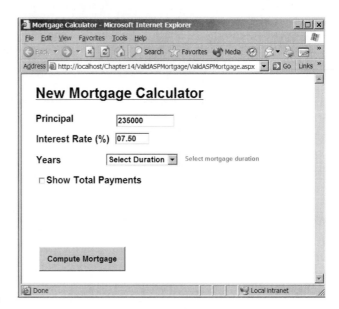

FIGURE 14.9B
Customvalidator at work.

14.8 OTHER CONTROLS IN ASP.NET

In this chapter, only three sets of server controls have been discussed: (1) HTML server controls, (2) Web form controls, and (3) validation controls. However, ASP.NET has more to offer. These are rich Web controls and user controls. Rich Web controls offer additional features and complex functionality. Although a detailed discussion of rich Web controls is beyond the scope of this book, they are as follows:

- `AdRotator` Web server control: To create dynamic ads to be displayed on the Web page.
- `Calendar` Web server control: Helps to develop interactive calendars on the Web page.
- `XML` Web server control: Helps to display XML documents on the Web page.

ASP.NET also allows developers to create custom user controls. Custom controls can be designed from the ground up, or existing controls can be modified to add more features. Alternatively, two or more controls can be combined together to form a new custom control. There is much more to ASP.NET than just Web forms and server controls. Several textbooks can be written on ASP.NET alone. The next chapter introduces more on ASP.NET and focuses on the development of dynamic Web pages using back-end databases.

SUGGESTED HOME ASSIGNMENTS

1. Design a Web form to check the validity of an email address. (Checking for @ and . characters is good enough.) Use validation controls.
2. Create a Web form project that would compute the price of a car based on the options selected and accessories chosen. Provide options for color (Red, Blue, Yellow, and Green),

capacity (4 Cyl., 6 Cyl.), and accessories (Leather seats, ABS, and Sun roof). Assume appropriate prices.

3. Design a Web form project to compute the letter grade for a student given the numeric grade. Use validation controls to check for numeric input.

TEST YOURSELF

1. What is the function of the Action attribute in the Form tag? Explain.
2. What is the difference between GET and POST methods of the Form tag?
3. What are the major benefits of ASP.NET when compared to ASP?
4. Briefly explain ASP.NET's two models of application development.
5. What is a round-trip? Explain.
6. Explain any three events of a page.
7. Compare and contrast the code-inline and code-behind models of programming.
8. Why is code-behind model preferred?
9. What is viewstate and how is viewstate maintained in ASP.NET pages?
10. When is HTML server controls preferred over ASP server controls?
11. Explain the `@Page` directive attribute `SmartNavigation`.
12. Identify events of server controls that trigger roundtrips. Name any three controls that can cause roundtrips.
13. What is the basic purpose of a validation control?
14. Briefly explain how the `RegularExpressionValidator` is used.
15. When should the `CustomValidator` control be used?
16. If a `RangeValidator` control is used, what happens if no value is entered in the control being validated?
17. What are the advantages of ASP Server controls over HTML server controls?
18. Compare `HTMLRadiobutton` control and `Radiobutton` server controls.
19. What are rich Web controls?
20. Describe custom controls.

Active Server Pages.NET and ActiveX Data Objects.NET

CHAPTER OBJECTIVES

After completing this chapter, students should understand

1. Specific intrinsic classes in ASP.NET—Request, Response, and Session
2. How state is maintained in Web pages
3. How ADO.NET is used in conjunction with ASP.NET (two lab sections are presented to enhance learning)
4. The `PlaceHolder` control that is unique to Web forms
5. How Web form controls can be created dynamically

15.1   AIMS OF CHAPTER

The ADO.NET provides many objects for interacting with databases such as the Connection, Command, and Data Reader objects. For a detailed review of ADO.NET, refer to the database chapters of this book. ADO.NET can be used in traditional Windows forms as well as in Web forms. ASP.NET, when used in conjunction with ADO.NET, can generate dynamic Web pages that can search for, add, modify, and delete records in a database. Most business-to-consumer (B-2-C) Web sites use modules such as the *Shopping Cart* that connect to a database on the backend to generate and display available products dynamically. Such sites also create instances of form controls dynamically. In the traditional ASP model, it is crucial, while designing Web pages, to plan for carrying information from one Web page to another. The reason is that the Web is *stateless*. ASP.NET can maintain the state of controls in a page automatically, thus reducing programming efforts to do so. Additionally, ASP.NET provides multiple ways to maintain state across pages. They involve using session variables, hidden form controls, cookies, etc. To gain a better understanding of Web application development using ASP.NET, a basic knowledge of Request and Response objects is necessary. Hence, this chapter focuses on three primary topics: (a) intrinsic classes in ASP.NET, (b) use of ADO.NET objects in ASP.NET applications, and (b) state maintenance techniques.

15.2   MORE ON ASP.NET

Before learning how to build ASP.NET pages that can display data using ADO.NET, it helps to understand three important intrinsic classes of ASP.NET: `HTTPRequest`, `HTTPResponse`, and `HTTPSessionState`. The `HTTPRequest` class is used to access information pertaining to a specific HTTP request from a client, and the `HTTPResponse` class is used to control the output, both text and binary, sent back to the client. The `HTTPSessionState` class is used mainly for storing and accessing information that is required across pages within a Web application. The `HTTPSessionState` class plays an important role in ASP.NET since the Web is stateless by design. Remember that HTTP used for Internet communications is a connectionless protocol.

15.2.1   `HTTPRequest` Class

When an HTTP request such as **http://www.prenhall.com** is made by a client to the Web server of a specific domain, it contains a wealth of information. This information includes, but is not limited to, cookies for the domain, Web forms control data in name–value pairs, and the IP address of the client machine, among others. The `HTTPRequest` class instance for an ASP.NET page is exposed as the `Request` property of the `Page` class. (See Table 14.3 of Chapter 14.) The information contained in an HTTP request can be accessed through the properties, collections, and methods of the `HTTPRequest` class. For example, the `Form` collection contains the values of all form controls in name/value pairs. The following code demonstrates how to access the value of one control (a textbox named `txtLastName`) in that collection:

```
Dim strLastName As String = Request.Form("txtLastName")
```

Note that Request.Form("txtLastName") in the preceding code can be replaced with txtLastName.Text since the form data is posted back to the same page in ASP.NET by default. This is possible in ASP.NET since the page object maintains the viewstate of its controls by default. Regardless of whether the viewstate of controls in a page are maintained, the Form collection of the Request property (of the page object) provides access to the value of the controls in the page when the form is posted. Table 15.1 lists some of the useful properties, collections, and methods of the HTTPRequest class. The properties of this class instance help determine many characteristics of the client, such as the type of browser, type of files accepted, and nature of the current connection (secure or not), among others. Such characteristics of the client help the developer to design Web applications appropriately.

15.2.2   `HTTPResponse` Class

Similar to `HTTPRequest` class, the `HTTPResponse` class instance for an ASP.NET page is exposed through the `Response` property of the `Page` class. There are several methods exposed by the `HTTPResponse` class instance that provide control over the output sent

TABLE 15.1   A Few of the `HTTPRequest` Class Properties, Collections, and Methods.

Property/Collection/Method	Description
`AcceptTypes` property	Returns a `String` array containing the MIME (Multipurpose Internet Mail Extension) types accepted by the client browser.
`Browser` property	Returns an instance of the `HttpBrowserCapabilities` class that helps to determine the characteristics of the client browser such as whether the browser supports background sounds, supports cookies, and Frames, among others.
`InputStream` property	Returns a stream object containing the body of the HTTP request.
`IsSecureConnection` property	Returns a Boolean indicating whether the current connection uses secure socket layers (SSL).
`TotalBytes` property	Returns an integer that gives the size of the HTTP request body.
`UserHostAddress` property	Returns the IP address of the client.
`Cookies` collection	Returns an instance of the `HttpCookieCollection` class that contains all the cookies present in the client request.
`Files` collection	Returns a collection of files uploaded as part of client's request.
`Form` collection	Returns an instance of the `NameValueCollection` class that contains all form control values (provided that the method attribute of the HTML form is set to POST).
`Params` collection	Returns an instance of the `NameValueCollection` class that contains name–value pairs for the `Cookies`, `Form`, `QueryString`, and the `ServerVariables` collection.
`SaveAs` method	Designed to save the HTTP request to disk. Accepts two arguments: filename and a second Boolean argument indicating whether to save the HTTP header information as part of the request.

to the browser. This class has only one collection—`Cookies`—which enables cookies to be set on the client during a response. The properties provide capabilities such as buffering the response, setting the MIME (Multipurpose Internet Mail Extensions) type, and determining whether the client is still connected. If the `BufferOutput` property is set to `False`, output is sent back to the client immediately as and when it is generated. This avoids long waits by the client if the response returns a large output. The default setting for the property is `True`, meaning that output is buffered. The `Clear` method clears the buffer as dictated by programming logic. To immediately send the buffered output to the client, `Flush` method is used. Table 15.2 lists some of the properties and methods of the `HTTPResponse` class, along with its single collection.

15.2.3   Maintaining State in Web Applications

As mentioned earlier, the Web is stateless; hence, state maintenance should be done so as to not lose information during postbacks and to carry information between pages. ASP.NET, as seen earlier, does state maintenance of controls in a page automatically by maintaining the viewstate of controls. However, the postback architecture in ASP.NET will *only* allow form data in a page to be posted back to the same page and

TABLE 15.2   A Few of the `HTTPResponse` Class Properties and Methods along with a Collection.

Property/Collection/Method	Description
`BufferOutput` property	Returns or sets a Boolean value to represent whether the output is buffered or sent back to the client immediately.
`Cache` property	Returns an instance of the `HTTPCachePolicy` class whose methods can be used for the cache settings of the page.
`ContentType` property	Returns or sets a string containing the MIME type of the current response.
`Expires` property	Returns or sets an integer representing the number of minutes to cache a page.
`IsClientConnected` property	Returns a Boolean indicating whether the client is still connected. It is useful to check this property before running processes that are highly resource intensive.
`Output` property	Returns a write-only `TextWriter` that can be used to write text to the output stream. This is an alternative to the `Write` method. The `TextWriter` provides its own methods, such as `Write` and `Close`.
`Cookies` collection	Returns an instance of the `HTTPCookieCollection` class containing cookies in the current request. Also used to set new or modified cookies on the client.
`AppendHeader` method	Adds an HTTP header with name and value to the output.
`Clear` method	Clears the content of the current output stream.
`End` method	Stops processing the current request and sends buffer to client immediately.
`Flush` method	Sends buffered output to client immediately.
`Redirect` method	Redirects execution to another page optionally terminating processing of the current page.
`Write` method	Used to write output including object data.
`WriteFile` method	Used to write the contents of the specified file to the output stream.

not to a different page.[36] This default behavior of ASP.NET architecture *cannot* be overridden. To pass a form control and other data to another page, they should be first processed in the page to store their values in cookies or session variables. Then, the `Redirect` method of the `Response` property of the page can be used to transfer control to a different page. Suppose there are two textboxes (`txtProductID` and `txtProductName`) on a Web form page. When a button on the page is clicked, the form data is posted back to the page. To pass the textbox values to a different page, add the following code to the button `Click` event handler:

```
Private Sub btnSubmit_Click(ByVal sender As System.Object, _
ByVal e As System.EventArgs) Handles btnSubmit.Click
    'Process Form Data and pass them to a different Page
```

---

[36]Thus, it is possible to create "a complete application in one page." Instead of designing different pages for different functionalities, different sections in the same page can be designed for different functionalities. If the `runat=server` attribute is removed from the `Form` tag, the form could be posted to another page given in the `action` attribute setting. However, Web form server controls cannot be used without this form attribute!

```
            Response.Cookies("ProductID") = txtProductID.Text
            Response.Cookies("ProductName") = txtProductName.Text
            Response.Redirect("SecondPage.aspx")
    End Sub
```

The code creates and assigns textbox values to two cookies—`ProductID` and `ProductName`—and then control is sent to the page `SecondPage.aspx`. Cookies are widely used to maintain state. Cookies are stored on the client, thus saving resources on the server. Since the client browser packages cookies as part of the HTTP request for a specific Web page, the page can access cookies through the `Cookies` collection of the `Request` property of the page object. Thus, information can be passed between pages, and the state is maintained. However, using cookies is subject to certain limitations. Some of the disadvantages of cookies are as follows:

- Cookies can store only text and the size in most browsers is limited to 4 kilobytes.
- Client browsers can be set to refuse cookies. In this scenario, Web applications that depend on cookies for state management will not work.
- Since cookies are stored on the client, they can be manipulated and an application may not function as designed. Also, regardless of whether cookies are required in a specific Web page, all the cookies for the specific domain are sent along with each HTTP request degrading performance.

Finally, for the preceding example, `SecondPage.aspx` page can access the cookies using the `Cookies` collection of the `Request` property:

```
lblProductID.Text = Request.Cookies("ProductID").Value
lblProductName.Text = Request.Cookies("ProductName").Value
```

Another way to pass information to a different page is to attach information at the end of URL requests:

http://localhost/SecondPage.aspx?ProductID=A123&ProductName=Book

There are two variables, `ProductID` and `ProductName`, attached at the end of the URL, and they carry the values of `A123` and `Book`, respectively. The name–value pairs are separated by &, and the string `ProductID=A123&ProductName=Book` is known as the `QueryString`. When the link is clicked, these name/value pairs can be accessed in `SecondPage.aspx` page through the `QueryString` collection of the `Request` property. The following syntax shows how to extract the value contained in the `QueryString` variable `ProductID`:

```
Dim strProdID As String = Request.QueryString("ProductID")
```

The demerits of this method are that the length of the URL has an upper limit of 2,048 characters (in Internet Explorer) and it is not advisable to use Login and Password information as part of `QueryString` for obvious reasons. Note that, while form data was automatically passed to SecondPage.aspx using Response.Redirect in the cookie example, user should click on the link to pass information in the QueryString example.[37]

Another popular method is to use session variables to maintain state and to pass form control information to other pages. The HTTPSessionState class is presented next.

15.2.4 HTTPSessionState Class

HTTPSessionState class is used mainly to store and share information across all Web pages in an application. Similar to HTTPRequest and HTTPResponse classes, the HTTPSessionState class instance for a page is exposed through the Session property of the page object. Session information for a client can be accessed through the properties, collections, and methods of this class. When a client visits a site, a new SessionID is created for the client for that session provided the EnableSessionState attribute of the @Page directive is not set to False. Clients are identified by the unique SessionID assigned to each. While using session variables for maintaining state, it is crucial to set the optimal default timeout value for the session. Since the Web is stateless, a Web server will not know whether a client is still interacting with the server. Hence, the session should automatically time out after specified minutes of client inactivity to release memory assigned to the session. The default is usually 20 minutes. Care should be taken not to set the session timeout value very high. At the same time, session timeout value should not be set too low as the client needs sufficient time to interact with a Web page. It is a balancing act and based on average amount of time clients spend on the site, an appropriate timeout value should be set. Although it is not always predictable when a client will leave the site, an explicit logout module can be provided and Session.Abandon method can be called to end the session freeing up the server resources. The Global.asax file, a file that contains code for responding to application-level events, can be used to define the session events. For example, when a client session is started, Session.Start event is invoked. Similarly, when a session ends Session.End event is fired. The following code in the Global.asax file demonstrates this:

```
Sub Session_Start(ByVal sender As Object, ByVal e As EventArgs)
    'Fires when the session is started
End Sub

Sub Session_End(ByVal sender As Object, ByVal e As EventArgs)
    'Fires when the session ends
End Sub
```

In ASP.NET, session is actually maintained through the use of a cookie called ASP.NET_SessionId. Browsers generally allow session cookies. However, ASP.NET supports both cookie and cookieless sessions. For cookieless sessions, ASP.NET automatically modifies the relative URLs to embed the SessionID and this helps the Web

---

[37]There are other ways to access form control data from other pages and to pass state information between pages. However, they are beyond the scope of this textbook.

TABLE 15.3 Some of the Properties, Collections, Methods, and Events of HTTPSessionState Class.

Properties/Collections/Methods	Description
Count property	Gets the number of items in the session-state collection.
IsCookieless property	Gets a value indicating whether the session ID is embedded in the URL or stored in an HTTP cookie.
IsNewSession property	Gets a value indicating whether the session was created with the current request.
SessionID property	Gets the unique SessionID used to identify the session.
Contents collection	Gets a reference to the current session-state object.
Keys collection	Gets a collection of the keys of all values stored in the session.
Abandon method	Cancels the current session.
Add method	Adds a new item to session state.
Clear method	Clears all values from session state.
CopyTo method	Copies the collection of session-state values to a one-dimensional array, starting at the specified index in the array.
Remove method	Deletes an item from the session-state collection by name.
RemoveAt method	Deletes an item at a specified index from the session-state collection.
Start event	Invoked when session is created. Should be defined in Global.asax file.
End event	Invoked when session is terminated. Should be defined in Global.asax file.

server to identify the specific client sending the request. Table 15.3 lists some of the properties, collections, methods, and events of the HTTPSessionState Class.

The cookie example in the previous section can be modified as follows to use session variables to pass form control information to the SecondPage.aspx page:

```
Private Sub btnSubmit_Click(ByVal sender As System.Object, _
ByVal e As System.EventArgs) Handles btnSubmit.Click
    'Process Form Data and pass them to a different Page

    Session("ProductID") = txtProductID.Text
    Session("ProductName") = txtProductName.Text
    Response.Redirect("SecondPage.aspx")
End Sub
```

In the SecondPage.aspx page, session variable values can be retrieved with the Session property of the page object, as in the following code:

```
lblProductID.Text = Session("ProductID")
lblProductName.Text = Session("ProductName")
```

15.2.5 Other Intrinsic Classes in ASP.NET

The intrinsic ASP.NET classes presented so far were intended only to give an idea about the capabilities of ASP.NET. The coverage of ASP.NET topics is limited in this textbook. There are several other intrinsic classes[38] in ASP.NET such as the `HTTPApplicationState` class, the `HTTPException` class, and the `HTTPServerUtility` class. Although detailed coverage of these classes is beyond the scope of this book, their purpose is as follows:

- `HTTPApplicationState` class: While `HTTPSessionState` class deals with session data (i.e., data specific to a single client across all pages during a session), `HTTPApplicationState` deals with global data—data required across all pages and to all clients. Typically, application objects can be used to store pieces of information such as the database `ConnectionString`. The `Application` property of the `Page` class refers to the `HTTPApplicationState` class.

- `HTTPException` class: This class provides a means of generating error information from various ASP.NET classes

- `HTTPServerUtility` class: As the name suggests, this class provides utility functions such as `URLEnconde` and `URLDecode` to encode and decode strings for use in URLs. The `Server` property of the `Page` class refers to this class.

15.3 ACTIVEX DATA OBJECTS.NET

ActiveX Data Objects.NET or simply ADO.NET is Microsoft's platform for data access. Since earlier database chapters have covered ADO.NET in detail, this section serves as a refresher before focusing on how ADO.NET is used in ASP.NET pages. The components of the ADO.NET object model are the DataSet and the .NET data providers.

15.3.1 The DataSet

The dataset contains the data retrieved from the data source such as Oracle, SQLServer, or MS Access and it stores the data in disconnected cache. These data include tables, constraints, and relationships between these tables. DataSet is one of the main objects of ADO.NET, and it is contained in the System.Data namespace. The DataSet class represents the dataset, and the main components of this class are as follows:

- **DataTableCollection**: A collection of data tables
- **DataTable**: Represents a table in the `DataSet`. The `DataTable` consists of the following collections representing the rows and columns in the `DataTable`
  - DataRowCollection: Represents the collection of rows in the `DataTable`
    - **DataRow**: Represents a single row in the `DataRowCollection`

---

[38]The `Page` class, covered in Chapter 14, is also an intrinsic class.

- ○ `DataColumnCollection`: Represents the collection of columns in the `DataTable`
  - ■ **`DataColumn`**: Represents a single column in the `DataColumnCollection`
- ○ `ConstraintCollection`: Represents a collection of constraints for a `DataTable`
  - ■ **`Constraint`**: Represents a constraint for one or more `DataColumn`
- **`DataRelationCollection`**: Represents the collection of data relations in a `DataSet`
- **`DataRelation`**: Represents the relationship between two `DataTable` objects

Datasets can be typed or untyped. A typed dataset is derived from the base `DataSet` class, and it contains an XML schema file. An untyped dataset does not contain a schema file; hence, the data tables, rows, and columns are exposed only as collections.

15.3.2 The .NET Data Providers

The .NET data provider acts as the "middleman" between a Windows or a Web application and the data source. It is used (a) to establish a connection with the data source, (b) to execute commands against the data source, and (c) to populate the dataset. After the application finishes its interaction with the dataset, the .NET data provider is used to update the data source with the changes made. Hence, the core components of the data provider are as follows:

- **The Connection object**: In order for an application to communicate with a data source, it needs to connect to the data source first. The connection object does just that.
- **The Command object**: Once a connection is made to the data source, data need to be retrieved by issuing commands to query the data source or to invoke stored procedures in the source. The command object also is useful to perform other data-manipulation tasks such as updating the data source and adding new data.
- **The Data Reader object**: Retrieving records from the data source and keeping them in memory is resource intensive. An application may not need to traverse the dataset forward and backward for its functionality. In such situations, the DataReader is the solution. This object stores only one record of data in memory at any given time. DataReader object reads data sequentially. This is basically a read-only, forward-only dataset, and it leads to better performance of the application.
- **The Data Adapter object**: This component provides the transfer mechanism for getting data from the data source to the dataset in the application. After the application modifies the data in the dataset, the DataAdapter object provides the mechanism to transfer the modified data back to the data source.

The .NET framework provides two data providers: OLEDB and SQL Server data providers.

TABLE 15.4   Some of the Classes of OLEDB.NET Data Provider.

Class	Description
OleDbConnection	Represents the connection object
OleDbCommand	Represents the command object
OleDbDataReader	Represents the DataReader object
OleDbDataAdapter	Represents the DataAdapter object
OleDbError	Represents the warnings and/or errors the data source returns

15.3.3   The OLE DB.NET Data Providers

The OLE DB.NET data providers are contained in the `System.Data.OleDb` namespace. OLEDB.NET data providers can be used to access both relational and nonrelational data sources including text and graphical data. However, OLEDB.NET does not support MSDASQL, the OLE DB provider for ODBC (Open DataBase Connectivity). Some of the classes of this data provider are listed in Table 15.4.

15.3.4   The SQL Server.NET Data Providers

The `System.Data.SqlClient` namespace contains the SQL Server.NET data providers, and these providers were specifically designed to access Microsoft SQL Server databases. Although, OLEDB.NET data providers can be used to access SQL Server data source, better performance can be achieved by using SQL Server.NET data providers. Like OLEDB.NET data provider, SQL Server.NET data provider also has classes for accessing the data sources. However, these classes have Sql prefix instead of OleDb prefix as in `SqlConnection, SqlCommand, SqlDataReader, SqlDataAdapter,` and `SqlError`.

LAB 15.1: THE FIRST ASP.NET/ADO.NET APPLICATION

Lab Objectives:

The main lab objectives are as follows:
- Learn how to retrieve data from a MS Access database and display it in an ASP.NET page
- Learn to display the data using a `DataGrid` control
- Learn to customize `DataGrid`
- Learn about `QueryString` method of maintaining state in Web pages

Application Overview:

In this lab, student data are retrieved from an MS Access database and displayed in a Web page by means of connection, command, and data grid objects. The `StudentID` field of the each retrieved student is hyperlinked to a second page. If the student's address is available in the database, it is displayed on the second page. As mentioned in Chapter 14, both the lab exercises in this chapter use the code-behind model.

Designing the Application

The labs in this chapter use a MS Access database. This database, `Course.mdb`, has three tables: `StudentInformation`, `StudentAddress`, and `VisualBasicQuizBank`. The sample records are shown in Figure 15.1. The tables are as follows:

`StudentInformation`: This table contains 10 student records in the following fields:

- `StudentID`: This is the primary key field containing the ID of the student
- `LastName`: Contains last name of the student
- `FirstMiddle`: Contains the first and middle name of the student
- `AppearedForExam`: A `Boolean` field that indicates whether the student has taken the exam.
- `StudentAnswers`: This contains a string representing the answers selected by the student.
- `NumericGrade`: Contains the numeric grade for the student.
- The last three fields are used in the Lab 15.2 (more on this in Lab 15.2).

`StudentAddress`: This table contains the addresses of six students.

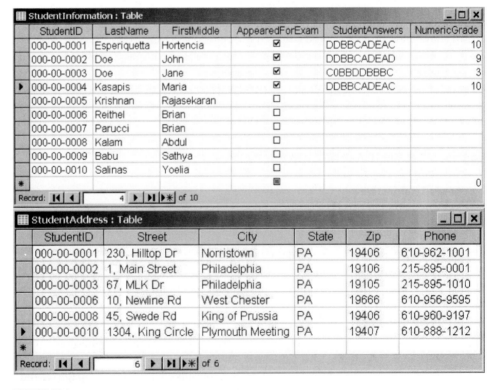

StudentInformation : Table

StudentID	LastName	FirstMiddle	AppearedForExam	StudentAnswers	NumericGrade
000-00-0001	Esperiquetta	Hortencia	☑	DDBBCADEAC	10
000-00-0002	Doe	John	☑	DDBBCADEAD	9
000-00-0003	Doe	Jane	☑	C0BBDDBBBC	3
000-00-0004	Kasapis	Maria	☑	DDBBCADEAC	10
000-00-0005	Krishnan	Rajasekaran	☐		
000-00-0006	Reithel	Brian	☐		
000-00-0007	Parucci	Brian	☐		
000-00-0008	Kalam	Abdul	☐		
000-00-0009	Babu	Sathya	☐		
000-00-0010	Salinas	Yoelia	☐		
			▣		0

Record: 4 of 10

StudentAddress : Table

StudentID	Street	City	State	Zip	Phone
000-00-0001	230, Hilltop Dr	Norristown	PA	19406	610-962-1001
000-00-0002	1, Main Street	Philadelphia	PA	19106	215-895-0001
000-00-0003	67, MLK Dr	Philadelphia	PA	19105	215-895-1010
000-00-0006	10, Newline Rd	West Chester	PA	19666	610-956-9595
000-00-0008	45, Swede Rd	King of Prussia	PA	19406	610-960-9197
000-00-0010	1304, King Circle	Plymouth Meeting	PA	19407	610-888-1212

Record: 6 of 6

FIGURE 15.1

The `StudentInformation` and `StudentAddress` tables.

- StudentID: Primary key field containing the ID of the student.
- Street: Contains the street address.
- City: City where the student resides.
- Zip: Contains the zip code.
- PhoneNumber: Contact number for the student.

VisualBasicQuizBank: Explained in Lab 15.2.

Create the sample access database with the specified tables here along with some dummy data as shown in Fig 15.1 and name the database Course.mdb. Open Visual Studio.NET and create a new ASP.NET application. Name the new project DataGrid in the popup New Project dialog box. Place a Label control for the heading and a DataGrid control on the Web form as shown in Fig 15.2. Name the DataGrid control grdStudent. Select the HeaderStyle property, and set the Font Bold to True so that the column headings of the data grid appear bold. Next, select the Data tab from the Toolbox and add an OleDbCommand object to the application (Figure 15.2). Name the OleDbCommand object cmdCommand in the properties window. Select the connection property of cmdCommand, and then select New from the dropdown list to create a new connection. From the Data Link Properties dialog box, select the Provider tab, and then select Microsoft Jet 4.0 OLE DB provider from the OLE DB Provider(s) list. In the Connection tab of the dialog box, provide the database name (Course.mdb) with its path information. Click Ok to close the Data Link Properties dialog box. This adds a new connection (OleDbConnection1) to the application. Rename the connection conConnection. The CommandText property of cmdCommand object has an associated Query Builder wizard. Using the wizard, build a query to retrieve all the records (and all the fields) from the StudentInformation table. Alternately, simply type in the

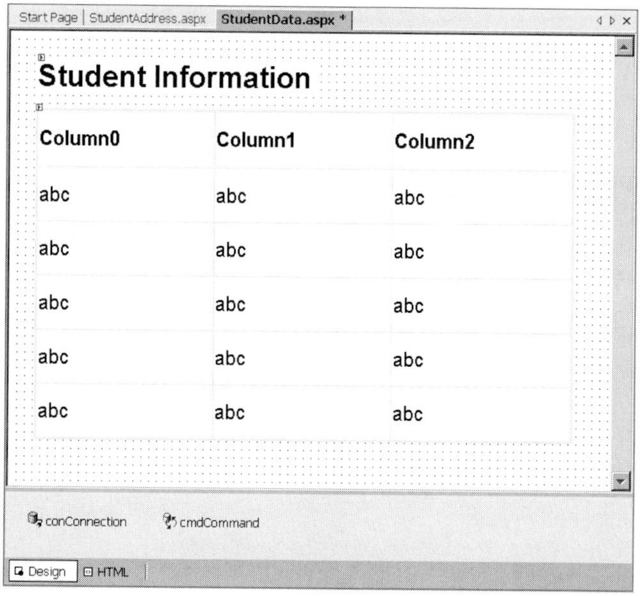

FIGURE 15.2
The StudentData.aspx interface.

following query in the `CommandText` property: `SELECT StudentInformation.* FROM StudentInformation`. Finally, change the name of the Web form to `StudentData.aspx`. The autogenerated HTML code for the `StudentData.aspx` page is as follows:

```
<%@ Page Language="vb" AutoEventWireup="false"
Codebehind="StudentData.aspx.vb" Inherits="DataGrid01.WebForm1"%>
<!DOCTYPE HTML PUBLIC "-//W3C//DTD HTML 4.0 Transitional//EN">
<HTML>
<HEAD>
      <title>Student Data</title>
      <meta name="GENERATOR" content="Microsoft Visual Studio.NET
7.0">
      <meta name="CODE_LANGUAGE" content="Visual Basic 7.0">
      <meta name="vs_defaultClientScript" content="JavaScript">
      <meta name="vs_targetSchema"
      content="http://schemas.microsoft.com/intellisense/ie5">
</HEAD>
<body MS_POSITIONING="GridLayout">
<form id="Form1" method="post" runat="server">
      <asp:Label id="lblHeading" style="Z-INDEX: 101; LEFT: 28px;
      POSITION: absolute; TOP: 27px" runat="server" Width="290px"
      Height="35px" Font-Bold="True" Font-Names="Arial" Font-
      Size="Large">Student Information</asp:Label>
      <asp:DataGrid id="grdStudent" style="Z-INDEX: 102; LEFT: 34px;
      POSITION: absolute; TOP: 83px" runat="server" Width="505px"
      Height="350px" BorderWidth="3px" BorderColor="WhiteSmoke" Font-
      Names="Arial">
      <HeaderStyle Font-Bold="True"
      BackColor="Transparent"></HeaderStyle>
      </asp:DataGrid>
</form>
</body>
</HTML>
```

Double-click an empty area of the Web form to open the code-behind file, `StudentData.aspx.vb`. Expand the `Web Form Designer Generated Code` region. This region will contain the autogenerated code for the `cmdCommand` and `conConnection` objects. The only thing left to do in code is to open the connection, execute the query using the command object, and bind the results with the data grid. Finally, the connection is closed and destroyed. Following is the code that performs these tasks (add it in the `Page_Load` event handler):

```
Private Sub Page_Load(ByVal sender As System.Object, ByVal e As _
System.EventArgs) Handles MyBase.Load
      'Get data and display in grid
      conConnection.Open()
      grdStudent.DataSource = cmdCommand.ExecuteReader()
      grdStudent.DataBind()
```

```
         conConnection.Close()
         conConnection.Dispose()
    End Sub
```

Once the `conConnection` connection has been opened using its `Open` method, `cmdCommand` object's `ExecuteReader` method is executed. The `DataReader` created is then assigned to the `DataSource` property of the data grid `grdStudent` and finally the `DataBind` method of the data grid is used to bind the grid to the data source. Run the application, and the Web page should appear as shown in Figure 15.3. The data grid automatically generates a table output with the field names as the first row. For a quick display of data, using the data grid may be highly desirable. The appearance of the output can be improved by customizing each column in the data grid control.

Enhancing the Application

The data grid output shown in Figure 15.2 is nothing but raw data in a table format. The output can be formatted for a more acceptable form of output by customizing each column. To do this, the `Columns` collection of the data grid needs to be configured. It is also possible to hyperlink data in specific columns. The focus of this part of the lab is to add the following features:

- Display only specific fields in the data grid with user-friendly column headings.
- Hyperlink the `StudentID` column to a second page (`StudentAddress.aspx`), and send the `StudentID` in a `QueryString` variable as input.
- Create the `StudentAddress.aspx` page, and display the address of the selected student if it is available in the `StudentAddress` table.

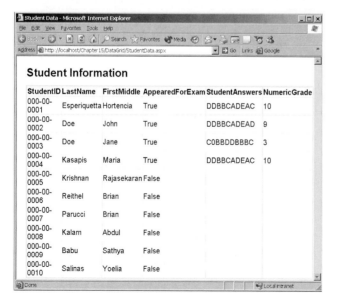

FIGURE 15.3
`StudentData.aspx` page with `DataGrid` control.

To display only specific fields from the `StudentInformation` table sorted by student ID, the `CommandText` property of the `cmdCommand` object should be changed to `SELECT StudentID, LastName, FirstMiddle, NumericGrade FROM StudentInforma-` `tion Order by StudentID`. This can be done either by using the `Query Builder` or by just entering the query in the `CommandText` property of the `cmdCommand` object. The next step is to customize each column. Click the icon in the `Columns` property of the data grid `grdStudent` to invoke the `Properties` popup dialog box. Select `Columns` from the menu on the top left-hand side of the window (Figure 15.4). Since the desired columns will be customized, make sure to uncheck *Create columns automatically at run time.* From the `Available columns` list, add three *Bound columns* and a *Hyperlink column* to the `Selected columns` list as shown in Figure 15.4. For each of the items in the `Selected columns` list, set the properties using the `BoundColumn` properties area. It is sufficient to edit the `Header text` and `Data Field` properties for each bound column. The `Header text` property is used to assign a heading for the specific column in the output and `Data Field` specifies the field name to which the column is bound. For example, the first bound column settings are `Header Text`: `Student ID` and `Data Field`: `StudentID`.

For the hyperlink column `LastName`, however, additional property settings are required. The property settings for this column are `Header text, Text field, URL field`, and `URL format string`. The `Text field` is the same as `Data Field`. The `URL field` specifies the field from which the hyperlink draws its data, and the `URL format string` is used to specify the linked page along with necessary `QueryString` variables.

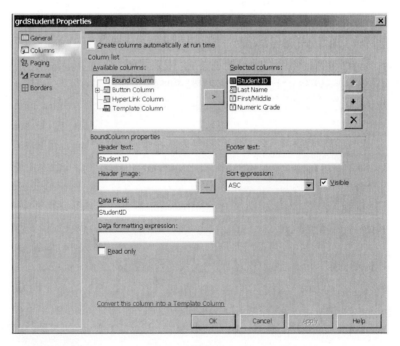

FIGURE 15.4
Data grid properties dialog box (bound column).

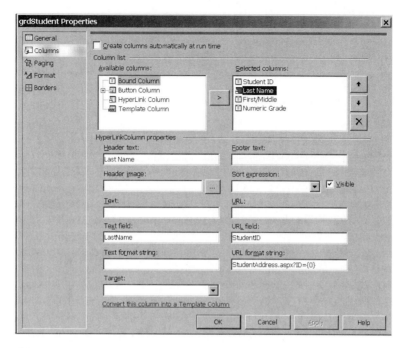

FIGURE 15.5
Data grid properties dialog box (hyperlink column).

In the current application, the LastName field is hyperlinked to StudentAddress.aspx page and it carries a QueryString variable, ID, which draws its value from field StudentID set in the URL field property. The URL format string used is StudentAddress.aspx?ID={0}. Figure 15.5 shows the property settings for the hyperlink column.

Add a Label at the top of the data grid to display an appropriate message to the user as shown in Figure 15.6. The next step is to create another Web form file, StudentAddress.aspx, to display student address, if available, for the selected student in StudentData.aspx file.

StudentAddress.aspx

Add a new Web form to the project by selecting Project from the main menu, and then Add New Item. From the popup Add New Item dialog box, select Web Form, and name it StudentAddress.aspx. Clicking Open will add a new Web form to the application. Add an OleDbConnection object and an OleDbCommand object to the Web form.[39] Next, these objects need to be configured. Name the objects conConnection and cmdCommand, respectively. Since these objects are on a different form, using the same name as the objects in StudentData.aspx page does not matter. Set the ConnectionString property of the connection object to the existing connection string shown in the dropdown list for the property. Set the Connection property of cmdCommand object to conConnection. The

---

[39]The data objects are added differently in this page. It is just another way to add the required data objects.

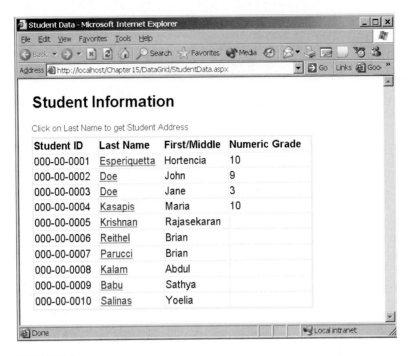

FIGURE 15.6
The `StudentData.aspx` page with a hyperlinked column.

`CommandText` property need not be set at design time. It will be modified during runtime. Add a `Label` for the title and another to display address as shown in Figure 15.7. The main function of the `StudentAddress.aspx` file is to retrieve the student's address from the `StudentAddress` table by querying the table using the `QueryString` variable supplied as part of the URL. To achieve this, add the following code to the `Page_Load` event handler in the code-behind file `StudentAddress.aspx.vb`:

```
Private Sub Page_Load(ByVal sender As System.Object, ByVal e As _
System.EventArgs) Handles MyBase.Load
      'Retrieve and Display Student's Address, if available, using ID

    Dim rdrReader As OleDb.OleDbDataReader
    Dim strID As String = Request.QueryString("ID")

    cmdCommand.CommandText = "Select * From StudentAddress " + _
    "Where StudentID ='" + strID + "'"
    conConnection.Open()
    rdrReader = cmdCommand.ExecuteReader()

    If rdrReader.Read Then
        lblAddress.Text = rdrReader("StudentID") + "<br>" + _
        rdrReader("Street") + "<br>" + rdrReader("City") + _
        ", " + rdrReader("State") + " " + rdrReader("Zip")
    Else
```

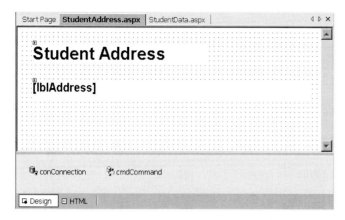

FIGURE 15.7
The StudentAddress.aspx interface.

```
        lblAddress.Text = strID + "<br>" + "Address NOT available"
End If

conConnection.Close()
cmdCommand.Dispose()
conConnection.Dispose()
End Sub
```

Before the code is discussed, note that Figure 15.6 shows the StudentData.aspx page with the last names hyperlinked. Move the mouse over any last name, and the associated hyperlink is displayed at the bottom of the browser. In the figure, the last name Doe has focus, and the hyperlink associated with Doe is **http://localhost/Chapter15/DataGrid/StudentAddress.aspx?ID=000-00-0002.** ID is the query string variable, and it is assigned the value of Doe's student ID. Similarly, every last name will have the ID variable (with the respective student ID assigned as its value) as part of the hyperlink. The ? character serves as the separator between the URL and the query string.

Returning to the Page_Load event handler for the code-behind file StudentAddress.aspx.vb, the value of the query string variable, ID, is retrieved from the QueryString collection[40] of the Request property of the page object, and the same is assigned to the variable strID. Next, a query is designed and assigned to the CommandText property of the cmdCommand object to retrieve the selected student's address from StudentAddress table. If the student address is found, it is displayed. Else an appropriate message is sent to the client. Figure 15.8 shows examples of outputs for two scenarios: when address is found and when it is not. Note the use of Read method of the Data Reader object.

For completeness, the code for the StudentAddress.aspx file is as follows:

```
<%@ Page Language="vb" AutoEventWireup="false"
Codebehind="StudentAddress.aspx.vb" Inherits="DataGrid.WebForm2" %>
```

---

[40]Note that the QueryString collection will contain only one variable: ID.

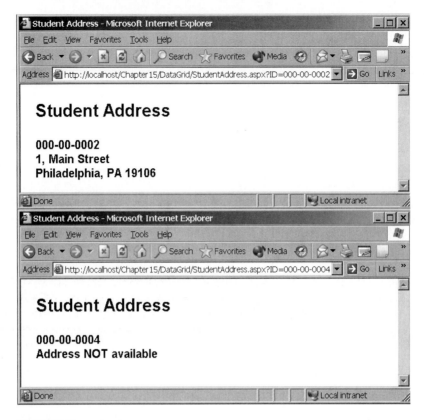

FIGURE 15.8
The StudentAddress.aspx page in action.

```
<!DOCTYPE HTML PUBLIC "-//W3C//DTD HTML 4.0 Transitional//EN">
<HTML>
<HEAD>
<title>Student Address</title>
<meta name="GENERATOR" content="Microsoft Visual Studio.NET 7.0">
<meta name="CODE_LANGUAGE" content="Visual Basic 7.0">
<meta name="vs_defaultClientScript" content="JavaScript">
<meta name="vs_targetSchema"
content="http://schemas.microsoft.com/intellisense/ie5">
</HEAD>
<body MS_POSITIONING="GridLayout">
<form id="Form1" method="post" runat="server">
<asp:Label id="Label1" style="Z-INDEX: 101; LEFT: 27px; POSITION:
absolute; TOP: 27px" runat="server" Width="313px" Height="30px"
Font-Names="Arial" Font-Bold="True" Font-Size="Large">Student
Address</asp:Label>
<asp:Label id="lblAddress" style="Z-INDEX: 102; LEFT: 27px;
POSITION: absolute; TOP: 91px" runat="server" Width="499px"
```

```
Height="32px" Font-Names="Arial" Font-Bold="True"></asp:Label>
</form>
</body>
</HTML>
```

15.4   INTRODUCTION LAB 15.2

The next lab exercise is designed to generate an online exam for students. The components of this lab and the knowledge gained can be useful in developing business applications such as online surveys and creating news Websites. In general, the code can be used to generate Web pages whose contents are generated using a data source. Such Web applications require minimal maintenance as long as the layout and the design need not be changed. Only the data source needs to be updated periodically.

This lab uses session variables for maintaining state. Also, the process of creating server controls dynamically is demonstrated. When Web form controls are created dynamically, they need to be placed inside a container to be rendered on the Web page. A `PlaceHolder` Web form control serves that purpose. In a simple Web page, placing of controls on a specific location can be fine-tuned using HTML tags. To do the same in a `PlaceHolder` control, one way is to use `LiteralControls`. ASP.NET compiles all HTML elements that do not require server-side processing into instances of the `LiteralControl` class.

15.4.1 The Processing Logic

The application presented in this lab, in short, requires students to log in to take the exam. After the exam is completed, it is immediately graded, and the numeric grade is displayed to students. The questions are generated in random order from a table that contains the questions. Dynamic Web form controls (mostly labels and radio buttons) are generated for the questions and answers and rendered on the client. The detailed processing logic is outlined as follows:

- Student provides last name and student ID to take the exam.
- The last name–student ID combination is checked against the data source to see whether they are valid.
- If valid and if the student had not taken the exam before, exam is generated and displayed. If the student had already taken the exam, an appropriate message is shown and the exam is neither generated nor shown to the student.
- Once the student completes the exam, submitting the exam (using a dynamically generated `Button` control) invokes a procedure that computes the exam grade, and the results are rendered. Also, appropriate fields in the data source are updated (a) to indicate that the student completed the exam, (b) to enter numeric grade, and (c) to store student answers.
- Since this is a Web application, care should be taken to account for possible user actions such as refreshing the Web page. Since a single page processes all of the

preceding functionalities in the `Page_Load` event handler, this is more of a concern. To direct the logic flow correctly, a session variable is used to determine when certain processes are invoked.

LAB 15.2: THE EXAM APPLICATION WITH DYNAMIC WEB FORM CONTROLS

Lab Objectives:
The main lab objectives are as follows:
- Learn how to create and use dynamic Web form controls
- Learn about `LiteralControl` and `PlaceHolder` controls
- Learn how Session variables are used
- Learn how to store database connection strings in the `Web.config` file

Application Overview

As mentioned in the last section, this application generates an exam from a data source and presents it to the student. The exam uses dynamic controls and when the student submits the exam it is graded and results are displayed. The application uses the data source for the following purposes:

- to check whether student last name/student ID combination is valid,
- to check whether the student had already taken the exam,
- to generate exam questions,
- to help in grading student exam once exam is submitted, and
- to update student exam status and to store student exam results.

Thus, the primary focus of this lab is to understand (a) how to create dynamic controls and work with them and (b) how ADO.NET components—Connection, Command, and Data Reader—are useful in interacting with a database. Also, use of session variables is demonstrated. The table `VisualBasicQuizBank` contains the exam questions and answers. The fields in this table are as follows:

- `ID`: Contains the question number. This is the primary key.
- `Question`: Contains the actual question.
- `Type`: Indicates whether the question is of type multiple choice (0) or type True/False (1). This is required to determine the number of answers options to be generated.
- `Group`: Although questions are displayed in the exam in random order, some of the questions may need to be displayed next to each other. For example, questions based on a code segment need to appear one after another instead of dispersed randomly. This field stores the `ID` of the last question in the sequence. In Figure 15.9, question 3's `Group` field has a value of 4, indicating that questions 3 and 4 should appear in order.
- `A`: Represents answer option A.
- `B`: Represents answer option B.
- `C`: Represents answer option C.

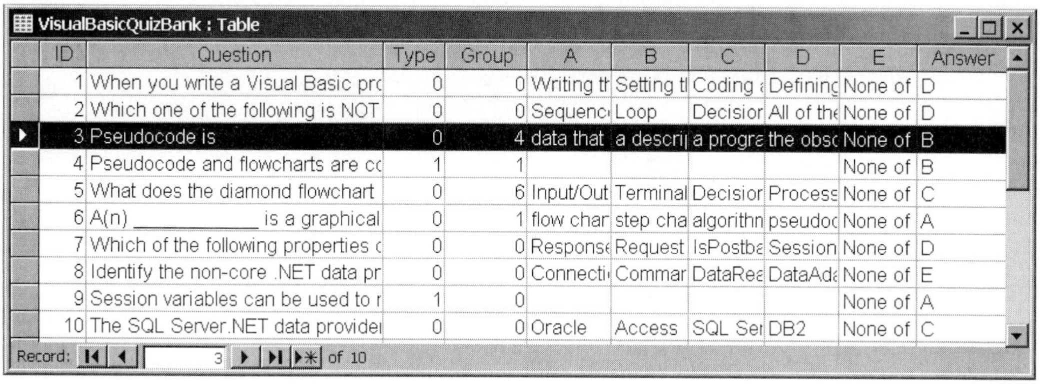

VisualBasicQuizBank : Table

ID	Question	Type	Group	A	B	C	D	E	Answer
1	When you write a Visual Basic prc	0	0	Writing th	Setting tl	Coding a	Defining	None of	D
2	Which one of the following is NOT	0	0	Sequenc	Loop	Decision	All of the	None of	D
3	Pseudocode is	0	4	data that	a descrij	a progra	the obsc	None of	B
4	Pseudocode and flowcharts are cc	1	1					None of	B
5	What does the diamond flowchart	0	6	Input/Out	Terminal	Decision	Process	None of	C
6	A(n) ____________ is a graphical	0	1	flow char	step cha	algorithn	pseudoc	None of	A
7	Which of the following properties c	0	0	Response	Request	IsPostba	Session	None of	D
8	Identify the non-core .NET data pr	0	0	Connecti	Commar	DataRea	DataAda	None of	E
9	Session variables can be used to r	1	0					None of	A
10	The SQL Server.NET data provider	0	0	Oracle	Access	SQL Ser	DB2	None of	C

Record: 3 of 10

FIGURE 15.9
The `VisualBasicQuizBank` table.

- `D`: Represents answer option D.
- `E`: Represents answer option E.
- `Answer`: This stores the correct answer option.

Designing the Application

Open Visual Studio.NET to create a new ASP.NET Web application. In the `Location` textbox, type the name `Exam`. Rename `WebForm1.aspx` to `Exam.aspx`. Place two `TextBox` controls, `txtLastName` and `txtPassword`, and appropriate `Label` controls on the Web form. Also, add a `PlaceHolder` control to the form (Figure 15.10). Rename it

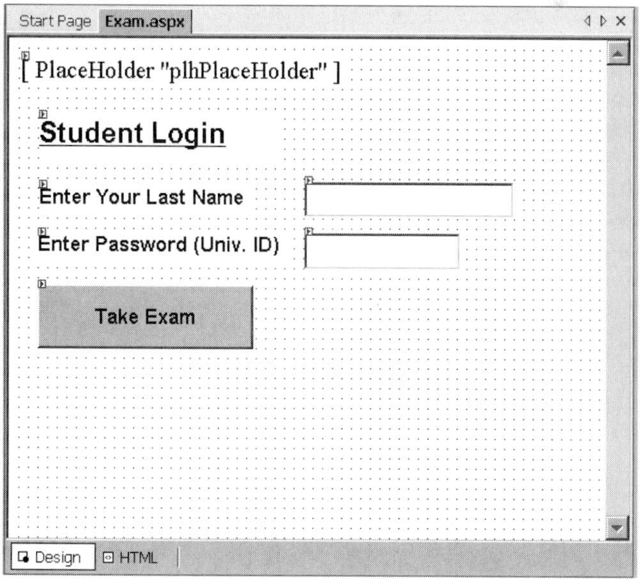

FIGURE 15.10
The `Exam.aspx` in design view.

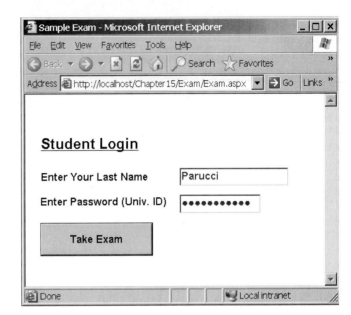

FIGURE 15.11
The `Exam.aspx` page with login interface.

`plhPlaceHolder`. This control will be the container for dynamically added controls. The student Login interface at runtime is shown in Figure 15.11.

The following is the HTML code listing for the `Exam.aspx` page:

```
<%@ Page Language="vb" AutoEventWireup="false"
Codebehind="Exam.aspx.vb" Inherits="Exam.WebForm1" %>
<!DOCTYPE HTML PUBLIC "-//W3C//DTD HTML 4.0 Transitional//EN">
<HTML>
<HEAD>
<title>Sample Exam</title>
<meta content="Microsoft Visual Studio.NET 7.0" name="GENERATOR">
<meta content="Visual Basic 7.0" name="CODE_LANGUAGE">
<meta content="JavaScript" name="vs_defaultClientScript">
<meta content=http://schemas.microsoft.com/intellisense/ie5
name="vs_targetSchema">
</HEAD>
<body MS_POSITIONING="GridLayout">
<!-- Declaration of Form elements starts -->
<form id="Form1" action="Exam.aspx" method="post" runat="server">
<asp:label id="lblHeading" style="Z-INDEX: 100; LEFT: 25px;
POSITION: absolute; TOP: 62px" runat="server" Font-
Underline="True" Font-Size="Medium" Font-Names="Arial" Font-
Bold="True" Height="39px" Width="203px">Student Login</asp:label>
<asp:label id="lblLastName" style="Z-INDEX: 101; LEFT: 25px;
POSITION: absolute; TOP: 118px" runat="server" Font-Size="X-
Small" Font-Names="Arial" Font-Bold="True" Height="20px"
Width="180px">Enter Your Last Name</asp:label>
```

```
<asp:label id="lblPassword" style="Z-INDEX: 102; LEFT: 24px;
POSITION: absolute; TOP: 156px" runat="server" Font-Size="X-
Small" Font-Names="Arial" Font-Bold="True" Height="23px"
Width="208px">Enter Password (Univ. ID)</asp:label>
<asp:textbox id="txtLastName" style="Z-INDEX: 106; LEFT: 249px;
POSITION: absolute; TOP: 114px" runat="server" Font-Size="X-
Small" Font-Names="Arial" Font-Bold="True" Height="28px"
Width="175px" ForeColor="Blue"></asp:textbox>
<asp:textbox id="txtPassword" style="Z-INDEX: 108; LEFT: 249px;
POSITION: absolute; TOP: 155px" runat="server" Font-Size="X-
Small" Font-Names="Arial" Font-Bold="True" Height="29px"
Width="130px" ForeColor="Blue" TextMode="Password"></asp:textbox>
<asp:button id="btnSubmit" style="Z-INDEX: 110; LEFT: 24px;
POSITION: absolute; TOP: 198px" runat="server" Font-Size="X-
Small" Font-Names="Arial" Font-Bold="True" Height="51px"
Width="182px" Text="Take Exam"></asp:button>
<asp:PlaceHolder id="plhPlaceHolder"
runat="server"></asp:PlaceHolder> </form>
</body>
</HTML>
```

Double-click the Web form to open the code window for the code-behind file,
Exam.aspx.vb. Add the following declarations in addition to the autogenerated declarations for the Web controls on the Exam.aspx file:

```
Protected mintComplete(9), mintActCount As Integer
Protected WithEvents plhPlaceHolder As _
System.Web.UI.WebControls.PlaceHolder
Protected mrdrReader As OleDb.OleDbDataReader
```

The mintComplete array and mintCount variable are required by the subprocedures (presented later in the lab). The mrdrReader is the DataReader object that will be
used for retrieving data from the data source. Add the following code for the
Page_Load event handler:

```
Private Sub Page_Load(ByVal objSender As System.Object, ByVal e As _
System.EventArgs) Handles MyBase.Load
  'Page_Load is used in this lab to display the exam and
  'to grade exam when exam is submitted
  If Page.IsPostBack Then

    'Hide Login Controls
    Call ControlsStatus()
    Dim strStatusResult As String = CheckStudent()

    'If Exam not taken, generate/Grade Exam, else
    'notify student and do nothing else
    If strStatusResult <> "Exam Already Taken" Then

      'If Exam submitted update session variable
```

```
        If Request.Form("btnExamSubmit") <> Nothing Then
            Session("ExamPosted") = "True"
        End If

        'Use session variable value to generate or grade exam
        If Session("ExamPosted") <> "True" Then
            Response.Write("<h3>Student Name: " + txtLastName.Text)
            Response.Write(" Student ID: " + txtPassword.Text + "</h3>")
            Response.Write("<hr>")
            Response.Write("<u><b>Answer all of the following")
            Response.Write("questions</u></b><br>")
            Call MakeExam()
        Else
            Call EditStudentExamData(txtPassword.Text)
            Call GradeExam()

            'Kill the session
            Session.Abandon()
        End If
    Else
            Response.Write(strStatusResult)
    End If
  End If
End Sub
```

After determining whether a postback had occurred, the login controls are immediately made invisible. Then, before making the exam, the first order of business is to determine whether the student had taken the exam, using the last name and student ID provided. If the student had already taken the exam, an appropriate message is displayed to the student by using the Write method of the Response property (an instance of HTTPResponse class) of the page object. If the student is yet to take the exam, the exam is generated and displayed after verifying the session variable; ExamPosted's value is not equal to "True". This step is required since the Page_Load event is fired every time the page is displayed. Postbacks cause the Page_Load event to execute twice: when the student submits the login information and when the student submits the exam. Hence, depending on when postback occurred, the exam needs to be either created and displayed or graded. If the student is submitting the exam, then the dynamically generated button, btnExamSubmit (presented later in code), will be part of the Form collection of the Request property of the page. If so, the exam should be graded. If it is not present, then exam should be generated and displayed to the student. Note that the use of session variable is redundant in the Page_Load event.[41] The logic does not require any session variables to be used. The only purpose of having it is to demonstrate how it is used. In this application, the Page_Load event acts as the control center invoking other subprograms.

---

[41]The code line If Session("ExamPosted") <> "True" Then can be replaced with If Request.Form ("btnExamSubmit") = Nothing Then. In this case, the If ... End If block that sets the session variable, ExamPosted to "True" can be removed.

The subprograms and their code are presented and discussed one by one. The various subprocedures used are as follows:

- ControlsStatus: This hides the login controls once the student logs in to take the exam
- CheckStudent: This function determines (a) whether last name–student ID combination is valid and (b) whether the student had already taken the exam.
- MakeExam: This is another important module, and it generates the exam by using CheckNumber() and WriteQuestion() subprograms
- CheckNumber: Since questions are picked randomly from the data source, this routine checks whether a selected question number had already been included in the exam
- WriteQuestion: This routine actually renders the question by generating dynamic RadioButton and Label controls. After CheckNumber() routine determines that the randomly generated question number had not been already selected, WriteQuestion() uses that number to send a query to the database to retrieve the question details and display accordingly using the dynamically generated controls.
- GradeExam: This subprogram grades the student results against the correct answers available in the data source. Also, the student record is updated

  - to indicate that exam had been taken by the student,
  - to enter his or her numeric grade, and
  - to enter the string that represent the student's answers.

- WriteResults: This subprogram displays the results of grading.

ControlsStatus

This subprogram hides the login controls after the student logs in. After the student clicks the Take Exam button on the login screen, see Figure 15.11, there is no need to display the login controls any more. Hence, in the Page_Load event, after detecting post back, the subprogram is called to make the controls invisible. The code is as follows:

```
Private Sub ControlsStatus()
    'Make the Login controls invisible
    lblHeading.Visible = False
    lblLastName.Visible = False
    lblPassword.Visible = False
    txtPassword.Visible = False
    txtLastName.Visible = False
    btnSubmit.Visible = False
End Sub
```

CheckStudent

This function uses last name and student ID to query the data source and determines whether the student had already taken the exam or not. It returns a string value. Unlike Lab 15.1, in this lab the required data objects are declared directly in code. This is yet another way of defining data objects in an ASP.NET application. Here is the code:

```
Private Function CheckStudent() As String
    'This routine checks whether student exists and if so whether exam
    'had already been taken

    Dim conConnection As New OleDb.OleDbConnection...42
    Dim cmdCommand As New OleDb.OleDbCommand()

    Dim strSQL As String = "Select * From StudentInformation" + _
    " Where LastName = '" & txtLN & "' And StudentID = '" + _
    txtPW + "'"

    cmdCommand.Connection = conConnection
    cmdCommand.CommandText = strSQL

    conConnection.Open()
    mrdrReader = cmdCommand.ExecuteReader()

    'Check whether record exists and if so student exam status
    If mrdrReader.Read() Then
        If mrdrReader("AppearedForExam") = True Then
            CheckStudent = mrdrReader("FirstMiddle") + _
            " " + txtLastName.Text + "<br>" + _
            "You already took the Exam!"
        Else
            CheckStudent = "Yet to Take Exam"
        End If
    Else
        CheckStudent = txtLastName.Text + "/" + txtPassword.Text + _
        "Combination Incorrect"
    End If

    mrdrReader.Close()
    conConnection.Close()
    conConnection.Dispose()
    cmdCommand.Dispose()
End Function
```

In the variables declaration part of the code, a connection object, conConnection is declared with the following syntax:

```
Dim conConnection As New _
OleDb.OleDbConnection(ConfigurationSettings.AppSettings("DataConnection"))
```

---

[42]**Dim** conConnection **As New** OleDb.OleDbConnection (ConfigurationSettings.AppSettings ("DataConnection"))

Since this application uses only one data source (Course.mdb), the Connection-String attribute of the connection objects used in the lab application will remain unchanged. In such a scenario, where the ConnectionString remains constant, it is better to place them in the AppSettings section of the Web.config file. This file allows you to establish application specific settings such as security, tracing, and error handling. Open the Web.config file (it should be listed in the Solution Explorer window), and add the following code in the Configuration section:

```
<appSettings>
   <add key="DataConnection"
   value="Provider=Microsoft.Jet.OleDB.4.0;Data
   Source=c:\Inetpub\wwwroot\Chapter15\Course.mdb;User Id=admin;
   Password=;"/>
</appSettings>
```

Note that the key DataConnection stores the connection string. The conConnection object, when created, is initialized with the connection string stored in the Web.config file. Student's last name and login ID information is used to build the SQL query. Using conConnection and cmdCommand objects, the data source is queried and the result is assigned to the DataReader, mrdrReader. The Read method of mrdrReader examines the student's row to determine his/her exam status. The Read method returns False if the ExecuteReader method returned no records. If the student information did exist in the database, CheckStudent returns 'Yet to Take Exam' provided the value of the field AppearedForExam is False. Finally, the conConnection and cmdCommand objects are disposed of, which is the suggested practice.

MakeExam

Next, add the subprogram MakeExam. This is an important subprogram designed to generate the exam by randomly picking the questions from the data source. The VisualBasicQuizBank contains 10 questions. All 10 questions will be retrieved (in random order) and used to make the exam. Essentially, the steps involved in this routine are as follows:

1. Use a loop to generate 10 questions. Before the loop starts, the Randomize() function is used to provide current system time as the seed for the Rnd() function.

2. The code inside the loop generates a random number between 1 and 10. This number represents the question to be retrieved from the data source.

3. The next step is to ensure that the question is not already present in the exam. If the newly generated number is not in the array, the WriteQuestion subroutine is invoked, as in the following code:

```
Private Sub MakeExam()
   'This Procedure Generates the Exam from Database
```

```
Dim intQueNumber, intCount As Integer
Dim bolFound As Boolean

'Seed for the random number
Randomize(Timer)

'Loop to generate 10 questions
Do While mintActCount <= 9
    intQueNumber = CInt(Int((10 * Rnd()) + 1))
    bolFound = False
    Call CheckNumber(intQueNumber, bolFound)

    'If the question is not already in the exam, add it
    If Not bolFound Then
        Call WriteQuestion(intQueNumber)
    End If
Loop
Dim praPara As LiteralControl = New LiteralControl("<p>")
plhPlaceHolder.Controls.Add(praPara)

'Generate and add a button to submit exam
Dim btnExamSubmit As New Button()
btnExamSubmit.Text = "Grade Exam"
btnExamSubmit.ToolTip = "Submit Exam"
btnExamSubmit.ID = "btnExamSubmit"
plhPlaceHolder.Controls.Add(btnExamSubmit)
End Sub
```

4. The loop terminates after 10 questions are generated. For this, a looping variable, `mintActCount` is used.

5. Once the exam is made, a final step is to add a button to submit the exam after the student completes the exam. The button should also be added to the `PlaceHolder` control, `plhPlaceHolder`, using its `Add` method.

CheckNumber

The `MakeExam` subprogram invokes this function, and it supplies one parameter—`intQNbr`—that contains the random number generated in `MakeExam`:

```
Private Function CheckNumber(ByVal intQNbr As Integer) As Boolean
    'Check whether question already included
    Dim intCount, intCheck As Integer

    For intCount = 0 To mintActCount - 1
        If mintComplete(intCount) = intQNbr Then
            'If question found, function returns true
            Return True
            Exit For
        End If
    Next
End Function
```

This function makes use of the `mintComplete()` array that contains the numbers of questions already in the exam to check whether its parameter value is already present in the array. The function returns a `Boolean` value. The `mintComplete()` array is updated *only* after the question is generated in the `WriteQuestion` subprogram.[43]

WriteQuestion

Invoked by the `MakeExam` routine, this subprogram is responsible for generating the question and adding it to the `plhPlaceHolder` control. It accepts a number (`intQNbr`) as its only parameter, representing the number of the question to be added. Any question that does not belong to a group is generated immediately. Grouped questions are generated and added to the placeholder control only if the parameter it receives represents the number of the first question in the group. The code is as follows:

```
Private Sub WriteQuestion(ByVal intQNbr As Integer)
Dim intCount, intGrpQues As Integer
Dim strGroupID As String

Dim strSQL As String = "Select * From VisualBasicQuizBank " + _
"Where ID = " + intQNbr.ToString

Dim conConnection As New OleDb.OleDbConnection.....

Dim cmdCommand As New OleDb.OleDbCommand(strSQL, conConnection)
conConnection.Open()
mrdrReader = cmdCommand.ExecuteReader

mrdrReader.Read()

'Group value 1 indicates that it is not the first question
'in a group of questions. Hence, do nothing
If mrdrReader("Group") = 1 Then
    conConnection.Close()
    Exit Sub
Else
    'If Group value field is > 1, then need to generate
    'more than one question. Else generate one question
    If mrdrReader("Group") > 1 Then
        intGrpQues = mrdrReader("Group") - mrdrReader("ID") + 1
    Else
        intGrpQues = 1
    End If
End If

'Generate 1 or more questions
For intCount = 1 To intGrpQues
```

[43]This is necessary because absence of the `intQNbr` in the array does not guarantee that the question will be generated. Since there are questions that should appear as a group, these questions are generated only if `intQNbr` is the same as the question number of the first question in the group. This is checked in the `WriteQuestion` subprogram.

```
strGroupID = "A" + CStr(mrdrReader("ID"))
mintComplete(mintActCount) = mrdrReader("ID")

'Create and Add label. Label represent the question
Dim lblQuestion As New Label()
'Declare literal controls required for positioning purposes
Dim praPara As LiteralControl = New LiteralControl("<p>")
lblQuestion.Text = "<b>" + CStr(mintActCount + 1) + _
". " + mrdrReader("Question") + "</b>"

plhPlaceHolder.Controls.Add(praPara)
plhPlaceHolder.Controls.Add(lblQuestion)
Dim lbrSpacer As LiteralControl = New LiteralControl("<br>")
plhPlaceHolder.Controls.Add(lbrSpacer)

'Check to see whether type is Multiple choice or True/False
If mrdrReader("Type") <> 1 Then
    'Declare 5 Radiobuttons for 5 choices
    Dim optAnswerA As New RadioButton()
    Dim optAnswerB As New RadioButton()
    Dim optAnswerC As New RadioButton()
    Dim optAnswerD As New RadioButton()
    Dim optAnswerE As New RadioButton()

    'Set properties of Radiobutton controls and
    'add to plhPlaceHolder
    optAnswerA.Text = "<b>A. </b>" + mrdrReader("A") + "<br>"
    optAnswerA.GroupName = strGroupID
    optAnswerA.ID = strGroupID + "A"
    plhPlaceHolder.Controls.Add(optAnswerA)

    optAnswerB.Text = "<b>B. </b>" + mrdrReader("B") + "<br>"
    optAnswerB.GroupName = strGroupID
    optAnswerB.ID = strGroupID + "B"
    plhPlaceHolder.Controls.Add(optAnswerB)

    optAnswerC.Text = "<b>C. </b>" + mrdrReader("C") + "<br>"
    optAnswerC.GroupName = strGroupID
    optAnswerC.ID = strGroupID + "C"
    plhPlaceHolder.Controls.Add(optAnswerC)

    optAnswerD.Text = "<b>D. </b>" + mrdrReader("D") + "<br>"
    optAnswerD.GroupName = strGroupID
    optAnswerD.ID = strGroupID + "D"
    plhPlaceHolder.Controls.Add(optAnswerD)

    optAnswerE.Text = "<b>E. </b>" + mrdrReader("E")
    optAnswerE.GroupName = strGroupID
    optAnswerE.ID = strGroupID + "E"
    plhPlaceHolder.Controls.Add(optAnswerE)
Else
    'Declare 2 Radiobuttons for True/False choices
    Dim optAnswerA As New RadioButton()
    Dim optAnswerB As New RadioButton()
```

```
            optAnswerA.Text = "<b>A. </b>" + "True" + "<br>"
            optAnswerA.GroupName = strGroupID
            optAnswerA.ID = strGroupID + "A"
            plhPlaceHolder.Controls.Add(optAnswerA)

            optAnswerB.Text = "<b>B. </b>" + "False"
            optAnswerB.GroupName = strGroupID
            optAnswerB.ID = strGroupID + "B"
            plhPlaceHolder.Controls.Add(optAnswerB)
    End If
    mrdrReader.Close()
    If intGrpQues > 1 And intCount < intGrpQues Then
        'Select the next question in group
        strSQL = "Select * From VisualBasicQuizBank " + _
        "Where ID = " + (intQNbr + intCount).ToString
        cmdCommand.CommandText = strSQL
        mrdrReader = cmdCommand.ExecuteReader()
        mrdrReader.Read()
    End If

    'Increment count of questions generated
    mintActCount += 1
    If mintActCount > 9 Then
        mrdrReader.Close()
        conConnection.Close()
        conConnection.Dispose()
        cmdCommand.Dispose()
        Exit Sub
    End If
Next

conConnection.Close()
conConnection.Dispose()
cmdCommand.Dispose()
End Sub
```

The local variable, intGrpQues, holds the value that indicates the number of questions to be generated during the current call to the subprogram. If the parameter received by the subprogram is not a group question, then intGrpQues is set to 1. Otherwise, it is set to the number of questions in the group. If intQNbr is not the first question in a group of questions (i.e., the field Group with value of 1), the subprogram is immediately terminated without generating any question. The For....Next loop is executed intGrpQues number of times. Within the loop, Radiobutton objects are instantiated and assigned values. Note that the GroupName attribute of Radiobutton objects for a question is assigned the same value. This is required so that the Radiobuttons can act as a single unit for that question. However, ID attribute is set to a unique value for the Radiobutton objects. The number of actual questions generated is stored in the variable, mintActCount and it is incremented as and when a question is made. After generating the first question in the group (if group question), a query is sent to the data source to

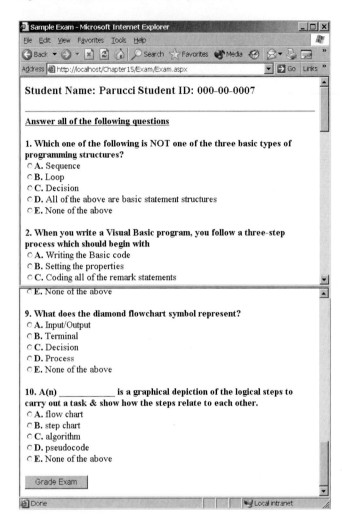

FIGURE 15.12
The Exam.aspx with dynamically generated exam.

retrieve the next question. The `LiteralControls` serve as useful purpose in positioning `Radiobutton` and `Label` controls within the `PlaceHolder` control. Finally, the objects are disposed of. Figure 15.12 shows questions with question numbers. Note that question numbers shown on the interface do not correspond to the `ID` field of questions in the data source. For example, question 1 shown on the interface is actually the second record in the data table.

GradeExam

Once the student submits the exam, this subprogram is invoked. The main function of this routine is to grade the exam by comparing student answers with correct answers in the data source:

```vbnet
Private Sub GradeExam()
  'Grade the Exam and Update Student File
  Dim strStudentAnswers, strAnswer As String
  Dim intCount As Integer = 1
  Dim intNoRight, intNotAnswered As Integer
  'Get the right answers from data source
  Dim strSQL As String = "Select Answer From " + _
  "VisualBasicQuizBank Order by ID"

  Dim conConnection As New OleDb.OleDbConnection.....

  Dim cmdCommand As New OleDb.OleDbCommand(strSQL, conConnection)
  conConnection.Open()

  mrdrReader = cmdCommand.ExecuteReader()

  'Grade Student answers
  While mrdrReader.Read()
      strAnswer = Right(Request.Form("A" & CStr(intCount)), 1)
      If mrdrReader("Answer") = strAnswer Then
          intNoRight += 1
      End If
      If strAnswer = "" Then
          strAnswer = "0"
          intNotAnswered += 1
      End If
      strStudentAnswers += strAnswer
      intCount += 1
  End While

  mrdrReader.Close()

  'Update student record to include student answers and exam status
  strSQL = "Update StudentInformation SET AppearedForExam = True, " + _
  "NumericGrade = " + intNoRight.ToString + ", StudentAnswers = '" + _
  strStudentAnswers + "' Where StudentID = '" + txtPassword.Text + "'"

  cmdCommand.CommandText = strSQL

  cmdCommand.ExecuteNonQuery()

  mrdrReader.Close()
  conConnection.Close()
  conConnection.Dispose()
  cmdCommand.Dispose()

  'Call subprogram to write results
  Call WriteResults(intNoRight, intCount, intNotAnswered)
End Sub
```

The local variables keep track of number of questions, number of questions correctly answered, number of questions not answered, and student answers in the variables `intCount`, `intNoRight`, `intNotAnswered`, and `strStudentAnswers`, respectively. When the exam is rendered on the browser, the .NET automatically renders them as HTML controls. The HTML output for question 1 rendered on the browser is as follows:

```
        <p><span><b>1. Which one of the following is NOT one of the three
basic types of programming structures?</b></span><br>
        <input id="A2A" type="radio" name="A2" value="A2A" /><label
for="A2A"><b>A. </b>Sequence<br></label>
        <input id="A2B" type="radio" name="A2" value="A2B" /><label
for="A2B"><b>B. </b>Loop<br></label>
        <input id="A2C" type="radio" name="A2" value="A2C" /><label
for="A2C"><b>C. </b>Decision<br></label>
        <input id="A2D" type="radio" name="A2" value="A2D" />
        <label for="A2D"><b>D. </b>All of the above are basic statement
structures<br></label>
        <input id="A2E" type="radio" name="A2" value="A2E" /><label
for="A2E"><b>E. </b>None of the above</label>
```

Note that the Name attributes of the rendered HTML Radio form controls for the answers are the same, but the Value attributes of the controls have different values that are the same as the ID attribute values. When the form is submitted, the values of the Radiobutton controls selected by the student become part of the Form collection, and they can be accessed using the Request property (an instance of HTTPRequest class) of the page. For example, to access and store the answer in a string variable for the preceding question, the code will be

```
strAnswer = Request.Form("A2")
```

This will assign 'A2D' to strAnswer if the student had correctly chosen option D as the answer. In the application, the Radiobutton control names were created dynamically. To access them in the GradeExam subprogram, a looping index (intCount) is used and this is appended to letter 'A' to produce the control names such as A1 the first time inside the loop, A2 the second time inside the loop, and so on. Then the Request property is used to retrieve the answers selected by students. The Right string function is used to strip 'D' out of the answer string 'A2D' (for question 2 in the data source). This is required since the last character in the answer string represent the student answer for a specific question. Once the loop terminates after all answers are checked, the student record is updated. Finally, the WriteResults subprogram is called.

WriteResults

Called from the GradeExam subprogram, this subprocedure accepts three parameters—intNumRight, intCnt, and intNA—containing values for number of correct answers, number of questions, and number of incorrect answers, respectively. These are displayed to the student with appropriate messages as shown in Figure 15.13. The code is as follows:

```
Private Sub WriteResults(ByVal intNumRight As Integer, _
ByVal intCnt As Integer, ByVal intNA As Integer)
```

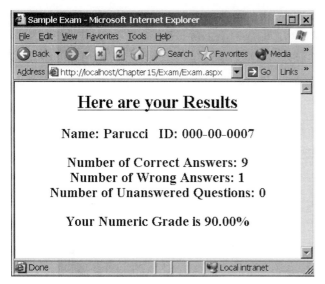

FIGURE 15.13
The Exam.aspx page with results of grading.

```
'Display results of grading to student
Response.Write("<h2><center><u>Here are your Results</u></h2>")
Response.Write("<h3>Name: " + txtLastName.Text + _
"   ID: " + txtPassword.Text + "<p>")
Response.Write("Number of Correct Answers: " + _
intNumRight.ToString + "<br>")
Response.Write("Number of Wrong Answers: " + _
(intCnt - (intNA + intNumRight)).ToString + "<br>")
Response.Write("Number of Unanswered Questions: " + _
intNA.ToString + "<p>")
Response.Write("Your Numeric Grade is " + _
FormatPercent(intNumRight / 10) + "</center></h3>")
End Sub
```

Notes:

1. The application is designed to generate an exam with only 10 questions. However, it can be modified easily to generate any number of questions.

2. Refreshing the page at any instant will not compromise the integrity of the page. Each page refresh invokes the Page_Load event, and during postbacks student exam status is checked first before generating or grading the exam. Hence, clicking *Refresh* button in the browser after results are displayed would result in an appropriate message (Figure 15.14). The same message would show when the student attempts to resubmit the exam with modified answers (after going back to the exam by clicking the *Back* button in the browser). When the exam is generated and shown to the student, clicking the Refresh button would regenerate the exam with questions in different order.

FIGURE 15.14
The Exam.aspx page response when student attempts to retake/resubmit the exam.

SUGGESTED HOME ASSIGNMENTS

1. Design a Web form project to Web-enable teacher evaluation form at your school. When the evaluation is submitted, write to a database. Create the appropriate database first.
2. Design a Web form project to search a student database. The search results should contain a link to retrieve detailed information about the student (similar to Lab 15.1). The database for Lab 15.1 can be used for this assignment
3. Design a Web form project to retrieve a quote from the database. Create a database, and name it QuoteOfTheDay.mdb. Each visit to the page should produce a different quote. Use random functions to select a quote.

TEST YOURSELF

1. What information is contained in the client's request to the Web server?
2. What property of the Page class exposes an instance of the HTTPRequest class?
3. What are cookies?
4. What does the Params collection of the HTTPRequest class contain?
5. Briefly explain the End method of HTTPResponse class.
6. How is an instance of the HTTPResponse class accessed by the page object?
7. Explain any two ways by which state can be maintained in Web applications.
8. In the site **http://www.mapquest.com**, when inputs of from and to addresses are provided to determine driving directions, how is this input information carried over to the directions page?
9. What is the main limitation of using cookies to maintain state?
10. Compare and contrast cookies and session variables.
11. How is an instance of HTTPSessionState class exposed to the page object?
12. Briefly explain the role of Global.asax file.
13. What are the benefits of using a DataReader object?

14. Which namespace contains the SQL server.NET data providers?

15. What purpose does the URL format string property of a field serve in a DataGrid control?

16. Literal controls help positioning of dynamic controls in place holders. Explain.

17. When should one use the PlaceHolder control?

18. How is the Web.Config file used in Lab 15.2?

19. Define the syntax to create and add a new Radiobutton control dynamically to a PlaceHolder control.

20. Consider the following code from Lab 15.2:

```
Dim lbrSpacer As LiteralControl = New LiteralControl("<br>")
plhPlaceHolder.Controls.Add(lbrSpacer)
```

Explain its purpose.

Web Services

CHAPTER OBJECTIVES

After completing this chapter, students should understand

1. The Web services framework
2. The components of Web services:
   - Extensible Markup Language (XML)
   - The XML Schema Definition (XSD)
   - Simple Object Access Protocol (SOAP)
   - Web Services Description Language (WSDL)
   - Universal Description, Discovery and Integration (UDDI) standard
3. How to create Web services
4. How these services are consumed by a client through the use of Proxy classes

16.1   AIMS OF CHAPTER

While Chapters 14 and 15 focused on the Web forms model of ASP.NET programming, this chapter focuses on the second model of programming, Web services. This is a very popular model that is expected to cause a major change in Web programming. The standards of this model such as SOAP and WSDL are still evolving. This chapter presents the components of the Web services model along with examples of how to create Web services and consume them. Since Web services use HTTP, they can go through firewalls, thus enhancing the possibility of widespread acceptance of Web services. In an oversimplified way, Web services can be thought of as subprograms or functions that generate required output after performing tasks using supplied inputs. However, unlike subprograms or functions, they reside on a remote server.

16.2   INTRODUCTION

Web development has come a long way. Since Tim Berners Lee created the World Wide Web concept, the Web browser has become a standard interface in Web application development—and a necessity in many aspects of life. Programming, in general, has gone through tremendous transformations, from command line languages (FORTRAN) to GUI languages (Visual Basic.NET). Similarly, in the world of Web development, it started from static Web pages to dynamic Web pages and currently Web services. Web services provide functionality and allow clients to consume the functionality regardless of where the application is located or the platform on which it is built. To achieve this, Web services use standard protocols such as HTTP. Businesses now can expose common functionalities to everyone or they can expose niche services to those who are in need of those services and ready to pay a price for it. Since firewalls allow HTTP traffic, consuming a Web service is easy. The functionalities of a Web service can range from simple services that return a single value to complex services that return a class or a dataset.

Once a Web service is made available on the Internet, a client should be able to locate the service—for example, via a directory. Once the service on a specific domain is located, clients must be able to discover all the Web services in that domain. After that, the description of each service and the parameters the service requires should be made available to the client. Finally, once a client understands the service description, the client can create applications to consume that service. In order to achieve all this, certain standards have been instituted.

16.2.1   XML Web Services—Established and Emerging Standards

The standards make it possible to create and consume Web services, irrespective of a user's location and platform constraints. There are various elements making up a Web service.\

Hypertext Transfer Protocol (HTTP)   This is the standard protocol of the World Wide Web. Most firewalls allow communications over TCP port 80, while they may close other ports such as 21 (for FTP). Since Web services use HTTP, clients and Web service providers can communicate without any hindrance.

Extensible Markup Language (XML**) and** XML **Schema Definition (**XSD**)**   XML, a derivative of Standard Generalized Markup Language (SGML), provides a standard way of representing data. The current version is XML 1.0, with version 1.1 currently (as of March 2003[4th] considered a work in progress. For more information, visit) http://www.w3.org/TR.[44] Since different platforms provide different types of type structures, this poses a problem in communications between the client and service provider. For example, an Integer data type on the client may use 16 bits, but the service provider may use 32 bits. While XML provides a way to represent data, the standard does not include standard data types and ways to extend them. The XML

---

[44]The World Wide Web Consortium (W3C), headed by Tim Berners-Lee, sets the standards for various protocols and languages used on the Internet.

schema (XSD) standard is the type system used by Web services. The XML schema allows simple and complex data types, and the tool used to create a Web service (VS.NET) usually converts the local data types used in the service to XSD types. The data are serialized and deserialized to text and transmitted using HTTP. XML is fast becoming the standard for data communications. In fact, Microsoft's use of XML for data communications in ADO.NET is an indication of the popularity and acceptance of XML.

Simple Object Access Protocol (SOAP).   When a Web service is available for use, clients should be able to send requests to and receive responses from the service. While XML provides means to represent the data structures and data, SOAP specifications provide the formats for the requests and the responses containing remote procedure call (RPC) or data or both. The specifications also provide standard rules for encoding data as XML so that data can be transferred across heterogeneous platforms. A SOAP message consists of a header and a body.

SOAP version 1.1 specifications are presented as a *NOTE* by W3C and hence are not yet a recommended standard. Version 1.2 is currently being drafted by W3C.

Web Services Description Language (WSDL).   The offerings of a Web service are outlined in a document using the Web Service Description Language. This is important, since a client must first understand what a service has to offer before consuming the service. Thus, XML-based WSDL provides a formal machine-readable (human-readable, too) description of the Web service that includes methods exposed, parameter inputs required, and data types of return values. When Web services are designed using VS.NET, the WSDL document for the Web service is automatically generated.

Once the location of the remote Web service is known to the client, VS.NET can automatically generate a proxy class for the service. The client application can then instantiate this class (as if it were a local class) and use its methods.

Universal Description, Discovery, and Integration (UDDI).   According to **http://www.uddi.org**, "The UDDI specification enables businesses to quickly, easily, and dynamically find and transact with one another. UDDI enables a business to (i) describe its business and its services, (ii) discover other businesses that offer desired services, and (iii) integrate with these other businesses." There are millions of businesses online, and the number is increasing every day. While not all of them offer Web services, it is still difficult for organizations to find the available Web services. Also, once a service is found there are no mechanisms available to determine how to conduct business electronically with the service provider. UDDI attempts to solve the issue of finding a service by creating a central UDDI registry for Web services and by organizing the different services into distinct groups. The UDDI registry also provides information on how the service provider prefers to conduct business with the business clients. Thus, UDDI helps to create a marketplace of Web services where service providers and potential clients can conduct business. Currently, the UDDI registry is jointly managed by IBM, Microsoft, and SAP and this shows the strong commitment of these corporations to the UDDI initiative. Once a service provider develops a Web service, it can be registered in the UDDI registry.

In order to completely describe the elements involved in a Web service and how they interact with each other, the next section demonstrates how to create a simple Web service and consume it.

16.3   DESIGNING A SIMPLE XML WEB SERVICE USING VISUAL STUDIO.NET

In this section, a Web service for computing mortgage payments will be built. A Web service file has an `.asmx` extension. Similar to Web forms programming, Web services programming has two coding models: code-inline and code-behind models. In the single file model, there will be only an `.asmx` file, whereas in the code-behind model, there are two files: an `.asmx` file and an `.asmx.vb` file. The code-behind model is recommended, as VS.NET IDE provides a lot of support for this model. Additionally, as mentioned in Chapter 14, the code-behind model is similar to Windows programming.

16.3.1   A Web Service New Project

Open VS.NET, and click `New Project`. Select `Visual Basic Projects` from the `New Project` window. Then, select `ASP.NET Web Service`, and enter `Mortgage` as the name of the service. This will create a solution file `Mortgage.sln` in the `Mortgage` folder (Figure 16.1). Click OK, and the resulting IDE will be as shown in Figure 16.2. Change the `Service1.asmx` filename to `Mortgage.asmx`. The files that appear in the `Solution Explorer` (automatically added by the IDE) are similar to the ones for a Web forms application:

- `AssemblyInfo.vb`: Describes the assembly and specifies the versioning information.
- `Global.asax`: Contains code for application-level events.
- `Mortgage.asmx`: This file in the code-behind model contains only a reference to code-behind file, the class name and the language used. A sample is `<%@`

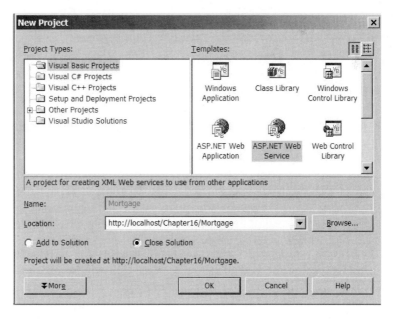

FIGURE 16.1
A new Web service project.

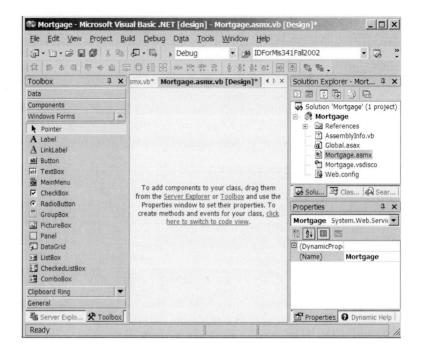

FIGURE 16.2
The VS.NET IDE for creating a Web service.

```
WebService Language="vb" Codebehind="Mortgage.asmx.vb" Class="Mort-
gage.Mortgage" %>
```

This file is the entry point for the Web service.

- `Mortgage.asmx.vb`: The code-behind file that contains the class definition for the Web service.

- `Mortgage.vsdisco`: This is a discovery file that helps clients to locate the Web service. This file contains links to the documents that describe the Web service using `WSDL`, documentation for the Web service, and references to other discovery documents. Discovery is a process of locating one or more related documents that describe a Web service. If the client knows the location of the service description, the discovery process can be bypassed. It is expected that the .vsdisco will become obsolete in favor of `UDDI`.

- `Web.Config`: Configuration settings for the service, such as mode of authentication and list of valid users.

Select the code view for the `Mortgage.asmx` file and add the following code to the existing code (the methods of a Web service that will be exposed to the client must have the `<WebMethod()>` processing directive):

```
Imports System.Web.Services

<WebService(Namespace:="http://tempuri.org/")> _
```

```
Public Class Mortgage
    Inherits System.Web.Services.WebService

#Region " Web Services Designer Generated Code "

    <WebMethod(Description:="This method accepts Loan Amount,
    Interest/year, and Period in Years to compute Monthly
    Mortgage Payments")> _
    Public Function MonthlyPayment(ByVal sngPrincipal As Single,_
    ByVal sngInterest As Single, ByVal intYears As Integer) _
    As Single
        'Compute and Return Monthly Payments
        sngInterest = sngInterest / 1200

        intYears = CInt(intYears * 12)

        Return sngPrincipal * (sngInterest _
    / (1 - (1 + sngInterest) ^ -intYears))
    End Function
End Class
```

The Web service classes belong to the System.Web.Services namespace and hence the Imports   System.Web.Services statement. The description of the MonthlyPayment function can be provided inside the <WebMethod()>, as shown in the previous code. The function accepts three parameters—sngPrincipal, sngInterest, and intYears, representing loan amount, annual interest rate, and loan period in years, respectively—to compute the monthly payment. To test the Web service, press F5 to run it. The resulting browser window should be as shown in Figure 16.3. The page

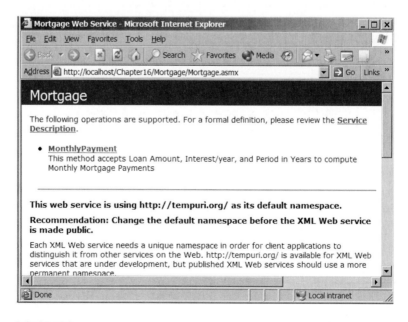

FIGURE 16.3
The mortgage Web service as seen in a browser.

shown in Figure 16.3 is automatically generated by ASP.NET runtime whenever a Web service file is called directly from a browser instead of through a SOAP request. The page displays a warning message for using **http://tempuri.org/** as the Web service's default namespace. A unique namespace should be used before deploying a Web service, since client applications need to distinguish it from other Web services on the Web. The page shows two important links: (1) a link to the method exposed by the Web service and (2) a link to the service description. If the Web service exposes more methods, there will be a link for each method.

Click the MonthlyPayment link to test this method. The resulting page contains textboxes to accept inputs for the method and also samples of a SOAP request and response, an HTTP GET request and response, and an HTTP POST request and response.

Provide sample inputs, and click the Invoke button. The HTTP GET protocol is used to invoke the method of the Web service as mentioned under Test sub heading in Figure 16.4. A new browser window will open, and the results in XML should be

```
<?xml version="1.0" encoding="utf-8" ?>
<float xmlns="http://tempuri.org/">2317.531</float>
```

Note that the Web service returned a float data value of 2317.531. Analysis of the URL in the resulting window shows the following, indicating that the values are indeed sent as QueryString variables:

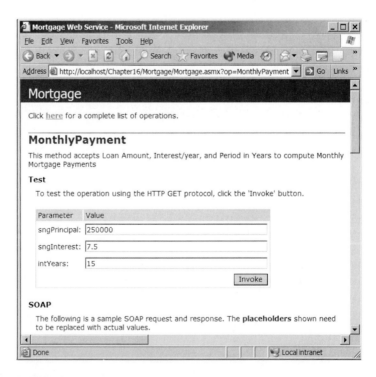

FIGURE 16.4
Testing the Web service method, MonthlyPayment.

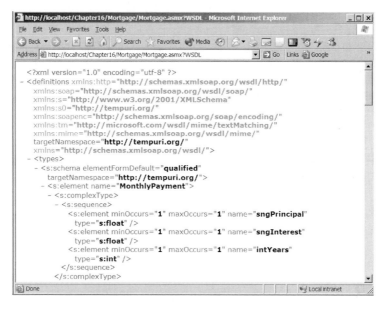

FIGURE 16.5
The service description in WSDL.

http://localhost/Chapter16/Mortgage/Mortgage.asmx/MonthlyPayment?
sngPrincipal=250000sngInterest=7.5intYears=15

Next, click the service description link in the main documentation page (Figure 16.3). The resulting page shows the WSDL contract of the Web service, which describes the methods exposed by the service, input parameters required, and the output the service generates.

The WSDL contract is a crucial document, since client applications use this contract to generate a proxy class through which they consume the service. The process of proxy class creation and Web service consumption is presented in the next section. Since the namespace of the Web service should be unique, modify the namespace of the service from[45]

```
<WebService(Namespace:="http://tempuri.org/")>
```

to

```
<WebService(Namespace:="http://your domain/Chapter16/Mortgage/")>
```

and rebuild the project so that the changes take effect. When the service is tested again, note that the warning message that appeared earlier (Figure 16.3) has disappeared. Refer to Figure 16.7 that shows the modified service.

---

[45]For this example, the domain name is Localhost.

16.3.2 Consuming the Web Service

This section focuses on understanding how Web services are consumed. Create an ASP.NET application, and name it `MortgageClient`. Name the Web form file `MortgageClient.aspx`. Add three `TextBox` controls to provide inputs for the loan amount, the interest rate, and the duration of the loan. Also, add a `Button` control. The next step is to create a proxy class based on the `WSDL` contract of the Web service created in the last section. When a Web reference to the Web service is added to the ASP.NET application, VS.NET IDE automatically creates the proxy class. Select `Add Web Reference` from the `Project` menu. In the resulting `Add Web Reference` popup window, type the address of the .asmx file as shown in Figure 16.6.

The address of the `.asmx` file created earlier is

http://localhost/Chapter16/Mortgage/Mortgage.asmx

Note that, for a production Web service, the domain name (localhost) should be replaced with the actual domain name hosting the service. Once the address of the `asmx` file is provided in the `Add Web Reference` window, clicking the button (or pressing `Enter` key) will retrieve the contract and the documentation for the Web service, as shown in Figure 16.7.

Click the `Add Reference` button, and this reference should appear in the `Solution Explorer` window. Select `Show All Files` option and expand `Web References`. It will

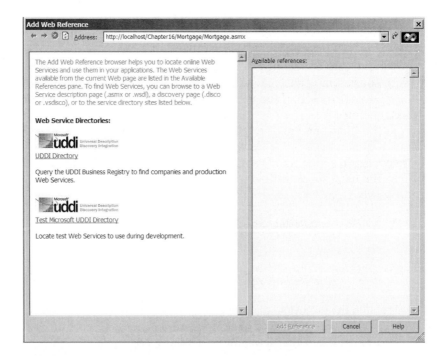

FIGURE 16.6
Add Web reference interface.

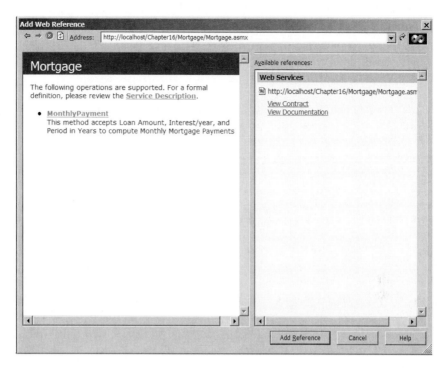

FIGURE 16.7
Mortgage Web service documentation.

show a new `.vb` file called `Reference.vb` containing the proxy class definitions for the Web service. Now, add the following code to the click event of the button on the Web forms page:

```
Private Sub btnSubmit_Click(ByVal sender As System.Object, _
ByVal e As System.EventArgs) Handles btnSubmit.Click

  'Create Proxy class instance and consume Web service
  Dim clsMortgage As New localhost.Mortgage()

  lblPayment.Text = "Monthly Payment " + "<Font color=Red>" + _
  FormatCurrency(clsMortgage.MonthlyPayment(CSng(txtPrincipal.Text, _
  CSng(txtInterest.Text), CInt(txtPeriod.Text))) + "</Font>"

  clsMortgage = Nothing
End Sub
```

Since a reference to the Web service has been added to the application, the namespace for the Web service will show in IntelliSense as shown in Figure 16.8. In the code, an instance of the Mortgage class belonging to the namespace Localhost is created, and its MonthlyPayment method is invoked. Although Mortgage is a proxy class, it acts as if it were a local class. The client application is transparent to the actual implementation of the method MonthlyPayment.

FIGURE 16.8
IntelliSense showing namespace and class of the referenced Web service.

Run the ASP.NET application, and the results should be as shown in Figure 16.9. Note that this is a simple application that does not check for validity of inputs. The communication between the ASP.NET client application and the Web service is through SOAP. The example Web service and the client application demonstrate how easy it is to create the service and consume it using the code-behind programming model in VS.NET IDE. For the single-page model, proxy classes are created using command line syntax. In this age of windows GUI, compiling with command lines is a little primitive, and the authors again strongly recommend using the code-behind model. The following is a summary of the concepts presented so far:

- Web services are easy to define. They are similar to a method definition, but with the WebMethod() directive.
- The namespace used should be unique to enable client applications to distinguish one Web service from another.
- Each Web service has a WSDL contract associated with it, and it is generated automatically by VS.NET.
- Communications between client applications and the Web services occur using SOAP.
- Web services can be registered in the UDDI registry, which is jointly hosted by Microsoft, IBM, and SAP.

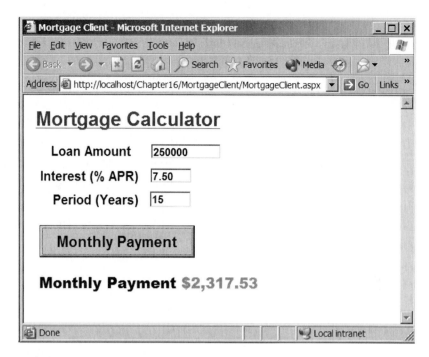

FIGURE 16.9
A client application consuming the Web service.

- Client applications create a proxy class based on the WSDL contract, and through this class, they consume the Web service. The WSDL contract that describes the Web service is crucial to understanding the services provided.
- Creation of proxy class is automatically done by the VS.NET IDE once a reference to the Web service is added to the application.
- The discovery files help the discovery process. However, it can be bypassed if the location of the WSDL contract is known.

The next two labs present more examples of Web services. In the first one, a Web service is designed to send email after validating the email addresses through another Web service. In the second, a client application is designed to consume Unisys weather Web service.

LAB 16.1 THE EMAIL WEB SERVICE

Lab Objectives:
The main lab objectives are as follows:

- Learn how to create a Web service that uses email features available in .NET
- Learn how to search Web services using the UDDI registry
- Learn how to use a remote Web service that returns a class containing information about the validity of email addresses

Application Overview

Web services can be used for several purposes, and this lab focuses on creating a Web service that sends out email. The parameters of the email such as From and To addresses, Subject, and Message body will be supplied by the client application consuming the service. The Web service utilizes a remote Web service to validate the email addresses. The remote Web service accepts one parameter, an email address, and returns a class containing information about the validity of the email address. Once the Web service is designed, a client application that consumes the Web service will be built.

Designing the email Web Service

From the `File` menu, select `New`, then `Project`, and finally `ASP.NET Web Service` under `Visual Basic Projects`. Type `FreeEMail` in the `Location` textbox, and create this in folder `Chapter16`. Rename the `.asmx` file `Email.asmx`. This file will contain a reference to the code-behind file `Email.asmx.vb`. The class definitions for the Web service should be added to the code-behind file. The code in `Email.asmx` is

```
<%@ WebService Language="vb" Codebehind="EMail.asmx.vb"
Class="FreeEMail.EMail" %>
```

Since this service will be using another remote Web service, a reference to the remote service should be added first to enable VS.NET IDE to create a proxy class. The available Web services can be searched using the `UDDI` registry jointly maintained by IBM, Microsoft, and SAP. Each company maintains a separate Web page for `UDDI` and the addresses are as follows:

IBM: **https://uddi.ibm.com/ubr/find**
Microsoft: **http://uddi.microsoft.com/**
SAP: **http://uddi.sap.com/**

Since they all contain the same data, any one of these sites can be used to search the available Web services and service providers. A quick search in IBM's UDDI site revealed the following entry point for an email verification service provided by CDYNE Systems—**http://www.cdyne.com** (Fig 16.10):

http://ws.cdyne.com/emailverify/ev.asmx

Select `Add Web Reference` from the `Project` menu, and add the preceding reference to the Web service project. The next step is to code the Web service. But first, the remote Web service must be thoroughly understood. Earlier, in the `Mortgage` example, it was known exactly what the Web service would return, since the service was built to demonstrate the concept of a Web service. The email verifier service, however, is remotely located; hence, a thorough understanding of what type of data the service returns is crucial before successfully consuming it. Such an understanding can be achieved in one of three ways: (a) by studying the `WSDL` contract of the service after clicking the Service Description link in the address **http://ws.cdyne.com/emailverify/ev.asmx**, (b) by invoking the methods (Figure 16.11) of the service and studying the results, and (c) by studying the proxy class contained in the `Reference.vb` file. A brief explanation of each is presented next:

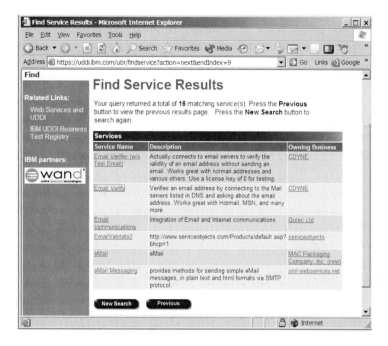

FIGURE 16.10
CDYNE's email verify service (found using IBM's UDDI Registry).

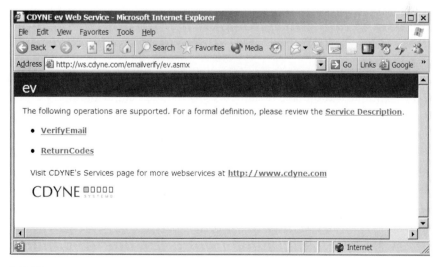

FIGURE 16.11
CDYNE's email Web service.

(a)   The WSDL contract is an XML document; hence, knowledge of XML is required to understand it. This contract is mainly intended for the VS.NET interface to generate the proxy class.

(b)   Invoking the VerifyEMail method of the service after providing **Chitti@drexel.edu** resulted in the following XML document:

```
<?xml version="1.0" encoding="utf-8" ?>
<ReturnIndicator xmlns:xsd="http://www.w3.org/2001/XMLSchema"
  xmlns:xsi="http://www.w3.org/2001/XMLSchema-instance"
  xmlns="http://ws.cdyne.com/">
<ResponseText>Mail Server will accept email</ResponseText>
<ResponseCode>3</ResponseCode>
<LastMailServer>glue.irt.drexel.edu</LastMailServer>
</ReturnIndicator>
```

In this XML document, there are three block tags—<ResponseText> </ResponseText>, <ResponseCode></ResponseCode>, and <LastMailServer> </LastMailServer>—contained within block tag <ReturnIndicator> </ReturnIndi-cator>. The tags are self-explanatory, except for ResponseCode. Invoking the second method returns another XML document with information about what those codes mean:

```
<?xml version="1.0" encoding="utf-8" ?>
http://ws.cdyne.com/emailverify/ev.asmx/ReturnCodes?
<ArrayOfAnyType xmlns:xsd="http://www.w3.org/2001/XMLSchema"
  xmlns:xsi="http://www.w3.org/2001/XMLSchema-instance"
  xmlns="http://ws.cdyne.com/">
<anyType xsi:type="xsd:string">0-Invalid Email Address</anyType>
<anyType xsi:type="xsd:string">1-Processing</anyType>
<anyType xsi:type="xsd:string">2-Verified Email Address</anyType>
<anyType xsi:type="xsd:string">3-Mail Server Accepted Email
  (awaiting verification)</anyType>
<anyType xsi:type="xsd:string">4-User not found</anyType>
<anyType xsi:type="xsd:string">5-Email Domain not found</anyType>
</ArrayOfAnyType>
```

(c)   Although these XML documents give an idea about the data returned by the service, the best way to learn more about the data structure of the results from the service is to study the proxy class contained in Reference.vb file. The Spe-cific contents of this file are as follows (the additional code present in the proxy class is not of importance in the current context):

```
Namespace com.cdyne.ws

Public Class ev
    Inherits ---

    Public Function VerifyEmail(ByVal email As String) As _
    ReturnIndicator
        Dim results() As Object = _
```

```
        Me.Invoke("VerifyEmail", New Object() {email})
        Return CType(results(0),ReturnIndicator)
    End Function
    ---

    Public Function ReturnCodes() As Object()
        Dim results() As Object = _
        Me.Invoke("ReturnCodes", New Object(-1) {})
        Return CType(results(0),Object())
    End Function
    ---

End Class
---

Public Class ReturnIndicator

    '<remarks/>
    Public ResponseText As String

    '<remarks/>
    Public ResponseCode As Integer

    '<remarks/>
     Public LastMailServer As String
End Class
End Namespace
```

Studying the preceding code gives a clear picture of the data types returned by the method. The VerifyEMail method returns a ReturnIndicator class. This class contains three Public properties ResponseText, ResponseCode, and LastMailServer. Note that the namespace is com.cdyne.ws and there are two classes in the namespace ev and ReturnIndicator. Thus, the proxy class contains the complete information required to understand the Web service.

Continuing with FreeEMail Web service project, double-click on the EMail.asmx.vb design interface, and add the following code for the SendMail method:

```
Imports System.Web.Services
Imports System.Web.Mail

<WebService(Namespace:="http://your domain/Chapter16")> _
Public Class EMail
        Inherits System.Web.Services.WebService
<WebMethod(Description:="This method sends free " & _
"e-mail")> Public Function SendMail(ByVal strFromAddr As String, _
ByVal strToAddr As String, ByVal strSubj As String, ByVal strMsg As _
String) As String
  'Free E-Mail Web Service
  Dim objCheck As New com.cdyne.ws.ev()

  Dim objFromAddr As com.cdyne.ws.ReturnIndicator = _
  objCheck.VerifyEmail(strFromAddr)
  Dim objToAddr As com.cdyne.ws.ReturnIndicator = _
  objCheck.VerifyEmail(strToAddr)
```

```
Dim intFromCode As Int16 = objFromAddr.ResponseCode
Dim intToCode As Int16 = objToAddr.ResponseCode

If intFromCode = 2 Or intFromCode = 3 Then
    If intToCode = 2 Or intToCode = 3 Then
        Dim objMail As New MailMessage()
        objMail.From = strFromAddr
        objMail.To = strToAddr

        'Syntax for cc
        'objMail.Cc = More Address

        'Syntax for Bcc
        'objMail.Bcc = More Address

        objMail.Subject = strSubj
        objMail.Body = strMsg
        SmtpMail.SmtpServer = "..mail server address here.."46
        SmtpMail.Send(objMail)
        objMail = Nothing
        Return "Mail Sent!"
    Else
        Return "Problem with To Address: " & objToAddr.ResponseText
    End If
Else
    Return "Problem with From Address: " & objFromAddr.ResponseText
End If
objCheck = Nothing
objFromAddr = Nothing
objToAddr = Nothing
End Function
End Class
```

In the preceding method, make sure to add code to (a) import the `System.Web.Mail` namespace and (b) change the name of the Web service's default namespace from **http://tempuri.org/** to something unique. Students are advised to use their school's domain name, with appropriate extensions (such as student ID) for the namespace. The Web service returns a string indicating whether the mail could be sent. If not, the incorrect email address is identified in the error message.

A new instance of the proxy class (`com.cdyne.ws.ev`) for the remote Web service is created in `objCheck`. Two more objects, `objFromAddr` and `objToAddr` of type `com.cdyne.ws.ReturnIndicator` class are created next. The `VerifyEMail` method of the remote Web service accepts an email address as the parameter and returns the `ReturnIndicator` class whose properties provide information about the validity of the email address. Two of the `SendMail` method's parameters, `strFromAddr` and `strToAddr`, are validated using the remote service. If the `ResponseCode` property value is either 2 or 3, then the email address is valid. This is checked for both the addresses. If both are valid addresses, then an instance of the `MailMessage` class is created in `objMail`. Once

---

[46]Students are advised to use their University's SMTP server address here.

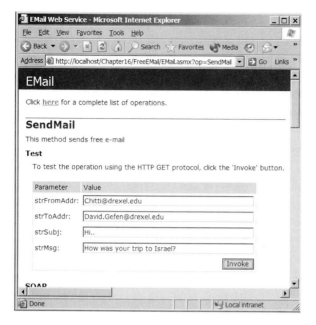

FIGURE 16.12A
Web service's `SendMail` method parameters.

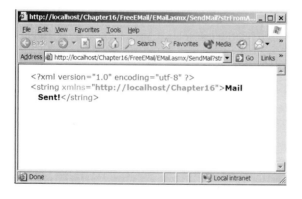

FIGURE 16.12B
XML result confirming status of email message.

the properties of this object are assigned with appropriate values, the email is sent. Finally, all the created objects are destroyed. Build and run the Web service by pressing F5. Sample inputs and results are shown in Figure 16.12.

The Client Application   Design a new ASP.NET application, and name the `aspx` page `FreeEMail.aspx`. In this lab, the client application will also be created in `Chapter16` folder. Add the appropriate controls (including validation controls) to build an interface for sending email as shown in Figure 16.13. Add a Web reference to the Web service created in the previous section. The Web address is

http://localhost/Chapter16/FreeEMail/EMail.asmx

FIGURE 16.13
Client application interface.

VS.NET IDE creates the necessary proxy class[47] for the service, and the next step is to add code to the `Click` event of the `Button` control.

If values are present for the From and To address `TextBox` controls,[48] an object of the proxy class is created and the Web service is consumed:

```
Private Sub btnSendMail_Click(ByVal sender As System.Object, ByVal e _
As System.EventArgs) Handles btnSendMail.Click
  'Send E-Mail

  Dim objEMail As New EMail.WebReference1.EMail()
  lblStatus.Text = _
  objEMail.SendMail(txtFromAddress.Text, txtToAddress.Text, _
  txtSubject.Text, txtMessage.Text)
  objEMail = Nothing
  If lblStatus.Text = "Mail Sent!" Then
     txtFromAddress.Text = ""
     txtToAddress.Text = ""
     txtSubject.Text = ""
     txtMessage.Text = ""
  End If
End Sub
```

A `Label` is used to display the status message of the email from the Web service. If the email is sent successfully, an appropriate message is shown in the label, and the

---

[47]The proxy class will be contained in `Reference.vb` file! It is left as an exercise for the student to study the contents of this file.

[48]Two `RequiredFieldValidators` are used to validate these two `TextBox` controls.

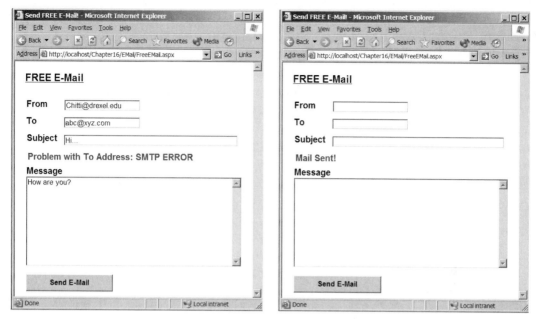

FIGURE 16.14
The client application at various stages.

contents of the textboxes are cleared. Note that, for the body of the message, a `TextBox` control is used with the `TextMode` property set to `MultiLine`. The autogenerated code is not shown here, since we have used similar code in previous labs. Figure 16.14 show sample interfaces after building and running the application.

In the next lab, another remote Web service is analyzed, and a client application to consume the service is designed. This remote Web service (Unisys Weather Web service) accepts the zip code as input and returns a class containing forecast for seven days. From a learning perspective, students should find this Web service very interesting.

LAB 16.2: UNISYS WEATHER WEB SERVICE

Lab Objectives:

The main lab objectives are as follows:

- Understand the data structure provided by Unisys Weather Web service
- Create a client application to consume the Web service

Application Overview

Unisys Corporation provides a Weather Web service that accepts zip code as input and returns weather forecast data for one week in two formats. There are two methods exposed by this service: `GetWeather` and `GetWeatherText`. The forecast data are returned as a string by `GetWeatherText` method while `GetWeather` returns a class. After studying proxy class for the Web service, a client application to consume the service will be built.

Unisys Weather Web Service

Searching the `UDDI` registry for weather-related Web services identified the Unisys service located at **http://weather.unisysfsp.com/PDCWebService/WeatherServices.asmx**[49] (Figure 16.15). Since the best way to understand the data returned by these services is to study the proxy class, the next section starts building the client application starting with adding a Web reference to the weather service.

The Client Application

Start a new `ASP.NET` Web Application named `Weather` in `Chapter16` folder. Rename `WebForm1.aspx` to `Weather.aspx`. Add a Web reference to the Unisys Weather Web service (**http://weather.unisysfsp.com/PDCWebService/WeatherServices.asmx**[50]) so that VS.NET can create a proxy class for this service. To study the proxy class, open the `Reference.vb` file (after selecting `Show All Files` icon in `Solution Explorer`). The following code shows selected parts of this proxy class:

```
Namespace com.unisysfsp.weather
    ---
Public Class WeatherServices
```

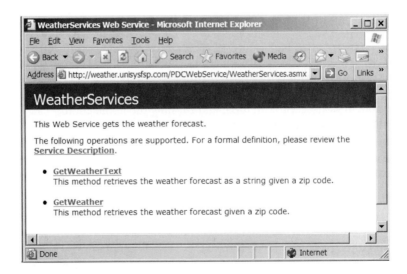

FIGURE 16.15
Unisys Weather Web service methods.

---

[49]Both the remote Web services in this chapter are free to consume. However, commercial Web services are not free and require a *License key* (given by the service provider) that should be passed as one of the method parameters to consume the service. Without the license key, the Web service methods will not work.

[50]More information about Unisys Weather services can be obtained from **http://Weather.unisys.com**.

```
Inherits System.Web.Services.Protocols.SoapHttpClientProtocol
    ---
Public Function GetWeather(ByVal ZipCode As String) As _
WeatherForecast
    Dim results() As Object = Me.Invoke("GetWeather", _
    New Object() {ZipCode})
    Return CType(results(0),WeatherForecast)
End Function

    ---
Public Function GetWeatherText(ByVal ZipCode As String) As String
    Dim results() As Object = Me.Invoke("GetWeatherText", _
    New Object() {ZipCode})
    Return CType(results(0),String)
End Function
    ---
End Class
```

The namespace for this service is `com.unisysfsp.weather`. The code shows the two exposed methods: `GetWeather` and `GetWeatherText`. `GetWeatherText` accepts `ZipCode` parameter and returns a `String` value. `GetWeather` also accepts `ZipCode` parameter, but returns a value of type `WeatherForecast`. Studying the proxy class further reveals that `WeatherForecast` is a class. Hence, `GetWeather` returns a class as output. Here is the code:

```
    ---
Public Class WeatherForecast

    '<remarks/>
    Public ZipCode As String

    '<remarks/>
    Public CityShortName As String

    '<remarks/>
    Public Time As String

    '<remarks/>
    Public Sunrise As String

    '<remarks/>
    Public Sunset As String

    '<remarks/>
    Public CurrentTemp As String

    '<remarks/>
    Public DayForecast() As DailyForecast
End Class
```

The `WeatherForecast` class exposes seven properties, the data type of the first six of which is `String`:

1. `ZipCode`—This contains the input parameter Zip code value.
2. `CityShortName`—Name of the City for the Zip code.

3. `Time`—The current time.
4. `Sunrise`—Time of Sunrise for the day.
5. `Sunset`—Time of Sunset for the day.
6. `CurrentTemp`—Current temperature information in Fahrenheit.
7. `DayForecast()`—This is an array of type `DailyForecast`. `DailyForecast` is another class defined in the proxy class. Its structure is as follows:

```
Public Class DailyForecast

    '<remarks/>
    Public Day As String

    '<remarks/>
    Public Forecast As String

    '<remarks/>
    Public Abbrev As String

    '<remarks/>
    Public HighTemp As String

    '<remarks/>
    Public LowTemp As String
End Class
```

The `DailyForecast` class exposes five variables, all of type `String`:

1. `Day`—Current day.
2. `Forecast`—Weather forecast for the day.
3. `Abbrev`—Abbreviation for forecast.
4. `HighTemp`—High temperature for the day in Fahrenheit.
5. `LowTemp`—Low temperature for the day in Fahrenheit.

Thus, the `GetWeather` method returns a class `WeatherForecast` that contains among other properties a `DayForecast()` array of type `DailyForecast` class. This `DailyForecast` class actually contains the forecast information for seven days. Actually, the `DayForecast()` array contains 10 objects of type `DailyForecast`, two each for the first three days and one each for the next four days. This can be tested by invoking the Web service directly using the following address of the `.asmx` file:

http://weather.unisysfsp.com/PDCWebService/WeatherServices.asmx

Now that the Web service methods and data types are clear, continue building the client application. Add appropriate controls to the Web form for providing inputs. Figure 16.16 shows a `CheckBox` control to provide input if the user preferred a simple forecast.

Add the following code to the `Click` event of the `Button` control `btnWeather`:

```
Private Sub btnWeather_Click(ByVal sender As System.Object, _
ByVal e As System.EventArgs) Handles btnWeather.Click
```

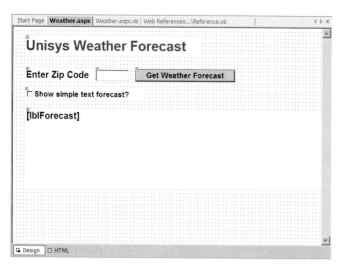

FIGURE 16.16
The client application interface.

```vb
'Gets the Weather for a Week
Dim objWeather As New com.unisysfsp.weather.WeatherServices()

If Not chkOutputOption.Checked Then
    'Show Forecast by Day
    Dim objForecast As New com.unisysfsp.weather.WeatherForecast()
    Dim objDayForecast() As com.unisysfsp.weather.DailyForecast

    Try
        objForecast = objWeather.GetWeather(txtZipCode.Text)
        objDayForecast = objForecast.DayForecast

        Dim intCount As Integer

        lblForecast.Text = "<Table><tr><td colspan=3>"
        lblForecast.Text += "<Font Color=Red>City: " & _
        objForecast.CityShortName & "</Font></td></tr>"
        lblForecast.Text += "<tr><td colspan=3>Sunrise: " & _
        objForecast.Sunrise
        lblForecast.Text += " Sunset: " & objForecast.Sunset & _
        "</td></tr>"
        lblForecast.Text += "<tr><td colspan=3>Current Time: " & _
        objForecast.Time & "</td></tr>"

        'This loop produces actual forecast contained
        'in objDayForecast array
        For intCount = 0 To UBound(objDayForecast)
            lblForecast.Text += "<tr>"
            lblForecast.Text += "<td><Font Color=Red>" & _
            objDayForecast(intCount).Day & "</Font></td>"
            lblForecast.Text += "<td>" & _
            GetImage(objDayForecast(intCount).Abbrev) & "</td>"
            lblForecast.Text += _
            "<td><Font Color=Blue>Forecast</Font>: " & _
            (objDayForecast(intCount).Forecast).ToLower
```

```vb
                        lblForecast.Text += " Low Temp: " & _
                        objDayForecast(intCount).LowTemp
                        lblForecast.Text += " High temp: " & _
                        objDayForecast(intCount).HighTemp & "</td>"
                        lblForecast.Text += "</tr>"
                Next
                lblForecast.Text += "</table>"
            Catch
                'Error Found! Zip code is invalid
                lblForecast.Text = "Invalid Zip Code! Please try again"
            Finally
                'Destroy the objects
                objWeather = Nothing
                objForecast = Nothing
            End Try
        Else
            Try
                'Show Raw Forecast
                lblForecast.Text = objWeather.GetWeatherText(txtZipCode.Text)
            Catch
                'Error Found! Zip code is invalid
                lblForecast.Text = "Invalid Zip Code! Please try again"
            Finally
                objWeather = Nothing
            End Try
        End If
    End Sub

    Private Function GetImage(ByVal strAbbv As String) As String
        'Return Image Name based on abbreviation

        Select Case strAbbv
            Case "SU"
                Return "<IMG SRC='.\Images\Sun.gif' ALT='Sunny'>"
            Case "PC"
                Return "<IMG SRC='.\Images\PartlyCloudy.gif' ALT='Partly
                Cloudy'>"
            Case "RA"
                Return "<IMG SRC='.\Images\Rain.gif' ALT='Rain'>"
            Case "TS"
                Return "<IMG SRC='.\Images\Thunder.gif' ALT='Thunderstorm'>"
            Case "SN"
                Return "<IMG SRC='.\Images\Snow.gif' ALT='Snow'>"
            Case "MO"
                Return "<IMG SRC='.\Images\Moon.gif' ALT='Clear'>"
            Case "MC"
                Return "<IMG SRC='.\Images\MoonCloudy.gif' ALT='Partly
                Cloudy'>"
            Case "FG"
                Return "<IMG SRC='.\Images\Fog.gif' ALT='Foggy'>"
        End Select
    End Function
```

The application returns the forecast in summary format (using GetWeatherText method) if the CheckBox is checked. Otherwise, forecast data are presented in a refined way (using GetWeather method).

First, an instance of the WeatherServices class is created in objWeather. If the user has checked the CheckBox control requesting simple text forecast, the GetWeatherText method of objWeather is invoked and results should appear as shown in Figure 16.17.

If the CheckBox has not been checked, an object objForecast of type WeatherForecast class is created. This object is required, since GetWeather method returns a class of type WeatherForecast. Also, an object array objDayForecast() of type DailyForecast is declared. This array, too, is required, because one of the properties of objForecast is an array of classes of type DailyForecast. Note the absence of New keyword; it is not allowed in arrays declaration.

Next, GetWeather method of objWeather object is invoked by passing Zip code in txtZipCode as its input parameter, and the results are assigned to the object objForecast. The DayForecast property array of objForecast is assigned to objDayForecast array. Finally, once the objects and the array have values, forecast data can be rendered on the client. First, the basic properties of objForecast object such as CityShortName, Sunrise, and Sunset are assigned to the output label lblForecast. The output is embedded in <table> and the associated <tr>, <td> tags so that the output is rendered in a table format. Next, a For...Next loop appends the contents of the

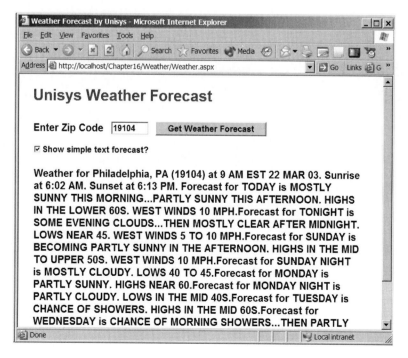

FIGURE 16.17
GetWeatherText method results.

array using <tr> and <td> tags to the Text property of lblForecast. The contents of the object array, objDayForecast, contains, for each day, forecast data, an abbreviation of the weather conditions, the high temperature, and the low temperature. The GetImage() method called from the loop accepts Abbrev as its parameter and returns the location of the appropriate image file.[51] The possible values[52] for the Abbrev property are SU-Sunny, PC-Partly Cloudy, MC-Moon Cloudy, MO-Moon, RA-Rain, TS-Thunderstorms, SN-Snow, and FG-Fog.

Figure 16.18 shows the results. If an invalid zip code is entered, the objDayForecast() array will be empty causing an exception. The Try...Catch...End Try blocks catches

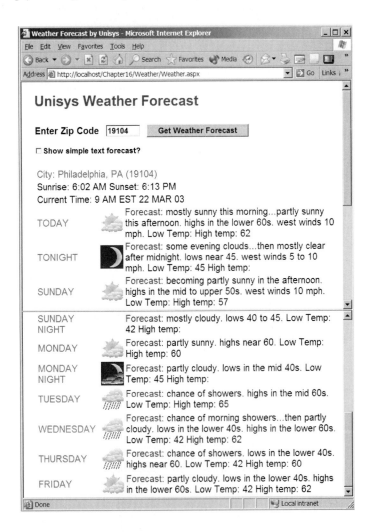

FIGURE 16.18
GetWeather method results.

---

[51]The images are located in a subfolder called Images under the Weather application folder. These images are courtesy of Unisys Corporation.

[52]Unisys Corporation provided all the possible values for the Abbrev property. However, these values can also be obtained by studying forecast data for different zip codes.

this exception and displays an appropriate error message. Build and run the application by pressing F5. The results should appear as in Figures 16.17 or 16.18.

SUGGESTED HOME ASSIGNMENTS

1. Design a simple Web service that provides a quote-of-the-day service. Also, design a client Web application to consume it.
2. Locate the CDYNE's credit card verifier Web service in one of the UDDI registries, and create a client application to consume it.
3. Search for a suitable Web service in IBM's UDDI registry (**https://uddi.ibm.com/ubr/find**) that would return location details given a zip code. Create a client Web application to consume it.

TEST YOURSELF

1. A Web service is nothing but a subprocedure. Explain.
2. Explain the role of XML in Web services
3. What is the meaning of the acronym XSD?
4. Where does SOAP fit in while using Web services?
5. What is W3C? Explain its role
6. Identify the primary role of a WSDL document.
7. What is UDDI registry? Outline the need for the same.
8. Using IBM's UDDI registry, locate any three Web services.
9. Explain the entry point to a Web service.
10. Identify the namespace for Web services.
11. Why is the syntax WebMethod() necessary in declaring Web methods?
12. What is **http://tempuri.org/**? Explain its role.
13. Explain the role of proxy classes and how they are generated.
14. What is a .vsdisco file? Outline its role.
15. How are Web services tested?
16. Briefly discuss the various data types that can be returned by a Web service.
17. What is a service contract? How does a client application use it?
18. Explain the System.Web.Mail namespace.
19. What is the data type returned by the remote method VerifyEMail in Lab 16.1?
20. How can two remote Web services with the same name be consumed in a client application?

Appendix: SQL

APPENDIX OBJECTIVES

1. Review of DDL commands
   - Create
   - Drop
2. Review of additional DML clauses
   - Where
   - Like
   - Order By
   - Top N
   - Top N Percent
   - Distinct
   - Group By
   - Having
3. Review of join and union
   - Embedded Select
   - Inner join
   - Outer join
   - Union
4. Review DML Action queries
   - Insert
   - Delete
   - Update
5. Understanding performance issues with SQL statements
   - Join strategies
   - Other performance considerations

A.1   AIMS OF APPENDIX

This appendix reviews SQL, Structured Query Language, which is at the base of all access to relational databases. As part of the review, performance issues are discussed.

A.2   SQL OVERVIEW

SQL is the interface language to relational DBMS. SQL has two components: the `Data Definition Language (DDL)` language and the `Data Manipulation Language (DML)`. DDL allows application programs to define the data structure: what tables there should be in the database, what fields each table should have, what the attributes (such as data type) of each field should be, how the tables relate to each other, and which group of users is allowed to do what on the data and its definition. In short, the DDL defines the database intention (structure) and security. The DML allows application programs to manipulate the data within the intention created by the DDL. There are four primary DML commands:

- `Select`—retrieves data from one or more rows and tables.
- `Update`—changes the value of specific attributes in a table.
- `Delete`—deletes whole rows of data.
- `Insert`—adds rows to a table.

In all of the examples that follow, the SQL keywords are presented in uppercase letters. This is purely a matter of presentation. SQL does not differentiate between uppercase and lowercase.

A.2.1   The Friends Database

All of the SQL statements that follow relate to the Friends database that comes with the CD accompanying this book. Friends contains six related tables: "Friends," with details of friends "Addresses," with the addresses of each friend; "Diary," with a list of meetings with these friends; "Topics," containing data for the lookup table in Diary with the topics that are discussed at each meeting; "Pets," with a list of the pets of each friend, and "Species," a lookup table with the list of species a pet can be. Friends are identified by a Friend ID, an autonumber. Address is identified by Friend ID and ZIP code. Diary is identified by Friend ID, date, time, and Topic ID. Pets are identified by Friend ID and the pet's name.

The diagrammatic representation of the database as generated by Access is shown in Figure A.1. The bold named attributes are the primary keys. The lines connecting the tables are the relationships. When these lines have a cardinality stated on them (▦), it means the referential integrity constraints are enforced. Referential integrity is a rule built into the data specifications that checks that a value in one table already exists in another. For example, the Titles table should not have a Publisher ID that does not already exist in the Publishers table. Referential integrity is how such references are specified and enforced in SQL.

You can open this Relationships window in Access 2002 by clicking the Relationships icon, ▦ , in the Database window. (See Figure A.2.)

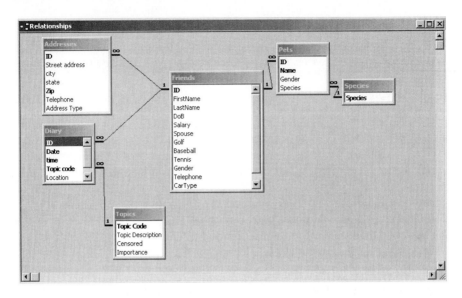

FIGURE A.1
The Friends Database Relationships window in Access.

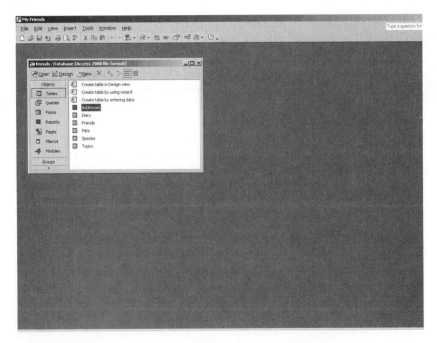

FIGURE A.2
Database window.

A.3 DDL

A.3.1 Create Table (DDL)

The Create Table command creates a new table:

```
Create Table <table-name>
        ([<attr> <data-type> [Not Null] [Default <value>],
         [<attr> <data-type> [Not Null] [Default <value>],
         ...
         [Primary Key (<attr>[,<attr>]...)]
         [,Unique(<attr>[,<attr>]...)]
         [,Foreign Key (<attr> References <table>(<attr>)]
         ...
         [,Foreign Key (<attr> References <table>(<attr>)]
         [,On Delete Cascade| Set Default| Set Null ]
         [,On Update Cascade| Set Default| Set Null]  );
```

The name of the new table is given in `<table-name>` and its list of attributes in `<attr>`. The data-type of the attributes can be `VarChar` (corresponding to the String data-type in Visual Basic), `Char (n)` (String with a fixed length), `Decimal (n,m)` (Currency), `Int` (Integer), `SmallInt` (Int16), `Float` (Double), `Date`, `Boolean`, `Byte`, `Short`, or `Long`.

The optional keyword "`Not Null`" specifies that the field cannot contain null. The optional keyword "`Default`" specifies the default value that will be placed in the field if no value is specified. The optional keyword "`Primary Key`" defines the primary key attributes, while the optional keyword "`Unique`" defines a unique index. "`Foreign Key`" defines the Referential Integrity relationships and "`On Delete`" and "`On Update`" define the operation associated with it.

Adding a new table through Access via the Create Table SQL command would look like Figure A.3. (To get to this window, in the main Database window, click the Queries tab and then Create Query in Design View. In the window that will open, click Close, and then, in the window behind it, the SQL button.) Run the query by clicking the Run icon ▣ .

A.3.2 Create Index (DDL)

The Create Index command creates a new index, `<index-name>`, on an existing table `<table>`, specifying the attribute, `<attr>`, or attributes it relates to:

```
Create [Unique] Index <index-name> On
        <table>(<attr> [,<attr>][...,<attr>]);
```

The optional keyword "Unique" means that there can be no duplicate entries in the index. The new index is added with Access. (See detail in Figure A.4.)

The new table will now appear in Access (Figure A.5). (In order to show the new table, click the Table name and then the Design button. Once the table is shown, click the Indexes button, ▣ , to show the Indexes window).

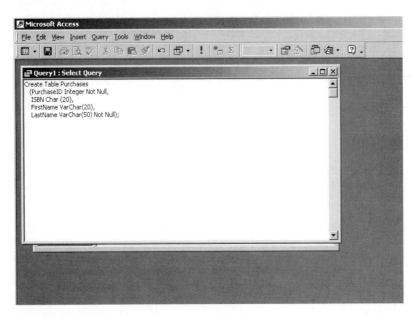

FIGURE A.3
Creating a table through the SQL view of Access Queries.

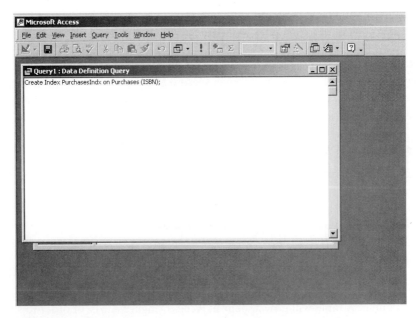

FIGURE A.4
Creating an index through the SQL view of Access Queries.

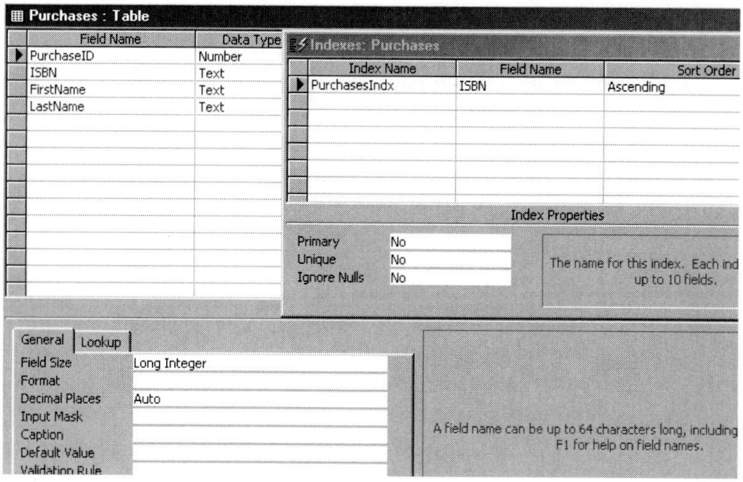

FIGURE A.5
The Table Design window in Access with its indexes shown in the Indexes window.

A.3.3   Drop Table (DDL)

The Drop command drops a table from a database. Both the data and the structure of the table will disappear:

```
Drop Table <table-name>;
```

A.3.4   Drop Index (DDL)

The Drop command can also be used to drop an index:

```
Drop Table <index-name> On <table-name>;
```

A.4   DML SELECT

While DDL defines data structures, DML manipulates the data within these structures. The most common DML command is Select, which retrieves data. All of the examples that follow can be entered into the same SQL window (Figure A.5).

A.4.1   Select

The Select command retrieves data from tables. This section will introduce the Select command gradually. Part 1 involves selecting data from a table. In order to retrieve all the data in a given table, such as Friends in the Friends database, simply type

```
SELECT * FROM Friends;
```

To limit the columns, just name the requested columns. Column names can be prefixed with the table name:

```
SELECT Friends.ID, Friends.FirstName, Friends.LastName
FROM Friends;
```

To limit the rows selected, the `Where` keyword should be used. The "where" clause supports all the logic operators: $>$, $<$, Not, =, (,), And, Or, $>=$, $<=$, $\sim=$, etc. In the following example, only male friends are selected:

```
SELECT Friends.ID, Friends.FirstName,
       Friends.LastName, Friends.Gender
FROM Friends
WHERE (((Friends.Gender)="male"));
```

The square brackets [ ] are necessary when the attribute name contains blanks, as in the case of "Company Name." Of course, there can be more than one element in the `Where` clause, as in the following code:

```
SELECT Addresses.ID, Addresses.[Street address],
       Addresses.state, Addresses.city
FROM Addresses
WHERE (((Addresses.state) Between "CA" And "IL" Or
       "City" Like "A*"));
```

The preceding SQL statement introduces two new keywords: `Between` and `Like`. The `Between` keyword can be used to simplify the SQL statement by replacing a "$>=$" and "$<=$" combination. The `Like` keyword allows the use of special "wildcard" characters when examining a string. The asterisk means "any character of any length." The "like" operator will select only the rows in which the "City" begins with an "A". Had the SQL statement been `"Like "*A*""`, all the rows in which "City" contains an "A" anywhere in the string would have been selected. Table A.1 shows the list of wildcard characters that the `Like` operator supports.

Accordingly, the following SQL statement will select the "City" of Friends that contain the letter "A" somewhere in their name, or have "B" as the second character, or contain a number, or start with the letters "C" through "E" and end with the letters "T" through "Z":

```
SELECT City
FROM Addresses
WHERE City Like "*A*" OR
      City Like "?B*" OR
      City Like "*#*" OR
      City Like "[C-E]*[T-Z]";
```

Note that the wildcard characters can be used in any combination with each other.

TABLE A.1   Wildcard Placeholders in SQL

Wildcard	Meaning
*	Placeholder for any number of any kind of character.
?	Placeholder for *one* character of any kind.
#	Placeholder for *one* digit.
[<from>-<to>]	Placeholder for *one* character by range of values.

Occasionally, it is also necessary to sort the output from the SQL statement. This is done using the `Order By` keyword. In the example that follows, the output is sorted by "State" in ascending order ("A" to "Z") and within each "State" by "City" in descending order:

```
SELECT State, City
FROM Addresses
WHERE Telephone Is Not Null
ORDER BY State, City DESC ;
```

The default `Order By` is ascending order. In order to specify a descending order, the `Desc` keyword should be added. Note that the `Where` clause is examining the value of "Telephone" even though its value is not being displayed. This is perfectly accepted in SQL.

Since the number of rows that can be returned from a `Select` statement can be large, the SQL statement can be set to show only the top (first) N rows or the first N% of the rows. In the following example, only the first 10 rows are shown and then only the top 15%:

```
SELECT TOP 10 State, City
FROM Addresses
WHERE Telephone Is Not Null
ORDER BY State, City DESC ;

SELECT TOP 15 PERCENT State, City
FROM Addresses
WHERE Telephone Is Not Null
ORDER BY State, City DESC ;
```

Occasionally, the output from a `Select` statement can contain double entries, as would happen in the following SQL statement, which inquires about which states have friends with telephone numbers:

```
SELECT Telephone, State
FROM Addresses
WHERE Telephone Is Not Null;
```

In order to show each row only once, the `Distinct` keyword is used:

```
SELECT DISTINCT Telephone, State
FROM Addresses
WHERE Telephone Is Not Null;
```

A.4.2   Select with Summation

The preceding SQL statements dealt with selecting data from single rows. SQL also allows summation of the data using `count` (to count the number of rows), `sum`, `min`, `max`, `avg`, `stDev`, `Var` (to show the sum, minimum, maximum, average, standard deviation, and variance, of numeric data), `First` and `Last` (to show the smallest and largest values also of nonnumeric data):

```
SELECT Count(ID) AS CountOfID,
Last(Telephone) AS LastOfTelephone,
First(Telephone) AS FirstOfTelephone
FROM Addresses
WHERE Telephone Is Not Null;
```

Note that the AS keyword names the new attributes.

With numeric data, the possibilities are greater:

```
SELECT Count(Friends.ID) AS CountOfID,
       First(Friends.FirstName) AS FirstOfFirstName,
       Last(Friends.LastName) AS LastOfLastName,
       Sum(Friends.DoB) AS SumOfDoB,
       Avg(Friends.DoB) AS AvgOfDoB,
       Min(Friends.DoB) AS MinOfDoB,
       Max(Friends.DoB) AS MaxOfDoB,
       StDev(Friends.DoB) AS StDevOfDoB,
       Var(Friends.DoB) AS VarOfDoB
FROM Friends;
```

The summarized data can also be shown by groupings (i.e., by a breakdown of the data). This is done using the Group By keyword. An example is given in the following SQL statement, which shows how many friends there are in each state:

```
SELECT Count(Addresses.ID) AS CountOfID, Addresses.state
FROM Addresses
GROUP BY Addresses.state;
```

The grouping can be limited with the Having keyword, just as the Where clause limits the selection of rows. The following SQL statement shows how many friends with a telephone number there are, grouped by and sorted by the state they are in, but only for states with a name code between "CA" and "IL":

```
SELECT Count(ID) AS CountOfID, State
FROM Addresses
WHERE Telephone Is Not Null
GROUP BY State
HAVING State Between "CA" And "IL"
ORDER BY State;
```

The HAVING keyword can also relate to the grouped values, as in the following SQL statement, where it limits the output to rows in which the count is more than 5:

```
SELECT Count(ID) AS CountOfID, Gender
FROM Friends
GROUP BY Gender
HAVING Count(ID)>5;
```

A.5   JOIN AND UNION IN THE SELECT COMMAND

A.5.1   Data from More Than One Table

The preceding SQL statements dealt with selecting data from a single table. Often, however, it is necessary to select data from more than one table: by join or by union. The result of *joining* tables is a view with columns from both tables. The tables in the join operation need not have the same attributes. The result of a *union* of tables is a view with rows from both tables. The tables in a union operation must be compatible.

When tables are joined, the number of columns or rows in the two tables can be different. When the tables are joined, there is usually a join criterion—a specification of which attribute to use when coupling the rows of the two tables. There are two types of join in SQL: *inner join* and *outer join*.

An inner join requires that every value of the join criterion in each table be matched by one or more values from the other table in order to be included. In Figure A.6, the two tables are joined by the values in Col1. Table 1 has values 1, 2, 3 and 4, while table 2 has values 1, 2, and 5. Consequently, the result of an inner join is that only the rows with values 1 and 2 (that appear in both tables) are included in the joined output.

On the other hand, in an *outer join*, every row in only one of tables must be matched by one or more values from the other table in order to be included, while all the rows of the other table are included, regardless of whether they are matched. According to which table's rows are always included, there are two types of outer join: left and right. A left outer join includes all the rows from Table 1 (the left table) and their matching values, where existing, from Table 2. Where there are no matching values in Table 2, the appropriate columns that are taken from Table 2 remain null. A right outer join includes all the rows from Table 2 (the right table) and their matching values, where existing, from Table 1, or, where there are no matching values, null. As can be seen in Figure A.7, not every row in one table must be matched by a row in another.

An inner join is written using the `Inner Join` keyword and specifying the tables involved and the join criteria. In the following SQL statement, there are two joins—one

Table 1

Col1	Col2	Col3
1	A	AA
2	B	BB
3	C	CC
4	D	DD

Table 2

Col4	Col5	Col6	Col7
1	Z	ZZ	Z1
2	Y	YY	Y1
5	X	XX	X1

Inner Join of Table 1 and Table 2 by Col1 and Col4

Col1	Col2	Col3	Col4	Col5	Col6	Col7
1	A	AA	1	Z	ZZ	Z1
2	B	BB	2	Y	YY	Y1

FIGURE A.6
Inner join.

Table 1

Col1	Col2	Col3
1	A	AA
2	B	BB
3	C	CC
4	D	DD

Table 2

Col4	Col5	Col6	Col7
1	Z	ZZ	Z1
2	Y	YY	Y1
5	X	XX	X1

Outer (left) Join of Table 1 and Table 2 by Col1 and Col4

Col1	Col2	Col3	Col4	Col5	Col6	Col7
1	A	AA	1	Z	ZZ	Z1
2	B	BB	2	Y	YY	Y1
3	C	CC	Null	Null	Null	Null
4	D	DD	Null	Null	Null	Null

Outer (right) Join of Table 1 and Table 2 by Col1 and Col4

Col1	Col2	Col3	Col4	Col5	Col6	Col7
1	A	AA	1	Z	ZZ	Z1
2	B	BB	2	Y	YY	Y1
Null	Null	Null	5	X	XX	X1

FIGURE A.7
Left outer join (above), and right outer join (below).

where the join criterion is the "ID" of the "Friends" table with the "ID" of the "Diary" Table and the other where the join criterion is the "Topic Code" of the "Diary" table with the "Topic Code" of the "Topics" Table:

```
SELECT DISTINCT Friends.FirstName, Friends.LastName,
       Topics.[Topic Description], Topics.Importance
FROM Topics INNER JOIN
       (Friends INNER JOIN Diary ON Friends.ID = Diary.ID)
           ON Topics.[Topic Code] = Diary.[Topic code]
ORDER BY Friends.LastName;
```

Needless to say, the Where, Group By, and all the other clauses apply here, too. Note that the attribute names are qualified (i.e., are prefixed by the table name). This is usually necessary in a join, because the tables being joined might have attributes with the same name.

Another way of performing an inner join is by using the Where clause to limit the results of a *Cartesian join*. (See Figure A.8.) A Cartesian join means joining every row in each table with every row in the other table.

The following SQL statement will produce an output equivalent to that produced by the inner join in the previous SQL statement, but because the Cartesian join must be performed before the Where limits the output, it is much more efficient to use an inner join:

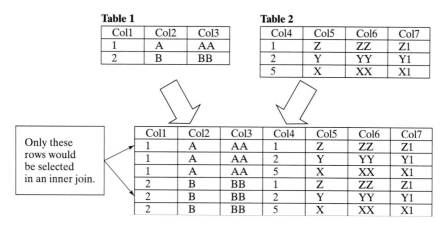

FIGURE A.8
Cartesian join.

```
SELECT DISTINCT Friends.FirstName, Friends.LastName,
       Topics.[Topic Description], Topics.Importance
FROM Topics, Friends, Diary
Where Friends.ID = Diary.ID and
   Diary.[Topic Code] = Topics.[Topic Code]
ORDER BY Friends.LastName;
```

Tables also can be inner joined with an *embedded select*. An embedded select uses a one-field output of one select statement as the input for another SQL statement using the IN keyword. The IN keyword chooses only values that are within a given list. In the following SQL statement, a list of all the "ID's" of Friends born during or after 1950 is created in the innermost select:

```
SELECT DISTINCT Addresses.ID,
       Addresses.city, Addresses.state, Addresses.Telephone
FROM Addresses
WHERE (((Addresses.ID) In
       select ID from Friends where Dob < #01/01/1950#)));
```

On the basis of the list created, only the matching ID in "Addresses" are selected. Again, using an inner join is more efficient and should always be preferred. Note the pound signs, #, that encapsulate the date. That is how date literals are handled.

An outer join SQL statement looks exactly like an inner join SQL statement except that the key words Inner Join are replaced with either Left Join or Right Join, depending on whether all the rows from the left-hand-side table are to be included or all the rows from the right-hand side, respectively. This is demonstrated in the following SQL statement:

```
SELECT DISTINCT Friends.ID,
       Friends.FirstName, Friends.LastName,
```

```
            Addresses.[Street address], Addresses.city,
            Addresses.state
FROM Friends LEFT JOIN Addresses
            ON Friends.ID = Addresses.ID
WHERE (((Friends.Golf)=True));
```

The SQL statement will select all the rows from the "Friends" table, but only those with a matching "ID" in "Addresses", and then only those rows in "Friends" dealing with Friends who play golf.

Another type of SQL statement that acquires data from two tables is the *union* statement. Union requires that the two tables have compatible structure: the same number of columns and the same data-types in each, albeit the attributes may have different names. See the example of union in Figure A.8.

Table 1

Col1	Col2	Col3
1	A	AA
2	B	BB
3	C	CC
4	D	DD

Table 2

Col1	Col2	Col3
5	Z	ZZ
6	Y	YY

Col1	Col2	Col3
1	A	AA
2	B	BB
3	C	CC
4	D	DD
5	Z	ZZ
6	Y	YY

FIGURE A.8
The result of a union between two tables.

The union statement in SQL is the combination of two SQL statements with the keyword Union. The following SQL statement creates a view with two columns—(1) first name and last name of a Friend and (2) city and state combinations:

```
SELECT Friends.FirstName, Friends.LastName
FROM Friends

Union

Select Addresses.City , Addresses.State
From Addresses
```

The union of the two SQL statements is possible, even though the columns deal with unrelated data, because the data-types are the same.

A.6   DML ACTION QUERIES

A.6.1   Insert

SQL statements can also be used to change data, inserting new rows, deleting existing rows, and updating attributes in existing rows. The `Insert` command, which, as its name implies, inserts new rows, has two formats. One is

```
Insert Into <table-name> Values (<values>);
```

where `<values>` is a list of values whose order corresponds to the order of the attributes in the table.

Alternatively, the list of attributes can be stated explicitly, in which case the order of the `<values>` should correspond to the order of the `<attribute-list>`:

```
Insert Into <table-name> (<attribute-list>) Values (<values>);
```

Accordingly, the two following SQL commands are equivalent:

```
INSERT Into Pets (ID, Name, Gender, Species)
     Values (12, "Bill", "Male", "Dog");
INSERT Into Pets Values (12, "Bilyl", "Male", "Cat");
```

Note that the order of the values in the preceding SQL statement corresponds to the order of the attributes in the table, while in the previous SQL statement it corresponded to the order of the attribute list in the SQL statement.

A.6.2   Insert with Select

The Insert SQL command can be used to insert values that are the result of a Select statement, too:

```
Select <fields>
     Into <table-name>
      <remainder of Select statement>;
```

An example is

```
SELECT Addresses.state, Friends.FirstName, Friends.LastName
    INTO [TX Friends]
FROM Friends INNER JOIN Addresses ON
     Friends.ID = Addresses.ID
WHERE (((Addresses.state)="TX"));
```

The foregoing set of SQL statements—best run, by the way, when the SQL commends are combined as one transaction—will create a new table in the Friends database and insert into it the results of the `Select` statement.

A.6.3   Delete

The Delete SQL command deletes rows from a table according to the `Where` clause. The syntax of the command is

```
Delete from <table-name>
        Where <Condition>;
```

The `<Condition>` of the `Delete` statement is identical to that of the `Select` statement. Omitting the `Where` clause will correspondingly delete all the rows in the table. Note that unlike the `Drop` command, the `Delete` command is a DML command; it only affects the data, not the structure of the table. For example, deleting all the rows of authors who were born in 1950 would be done like this:

```
DELETE FROM Friends
    WHERE [DoB] BETWEEN #01/01/1950# and #12/31/1950#;
```

A.6.4   Update

The Update SQL command updates the values of a given attribute in a table according to the `Where` clause. The syntax of the command is

```
Update <table-name>
        Set <attribute> = <value>
        Where <Condition>;
```

The `<Condition>` of the `Update` statement is identical to that of the `Select` statement. Omitting the `Where` clause will update the values of the attribute throughout the table. For example, updating the "Car Type" of all the authors who were born in the 1950s would be done with the following command:

```
UPDATE Friends SET Friends.CarType = "Old Car"
WHERE (((Friends.DoB)
    Between #1/1/1950# And #12/31/1959#));
```

A.7   PERFORMANCE CONSIDERATIONS IN SQL

A.7.1   Join Strategies

Joining tables is one of the most expensive operations in SQL. Consequently, choosing which indexes to declare and so guiding the DBMS to choose the best join strategy is often a major consideration in database design. Accordingly, make sure that there are indexes on join columns in both tables and that the indexes are complete (i.e., that they represent the whole logical key involved). For example, when indexing by a customer's name, make the index on both "Last Name" and "First Name." We next examine examples of several join strategies with the following SQL statement:

```
SELECT *
FROM Table1 INNER JOIN Table2 On
    Table1.key = Table2.key;
```

The choice of join strategy is in the hands of the DBMS alone, but the addition of indexes can influence the DBMS.

1. *Nested Iteration Join.* This is the last-resort algorithm. It is performed when none of the other algorithms can be used, usually because there are no appropriate indexes. This algorithm is also used when the tables involved contain few rows. The nested iteration join algorithm pairs each outer table record with its matching pair in the inner table and retains only those pairs that match the Where clause and the record selected if the clause is true. No indexes are used in this algorithm.

2. *Index Join.* This algorithm is used when there is an appropriate index on the join criteria in the inner table. The algorithm reads all the records of the outer table. Then, for each record, it examines in the inner table's index whether it is matched in the inner table. If so, the appropriate record is read from the inner table and the Where is clause examined and the record selected if the clause is true.

3. *Lookup Join.* This algorithm works like the indexed join algorithm, except that the appropriate columns of the inner table are projected (copied) to a new temporary table and indexed there according to the join criteria before an indexed join is performed. (See Figure A.9.)

4. *Merge Join.* First the tables are merged, then the rows are paired and the Where clause is examined, and finally the record is selected if the clause is true. This algorithm is used primarily when large tables are involved and where merge can avoid the need to sort the output.

5. *Index–Merge Join.* This algorithm reads the outer table in the sequence of the index used in the join operation. For each row, the algorithm reads the inner table according to the index used for the join. If the two keys match, the Where clause is examined and the record is selected if the clause is true. Otherwise, the smaller of the two keys (the outer table or the inner table key) is advanced, and the next record with the key is read:

```
oledbDataReader1.Read
oledbDataReader2.Read

While Not EOF(Table1) and Not EOF(Table2)
     If Table1.key = Table2.Key Then
```

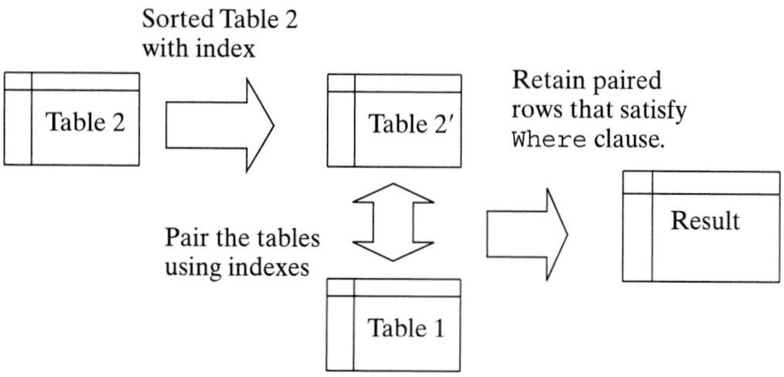

FIGURE A.9
Lookup join.

```
                        Call Examine_Where_Clause
            Else
                    If Table1.Key > Table2.Key Then
                            OledbDataReader2.Read
                    Else
                            oledbDataReader1.Read
                    End If
            End If
    Wend
```

A.7.2   More Considerations in SQL

Another important set of performance considerations that relates to one of the basic rules of programming is "KISS": "Keep it simple, stupid." This rule is especially appropriate when it comes to query optimization, because the complier can be easily "deceived" into performing a nonoptimal algorithm by unnecessarily complex queries:

- Adding an `IIF` expression in an SQL statement should be avoided because some DBMS (such as Access) cannot optimize the `IIF` expression. If an `IF` statement is necessary, the best place to put it is in a subroutine connected to the control of the form.

- Reduce the number of columns in the Group By clause to the necessary minimum. When both `Inner Join` and `Group By` are used in the same SQL statement, it is best to `Group By` before the `Inner Join` by splitting the SQL statement into two statements.

- Avoid unneeded tables in the join. In some cases, additional tables are added to an SQL statement because logically they seem to belong in the SQL statement, even though the data already exist in other tables that are already in the SQL statement. For example, suppose a query is seeking to identify all the City values of Friends with whom one speaks about soccer. On a first examination, the data should come from the "Friends," "Addresses," and "Diary" tables, as in the following SQL statement:

```
SELECT DISTINCT Addresses.city
FROM (Friends INNER JOIN Addresses ON
    Friends.ID = Addresses.ID) INNER JOIN Diary ON
    Friends.ID = Diary.ID
WHERE (((Diary.[Topic code])="Soccer"));
```

But this statement unnecessarily joins the "Friends" table to the SQL statement, because no new data are referenced in it. Dropping the table will, accordingly, result in a (cheaper) join of just two, rather than three, tables:

```
SELECT DISTINCT Addresses.city
FROM Addresses INNER JOIN Diary ON
    Addresses.ID = Diary.ID
WHERE (((Diary.[Topic code])="Soccer"));
```

- Do not be greedy. Request only the rows and columns that are necessary. Requesting too much information will add unnecessary traffic on the network.

Index